Python

E S S E N T I A L   R E F E R E N C E

Third Edition

David Beazley

DEVELOPER'S
LIBRARY

Sams Publishing, 800 East 96th Street, Indianapolis, Indiana 46240 USA

Python Essential Reference, Third Edition

International Standard Book Number: 0-672-32862-3

Library of Congress Catalog Card Number: 200593277

Printed in the United States of America

Sixth Printing: April 2008

10   09   08   6   7   8   9

Trademarks

Warning and Disclaimer

Bulk Sales

Sams Publishing offers excellent discounts on this book when ordered in quantity for bulk purchases or special sales. For more information, please contact

U.S. Corporate and Government Sales

1-800-382-3419

corpsales@pearsontechgroup.com

For sales outside of the U.S., please contact

International Sales

international@pearsoned.com

Acquisitions Editor
Jenny Watson

Development Editor
Scott Meyers

Managing Editor
Charlotte Clapp

Project Editor
Andy Beaster

Copy Editor
Bart Reed

Proofreader
Paula Lowell

Indexer
David Beazley

Technical Editor
Timothy Boronczyk

Publishing Coordinator
Vanessa Evans

Book Designer
Gary Adair

Page Layout
Michelle Mitchell

❖

This book is dedicated to "The Plan."

❖

Contents at a Glance

Table of Contents

About the Author

David M. Beazley is a long-time Python enthusiast, having been involved with the Python community since 1996. He is probably best known for his work on SWIG, a popular software package for integrating C/C++ programs with other programming languages, including Python, Perl, Ruby, Tcl, and Java. He has also written a number of other programming tools, including PLY, a Python implementation of lex and yacc. Dave spent seven years working in the Theoretical Physics Division at Los Alamos National Laboratory, where he helped pioneer the use of Python with massively parallel supercomputers. After that, Dave went off to work as an evil professor, where he briefly enjoyed tormenting college students with a variety of insane programming projects. However, he has since seen the error of his ways and is now working as a professional musician and occasional software consultant in Chicago. He can be contacted at http://www.dabeaz.com.

Acknowledgments

This book would not be possible without the support of many people. First, I'd like to thank Timothy Boronczyk for his feedback regarding the third edition. I'd also like to acknowledge past technical reviewers Paul DuBois, Mats Wichmann, David Ascher, and Tim Bell for their valuable comments and advice that made earlier editions a success. Guido van Rossum, Jeremy Hylton, Fred Drake, Roger Masse, and Barry Warsaw also provided tremendous assistance with the first edition while hosting me for a few weeks back in the hot summer of 1999. Last, but not least, this book would not be possible without all of the feedback I received from readers. There are far too many people to list individually, but I have done my best to incorporate your suggestions for making the book even better. I'd also like to thank all the folks at Sams Publishing and Pearson Education for their continued commitment to the project and assistance. Jenny Watson, Scott Meyers, Andy Beaster, and Bart Reed all helped out to get this edition out the door in good shape. A special thanks is in order for Robin Drake, whose tremendous effort in editing previous editions made the third edition possible. Finally, I'd like to offer a special acknowledgment to my musical partners in crime: Jim Trompeter, David Bloom, Thomas Mucha, Trent Harris, Matt Mayes, Marc Piane, and Alex Alvarado. They had absolutely nothing whatsoever to do with Python or this book, but they put up with me when I was spending far too much time working on the book and not enough time working on interesting new bebop lines. Thanks guys.

We Want to Hear from You!

As the reader of this book, *you* are our most important critic and commentator. We value your opinion and want to know what we're doing right, what we could do better, what areas you'd like to see us publish in, and any other words of wisdom you're willing to pass our way.

You can email or write me directly to let me know what you did or didn't like about this book—as well as what we can do to make our books stronger.

Please note that I cannot help you with technical problems related to the topic of this book, and that due to the high volume of mail I receive, I might not be able to reply to every message.

When you write, please be sure to include this book's title and author as well as your name and phone or email address. I will carefully review your comments and share them with the author and editors who worked on the book.

E-mail: opensource@samspublishing.com
Mail: Mark Taber
            Associate Publisher
            Sams Publishing
            800 East 96th Street
            Indianapolis, IN 46240 USA

Reader Services

Visit our website and register this book at www.samspublishing.com/register for convenient access to any updates, downloads, or errata that might be available for this book.

Introduction

THIS BOOK IS INTENDED TO BE A CONCISE REFERENCE to the Python programming language. Although an experienced programmer will probably be able to learn Python from this book, it's not intended to be an extended tutorial or a treatise on how to program. Rather, the goal is to present the core Python language, the contents of the Python library, and the Python extension API in a manner that's accurate and concise. This book assumes that the reader has prior programming experience with Python or another language such as C or Java. In a addition, a general familiarity with systems programming topics (for example, basic operating system concepts and network programming) may be useful in understanding certain parts of the library reference.

Python is freely available for download at http://www.python.org. Versions are available for almost every operating system, including UNIX, Windows, Macintosh, and Java. In addition, the Python website includes links to documentation, how-to guides, and a wide assortment of third-party software.

The contents of this book are based on Python 2.4. However, readers should be aware that Python is a constantly evolving language. Most of the topics described herein are likely to be applicable to future versions of Python 2.x. In addition, much of the material is applicable to earlier releases. To a lesser extent, the topics in this book also apply to alternative Python implementations such as Jython (an implementation of Python in Java) and IronPython (an implementation of Python for .NET). However, those implementations are not the primary focus.

Just as Python is an evolving language, the third edition of *Python Essential Reference* has evolved to make use of new language features and new library modules. In fact, since the publication of the second edition, Python has undergone a dramatic transformation involving significant changes to core parts of the language. In addition, a wide variety of new and interesting features have been added. Rather than discussing these changes as a mere afterthought, the entire text has been updated to reflect the modern state of Python programming. Although no distinction is given to new features, detailed descriptions of language changes can be found at http://www.python.org.

Finally, it should be noted that Python already includes thousands of pages of useful documentation. The contents of this book are largely based on that documentation, but with a number of key differences. First, this reference presents most of the same information in a much more compact form, with different examples, and alternative descriptions of many topics. Second, a significant number of topics in the library reference have been expanded to include outside reference material. This is especially true for low-level system and networking modules in which effective use of a module normally relies on a myriad of options listed in manuals and outside references. In addition, in order to produce a more concise reference, a number of deprecated and relatively obscure library modules have been omitted. Finally, this reference doesn't attempt to cover large frameworks such as Tkinter, XML, and the COM extensions, as these topics are beyond the scope of this book and are described in books of their own.

In writing this book, it has been my goal to produce a reference containing virtually everything I have needed to use Python and its large collection of modules. Although this is by no means a gentle introduction to the Python language, I hope that you find the contents of this book to be a useful addition to your programming reference library for many years to come. I welcome your comments.

David Beazley
Chicago, Illinois
November 27, 2005

I

The Python Language

A Tutorial Introduction

THIS CHAPTER PROVIDES A QUICK INTRODUCTION to Python. The goal is to illustrate Python's essential features without getting too bogged down in special rules or details. To do this, the chapter briefly covers basic concepts such as variables, expressions, control flow, functions, classes, and input/output. This chapter is not intended to provide comprehensive coverage, nor does it cover all of Python's more advanced features. However, experienced programmers should be able to extrapolate from the material in this chapter to create more advanced programs. Beginners are encouraged to try a few examples to get a feel for the language.

Running Python

Python programs are executed by an interpreter. On most machines, the interpreter can be started by simply typing **python**. However, many different programming environments for Python are currently available (for example, ActivePython, PythonWin, IDLE, and PythonIDE). In this case, Python is started by launching the appropriate application. When the interpreter starts, a prompt appears at which you can start typing programs into a simple read-evaluation loop. For example, in the following output, the interpreter displays its copyright message and presents the user with the >>> prompt, at which the user types the familiar "Hello World" command:

```
Python 2.4.1 (#2, Mar 31 2005, 00:05:10)
[GCC 3.3 20030304 (Apple Computer, Inc. build 1666).] on darwin
Type "help", "copyright", "credits" or "license" for more information.
>>> print "Hello World"
Hello World
>>>
```

Programs can also be placed in a file such as the following:

```
# helloworld.py
print "Hello World"
```

Python source files are ordinary text files and normally have a .py suffix. The # character denotes a comment that extends to the end of the line.

To execute the helloworld.py file, you provide the filename to the interpreter as follows:

```
% python helloworld.py
Hello World
%
```

On Windows, Python programs can be started by double-clicking a `.py` file or typing the name of the program into the "run" command on the Windows "Start" menu. This launches the interpreter and runs the program in a console window. In this case, the console window disappears immediately after the program completes its execution (often before you can read its output). To prevent this problem, you should use an integrated development environment such as PythonWin. An alternative approach is to launch the program using a `.bat` file containing a statement such as `python -i helloworld.py` that instructs the interpreter to enter interactive mode after program execution.

Within the interpreter, the `execfile()` function runs a program, as in the following example:

```
>>> execfile("helloworld.py")
Hello World
```

On UNIX, you can also invoke Python using `#!` in a shell script:

```
#!/usr/local/bin/python
print "Hello World"
```

The interpreter runs until it reaches the end of the input file. If it's running interactively, you can exit the interpreter by typing the EOF (end of file) character or by selecting Exit from a pull-down menu. On UNIX, EOF is Ctrl+D; on Windows, it's Ctrl+Z. A program can also exit by calling the `sys.exit()` function or raising the `SystemExit` exception. For example:

```
>>> import sys
>>> sys.exit()
```

or

```
>>> raise SystemExit
```

Variables and Arithmetic Expressions

The program in Listing 1.1 shows the use of variables and expressions by performing a simple compound-interest calculation.

Listing 1.1   **Simple Compound-Interest Calculation**

```
principal = 1000       # Initial amount
rate = 0.05            # Interest rate
numyears = 5           # Number of years
year = 1
while year <= numyears:
        principal = principal*(1+rate)
        print year, principal
        year += 1
```

The output of this program is the following table:

```
1 1050.0
2 1102.5
3 1157.625
4 1215.50625
5 1276.2815625
```

Python is a dynamically typed language in which names can represent values of different types during the execution of a program. In fact, the names used in a program are really just labels for various quantities and objects. The assignment operator simply creates an association between a name and a value. This is different from C, for example, in which a name represents a fixed size and location in memory into which results are placed. The dynamic behavior of Python can be seen in Listing 1.1 with the `principal` variable. Initially, it's assigned to an integer value. However, later in the program it's reassigned as follows:

```
principal = principal*(1+rate)
```

This statement evaluates the expression and reassociates the name `principal` with the result. When this occurs, the original binding of `principal` to the integer `1000` is lost. Furthermore, the result of the assignment may change the type of the variable. In this case, the type of `principal` changes from an integer to a floating-point number because `rate` is a floating-point number.

A newline terminates each individual statement. You also can use a semicolon to separate statements, as shown here:

```
principal = 1000; rate = 0.05; numyears = 5;
```

The `while` statement tests the conditional expression that immediately follows. If the tested statement is true, the body of the `while` statement executes. The condition is then retested and the body executed again until the condition becomes false. The body of the loop is denoted by indentation; the three statements following `while` in Listing 1.1 execute on each iteration. Python doesn't specify the amount of required indentation, as long as it's consistent within a block.

One problem with the program in Listing 1.1 is that the output isn't very pretty. To make it better, you could right-align the columns and limit the precision of `principal` to two digits by modifying `print` to use a format string, like this:

```
print "%3d  %0.2f" % (year, principal)
```

Now the output of the program looks like this:

```
1   1050.00
2   1102.50
3   1157.63
4   1215.51
5   1276.28
```

Format strings contain ordinary text and special formatting-character sequences such as `"%d"`, `"%s"`, and `"%f"`. These sequences specify the formatting of a particular type of data such as an integer, string, or floating-point number, respectively. The special-character sequences can also contain modifiers that specify a width and precision. For example, `"%3d"` formats an integer right-aligned in a column of width 3, and `"%0.2f"` formats a floating-point number so that only two digits appear after the decimal point. The behavior of format strings is almost identical to the C `sprintf()` function and is described in detail in Chapter 4, "Operators and Expressions."

Conditionals

The `if` and `else` statements can perform simple tests. Here's an example:

```
# Compute the maximum (z) of a and b
if a < b:
    z = b
```

```
else:
        z = a
```

The bodies of the `if` and `else` clauses are denoted by indentation. The `else` clause is optional.

To create an empty clause, use the `pass` statement as follows:

```
if a < b:
        pass        # Do nothing
else:
        z = a
```

You can form Boolean expressions by using the `or`, `and`, and `not` keywords:

```
if b >= a and b <= c:
        print "b is between a and c"
if not (b < a or b > c):
        print "b is still between a and c"
```

To handle multiple-test cases, use the `elif` statement, like this:

```
if a == '+':
        op = PLUS
elif a == '-':
        op = MINUS
elif a == '*':
        op = MULTIPLY
else:
        raise RuntimeError, "Unknown operator"
```

To denote truth values, you can use the Boolean values `True` and `False`. Here's an example:

```
if c in '0123456789':
    isdigit = True
else:
    isdigit = False
```

File Input and Output

The following program opens a file and reads its contents line by line:

```
f = open("foo.txt")          # Returns a file object
line = f.readline()          # Invokes readline() method on file
while line:
        print line,          # trailing ',' omits newline character
        line = f.readline()
f.close()
```

The `open()` function returns a new file object. By invoking methods on this object, you can perform various file operations. The `readline()` method reads a single line of input, including the terminating newline. An empty string is returned at the end of the file.

In the example, the program is simply looping over all the lines in the file `foo.txt`. Whenever a program loops over a collection of data like this (for instance input lines, numbers, strings, and so on), it is commonly known as "iteration." Because iteration is such a common operation, Python provides a number of shortcuts for simplifying the process. For instance, the same program can be written much more succinctly as follows:

```
for line in open("foo.txt"):
    print line,
```

To make the output of a program go to a file, you can supply a file to the print statement using >>, as shown in the following example:

```
f = open("out","w")        # Open file for writing
while year <= numyears:
        principal = principal*(1+rate)
        print >>f,"%3d    %0.2f" % (year,principal)
        year += 1
f.close()
```

In addition, file objects support a write() method that can be used to write raw data. For example, the print statement in the previous example could have been written this way:

```
f.write("%3d    %0.2f\n" % (year,principal))
```

Although these examples have worked with files, the same techniques apply to the standard output and input streams of the interpreter. For example, if you wanted to read user input interactively, you can read from the file sys.stdin. If you want to write data to the screen, you can write to sys.stdout, which is the same file used to output data produced by the print statement. For example:

```
import sys
sys.stdout.write("Enter your name :")
name = sys.stdin.readline()
```

The preceding code can also be shortened to the following:

```
name = raw_input("Enter your name :")
```

Strings

To create string literals, enclose them in single, double, or triple quotes as follows:

```
a = "Hello World"
b = 'Python is groovy'
c = """What is footnote 5?"""
```

The same type of quote used to start a string must be used to terminate it. Triple-quoted strings capture all the text that appears prior to the terminating triple quote, as opposed to single- and double-quoted strings, which must be specified on one logical line. Triple-quoted strings are useful when the contents of a string literal span multiple lines of text such as the following:

```
print '''Content-type: text/html

<h1> Hello World </h1>
Click <a href="http://www.python.org">here</a>.
'''
```

Strings are sequences of characters indexed by integers, starting at zero. To extract a single character, use the indexing operator s[i] like this:

```
a = "Hello World"
b = a[4]              # b = 'o'
```

To extract a substring, use the slicing operator s[i:j]. This extracts all elements from s whose index k is in the range i <= k < j. If either index is omitted, the beginning or end of the string is assumed, respectively:

```
c = a[:5]               # c = "Hello"
d = a[6:]               # d = "World"
e = a[3:8]              # e = "lo Wo"
```

Strings are concatenated with the plus (+) operator:

```
g = a + " This is a test"
```

Other data types can be converted into a string by using either the str() or repr() function or backquotes (`), which are a shortcut notation for repr(). For example:

```
s = "The value of x is " + str(x)
s = "The value of y is " + repr(y)
s = "The value of y is " + `y`
```

In many cases, str() and repr() return identical results. However, there are subtle differences in semantics that are described in later chapters.

Lists

Lists are sequences of arbitrary objects. You create a list as follows:

```
names = [ "Dave", "Mark", "Ann", "Phil" ]
```

Lists are indexed by integers, starting with zero. Use the indexing operator to access and modify individual items of the list:

```
a = names[2]            # Returns the third item of the list, "Ann"
names[0] = "Jeff"       # Changes the first item to "Jeff"
```

To append new items to the end of a list, use the append() method:

```
names.append("Kate")
```

To insert an item in the list, use the insert() method:

```
names.insert(2, "Sydney")
```

You can extract or reassign a portion of a list by using the slicing operator:

```
b = names[0:2]                       # Returns [ "Jeff", "Mark" ]
c = names[2:]                        # Returns [ "Sydney", "Ann", "Phil", "Kate" ]
names[1] = 'Jeff'                    # Replace the 2nd item in names with 'Jeff'
names[0:2] = ['Dave','Mark','Jeff']  # Replace the first two items of
                                     # the list with the list on the right.
```

Use the plus (+) operator to concatenate lists:

```
a = [1,2,3] + [4,5]     # Result is [1,2,3,4,5]
```

Lists can contain any kind of Python object, including other lists, as in the following example:

```
a = [1,"Dave",3.14, ["Mark", 7, 9, [100,101]], 10]
```

Nested lists are accessed as follows:

```
a[1]                    # Returns "Dave"
a[3][2]                 # Returns 9
a[3][3][1]              # Returns 101
```

The program in Listing 1.2 illustrates a few more advanced features of lists by reading a list of numbers from a file specified on the command line and outputting the minimum and maximum values.

Listing 1.2 **Advanced List Features**

```
import sys                        # Load the sys module
if len(sys.argv) != 2            # Check number of command line arguments :
    print "Please supply a filename"
    raise SystemExit
f = open(sys.argv[1])            # Filename on the command line
svalues = f.readlines()          # Read all lines into a list
f.close()

# Convert all of the input values from strings to floats
fvalues = [float(s) for s in svalues]

# Print min and max values
print "The minimum value is ", min(fvalues)
print "The maximum value is ", max(fvalues)
```

The first line of this program uses the import statement to load the sys module from the Python library. This module is being loaded in order to obtain command-line arguments.

The open() method uses a filename that has been supplied as a command-line option and stored in the list sys.argv. The readlines() method reads all the input lines into a list of strings.

The expression [float(s) for s in svalues] constructs a new list by looping over all the strings in the list svalues and applying the function float() to each element. This particularly powerful method of constructing a list is known as a *list comprehension*.

After the input lines have been converted into a list of floating-point numbers, the built-in min() and max() functions compute the minimum and maximum values.

Tuples

Closely related to lists is the tuple data type. You create tuples by enclosing a group of values in parentheses, like this:

```
a = (1,4,5,-9,10)
b = (7,)                                      # Singleton (note extra ,)
person = (first_name, last_name, phone)
```

Sometimes Python recognizes that a tuple is intended, even if the parentheses are missing:

```
a = 1,4,5,-9,10
b = 7,
person = first_name, last_name, phone
```

Tuples support most of the same operations as lists, such as indexing, slicing, and concatenation. The only difference is that you cannot modify the contents of a tuple after creation (that is, you cannot modify individual elements or append new elements to a tuple).

Sets

A set is used to contain an unordered collection of objects. To create a set, use the
`set()` function and supply a sequence of items such as follows:

```
s = set([3,5,9,10])      # Create a set of numbers
t = set("Hello")         # Create a set of characters
```

Unlike lists and tuples, sets are unordered and cannot be indexed in the same way. More
over, the elements of a set are never duplicated. For example, if you print the value of t
from the preceding code, you get the following:

```
>>> print t
set(['H', 'e', 'l', 'o'])
```

Notice that only one `'l'` appears.

Sets support a standard collection of set operations, including union, intersection, difference, and symmetric difference. For example:

```
a = t | s      # Union of t and s
b = t & s      # Intersection of t and s
c = t - s      # Set difference (items in t, but not in s)
d = t ^ s      # Symmetric difference (items in t or s, but not both)
```

New items can be added to a set using `add()` or `update()`:

```
t.add('x')
s.update([10,37,42])
```

An item can be removed using `remove()`:

```
t.remove('H')
```

Dictionaries

A *dictionary* is an associative array or hash table that contains objects indexed by keys.
You create a dictionary by enclosing the values in curly braces ({ }) like this:

```
a = {
       "username" : "beazley",
       "home" : "/home/beazley",
       "uid" : 500
    }
```

To access members of a dictionary, use the key-indexing operator as follows:

```
u = a["username"]
d = a["home"]
```

Inserting or modifying objects works like this:

```
a["username"] = "pxl"
a["home"] = "/home/pxl"
a["shell"] = "/usr/bin/tcsh"
```

Although strings are the most common type of key, you can use many other Python
objects, including numbers and tuples. Some objects, including lists and dictionaries,
cannot be used as keys, because their contents are allowed to change.

Dictionary membership is tested with the `has_key()` method, as in the following
example:

```
if a.has_key("username"):
    username = a["username"]
else:
    username = "unknown user"
```

This particular sequence of steps can also be performed more compactly as follows:

```
username = a.get("username", "unknown user")
```

To obtain a list of dictionary keys, use the keys() method:

```
k = a.keys()              # k = ["username","home","uid","shell"]
```

Use the del statement to remove an element of a dictionary:

```
del a["username"]
```

Iteration and Looping

The simple loop shown earlier used the while statement. The other looping construct is the for statement, which is used to iterate over a collection of items. Iteration is one of Python's most rich features. However, the most common form of iteration is to simply loop over all the members of a sequence such as a string, list, or tuple. Here's an example:

```
for i in range(1,10):
        print "2 to the %d power is %d" % (i, 2**i)
```

The range(i, j) function constructs a list of integers with values from i to j-1. If the starting value is omitted, it's taken to be zero. An optional stride can also be given as a third argument. For example:

```
a = range(5)         # a = [0,1,2,3,4]
b = range(1,8)       # b = [1,2,3,4,5,6,7]
c = range(0,14,3)    # c = [0,3,6,9,12]
d = range(8,1,-1)    # d = [8,7,6,5,4,3,2]
```

The range() function works by constructing a list and populating it with values according to the starting, ending, and stride values. For large ranges, this process is expensive in terms of both memory and runtime performance. To avoid this, you can use the xrange() function, as shown here:

```
for i in xrange(1,10):
        print "2 to the %d power is %d" % (i, 2**i)

a = xrange(100000000)        # a = [0,1,2, ..., 99999999]
b = xrange(0,100000000,5)    # b = [0,5,10, ...,99999995]
```

Rather than creating a sequence populated with values, the sequence returned by xrange() computes its values from the starting, ending, and stride values whenever it's accessed.

The for statement is not limited to sequences of integers and can be used to iterate over many kinds of objects, including strings, lists, and dictionaries. For example:

```
a = "Hello World"
# Print out the characters in a
for c in a:
        print c

b = ["Dave","Mark","Ann","Phil"]
```

```
# Print out the members of a list
for name in b:
        print name

c = { 'a' : 3, 'name': 'Dave', 'x': 7.5 }
# Print out all of the members of a dictionary
for key in c:
        print key, c[key]
```

In addition, the `for` statement can be applied to any object that supports a special iteration protocol. In an earlier example, iteration was used to loop over all the lines in a file:

```
for line in open("foo.txt"):
print line,
```

This works because files provide special iteration methods that work as follows:

```
>>> i = f.__iter__()    # Return an iterator object
>>> i.next()            # Return first line
>>> i.next()            # Return next line
... continues ...
>>> i.next()            # No more data
Traceback (most recent call last):
  File "<stdin>", line 1, in ?
StopIteration
>>>
```

Underneath the covers, the `for` statement relies on these methods to iterate over lines in the file.

Instead of iterating over a collection of items such as the elements of a list, it is also possible to iterate over an object that knows how to generate items on demand. This sort of object is called a *generator* and is defined using a function. For example, if you wanted to iterate over the Fibonacci numbers, you could do this:

```
# Generate fibonacci numbers
def fibonacci(max):
    s = 1
    t = 1
    while s < max:
        yield s          # Produce a value
        w = s + t
        s = t
        t = w
    return

# Print fibonacci numbers less than 1000
for n in fibonacci(1000):
    print n
```

In this case, the `yield` statement produces a value used in iteration. When the next value is requested, the function resumes execution right after `yield`. Iteration stops when the generator function returns. More details about iterators and generators can be found in Chapter 6, "Functions and Functional Programming."

Functions

You use the `def` statement to create a function, as shown in the following example:

```
def remainder(a,b):
      q = a // b          # // is truncating division.
      r = a - q*b
      return r
```

To invoke a function, simply use the name of the function followed by its arguments enclosed in parentheses, such as `result = remainder(37,15)`. You can use a tuple to return multiple values from a function, as shown here:

```
def divide(a,b):
      q = a // b          # If a and b are integers, q is integer
      r = a - q*b
      return (q,r)
```

When returning multiple values in a tuple, it's often useful to invoke the function as follows:

```
quotient, remainder = divide(1456,33)
```

To assign a default value to a parameter, use assignment:

```
def connect(hostname,port,timeout=300):
   # Function body
```

When default values are given in a function definition, they can be omitted from subsequent function calls. When omitted, the argument will simply take on the default value. For example:

```
connect('www.python.org', 80)
```

You also can invoke functions by using keyword arguments and supplying the arguments in arbitrary order. However, this requires you to know the names of the arguments in the function definition. For example:

```
connect(port=80,hostname="www.python.org")
```

When variables are created or assigned inside a function, their scope is local. That is, the variable is only defined inside the body of the function and is destroyed when the function returns. To modify the value of a global variable from inside a function, use the `global` statement as follows:

```
a = 4.5
...
def foo():
      global a
      a = 8.8              # Changes the global variable a
```

Classes

The `class` statement is used to define new types of objects and for object-oriented programming. For example, the following class defines a simple stack with `push()`, `pop()`, and `length()` operations:

```
class Stack(object):
      def __init__(self):              # Initialize the stack
            self.stack = [ ]
      def push(self,object):
            self.stack.append(object)
      def pop(self):
            return self.stack.pop()
```

```
def length(self):
        return len(self.stack)
```

In the first line of the class definition, the statement class Stack(object) declares Stack to be an object. The use of parentheses is how Python specifies inheritance—in this case, Stack inherits from object, which is the root of all Python types. Inside the class definition, methods are defined using the def statement. The first argument in each method always refers to the object itself. By convention, self is the name used for this argument. All operations involving the attributes of an object must explicitly refer to the self variable. Methods with leading and trailing double underscores are special methods. For example, __init__ is used to initialize an object after it's created.

To use a class, write code such as the following:

```
s = Stack()              # Create a stack
s.push("Dave")           # Push some things onto it
s.push(42)
s.push([3,4,5])
x = s.pop()              # x gets [3,4,5]
y = s.pop()              # y gets 42
del s                    # Destroy s
```

In this example, an entirely new object was created to implement the stack. However, a stack is almost identical to the built-in list object. Therefore, an alternative approach would be to inherit from list and add an extra method:

```
class Stack(list):
        # Add push() method for stack interface
        # Note: lists already provide a pop() method.
        def push(self,object):
                self.append(object)
```

Normally, all of the methods defined within a class apply only to instances of that class (that is, the objects that are created). However, different kinds of methods can be defined, such as static methods familiar to C++ and Java programmers. For example:

```
class EventHandler(object):
        @staticmethod
        def dispatcherThread():
                while (1):
                        # Wait for requests
                    ...

EventHandler.dispatcherThread()         # Call method as a function
```

In this case, @staticmethod declares the method that follows to be a static method. @staticmethod is actually an example of using an object known as a decorator—a topic that is discussed further in the chapter on functions and functional programming.

Exceptions

If an error occurs in your program, an exception is raised and an error message such as the following appears:

```
Traceback (innermost last):
 File "<interactive input>", line 42, in foo.py
NameError: a
```

The error message indicates the type of error that occurred, along with its location. Normally, errors cause a program to terminate. However, you can catch and handle exceptions using the try and except statements, like this:

```
try:
    f = open("file.txt","r")
except IOError, e:
    print e
```

If an IOError occurs, details concerning the cause of the error are placed in e and control passes to the code in the except block. If some other kind of exception is raised, it's passed to the enclosing code block (if any). If no errors occur, the code in the except block is ignored. When an exception is handled, program execution resumes with the statement that immediately follows the except block. The program does not return back to the location where the exception occurred.

The raise statement is used to signal an exception. When raising an exception, you can use one of the built-in exceptions, like this:

```
raise RuntimeError, "Unrecoverable error"
```

Or you can create your own exceptions, as described in the section "Defining New Exceptions" in Chapter 5, "Control Flow."

Modules

As your programs grow in size, you'll probably want to break them into multiple files for easier maintenance. To do this, Python allows you to put definitions in a file and use them as a module that can be imported into other programs and scripts. To create a module, put the relevant statements and definitions into a file that has the same name as the module. (Note that the file must have a .py suffix.) Here's an example:

```
# file :  div.py
def divide(a,b):
    q = a//b         # If a and b are integers, q is an integer
    r = a - q*b
    return (q,r)
```

To use your module in other programs, you can use the import statement:

```
import div
a, b = div.divide(2305, 29)
```

The import statement creates a new namespace that contains all the objects defined in the module. To access this namespace, simply use the name of the module as a prefix, as in div.divide() in the preceding example.

If you want to import a module using a different name, supply the import statement with an optional as qualifier, as follows:

```
import div as foo
a,b = foo.divide(2305,29)
```

To import specific definitions into the current namespace, use the from statement:

```
from div import divide
a,b = divide(2305,29)        # No longer need the div prefix
```

To load all of a module's contents into the current namespace, you can also use the following:

```
from div import *
```

Finally, the `dir()` function lists the contents of a module and is a useful tool for interactive experimentation, because it can be used to provide a list of available functions and variables:

```
>>> import string
>>> dir(string)
['__builtins__', '__doc__', '__file__', '__name__', '_idmap',
 '_idmapL', '_lower', '_swapcase', '_upper', 'atof', 'atof_error',
 'atoi', 'atoi_error', 'atol', 'atol_error', 'capitalize',
 'capwords', 'center', 'count', 'digits', 'expandtabs', 'find',
...
>>>
```

Getting Help

When working with Python, you have several sources of quickly available information. First, when Python is running in interactive mode, you can use the `help()` command to get information about built-in modules and other aspects of Python. Simply type **help()** by itself for general information or **help('*modulename*')** for information about a specific module. The `help()` command can also be used to return information about specific functions if you supply a function name.

Most Python functions have documentation strings that describe their usage. To print the doc string, simply print the __doc__ attribute. Here's an example:

```
>>> print issubclass.__doc__
issubclass(C, B) -> bool

Return whether class C is a subclass (i.e., a derived class) of class B.
When using a tuple as the second argument issubclass(X, (A, B, ...)),
is a shortcut for issubclass(X, A) or issubclass(X, B) or ... (etc.).
>>>
```

Last, but not least, most Python installations also include the command pydoc, which can be used to return documentation about Python modules. Simply type **pydoc** *topic* at a command prompt (for example, in the Unix command shell).

## 2

Lexical Conventions and Syntax

THIS CHAPTER DESCRIBES THE SYNTACTIC AND LEXICAL CONVENTIONS of a Python program. Topics include line structure, grouping of statements, reserved words, literals, operators, tokens, and source code encoding. In addition, the use of Unicode string literals is described in detail.

Line Structure and Indentation

Each statement in a program is terminated with a newline. Long statements can span multiple lines by using the line-continuation character (\), as shown in the following example:

```
a = math.cos(3*(x-n)) + \
    math.sin(3*(y-n))
```

You don't need the line-continuation character when the definition of a triple-quoted string, list, tuple, or dictionary spans multiple lines. More generally, any part of a program enclosed in parentheses (. . .), brackets [. . .], braces { . . . }, or triple quotes can span multiple lines without use of the line-continuation character because they denote the start and end of a definition.

Indentation is used to denote different blocks of code, such as the bodies of functions, conditionals, loops, and classes. The amount of indentation used for the first statement of a block is arbitrary, but the indentation of the entire block must be consistent. For example:

```
if a:
    statement1      # Consistent indentation
    statement2
else:
    statement3
      statement4    # Inconsistent indentation (error)
```

If the body of a function, conditional, loop, or class is short and contains only a few statements, they can be placed on the same line, like this:

```
if a:    statement1
else:    statement2
```

To denote an empty body or block, use the pass statement. For example:

```
if a:
    pass
else:
    statements
```

Although tabs can be used for indentation, this practice is discouraged. The use of spaces is universally preferred (and encouraged) by the Python programming community. When tab characters are encountered, they're converted into the number of spaces required to move to the next column that's a multiple of 8 (for example, a tab appearing in column 11 inserts enough spaces to move to column 16). Running Python with the -t option prints warning messages when tabs and spaces are mixed inconsistently within the same program block. The -tt option turns these warning messages into TabError exceptions.

To place more than one statement on a line, separate the statements with a semicolon (;). A line containing a single statement can also be terminated by a semicolon, although this is unnecessary and considered poor style.

The # character denotes a comment that extends to the end of the line. A # appearing inside a quoted string doesn't start a comment, however.

Finally, the interpreter ignores all blank lines except when running in interactive mode. In this case, a blank line signals the end of input when typing a statement that spans multiple lines.

Identifiers and Reserved Words

An *identifier* is a name used to identify variables, functions, classes, modules, and other objects. Identifiers can include letters, numbers, and the underscore character (_), but must always start with a nonnumeric character. Letters are currently confined to the characters A–Z and a–z in the ISO-Latin character set. Because identifiers are case sensitive, FOO is different from foo. Special symbols such as $, %, and @ are not allowed in identifiers. In addition, words such as if, else, and for are reserved and cannot be used as identifier names. The following list shows all the reserved words:

and	elif	global	or	yield
assert	else	if	pass	
break	except	import	print	
class	exec	in	raise	
continue	finally	is	return	
def	for	lambda	try	
del	from	not	while	

Identifiers starting or ending with underscores often have special meanings. For example, identifiers starting with a single underscore such as _foo are not imported by the from module import * statement. Identifiers with leading and trailing double underscores such as __init__ are reserved for special methods, and identifiers with leading double underscores such as __bar are used to implement private class members, as described in Chapter 7, "Classes and Object-Oriented Programming." General-purpose use of similar identifiers should be avoided.

Literals

There are five built-in numeric types:

- Booleans
- Integers
- Long integers
- Floating-point numbers
- Complex numbers

The identifiers `True` and `False` are interpreted as Boolean values with the integer values of 0 and 1, respectively. A number such as `1234` is interpreted as a decimal integer. To specify an octal or hexadecimal integer, precede the value with `0` or `0x`, respectively (for example, `0644` or `0x100fea8`). Long integers are typically written with a trailing `l` (ell) or `L` character, as in `1234567890L`. Unlike integers, which are limited by machine precision, long integers can be of any length (up to the maximum memory of the machine). Although the trailing `L` is used to denote long integers, it may be omitted. In this case, a large integer value will automatically be converted into a long integer if it exceeds the precision of the standard integer type. Numbers such as `123.34` and `1.2334e+02` are interpreted as floating-point numbers. An integer or floating-point number with a trailing `j` or `J`, such as `12.34J`, is a complex number. You can create complex numbers with real and imaginary parts by adding a real number and an imaginary number, as in `1.2 + 12.34J`.

Python currently supports two types of string literals:

- 8-bit character data (ASCII)
- Unicode (16-bit-wide character data)

The most commonly used string type is 8-bit character data, because of its use in representing characters from the ASCII or ISO-Latin character set as well as representing raw binary data as a sequence of bytes. By default, 8-bit string literals are defined by enclosing text in single (`'`), double (`"`), or triple (`'''` or `"""`) quotes. You must use the same type of quote to start and terminate a string. The backslash (`\`) character is used to escape special characters such as newlines, the backslash itself, quotes, and nonprinting characters. Table 2.1 shows the accepted escape codes. Unrecognized escape sequences are left in the string unmodified and include the leading backslash. Furthermore, it's legal for strings to contain embedded null bytes and binary data. Triple-quoted strings can span multiple lines and include unescaped newlines and quotes.

Table 2.1 **Standard Character Escape Codes**

Character	Description
\	Newline continuation
\\	Backslash
\'	Single quote
\"	Double quote

Table 2.1   **Continued**

Character	Description
\a	Bell
\b	Backspace
\e	Escape
\0	Null
\n	Line feed
\v	Vertical tab
\t	Horizontal tab
\r	Carriage return
\f	Form feed
\ooo	Octal value (\000 to \377)
\xhh	Hexadecimal value (\x00 to \xff)

Unicode strings are used to represent multibyte international character sets and allow for 65,536 unique characters. Unicode string literals are defined by preceding an ordinary string literal with a u or U, such as in u"hello". In Unicode, each character is internally represented by a 16-bit integer value. For the purposes of notation, this value is written as U+XXXX, where XXXX is a four-digit hexadecimal number. (Note that this notation is only a convention used to describe Unicode characters and is not Python syntax.) For example, U+0068 is the Unicode character for the letter *h* in the Latin-1 character set. When Unicode string literals are defined, standard characters and escape codes are directly mapped as Unicode ordinals in the range [U+0000, U+00FF]. For example, the string "hello\n" is mapped to the sequence of ASCII values 0x68, 0x65, 0x6c, 0x6c, 0x6f, 0x0a, whereas the Unicode string u"hello\n" is mapped to the sequence U+0068, U+0065, U+006C, U+006C, U+006F, U+000A. Arbitrary Unicode characters are defined using the \uXXXX escape sequence. This sequence can only appear inside a Unicode string literal and must always specify a four-digit hexadecimal value. For example:

```
s = u"\u0068\u0065\u006c\u006c\u006f\u000a"
```

In older versions of Python, the \xXXXX escape sequence could be used to define Unicode characters. Although this is still allowed, the \uXXXX sequence should be used instead. In addition, the \ooo octal escape sequence can be used to define Unicode characters in the range [U+0000, U+01FF]. If you know the standard Unicode name for a character (consult http://www.unicode.org/charts for reference), it can be included using the special \N{character name} escape sequence. For example:

```
s = u"M\N{LATIN SMALL LETTER U WITH DIAERESIS}ller"
```

Unicode string literals should not be defined using a sequence of raw bytes that correspond to a multibyte Unicode data encoding such as UTF-8 or UTF-16. For example, writing a raw UTF-8 encoded string such as u'M\303\274ller' produces the seven-character Unicode sequence U+004D, U+00C3, U+00BC, U+006C, U+006C, U+0065, U+0072, which is probably not what you want. This is because in UTF-8, the multibyte sequence \303\274 is supposed to represent the single character U+00FC, not the two characters U+00C3 and U+00BC. However, Python programs can specify a source code encoding that allows UTF-8, UTF-16, and other encoded strings to appear directly in the source code. This is described in the "Source Code Encoding" section at the end of this chapter. For more details about Unicode encodings, see Chapter 3, "Types and Objects" Chapter 4, "Operators and Expressions," and Chapter 9, "Input and Output."

Optionally, you can precede a string with an r or R, such as in r'\n\"'. These strings are known as *raw strings* because all their backslash characters are left intact—that is, the string literally contains the enclosed text, including the backslashes. Raw strings cannot end in a single backslash, such as r"\". When raw Unicode strings are defined, \u*XXXX* escape sequences are still interpreted as Unicode characters, provided that the number of preceding \ characters is odd. For instance, ur"\u1234" defines a raw Unicode string with the character U+1234, whereas ur"\\u1234" defines a seven-character Unicode string in which the first two characters are slashes and the remaining five characters are the literal "u1234". Also, when defining raw Unicode string literals the "r" must appear after the "u" as shown.

Adjacent strings (separated by whitespace or a newline) such as "hello" 'world' are concatenated to form a single string: "helloworld". String concatenation works with any mix of ordinary, raw, and Unicode strings. However, whenever one of the strings is Unicode, the final result is always coerced to Unicode. Therefore, "hello" u"world" is the same as u"hello" + u"world". In addition, due to subtle implementation aspects of Unicode, writing "s1" u"s2" may produce a result that's different from writing u"s1s2". The details of this coercion process are described further in Chapter 4.

If Python is run with the -U command-line option, all string literals are interpreted as Unicode.

Values enclosed in square brackets [...], parentheses (...), and braces {...} denote lists, tuples, and dictionaries, respectively, as in the following example:

```
a = [ 1, 3.4, 'hello' ]      # A list
b = ( 10, 20, 30 )           # A tuple
c = { 'a': 3, 'b':42 }       # A dictionary
```

Operators, Delimiters, and Special Symbols

The following operators are recognized:

```
+      -      *      **     /      //     %      <<     >>     &      |
^      ~      <      >      <=     >=     ==     !=     <>     +=
-=     *=     /=     //=    %=     **=    &=     |=     ^=     >>=    <<=
```

The following tokens serve as delimiters for expressions, lists, dictionaries, and various parts of a statement:

```
(      )      [      ]      {      }      ,      :      .      `      =      ;
```

For example, the equal (=) character serves as a delimiter between the name and value of an assignment, whereas the comma (,) character is used to delimit arguments to a function, elements in lists and tuples, and so on. The period (.) is also used in floating-point numbers and in the ellipsis (...) used in extended slicing operations.

Finally, the following special symbols are also used:

```
'      "      #      \      @
```

The characters $ and ? have no meaning in Python and cannot appear in a program except inside a quoted string literal.

Documentation Strings

If the first statement of a module, class, or function definition is a string, that string becomes a documentation string for the associated object, as in the following example:

```
def fact(n):
    "This function computes a factorial"
    if (n <= 1): return 1
    else: return n*fact(n-1)
```

Code-browsing and documentation-generation tools sometimes use documentation strings. The strings are accessible in the __doc__ attribute of an object, as shown here:

```
>>> print fact.__doc__
This function computes a factorial
>>>
```

The indentation of the documentation string must be consistent with all the other statements in a definition.

Decorators

Any function or method may be preceded by a special symbol known as a decorator, the purpose of which is to modify the behavior of the definition that follows. Decorators are denoted with the @ symbol and must be placed on a separate line immediately before the corresponding function or method. For example:

```
class Foo(object):
    @staticmethod
    def bar():
        pass
```

More than one decorator can be used, but each one must be on a separate line. For example:

```
@foo
@bar
def spam():
    pass
```

More information about decorators can be found in Chapter 6, "Functions and Functional Programming," and Chapter 7, "Classes and Object-Oriented Programming."

Source Code Encoding

Python source programs are normally written in standard 7-bit ASCII. However, users working in Unicode environments may find this awkward—especially if they must write a lot of string literals.

It is possible to write Python source code in a different encoding by including a special comment in the first or second line of a Python program:

```
#!/usr/bin/env python
# -*- coding: UTF-8 -*-

name = u'M\303\274ller'  # String in quotes is directly encoded in UTF-8.
```

When the special coding: comment is supplied, Unicode string literals may be specified directly in the specified encoding (using a Unicode-aware editor program for
instance). However, other elements of Python, including identifier names and reserved
words, are still restricted to ASCII characters.

3

Types and Objects

ALL THE DATA STORED IN A PYTHON program is built around the concept of an *object*. Objects include fundamental data types such as numbers, strings, lists, and dictionaries. It's also possible to create user-defined objects in the form of classes or extension types. This chapter describes the Python object model and provides an overview of the built-in data types. Chapter 4, "Operators and Expressions," further describes operators and expressions.

Terminology

Every piece of data stored in a program is an object. Each object has an identity, a type, and a value.

For example, when you write a = 42, an integer object is created with the value of 42. You can view the *identity* of an object as a pointer to its location in memory. a is a name that refers to this specific location.

The *type* of an object (which is itself a special kind of object) describes the internal representation of the object as well as the methods and operations that it supports. When an object of a particular type is created, that object is sometimes called an *instance* of that type. After an object is created, its identity and type cannot be changed. If an object's value can be modified, the object is said to be *mutable*. If the value cannot be modified, the object is said to be *immutable*. An object that contains references to other objects is said to be a *container* or *collection*.

In addition to holding a value, many objects define a number of data attributes and methods. An *attribute* is a property or value associated with an object. A *method* is a function that performs some sort of operation on an object when the method is invoked. Attributes and methods are accessed using the dot (.) operator, as shown in the following example:

```
a = 3 + 4j        # Create a complex number
r = a.real        # Get the real part (an attribute)

b = [1, 2, 3]     # Create a list
b.append(7)       # Add a new element using the append method
```

Object Identity and Type

The built-in function id() returns the identity of an object as an integer. This integer usually corresponds to the object's location in memory, although this is specific to the

Python implementation and the platform being used. The is operator compares the identity of two objects. The built-in function type() returns the type of an object. For example:

```
# Compare two objects
def compare(a,b):
    print 'The identity of a is ', id(a)
    print 'The identity of b is ', id(b)
    if a is b:
        print 'a and b are the same object'
    if a == b:
        print 'a and b have the same value'
    if type(a) is type(b):
        print 'a and b have the same type'
```

The type of an object is itself an object. This type object is uniquely defined and is always the same for all instances of a given type. Therefore, the type can be compared using the is operator. All type objects are assigned names that can be used to perform type checking. Most of these names are built-ins, such as list, dict, and file. For example:

```
if type(s) is list:
    print 'Is a list'

if type(f) is file:
    print 'Is a file'
```

However, some type names are only available in the types module. For example:

```
import types
if type(s) is types.NoneType:
    print "is None"
```

Because types can be specialized by defining classes, a better way to check types is to use the built-in isinstance(*object*, *type*) function. For example:

```
if isinstance(s,list):
    print 'Is a list'

if isinstance(f,file):
    print 'Is a file'

if isinstance(n,types.NoneType):
    print "is None"
```

The isinstance() function also works with user-defined classes. Therefore, it is a generic, and preferred, way to check the type of any Python object.

Reference Counting and Garbage Collection

All objects are reference-counted. An object's reference count is increased whenever it's assigned to a new name or placed in a container such as a list, tuple, or dictionary, as shown here:

```
a = 3.4        # Creates an object '3.4'
b = a          # Increases reference count on '3.4'
c = []
c.append(b)    # Increases reference count on '3.4'
```

This example creates a single object containing the value 3.4. a is merely a name that refers to the newly created object. When b is assigned a, b becomes a new name for the same object, and the object's reference count increases. Likewise, when you place b into a list, the object's reference count increases again. Throughout the example, only one object contains 3.4. All other operations are simply creating new references to the object.

An object's reference count is decreased by the del statement or whenever a reference goes out of scope (or is reassigned). For example:

```
del a        # Decrease reference count of 3.4
b = 7.8      # Decrease reference count of 3.4
c[0]=2.0     # Decrease reference count of 3.4
```

When an object's reference count reaches zero, it is garbage-collected. However, in some cases a circular dependency may exist among a collection of objects that are no longer in use. For example:

```
a = { }
b = { }
a['b'] = b       # a contains reference to b
b['a'] = a       # b contains reference to a
del a
del b
```

In this example, the del statements decrease the reference count of a and b and destroy the names used to refer to the underlying objects. However, because each object contains a reference to the other, the reference count doesn't drop to zero and the objects remain allocated (resulting in a memory leak). To address this problem, the interpreter periodically executes a cycle-detector that searches for cycles of inaccessible objects and deletes them. The cycle-detection algorithm can be fine-tuned and controlled using functions in the gc module.

References and Copies

When a program makes an assignment such as a = b, a new reference to b is created. For immutable objects such as numbers and strings, this assignment effectively creates a copy of b. However, the behavior is quite different for mutable objects such as lists and dictionaries. For example:

```
b = [1,2,3,4]
a = b            # a is a reference to b
a[2] = -100      # Change an element in 'a'
print b          # Produces '[1, 2, -100, 4]'
```

Because a and b refer to the same object in this example, a change made to one of the variables is reflected in the other. To avoid this, you have to create a copy of an object rather than a new reference.

Two types of copy operations are applied to container objects such as lists and dictionaries: a shallow copy and a deep copy. A *shallow copy* creates a new object, but populates it with references to the items contained in the original object. For example:

```
b = [ 1, 2, [3,4] ]
a = b[:]         # Create a shallow copy of b.
a.append(100)    # Append element to a.
print b          # Produces '[1,2, [3,4]]'. b unchanged.
a[2][0] = -100   # Modify an element of a.
print b          # Produces '[1,2, [-100,4]]'.
```

In this case, a and b are separate list objects, but the elements they contain are shared. Therefore, a modification to one of the elements of a also modifies an element of b, as shown.

A *deep copy* creates a new object and recursively copies all the objects it contains. There is no built-in function to create deep copies of objects. However, the copy.deepcopy() function in the standard library can be used, as shown in the following example:

```
import copy
b = [1, 2, [3, 4] ]
a = copy.deepcopy(b)

a[2] = -100

print a     # produces [1,2, -100, 4]

print b     # produces [1,2,3,4]
```

Built-in Types

Approximately two dozen types are built into the Python interpreter and grouped into a few major categories, as shown in Table 3.1. The Type Name column in the table lists the name that can be used to check for that type using isinstance() and other type-related functions. Types include familiar objects such as numbers and sequences. Others are used during program execution and are of little practical use to most programmers. The next few sections describe the most commonly used built-in types.

Table 3.1   **Built-in Python Types**

Type Category	Type Name	Description
None	types.NoneType	The null object None
Numbers	int	Integer
	long	Arbitrary-precision integer
	float	Floating point
	complex	Complex number
	bool	Boolean (True or False)
Sequences	str	Character string
	unicode	Unicode character string
	basestring	Abstract base type for all strings
	list	List
	tuple	Tuple
	xrange	Returned by xrange()
Mapping	dict	Dictionary
Sets	set	Mutable set
	frozenset	Immutable set

Table 3.1 **Continued**

Type Category	Type Name	Description
Callable	`types.BuiltinFunctionType`	Built-in functions
	`types.BuiltinMethodType`	Built-in methods
	`type`	Type of built-in types and classes
	`object`	Ancestor of all types and classes
	`types.FunctionType`	User-defined function
	`types.InstanceType`	Class object instance
	`types.MethodType`	Bound class method
	`types.UnboundMethodType`	Unbound class method
Modules	`types.ModuleType`	Module
Classes	`object`	Ancestor of all types and classes
Types	`type`	Type of built-in types and classes
Files	`file`	File
Internal	`types.CodeType`	Byte-compiled code
	`types.FrameType`	Execution frame
	`types.GeneratorType`	Generator object
	`types.TracebackType`	Stacks traceback of an exception
	`types.SliceType`	Generated by extended slices
	`types.EllipsisType`	Used in extended slices
Classic Classes	`types.ClassType`	Old-style class definition
	`types.InstanceType`	Old-style class instance

Note that `object` and `type` appear twice in Table 3.1 because classes and types are both callable. The types listed for "Classic Classes" refer to an obsolete, but still supported object-oriented interface. More details about this can be found later in this chapter and in Chapter 7, "Classes and Object-Oriented Programming."

The None Type

The `None` type denotes a null object (an object with no value). Python provides exactly one null object, which is written as `None` in a program. This object is returned by functions that don't explicitly return a value. None is frequently used as the default value of optional arguments, so that the function can detect whether the caller has actually passed a value for that argument. `None` has no attributes and evaluates to `False` in Boolean expressions.

Numeric Types

Python uses five numeric types: Booleans, integers, long integers, floating-point numbers, and complex numbers. Except for Booleans, all numeric objects are signed. All numeric types are immutable.

Booleans are represented by two values: True and False. The names True and False are respectively mapped to the numerical values of 1 and 0.

Integers represent whole numbers in the range of -2147483648 to 2147483647 (the range may be larger on some machines). Internally, integers are stored as 2's complement binary values, in 32 or more bits. Long integers represent whole numbers of unlimited range (limited only by available memory). Although there are two integer types, Python tries to make the distinction seamless. Most functions and operators that expect integers work with any integer type. Moreover, if the result of a numerical operation exceeds the allowed range of integer values, the result is transparently promoted to a long integer (although in certain cases, an OverflowError exception may be raised instead).

Floating-point numbers are represented using the native double-precision (64-bit) representation of floating-point numbers on the machine. Normally this is IEEE 754, which provides approximately 17 digits of precision and an exponent in the range of -308 to 308. This is the same as the double type in C. Python doesn't support 32-bit single-precision floating-point numbers. If space and precision are an issue in your program, consider using Numerical Python (http://numpy.sourceforge.net).

Complex numbers are represented as a pair of floating-point numbers. The real and imaginary parts of a complex number z are available in z.real and z.imag.

Sequence Types

Sequences represent ordered sets of objects indexed by nonnegative integers and include strings, Unicode strings, lists, and tuples. Strings are sequences of characters, and lists and tuples are sequences of arbitrary Python objects. Strings and tuples are immutable; lists allow insertion, deletion, and substitution of elements. All sequences support iteration.

Table 3.2 shows the operators and methods that you can apply to all sequence types. Element i of sequence s is selected using the indexing operator s[i], and subsequences are selected using the slicing operator s[i:j] or extended slicing operator s[i:j:stride] (these operations are described in Chapter 4). The length of any sequence is returned using the built-in len(s) function. You can find the minimum and maximum values of a sequence by using the built-in min(s) and max(s) functions. However, these functions only work for sequences in which the elements can be ordered (typically numbers and strings).

Table 3.3 shows the additional operators that can be applied to mutable sequences such as lists.

Table 3.2   **Operations and Methods Applicable to All Sequences**

Item	Description
s[i]	Returns element i of a sequence
s[i:j]	Returns a slice
s[i:j:stride]	Returns an extended slice
len(s)	Number of elements in s

Table 3.2 **Continued**

Item	Description
min(s)	Minimum value in s
max(s)	Maximum value in s

Table 3.3 **Operations Applicable to Mutable Sequences**

Item	Description
s[i] = v	Item assignment
s[i:j] = t	Slice assignment
s[i:j:stride] = t	Extended slice assignment
del s[i]	Item deletion
del s[i:j]	Slice deletion
del s[i:j:stride]	Extended slice deletion

Additionally, lists support the methods shown in Table 3.4. The built-in function list(s) converts any iterable type to a list. If s is already a list, this function constructs a new list that's a shallow copy of s. The s.append(x) method appends a new element, x, to the end of the list. The s.index(x) method searches the list for the first occurrence of x. If no such element is found, a ValueError exception is raised. Similarly, the s.remove(x) method removes the first occurrence of x from the list. The s.extend(t) method extends the list s by appending the elements in sequence t. The s.sort() method sorts the elements of a list and optionally accepts a comparison function, key function, and reverse flag. The comparison function should take two arguments and return negative, zero, or positive, depending on whether the first argument is smaller, equal to, or larger than the second argument, respectively. The key function is a function that is applied to each element prior to comparison during sorting. Specifying a key function is useful if you want to perform special kinds of sorting operations, such as sorting a list of strings, but with case insensitivity. The s.reverse() method reverses the order of the items in the list. Both the sort() and reverse() methods operate on the list elements in place and return None.

Table 3.4 **List Methods**

Method	Description
list(s)	Converts s to a list.
s.append(x)	Appends a new element, x, to the end of s.
s.extend(t)	Appends a new list, t, to the end of s.
s.count(x)	Counts occurrences of x in s.
s.index(x [,start [,stop]])	Returns the smallest i where s[i] ==x. start and stop optionally specify the starting and ending index for the search.
s.insert(i,x)	Inserts x at index i.

Table 3.4 **Continued**

Method	Description
`s.pop([i])`	Returns the element i and removes it from the list. If i is omitted, the last element is returned.
`s.remove(x)`	Searches for x and removes it from s.
`s.reverse()`	Reverses items of s in place.
`s.sort([cmpfunc` `[, keyf [, reverse]]])`	Sorts items of s in place. `cmpfunc` is a comparison function. `keyf` is a key function. `reverse` is a flag that sorts the list in reverse order.

Python provides two string object types. Standard strings are sequences of bytes containing 8-bit data. They may contain binary data and embedded NULL bytes. Unicode strings are sequences of 16-bit characters encoded in a format known as UCS-2. This allows for 65,536 unique character values. Although the latest Unicode standard supports up to 1 million unique character values, these extra characters are not supported by Python by default. Instead, they must be encoded as a special two-character (4-byte) sequence known as a *surrogate pair*—the interpretation of which is up to the application. Python does not check data for Unicode compliance or the proper use of surrogates. As an optional feature, Python may be built to store Unicode strings using 32-bit integers (UCS-4). When enabled, this allows Python to represent the entire range of Unicode values from U+000000 to U+110000. All Unicode-related functions are adjusted accordingly.

Both standard and Unicode strings support the methods shown in Table 3.5. Although these methods operate on string instances, none of these methods actually modifies the underlying string data. Thus, methods such as `s.capitalize()`, `s.center()`, and `s.expandtabs()` always return a new string as opposed to modifying the string s. Character tests such as `s.isalnum()` and `s.isupper()` return `True` or `False` if all the characters in the string s satisfy the test. Furthermore, these tests always return `False` if the length of the string is zero. The `s.find()`, `s.index()`, `s.rfind()`, and `s.rindex()` methods are used to search s for a substring. All these functions return an integer index to the substring in s. In addition, the `find()` method returns `-1` if the substring isn't found, whereas the `index()` method raises a `ValueError` exception. Many of the string methods accept optional `start` and `end` parameters, which are integer values specifying the starting and ending indices in s. In most cases, these values may given negative values, in which case the index is taken from the end of the string. The `s.translate()` method is used to perform character substitutions. The `s.encode()` and `s.decode()` methods are used to transform the string data to and from a specified character encoding. As input it accepts an encoding name such as `'ascii'`, `'utf-8'`, or `'utf-16'`. This method is most commonly used to convert Unicode strings into a data encoding suitable for I/O operations and is described further in Chapter 9, "Input and Output." More details about string methods can be found in the documentation for the `string` module.

Table 3.5   **String Methods**

Method	Description
s.capitalize()	Capitalizes the first character.
s.center(width [, pad])	Centers the string in a field of length width. pad is a padding character.
s.count(sub [,start [,end]])	Counts occurrences of the specified substring sub.
s.decode([encoding [,errors]])	Decodes a string and returns a Unicode string.
s.encode([encoding [,errors]])	Returns an encoded version of the string.
s.endswith(suffix [,start [,end]])	Checks the end of the string for a suffix.
s.expandtabs([tabsize])	Replaces tabs with spaces.
s.find(sub [, start [,end]])	Finds the first occurrence of the specified substring sub.
s.index(sub [, start [,end]])	Finds the first occurrence or error in the specified substring sub.
s.isalnum()	Checks whether all characters are alphanumeric.
s.isalpha()	Checks whether all characters are alphabetic.
s.isdigit()	Checks whether all characters are digits.
s.islower()	Checks whether all characters are lowercase.
s.isspace()	Checks whether all characters are whitespace.
s.istitle()	Checks whether the string is a title-cased string (first letter of each word capitalized).
s.isupper()	Checks whether all characters are uppercase.
s.join(t)	Joins the strings s and t.
s.ljust(width [, fill])	Left-aligns s in a string of size width.
s.lower()	Converts to lowercase.
s.lstrip([chrs])	Removes leading whitespace or characters supplied in chrs.
s.replace(old, new [,maxreplace])	Replaces the substring.
s.rfind(sub [,start [,end]])	Finds the last occurrence of a substring.
s.rindex(sub [,start [,end]])	Finds the last occurrence or raises an error.
s.rjust(width [, fill])	Right-aligns s in a string of length width.
s.rsplit([sep [,maxsplit]])	Splits a string from the end of the string using sep as a delimiter. maxsplit is the maximum number of splits to perform. If maxsplit is omitted, the result is identical to the split() method.
s.rstrip([chrs])	Removes trailing whitespace or characters supplied in chrs.

Table 3.5   **Continued**

Method	Description
`s.split([sep [,maxsplit]])`	Splits a string using *sep* as a delimiter. *maxsplit* is the maximum number of splits to perform.
`s.splitlines([keepends])`	Splits a string into a list of lines. If *keepends* is 1, trailing newlines are preserved.
`s.startswith(prefix [,start [,end]])`	Checks whether a string starts with *prefix*.
`s.strip([chrs])`	Removes leading and trailing whitespace or characters supplied in *chrs*.
`s.swapcase()`	Converts uppercase to lowercase, and vice versa.
`s.title()`	Returns a title-cased version of the string.
`s.translate(table [,deletechars])`	Translates a string using a character translation table *table*, removing characters in *deletechars*.
`s.upper()`	Converts a string to uppercase.
`s.zfill(width)`	Pads a string with zeros on the left up to the specified *width*.

Because there are two different string types, Python provides an abstract type, `basestring`, that can be used to test if an object is any kind of string. Here's an example:

```
if isinstance(s,basestring):
    print "is some kind of string"
```

The built-in function `range([i,]j [,stride])` constructs a list and populates it with integers *k* such that $i <= k < j$. The first index, *i*, and the *stride* are optional and have default values of 0 and 1, respectively. The built-in `xrange([i,] j [,stride])` function performs a similar operation, but returns an immutable sequence of type `xrange`. Rather than storing all the values in a list, this sequence calculates its values whenever it's accessed. Consequently, it's much more memory-efficient when working with large sequences of integers. However, the `xrange` type is much more limited than its list counterpart. For example, none of the standard slicing operations are supported. This limits the utility of `xrange` to only a few applications such as iterating in simple loops. The `xrange` type provides a single method, `s.tolist()`, that converts its values to a list.

Mapping Types

A *mapping object* represents an arbitrary collection of objects that are indexed by another collection of nearly arbitrary key values. Unlike a sequence, a mapping object is unordered and can be indexed by numbers, strings, and other objects. Mappings are mutable.

Dictionaries are the only built-in mapping type and are Python's version of a hash table or associative array. You can use any immutable object as a dictionary key value (strings, numbers, tuples, and so on). Lists, dictionaries, and tuples containing mutable objects cannot be used as keys (the dictionary type requires key values to remain constant).

To select an item in a mapping object, use the key index operator $m[k]$, where k is a key value. If the key is not found, a KeyError exception is raised. The len(m) function returns the number of items contained in a mapping object. Table 3.6 lists the methods and operations.

Table 3.6   **Methods and Operations for Dictionaries**

Item	Description
len(*m*)	Returns the number of items in *m*.
m[*k*]	Returns the item of *m* with key *k*.
m[*k*]=*x*	Sets *m*[*k*] to *x*.
del *m*[*k*]	Removes *m*[*k*] from *m*.
m.clear()	Removes all items from *m*.
m.copy()	Makes a shallow copy of *m*.
m.has_key(*k*)	Returns True if *m* has key *k*; otherwise, returns False.
m.items()	Returns a list of (*key*, *value*) pairs.
m.iteritems()	Returns an iterator that produces (*key*, *value*) pairs.
m.iterkeys()	Returns an iterator that produces dictionary keys.
m.itervalues()	Returns an iterator that produces dictionary values.
m.keys()	Returns a list of key values.
m.update(*b*)	Adds all objects from *b* to *m*.
m.values()	Returns a list of all values in *m*.
m.get(*k* [,*v*])	Returns *m*[*k*] if found; otherwise, returns *v*.
m.setdefault(*k* [, *v*])	Returns *m*[*k*] if found; otherwise, returns *v* and sets *m*[*k*] = *v*.
m.pop(*k* [,*default*])	Returns *m*[*k*] if found and removes it from *m*; otherwise, returns *default* if supplied or raises KeyError if not.
m.popitem()	Removes a random (*key*, *value*) pair from *m* and returns it as a tuple.

The *m*.clear() method removes all items. The *m*.copy() method makes a shallow copy of the items contained in a mapping object and places them in a new mapping object. The *m*.items() method returns a list containing (*key*, *value*) pairs. The *m*.keys() method returns a list with all the key values, and the *m*.values() method returns a list with all the objects. The *m*.update(*b*) method updates the current mapping object by inserting all the (*key*, *value*) pairs found in the mapping object *b*. The *m*.get(*k* [,*v*]) method retrieves an object, but allows for an optional default value, *v*, that's returned if no such object exists. The *m*.setdefault(*k* [,*v*]) method is similar to *m*.get(), except that in addition to returning *v* if no object exists, it sets *m*[*k*] = *v*. If *v* is omitted, it defaults to None. The *m*.pop() method returns an item from a dictionary and removes it at the same time. The *m*.popitem() method is used to iteratively destroy the contents of a dictionary. The *m*.iteritems(), *m*.iterkeys(), and *m*.itervalues() methods return iterators that allow looping over all the dictionary items, keys, or values, respectively.

Set Types

A *set* is an unordered collection of unique items. Unlike sequences, sets provide no indexing or slicing operations. They are also unlike dictionaries in that there are no key values associated with the objects. In addition, the items placed into a set must be immutable. Two different set types are available: set is a mutable set, and frozenset is an immutable set. Both kinds of sets are created using a pair of built-in functions:

```
s = set([1,5,10,15])
f = frozenset(['a',37,'hello'])
```

Both set() and frozenset() populate the set by iterating over the supplied argument. Both kinds of sets provide the methods outlined in Table 3.7

Table 3.7   **Methods and Operations for Set Types**

Item	Description
len(*s*)	Return number of items in *s*.
s.copy()	Makes a shallow copy of *s*.
s.difference(*t*)	Set difference. Returns all the items in *s*, but not in *t*.
s.intersection(*t*)	Intersection. Returns all the items that are both in *s* and in *t*.
s.issubbset(*t*)	Returns True if *s* is a subset of *t*.
s.issuperset(*t*)	Returns True if *s* is a superset of *t*.
s.symmetric_difference(*t*)	Symmetric difference. Returns all the items that are in *s* or *t*, but not in both sets.
s.union(*t*)	Union. Returns all items in *s* or *t*.

The *s*.difference(*t*), *s*.intersection(*t*), *s*.symmetric_difference(*t*), and *s*.union(*t*) methods provide the standard mathematical operations on sets. The returned value has the same type as *s* (set or frozenset). The parameter *t* can be any Python object that supports iteration. This includes sets, lists, tuples, and strings. These set operations are also available as mathematical operators, as described further in Chapter 4.

Mutable sets (set) additionally provide the methods outlined in Table 3.8.

Table 3.8   **Methods for Mutable Set Types**

Item	Description
s.add(*item*)	Adds *item* to *s*. Has no effect if *item* is already in *s*.
s.clear()	Removes all items from *s*.
s.difference_update(*t*)	Removes all the items from *s* that are also in *t*.
s.discard(*item*)	Removes *item* from *s*. If *item* is not a member of *s*, nothing happens.

Table 3.8   **Continued**

Item	Description
`s.intersection_update(t)`	Computes the intersection of *s* and *t* and leaves the result in *s*.
`s.pop()`	Returns an arbitrary set element and removes it from *s*.
`s.remove(item)`	Removes *item* from *s*. If *item* is not a member, `KeyError` is raised.
`s.symmetric_difference_update(t)`	Computes the symmetric difference of *s* and *t* and leaves the result in *s*.
`s.update(t)`	Adds all the items in *t* to *s*. *t* may be another set, a sequence, or any object that supports iteration.

All these operations modify the set *s* in place. The parameter *t* can be any object that supports iteration.

Callable Types

Callable types represent objects that support the function call operation. There are several flavors of objects with this property, including user-defined functions, built-in functions, instance methods, and classes.

User-defined functions are callable objects created at the module level by using the `def` statement, at the class level by defining a static method, or with the `lambda` operator. Here's an example:

```
def foo(x,y):
    return x+y

class A(object):
    @staticmethod
    def foo(x,y):
        return x+y

bar = lambda x,y: x + y
```

A user-defined function *f* has the following attributes:

Attribute(s)	Description
`f.__doc__` or `f.func_doc`	Documentation string
`f.__name__` or `f.func_name`	Function name
`f.__dict__` or `f.func_dict`	Dictionary containing function attributes
`f.func_code`	Byte-compiled code
`f.func_defaults`	Tuple containing the default arguments
`f.func_globals`	Dictionary defining the global namespace
`f.func_closure`	Tuple containing data related to nested scopes

Methods are functions that operate only on instances of an object. Two types of methods—instance methods and class methods—are defined inside a class definition, as shown here:

```
class Foo(object):
        def __init__(self):
          self.items = [ ]
        def update(self, x):
          self.items.append(x)
        @classmethod
        def whatami(cls):
          return cls
```

An instance method is a method that operates on an instance of an object. The instance is passed to the method as the first argument, which is called `self` by convention. Here's an example:

```
f = Foo()
f.update(2)       # update() method is applied to the object f
```

A class method operates on the class itself. The class object is passed to a class method in the first argument, `cls`. Here's an example:

```
Foo.whatami()   # Operates on the class Foo
f.whatami()     # Operates on the class of f (Foo)
```

A bound method object is a method that is associated with a specific object instance. Here's an example:

```
a = f.update       # a is a method bound to f
b = Foo.whatami    # b is method bound to Foo (classmethod)
```

In this example, the objects a and b can be called just like a function. When invoked, they will automatically apply to the underlying object to which they were bound. Here's an example:

```
a(4)        # Calls f.update(4)
b()         # Calls Foo.whatami()
```

Bound and unbound methods are no more than a thin wrapper around an ordinary function object. The following attributes are defined for method objects:

Attribute	Description
m.__doc__	Documentation string
m.__name__	Method name
m.im_class	Class in which this method was defined
m.im_func	Function object implementing the method
m.im_self	Instance associated with the method (None if unbound)

So far, this discussion has focused on functions and methods, but class objects (described shortly) are also callable. When a class is called, a new class instance is created. In addition, if the class defines an __init__() method, it's called to initialize the newly created instance.

An object instance is also callable if it defines a special method, __call__(). If this method is defined for an instance, *x*, then *x*(*args*) invokes the method *x*.__call__(*args*).

The final types of callable objects are built-in functions and methods, which correspond to code written in extension modules and are usually written in C or C++. The following attributes are available for built-in methods:

Attribute	Description
b.__doc__	Documentation string
b.__name__	Function/method name
b.__self__	Instance associated with the method

For built-in functions such as len(), __self__ is set to None, indicating that the function isn't bound to any specific object. For built-in methods such as x.append(), where x is a list object, __self__ is set to x.

Finally, it is important to note that all functions and methods are first-class objects in Python. That is, function and method objects can be freely used like any other type. For example, they can be passed as arguments, placed in lists and dictionaries, and so forth.

Classes and Types

When you define a class, the class definition normally produces an object of type type. Here's an example:

```
>>> class Foo(object):
...     pass
...
>>> type(Foo)
<type 'type'>
```

When an object instance is created, the type of the instance is the class that defined it. Here's an example:

```
>>> f = Foo()
>>> type(f)
<class '__main__.Foo'>
```

More details about the object-oriented interface can be found in Chapter 7. However, there are a few attributes of types and instances that may be useful. If t is a type or class, then the attribute t.__name__ contains the name of the type. The attributes t.__bases__ contains a tuple of base classes. If o is an object instance, the attribute o.__class__ contains a reference to its corresponding class and the attribute o.__dict__ is a dictionary used to hold the object's attributes.

Modules

The *module* type is a container that holds objects loaded with the import statement. When the statement import foo appears in a program, for example, the name foo is assigned to the corresponding module object. Modules define a namespace that's implemented using a dictionary accessible in the attribute __dict__. Whenever an attribute of a module is referenced (using the dot operator), it's translated into a dictionary lookup. For example, m.x is equivalent to m.__dict__["x"]. Likewise, assignment to an attribute such as m.x = y is equivalent to m.__dict__["x"] = y. The following attributes are available:

Attribute	Description
m.__dict__	Dictionary associated with the module
m.__doc__	Module documentation string
m.__name__	Name of the module
m.__file__	File from which the module was loaded
m.__path__	Fully qualified package name, defined when the module object refers to a package

Files

The file object represents an open file and is returned by the built-in open() function (as well as a number of functions in the standard library). The methods on this type include common I/O operations such as read() and write(). However, because I/O is covered in detail in Chapter 9, readers should consult that chapter for more details.

Internal Types

A number of objects used by the interpreter are exposed to the user. These include traceback objects, code objects, frame objects, generator objects, slice objects, and the Ellipsis object. It is rarely necessary to manipulate these objects directly. However, their attributes are provided in the following sections for completeness.

Code Objects

Code objects represent raw byte-compiled executable code, or bytecode, and are typically returned by the built-in compile() function. Code objects are similar to functions except that they don't contain any context related to the namespace in which the code was defined, nor do code objects store information about default argument values. A code object, c, has the following read-only attributes:

Attribute	Description
c.co_name	Function name.
c.co_argcount	Number of positional arguments (including default values).
c.co_nlocals	Number of local variables used by the function.
c.co_varnames	Tuple containing names of local variables.
c.co_cellvars	Tuple containing names of variables referenced by nested functions.
c.co_freevars	Tuple containing names of free variables used by nested functions.
c.co_code	String representing raw bytecode.
c.co_consts	Tuple containing the literals used by the bytecode.
c.co_names	Tuple containing names used by the bytecode.
c.co_filename	Name of the file in which the code was compiled.
c.co_firstlineno	First line number of the function.
c.co_lnotab	String encoding bytecode offsets to line numbers.

Attribute	Description
`c.co_stacksize`	Required stack size (including local variables).
`c.co_flags`	Integer containing interpreter flags. Bit 2 is set if the function uses a variable number of positional arguments using `"*args"`. Bit 3 is set if the function allows arbitrary keyword arguments using `"**kwargs"`. All other bits are reserved.

Frame Objects

Frame objects are used to represent execution frames and most frequently occur in traceback objects (described next). A frame object, `f`, has the following read-only attributes:

Attribute	Description
`f.f_back`	Previous stack frame (toward the caller).
`f.f_code`	Code object being executed.
`f.f_locals`	Dictionary used for local variables.
`f.f_globals`	Dictionary used for global variables.
`f.f_builtins`	Dictionary used for built-in names.
`f.f_restricted`	Set to 1 if executing in restricted execution mode.
`f.f_lineno`	Line number.
`f.f_lasti`	Current instruction. This is an index into the bytecode string of f_code.

The following attributes can be modified (and are used by debuggers and other tools):

Attribute	Description
`f.f_trace`	Function called at the start of each source code line
`f.f_exc_type`	Most recent exception type
`f.f_exc_value`	Most recent exception value
`f.f_exc_traceback`	Most recent exception traceback

Traceback Objects

Traceback objects are created when an exception occurs and contains stack trace information. When an exception handler is entered, the stack trace can be retrieved using the `sys.exc_info()` function. The following read-only attributes are available in traceback objects:

Attribute	Description
`t.tb_next`	Next level in the stack trace (toward the execution frame where the exception occurred)
`t.tb_frame`	Execution frame object of the current level
`t.tb_line`	Line number where the exception occurred
`t.tb_lasti`	Instruction being executed in the current level

Generator Objects

Generator objects are created when a generator function is invoked (see Chapter 6, "Functions and Functional Programming"). A generator function is defined whenever a function makes use of the special `yield` keyword. The generator object serves as both an iterator and a container for information about the generator function itself. The following attributes and methods are available:

Attribute	Description
`g.gi_frame`	Execution frame of the generator function.
`g.gi_running`	Integer indicating whether or not the generator function is currently running.
`g.next()`	Execute the function until the next yield statement and return the value.

Slice Objects

Slice objects are used to represent slices given in extended slice syntax, such as `a[i:j:stride]`, `a[i:j, n:m]`, or `a[..., i:j]`. Slice objects are also created using the built-in `slice([i,] j [,stride])` function. The following read-only attributes are available:

Attribute	Description
`s.start`	Lower bound of the slice; None if omitted
`s.stop`	Upper bound of the slice; None if omitted
`s.step`	Stride of the slice; None if omitted

Slice objects also provide a single method, `s.indices(length)`. This function takes a length and returns a tuple `(start,stop,stride)` that indicates how the slice would be applied to a sequence of that length. For example:

```
s = slice(10,20)   #  Slice object represents [10:20]
s.indices(100)     #  Returns (10,20,1) --> [10:20]
s.indices(15)      #  Returns (10,15,1) --> [10:15]
```

Ellipsis Object

The Ellipsis object is used to indicate the presence of an ellipsis (. . .) in a slice. There is a single object of this type, accessed through the built-in name `Ellipsis`. It has no attributes and evaluates as `True`. None of Python's built-in types makes use of `Ellipsis`, but it may be used in third-party applications.

Classic Classes

In versions of Python prior to version 2.2, classes and objects were implemented using an entirely different mechanism that is now deprecated. For backward compatibility, however, these classes, called *classic classes* or *old-style classes*, are still supported.

The reason that classic classes are deprecated is due to their interaction with the Python type system. Classic classes do not define new data types, nor is it possible to specialize any of the built-in types such as lists or dictionaries. To overcome this limitation, Python 2.2 unified types and classes while introducing a different implementation of user-defined classes.

A classic class is created whenever an object *does not* inherit (directly or indirectly) from object. For example:

```
# A modern class
class Foo(object):
    pass

# A classic class.  Note: Does not inherit from object
class Bar:
    pass
```

Classic classes are implemented using a dictionary that contains all the objects defined within the class and defines a namespace. References to class attributes such as c.x are translated into a dictionary lookup, c.__dict__["x"]. If an attribute isn't found in this dictionary, the search continues in the list of base classes. This search is depth first in the order that base classes were specified in the class definition. An attribute assignment such as c.y = 5 always updates the __dict__ attribute of c, not the dictionaries of any base class.

The following attributes are defined by class objects:

Attribute	Description
c.__dict__	Dictionary associated with the class
c.__doc__	Class documentation string
c.__name__	Name of the class
c.__module__	Name of the module in which the class was defined
c.__bases__	Tuple containing base classes

A *class instance* is an object created by calling a class object. Each instance has its own local namespace that's implemented as a dictionary. This dictionary and the associated class object have the following attributes:

Attribute	Description
x.__dict__	Dictionary associated with an instance
x.__class__	Class to which an instance belongs

When the attribute of an object is referenced, such as in x.a, the interpreter first searches in the local dictionary for x.__dict__["a"]. If it doesn't find the name locally, the search continues by performing a lookup on the class defined in the __class__ attribute. If no match is found, the search continues with base classes, as described earlier. If still no match is found and the object's class defines a __getattr__() method, it's used to perform the lookup. The assignment of attributes such as x.a = 4 always updates x.__dict__, not the dictionaries of classes or base classes.

Special Methods

All the built-in data types implement a collection of special object methods. The names of special methods are always preceded and followed by double underscores (__). These methods are automatically triggered by the interpreter as a program executes. For example, the operation x + y is mapped to an internal method, x.__add__(y), and an indexing operation, x[k], is mapped to x.__getitem__(k). The behavior of each data type depends entirely on the set of special methods that it implements.

User-defined classes can define new objects that behave like the built-in types simply by supplying an appropriate subset of the special methods described in this section. In addition, built-in types such as lists and dictionaries can be specialized (via inheritance) by redefining some of the special methods.

Object Creation, Destruction, and Representation

The methods in Table 3.9 create, initialize, destroy, and represent objects. `__new__()` is a static method that is called to create an instance (although this method is rarely redefined). The `__init__()` method initializes the attributes of an object and is called immediately after an object has been newly created. The `__del__()` method is invoked when an object is about to be destroyed. This method is invoked only when an object is no longer in use. It's important to note that the statement del x only decrements an object's reference count and doesn't necessarily result in a call to this function. Further details about these methods can be found in Chapter 7.

Table 3.9 **Special Methods for Object Creation, Destruction, and Representation**

Method	Description
`__new__(cls [,*args [,**kwargs]])`	A static method called to create a new instance
`__init__(self [,*args [,**kwargs]])`	Called to initialize a new instance
`__del__(self)`	Called to destroy an instance
`__repr__(self)`	Creates a full string representation of an object
`__str__(self)`	Creates an informal string representation
`__cmp__(self,other)`	Compares two objects and returns negative, zero, or positive
`__hash__(self)`	Computes a 32-bit hash index
`__nonzero__(self)`	Returns 0 or 1 for truth-value testing
`__unicode__(self)`	Creates a Unicode string representation

The `__new__()` and `__init__()` methods are used to create and initialize new instances. When an object is created by calling A(args), it is translated into the following steps:

```
x = A.__new__(A,args)
is isinstance(x,A): x.__init__(args)
```

The `__repr__()` and `__str__()` methods create string representations of an object. The `__repr__()` method normally returns an expression string that can be evaluated to re-create the object. This method is invoked by the built-in repr() function and by the backquotes operator (`` ` ``). For example:

```
a = [2,3,4,5]      # Create a list
s = repr(a)        # s = '[2, 3, 4, 5]'
                   # Note : could have also used s = `a`
b = eval(s)        # Turns s back into a list
```

If a string expression cannot be created, the convention is for __repr__() to return a string of the form <...*message*...>, as shown here:

```
f = open("foo")
a = repr(f)        # a = "<open file 'foo', mode 'r' at dc030>"
```

The __str__() method is called by the built-in str() function and by the print statement. It differs from __repr__() in that the string it returns can be more concise and informative to the user. If this method is undefined, the __repr__() method is invoked.

The __cmp__(*self,other*) method is used by all the comparison operators. It returns a negative number if *self* < *other*, zero if *self* == *other*, and positive if *self* > *other*. If this method is undefined for an object, the object will be compared by object identity. In addition, an object may define an alternative set of comparison functions for each of the relational operators. These are known as rich comparisons and are described shortly. The __nonzero__() method is used for truth-value testing and should return 0 or 1 (or True or False). If undefined, the __len__() method is invoked to determine truth.

Finally, the __hash__() method computes an integer hash key used in dictionary operations (the hash value can also be returned using the built-in function hash()). The value returned should be identical for two objects that compare as equal. Furthermore, mutable objects should not define this method; any changes to an object will alter the hash value and make it impossible to locate an object on subsequent dictionary lookups. An object should not define a __hash__() method without also defining __cmp__().

Attribute Access

The methods in Table 3.10 read, write, and delete the attributes of an object using the dot (.) operator and the del operator, respectively.

Table 3.10   **Special Methods for Attribute Access**

Method	Description
__getattribute__(*self,name*)	Returns the attribute *self.name*.
__getattr__(*self, name*)	Returns the attribute *self.name* if not found through normal attribute lookup.
__setattr__(*self, name, value*)	Sets the attribute *self.name = value*. Overrides the default mechanism.
__delattr__(*self, name*)	Deletes the attribute *self.name*.

An example will illustrate:

```
class Foo(object):
    def __init__(self):
        self.x = 37

f = Foo()

a = f.x        # Invokes __getattribute__(f,"x")
b = f.y        # Invokes __getattribute__(f,"y") --> Not found
               # Then invokes __getattr__(f,"y")
```

```
f.x = 42        # Invokes __setattr__(f,"x",42)
f.y = 93        # Invokes __setattr__(f,"y",93)

del f.y         # Invokes __delattr__(f,"y")
```

Whenever an attribute is accessed, the `__getattribute__`() method is always invoked. If the attribute is located, it is returned. Otherwise, the `__getattr__`() method is invoked. The default behavior of `__getattr__`() is to raise an `AttributeError` exception. The `__setattr__`() method is always invoked when setting an attribute, and the `__delattr__`() method is always invoked when deleting an attribute.

A subtle aspect of attribute access concerns a special kind of attribute known as a *descriptor*. A descriptor is an object that implements one or more of the methods in Table 3.11.

Table 3.11   **Special Methods for Descriptor Attributes**

Method	Description
`__get__`(*self, instance, owner*)	Returns an attribute value or raises `AttributeError`
`__set__`(*self, instance, value*)	Sets the attribute to `value`
`__delete__`(*self, instance*)	Deletes the attribute

Essentially, a descriptor attribute knows how to compute, set, and delete its own value whenever it is accessed. Typically, it is used to provide advanced features of classes such as static methods and properties. For example:

```
class SimpleProperty(object):
    def __init__(self,fget,fset):
        self.fget = fget
        self.fset = fset
    def __get__(self,instance,cls):
        return self.fget(instance)        # Calls instance.fget()
    def __set__(self,instance,value)
        return self.fset(instance,value)  # Calls instance.fset(value)

class Circle(object):
    def __init__(self,radius):
        self.radius = radius
    def getArea(self):
        return math.pi*self.radius**2
    def setArea(self):
        self.radius = math.sqrt(area/math.pi)
    area = SimpleProperty(getArea,setArea)
```

In this example, the class `SimpleProperty` defines a descriptor in which two functions, `fget` and `fset`, are supplied by the user to get and set the value of an attribute (note that a more advanced version of this is already provided using the `property`() function described in Chapter 7). In the `Circle` class that follows, these functions are used to create a descriptor attribute called `area`. In subsequent code, the `area` attribute is accessed transparently.

```
c = Circle(10)
a = c.area         # Implicitly calls c.getArea()
c.area = 10.0      # Implicitly calls c.setArea(10.0)
```

Underneath the covers, access to the attribute c.area is being translated into an operation such as Circle.__dict__['area'].__get__(c,Circle).

It is important to emphasize that descriptors can only be created at the class level. It is not legal to create descriptors on a per-instance basis by defining descriptor objects inside __init__() and other methods.

Sequence and Mapping Methods

The methods in Table 3.12 are used by objects that want to emulate sequence and mapping objects.

Table 3.12   **Methods for Sequences and Mappings**

Method	Description
__len__(self)	Returns the length of self
__getitem__(self, key)	Returns self[key]
__setitem__(self, key, value)	Sets self[key] = value
__delitem__(self, key)	Deletes self[key]
__getslice__(self,i,j)	Returns self[i:j]
__setslice__(self,i,j,s)	Sets self[i:j] = s
__delslice__(self,i,j)	Deletes self[i:j]
__contains__(self,obj)	Returns True if obj is in self; otherwise, returns False

Here's an example:

```
a = [1,2,3,4,5,6]
len(a)                  # __len__(a)
x = a[2]                # __getitem__(a,2)
a[1] = 7                # __setitem__(a,1,7)
del a[2]                # __delitem__(a,2)
x = a[1:5]              # __getslice__(a,1,5)
a[1:3] = [10,11,12]     # __setslice__(a,1,3,[10,11,12])
del a[1:4]              # __delslice__(a,1,4)
```

The __len__ method is called by the built-in len() function to return a nonnegative length. This function also determines truth values unless the __nonzero__() method has also been defined.

For manipulating individual items, the __getitem__() method can return an item by key value. The key can be any Python object, but is typically an integer for sequences. The __setitem__() method assigns a value to an element. The __delitem__() method is invoked whenever the del operation is applied to a single element.

The slicing methods support the slicing operator s[i:j]. The __getslice__() method returns a slice, which is normally the same type of sequence as the original object. The indices i and j must be integers, but their interpretation is up to the method. Missing values for i and j are replaced with 0 and sys.maxint, respectively. The __setslice__() method assigns values to a slice. Similarly, __delslice__() deletes all the elements in a slice.

The __contains__() method is used to implement the in operator.

In addition to implementing the methods just described, sequences and mappings implement a number of mathematical methods, including __add__(), __radd__(), __mul__(), and __rmul__() to support concatenation and sequence replication. These methods are described shortly.

Finally, Python supports an extended slicing operation that's useful for working with multidimensional data structures such as matrices and arrays. Syntactically, you specify an extended slice as follows:

```
a = m[0:100:10]             # Strided slice (stride=10)
b = m[1:10, 3:20]           # Multidimensional slice
c = m[0:100:10, 50:75:5]    # Multiple dimensions with strides
m[0:5, 5:10] = n            # extended slice assignment
del m[:10, 15:]             # extended slice deletion
```

The general format for each dimension of an extended slice is $i:j[:stride]$, where $stride$ is optional. As with ordinary slices, you can omit the starting or ending values for each part of a slice. In addition, a special object known as the Ellipsis and written as ... is available to denote any number of trailing or leading dimensions in an extended slice:

```
a = m[..., 10:20]      # extended slice access with Ellipsis
m[10:20, ...] = n
```

When using extended slices, the __getitem__(), __setitem__(), and __delitem__() methods implement access, modification, and deletion, respectively. However, instead of an integer, the value passed to these methods is a tuple containing one or more slice objects and at most one instance of the Ellipsis type. For example,

```
a = m[0:10, 0:100:5, ...]
```

invokes __getitem__() as follows:

```
a = __getitem__(m, (slice(0,10,None), slice(0,100,5), Ellipsis))
```

Python strings, tuples, and lists currently provide some support for extended slices, which is described in Chapter 4. Special-purpose extensions to Python, especially those with a scientific flavor, may provide new types and objects with advanced support for extended slicing operations.

Iteration

If an object, obj, supports iteration, it must provide a method, obj.__iter__(), that returns an iterator object. The iterator object iter, in turn, must implement a single method, iter.next(), that returns the next object or raises StopIteration to signal the end of iteration. Both of these methods are used by the implementation of the for statement as well as other operations that implicitly perform iteration. For example, the statement for x in s is carried out by performing steps equivalent to the following:

```
_iter = s.__iter__()
while 1:
    try:
        x = _iter.next()
    except StopIteration:
        break
    # Do statements in body of for loop
    ...
```

Mathematical Operations

Table 3.13 lists special methods that objects must implement to emulate numbers. Mathematical operations are always evaluated from left to right; when an expression such as $x + y$ appears, the interpreter tries to invoke the method $x.$__add__(y). The special methods beginning with r support operations with reversed operands. These are invoked only if the left operand doesn't implement the specified operation. For example, if x in $x + y$ doesn't support the __add__() method, the interpreter tries to invoke the method $y.$__radd__(x).

Table 3.13   **Methods for Mathematical Operations**

Method	Result
__add__(self,other)	self + other
__sub__(self,other)	self - other
__mul__(self,other)	self * other
__div__(self,other)	self / other
__truediv__(self,other)	self / other (future)
__floordiv__(self,other)	self // other
__mod__(self,other)	self % other
__divmod__(self,other)	divmod(self,other)
__pow__(self,other [,modulo])	self ** other, pow(self, other, modulo)
__lshift__(self,other)	self << other
__rshift__(self,other)	self >> other
__and__(self,other)	self & other
__or__(self,other)	self | other
__xor__(self,other)	self ^ other
__radd__(self,other)	other + self
__rsub__(self,other)	other - self
__rmul__(self,other)	other * self
__rdiv__(self,other)	other / self
__rtruediv__(self,other)	other / self (future)
__rfloordiv__(self,other)	other // self
__rmod__(self,other)	other % self
__rdivmod__(self,other)	divmod(other,self)
__rpow__(self,other)	other ** self
__rlshift__(self,other)	other << self
__rrshift__(self,other)	other >> self
__rand__(self,other)	other & self
__ror__(self,other)	other | self
__rxor__(self,other)	other ^ self
__iadd__(self,other)	self += other

Table 3.13   **Continued**

Method	Result
__isub__(*self*,*other*)	*self* -= *other*
__imul__(*self*,*other*)	*self* *= *other*
__idiv__(*self*,*other*)	*self* /= *other*
__itruediv__(*self*,*other*)	*self* /= *other* (future)
__ifloordiv__(*self*,*other*)	*self* //= *other*
__imod__(*self*,*other*)	*self* %= *other*
__ipow__(*self*,*other*)	*self* **= *other*
__iand__(*self*,*other*)	*self* &= *other*
__ior__(*self*,*other*)	*self* |= *other*
__ixor__(*self*,*other*)	*self* ^= *other*
__ilshift__(*self*,*other*)	*self* <<= *other*
__irshift__(*self*,*other*)	*self* >>= *other*
__neg__(*self*)	-*self*
__pos__(*self*)	+*self*
__abs__(*self*)	abs(*self*)
__invert__(*self*)	~*self*
__int__(*self*)	int(*self*)
__long__(*self*)	long(*self*)
__float__(*self*)	float(*self*)
__complex__(*self*)	complex(*self*)
__oct__(*self*)	oct(*self*)
__hex__(*self*)	hex(*self*)
__coerce__(*self*,*other*)	Type coercion

The methods __iadd__(), __isub__(), and so forth are used to support in-place arithmetic operators such as a+=b and a-=b (also known as *augmented assignment*). A distinction is made between these operators and the standard arithmetic methods because the implementation of the in-place operators might be able to provide certain customizations such as performance optimizations. For instance, if the `self` parameter is not shared, it might be possible to modify its value in place without having to allocate a newly created object for the result.

The three flavors of division operators, __div__(), __truediv__(), and __floordiv__(), are used to implement true division (/) and truncating division (//) operations. The separation of division into two types of operators is a relatively recent change to Python that was started in Python 2.2, but which has far-reaching effects. As of this writing, the default behavior of Python is to map the / operator to __div__(). In the future, it will be remapped to __truediv__(). This latter behavior can currently be enabled as an optional feature by including the statement from __future__ import division in a program.

The conversion methods __int__(), __long__(), __float__(), and __complex__() convert an object into one of the four built-in numerical types. The __oct__() and __hex__() methods return strings representing the octal and hexa-decimal values of an object, respectively.

The __coerce__(x, y) method is used in conjunction with mixed-mode numeri-cal arithmetic. This method returns either a 2-tuple containing the values of x and y converted to a common numerical type, or NotImplemented (or None) if no such con-version is possible. To evaluate the operation x op y, where op is an operation such as +, the following rules are applied, in order:

1. If x has a __coerce__() method, replace x and y with the values returned by x.__coerce__(y). If None is returned, skip to step 3.

2. If x has a method __op__(), return x.__op__(y). Otherwise, restore x and y to their original values and continue.

3. If y has a __coerce__() method, replace x and y with the values returned by y.__coerce__(x). If None is returned, raise an exception.

4. If y has a method __rop__(), return y.__rop__(x). Otherwise, raise an excep-tion.

Although strings define a few arithmetic operations, the __coerce__() method is not used in mixed-string operations involving standard and Unicode strings.

The interpreter supports only a limited number of mixed-type operations involving the built-in types, in particular the following:

- If x is a string, x % y invokes the string-formatting operation, regardless of the type of y.
- If x is a sequence, x + y invokes sequence concatenation.
- If either x or y is a sequence and the other operand is an integer, x * y invokes sequence repetition.

Comparison Operations

Table 3.14 lists special methods that objects can implement to provide individualized versions of the relational operators (<, >, <=, >=, ==, !=). These are known as rich com-parisons. Each of these functions takes two arguments and is allowed to return any kind of object, including a Boolean value, a list, or any other Python type. For instance, a numerical package might use this to perform an element-wise comparison of two matrices, returning a matrix with the results. If a comparison can't be made, these func-tions may also raise an exception.

Table 3.14 **Methods for Comparisons**

Method	Result
__lt__(self, other)	self < other
__le__(self, other)	self <= other
__gt__(self, other)	self > other
__ge__(self, other)	self >= other
__eq__(self, other)	self == other
__ne__(self, other)	self != other

Callable Objects

Finally, an object can emulate a function by providing the __call__(*self* [,*args* [, **kwargs*]]) method. If an object, *x*, provides this method, it can be invoked like a function. That is, *x*(*arg1*, *arg2*, ...) invokes *x*.__call__(*self*, *arg1*, *arg2*, ...).

Performance Considerations

The execution of a Python program is mostly a sequence of function calls involving the special methods described in the earlier section "Special Methods." If you find that a program runs slowly, you should first check to see if you're using the most efficient algorithm. After that, considerable performance gains can be made simply by understanding Python's object model and trying to eliminate the number of special method calls that occur during execution.

For example, you might try to minimize the number of name lookups on modules and classes. For example, consider the following code:

```
import math
d= 0.0
for i in xrange(1000000):
    d = d + math.sqrt(i)
```

In this case, each iteration of the loop involves two name lookups. First, the math module is located in the global namespace; then it's searched for a function object named sqrt. Now consider the following modification:

```
from math import sqrt
d = 0.0
for i in xrange(1000000):
    d = d + sqrt(i)
```

In this case, one name lookup is eliminated from the inner loop, resulting in a considerable speedup.

Unnecessary method calls can also be eliminated by making careful use of temporary values and avoiding unnecessary lookups in sequences and dictionaries. For example, consider the following two classes:

```
class Point(object):
    def __init__(self,x,y,z):
        self.x = x
        self.y = y
        self.z = z

class Poly(object):
    def __init__(self):
        self.pts = [ ]
    def addpoint(self,pt):
        self.pts.append(pt)
    def perimeter(self):
        d = 0.0
        self.pts.append(self.pts[0])       # Temporarily close the polygon
        for i in xrange(len(self.pts)-1):
            d2 = (self.pts[i+1].x - self.pts[i].x)**2 + \
                 (self.pts[i+1].y - self.pts[i].y)**2 + \
                 (self.pts[i+1].z - self.pts[i].z)**2
            d = d + math.sqrt(d2)
        self.pts.pop()                     # Restore original list of points
        return d
```

In the `perimeter()` method, each occurrence of `self.pts[i]` involves two special-method lookups—one involving a dictionary and another involving a sequence. You can reduce the number of lookups by rewriting the method as follows:

```
class Poly(object):
    ...
    def perimeter(self):
        d = 0.0
        pts = self.pts
        pts.append(pts[0])
        for i in xrange(len(pts)-1):
            p1 = pts[i+1]
            p2 = pts[i]
            d2 = (p1.x - p2.x)**2 + \
                 (p1.y - p2.y)**2 + \
                 (p1.z - p2.z)**2
            d = d + math.sqrt(d2)
        pts.pop()
        return d
```

Although the performance gains made by such modifications are often modest (15%–20%), an understanding of the underlying object model and the manner in which special methods are invoked can result in faster programs. Of course, if performance is extremely critical, you often can export functionality to a Python extension module written in C or C++.

4

Operators and Expressions

THIS CHAPTER DESCRIBES PYTHON'S BUILT-IN OPERATORS as well as the precedence rules used in the evaluation of expressions.

Operations on Numbers

The following operations can be applied to all numeric types:

Operation	Description
x + y	Addition
x - y	Subtraction
x * y	Multiplication
x / y	Division
x // y	Truncating division
x ** y	Power (x^y)
x % y	Modulo (x mod y)
-x	Unary minus
+x	Unary plus

The truncating division operator (also known as *floor division*) truncates the result to an integer and works with both integers and floating-point numbers. As of this writing, the true division operator (/) also truncates the result to an integer if the operands are integers. Therefore, 7/4 is 1, not 1.75. However, this behavior is scheduled to change in a future version of Python, so you will need to be careful. The modulo operator returns the remainder of the division x // y. For example, 7 % 4 is 3. For floating-point numbers, the modulo operator returns the floating-point remainder of x // y, which is x - (x // y) * y. For complex numbers, the modulo (%) and truncating division operators (//) are invalid.

The following shifting and bitwise logical operators can only be applied to integers and long integers:

Operation	Description
x << y	Left shift
x >> y	Right shift
x & y	Bitwise AND

Operation	Description
x | y	Bitwise OR
x ^ y	Bitwise XOR (exclusive OR)
~x	Bitwise negation

The bitwise operators assume that integers are represented in a 2's complement binary representation. For long integers, the bitwise operators operate as if the sign bit is infinitely extended to the left. Some care is required if you are working with raw bit-patterns that are intended to map to native integers on the hardware. This is because Python does not truncate the bits or allow values to overflow—instead, a result is promoted to a long integer.

In addition, you can apply the following built-in functions to all the numerical types:

Function	Description
abs(x)	Absolute value
divmod(x, y)	Returns (x // y, x % y)
pow(x, y [, modulo])	Returns (x ** y) % modulo
round(x, [n])	Rounds to the nearest multiple of 10^{-n} (floating-point numbers only)

The abs() function returns the absolute value of a number. The divmod() function returns the quotient and remainder of a division operation. The pow() function can be used in place of the ** operator, but also supports the ternary power-modulo function (often used in cryptographic algorithms). The round() function rounds a floating-point number, x, to the nearest multiple of 10 to the power minus n. If n is omitted, it's set to 0. If x is equally close to two multiples, rounding is performed away from zero (for example, 0.5 is rounded to 1 and -0.5 is rounded to -1).

When working with integers, the result of an expression is automatically promoted to a long integer if it exceeds the precision available in the integer type. In addition, the Boolean values True and False can be used anywhere in an expression and have the values 1 and 0, respectively.

The following comparison operators have the standard mathematical interpretation and return a Boolean value of True for true, False for false:

Operation	Description
x < y	Less than
x > y	Greater than
x == y	Equal to
x != y	Not equal to (same as <>)
x >= y	Greater than or equal to
x <= y	Less than or equal to

Comparisons can be chained together, such as in w < x < y < z. Such expressions are evaluated as w < x and x < y and y < z. Expressions such as x < y > z are legal, but are likely to confuse anyone else reading the code (it's important to note that no comparison is made between x and z in such an expression). Comparisons other than equality involving complex numbers are undefined and result in a TypeError.

Operations involving numbers are valid only if the operands are of the same type. If the types differ, a coercion operation is performed to convert one of the types to the other, as follows:

1. If either operand is a complex number, the other operand is converted to a complex number.

2. If either operand is a floating-point number, the other is converted to a float.

3. If either operand is a long integer, the other is converted to a long integer.

4. Otherwise, both numbers must be integers and no conversion is performed.

Operations on Sequences

The following operators can be applied to sequence types, including strings, lists, and tuples:

Operation	Description
s + r	Concatenation
s * n, n * s	Makes n copies of s, where n is an integer
s % d	String formatting (strings only)
s[i]	Indexing
s[i:j]	Slicing
s[i:j:stride]	Extended slicing
x in s, x not in s	Membership
for x in s:	Iteration
len(s)	Length
min(s)	Minimum item
max(s)	Maximum item

The + operator concatenates two sequences of the same type. The s * n operator makes n copies of a sequence. However, these are shallow copies that replicate elements by reference only. For example, consider the following code:

```
a = [3,4,5]        # A list
b = [a]            # A list containing a
c = 4*b            # Make four copies of b

# Now modify a
a[0] = -7

# Look at c
print c
```

The output of this program is the following:

```
[[-7, 4, 5], [-7, 4, 5], [-7, 4, 5], [-7, 4, 5]]
```

In this case, a reference to the list a was placed in the list b. When b was replicated, four additional references to a were created. Finally, when a was modified, this change was propagated to all the other "copies" of a. This behavior of sequence multiplication is often unexpected and not the intent of the programmer. One way to work around the problem is to manually construct the replicated sequence by duplicating the contents of a. For example:

```
a = [ 3, 4, 5 ]
c = [a[:] for j in range(4)]   # [:] makes a copy of a list
```

The copy module in the standard library can also be used to make copies of objects.

The indexing operator s[n] returns the nth object from a sequence in which s[0] is the first object. Negative indices can be used to fetch characters from the end of a sequence. For example, s[-1] returns the last item. Otherwise, attempts to access elements that are out of range result in an IndexError exception.

The slicing operator s[i:j] extracts a subsequence from s consisting of the elements with index k, where i <= k < j. Both i and j must be integers or long integers. If the starting or ending index is omitted, the beginning or end of the sequence is assumed, respectively. Negative indices are allowed and assumed to be relative to the end of the sequence. If i or j is out of range, they're assumed to refer to the beginning or end of a sequence, depending on whether their value refers to an element before the first item or after the last item, respectively.

The slicing operator may be given an optional stride, s[i:j:stride], that causes the slice to skip elements. However, the behavior is somewhat more subtle. If a stride is supplied, i is the starting index, j is the ending index, and the produced subsequence is the elements s[i], s[i+stride], s[i+2*stride], and so forth until index j is reached (which is not included). The stride may also be negative. If the starting index i is omitted, it is set to the beginning of the sequence if stride is positive or the end of the sequence if stride is negative. If the ending index j is omitted, it is set to the end of the sequence if stride is positive or the beginning of the sequence if stride is negative. Here are some examples:

```
a = [0, 1, 2, 3, 4, 5, 6, 7, 8, 9]

b = a[::2]      # b = [0, 2, 4, 6, 8 ]
c = a[::-2]     # c = [9, 7, 5, 3, 1 ]
d = a[0:5:2]    # d = [0,2,4]
e = a[5:0:-2]   # e = [5,3,1]
f = a[:5:1]     # f = [0,1,2,3,4]
g = a[:5:-1]    # g = [9,8,7,6]
h = a[5::1]     # h = [5,6,7,8,9]
i = a[5::-1]    # i = [5,4,3,2,1,0]
j = a[5:0:-1]   # j = [5,4,3,2,1]
```

The x in s operator tests to see whether the object x is in the sequence s and returns True or False. Similarly, the x not in s operator tests whether x is not in the sequence s. For strings, the in and not in operators accept subtrings. For example, 'hello' in 'hello world' produces True.

The for x in s operator iterates over all the elements of a sequence and is described further in Chapter 5, "Control Flow." len(s) returns the number of elements in a sequence. min(s) and max(s) return the minimum and maximum values of a sequence, respectively, although the result may only make sense if the elements can be ordered with respect to the < operator (for example, it would make little sense to find the maximum value of a list of file objects).

Strings and tuples are immutable and cannot be modified after creation. Lists can be modified with the following operators:

Operation	Description
s[i] = x	Index assignment
s[i:j] = r	Slice assignment
s[i:j:stride] = r	Extended slice assignment
del s[i]	Deletes an element
del s[i:j]	Deletes a slice
del s[i:j:stride]	Deletes an extended slice

The s[i] = x operator changes element i of a list to refer to object x, increasing the reference count of x. Negative indices are relative to the end of the list and attempts to assign a value to an out-of-range index result in an IndexError exception. The slicing assignment operator s[i:j] = r replaces elements k, where i <= k < j, with elements from sequence r. Indices may have the same values as for slicing and are adjusted to the beginning or end of the list if they're out of range. If necessary, the sequence s is expanded or reduced to accommodate all the elements in r. Here's an example:

```
a = [1,2,3,4,5]
a[1] = 6                        # a = [1,6,3,4,5]
a[2:4] = [10,11]      # a = [1,6,10,11,5]
a[3:4] = [-1,-2,-3]   # a = [1,6,10,-1,-2,-3,5]
a[2:] = [0]           # a = [1,6,0]
```

Slicing assignment may be supplied with an optional stride argument. However, the behavior is somewhat more restricted in that the argument on the right side must have exactly the same number of elements as the slice that's being replaced. Here's an example:

```
a = [1,2,3,4,5]
a[1::2] = [10,11]      # a = [1,10,3,11,5]
a[1::2] = [30,40,50]   # ValueError.  Only two elements in slice on left
```

The del s[i] operator removes element i from a list and decrements its reference count. del s[i:j] removes all the elements in a slice. A stride may also be supplied, as in del s[i:j:stride].

Sequences are compared using the operators <, >, <=, >=, ==, and !=. When comparing two sequences, the first elements of each sequence are compared. If they differ, this determines the result. If they're the same, the comparison moves to the second element of each sequence. This process continues until two different elements are found or no more elements exist in either of the sequences. If the end of both sequences is reached, the sequences are considered equal. If a is a subsequence of b, then a < b. Strings are compared using lexicographical ordering. Each character is assigned a unique index determined by the machine's character set (such as ASCII or Unicode). A character is less than another character if its index is less.

The modulo operator (s % d) produces a formatted string, given a format string, s, and a collection of objects in a tuple or mapping object (dictionary). The string s may be a standard or Unicode string. The behavior of this operator is similar to the C sprintf() function. The format string contains two types of objects: ordinary characters (which are left unmodified) and conversion specifiers, each of which is replaced with a formatted string representing an element of the associated tuple or mapping. If d is a tuple, the number of conversion specifiers must exactly match the number of objects in d. If d is a mapping, each conversion specifier must be associated with a valid

key name in the mapping (using parentheses, as described shortly). Each conversion specifier
starts with the % character and ends with one of the conversion characters shown in Table 4.1.

Table 4.1   **String Formatting Conversions**

Character	Output Format
d, i	Decimal integer or long integer.
u	Unsigned integer or long integer.
o	Octal integer or long integer.
x	Hexadecimal integer or long integer.
X	Hexadecimal integer (uppercase letters).
f	Floating point as [-]m.dddddd.
e	Floating point as [-]m.dddddde±xx.
E	Floating point as [-]m.ddddddE±xx.
g, G	Use %e or %E for exponents less than −4 or greater than the precision; otherwise use %f.
s	String or any object. The formatting code uses str() to generate strings.
r	Produces the same string as produced by repr().
c	Single character.
%	Literal %.

Between the % character and the conversion character, the following modifiers may appear, in this order:

1. A key name in parentheses, which selects a specific item out of the mapping object. If no such element exists, a KeyError exception is raised.
2. One or more of the following:
    - − sign, indicating left alignment. By default, values are right-aligned.
    - + sign, indicating that the numeric sign should be included (even if positive).
    - 0, indicating a zero fill.

3. A number specifying the minimum field width. The converted value will be printed in a field at least this wide and padded on the left (or right if the − flag is given) to make up the field width.
4. A period separating the field width from a precision.
5. A number specifying the maximum number of characters to be printed from a string, the number of digits following the decimal point in a floating-point number, or the minimum number of digits for an integer.

In addition, the asterisk (*) character may be used in place of a number in any width field. If present, the width will be read from the next item in the tuple.

The following code illustrates a few examples:

```
a = 42
b = 13.142783
c = "hello"
d = {'x':13, 'y':1.54321, 'z':'world'}
e = 5628398123741234L

print 'a is %d' % a          #  "a is 42"
print '%10d %f' % (a,b)      #  "        42 13.142783"
print '%+010d %E' % (a,b)    #  "+000000042 1.314278E+01"
print '%(x)-10d  %(y)0.3g' % d  #  "13        1.54"
print '%0.4s %s' % (c, d['z'])  #  "hell world"
print '%*.*f' % (5,3,b)      #  "13.143"
print 'e = %d' % e           #  "e = 5628398123741234"
```

Operations on Dictionaries

Dictionaries provide a mapping between names and objects. You can apply the following operations to dictionaries:

Operation	Description
x = d[k]	Indexing by key
d[k] = x	Assignment by key
del d[k]	Deletes an item by key
len(d)	Number of items in the dictionary

Key values can be any immutable object, such as strings, numbers, and tuples. In addition, dictionary keys can be specified as a comma-separated list of values, like this:

```
d = { }
d[1,2,3] = "foo"
d[1,0,3] = "bar"
```

In this case, the key values represent a tuple, making the preceding assignments identical to the following:

```
d[(1,2,3)] = "foo"
d[(1,0,3)] = "bar"
```

Operations on Sets

The set and frozenset type support a number of common set operations:

Operation	Description
s | t	Union of s and t
s & t	Intersection of s and t
s - t	Set difference
s ^ t	Symmetric difference
len(s)	Number of items in the set
max(s)	Maximum value
min(s)	Minimum value

Augmented Assignment

Python provides the following set of augmented assignment operators:

Operation	Description
x += y	x = x + y
x -= y	x = x - y
x *= y	x = x * y
x /= y	x = x / y
x //= y	x = x // y
x **= y	x = x ** y
x %= y	x = x % y
x &= y	x = x & y
x |= y	x = x | y
x ^= y	x = x ^ y
x >>= y	x = x >> y
x <<= y	x = x << y

These operators can be used anywhere that ordinary assignment is used. For example:

```
a = 3
b = [1,2]
c = "Hello %s %s"
a += 1                     # a = 4
b[1] += 10                 # b = [1, 12]
c %= ("Monty", "Python")   # c = "Hello Monty Python"
```

Augmented assignment doesn't violate mutability or perform in-place modification of objects. Therefore, writing x += y creates an entirely new object x with the value x + y. User-defined classes can redefine the augmented assignment operators using the special methods described in Chapter 3, "Types and Objects."

The Attribute (.) Operator

The dot (.) operator is used to access the attributes of an object. For example:

```
foo.x = 3
print foo.y
a = foo.bar(3,4,5)
```

More than one dot operator can appear in a single expression, such as in foo.y.a.b. The dot operator can also be applied to the intermediate results of functions, as in a = foo.bar(3,4,5).spam.

Type Conversion

Sometimes it's necessary to perform conversions between the built-in types. To convert between types you simply use the type name as a function. In addition, several built-in functions are supplied to perform special kinds of conversions. All of these functions return a new object representing the converted value.

Function	Description
int(x [,base])	Converts x to an integer. base specifies the base if x is a string.
long(x [,base])	Converts x to a long integer. base specifies the base if x is a string.
float(x)	Converts x to a floating-point number.
complex(real [,imag])	Creates a complex number.
str(x)	Converts object x to a string representation.
repr(x)	Converts object x to an expression string.
eval(str)	Evaluates a string and returns an object.
tuple(s)	Converts s to a tuple.
list(s)	Converts s to a list.
set(s)	Converts s to a set.
dict(d)	Creates a dictionary. d must be a sequence of (key,value) tuples.
frozenset(s)	Converts s to a frozen set.
chr(x)	Converts an integer to a character.
unichr(x)	Converts an integer to a Unicode character.
ord(x)	Converts a single character to its integer value.
hex(x)	Converts an integer to a hexadecimal string.
oct(x)	Converts an integer to an octal string.

You also can write the repr(x) function using backquotes as `x`. Note that the str() and repr() functions may return different results. repr() typically creates an expression string that can be evaluated with eval() to re-create the object. On the other hand, str() produces a concise or nicely formatted representation of the object (and is used by the print statement). The ord() function returns the integer ordinal value for a standard or Unicode character. The chr() and unichr() functions convert integers back into standard or Unicode characters, respectively.

To convert strings back into numbers and other objects, use the int(), long(), and float() functions. The eval() function can also convert a string containing a valid expression to an object. Here's an example:

```
a = int("34")               # a = 34
b = long("0xfe76214", 16)   # b = 266822164L  (0xfe76214L)
b = float("3.1415926")      # b = 3.1415926
c = eval("3, 5, 6")         # c = (3,5,6)
```

In functions that create containers (list(), tuple(), set(), and so on), the argument may be any object that supports iteration that is used to generate all the items used to populate the object that's being created.

Unicode Strings

The use of standard strings and Unicode strings in the same program presents a number of subtle complications. This is because such strings may be used in a variety of operations, including string concatenation, comparisons, dictionary key lookups, and as arguments to built-in functions.

To convert a standard string, *s*, to a Unicode string, the built-in unicode(*s* [, *encoding* [,*errors*]]) function is used. To convert a Unicode string, *u*, to a standard string, the string method *u*.encode([*encoding* [, *errors*]]) is used. Both of these conversion operators require the use of a special encoding rule that specifies how 16-bit Unicode character values are mapped to a sequence of 8-bit characters in standard strings, and vice versa. The encoding parameter is specified as a string and is one of the following values:

Value	Description
'ascii'	7-bit ASCII
'latin-1' or 'iso-8859-1'	ISO 8859-1 Latin-1
'utf-8'	8-bit variable-length encoding
'utf-16'	16-bit variable-length encoding (may be little or big endian)
'utf-16-le'	UTF-16, little endian encoding
'utf-16-be'	UTF-16, big endian encoding
'unicode-escape'	Same format as Unicode literals u"string"
'raw-unicode-escape'	Same format as raw Unicode literals ur"string"

The default encoding is set in the site module and can be queried using sys. getdefaultencoding(). In most cases, the default encoding is 'ascii', which means that ASCII characters with values in the range [0x00,0x7f] are directly mapped to Unicode characters in the range [U+0000, U+007F]. Details about the other encodings can be found in Chapter 9, "Input and Output."

When string values are being converted, a UnicodeError exception may be raised if a character that can't be converted is encountered. For instance, if the encoding rule is 'ascii', a Unicode character such as U+1F28 can't be converted because its value is too large. Similarly, the string "\xfc" can't be converted to Unicode because it contains a character outside the range of valid ASCII character values. The errors parameter determines how encoding errors are handled. It's a string with one of the following values:

Value	Description
'strict'	Raises a UnicodeError exception for decoding errors.
'ignore'	Ignores invalid characters.
'replace'	Replaces invalid characters with a replacement character (U+FFFD in Unicode, '?' in standard strings).
'backslashreplace'	Replaces invalid characters with a Python character escape sequence. For example, the character U+1234 is replaced by '\u1234'.
'xmlcharrefreplace'	Replaces invalid characters with an XML character reference. For example, the character U+1234 is replaced by 'ሴ'.

The default error handling is 'strict'.

When standard strings and Unicode strings are mixed in an expression, standard strings are automatically coerced to Unicode using the built-in unicode() function. For example:

```
s = "hello"
t = u"world"
w = s + t            # w = unicode(s) + t
```

When Unicode strings are used in string methods that return new strings (as described in Chapter 3), the result is always coerced to Unicode. Here's an example:

```
a = "Hello World"
b = a.replace("World", u"Bob")   # Produces u"Hello Bob"
```

Furthermore, even if zero replacements are made and the result is identical to the original string, the final result is still a Unicode string.

If a Unicode string is used as the format string with the % operator, all the arguments are first coerced to Unicode and then put together according to the given format rules. If a Unicode object is passed as one of the arguments to the % operator, the entire result is coerced to Unicode at the point at which the Unicode object is expanded. For example:

```
c = "%s %s" % ("Hello", u"World") # c = "Hello " + u"World"
d = u"%s %s" % ("Hello", "World") # d = u"Hello " + u"World"
```

When applied to Unicode strings, the str() and repr() functions automatically coerce the value back to a standard string. For Unicode string u, str(u) produces the value u.encode() and repr(u) produces u"%s" % repr(u.encode('unicode-escape')).

In addition, most library and built-in functions that only operate with standard strings will automatically coerce Unicode strings to a standard string using the default encoding. If such a coercion is not possible, a UnicodeError exception is raised.

Standard and Unicode strings can be compared. In this case, standard strings are coerced to Unicode using the default encoding before any comparison is made. This coercion also occurs whenever comparisons are made during list and dictionary operations. For example, 'x' in [u'x', u'y', u'z'] coerces 'x' to Unicode and returns True. For character containment tests such as 'W' in u'Hello World', the character 'W' is coerced to Unicode before the test.

When computing hash values with the hash() function, standard strings and Unicode strings produce identical values, provided that the Unicode string only contains characters in the range [U+0000, U+007F]. This allows standard strings and Unicode strings to be used interchangeably as dictionary keys, provided that the Unicode strings are confined to ASCII characters. For example:

```
a = { }
a[u"foo"] = 1234
print a["foo"]        # Prints 1234
```

However, it should be noted that this dictionary key behavior may not hold if the default encoding is ever changed to something other than 'ascii' or if Unicode strings contain non-ASCII characters. For example, if 'utf-8' is used as a default character encoding, it's possible to produce pathological examples in which strings compare as equal, but have different hash values. For example:

```
a = u"M\u00fcller"      # Unicode string
b = "M\303\274ller"     # utf-8 encoded version of a
print a == b            # Prints '1', true
print hash(a)==hash(b)  # Prints '0', false
```

Boolean Expressions and Truth Values

The and, or, and not keywords can form Boolean expressions. The behavior of these operators is as follows:

Operator	Description
x or y	If x is false, return y; otherwise, return x.
x and y	If x is false, return x; otherwise, return y.
not x	If x is false, return 1; otherwise, return 0.

When you use an expression to determine a true or false value, True, any nonzero number, nonempty string, list, tuple, or dictionary is taken to be true. False, zero, None, and empty lists, tuples, and dictionaries evaluate as false. Boolean expressions are evaluated from left to right and consume the right operand only if it's needed to determine the final value. For example, a and b evaluates b only if a is true.

Object Equality and Identity

The equality operator (x == y) tests the values of x and y for equality. In the case of lists and tuples, all the elements are compared and evaluated as true if they're of equal value. For dictionaries, a true value is returned only if x and y have the same set of keys and all the objects with the same key have equal values. Two sets are equal if they have the same elements, which are compared using equality (==).

The identity operators (x is y and x is not y) test two objects to see whether they refer to the same object in memory. In general, it may be the case that x == y, but x is not y.

Comparison between objects of noncompatible types, such as a file and a floating-point number, may be allowed, but the outcome is arbitrary and may not make any sense. In addition, comparison between incompatible types may result in an exception.

Order of Evaluation

Table 4.2 lists the order of operation (precedence rules) for Python operators. All operators except the power (**) operator are evaluated from left to right and are listed in the table from highest to lowest precedence. That is, operators listed first in the table are evaluated before operators listed later. (Note that operators included together within subsections, such as x * y, x / y, x // y, and x % y, have equal precedence.)

Table 4.2   Order of Evaluation (Highest to Lowest)

Operator	Name
(...), [...], {...}	Tuple, list, and dictionary creation
`...`	String conversion

Table 4.2 **Continued**

Operator	Name
`s[i]`, `s[i:j]`	Indexing and slicing
`s.attr`	Attributes
`f(...)`	Function calls
`+x`, `-x`, `~x`	Unary operators
`x ** y`	Power (right associative)
`x * y`, `x / y`, `x // y`, `x % y`	Multiplication, division, floor division, modulo
`x + y`, `x - y`	Addition, subtraction
`x << y`, `x >> y`	Bit-shifting
`x & y`	Bitwise and
`x ^ y`	Bitwise exclusive or
`x	y`	Bitwise or
`x < y`, `x <= y`,	Comparison, identity, and sequence
`x > y`, `x >= y`,	membership tests
`x == y`, `x != y`	
`x <> y`	
`x is y`, `x is not y`	
`x in s`, `x not in s`	
`not x`	Logical negation
`x and y`	Logical and
`x or y`	Logical or
`lambda args: expr`	Anonymous function

5

Control Flow

T HIS CHAPTER DESCRIBES STATEMENTS RELATED TO the control flow of a program. Topics include conditionals, iteration, and exceptions.

Conditionals

The if, else, and elif statements control conditional code execution. The general format of a conditional statement is as follows:

```
if expression:
    statements
elif expression:
    statements
elif expression:
    statements
...
else:
    statements
```

If no action is to be taken, you can omit both the else and elif clauses of a conditional. Use the pass statement if no statements exist for a particular clause:

```
if expression:
    pass            # Do nothing
else:
    statements
```

Loops and Iteration

You implement loops using the for and while statements. For example:

```
while expression:
    statements

for i in s:
    statements
```

The while statement executes statements until the associated expression evaluates to false. The for statement iterates over all the elements of s until no more elements are available. The for statement works with any object that supports iteration. This obviously includes the built-in sequence types such as lists, tuples, and strings, but also any object that implements the iterator protocol.

An object, s, supports iteration if it can be used with the following code, which mirrors the implementation of the for statement:

```
it = s.__iter__()          # Get an iterator for s
while 1:
    try:
        i = it.next()      # Get next item
    except StopIteration:  # No more items
        break
    # Perform operations on i
    ...
```

If the elements used in iteration are tuples of identical size, you can use the following variation of the for statement:

```
for x,y,z in s:
    statements
```

In this case, s must contain or produce tuples, each with three elements. On each iteration, the contents of the variables x, y, and z are assigned the contents of the corresponding tuple.

When looping, it is sometimes useful to keep track of a numerical index in addition to the data values. For example:

```
i = 0
for x in s:
    print i, x
    i += 1

# An alternative
for i in range(len(s)):
    print s[i]
```

Python provides a built-in function, enumerate(), that can be used for this purpose:

```
for i,x in enumerate(s):
    print i,x
```

enumerate(s) creates an iterator that simply returns (0, s[0]), (1, s[1]), (2, s[2]), and so on.

To break out of a loop, use the break statement. For example, the following function reads lines of text from the user until an empty line of text is entered:

```
while 1:
    cmd = raw_input('Enter command > ')
    if not cmd:
        break                # No input, stop loop
    # process the command
    ...
```

To jump to the next iteration of a loop (skipping the remainder of the loop body), use the continue statement. This statement tends to be used less often, but is sometimes useful when the process of reversing a test and indenting another level would make the program too deeply nested or unnecessarily complicated. As an example, the following loop prints only the nonnegative elements of a list:

```
for a in s:
    if a < 0:
        continue           # Skip negative elements
    print a
```

The break and continue statements apply only to the innermost loop being executed. If it's necessary to break out of a deeply nested loop structure, you can use an exception. Python doesn't provide a "goto" statement.

You can also attach the else statement to loop constructs, as in the following example:

```
# while-else
while i < 10:
    do something
    i = i + 1
else:
    print 'Done'

# for-else
for a in s:
    if a == 'Foo':
        break
else:
    print 'Not found!'
```

The else clause of a loop executes only if the loop runs to completion. This either occurs immediately (if the loop wouldn't execute at all) or after the last iteration. On the other hand, if the loop is terminated early using the break statement, the else clause is skipped.

Exceptions

Exceptions indicate errors and break out of the normal control flow of a program. An exception is raised using the raise statement. The general format of the raise statement is raise Exception [, value] where Exception is the exception type and value is an optional value giving specific details about the exception. For example:

```
raise RuntimeError, "Unrecoverable Error"
```

If the raise statement is used without any arguments, the last exception generated is raised again (although this works only while handling a previously raised exception).

To catch an exception, use the try and except statements, as shown here:

```
try:
    f = open('foo')
except IOError, e:
    print "Unable to open 'foo': ", e
```

When an exception occurs, the interpreter stops executing statements in the try block and looks for an except clause that matches the exception that has occurred. If one is found, control is passed to the first statement in the except clause. After the except clause is executed, control continues with the first statement that appears after the try-except block. Otherwise, the exception is propagated up to the block of code in which the try statement appeared. This code may itself be enclosed in a try-except that can handle the exception. If an exception works its way up to the top level of a program without being caught, the interpreter aborts with an error message. If desired, uncaught exceptions can also be passed to a user-defined function, sys.excepthook(), as described in Chapter 13, "Python Runtime Service."

The optional second argument to the except statement is the name of a variable in which the argument supplied to the raise statement is placed if an exception occurs.

Exception handlers can examine this value to find out more about the cause of the
exception.

Multiple exception-handling blocks are specified using multiple except clauses, as in
the following example:

```
try:
    do something
except IOError, e:
    # Handle I/O error
    ...
except TypeError, e:
    # Handle Type error
    ...
except NameError, e:
    # Handle Name error
    ...
```

A single handler can catch multiple exception types like this:

```
try:
    do something
except (IOError, TypeError, NameError), e:
    # Handle I/O, Type, or Name errors
    ...
```

To ignore an exception, use the pass statement as follows:

```
try:
    do something
except IOError:
    pass                 # Do nothing (oh well).
```

To catch all exceptions, omit the exception name and value:

```
try:
    do something
except:
    print 'An error occurred'
```

The try statement also supports an else clause, which must follow the last except
clause. This code is executed if the code in the try block doesn't raise an exception.
Here's an example:

```
try:
    f = open('foo', 'r')
except IOError:
    print 'Unable to open foo'
else:
    data = f.read()
    f.close()
```

The finally statement defines a cleanup action for code contained in a try block. For
example:

```
f = open('foo','r')
try:
    # Do some stuff
    ...
finally:
    f.close()
    print "File closed regardless of what happened."
```

The finally clause isn't used to catch errors. Rather, it's used to provide code that must always be executed, regardless of whether an error occurs. If no exception is raised, the code in the finally clause is executed immediately after the code in the try block. If an exception occurs, control is first passed to the first statement of the finally clause. After this code has executed, the exception is re-raised to be caught by another exception handler. The finally and except statements cannot appear together within a single try statement.

Python defines the built-in exceptions listed in Table 5.1. (For specific details about these exceptions, see Chapter 11.)

Table 5.1   **Built-in Exceptions**

Exception	Description
Exception	The root of all exceptions
SystemExit	Generated by sys.exit()
StopIteration	Raised to stop iteration
StandardError	Base for all built-in exceptions
ArithmeticError	Base for arithmetic exceptions
FloatingPointError	Failure of a floating-point operation
OverflowError	Arithmetic overflow
ZeroDivisionError	Division or modulus operation with 0
AssertionError	Raised by the assert statement
AttributeError	Raised when an attribute name is invalid
EnvironmentError	Errors that occur externally to Python
IOError	I/O or file-related error
OSError	Operating system error
EOFError	Raised when the end of the file is reached
ImportError	Failure of the import statement
KeyboardInterrupt	Generated by the interrupt key (usually Ctrl+C)
LookupError	Indexing and key errors
IndexError	Out-of-range sequence offset
KeyError	Nonexistent dictionary key
MemoryError	Out of memory
NameError	Failure to find a local or global name
UnboundLocalError	Unbound local variable
ReferenceError	Weak reference used after referent destroyed
RuntimeError	A generic catchall error
NotImplementedError	Unimplemented feature

Table 5.1   **Continued**

Exception	Description
SyntaxError	Parsing error
IndentationError	Indentation error
TabError	Inconsistent tab usage (generated with -tt option)
SystemError	Nonfatal system error in the interpreter
TypeError	Passing an inappropriate type to an operation
ValueError	Invalid type
UnicodeError	Unicode error
UnicodeDecodeError	Unicode decoding error
UnicodeEncodeError	Unicode encoding error
UnicodeTranslateError	Unicode translation error

Exceptions are organized into a hierarchy as shown in the table. All the exceptions in a particular group can be caught by specifying the group name in an except clause. For example:

```
try:
    statements
except LookupError:      # Catch IndexError or KeyError
    statements
```

or

```
try:
    statements
except StandardError:    # Catch any built-in exception
    statements
```

Defining New Exceptions

All the built-in exceptions are defined in terms of classes. To create a new exception, create a new class definition that inherits from exceptions.Exception, such as the following:

```
import exceptions
# Exception class
class NetworkError(exceptions.Exception):
    def __init__(self,args=None):
        self.args = args
```

The name args should be used as shown. This allows the value used in the raise statement to be properly printed in tracebacks and other diagnostics. In other words,

```
raise NetworkError, "Cannot find host."
```

creates an instance of NetworkError using the following call:

```
NetworkError("Cannot find host.")
```

The object that is created will print itself as "NetworkError: Cannot find host." If you use a name other than the self.args name or don't store the argument, this feature won't work correctly.

When an exception is raised, the optional value supplied in the `raise` statement is used as the argument to the exception's class constructor. If the constructor for an exception requires more than one argument, it can be raised in two ways:

```
import exceptions
# Exception class
class NetworkError(exceptions.Exception):
     def __init__(self,errno,msg):
          self.args = (errno, msg)
          self.errno = errno
          self.errmsg = msg

# Raises an exception (multiple arguments)
def error2():
     raise NetworkError(1, 'Host not found')

# Raises an exception (multiple arguments supplied as a tuple)
def error3():
     raise NetworkError, (1, 'Host not found')
```

Exceptions can be organized into a hierarchy using inheritance. For instance, the `NetworkError` exception defined earlier could serve as a base class for a variety of more specific errors. For example:

```
class HostnameError(NetworkError):
    pass

class TimeoutError(NetworkError):
    pass

def error3():
    raise HostnameError

def error4():
    raise TimeoutError

try:
    error3()
except NetworkError:
    import sys
    print sys.exc_type     # Prints exception type
```

In this case, the `except NetworkError` statement catches any exception derived from `NetworkError`. To find the specific type of error that was raised, examine the variable `sys.exc_type`. Similarly, the `sys.exc_value` variable contains the value of the last exception. Alternatively, the `sys.exc_info()` function can be used to retrieve exception information in a manner that doesn't rely on global variables and is thread-safe.

Assertions and __debug__

The `assert` statement can introduce debugging code into a program. The general form of `assert` is

```
assert test [, data]
```

where *test* is an expression that should evaluate to true or false. If *test* evaluates to false, `assert` raises an `AssertionError` exception with the optional *data* supplied to the `assert` statement. For example:

```
def write_data(file,data):
    assert file, "write_data: file is None!"
    ...
```

Assertions are not checked when Python runs in optimized mode (specified with the -O option).

In addition to `assert`, Python provides the built-in read-only variable `__debug__`, which is set to 1 unless the interpreter is running in optimized mode (specified with the -O option). Programs can examine this variable as needed—possibly running extra error-checking procedures if set.

The `assert` statement should not be used for code that must be executed to make the program correct, because it won't be executed if Python is run in optimized mode. In particular, it's an error to use `assert` to check user input. Instead, `assert` statements are used to check things that should always be true; if one is violated, it represents a bug in the program, not an error by the user.

For example, if the function `write_data()`, shown previously, were intended for use by an end user, the `assert` statement should be replaced by a conventional `if` statement and the desired error-handling.

6

Functions and Functional Programming

MOST SUBSTANTIAL PROGRAMS ARE BROKEN UP into functions for better modularity and ease of maintenance. Python makes it easy to define functions, but borrows a number of ideas from functional programming languages that simplify certain tasks. This chapter describes functions, anonymous functions, generators, and functional programming features, as well as the eval() and execfile() functions and the exec statement. It also describes list comprehensions, a powerful list-construction technique.

Functions

Functions are defined with the def statement:

```
def add(x,y):
    return x+y
```

You invoke a function by writing the function name followed by a tuple of function arguments, such as a = add(3,4). The order and number of arguments must match those given in the function definition. If a mismatch exists, a TypeError exception is raised.

You can attach default arguments to function parameters by assigning values in the function definition. For example:

```
def foo(x,y,z = 42):
```

When a function defines a parameter with a default value, that parameter and all the parameters that follow are optional. If values are not assigned to all the optional parameters in the function definition, a SyntaxError exception is raised.

Default parameter values are always set to the objects that were supplied as values when the function was defined. For example:

```
a = 10
def foo(x = a):
    print x

a = 5                # Reassign 'a'.
foo()                # Prints '10' (default value not changed)
```

However, the use of mutable objects as default values may lead to unintended behavior:

```
a = [10]
def foo(x = a):
    print x
a.append(20)
foo()                   # Prints '[10, 20]'
```

A function can accept a variable number of parameters if an asterisk (*) is added to the last parameter name:

```
def fprintf(file, fmt, *args):
    file.write(fmt % args)

# Use fprintf. args gets (42,"hello world", 3.45)
fprintf(out,"%d %s %f", 42, "hello world", 3.45)
```

In this case, all the remaining arguments are placed into the *args* variable as a tuple. To pass the tuple *args* to another function as if they were parameters, the *args syntax can be used as follows:

```
def printf(fmt, *args):
        # Call another function and pass along args
        fprintf(sys.stdout,fmt, *args)
```

You can also pass function arguments by explicitly naming each parameter and specifying a value, as follows:

```
def foo(w,x,y,z):
    print w,x,y,z

# Keyword invocation
foo(x=3, y=22, w='hello', z=[1,2])
```

With keyword arguments, the order of the parameters doesn't matter. However, unless you're using default values, you must explicitly name all the function parameters. If you omit any of the required parameters or if the name of a keyword doesn't match any of the parameter names in the function definition, a `TypeError` exception is raised.

Positional arguments and keyword arguments can appear in the same function call, provided that all the positional arguments appear first, values are provided for all non-optional arguments, and no argument value is defined more than once. For example:

```
foo('hello',3, z=[1,2], y=22)
foo(3,22, w='hello', z=[1,2])    # TypeError. Multiple values for w
```

If the last argument of a function definition begins with **, all the additional keyword arguments (those that don't match any of the parameter names) are placed in a dictionary and passed to the function. For example:

```
def spam(**parms):
    print "You supplied the following args:"
    for k in parms.keys():
        print "%s = %s" % (k, parms[k])

spam(x=3, a="hello", foobar=(2,3))
```

You can combine extra keyword arguments with variable-length argument lists, as long as the ** parameter appears last:

```
# Accept variable number of positional or keyword arguments
def spam(x, *args, **keywords):
    print x, args, keywords
```

Keywords arguments can also be passed to another function using the `**keywords` syntax:

```
def callfunc(func, *args, **kwargs):
    print args
    print kwargs
    func(*args,**kwargs)
```

Finally, functions can have arbitrary attributes attached to them. For example:

```
def foo():
    print "Hello world"

foo.secure = 1
foo.private = 1
```

Function attributes are stored in a dictionary that is available as the `__dict__` attribute of a function.

The primary use of function attributes is in specialized applications such as parser generators and network applications that would like to attach additional information to a function. They may also be set by the function itself to hold information that carries through to the next invocation of the function.

Parameter Passing and Return Values

When a function is invoked, its parameters are passed by reference. If a mutable object (such as a list or dictionary) is passed to a function where it's then modified, those changes will be reflected in the caller. For example:

```
a = [1,2,3,4,5]
def foo(x):
    x[3] = -55      # Modify an element of x

foo(a)              # Pass a
print a             # Produces [1,2,3,-55,5]
```

The `return` statement returns a value from a function. If no value is specified or you omit the `return` statement, the `None` object is returned. To return multiple values, place them in a tuple:

```
def factor(a):
    d = 2
    while (d <= (a/2)):
        if ((a/d)*d == a):
            return ((a/d),d)
        d = d + 1
    return (a,1)
```

Multiple return values returned in a tuple can be assigned to individual variables:

```
x,y = factor(1243)      # Return values placed in x and y.
```

or

```
(x,y) = factor(1243)    # Alternate version. Same behavior.
```

Scoping Rules

Each time a function executes, a new local namespace is created. This namespace contains the names of the function parameters, as well as the names of variables that are assigned inside the function body. When resolving names, the interpreter first searches the local namespace. If no match exists, it searches the global namespace. The global namespace for a function is always the module in which the function was defined. If the interpreter finds no match in the global namespace, it makes a final check in the built-in namespace. If this fails, a `NameError` exception is raised.

One peculiarity of namespaces is the manipulation of global variables from within a function. For example, consider the following code:

```
a = 42
def foo():
    a = 13
foo()
print a
```

When this code is executed, the value `42` prints, despite the appearance that we might be modifying the variable a inside the function `foo`. When variables are assigned inside a function, they're always bound to the function's local namespace; as a result, the variable a in the function body refers to an entirely new object containing the value `13`. To alter this behavior, use the `global` statement. `global` simply marks a list of names as belonging to the global namespace, and it's necessary only when global variables will be modified. It can be placed anywhere in a function body and used repeatedly. For example:

```
a = 42
b = 13
def foo():
    global a, b      # 'a' is in global namespace
    a = 13
    b = 0
foo()
print a
```

Python supports nested function definitions. For example:

```
def bar():
    x = 10
    def spam():              # Nested function definition
        print 'x is ', x
    while x > 0:
        spam()
        x -= 1
```

With nested scopes, names are resolved by first checking the local scope and then all enclosing scopes from the innermost scope to the outermost scope. If no match is found, the global and built-in namespaces are checked as before. Although names in enclosing scopes are available, Python only allows variables to be reassigned in the innermost scope (local variables) and the global namespace (using `global`). Therefore, an inner function can't reassign the value of a local variable defined in an outer function.

If a local variable is used before it's assigned a value, an `UnboundLocalError` exception is raised. For example:

```
def foo():
    print i        # Results in UnboundLocalError exception
    i = 0
```

Functions as Objects

Functions are first-class objects in Python. This means that they can be passed around and used just like any other data type. For example, a function can be returned as a result:

```
def derivative(f):
    def compute(x):
        return (f(x+dx) - f(x))/dx
    return compute
```

In this example, the `compute()` function is returned as a result. Within this function, the variable dx is a free variable that will be bound when the function actually executes. The variable f was originally passed to the function `derivative()` and remains bound to that value in the function `compute()`. In addition, you can pass a function as an argument to another function:

```
# Find the zero of a function using Newton's method
#     f is a function object representing a mathematical function
#     x is an initial guess for the root
#     dx is a delta used when approximating the derivative
#     tol is a tolerance that determines when iteration stops
def newtons_method(f,x,dx, tol):
    df = derivative(f)          # Returns a function df that computes
                                # the derivative
    while 1:
        x1 = x - f(x)/df(x)     # Calls the df function above.
        t = abs(x1 - x)
        if t < tol: break
        x = x1
    return x
# Example of use
def f(x):
    return 3*x**5 - 2*x**3 + 1*x - 37

zero = newtons_method(f,1,0.000001,0.000001)
```

Recursion

Python places a limit on the depth of recursive function calls. The function `sys.getrecursionlimit()` returns the current maximum recursion depth, and the function `sys.setrecursionlimit()` can be used to change the value. The default value is 1000. When the recursion depth is exceeded, a `RuntimeError` exception is raised.

The `apply()` Function

The `apply(funcname, [, args [, kwargs]])` function is used to invoke a function indirectly where the arguments have been constructed in the form of a tuple or dictionary. `args` is a tuple containing the positional argument to be supplied to the function. If omitted, no arguments are passed. *kwargs* is a dictionary containing keyword arguments. The following statements produce identical results:

```
foo(3,"x", name='Dave', id=12345)
```

or

```
apply(foo, (3,"x"), { 'name': 'Dave', 'id': 12345 })
```

In older versions of Python, apply() was the only mechanism for calling a function in which the arguments were contained in a tuple or dictionary. This capability is now handled by the following syntax:

```
a = (3,"x")
b = { 'name' : 'Dave', 'id': 12345 }
foo(*a,**b)     # Same as code above
```

The lambda Operator

To create an anonymous function in the form of an expression, use the lambda statement:

```
lambda args : expression
```

args is a comma-separated list of arguments, and *expression* is an expression involving those arguments. For example:

```
a = lambda x,y : x+y
print a(2,3)                # produces 5
```

The code defined with lambda must be a valid expression. Multiple statements and other non-expression statements, such as print, for, and while, cannot appear in a lambda statement. lambda expressions follow the same scoping rules as functions.

map(), zip(), reduce(), and filter()

The t = map(*func, s*) function applies the function *func* to each of the elements in *s* and returns a new list, *t*. Each element of *t* is t[i] = func(s[i]). The function given to map() should require only one argument. For example:

```
a = [1, 2, 3, 4, 5, 6]
def foo(x):
    return 3*x

b = map(foo,a)    # b = [3, 6, 9, 12, 15, 18]
```

Alternatively, this could be calculated using an anonymous function, as follows:

```
b = map(lambda x: 3*x, a)    # b = [3, 6, 9, 12, 15, 18]
```

The map() function can also be applied to multiple lists, such as t = map(*func, s1, s2, ..., sn*). In this case, each element of *t* is t[i] = func(s1[i], s2[i], ..., sn[i]), and the function given to map() must accept the same number of arguments as the number of lists given. The result has the same number of elements as the longest list in *s1, s2, ... sn*. During the calculation, short lists are extended with values of None to match the length of the longest list, if necessary.

If the function is set to None, the identity function is assumed. If multiple lists are passed to map(None, s1, s2, ... sn), the function returns a list of tuples in which each tuple contains an element from each list. For example:

```
a = [1,2,3,4]
b = [100,101,102,103]
c = map(None, a, b)   # c = [(1,100), (2,101), (3,102), (4,103)]
```

As an alternative to map(), a list of tuples can also be created using the zip(s1,s2,...,sn) function. zip() takes a collection of sequences and returns a new list, t, in which each element of t is t[i] = (s1[i], s2[i], ..., sn[i]). Unlike map(), zip() truncates the length of t to the shortest sequence in s1, s2, ... sn. Here's an example:

```
d = [1,2,3,4,5]
e = [10,11,12]
f = zip(d,e)    # f = [(1,10), (2,11), (3,12)]
g = map(None,d,e)  # g = [(1,10), (2,11), (3,12), (4,None), (5,None)]
```

The reduce(func, s) function collects information from a sequence and returns a single value (for example, a sum, maximum value, and so on). reduce() works by applying the function func to the first two elements of s. This value is then combined with the third element to yield a new value. This result is then combined with the fourth element, and so forth until the end of the sequence. The function func must accept two arguments and return a single value. For example:

```
def sum(x,y):
    return x+y

b = reduce(sum, a)    # b = (((1+2)+3)+4) = 10
```

The filter(func,s) function filters the elements of s using a filter function, func(), that returns true or false. A new sequence is returned consisting of all elements, x of s, for which func(x) is true. For example:

```
c = filter(lambda x: x < 4, a)    # c = [1, 2, 3]
```

If func is set to None, the identity function is assumed and filter() returns all elements of s that evaluate to true.

List Comprehensions

Many operations involving map() and filter() can be replaced with a list-construction operator known as a *list comprehension*. The syntax for a list comprehension is as follows:

```
[expression for item1 in iterable1
            for item2 in iterable2
            ...
            for itemN in iterableN
            if condition ]
```

This syntax is roughly equivalent to the following code:

```
s = []
for item1 in iterable1:
    for item2 in iterable2:
        ...
            for itemN in iterableN:
                if condition: s.append(expression)
```

To illustrate, consider the following example:

```
a = [-3,5,2,-10,7,8]
b = 'abc'

c = [2*s for s in a]        # c = [-6,10,4,-20,14,16]
d = [s for s in a if s >= 0]  # d = [5,2,7,8]
e = [(x,y) for x in a       # e = [(5,'a'),(5,'b'),(5,'c'),
           for y in b       #      (2,'a'),(2,'b'),(2,'c'),
           if x > 0 ]       #      (7,'a'),(7,'b'),(7,'c'),
                            #      (8,'a'),(8,'b'),(8,'c')]

f = [(1,2), (3,4), (5,6)]
g = [math.sqrt(x*x+y*y)     # f = [2.23606, 5.0, 7.81024]
     for x,y in f]

h = reduce(lambda x,y: x+y,   # Sum of squares
           [math.sqrt(x*x+y*y)
            for x,y in f])
```

The sequences supplied to a list comprehension don't have to be the same length because they're iterated over their contents using a nested set of `for` loops, as previously shown. The resulting list contains successive values of expressions. The `if` clause is optional; however, if it's used, *expression* is evaluated and added to the result only if *condition* is true.

Finally, if a list comprehension is used to construct a list of tuples, the tuple values must be enclosed in parentheses. For example, `[(x,y) for x in a for y in b]` is legal syntax, whereas `[x,y for x in a for y in b]` is not.

Generators and `yield`

If a function uses the `yield` keyword, it defines an object known as a *generator*. A generator is a function that produces values for use in iteration. For example:

```
def count(n):
    print "starting to count"
    i = 0
    while i < n:
        yield i
        i += 1
    return
```

If you call this function, you will find that none of its code executes. For example:

```
>>> c = count(100)
>>>
```

Instead of the function executing, an iterator object is returned. The iterator object, in turn, executes the function whenever `next()` is called. For example:

```
>>> c.next()
0
>>> c.next()
1
```

When `next()` is invoked on the iterator, the generator function executes statements until it reaches a `yield` statement. The `yield` statement produces a result at which point execution of the function stops until `next()` is invoked again. Execution then resumes with the statement following `yield`.

The primary use of generators is looping with the `for` statement. For example:

```
for n in count(100):
    print n
```

A generator function terminates by calling `return` or raising `StopIteration`, at which point iteration will stop. It is never legal for a generator to return a value upon completion.

Generator Expressions

A generator expression is an object that performs the same kind of function as a list comprehension. The syntax is the same as for list comprehensions except that you use parentheses instead of square brackets. For example:

```
(expression for item1 in iterable1
            for item2 in iterable2
            ...
            for itemN in iterableN
            if condition )
```

Unlike a list comprehension, a generator expression does not actually create a list or immediately evaluate the expression inside the parentheses. Instead, it creates a generator object that produces the values on demand via iteration. For example:

```
>>> a = [1, 2, 3, 4]
>>> b = (10*i for i in a)
>>> b
<generator object at 0x590a8>
>>> b.next()
10
>>> b.next()
20
...
```

The difference between list and generator expressions is important, but subtle. With a list comprehension, Python actually creates a sequence that contains the resulting data. With a generator expression, Python creates a generator that merely knows how to produce data on demand. In certain applications, this can greatly improve performance and memory use. For example:

```
# Read a file
f = open("data.txt")                       # Open a file
lines = (t.strip() for t in f)             # Read lines, strip
                                           # trailing/leading whitespace
comments = (t for t in lines if t[0] == '#') # All comments
for c in comments:
    print c
```

In this example, the generator expression that extracts lines and strips whitespace does not actually read the file into memory. The same is true of the expression that extracts comments. Instead, the lines of the file are actually read when the program starts iterating in the `for` loop that follows. During this iteration, the lines of the file are produced upon demand and filtered accordingly. In fact, at no time will the entire file be loaded into memory during this process. Therefore, this would be a highly efficient way to extract comments from a gigabyte-sized Python source file.

Unlike a list comprehension, a generator expression does not create an object that works like a sequence. It can't be indexed and none of the usual list operations will work (for example, append()). However, a generator expression can be converted into a list using the built-in list() function:

```
clist = list(comments)
```

Function Decorators

Function decorators are used to modify what happens when a function is defined. That is, they affect the behavior of the def statement itself. Decorators are denoted using the special @ symbol, as follows:

```
@foo
def bar(x):
    return x*2
```

The preceding code is shorthand for the following:

```
def bar(x):
    return x*2
bar = foo(bar)
```

In the example, a function bar() is defined. However, immediately after its definition, the function object itself is passed to the function foo(), which returns an object that replaces the original bar. An example will clarify:

```
def foo(f):
    def wrapper(*x,**y):
        print "Calling", f.__name__
        return f(*x,**y)
    return wrapper
```

In this case, foo() places a wrapper function around the original function object. If you call bar(), you will see the output of the print statement.

When decorators are used, they must appear on their own line immediately prior to a function definition declared with def. More than one decorator can also be applied. For example:

```
@foo
@bar
@spam
def grok(x):
    pass
```

In this case, the decorators are applied in order. The result is the same as this:

```
def grok(x):
    pass
grok = foo(bar(spam(grok)))
```

A decorator can also accept arguments. For example:

```
@eventhandler(BUTTON)
def handle_button(msg):
    ...
@eventhandler(RESET)
def handle_reset(msg):
    ...
```

If arguments are supplied, the semantics of the decorator is as follows:

```
def handle_button(msg):
    ...
temp = eventhandler(BUTTON)              # Call decorator with supplied arguments
handle_button = temp(handle_button)     # Call the function returned by the decorator
```

In this case, the decorator function only accepts the arguments supplied with the @ specifier. It then returns a function that is called with the function as an argument. For example:

```
# Event handler decorator
def eventhandler(event):
    def register_function(f):
        event_handlers[event] = f
        return f
    return register_function
```

eval(), exec, execfile(), **and** compile()

The eval(*str* [,*globals* [,*locals*]]) function executes an expression string and returns the result. For example:

```
a = eval('3*math.sin(3.5+x) + 7.2')
```

Similarly, the exec statement executes a string containing arbitrary Python code. The code supplied to exec is executed as if the code actually appeared in place of the exec statement. For example:

```
a = [3, 5, 10, 13]
exec "for i in a: print i"
```

Finally, the execfile(*filename* [,globals [,locals]]) function executes the contents of a file. For example:

```
execfile("foo.py")
```

All these functions execute within the namespace of the caller (which is used to resolve any symbols that appear within a string or file). Optionally, eval(), exec, and execfile() can accept one or two dictionaries that serve as the global and local namespaces for the code to be executed, respectively. For example:

```
globals = {'x': 7,
           'y': 10,
           'birds': ['Parrot', 'Swallow', 'Albatross']
          }

locals = { }

# Execute using the above dictionaries as the global and local namespace
a = eval("3*x + 4*y", globals, locals)
exec "for b in birds: print b" in globals, locals    # Note unusual syntax
execfile("foo.py", globals, locals)
```

If you omit one or both namespaces, the current values of the global and local namespaces are used. Also, due to issues related to nested scopes, the use of exec or execfile() inside of a function body may result in a SyntaxError exception if that function also contains nested function definitions or uses the lambda operator.

Note that the syntax of the exec statement in the example is different from that of eval() and execfile(). exec is a statement (much like print or while), whereas eval() and execfile() are built-in functions.

When a string is passed to exec, eval(), or execfile(), the parser first compiles it into bytecode. Because this process is expensive, it may be better to precompile the code and reuse the bytecode on subsequent calls if the code will be executed multiple times.

The compile(str, filename, kind) function compiles a string into bytecode in which str is a string containing the code to be compiled and filename is the file in which the string is defined (for use in traceback generation). The kind argument specifies the type of code being compiled—'single' for a single statement, 'exec' for a set of statements, or 'eval' for an expression. The code object returned by the compile() function can also be passed to the eval() function and exec statement. For example:

```
str = "for i in range(0,10): print i"
c = compile(str,'','exec')       # Compile into a code object
exec c                           # Execute it

str2 = "3*x + 4*y"
c2 = compile(str2, '', 'eval')   # Compile into an expression
result = eval(c2)                # Execute it
```

7

Classes and Object-Oriented Programming

CLASSES ARE THE PRIMARY MECHANISM USED to create data structures and new kinds of objects. This chapter covers the details of classes, but is not intended to be an introduction to object-oriented programming and design. It's assumed that the reader has prior experience with data structures and object-oriented programming in other languages such as C or Java. (Chapter 3, "Types and Objects," contains additional information about the terminology and internal implementation of objects.)

The class Statement

A *class* defines a set of attributes associated with a collection of objects known as *instances*. These attributes typically include functions, which are known as *methods*, variables, which are known as *class variables*, and computed attributes, which are known as *properties*.

Classes are defined using the class statement. The body of a class contains a series of statements that is executed when the class is first defined. Here's an example:

```
class Account(object):
    "A simple class"
    num_accounts = 0
    def __init__(self,name,balance):
        "Initialize a new Account instance"
        self.name = name
        self.balance = balance
        Account.num_accounts += 1
    def __del__(self):
        Account.num_accounts -= 1
    def deposit(self,amt):
        "Add to the balance"
        self.balance = self.balance + amt
    def withdraw(self,amt):
        "Subtract from the balance"
        self.balance = self.balance - amt
    def inquiry(self):
        "Return the current balance"
        return self.balance
```

The objects created during the execution of the class body are placed into a class object that serves as a namespace. For example, the members of the Account class are accessible as follows:

```
Account.num_accounts
Account.__init__
Account.__del__
Account.deposit
Account.withdraw
Account.inquiry
```

It's important to note that a `class` statement doesn't create any instances of a class (for example, no accounts are actually created in the preceding example). Rather, a class defines a set of attributes shared by all the instances that will be created later. In this sense, you might think of it as a blueprint that is used to construct instances of an object.

The functions defined inside a class are known as *methods*. An instance method is a function that operates on an instance of the class, which is passed as the first argument. By convention, this argument is called `self`, although any legal identifier name can be used. In the preceding example, `deposit()`, `withdraw()`, and `inquiry()` are examples of instance methods.

If a method is defined with an `@staticmethod` decorator, it is called a *static method*. A static method is merely a function that is packaged with the class but is not associated with instances. Because no instance is involved, a static method does not have a `self` parameter. If a method is defined with an `@classmethod` decorator, it is called a *class method*. A class method receives the class object itself as the first argument, which is called `cls` by convention. The following example shows static and class methods:

```
class Foo(object):
    @staticmethod
    def bar(x):
        print "I'm bar, x is", x
    @classmethod
    def spam(cls):
        print cls

Foo.bar(3)      # Call static method
Foo.spam()      # Call class method.  Foo gets passed as an argument
```

It should be noted that static and class methods can be created by calling the built-in functions `staticmethod()` and `classmethod()` instead of using decorators. For example:

```
class Foo(object):
    def bar(x):
        print "I'm bar, x is", x
    bar = staticmethod(bar)
    def spam(cls):
        print cls
    spam = classmethod(spam)
```

Class variables such as num_accounts, defined in an earlier example, are shared among all instances of a class (that is, they're not individually assigned to each instance).

Properties are attributes that look like simple variables but are actually managed by methods. For example:

```
class Circle(object):
    def __init__(self,radius):
        self.radius = radius
    def getArea(self):
        return math.pi*self.radius**2
    def setArea(self,area):
```

```
        self.radius = math.sqrt(area/math.pi)
    area = property(getArea, setArea, doc='area of circle')
```

In this example, the attribute area is defined as a property with the built-in property(*getf*=None, *setf*=None, *delf*=None, *doc*=None) function. Whenever area is accessed, it will use the methods getArea() and setArea() to read and modify the value, respectively.

Finally, although a class defines a namespace, this namespace is not a scope for code appearing inside the class body. Therefore, references to other attributes of a class must use a fully qualified name, as shown in the following example:

```
class Foo(object):
    def bar(self):
        print "bar!"
    def spam(self):
        bar(self)       # Incorrect! 'bar' generates a NameError
        Foo.bar(self) # This works
```

Class Instances

Instances of a class are created by calling a class object as a function. This first creates a new instance by calling the static method __new__(), which is rarely defined by the user, but implemented as part of object. This, in turn, calls the __init__() method of the class, which is almost always defined by a user to initialize the contents of an instance. For example:

```
# Create a few accounts
a = Account("Guido", 1000.00)  # Invokes Account.__init__(a,"Guido",1000.00)
b = Account("Bill", 10.00)
```

The attributes and methods of the newly created instances are accessible using the dot (.) operator as follows:

```
a.deposit(100.00)       # Calls Account.deposit(a,100.00)
b.withdraw(50.00)       # Calls Account.withdraw(b,50.00)
name = a.name           # Get account name
print a.num_accounts    # Number of accounts(class variable)
```

Internally, instances are implemented using a dictionary that's accessible as the instance's __dict__ attribute. This dictionary contains the information that's unique to each instance. For example:

```
>>> print a.__dict__
{'balance': 1100.0, 'name': 'Guido'}
```

Whenever the attributes of an instance are modified, these changes are made to the instance's local dictionary. Within methods defined in the class, attributes are changed through assignment to the self variable, as shown in the __init__(), deposit(), and withdraw() methods of Account. In addition, new attributes can be added to an instance at any time, like this:

```
a.number = 123456     # Add attribute 'number' to a.__dict__
```

Although the assignment of attributes is always performed on the local dictionary of an instance, attribute access is more complicated. Whenever an attribute *name* is accessed, the interpreter calls a special method, __getattribute__(*self,name*). The default behavior of __getattribute__() is to look for a match in the instance dictionary. If no match is found, the interpreter searches the dictionary of the class object used to create the instance. If this fails, a search of base classes is performed. If this fails, a final attempt to find the attribute is made by trying to invoke the __getattr__() method of the class (if defined). If this fails, an AttributeError exception is raised.

The fact that new attributes can be arbitrarily added to an instance is probably surprising to programmers familiar with other programming languages. However, the dynamic nature of Python makes this easy. If necessary, a class may specify a legal set of attribute names by defining a special variable called __slots__. For example:

```
class Account(object):
    __slots__ = 'name','balance'   # Note: a tuple ('name','balance')
    ...
```

When __slots__ is defined, the attribute names on instances are restricted to the names specified. Otherwise, an AttributeError exception is raised. In addition, the Python interpreter uses __slots__ to perform some optimizations. For example, the attributes may be stored in a more efficient data structure than a dictionary. The presence of __slots__ has no effect on the invocation of methods such as __getattribute__(), __getattr__(), and __setattr__() should they be redefined in a class. However, the default behavior of these methods will take __slots__ into account if it is defined.

Reference Counting and Instance Destruction

All instances have a reference count. If the reference count reaches zero, the instance is destroyed. When the instance is about to be destroyed, the interpreter looks for a __del__() method associated with the object and calls it. In practice, it's rarely necessary for a class to define a __del__() method. The only exception is when the destruction of an object requires a cleanup action such as closing a file, shutting down a network connection, or releasing other system resources. Even in these cases, it's dangerous to rely on __del__() for a clean shutdown because there's no guarantee that this method will be called when the interpreter exits. A better approach may be to define a method such as close() that a program can use to explicitly perform a shutdown. Finally, it should be noted that instances for which __del__() is defined cannot be collected by Python's cyclic garbage collector (which is a strong reason not to define __del__ unless you need to). See Chapter 11, "Introduction to the Python Standard Library," for details.

Occasionally, a program will use the del statement to delete a reference to an object. If this causes the reference count of the object to reach zero, the __del__() method is called. However, in general, the del statement doesn't directly call __del__().

Inheritance

Inheritance is a mechanism for creating a new class that specializes or modifies the behavior of an existing class. The original class is called a *base class* or a *superclass*. The new class is called a *derived class* or a *subclass*. When a class is created via inheritance, it "inherits" the attributes defined by its base classes. However, a derived class may redefine any of these attributes and add new attributes of its own.

Inheritance is specified with a comma-separated list of base-class names in the class statement. If there is no logical base class, a class inherits from object, as has been shown in prior examples. object is an abstract type that is the root of all Python objects and provides the default implementation of common methods such as __new__(), which creates new instances. For example:

```
class A(object):
    def method1(self):
        print "Class A : method1"

class B(A):         # Inherits from A
    def method1(self):
        print "Class B : method1"
    def method2(self):
        print "Class B : method2"

class C(B):         # Inherits from B
    def method3(self):
        print "Class C: method 3"

class D(A):
    def method1(self):
        print "Class D: method 1"

class E(B,D):       # Inherits from B and D (multiple inheritance)
    pass
```

When searching for attributes, Python first checks the class definition itself, followed by a search of the base classes:

```
c = C()             # Create a 'C'
c.method3()         # Invokes C.method3(c)
c.method1()         # Invokes B.method1(c)

e = E()             # Create a 'E'
e.method1()         # Invokes B.method1(e).   See discussion below.
```

For simple class hierarchies involving single inheritance, Python searches for attributes by walking up the inheritance hierarchy until it finds the first definition. For example, in the class C example, Python searches the classes in the order C, B, A. When multiple inheritance is used, attribute resolution becomes considerably more complicated. In this case, all the base classes are ordered in a list from the "most specialized" class to the "least specialized" class. Then this list is searched in order until the first definition of the attribute is found. In the example, the class A is the least specialized because it is at the top of the hierarchy. The class B is more specialized than A because it inherits from A. For a given class, the ordering of base classes can be viewed by printing its __mro__ attribute. For example:

```
>>> print E.__mro__
(<class '__main__.E'>, <class '__main__.B'>, <class '__main__.D'>,
<class '__main__.A'>, <type 'object'>)
```

In most cases, this list should simply "make sense." That is, the list will look a lot like a topological sort of the base classes going from the bottom of the hierarchy (most specialized) to the top (least specialized). However, the actual construction of the list is performed according to the C3 linearization algorithm, which is described in the paper "A Monotonic Superclass Linearization for Dylan" (K. Barrett, et al, presented at OOPSLA'96). Usually, this algorithm orders the base classes exactly like you would expect. However, a subtle aspect of this algorithm is that certain class hierarchies will be rejected by Python with a TypeError. For example:

```
class X(object): pass
class Y(X): pass
class Z(X,Y): pass  # TypeError.
                    # Can't create consistent method resolution order
```

In this case, the method resolution algorithm has rejected class Z because it can't determine an ordering of the base classes that makes sense. For example, the class X appears before class Y in the inheritance list, so it must be checked first. However, class Y is more specialized because it inherits from X. Therefore, if X is checked first, it would not be possible to resolve specialized methods in Y. In practice, these issues should rarely arise—and if they do, it usually indicates a more serious design problem with a program.

If a derived class defines an attribute with the same name as an attribute in a base class, instances of the derived class use the attributes in the derived class. If it's ever necessary to access the original attribute, a fully qualified name can be used as follows:

```
class D(A):
    def method1(self):
        print "Class D : method1"
        A.method1(self)          # Invoke base class method
```

One of the most common applications of this is in the initialization of class instances. When an instance is created, the `__init__()` methods of base classes are not invoked. Therefore, it's up to a derived class to perform the proper initialization of its base classes, if necessary. For example:

```
class D(A):
    def __init__(self, args1):
        # Initialize the base class
        A.__init__(self)
        # Initialize myself
        ...
```

Similar steps may also be necessary when defining cleanup actions in the `__del__()` method.

Python provides a function, `super(class,obj)`, that can be used to call methods in a superclass. This function is most useful if you want to invoke a method in one of the parent classes without having to reimplement Python's method resolution algorithm. For example:

```
class D(A,B):
    def method1(self):
        print "Class D : method1"
        super(D,self).method1()   # Invoke appropriate base class method
```

Polymorphism

Polymorphism, or *dynamic binding*, is the ability to use an instance without regard for its type. It is handled entirely through the attribute lookup process described for inheritance in the preceding section. Whenever a method is accessed as `obj.method()`, *method* is located by searching within the instance itself, the instance's class definition, and then base classes, in that order. The first match found is used as the method. For special methods such as `__getattr__()`, Python first searches in the instance's class definition, followed by base classes.

Information Hiding

By default, all attributes are "public." This means that all attributes of a class instance are accessible without any restrictions. It also implies that everything defined in a base class is inherited and accessible within a derived class. This behavior is often undesirable in object-oriented applications because it exposes the internal implementation of an object and can lead to namespace conflicts between objects defined in a derived class and those defined in a base class.

To fix this problem, all names in a class that start with a double underscore, such as __Foo, are automatically mangled to form a new name of the form _Classname__Foo. This effectively provides a way for a class to have private attributes, because private names used in a derived class won't collide with the same private names used in a base class. For example:

```
class A(object):
    def __init__(self):
        self.__X = 3          # Mangled to self._A__X

class B(A):
    def __init__(self):
        A.__init__(self)
        self.__X = 37         # Mangled to self._B__X
```

Although this scheme provides the illusion of data hiding, there's no strict mechanism in place to prevent access to the "private" attributes of a class. In particular, if the name of the class and corresponding private attribute are known, they can be accessed using the mangled name.

Operator Overloading

User-defined objects can be made to work with all of Python's built-in operators by adding implementations of the special methods described in Chapter 3 to a class. For example, if you wanted to add a new kind of number to Python, you could define a class in which special methods such as __add__() were defined to make instances work with the standard mathematical operators.

The following example shows how this works by defining a class that implements the complex numbers with some of the standard mathematical operators and type-coercion methods to allow complex numbers to be mixed with integers and floats. Note that because Python already provides a complex number type, this class is only provided for the purpose of illustration.

```
class Complex(object):
    def __init__(self,real,imag=0):
        self.real = float(real)
        self.imag = float(imag)
    def __repr__(self):
        return "Complex(%s,%s)" % (self.real, self.imag)
    def __str__(self):
        return "(%g+%gj)" % (self.real, self.imag)
    # self + other
    def __add__(self,other):
        return Complex(self.real + other.real, self.imag + other.imag)
    # self - other
    def __sub__(self,other):
        return Complex(self.real - other.real, self.imag - other.imag)
    # -self
```

```
def __neg__(self):
    return Complex(-self.real, -self.imag)
# other + self
def __radd__(self,other):
    return Complex.__add__(other,self)
# other - self
def __rsub__(self,other):
    return Complex.__sub__(other,self)
# Coerce other numerical types to complex
def __coerce__(self,other):
    if isinstance(other,Complex):
        return self,other
    try:   # See if it can be converted to float
        return self, Complex(float(other))
    except ValueError:
        pass
```

This example contains a few items of interest:

- First, the normal behavior of `__repr__()` is to create a string that can be evaluated to re-create the object. In this case, a string of the form `"Complex(r,i)"` is created. On the other hand, the `__str__()` method creates a string that's intended for nice output formatting (this is the string that would be produced by the `print` statement).

- Second, to handle operators in which complex numbers appear on both the left and right side of operators, both the `__op__()` and `__rop__()` methods for each operation must be provided.

- Finally, the `__coerce__` method is used to handle operations involving mixed types. In this case, other numeric types are converted to complex numbers so that they can be used in the complex arithmetic methods.

Types and Class Membership Tests

When you create an instance of a class, the type of that instance is the class itself. To test for membership in a class, use the built-in function `isinstance(obj,cname)`. This function returns `True` if an object, `obj`, belongs to the class `cname` or any class derived from `cname`. For example:

```
class A(object): pass
class B(A): pass
class C(object): pass

a = A()            # Instance of 'A'
b = B()            # Instance of 'B'
c = C()            # Instance of 'C'

type(a)            # Returns the class object A
isinstance(a,A)    # Returns True
isinstance(b,A)    # Returns True, B derives from A
isinstance(b,C)    # Returns False, C not derived from A
```

Similarly, the built-in function `issubclass(A,B)` returns `True` if the class `A` is a subclass of class `B`. For example:

```
issubclass(B,A)    # Returns True
issubclass(C,A)    # Returns False
```

Classic Classes

Python 2.1 and earlier versions implemented classes using a different mechanism than what is currently used. However, these old-style or classic classes are still supported for backward compatibility. A classic class is defined whenever a class does *not* inherit (directly or indirectly) from `object`. For example:

```
class A:                    # A classic class
    def __init__(self,x):
        self.x = x

class B(A): pass            # A classic class--inherits from A
```

Almost all the basic principles discussed in this chapter apply to classic classes. However, these classes are somewhat more limited in their features. The following list briefly outlines some of the differences.

- Classic classes do not define new types. In fact, the type of all instances regardless of class is `type.InstanceType`.
- `__slots__` has no effect on classic classes.
- Inheritance is handled by performing a depth-first search of the base classes and returning the first match found.

The primary problem with classic classes is their poor integration with the rest of the Python type system. In the future, classic classes are likely to be deprecated entirely. Therefore, there's little benefit in using them.

Metaclasses

When you define a class in Python, the class definition itself becomes an object. For example:

```
class Foo(object): pass
isinstance(Foo,object)      # Returns True
```

If you think about this long enough, you will realize that something had to create the `Foo` object. This creation of the class object is controlled by a special kind of object called a *metaclass*. Simply stated, a metaclass is an object that knows how to create and manage classes.

In the preceding example, the metaclass that is controlling the creation of `Foo` is a class called `type`. In fact, if you display the type of `Foo`, you will find out that it *is* a type:

```
>>> print type(Foo)
<type 'type'>
```

When a new class is defined with the `class` statement, a number of things happen. First, the body of the class is executed as series of statements within its own private dictionary, d. Next, the name of the class, the list of base classes, and the dictionary d are passed to the constructor of a metaclass to create the corresponding class object. Here is an example of how it works:

```
class_name = "Foo"          # Name of class
class_parents = (object,)   # Base classes
class_body = """            # Class body
def __init__(self,x):
```

```
    self.x = x
def blah(self):
    print "Hello World"
"""

class_dict = { }
# Execute the body in the local dictionary class_dict
exec class_body in globals(), class_dict

# Create the class object Foo
Foo = type(class_name,class_parents,class_dict)
```

This procedure creates a modern class. However, it is exactly the same for classic classes. The only difference would be in the last step, which would be modified as follows:

```
# Create a classic class object Foo
Foo = types.ClassType(class_name,class_parents,class_dict)
```

In the final step of defining a class, the class statement must choose an appropriate metaclass that will be used to create the class object. This choice is controlled in a number of ways. First, the class dictionary *d* is examined for the existence of a __metaclass__ attribute. If present, it is used as the metaclass. For example:

```
class Foo:
    __metaclass__ = type    # Specifies what kind of class this is
    ...
```

If no __metaclass__ attribute is defined, the class statement examines the first entry in the tuple of base classes (if any). In this case, the metaclass is the same as the type of the first base class. Therefore, when you write

```
class Foo(object): pass
```

Foo is the same type of class as object.

If no base classes are specified, the class statement checks for the existence of a global variable called __metaclass__. If this variable is found, it will be used to create classes. If you set this variable, it will control how classes are created when a simple class statement is used. For example:

```
__metaclass__ = type
class Foo:
    pass
```

In this example, the class Foo is created as a modern class even though its class definition looks like the older class style.

Finally, if no __metaclass__ value can be found anywhere, Python defaults to using types.ClassType as the metaclass. This metaclass corresponds to the older classic-class implementation.

If desired, you can create your own metaclass objects—something that allows you to control the Python class/object framework in very interesting ways. To do this, you typically inherit from one of the existing metaclasses (type or types.ClassType):

```
# This very evil meta-class enforces a "minimum length identifier" rule
class verboseclass(type):
    def __init__(self, name, bases, dict):
        # Create the class, but first make sure attribute names are extra long
        for key,value in dict.items():
            # ignore special methods
            if key.startswith("__") and key.endswith("__"): continue
            if len(key) < 16: raise TypeError,\
```

```
                   "All class attribute names must be at least 16 letters"
          type.__init__(self,name,bases,dict)

# Create a root class from which other classes can inherit to be verbose
class verbose(object):
    __metaclass__ = verboseclass

# Here's a user-defined class that uses the metaclass
class foo(verbose):
    def aVerySimpleMethodCalledBar(self):  # Ah yes, an acceptably long method name
        print "Hello world"
    def spam(self):                # An unacceptably short name (raises TypeError)
        print "Sorry"
```

Within the metaclass, you would generally define or specialize the default behavior of the general-purpose special methods as needed (that is, `__getattribute__()`, `__setattr__()`, and so on).

To use your metaclass, you would either create a root object from which subsequent objects would inherit (like `object`) or have users specify the metaclass with the `__metaclass__` attribute or variable.

8

Modules and Packages

LARGE PYTHON PROGRAMS ARE OFTEN ORGANIZED as a package of modules. In addition, a large number of modules are included in the Python library. This chapter describes the module and package system in more detail.

Modules

You can turn any valid source file into a module by loading it with the `import` statement. For example, consider the following code:

```
# file : spam.py
a = 37                    # A variable
def foo:                  # A function
    print "I'm foo"
class bar:                # A class
    def grok(self):
        print "I'm bar.grok"
b = bar()                 # Create an instance
```

To load this code as a module, you use the statement `import spam`. The first time `import` is used to load a module, it does three things:

1. It creates a new namespace that serves as a namespace to all the objects defined in the corresponding source file. This is the namespace accessed when functions and methods defined within the module use the `global` statement.

2. It executes the code contained in the module within the newly created namespace.

3. It creates a name within the caller that refers to the module namespace. This name matches the name of the module and is used as follows:

   ```
   import spam           # Loads and executes the module 'spam'
   print spam.a          # Accesses a member of module 'spam'
   spam.foo()
   c = spam.bar()
   ...
   ```

To import multiple modules, supply `import` with a comma-separated list of module names, like this:

```
import socket, os, re
```

Modules can be imported using alternative names by using the `as` qualifier. For example:

```
import os as system
import socket as net, thread as threads
system.chdir("..")
net.gethostname()
```

Use the `from` statement to load specific definitions within a module into the current namespace. The `from` statement is identical to `import` except that instead of creating a name referring to the newly created module namespace, it places references to one or more of the objects defined in the module into the current namespace:

```
from socket import gethostname # Imports 'socket'
                               # Put gethostname in current namespace

print gethostname()            # Use without module name
socket.gethostname()           # NameError: socket
```

The `from` statement also accepts a comma-separated list of object names. For example:

```
from socket import gethostname, socket
```

If you have a very long list of names to import, you can enclose the names in parentheses, which makes it easier to break the `import` statement across multiple lines. For example:

```
from socket import (socket,
                    gethostname,
                    AF_INET,
                    SOCK_STREAM )
```

The asterisk (*) wildcard character can also be used to load all the definitions in a module, except those that start with an underscore. For example:

```
from socket import *   # Load all definitions into current namespace
```

Modules can more precisely control the set of names imported by `from module import *` by defining the list `__all__`. For example:

```
# module: foo.py
__all__ = [ 'bar', 'spam' ]     # Names I will import when * wildcard used
```

In addition, the `as` qualifier can be used to rename specific objects imported with `from`. For example:

```
from socket import gethostname as hostname
h = hostname()
```

The `import` statement can appear at any point in a program. However, the code in each module is loaded and executed only once, regardless of how often you use the `import` statement. Subsequent `import` statements simply create a reference to the module namespace created on a previous import. You can find a dictionary containing all currently loaded modules in the variable `sys.modules`, which is a dictionary that maps module names to module objects. The contents of this dictionary are used to determine whether `import` loads a fresh copy of a module.

The `from module import *` statement may only be used at the top level of a module. In particular, it is illegal to use this form of import inside function bodies due to the way in which it interacts with function scoping rules.

Each module defines a variable, `__name__`, that contains the module name. Programs can examine this variable to determine the module in which they're executing. The top-level module of the interpreter is named `__main__`. Programs specified on the command line or entered interactively run inside the __main__ module. Sometimes, a program may alter its behavior, depending on whether it has been imported as a module or is running in __main__. For example, a module may include some testing code that is executed if the module is used as the main program, but is not executed if the module is simply imported by another module. This can be done as follows:

```
# Check if running as a program
if __name__ == '__main__':
    # Yes
    statements
else:
    # No, I must have been imported as a module
    statements
```

The Module Search Path

When loading modules, the interpreter searches the list of directories in sys.path. The following is a typical value of sys.path:

```
['', '/usr/local/lib/python2.0',
    '/usr/local/lib/python2.0/plat-sunos5',
    '/usr/local/lib/python2.0/lib-tk',
    '/usr/local/lib/python2.0/lib-dynload',
    '/usr/local/lib/python2.0/site-packages']
```

The empty string ' ' refers to the current directory.

To add new directories to the search path, simply append them to this list.

In addition to directories, ZIP archive files containing Python modules can be added to the search path. This can be a convenient way to package a collection of modules as a single file. For example, suppose you created two modules, foo.py and bar.py, and placed them in a zip file called mymodules.zip. The file could be added to the Python search path as follows:

```
>>> import sys
>>> sys.path.append("mymodules.zip")
>>> import foo, bar
```

Specific locations within the directory structure of a zip file can also be used. In addition, zip files can be mixed with regular pathname components. Here's an example:

```
sys.path.append("/tmp/modules.zip/lib/python")
```

Despite support for zip file imports, there are some restrictions to be aware of. First, it is only possible import .py, .pyw, .pyc, and .pyo files from an archive. Shared libraries and extension modules written in C cannot be loaded from archives. Moreover, Python will not create .pyc and .pyo files when .py files are loaded from an archive (described next). This may greatly reduce performance.

Module Loading and Compilation

So far, this chapter has presented modules as files containing Python code. However, modules loaded with import really fall into four general categories:

- Code written in Python (.py files)
- C or C++ extensions that have been compiled into shared libraries or DLLs

- Packages containing a collection of modules
- Built-in modules written in C and linked into the Python interpreter

When looking for a module (for example, `foo`), the interpreter searches each of the directories in `sys.path` for the following files (listed in search order):

1. A directory, `foo`, defining a package.
2. `foo.so`, `foomodule.so`, `foomodule.sl`, or `foomodule.dll` (compiled extensions).
3. `foo.pyo` (only if the `-O` or `-OO` option has been used).
4. `foo.pyc`.
5. `foo.py`. (On Windows, Python also checks for `.pyw` files.)

Packages are described shortly; compiled extensions are described in Chapter 27, "Extending and Embedding Python." For `.py` files, when a module is first imported, it's compiled into bytecode and written back to disk as a `.pyc` file. On subsequent imports, the interpreter loads this precompiled bytecode unless the modification date of the `.py` file is more recent (in which case, the `.pyc` file is regenerated). `.pyo` files are used in conjunction with the interpreter's `-O` option. These files contain bytecode stripped of line numbers, assertions, and other debugging information. As a result, they're somewhat smaller and allow the interpreter to run slightly faster. If the `-OO` option is specified instead of `-O`, documentation strings are also stripped from the file. This removal of documentation strings occurs only when `.pyo` files are created—not when they're loaded. If none of these files exists in any of the directories in `sys.path`, the interpreter checks whether the name corresponds to a built-in module name. If no match exists, an `ImportError` exception is raised.

The compilation of files into `.pyc` and `.pyo` files occurs only in conjunction with the `import` statement. Programs specified on the command line or standard input don't produce such files. In addition, these files aren't created if a module is loaded from a zip archive.

When `import` searches for files, it matches filenames in a case-sensitive manner—even on machines where the underlying file system is case-insensitive, such as on Windows and OS X (such systems are case-preserving, however). Therefore, `'import foo'` will only import the file `'foo.py'` and not the file `'FOO.PY'`. However, as a general rule, you should avoid the use of module names that differ in case only.

Module Reloading

The built-in function `reload()` can be used to reload and execute the code contained within a module previously loaded with `import`. It accepts a module object as a single argument. For example:

```
import foo
... some code ...
reload(foo)          # Reloads foo
```

All operations involving the module after the execution of `reload()` will utilize the newly loaded code. However, `reload()` doesn't retroactively update objects created using the old module. Therefore, it's possible for references to coexist for objects in both the old and new versions of a module. Furthermore, compiled extensions written in C or C++ cannot be reloaded using `reload()`.

As a general rule, avoid module reloading except during debugging and development.

Packages

Packages allow a collection of modules to be grouped under a common package name. This technique helps resolve namespace conflicts between module names used in different applications. A package is defined by creating a directory with the same name as the package and creating the file __init__.py in that directory. You can then place additional source files, compiled extensions, and subpackages in this directory, as needed. For example, a package might be organized as follows:

```
Graphics/
    __init__.py
    Primitive/
        __init__.py
        lines.py
        fill.py
        text.py
        ...
    Graph2d/
        __init__.py
        plot2d.py
        ...
    Graph3d/
        __init__.py
        plot3d.py
        ...
    Formats/
        __init__.py
        gif.py
        png.py
        tiff.py
        jpeg.py
```

The import statement is used to load modules from a package in a number of ways:

- import Graphics.Primitive.fill

  This loads the submodule Graphics.Primitive.fill. The contents of this module have to be explicitly named, such as
  Graphics.Primitive.fill.floodfill(img,x,y,color).

- from Graphics.Primitive import fill

  This loads the submodule fill but makes it available without the package prefix; for example, fill.floodfill(img,x,y,color).

- from Graphics.Primitive.fill import floodfill

  This loads the submodule fill but makes the floodfill function directly accessible; for example, floodfill(img,x,y,color).

Whenever any part of a package is imported, the code in the file __init__.py is executed. Minimally, this file may be empty, but it can also contain code to perform package-specific initializations. All the __init__.py files encountered during an import are executed. Therefore, the statement import Graphics.Primitive.fill, shown earlier, would first execute the __init__.py file in the Graphics directory and then the __init__.py file in the Primitive directory.

One peculiar problem with packages is the handling of this statement:

```
from Graphics.Primitive import *
```

The intended outcome of this statement is to import all the modules associated with a package into the current namespace. However, because filename conventions vary from system to system (especially with regard to case sensitivity), Python cannot accurately determine what modules those might be. As a result, this statement just imports all the references defined in the __init__.py file in the Primitive directory. This behavior can be modified by defining a list, __all__, that contains all the module names associated with the package. This list should be defined in the package __init__.py file, like this:

```
# Graphics/Primitive/__init__.py
__all__ = ["lines","text","fill",...]
```

Now when the user issues a from Graphics.Primitive import * statement, all the listed submodules are loaded as expected.

Importing a package name alone doesn't import all the submodules contained in the package. For example, the following code doesn't work:

```
import Graphics
Graphics.Primitive.fill.floodfill(img,x,y,color)   # Fails!
```

However, because the import Graphics statement executes the __init__.py file in the Graphics directory, it could be modified to import all the submodules automatically, as follows:

```
# Graphics/__init__.py
import Primitive, Graph2d, Graph3d

# Graphics/Primitive/__init__.py
import lines, fill, text, ...
```

Now the import Graphics statement imports all the submodules and makes them available using their fully qualified names.

The modules contained within the same directory of a package can refer to each other without a full package name being supplied. For example, the Graphics.Primitive.fill module could import the Graphics.Primitive.lines module simply by using import lines. However, if a module is located in a different subdirectory, its full package name must be used. For example, if the plot2d module of Graphics.Graph2d needs to use the lines module of Graphics.Primitive, it must use a statement such as from Graphics.Primitive import lines. If necessary, a module can examine its __name__ variable to find its fully qualified module name. For example, the following code imports a module from a sibling subpackage knowing only the name of the sibling (and not that of its top-level package):

```
# Graphics/Graph2d/plot2d.py

# Determine the name of the package where my package is located
import string
base_package = string.join(string.split(__name__,'.')[:-2],'.')

# Import the ../Primitive/fill.py module
exec "from %s.Primitive import fill" % (base_package,)
```

Finally, when Python imports a package, it defines a special variable, __path__, that contains a list of directories that are searched when looking for package submodules (__path__ is a package-specific version of the sys.path variable). __path__ is accessible to the code contained in __init__.py files and initially contains a single item with the directory name of the package. If necessary, a package can supply additional directories to the __path__ list to alter the search path used for finding submodules.

## 9

Input and Output

THIS CHAPTER DESCRIBES THE DETAILS OF PYTHON input and output (I/O), including command-line options, environment variables, file I/O, Unicode, and object persistence.

Reading Options and Environment Variables

When the interpreter starts, command-line options are placed in the list sys.argv. The first element is the name of the program. Subsequent elements are the options presented on the command line *after* the program name. The following program shows how to access command-line options:

```
# printopt.py
# Print all of the command-line options
import sys
for i in range(len(sys.argv)):
    print "sys.argv[%d] = %s" % (i, sys.argv[i])
```

Running the program produces the following:

```
% python printopt.py foo bar -p
sys.argv[0] = printopt.py
sys.argv[1] = foo
sys.argv[2] = bar
sys.argv[3] = -p
%
```

Environment variables are accessed in the dictionary os.environ. For example:

```
import os
path = os.environ["PATH"]
user = os.environ["USER"]
editor = os.environ["EDITOR"]
... etc ...
```

To modify the environment variables, set the os.environ variable. Alternatively, you can use the os.putenv() function. For example:

```
os.environ["FOO"] = "BAR"
```

```
os.putenv("FOO","BAR")
```

Files and File Objects

The built-in function open(*name* [,*mode* [,*bufsize*]]) opens and creates a file object, as shown here:

```
f = open('foo')           # Opens 'foo' for reading
f = open('foo','r')       # Opens 'foo' for reading (same as above)
f = open('foo','w')       # Open for writing
```

Although less common, files can also be created by calling the file object constructor, which is identical to open(). For example:

```
f = file('foo')           # Opens 'foo' for reading
f = file('foo','w')       # Open for writing
```

The file mode is 'r' for read, 'w' for write, or 'a' for append. The mode character can be followed by 'b' for binary data, such as 'rb' or 'wb'. This is optional on UNIX, but it's required on Windows and should be included if you are concerned about portability. In addition, a file can be opened for updates by supplying a plus (+) character, such as 'r+' or 'w+'. When a file is opened for update, you can perform both input and output, as long as all output operations flush their data before any subsequent input operations. If a file is opened using 'w+' mode, its length is first truncated to zero. If a file is opened with mode 'U' or 'rU', it provides universal newline support for reading. This feature simplifies cross-platform work by translating different newline encodings (such as '\n', '\r', and '\r\n') to a standard '\n' character in the strings returned by various file I/O functions.

The optional *bufsize* parameter controls the buffering behavior of the file, where 0 is unbuffered, 1 is line buffered, and a negative number requests the system default. Any other positive number indicates the approximate buffer size in bytes that will be used.

Table 9.1 shows the methods supported by file objects.

Table 9.1 **File Methods**

Method	Description
f.read([n])	Reads at most n bytes.
f.readline([n])	Reads a single line of input up to n characters. If n is omitted, this method reads the entire line.
f.readlines([size])	Reads all the lines and returns a list. size optionally specifies the approximate number of bytes to read before stopping.
f.xreadlines()	Returns an iterator that reads lines from the file. (Obsolete.)
f.write(S)	Writes string S.
f.writelines(L)	Writes all strings in list L.
f.close()	Closes the file.
f.tell()	Returns the current file pointer.
f.seek(offset [, where])	Seeks to a new file position.
f.isatty()	Returns 1 if f is an interactive terminal.
f.flush()	Flushes the output buffers.

Table 9.1 **Continued**

Method	Description
f.truncate([size])	Truncates the file to at most size bytes.
f.fileno()	Returns an integer file descriptor.
f.next()	Returns the next line or raises StopIteration.

The read() method returns the entire file as a string unless an optional *length* parameter is given specifying the maximum number of bytes. The readline() method returns the next line of input, including the terminating newline; the readlines() method returns all the input lines as a list of strings. The readline() method optionally accepts a maximum line length, *n*. If a line longer than *n* bytes is read, the first *n* bytes are returned. The remaining line data is not discarded and will be returned on subsequent read operations. The readlines() method accepts a size parameter that specifies the approximate number of bytes to read before stopping. The actual number of bytes read may be larger than this depending on how much data has been buffered.

Both the readline() and readlines() methods are platform-aware and handle different representations of newlines properly (for example, '\n' versus '\r\n'). If the file is opened in universal newline mode ('U' or 'rU'), newlines are converted to '\n'.

The xreadlines() method returns an iterator for reading the file line by line. However, this method is only provided for backward compatibility because files can already be used as iterators. For example:

```
for line in f:        # Iterate over all lines in the file
    # Do something with line
    ...
```

The write() method writes a string to the file, and the writelines() method writes a list of strings to the file. In all these cases, the string can contain binary data, including embedded NULL characters. writelines() does not add newline characters to the output, so the supplied list of output strings should already be formatted as necessary.

The seek() method is used to randomly access parts of a file given an *offset* and a placement rule in *where*. If *where* is 0 (the default), seek() assumes that *offset* is relative to the start of the file; if *where* is 1, the position is moved relative to the current position; and if *where* is 2, the offset is taken from the end of the file. The tell() method returns the current position in a file. On machines that support large files (greater than 2GB), the seek() and tell() methods may use long integers. The fileno() method returns the integer file descriptor for a file and is sometimes used in low-level I/O operations in certain library modules.

File objects also have the read-only data attributes shown here:

Attribute	Description
f.closed	Boolean value indicates the file state: False if the file is open, True if closed.
f.mode	The I/O mode for the file.
f.name	Name of the file if created using open(). Otherwise, it will be a string indicating the source of the file.

Attribute	Description
f.softspace	Boolean value indicating whether a space character needs to be printed before another value when using the print statement. Classes that emulate files must provide a writable attribute of this name that's initially initialized to zero.
f.newlines	When a file is opened in universal newline mode, this attribute contains the newline representation actually found in the file. The value is either None if no newlines have been encountered, a string containing '\n', '\r', or '\r\n', or a tuple containing all the different newline encodings seen.
f.encoding	A string that indicates file encoding, if any (for example, 'latin-1' or 'utf-8'). The value is None if no encoding is being used.

Standard Input, Output, and Error

The interpreter provides three standard file objects, known as *standard input, standard output,* and *standard error,* which are available in the sys module as sys.stdin, sys.stdout, and sys.stderr, respectively. stdin is a file object corresponding to the stream of input characters supplied to the interpreter. stdout is the file object that receives output produced by print. stderr is a file that receives error messages. More often than not, stdin is mapped to the user's keyboard, whereas stdout and stderr produce text onscreen.

The methods described in the preceding section can be used to perform raw I/O with the user. For example, the following function reads a line of input from standard input:

```
def gets():
    text = ""
    while 1:
        c = sys.stdin.read(1)
        text = text + c
        if c == '\n': break
    return text
```

Alternatively, the built-in function raw_input(*prompt*) can read a line of text from stdin:

```
s = raw_input("type something : ")
print "You typed '%s'" % (s,)
```

Finally, keyboard interrupts (often generated by Ctrl+C) result in a KeyboardInterrupt exception that can be caught using an exception handler.

If necessary, the values of sys.stdout, sys.stdin, and sys.stderr can be replaced with other file objects, in which case the print statement and raw input functions use the new values. Should it ever be necessary to restore the original value of sys.stdout, it should be saved first. The original values of sys.stdout, sys.stdin, and sys.stderr at interpreter startup are also available in sys.__stdout__, sys.__stdin__, and sys.__stderr__, respectively.

Note that in some cases `sys.stdin`, `sys.stdout`, and `sys.stderr` may be altered by the use of an integrated development environment (IDE). For example, when Python is run under Idle, `sys.stdin` is replaced with an object that behaves like a file, but is really an object in the development environment. In this case, certain low-level methods, such as `read()` and `seek()`, may be unavailable.

The print Statement

The `print` statement produces output on the file contained in `sys.stdout`. `print` accepts a comma-separated list of objects such as the following:

```
print "The values are", x, y, z
```

For each object, the `str()` function is invoked to produce an output string. These output strings are then joined and separated by a single space to produce the final output string. The output is terminated by a newline unless a trailing comma is supplied to the print statement. In this case, only a trailing space is printed. For example:

```
print "The values are ", x, y, z, w
# Print the same text, using two print statements
print "The values are ", x, y,    # Omits trailing newline
print z, w
```

To produce formatted output, use the string-formatting operator (`%`) as described in Chapter 4, "Operators and Expressions." For example:

```
print "The values are %d %7.5f %s" % (x,y,z) # Formatted I/O
```

You can change the destination of the `print` statement by adding the special `>>file` modifier followed by a comma, where *file* is a file object that allows writes. Here's an example:

```
f = open("output","w")
print >>f, "hello world"
...
f.close()
```

Combining formatted I/O using dictionaries with triple-quoted strings is a powerful way to write computer-generated text. For example, you could write a short form letter, filling in a name, an `item` name, and an `amount`, as shown in the following example:

```
Dear Mr. Bush,

Please send back my blender or pay me $50.00.

                            Sincerely yours,


                            Joe Python User
```

To do this, you can form a triple-quoted string containing text and dictionary-based format specifiers such as the following:

```
# Note: trailing slash right after """ prevents a blank line
# from appearing as the first line
form = """\
Dear %(name)s,
Please send back my %(item)s or pay me $%(amount)0.2f.
                            Sincerely yours,
```

```
                                        Joe Python User
"""
print form % { 'name': 'Mr. Bush',
               'item': 'blender',
               'amount': 50.00,
                  }
```

For forms involving many lines and many items to be substituted, this is much clearer than using one `print` statement per line or a large tuple of items to format.

For certain kinds of forms, it may be even easier to use `Template` strings, as follows:

```
import string
form = string.Template("""\
Dear $name,
Please send back my $item or pay me $amount.
                              Sincerely yours,


                                        Joe Python User
""")
print form.substitute({'name': 'Mr. Bush',
                       'item': 'blender',
                       'amount': "%0.2f" % 50.0})
```

In this case, special $ variables in the string indicate substitutions. The `form.substitute()` method takes a dictionary of replacements and returns a new string. `Template` strings are always Unicode.

Persistence

It's often necessary to save and restore the contents of an object to a file. One approach to this problem is to write a pair of functions that read and write data from a file in a special format. An alternative approach is to use the `pickle` and `shelve` modules.

The `pickle` module serializes an object into a stream of bytes that can be written to a file. For example, the following code writes an object to a file:

```
import pickle
object = someObject()
f = open(filename,'w')
pickle.dump(object, f)       # Save object
```

To restore the object, you can use the following code:

```
import pickle
f = open(filename,'r')
object = pickle.load(f)    # Restore the object
```

The `shelve` module is similar, but saves objects in a dictionary-like database:

```
import shelve
object = someObject()
dbase = shelve.open(filename)      # Open a database
dbase['key'] = object              # Save object in database
...
object = dbase['key']              # Retrieve it
dbase.close()                      # Close the database
```

In both cases, only serializable objects can be saved to a file. Most Python objects can be serialized, but special-purpose objects such as files maintain an internal state that cannot be saved and restored in this manner. For more details about the `pickle` and `shelve` modules, see Chapter 13, "Python Runtime Services."

Unicode I/O

Internally, Unicode strings are represented as sequences of 16-bit (UCS-2) or 32-bit (UCS-4) integer character values, depending on how Python is built. As in 8-bit strings, all characters are the same size, and most common string operations are simply extended to handle strings with a larger range of character values. However, whenever Unicode strings are converted to a stream of bytes, a number of issues arise. First, to preserve compatibility with existing software, it may be desirable to convert Unicode to an 8-bit representation compatible with software that expects to receive ASCII or other 8-bit data. Second, the use of 16-bit or 32-bit characters introduces problems related to byte ordering. For the Unicode character U+HHLL, "little endian" encoding places the low-order byte first, as in LL HH. "Big endian" encoding, on the other hand, places the high-order byte first, as in HH LL. Because of this difference, it's generally not possible to simply write raw Unicode data to a file without also specifying the encoding used.

To address these problems, external representation of Unicode strings is always done according to a specific encoding rule. This rule precisely defines how Unicode characters are to be represented as a byte sequence. In Chapter 4, encoding rules were first described for the unicode() function and the s.encode() string method. Here's an example:

```
a = u"M\u00fcller"
b = "Hello World"
c = a.encode('utf-8')     # Convert a to a UTF-8 string
d = unicode(b)            # Convert b to a Unicode string
```

To support Unicode I/O, these encoding and decoding concepts are extended to files. The built-in codecs module contains a collection of functions for converting byte-oriented data to and from Unicode strings according to a variety of different data-encoding schemes.

Perhaps the most straightforward way to handle Unicode files is to use the codecs.open(*filename* [, *mode* [, *encoding* [, *errors*]]]) function, as follows:

```
f = codecs.open('foo.txt','r','utf-8','strict')     # Reading
g = codecs.open('bar.txt','w','utf-16-le')          # Writing
```

This creates a file object that reads or writes Unicode strings. The encoding parameter specifies the underlying character encoding that will be used to translate data as it is read or written to the file. The *errors* parameter determines how errors are handled and is one of 'strict', 'ignore', 'replace', 'backslashreplace', or 'xmlcharrefreplace'. In 'strict' mode, encoding errors raise a UnicodeError exception. In 'ignore' mode, encoding errors are ignored. In 'replace' mode, characters that can't be converted are replaced by a replacement character. The replacement character is U+FFFD in Unicode and '?' in 8-bit strings. In 'backslashreplace' mode, characters that can't be encoded are replaced by Python backslash quoting (for example, '\u1234'), and in 'xmlcharrefreplace' mode, characters are replaced by XML character references (for example, 'ሴ').

If you already have a file object, the codecs.EncodedFile(*file*, *inputenc* [, *outputenc* [, *errors*]]) function can be used to place an encoding wrapper around it. Here's an example:

```
f = open("foo.txt","r")
...
fenc = codecs.EncodedFile(f,'utf-8')
```

In this case, data read from the file will be interpreted according to the encoding supplied in *inputenc*. Data written to the file will be interpreted according to the encoding in *inputenc* and written according to the encoding in *outputenc*. If *outputenc* is omitted, it defaults to the same as *inputenc*. *errors* has the same meaning as described earlier.

If you should need more fine-grained control over Unicode I/O, the codecs module provides a lower-level interface that can be used. A specific codec is selected by calling the codecs.lookup(*encoding*) function. This function returns a four-element tuple: (*enc_func, decode_func, stream_reader, stream_writer*). Here's an example:

```
import codecs
(utf8_encode, utf8_decode, utf8_reader, utf8_writer) = \
        codecs.lookup('utf-8')
```

The *enc_func(u* [*,errors*]) function takes a Unicode string, *u*, and returns a tuple (*s, len*) in which *s* is an 8-bit string containing a portion or all of the Unicode string *u*, converted into the desired encoding, and *len* contains the number of Unicode characters converted. The *decode_func(s* [*,errors*]) function takes an 8-bit string, *s*, and returns a tuple (*u, len*) containing a Unicode string, *u*, and the number of characters in *s* that were converted. The *errors* parameter determines how errors are handled and is the same as described earlier.

stream_reader is a class that implements a wrapper for reading Unicode data from a file object. Calling *stream_reader(file)* returns an object in which the read(), readline(), and readlines() methods read Unicode string data. *stream_writer* is a class that provides a wrapper for writing Unicode to a file object. Calling *stream_writer(file)* returns a file object in which the write() and writelines() methods translate Unicode strings to the given encoding on the output stream.

The following example illustrates how to read and write UTF-8 encoded Unicode data using these functions:

```
# Output Unicode data to a file
ustr = u'M\u00fcller'          # A Unicode string

outf = utf8_writer(open('foo','w'))   # Create UTF-8 output stream
outf.write(ustr)
outf.close()

# Read Unicode data from a file
infile = utf8_reader(open('bar'))
ustr = infile.read()
infile.close()
```

When you're working with Unicode files, the data encoding is usually embedded in the file itself. For example, XML parsers may look at the first few bytes of the string '<?xml ...>' to determine the document encoding. If the first four values are 3C 3F 78 6D ('<?xm'), the encoding is assumed to be UTF-8. If the first four values are 00 3C 00 3F or 3C 00 3F 00, the encoding is assumed to be UTF-16 big endian or UTF-16 little endian, respectively. Alternatively, a document encoding may appear in MIME headers or as an attribute of other document elements. Here's an example:

```
<?xml ... encoding="ISO-8859-1" ... ?>
```

Similarly, Unicode files may also include special byte-order markers (BOM) that indicate properties of the character encoding. The Unicode character U+FEFF is reserved for this purpose. Typically, the marker is written as the first character in the file. Programs then read this character and look at the arrangement of the bytes to determine encoding (for example, '\xff\xfe' for UTF-16-LE or '\xfe\xff' UTF-16-BE). Once the encoding is determined, the BOM character is discarded and the remainder of the file is processed.

When the encoding is read from a document, code similar to the following might be used:

```
f = open("somefile","r")
# Determine encoding of the file
...
# Put an appropriate encoding wrapper on the file
fenc = codecs.EncodedFile(f,encoding)
data = fenc.read()
```

Unicode Data Encoding

Table 9.2 lists some of the currently available encoders in the codecs module.

Table 9.2   **Encoders in the** codecs **Module**

Encoder	Description
'ascii'	ASCII encoding
'latin-1', 'iso-8859-1'	ISO-8859-1 or Latin-1 encoding
'utf-8'	8-bit variable-length encoding
'utf-16'	16-bit variable-length encoding
'utf-16-le'	UTF-16, but with explicit little endian encoding
'utf-16-be'	UTF-16, but with explicit big endian encoding
'unicode-escape'	Same format as u"*string*"
'raw-unicode-escape'	Same format as ur"*string*"

The following sections describe each of the encoders in more detail.

'ascii' **Encoding**

In 'ascii' encoding, character values are confined to the ranges [0x00,0x7f] and [U+0000, U+007F]. Any character outside this range is invalid.

'iso-8859-1' **or** 'latin-1' **Encoding**

Characters can be any 8-bit value in the ranges [0x00,0xff] and [U+0000, U+00FF]. Values in the range [0x00,0x7f] correspond to characters from the ASCII character set. Values in the range [0x80,0xff] correspond to characters from the ISO-8859-1 or extended ASCII character set. Any characters with values outside the range [0x00,0xff] result in an error.

'utf-8' **Encoding**

UTF-8 is a variable-length encoding that allows all Unicode characters to be represented. A single byte is used to represent ASCII characters in the range 0–127. All other characters are represented by multibyte sequences of two or three bytes. The encoding of these bytes is shown here:

Unicode Characters	Byte 0	Byte 1	Byte 2
U+0000 - U+007F	0nnnnnnn		
U+007F - U+07FF	110nnnnn	10nnnnnn	
U+0800 - U+FFFF	1110nnnn	10nnnnnn	10nnnnnn

For two-byte sequences, the first byte always starts with the bit sequence 110. For three-byte sequences, the first byte starts with the bit sequence 1110. All subsequent data bytes in multibyte sequences start with the bit sequence 10.

In full generality, the UTF-8 format allows for multibyte sequences of up to six bytes. In Python, four-byte UTF-8 sequences are used to encode a pair of Unicode characters known as a *surrogate pair*. Both characters have values in the range [U+D800, U+DFFF] and are combined to encode a 20-bit character value. The surrogate encoding is as follows: The four-byte sequence 11110nnn 10nnnnnn 10nmmmm 10mmmmm is encoded as the pair U+D800 + N, U+DC00 + M, where N is the upper 10 bits and M is the lower 10 bits of the 20-bit character encoded in the four-byte UTF-8 sequence. Five- and six-byte UTF-8 sequences (denoted by starting bit sequences of 111110 and 1111110, respectively) are used to encode character values up to 32 bits in length. These values are not supported by Python and currently result in a UnicodeError exception if they appear in an encoded data stream.

UTF-8 encoding has a number of useful properties that allow it to be used by older software. First, the standard ASCII characters are represented in their standard encoding. This means that a UTF-8 encoded ASCII string is indistinguishable from a traditional ASCII string. Second, UTF-8 doesn't introduce embedded NULL bytes for multibyte character sequences. Therefore, existing software based on the C library and programs that expect NULL-terminated 8-bit strings will work with UTF-8 strings. Finally, UTF-8 encoding preserves the lexicographic ordering of strings. That is, if a and b are Unicode strings and a < b, then a < b also holds when a and b are converted to UTF-8. Therefore, sorting algorithms and other ordering algorithms written for 8-bit strings will also work for UTF-8.

'utf-16', 'utf-16-be', and 'utf-16-le' Encoding

UTF-16 is a variable-length 16-bit encoding in which Unicode characters are written as 16-bit values. Unless a byte ordering is specified, big endian encoding is assumed. In addition, a byte-order marker of U+FEFF can be used to explicitly specify the byte ordering in a UTF-16 data stream. In big endian encoding, U+FEFF is the Unicode character for a zero-width nonbreaking space, whereas the reversed value U+FFFE is an illegal Unicode character. Thus, the encoder can use the byte sequence FE FF or FF FE to determine the byte ordering of a data stream. When reading Unicode data, Python removes the byte-order markers from the final Unicode string.

'utf-16-be' encoding explicitly selects UTF-16 big endian encoding. 'utf-16-le' encoding explicitly selects UTF-16 little ending encoding.

Although there are extensions to UTF-16 to support character values greater than 16 bits, none of these extensions are currently supported.

'unicode-escape' and 'raw-unicode-escape' Encoding

These encoding methods are used to convert Unicode strings to the same format as used in Python Unicode string literals and Unicode raw string literals. Here's an example:

```
s = u'u\14a8\u0345\u2a34'
t = s.encode('unicode-escape')    #t = '\u14a8\u0345\u2a34'
```

Unicode Character Properties

In addition to performing I/O, programs that use Unicode may need to test Unicode characters for various properties such as capitalization, numbers, and whitespace. The unicodedata module provides access to a database of character properties. General character properties can be obtained with the unicodedata.category(c) function. For example, unicodedata.category(u"A") returns 'Lu', signifying that the character is an uppercase letter. Further details about the Unicode character database and the unicodedata module can be found in Chapter 16, "String and Text Handling."

10

Execution Environment

THIS CHAPTER DESCRIBES THE ENVIRONMENT IN WHICH Python programs are executed. The goal is to describe the runtime behavior of the interpreter, including program startup, configuration, and program termination.

Interpreter Options and Environment

The interpreter has a number of options that control its runtime behavior and environment. Options are given to the interpreter on the command line as follows:

```
python [options] [-c cmd | filename | - ] [args]
```

Here's a list of the available command-line options:

Option	Description
-d	Generates parser debugging information.
-E	Ignores environment variables.
-h	Prints a list of all available command-line options.
-i	Enters interactive mode after program execution.
-m module	Runs library module module as a script.
-O	Optimized mode.
-OO	Optimized mode plus removal of documentation strings.
-Q arg	Specifies the behavior of the division operator. One of -Qold (the default), -Qnew, -Qwarn, or -Qwarnall.
-S	Prevents inclusion of the site initialization module.
-t	Reports warnings about inconsistent tab usage.
-tt	Inconsistent tab usage results in a TabError exception.
-u	Unbuffered binary stdout and stdin.
-U	Unicode literals. All string literals are handled as Unicode.
-v	Verbose mode.
-V	Prints the version number and exits.
-x	Skip the first line of the source program.
-c cmd	Executes cmd as a string.
-Wfilter	Adds a warning filter (see warnings module, p.174).

The -d option debugs the interpreter and is of limited use to most programmers. Instead, -i may be more useful because it starts an interactive session immediately after a program has finished execution and is useful for debugging. The -m option runs a library module as a script. The -O and -OO options apply some optimization to byte-compiled files and are described in Chapter 8, "Modules and Packages." The -Q option is used to specify the behavior of the division operator. With -Qold, integer division truncates the result. With -Qnew, integer division results in a floating-point number if the result would have a fractional component. The -S option omits the site initialization module described in the later section "Site Configuration Files." The -t, -tt, and -v options report additional warnings and debugging information. -x ignores the first line of a program in the event that it's not a valid Python statement (for example, when the first line starts the Python interpreter in a script). The -U option forces the interpreter to treat all string literals as Unicode.

The program name appears after all the interpreter options. If no name is given, or the hyphen (-) character is used as a filename, the interpreter reads the program from standard input. If standard input is an interactive terminal, a banner and prompt are presented. Otherwise, the interpreter opens the specified file and executes its statements until an end-of-file marker is reached. The -c *cmd* option can be used to execute short programs in the form of a command-line option (for example, python -c "print 'hello world'").

Command-line options appearing after the program name or hyphen (-) are passed to the program in sys.argv, as described in the section "Reading Options and Environment Variables" in Chapter 9, "Input and Output."

Additionally, the interpreter reads the following environment variables:

Variable	Description
PYTHONPATH	Colon-separated module search path
PYTHONSTARTUP	File executed on interactive startup
PYTHONHOME	Location of the Python installation
PYTHONINSPECT	Implies the -i option
PYTHONUNBUFFERED	Implies the -u option
PYTHONCASEOK	Indicates to use case-insensitive matching for module names used by import

PYTHONPATH specifies a module search path that is inserted into the beginning of sys.path, which is described in Chapter 8. PYTHONSTARTUP specifies a file to execute when the interpreter runs in interactive mode. The PYTHONHOME variable is used to set the location of the Python installation but is rarely needed, because Python knows how to find its own libraries and the site-packages directory where extensions are normally installed. If a single directory such as /usr/local is given, the interpreter expects to find all files in that location. If two directories are given, such as /usr/local:/usr/local/sparc-solaris-2.6, the interpreter searches for platform-independent files in the first directory and platform-dependent files in the second. PYTHONHOME has no effect if no valid Python installation exists at the specified location.

On Windows, some of the environment variables such as PYTHONPATH are additionally read from Registry entries found in HKEY_LOCAL_MACHINE/Software/Python.

Interactive Sessions

If no program name is given and the standard input to the interpreter is an interactive terminal, Python starts in interactive mode. In this mode, a banner message is printed and the user is presented with a prompt. In addition, the interpreter evaluates the script contained in the PYTHONSTARTUP environment variable (if set). This script is evaluated as if it's part of the input program (that is, it isn't loaded using an import statement). One application of this script might be to read a user configuration file such as .pythonrc.

When interactive input is being accepted, two user prompts appear. The >>> prompt appears at the beginning of a new statement; the ... prompt indicates a statement continuation. For example:

```
Python 2.0 (#1, Oct 27 2000, 14:34:45)
[GCC 2.95.2 19991024 (release)] on sunos5
Type "copyright", "credits" or "license" for more information.
>>> for i in range(0,4):
...     print i
...
0
1
2
3
>>>
```

In customized applications, you can change the prompts by modifying the values of sys.ps1 and sys.ps2.

On some systems, Python may be compiled to use the GNU readline library. If enabled, this library provides command histories, completion, and other additions to Python's interactive mode.

By default, the output of commands issued in interactive mode is generated by printing the output of the built-in repr() function on the result. Starting with Python 2.1, this can be changed by setting the variable sys.displayhook to a function responsible for displaying results. For example:

```
>>> def my_display(x):
...     print "result = %s" % repr(x)
...
>>> sys.displayhook = my_display
>>> 3+4
result = 7
>>>
```

Finally, in interactive mode, it is useful to know that the result of the last operation is stored in a special variable (_). This variable can be used to retrieve the result should you need to use it in subsequent operations. For example:

```
>>> 7 + 3
10
>>> print _ + 2
12
>>>
```

Launching Python Applications

In most cases, you'll want programs to start the interpreter automatically, rather than first having to start the interpreter manually. On UNIX, this is done by giving the program execute permission and setting the first line of a program to something like this:

```
#!/usr/local/bin/python
# Python code from this point on...
import string
print "Hello world"
...
```

On Windows, double-clicking a `.py`, `.pyw`, `.wpy`, `.pyc`, or `.pyo` file automatically launches the interpreter. Normally, programs run in a console window unless they're renamed with a `.pyw` suffix (in which case the program runs silently). If it's necessary to supply options to the interpreter, Python can also be started from a `.bat` file. For example, this `.bat` file simply runs Python on a script and passes any options supplied on the command prompt along to the interpreter:

```
:: foo.bat
:: Runs foo.py script and passes supplied command line options along (if any)
c:\python24\python.exe c:\pythonscripts\foo.py %*
```

Site Configuration Files

A typical Python installation may include a number of third-party modules and packages. To configure these packages, the interpreter first imports the module `site`. The role of `site` is to search for package files and to add additional directories to the module search path `sys.path`. In addition, the `site` module sets the default encoding for Unicode string conversions. For details on the `site` module, see Chapter 13, "Python Runtime Services."

Enabling Future Features

New language features that affect compatibility with older versions of Python are often disabled when they first appear in a release. To enable these features, the statement `from __future__ import feature` can be used. For example:

```
# Enable new division semantics
from __future__ import division
```

When used, this statement should appear as the first statement of a module or program. Furthermore, the intent of the `__future__` module is to introduce features that will eventually be a standard part of the Python language (in which case the use of `__future__` will not be required).

Program Termination

A program terminates when no more statements exist to execute in the input program, when an uncaught `SystemExit` exception is raised (as generated by `sys.exit()`), or when the interpreter receives a `SIGTERM` or `SIGHUP` signal (on UNIX). On exit, the interpreter decrements the reference count of all objects in all the currently known namespaces (and destroys each namespace as well). If the reference count of an object reaches zero, the object is destroyed and its `__del__()` method is invoked.

It's important to note that in some cases the __del__() method might not be invoked at program termination. This can occur if circular references exist between objects (in which case objects may be allocated, but accessible from no known namespace). Although Python's garbage collector can reclaim unused circular references during execution, it isn't normally invoked on program termination.

Because there's no guarantee that __del__() will be invoked at termination, it may be a good idea to explicitly clean up certain objects, such as open files and network connections. To accomplish this, add specialized cleanup methods (for example, close()) to user-defined objects. Another possibility is to write a termination function and register it with the atexit module, as follows:

```
import atexit
connection = open_connection("deaddot.com")

def cleanup():
    print "Going away..."
    close_connection(connection)

atexit.register(cleanup)
```

The garbage collector can also be invoked in this manner:

```
import atexit, gc
atexit.register(gc.collect)
```

One final peculiarity about program termination is that the __del__ method for some objects may try to access global data or methods defined in other modules. Because these objects may already have been destroyed, a NameError exception occurs in __del__, and you may get an error such as the following:

```
Exception exceptions.NameError: 'c' in <method Bar.__del__
of Bar instance at c0310> ignored
```

If this occurs, it means that __del__ has aborted prematurely. It also implies that it may have failed in an attempt to perform an important operation (such as cleanly shutting down a server connection). If this is a concern, it's probably a good idea to perform an explicit shutdown step in your code, rather than relying on the interpreter to destroy objects cleanly at program termination. The peculiar NameError exception can also be eliminated by declaring default arguments in the declaration of the __del__() method:

```
import foo
class Bar(object):
    def __del__(self, foo=foo):
        foo.bar()          # Use something in module foo
```

In some cases, it may be useful to terminate program execution without performing any cleanup actions. This can be accomplished by calling os._exit(*status*). This function provides an interface to the low-level exit() system call responsible for killing the Python interpreter process. When it's invoked, the program immediately terminates without any further processing or cleanup.

The Python Library

11

Introduction to the Python Standard Library

P YTHON IS BUNDLED WITH A LARGE COLLECTION of modules collectively known as
the Python library. Library modules are used simply via an `import` statement. For
example:

```
import socket
```

Automatically generated documentation, collected from documentation strings and
source code, can be obtained using the `pydoc` command (executed as a shell command)
or the `help()` command if running interactively in the Python interpreter. For
example:

```
>>> help(re)
Help on module re:

NAME
    re - Minimal "re" compatibility wrapper.  See "sre" for documentation.

FILE
    /Library/Frameworks/Python.framework/Versions/2.4/lib/python2.4/re.py

MODULE DOCS
    http://www.python.org/doc/current/lib/module-re.html

CLASSES
    exceptions.Exception
        sre_constants.error

    class error(exceptions.Exception)
     |  Methods inherited from exceptions.Exception:
     |
     |  __getitem__(...)
     |
     |  __init__(...)
     |
     |  __str__(...)

FUNCTIONS
    compile(pattern, flags=0)
        Compile a regular expression pattern, returning a pattern object.

...
```

In addition, online documentation for all modules can almost always be found at the following URL:

http://www.python.org/doc/current/lib/modindex.html

Documentation for a specific module can be found at the following URL:

http://www.python.org/doc/current/lib/module-*modname*.html

Simply replace *modname* with the name of the module in the preceding URL.

Library Overview

The Python library is strongly focused on the following areas:

- **Systems programming**   Python provides access to a wide variety of operating system interfaces, including low-level system calls, system administration tools, file handling, threads, locking, and interprocess communication.

- **Network programming**   Support for programming with sockets and a wide variety of network protocols is provided.

- **Text and string processing**   A large number of modules related to basic text and string processing are provided. These include support for regular expression parsing, string formatting, Unicode, and internationalization.

- **Data encoding and decoding**   A wide variety of modules are included for dealing with various types of files and data formats (for example, support for reading and writing zip, tar, gzip, and bz2 encoded files as well as dealing with common data formats such as base 64).

- **Internet application programming**   A large number of modules provide support for various Internet application protocols (HTTP, email, news, and so on). In addition, a large number of modules are provided for working with common Internet data encodings.

- **Data structures and algorithms**   A number of modules implement new data structures (queues, heaps, and so on).

To understand the full contents of the library, it is useful to have a basic understanding of application programming. In addition, because many of the library modules are based on C programming interfaces, a good book on C programming may be useful in understanding the finer points of certain library modules.

Preview

The remaining chapters of this book focus on the different areas of the Python library.
   Most of the material presented is based on Python's online documentation.
However, a number of significant changes have been made:

- In some cases, the documentation has been condensed to fit in a more compact format. This has been done to streamline the discussion and make the book more "portable."

- In certain cases, the documentation has been greatly expanded. For instance, coverage of operating systems and network-related modules includes additional information drawn from standards documents and systems programming texts. In the online documentation, much of this information is only referred to by reference.

- In most cases, different examples have been provided in order to complement or expand upon examples in the online documentation.

- Special-purpose modules applicable to a single platform are omitted (for instance, SGI multimedia extensions).

- Large frameworks such as Tkinter are omitted because they are beyond the scope of this book and they're already covered in books of their own.

- Obsolete modules are not covered, even though they are still included in the standard library. A list of omitted modules can be found in Chapter 25, "Miscellaneous Modules."

12

Built-in Functions and Exceptions

THIS CHAPTER DESCRIBES PYTHON'S BUILT-IN FUNCTIONS and exceptions. Much of this material is covered less formally in earlier chapters of this book. This chapter consolidates all this information and expands upon some of the more subtle features of certain functions.

Built-in Functions

The functions in this section are always available to the interpreter and are contained within the __builtin__ module. In addition, the __builtins__ attribute of each module usually refers to this module.

_ (underscore)

By default, the _ variable is set to the result of the last expression evaluated when the interpreter is running in interactive mode.

> **See Also:**
> sys.displayhook (p. 166)

__import__(*name* [, *globals* [, *locals* [, *fromlist*]]])

This function is invoked by the import statement to load a module. *name* is a string containing the module name, *globals* is an optional dictionary defining the global namespace, *locals* is a dictionary defining the local namespace, and *fromlist* is a list of targets given to the from statement. For example, the statement import spam results in a call to __import__('spam', globals(), locals(), []), whereas the statement from spam import foo results in the call __import__ ('spam', globals(), locals(), ['foo']). If the module name is prefixed by a package name, such as foo.bar, and *fromlist* is empty, the corresponding module object is returned. If *fromlist* is not empty, only the top-level package is returned.

This function is intended to be a low-level interface to the module loader. It doesn't perform all the steps performed by an import statement (in particular, the local namespace is not updated with names referring to objects contained within the module). This function can be redefined by the user to implement new behaviors for import.

The default implementation doesn't even look at the *locals* parameter, whereas *globals* is only used to determine package context (these parameters are supplied so that alternative implementations of __import__() have full access to the global and local namespace information where import statements appear). Note that the imp module contains a variety of functions that are used in implementing import.

abs(*x*)

Returns the absolute value of *x*.

apply(*func* [, *args* [, *keywords*]])

Performs a function call operation on a callable object, *func*. *args* is a tuple containing positional arguments, and *keywords* is a dictionary containing keyword arguments. The apply() function can also be written as *func(*args, **keywords)*.

basestring

This is an abstract data type that is the superclass of all strings (str and unicode). It is primarily used for type testing. For example, isinstance(*s*,basestring) returns True if *s* is either kind of string.

bool([*x*])

Converts the object *x* to a Boolean. Returns True if *x* evaluates to true using the usual truth-testing semantics (that is, nonzero number, non-empty list, and so on). Otherwise, False is returned. False is also returned if *x* is omitted. bool is implemented as a class that inherits from int.

callable(*object*)

Returns True if *object* is a callable object. Otherwise, False is returned.

chr(*i*)

Converts an integer value, *i* (where 0 <= *i* <= 255), into a one-character string. Raises ValueError if *i* is outside this range.

classmethod(func)

This function creates a class method for the function *func*. It is typically only used inside class definitions where it is implicitly invoked by the @classmethod decorator. Unlike a normal method, a class method receives the class as the first argument, not an instance. For example, if you had an object, f, that is an instance of class Foo, invoking a class method on f will pass the class Foo as the first argument to the method, not the instance f.

cmp(*x*, *y*)

Compares *x* and *y* and returns a negative number if *x* < *y*, a positive number if *x* > *y*, or 0 if *x* == *y*. Any two objects can be compared, although the result may be meaningless if the two objects have no meaningful comparison method defined (for example, comparing a number with a file object). In certain circumstances, such comparisons may also raise an exception.

coerce(*x*, *y*)

Returns a tuple containing the values of *x* and *y* converted to a common numerical type. See the section "Mathematical Operations" in Chapter 3, "Types and Objects."

`compile(`*`string, filename, kind`* `[,` *`flags`* `[,` *`dont_inherit`*`]])`

Compiles *string* into a code object for use with exec or eval(). *string* is a string containing valid Python code. If this code spans multiple lines, the lines must be terminated by a single newline ('\n') and not platform-specific variants (for example, '\r\n' on Windows). *filename* is a string containing the name of the file in which the string was defined. *kind* is 'exec' for a sequence of statements, 'eval' for a single expression, or 'single' for a single executable statement. The *flags* parameter determines which optional features (associated with the __future__ module) are enabled. Features are specified using the bitwise OR of flags defined in the __future__ module. For example, if you wanted to enable new division semantics, you would set *flags* to __future__.division.compiler_flag. If *flags* is omitted or set to 0, the code is compiled with whatever features are currently in effect. If *flags* is supplied, the features specified are added to those features already in effect. If dont_inherit is set, only those features specified in *flags* are enabled—features currently enabled are ignored.

`complex([`*`real`* `[,` *`imag`*`]])`

Creates a complex number with real and imaginary components, *real* and *imag*, which can be supplied as any numeric type. If *imag* is omitted, the imaginary component is set to zero. If *real* is passed as a string, the string is parsed and converted to a complex number. In this case, *imag* should be omitted. If no arguments are given, 0j is returned.

`delattr(`*`object, attr`*`)`

Deletes an attribute of an object. *attr* is a string. Same as del *object.attr*.

`dict([`*`m`*`])` or `dict(`*`key1 = value1, key2 = value2, ...`*`)`

Creates a new dictionary. If no argument is given, an empty dictionary is returned. If *m* is a mapping object (such as a dictionary), a new dictionary having the same keys and same values as *m* is returned. For example, if *m* is a dictionary, dict(*m*) simply makes a copy of it. If *m* is not a mapping, it must support iteration in which a sequence of (*key, value*) pairs is produced. These pairs are used to populate the dictionary. dict() can also be called with keyword arguments. For example, dict(foo=3, bar=7) creates the dictionary { 'foo' : 3, 'bar' : 7 }.

`dir([`*`object`*`])`

Returns a sorted list of attribute names. If *object* is a module, it contains the list of symbols defined in that module. If *object* is a type or class object, it returns a list of attribute names. The names are typically obtained from the object's __dict__ attributed if defined, but other sources may be used. If no argument is given, the names in the current local symbol table are returned. It should be noted that this function is primarily used for informational purposes (for example, used interactively at the command line). It should not be used for formal program analysis because the information obtained may be incomplete.

`divmod(`*`a, b`*`)`

Returns the quotient and remainder of long division as a tuple. For integers, the value (*a* // *b*, *a* % *b*) is returned. For floats, (math.floor(*a* / *b*), *a* % *b*) is returned. This function may not be called with complex numbers.

`enumerate(iter)`

Given an iterable object, *iter*, returns a new iterator that produces tuples containing a count and the value produced from *iter*. For example, if *iter* produces a, b, c, then enumerate(iter) produces (0,a), (1,b), (2,c).

`eval(expr [, globals [, locals]])`

Evaluates an expression. *expr* is a string or a code object created by compile(). *globals* and *locals* define the global and local namespaces, respectively, for the operation. If omitted, the expression is evaluated in the namespace of the caller. If given, *globals* must be a dictionary. *locals* may be any kind of mapping object.

`execfile(filename [, globals [, locals]])`

Executes the statements in the file *filename*. *globals* and *locals* define the global and local namespaces, respectively, in which the file is executed. If only *globals* is provided, it serves as both the global and local namespace. If both parameters are omitted, the file's contents are executed in the namespace of the caller. If given, *globals* must be a dictionary. *locals* may be any kind of mapping object. This function should not be used inside of other functions or methods (although supported in certain cases, it may be illegal in others).

`file(filename [, mode [, bufsize]])`

Creates a new file object. This function is exactly the same as the more commonly used open() function. See the description of open() for an explanation of the parameters. file is more commonly used for type testing. For example, isinstance(f, file) tests if f is a file.

`filter(function, iterable)`

Creates a list consisting of the objects from *iterable* for which *function* evaluates to true. If *function* is None, the identity function is used and all the elements of *iterable* that are false are removed. *iterable* can be any object that supports iteration. Note that filtering is often performed using list comprehensions instead (see Chapter 6, "Functions and Functional Programming").

`float([x])`

Converts x to a floating-point number. If x is a string, it is parsed and converted to a float. If no argument is supplied, 0.0 is returned.

`frozenset([iterable])`

Creates an immutable set object populated with items taken from *iterable*. These items must also be immutable. If no argument is given, an empty set is returned.

`getattr(object, name [,default])`

Returns the value of a named attribute of an object. *name* is a string containing the attribute name. *default* is an optional value to return if no such attribute exists. Otherwise, AttributeError is raised. Same as *object.name*.

`globals()`

Returns the dictionary of the current module that represents the global namespace. When called inside another function or method, it returns the global namespace of the module in which the function or method was defined.

hasattr(*object*, *name*)

Returns True if *name* is the name of an attribute of *object*. False is returned otherwise. *name* is a string.

hash(*object*)

Returns an integer hash value for an object (if possible). The hash value is primarily used in the implementation of dictionaries and other mapping objects. The hash value is the same for any two objects that compare as equals. Mutable objects don't define a hash value.

help([*object*])

Calls the built-in help system during interactive sessions. *object* may be a string representing the name of a module, class, function, method, keyword, or documentation topic. If it is any other kind of object, a help screen related to that object will be produced. If no argument is supplied, an interactive help tool will start and provide more information.

hex(*x*)

Converts an integer, *x*, to a hexadecimal string.

id(*object*)

Returns the unique integer identity of *object*.

input([*prompt*])

Same as eval(raw_input(*prompt*)).

int(*x* [,*base*])

Converts a number or string, *x*, to an integer. *base* optionally specifies a base when converting from a string. If the result exceeds the precision of the integer type, a long integer is returned instead.

intern(*string*)

Checks to see whether *string* is contained in an internal table of strings. If found, a copy of the internal string is returned. If not, *string* is added to the internal table and returned. This function is primarily used to get better performance in operations involving dictionary lookups. Not applicable to Unicode strings. Interned strings are still garbage-collected. Therefore, the returned value must be stored someplace in order for this function to be of any practical use.

isinstance(*object*, *classobj*)

Returns True if *object* is an instance of *classobj* or a subclass of *classobj*. The *classobj* parameter can also be a tuple of possible types or classes. For example, isinstance(*s*, (list,tuple)) returns True if *s* is a tuple or a list.

issubclass(*class1*, *class2*)

Returns True if *class1* is a subclass of (derived from) *class2*. *class2* can also be a tuple of possible classes, in which case each class will be checked. Note that issubclass(*A*, *A*) is true.

`iter(object [,sentinel])`

Returns an iterator for producing items in `object`. If the `sentinel` parameter is omitted, the object must either provide the method `__iter__()`, which creates an iterator, or the object must implement `__getitem__()`, which accepts integer arguments starting at 0. If `sentinel` is specified, `object` is interpreted differently. Instead, `object` should be a callable object that takes no parameters. The returned iterator object will call this function repeatedly until the returned value is equal to `sentinel`, at which point iteration will stop. A `TypeError` will be generated if `object` does not support iteration.

`len(s)`

Returns the number of items contained in `s`. `s` is usually a list, tuple, string, set, or dictionary.

`list([s])`

Returns a new list consisting of the items in `s`. `s` may be any object that supports iteration. If `s` is already a list, a copy is made. If no argument is given, an empty list is returned.

`locals()`

Returns a dictionary corresponding to the local namespace of the caller.

`long([x [, base]])`

Converts a number or string, `x`, to a long integer. `base` optionally specifies the base of the conversion when converting from a string. If no argument is given, this function returns `0L`.

`map(function, list, ...)`

Applies `function` to every item of `list` and returns a list of results. If multiple lists are supplied, `function` is assumed to take that many arguments, with each argument taken from a different list. If `function` is `None`, the identity function is assumed. If `None` is mapped to multiple lists, a list of tuples is returned, wherein each tuple contains an element from each list. Short lists are extended with values of `None` to match the length of the longest list, if necessary. Consider using list comprehensions instead of `map`. For example, `map(function, alist)` can be replaced by `[function(x) for x in alist]`.

See Also:
zip (p. 144)

`max(s [, args, ...])`

For a single argument, `s`, this function returns the maximum value of the items in `s`, which may be any iterable object. For multiple arguments, it returns the largest of the arguments.

`min(s [, args, ...])`

For a single argument, `s`, this function returns the minimum value of the items in `s`, which may be able iterable object. For multiple arguments, it returns the smallest of the arguments.

`object()`

Returns a bland uninteresting object. `object` is the abstract base class for all classes and types. No arguments are accepted.

`oct(x)`

Converts an integer, *x*, to an octal string.

`open(filename [, mode [, bufsize]])`

Opens the file `filename` and returns a new file object (see Chapter 10, "Execution Environment"). `mode` indicates how the file should be opened: `'r'` for reading, `'w'` for writing, and `'a'` for appending. An optional `'+'` can be added to the mode to open the file for updating (which allows both reading and writing). A mode of `'w+'` truncates the file to zero length if it already exists. A mode of `'r+'` or `'a+'` opens the file for both reading and writing, but leaves the original contents intact when the file is opened. Append `'b'` to the mode to indicate binary mode on platforms such as Windows, where a distinction is made between text and binary files. If a mode of `'U'` or `'rU'` is specified, the file is opened in universal newline mode. In this mode, all variants of a newline (`'\n'`, `'\r'`, `'\r\n'`) are converted to the standard `'\n'` character. If the mode is omitted, a mode of `'r'` is assumed. The `bufsize` argument specifies the buffering behavior, where 0 is unbuffered, 1 is line buffered, and any other positive number indicates an approximate buffer size in bytes. A negative number indicates that the system default buffering should be used (this is the default behavior). Note that this function is an alias for `file()`.

`ord(c)`

Returns the integer ordinal value of a single character, *c*. For ordinary characters, a value in the range `[0,255]` is returned. For Unicode characters, a value in the range `[0,65535]` is returned.

`pow(x, y [, z])`

Returns $x ** y$. If *z* is supplied, this function returns $(x ** y) \% z$. If all three arguments are given, they must be integers and *y* must be nonnegative.

`property([fget [,fset [,fdel [,doc]]]])`

Creates a property attribute for classes. `fget` is a function that returns the attribute value, `fset` sets the attribute value, and `fdel` deletes an attribute. `doc` provides a documentation string. These parameters may be supplied using keyword arguments—for example, `property(fget=getX, doc="some text")`.

`range([start,] stop [, step])`

Creates a list of integers from `start` to `stop`. `step` indicates a stride and is set to 1 if omitted. If `start` is omitted (when `range()` is called with one argument), it defaults to 0. A negative `step` creates a list of numbers in descending order.

See Also:

xrange (p. 144)

`raw_input([`*`prompt`*`])`

Reads a line of input from standard input (`sys.stdin`) and returns it as a string. If *prompt* is supplied, it's first printed to standard output (`sys.stdout`). Trailing newlines are stripped and an `EOFError` exception is raised if an EOF is read. If the `readline` module is loaded, this function will use it to provide advanced line-editing and command-completion features.

`reduce(`*`func, seq`* `[,` *`initializer`*`])`

Applies a function, *func*, cumulatively to the items in the sequence *seq* and returns a single value. *func* is expected to take two arguments and is first applied to the first two items of *seq*. This result and subsequent elements of *seq* are then combined one at a time in a similar manner, until all elements of *seq* have been consumed. *initializer* is an optional starting value used in the first computation and when *seq* is empty.

`reload(`*`module`*`)`

Reloads an already imported module. *module* must refer to an existing module object. The use of this function is discouraged except for debugging. Keep the following issues in mind:

- When a module is reloaded, the dictionary defining its global namespace is retained. Thus, definitions in the old module that aren't part of the newly reloaded module are retained. Modules can exploit this to see if they have been previously loaded.

- It's usually illegal to reload dynamically loaded modules written in C.

- If any other modules have imported this module by using the `from` statement, they'll continue to use the definitions in the previously imported module. This problem can be avoided by either reissuing the `from` statement after a module has been reloaded or using fully qualified names such as *module.name*.

- If there are any object instances created by classes in the old module, they'll continue to use methods defined in the old module.

`repr(`*`object`*`)`

Returns a string representation of *object*. This is the same string generated by backquotes (``` `` ```). In most cases, the returned string is an expression that can be passed to `eval()` to re-create the object.

`reversed(`*`s`*`)`

Creates a reverse iterator for sequence *s*. This function only works if *s* implements the sequence methods `__len__()` and `__getitem__()`. In addition, *s* must index items starting at 0.

`round(`*`x`* `[,` *`n`*`])`

Rounds the result of rounding the floating-point number *x* to the closest multiple of 10 to the power minus *n*. If *n* is omitted, it defaults to 0. If two multiples are equally close, rounding is done away from 0 (for example, 0.5 is rounded to 1.0 and -0.5 is rounded to -1.0).

`set([iterable])`

Creates a set populated with items taken from *iterable*. The items must be immutable. If *iterable* contains other sets, those sets must be of type *frozenset*. If *iterable* is omitted an empty set is returned.

`setattr(object, name, value)`

Sets an attribute of an object. *name* is a string. Same as *object.name* = *value*.

`slice([start,] stop [, step])`

Returns a slice object representing integers in the specified range. Slice objects are also generated by the extended slice syntax `a[i:i:k]`. See the section "Sequence and Mapping Methods" in Chapter 3 for details.

`sorted(iterable [,cmp [, key [, reverse]]])`

Creates a sorted list from items in *iterable*. $cmp(x, y)$ is a comparison function that returns –1 if $x < y$, 0 if $x == y$, or 1 if $x > y$. $key(x)$ is a function that transforms values before they are passed to the compare function. If *reverse* is True, the list is sorted in reverse order. The arguments can be specified using keywords. For example, `sorted(a, reverse=True)` creates a list sorted in reverse order.

`staticmethod(func)`

Creates a static method for use in classes. This function is implicitly invoked by the `@staticmethod` decorator.

`str([object])`

Returns a string representing the printable form of an object. This is the same string as would be produced by the *print* statement. If no argument is given, an empty string is returned.

`sum(iterable [,initial])`

Computes the sum of a sequence of items taken from *iterable*. *initial* provides the starting value and defaults to 0. This function only works with numbers.

`super(type [, object])`

Returns a special super-object that represents the superclasses of *type*. The primary purpose of this object is to invoke methods in base classes. Here's an example:

```
class B(A):
    def foo(self):
        super(B,self).foo()
```

If *object* is an object, then `isinstance(object, type)` must be true. If *object* is a type, then it must be a subclass of *type*. See Chapter 7, "Classes and Object-Oriented Programming," for more details.

`tuple([s])`

Creates a tuple whose items are taken from *s*, which may be any iterable object. If *s* is already a tuple, it's returned unmodified. If no argument is given, an empty tuple is returned.

type(*object*)

Returns the type of *object*. The type is returned as a type object as defined as a built-in object or in the types module. For common types such as integers, floats, and lists, the type is the same as the conversion functions int, float, list, and so forth (in fact, the conversion function is really just a constructor for the type).

See Also:
isinstance (p. 139)

type(name,bases,dict)

Creates a new *type* object (which is the same as defining a new class). *name* is the name of the type, *bases* is a tuple of base classes, and *dict* is a dictionary containing definitions corresponding to a class body. This function is most commonly used when working with metaclasses. This is described further in Chapter 7.

unichr(i)

Converts the integer or long integer *i*, where 0 <= i <= 65535, to a single Unicode character.

unicode(*string* [,*encoding* [,*errors*]])

Converts *string* to a Unicode string. *encoding* specifies the data encoding of *string*. If omitted, the default encoding as returned by sys.getdefaultencoding() is used. *errors* specifies how encoding errors are handled and is one of 'strict', 'ignore', 'replace', 'backslashreplace', or 'xmlcharrefreplace'. See Chapter 9, "Input and Output," and Chapter 3, "Types and Objects," for details.

vars([*object*])

Returns the symbol table of *object* (usually found in its __dict__ attribute). If no argument is given, a dictionary corresponding to the local namespace is returned.

xrange([*start*,] *stop* [, *step*])

Works like range(), except that an xrange object is returned. This object produces the same values as stored in the list created by range(), but without actually storing them. This is useful when working with very large ranges of integers that would consume a large amount of memory. *start*, *stop*, and *step* are limited to the set of values supported by integers (not long integers). xrange objects do not provide most list methods and operators (for example, slicing).

zip([*s1* [, *s2* [,..]]])

Returns a list of tuples where the *n*th tuple is (*s1*[n], *s2*[n], ...). The resulting list is truncated to the length of the shortest argument sequence. If no arguments are given, an empty list is returned.

Built-in Exceptions

Built-in exceptions are contained in the exceptions module, which is always loaded prior to the execution of any program. Exceptions are defined as classes. The following exceptions serve as base classes for all the other exceptions:

Exception

The root class for all exceptions. All built-in exceptions are derived from this class. User-defined exceptions should use this as a base class.

StandardError

The base class for all built-in exceptions except for SystemExit and StopIteration.

ArithmeticError

The base class for arithmetic exceptions, including OverflowError, ZeroDivisionError, and FloatingPointError.

LookupError

The base class for indexing and key errors, including IndexError and KeyError.

EnvironmentError

The base class for errors that occur outside Python, including IOError and OSError.

The preceding exceptions are never raised explicitly. However, they can be used to catch certain classes of errors. For instance, the following code would catch any sort of numerical error:

```
try:
    # Some operation
    ...
except ArithmeticError, e:
    # Math error
```

When an exception is raised, an instance of an exception class is created. This instance is placed in the optional variable supplied to the except statement. For example:

```
except IOError, e:
    # Handle error
    # 'e' has an instance of IOError
```

Most exceptions have an associated value that can be found in the args attribute of the exception instance ('e.args' in the preceding example). In most cases, this is a string describing the error. For EnvironmentError exceptions, the value is a 2-tuple or 3-tuple containing an integer error number, string error message, and an optional filename (these values are also available as exception attributes, as described next).

The following exceptions are raised by programs:

AssertionError

Failed assert statement.

AttributeError

Failed attribute reference or assignment.

EOFError

End of file. Generated by the built-in functions input() and raw_input().

Note

A number of I/O methods, such as read() and readlines(), return an empty string for EOF.

FloatingPointError

Failed floating-point operation. Note that this is only raised if Python is configured to handle floating-point exceptions.

IOError

Failed I/O operation. The value is an `IOError` instance with the attributes `errno`, `strerror`, and `filename`. `errno` is an integer error number, `strerror` is a string error message, and `filename` is an optional filename.

ImportError

Raised when an `import` statement can't find a module or when `from` can't find a name in a module.

IndentationError

Indentation error. A subclass of `SyntaxError`.

IndexError

Sequence subscript out of range.

KeyError

Key not found in a dictionary.

KeyboardInterrupt

Raised when the user presses the interrupt key (usually Ctrl+C).

MemoryError

Recoverable out-of-memory error.

NameError

Name not found in local or global namespaces.

NotImplementedError

Unimplemented feature. Can be raised by base classes that require derived classes to implement certain methods. A subclass of `RuntimeError`.

OSError

Operating system error. Primarily raised by functions in the `os` module. The value is the same as for `IOError`.

OverflowError

Result of an arithmetic operation being too large to be represented. This exception is no longer generated in most cases because the large integer results are promoted to long integers instead.

ReferenceError

Result of accessing a weak reference after the underlying object has been destroyed. See the `weakref` module (p. 176)

RuntimeError

A generic error not covered by any of the other categories.

`StopIteration`

Raised to signal the end of iteration. This normally happens in the `next()` method of an object or in a generator function.

`SyntaxError`

Parser syntax error. Instances have the attributes `filename`, `lineno`, `offset`, and `text`, which can be used to gather more information.

`SystemError`

Internal error in the interpreter. The value is a string indicating the problem.

`SystemExit`

Raised by the `sys.exit()` function. The value is an integer indicating the return code. If it's necessary to exit immediately, `os._exit()` can be used.

`TabError`

Inconsistent tab usage. Generated when Python is run with the `-tt` option. A subclass of `SyntaxError`.

`TypeError`

Occurs when an operation or function is applied to an object of an inappropriate type.

`UnboundLocalError`

Unbound local variable referenced. This error occurs if a variable is referenced before it's defined in a function. A subclass of `NameError`.

`UnicodeError`

Unicode encoding or decoding error. A subclass of `ValueError`.

`UnicodeEncodeError`

Unicode encoding error. A subclass of `UnicodeError`.

`UnicodeDecodeError`

Unicode decoding error. A subclass of `UnicodeError`.

`UnicodeTranslateError`

Unicode error occurred during translation. A subclass of `UnicodeError`.

`ValueError`

Generated when the argument to a function or operation is the right type but an inappropriate value.

`WindowsError`

Generated by failed system calls on Windows. A subclass of `OSError`.

`ZeroDivisionError`

Dividing by zero.

The exceptions module also defines the exception objects Warning, UserWarning, DeprecationWarning, FutureWarning, PendingDeprecationWarning, RuntimeWarning, and SyntaxWarning. These exceptions are used as part of the Python warning framework and are described further in the warnings module (**p. 174**).

## 13

Python Runtime Services

THIS CHAPTER DESCRIBES MODULES THAT CONTROL the Python interpreter and its environment. Topics include garbage collection, basic management of objects (copying, marshalling, and so on), weak references, and system parameters.

atexit

The atexit module is used to register functions to execute when the Python interpreter exits. A single function is provided:

register(*func* [, *args* [, *kwargs*]])

Adds function *func* to a list of functions that will execute when the interpreter exits. *args* is tuple of arguments to pass to the function. *kwargs* is a dictionary of keyword arguments. The function is invoked as *func*(*args*, **kwargs*). Upon exit, functions are invoked in reverse order of registration (the most recently added exit function is invoked first). If an error occurs, an exception message will be printed to standard error, but will otherwise be ignored.

> **Note**
> The atexit module should be used instead of setting the sys.exitfunc variable directly because doing so may interfere with other modules that have defined cleanup actions.

> **See Also:**
> sys (p. 166)

code

The code module defines classes and functions that may be useful in implementing interactive new read-eval loops (for instance, if you wanted to provide a different interactive interface to the Python interpreter).

compile_command(*source* [, *filename* [, *symbol*]])

Compiles Python code in the string *source* and returns a code object if *source* is complete and valid. Returns None if *source* is syntactically correct but incomplete.

`SyntaxError` is raised if *source* is complete but contains a syntax error. Raises
`OverflowError` or `ValueError` if any literal values are invalid. *filename* is an optional filename that can be associated with *source* and defaults to `'<input>'`. The
filename is most commonly used to set the filename that appears in error messages.
symbol is an optional start symbol for the grammar, which is either `'single'` (the
default) or `'eval'`.

interact([*banner* [, *readfunc* [, *local*]]])

Runs an instance of the interactive interpreter. *banner* is a message to print upon startup. *readfunc* is a function that is used to prompt and read input lines. It defaults to
`raw_input()`. *local* is a dictionary that serves as the namespace in which the code
will execute. By default, it is set to a dictionary where key `'__name__'` is set to
`'__console__'` and key `'__doc__'` is set to None.

InteractiveInterpreter([*locals*])

Creates an `InteractiveInterpreter` instance that implements an interactive interpreter. This class contains the machinery that's used to implement the part of the
`interact()` function that compiles and runs Python code. *locals* has the same meaning as for the `interact()` function.

An instance, *i*, of `InteractiveInterpreter` has the following methods:

i.runsource(*source* [, *filename* [, *symbol*]])

Runs Python source code in *source*. *filename* is the filename associated with *source*
and defaults to `'<input>'`. *symbol* is either `'single'` (the default) or `'eval'`. If
source is complete and syntactically valid, it is executed using the `runcode()` method
and `False` is returned. If *source* is complete, but contains some kind of syntax-related
error (`SyntaxError`, `ValueError`, and so on), the `showSyntaxError()` method is
called and `False` is returned. If *source* is incomplete, `True` is returned to indicate that
more input is necessary.

i.runcode(*code*)

Executes a code object. If an exception occurs, it is caught and passed to the
`showtraceback()` method. All exceptions are caught except for `SystemExit`.

i.showsyntaxError([*filename*])

Displays information about the syntax error that just occurred. Output is generated
using the `write()` method. *filename* is a filename that's placed into the exception
object.

i.showtraceback()

Displays traceback information for an exception. Traceback is output using the `write()`
method.

i.write(*data*)

Writes the string *data* to standard error (`sys.stderr`). This can be redefined in subclasses to redirect error output elsewhere.

InteractiveConsole([*banner* [, *readfunc* [, *local*]]])

Creates an `InteractiveConsole` object that provides features of the Python console. It
provides functionality related to interactive input of Python programs such as prompting

and a read-eval loop. *banner* is a message to display on console startup; *readfunc* is a function to use for input and defaults to the built-in function raw_input(). *local* is a dictionary to use for the local namespace. InteractiveConsole inherits from InteractiveInterpreter.

   An instance, *c*, of InteractiveConsole has the same methods as InteractiveInterpreter in addition to the following methods:

c.interact([*banner*])

Starts the interactive console. *banner* is an optional banner message that's printed upon startup.

c.push(*line*)

Pushes a line of input source onto the console input buffer. *line* is appended to any source already present in the input, and runsource() is used to run the new input buffer. Returns True if more input is required and False if the *line* was processed. The *line* that's added may have internal newlines, but should not be terminated by a newline. The input buffer is cleared whenever the input is successfully processed (and False is returned).

c.resetbuffer()

Clears all unprocessed source text from the input buffer.

c.raw_input([*prompt*])

This method is used for prompting and reading of input. Input lines are stripped of trailing newlines. If the EOF character is entered, EOFError is raised. By default, the built-in raw_input() function is used for input, but this can be changed in derived classes.

> **Note**
>
> InteractiveInterpreter and InteractiveConsole can be subclassed and modified as necessary for a particular application.

copy

The copy module provides functions for making shallow and deep copies of compound objects, including lists, tuples, dictionaries, and class instances.

copy(*x*)

Makes a shallow copy of *x* by creating a new compound object and duplicating the members of *x* by reference.

deepcopy(*x* [, *visit*])

Makes a deep copy of *x* by creating a new compound object and recursively duplicating all the members of *x*. *visit* is an optional dictionary that's used to keep track of visited objects in order to detect and avoid cycles in recursively defined data structures. This argument is typically only supplied if deepcopy() is being called recursively, as described later.

A class can implement its own copy methods by implementing the methods
__copy__(self) and __deepcopy__(self, visit). Both methods should return a
copy of the object. In addition, the __deepcopy__() method must accept a dictionary,
visit, as described for the deepcopy() function. When writing __deepcopy__(), it's
not necessary to modify visit. However, visit should be passed to subsequent calls to
deepcopy() (if any) performed inside the __deepcopy__() method.

Notes

- This module can be used with simple types such as integers and strings, but
  there's little need to do so.
- The copy functions don't work with modules, class objects, functions, methods,
  tracebacks, stack frames, files, sockets, and other similar types. When an object
  can't be copied, the copy.error exception is raised.
- The copy_reg module is not used by this module.

See Also:
pickle (p. 162)

copy_reg

The copy_reg module extends the capabilities of the pickle and cPickle modules to
handle the serialization of objects described by extension types (as defined in C extension modules). To do this, extension writers use this module to register reduction and
construction functions that are used to serialize and unserialize an object, respectively.

constructor(cfunc)

Declares cfunc to be a valid constructor function. cfunc must be a callable object that
accepts the tuple of values returned by the reduction function given to the pickle()
function.

pickle(type, rfunc [, cfunc])

Registers rfunc as a reduction function for objects of type type. rfunc is a function
that takes an object of the specified type and returns a tuple containing the constructor
function and a tuple of arguments to pass to that function in order to reassemble the
object. If supplied, cfunc is the constructor function that's registered using the
constructor() function.

Example

The following example shows how this module would be used to pickle complex numbers. (Note that because complex numbers are already pickleable, this example is only
intended to illustrate the use of this module.)

```
# Register a method for pickling complex numbers
import copy_reg

# Create a complex number from two reals
def construct_complex(real,imag):
```

```
        return complex(real,imag)        # Built-in function
# Take a complex number 'c' and turn it into a tuple of floats
def reduce_complex(c):
        return construct_complex, (c.real, c.imag)

# Register our handler
copy_reg.pickle(complex,reduce_complex, construct_complex)
```

When complex numbers are pickled, the reduce_complex() function is called. When the object is later unpickled, the function construct_complex() is called, using the tuple of values originally returned by reduce_complex().

Notes

- copy_reg is a misnomer—this module isn't used by the copy module.
- It's not necessary to use this module when pickling instances of user-defined classes unless you want to customize the way in which a class is normally pickled.

See Also:
pickle (p. 164)

__future__

The __future__ module is used to enable features that are new but not yet turned on by default. Typically these features change an important aspect of the Python interpreter that could potentially break a lot of old code if they were turned on right away. Therefore, new features are introduced gradually—first as optional features and then as standard features in later releases.

Optional features are enabled by including a statement such as

```
from __future__ import featurename
```

at the top of a source file that uses the feature.

Currently, the following features have been defined:

nested_scopes

Support for nested scopes in functions. First introduced in Python 2.1 and made the default behavior in Python 2.2.

generators

Support for generators. First introduced in Python 2.2 and made the default behavior in Python 2.3.

division

Modified division semantics where integer division returns a fractional result. For example, 1/4 yields 0.25 instead of 0. First introduced in Python 2.2 and is still an optional feature as of Python 2.4. Will be the default behavior in a later release (purportedly Python 3.0).

Notes

- No feature name is ever deleted from `__future__`. Therefore, even if a feature is turned on by default in a later Python version, no existing code that uses that feature name will break.
- A list of all feature names can be found in `__future__.all_feature_names`.

gc

The `gc` module provides an interface for controlling the garbage collector used to collect cycles in objects such as lists, tuples, dictionaries, and instances. As various types of container objects are created, they're placed on a list that's internal to the interpreter. Whenever container objects are deallocated, they're removed from this list. If the number of allocations exceeds the number of deallocations by a user-definable threshold value, the garbage collector is invoked. The garbage collector works by scanning this list and identifying collections of objects that are no longer being used but haven't been deallocated due to circular dependencies. In addition, the garbage collector uses a three-level generational scheme in which objects that survive the initial garbage-collection step are placed onto lists of objects that are checked less frequently. This provides better performance for programs that have a large number of long-lived objects.

`collect()`

Runs a full garbage collection. This function checks all generations and returns the number of unreachable objects found.

`disable()`

Disables garbage collection.

`enable()`

Enables garbage collection.

`garbage`

A variable containing a read-only list of the uncollectable objects that the garbage collector could not release for some reason. See the notes for this module.

`get_debug()`

Returns the debugging flags currently set.

`get_objects()`

Returns a list of all objects being tracked by the garbage collector. Does not include the returned list.

`get_referrers(obj1, obj2, ...)`

Returns a list of all objects that directly refer to the objects *obj1*, *obj2*, and so on. The returned list may include objects that have not yet been garbage collected as well as partially constructed objects.

`get_referents(obj1, obj2, ...)`

Returns a list of objects that the objects `obj1`, `obj2`, and so on refer to. For example, if `obj1` is a container, this would return a list of the objects in the container.

`get_threshold()`

Returns the current collection threshold as a tuple.

`isenabled()`

Returns `True` if garbage collection is enabled.

`set_debug(flags)`

Sets the garbage-collection debugging flags, which can be used to debug the behavior of the garbage collector. `flags` is the bitwise OR of the constants DEBUG_STATS, DEBUG_COLLECTABLE, DEBUG_UNCOLLECTABLE, DEBUG_INSTANCES, DEBUG_OBJECTS, DEBUG_SAVEALL, and DEBUG_LEAK. The DEBUG_LEAK flag is probably the most useful because it will have the collector print information useful for debugging programs with memory leaks.

`set_threshold(threshold0 [, threshold1[, threshold2]])`

Sets the collection frequency of garbage collection. Objects are classified into three generations, where generation 0 contains the youngest objects and generation 2 contains the oldest objects. Objects that survive a garbage-collection step are moved to the next-oldest generation. Once an object reaches generation 2, it stays in that generation. `threshold0` is the difference between the number of allocations and deallocations that must be reached before garbage collection occurs in generation 0. `threshold1` is the number of collections of generation 0 that must occur before generation 1 is scanned. `threshold2` is the number of collections that must occur in generation 1 before generation 2 is collected. The default threshold is currently set to (700, 10, 10). Setting `threshold0` to zero disables garbage collection.

Notes

- Circular references involving objects with a `__del__()` method are not garbage-collected and are placed on the list `gc.garbage` (uncollectable objects). These objects are not collected due to difficulties related to object finalization.

- The functions `get_referrers()` and `get_referents()` only apply to objects that support garbage collection. In addition, these functions are only intended for debugging. They should not be used for other purposes.

inspect

The `inspect` module is used to gather information about live Python objects such as attributes, documentation strings, source code, and so on.

`currentframe()`

Returns the frame object corresponding to the caller's stack frame.

`formatargspec(args [, varags [, varkw [, defaults]]])`

Produces a nicely formatted string representing the values returned by `getargspec()`.

`formatargvalues(args [, varargs [, varkw [, locals]]])`

Produces a nicely formatted string representing the values returned by
`getargvalues()`.

`getargspec(func)`

Given a function, `func`, returns a tuple (`args, varargs, varkw, defaults`).
`args` is a list of argument names, `varargs` is the name of the `*` argument (if any).
`varkw` is the name of the `**` argument (if any), and `defaults` is a tuple of default
argument values or `None` if there are no default argument values. If there are default
argument values, the `defaults` tuple represents the values of the last *n* arguments in
`args`, where *n* is `len(defaults)`.

`getargvalues(frame)`

Returns the values of arguments supplied to a function with execution frame `frame`.
Returns a tuple (`args, varargs, varkw, locals`). `args` is a list of argument
names, `varargs` is the name of the `*` argument (if any), and `varkw` is the name of the
`**` argument (if any). `locals` is the local dictionary of the frame.

`getclasstree(classes [, unique])`

Given a list of related classes, `classes`, this function organizes the classes into a hierarchy based on inheritance. The hierarchy is represented as a collection of nested lists,
where each entry in the list is a list of classes that inherit from the class that immediately precedes the list. Each entry in the list is a 2-tuple (`cls, bases`), where `cls` is the
class object and `bases` is a tuple of base classes. If `unique` is `True`, each class only
appears once in the returned list. Otherwise, a class may appear multiple times if
multiple inheritance is being used.

`getcomments(object)`

Returns a string consisting of comments that immediately precede the definition of
`object` in Python source code. If `object` is a module, comments defined at the top of
the module are returned. Returns `None` if no comments are found.

`getdoc(object)`

Returns the documentation string for `object`. Tabs are expanded to spaces in the
returned string. Whitespace indenting used to align the documentation string within the
code block is also removed. Returns `None` if no documentation string is defined.

`getfile(object)`

Returns the name of the file in which `object` was defined. May return `TypeError` if
this information is not applicable or available (for example, for built-in functions).

`getframeinfo(frame [, context])`

Returns a tuple (`filename, line, funcname, contextlist, index`) containing
information about the frame object `frame`. `filename` and `line` specify a source code
location. The `context` parameter specifies the number of lines of context from the
source code to retrieve. The `contextlist` field in the returned tuple contains a list of
source lines corresponding to this context. The `index` field is a numerical index within
this list for the line corresponding to `frame`.

getinnerframes(*traceback* [, *context*])

Returns a list of frame records for the frame of a traceback and all inner frames. Each frame-record is a 6-tuple consisting of (*frame*, *filename*, *line*, *funcname*, *contextlist*, *index*). *filename*, *line*, *context*, *contextlist*, and *index* have the same meaning as with getframeinfo().

getmembers(*object* [, *predicate*])

Returns all of the members of *object*. Typically, the members are obtained by looking in the __dict__ attribute of an object, but this function may return attributes of *object* stored elsewhere (for example, docstrings in __doc__, objects' names in __name__, and so on). The members are returned a list of (*name*, *value*) pairs. *predicate* is an optional function that accepts a member object as an argument and returns True or False. Only members for which *predicate* returns True are returned. Functions such as isfunction() and isclass() can be used as predicate functions.

getmodule(*object*)

Returns the module in which *object* was defined (if possible).

getmoduleinfo(*path*)

Returns information about how Python would interpret the file *path*. If *path* is not a Python module, None is returned. Otherwise, a tuple (*name*, *suffix*, *mode*, *mtype*) is returned where *name* is the name of the module, *suffix* is the filename suffix, *mode* is the file mode that would be used to open the module, and *mtype* is an integer code specifying the module type. Module type codes are defined in the imp module as follows:

Module Type	Description
imp.PY_SOURCE	Python source file
imp.PY_COMPILED	Python compiled object file (.pyc)
imp.C_EXTENSION	Dynamically loadable C extension
imp.PKG_DIRECTORY	Package directory
imp.C_BUILTIN	Built-in module
imp.PY_FROZEN	Frozen module

getmodulename(*path*)

Returns the name of the module that would be used for the file *path*. If *path* does not look like a Python module, None is returned.

getmro(*cls*)

Returns a tuple of classes that represent the method-resolution ordering used to resolve methods in class *cls*. See Chapter 7, "Classes and Object-Oriented Programming," for further details.

getouterframes(*frame* [, *context*])

Returns a list of frame records for *frame* and all outer frames. This list represents the calling sequence where the first entry contains information for *frame*. Each frame record is a 6-tuple (*frame*, *filename*, *line*, *funcname*, *contextlist*, *index*) where the fields have the same meaning as for getinnerframes(). The *context* argument has the same meaning as for getframeinfo().

getsourcefile(*object*)

Returns the name of the Python source file in which *object* was defined.

getsourcelines(*object*)

Returns a tuple (*sourcelines*, *firstline*) corresponding to the definition of *object*. *sourcelines* is a list of source code lines, and *firstline* is the line number of the first source code line. Raises IOError if source code can't be found.

getsource(*object*)

Returns source code of *object* as a single string. Raises IOError if the source code can't be found.

isbuiltin(*object*)

Returns True if *object* is a built-in function.

isclass(*object*)

Returns True if *object* is a class.

iscode(*object*)

Returns True if *object* is a code object.

isframe(*object*)

Returns True if *object* is a frame object.

isfunction(*object*)

Returns True if *object* is a function object.

ismethod(*object*)

Returns True if *object* is a method.

isdatadescriptor(*object*)

Returns True if *object* is a data descriptor object. This is the case if *object* defines both a __get__() and __set__() method.

ismethoddescriptor(*object*)

Returns True if *object* is a method descriptor object. This is the case if *object* is not a method, class, or function and it defines a __get__() method but does not define __set__().

ismodule(*object*)

Returns True if *object* is a module object.

isroutine(*object*)

Returns True if *object* is a user-defined or built-in function or method.

istraceback(*object*)

Returns True if *object* is a traceback object.

`stack([context])`

Returns a list of frame records corresponding to the stack of the caller. Each frame record is a 6-tuple (`frame`, `filename`, `line`, `funcname`, `contextlist`, `index`), which contains the same information as returned by `getinnerframes()`. `context` specifies the number of lines of source context to return in each frame record.

`trace([context])`

Returns a list of frame records for the stack between the current frame and the frame in which the current exception was raised. The first frame record is the caller, and the last frame record is the frame where the exception occurred. `context` specifies the number of lines of source context to return in each frame record.

marshal

The `marshal` module is used to serialize Python objects in an "undocumented" Python-specific data format. `marshal` is similar to the `pickle` and `shelve` modules, but it is less powerful and intended for use only with simple objects. It shouldn't be used to implement persistent objects in general (use `pickle` instead).

`dump(value, file [, version])`

Writes the object value to the open file object `file`. If `value` is an unsupported type, a `ValueError` exception is raised. `version` is an integer that specifies the data format to use. The default output format is found in `marshal.version` and is currently set to 1. Version 0 is an older format used by earlier versions of Python.

`dumps(value [,version])`

Returns the string written by the `dump()` function. If `value` is an unsupported type, a `ValueError` exception is raised. `version` is the same as described previously.

`load(file)`

Reads and returns the next value from the open file object `file`. If no valid value is read, an `EOFError`, `ValueError`, or `TypeError` exception will be raised. The format of the input data is automatically detected.

`loads(string)`

Reads and returns the next value from the string `string`.

Notes

- Data is stored in a binary architecture-independent format.
- Only `None`, integers, long integers, floats, complex numbers, strings, Unicode strings, tuples, lists, dictionaries, and code objects are supported. Lists, tuples, and dictionaries can only contain supported objects. Class instances and recursive references in lists, tuples, and dictionaries are not supported.
- Integers may be promoted to long integers if the built-in integer type doesn't have enough precision—for example, if the marshalled data contains a 64-bit integer, but the data is being read on a 32-bit machine.

- marshal is not intended to be secure against erroneous or maliciously construct-ed data and should not be used to unmarshal data from untrusted sources.
- marshal is significantly faster than pickle, but it isn't as flexible.

See Also:
pickle (p. 162), shelve (p. 242)

new

The new module is used to create various types of objects used by the interpreter. The primary use of this module is by applications that need to create objects in a nonstan-dard manner (such as when unmarshalling data).

instance(class, dict)

Creates an old-style class instance of *class* with dictionary *dict* without calling the __init__() method. Does not work with classes that inherit from object (new-style classes).

instancemethod(function, instance, class)

Creates a method object, bound to *instance*. *function* must be a callable object. If *instance* is None, an unbound instance method is created.

function(code, globals [, name [, argdefs]])

Creates a function object with the given *code* object and global namespace. *name* is the name of the function or None (in which case the function name is taken from *code*.co_name). *argdefs* is a tuple containing default parameter values.

code(argcount, nlocals, stacksize, flags, codestring, constants, names, varnames, filename, name, firstlineno, lnotab)

Creates a new Code object. See the section "Code Objects" in Chapter 3, "Types and Objects," for a description of the arguments.

module(name)

Creates a new module object. *name* is the module name.

classobj(name, baseclasses, dict)

Creates an old-style class object. *name* is the class name, *baseclasses* is a tuple of base classes, and *dict* is a dictionary defining the class namespace.

Note
Use of this module is rarely necessary because most objects can be constructed using their type name instead. For example, to create a new module object, simply use types.ModuleType("name") instead of calling new.module("name").

See Also:
Chapter 3 and the types module (p. 172)

operator

The operator module provides functions that access the built-in operators and special methods of the interpreter described in Chapter 3. For example, add(3, 4) is the same as 3 + 4. When the name of a function matches the name of a special method, it can also be invoked using its name with double underscores—for example, __add__ (3, 4).

Function	Description
add(a, b)	Returns a + b for numbers
sub(a, b)	Returns a - b
mul(a, b)	Returns a * b for numbers
div(a, b)	Returns a / b (old division)
floordiv(a, b)	Returns a // b
truediv(a, b)	Returns a / b (new division)
mod(a, b)	Returns a % b
neg(a)	Returns -a
pos(a)	Returns +a
abs(a)	Returns the absolute value of a
inv(a), invert(a)	Returns the inverse of a (~a)
lshift(a, b)	Returns a << b
rshift(a, b)	Returns a >> b
and_(a, b)	Returns a & b (bitwise AND)
or_(a, b)	Returns a | b (bitwise OR)
xor(a, b)	Returns a ^ b (bitwise XOR)
not_(a)	Returns not a
lt(a, b)	Returns a < b
le(a, b)	Returns a <= b
eq(a, b)	Returns a == b
ne(a, b)	Returns a != b
gt(a, b)	Returns a > b
ge(a, b)	Returns a >= b
truth(a)	Returns True if a is true, False otherwise
concat(a, b)	Returns a + b for sequences
repeat(a, b)	Returns a * b for sequence a and integer b
contains(a, b)	Returns the result of b in a
countOf(a, b)	Returns the number of occurrences of b in a
indexOf(a, b)	Returns the index of the first occurrence of b in a
getitem(a, b)	Returns a[b]
setitem(a, b, c)	a[b] = c
delitem(a, b)	del a[b]

Function	Description
getslice(a, b, c)	Returns a[b:c]
setslice(a, b, c, v)	Sets a[b:c] = v
delslice(a, b, c)	del a[b:c]
is_(a, b)	a is b
is_not(a, b)	a is not b

In addition, the operator module defines the following functions for testing object properties. Note that these functions are not entirely reliable for user-defined instances because they don't perform an exhaustive test of the interface to see whether all functions are implemented.

Function	Description
isMappingType(o)	Tests whether o supports the mapping interface
isNumberType(o)	Tests whether o supports the number interface
isSequenceType(o)	Tests whether o supports the sequence interface

The following functions are used to create wrappers around attribute lookup and access to items:

attrgetter(attrname)

Creates a callable object, f, where a call to f(obj) returns obj.attrname.

itemgetter(item)

Creates a callable object, f, where a call to f(obj) returns obj[item].

> **Note**
>
> The semantics of division are being changed in a future Python version. The div() function corresponds to the old behavior (which truncates integers). The truediv() corresponds to the new semantics, which are enabled using from __future__ import division.

> **See Also:**
>
> "Special Methods" in Chapter 3 (p. 45)

pickle **and** cPickle

The pickle and cPickle modules are used to serialize Python objects into a stream of bytes suitable for storing in a file, transferring across a network, or placing in a database. This process is variously called *pickling, serializing, marshalling,* or *flattening.* The resulting byte stream can also be converted back into a series of Python objects using an unpickling process.

The pickling and unpickling processes are controlled by using Pickler and Unpickler objects, as created by the following two functions:

```
Pickler(file [, protocol ])
```

Creates a pickling object that writes data to the file object `file`. `protocol` specifies the output format of the data. Protocol 0 (the default) is a text-based format that is backward compatible with earlier versions of Python. Protocol 1 is a binary protocol that is also compatible with most earlier Python versions. Protocol 2 is a newer protocol that provides more efficient pickling of classes and instances. If `protocol` is negative, the most modern protocol will be selected. The variable `pickle.HIGHEST_PROTOCOL` contains the highest protocol available.

```
Unpickler(file)
```

Creates an unpickling object that reads data from the file object `file`. The unpickler automatically detects the protocol of the incoming data.

To serialize an object, x, onto a file, f, the dump() method of the pickler object is used. For example:

```
f = open('myfile', 'w')
p = pickle.Pickler(f)      # Send pickled data to file f
p.dump(x)                  # Dump x
```

To later unpickle the object from the file, do the following:

```
f = open('myfile')
u = pickle.Unpickler(f)
x = u.load()               # Restore x from file f
```

Multiple calls to the dump() and load() methods are allowed, provided that the sequence of load() calls used to restore a collection of previously stored objects matches the sequence of dump() calls used during the pickling process.

The `Pickler` object keeps track of the objects that have been previously pickled and ignores duplicates. This can be reset by calling the `p.clear_memo()` method of a `Pickler` object, p.

The following functions are available as shortcuts to common pickling operations:

```
dump(object, file [, protocol ])
```

Dumps a pickled representation of `object` to the file object `file`. Same as `Pickler(file, bin).dump(object)`.

```
dumps(object [, protocol [, bin]])
```

Same as dump(), but returns a string containing the pickled data.

```
load(file)
```

Loads a pickled representation of an object from the file object `file`. Same as `Unpickler(file).load()`.

```
loads(string)
```

Same as load(), but reads the pickled representation of an object from a string.

The following objects can be pickled:

- None
- Integers, long integers, floating-point, and complex numbers
- Tuples, lists, and dictionaries containing only pickleable objects
- Classes defined at the top level of a module
- Instances of classes defined at the top level of a module

When class instances are pickled, their corresponding class definition must appear at the top level of a module (that is, no nested classes). When instances are unpickled, the module in which their class definition appeared is automatically imported. In addition, when instances are re-created, their __init__() method is not invoked. If it's necessary to call __init__() when unpickling, the class must define a special method, __getnewargs__(), that returns a tuple of arguments, args, that will be placed into the byte stream when pickling. When the object X is reconstructed, the object will be re-created by calling X.__new__(X, *args), which will, in turn, call __init__() with the appropriate arguments. It should be noted that this technique only works with modern classes. If a program uses old-style classes, it implements the function __getinitargs__() instead.

It's also worth noting that when pickling class instances in which the corresponding class definition appears in __main__, that class definition must be manually reloaded prior to unpickling a saved object (because there's no way for the interpreter to know how to automatically load the necessary class definitions back into __main__ when unpickling).

A class can define customized methods for saving and restoring its state by implementing the special methods __getstate__() and __setstate__(). The __getstate__() method must return a pickleable object (such as a string) representing the state of the object. The __setstate__() method accepts the pickled object and restores its state. If no __getstate__() method is found, pickle simply pickles an object's __dict__ attribute.

When an attempt is made to pickle an unsupported object type, the pickle.PicklingError exception is raised. If an error occurs while unpickling, the pickle.UnpicklingError exception is raised.

Notes

- Recursive objects (objects containing references to themselves) and object sharing are handled correctly. However, if the same object is dumped to a Pickler object more than once, only the first instance is saved (even if the object has changed between dumps).

- When class instances are pickled, their class definitions and associated code for methods are not saved. This allows classes to be modified or upgraded while still being able to read data saved from older versions.

- pickle defines Pickler and Unpickler as classes that can be subclassed if necessary.

- The cPickle module is up to 1,000 times faster than pickle, but it doesn't allow subclassing of the Pickler and Unpickler objects.

- The data format used by pickle is Python-specific and shouldn't be assumed to be compatible with any external standards such as XDR.

- Any object that provides write(), read(), and readline() methods can be used in place of a file.

- Whenever possible, the pickle module should be used instead of the marshal module because pickle is more flexible, the data encoding is documented, and additional error checking is performed.

- Due to security concerns, programs should not unpickle data received from untrusted sources.

- The copy_reg moduleis used to register new types with the pickle module.

See Also:

shelve **(p. 242)**, marshal **(p. 159)**, copy_reg **(p. 152)**

site

The site module is automatically imported when the interpreter starts and is used to perform sitewide initialization of packages and to set the default Unicode encoding. The module works by first creating a list of up to four directory names created from the values of sys.prefix and sys.exec_prefix. On Windows, the list of directories is as follows:

```
[ sys.prefix,
  sys.exec_prefix ]
```

On UNIX, the directories are as follows:

```
[ sys.prefix + 'lib/pythonvers/site-packages',
  sys.prefix + 'lib/site-python',
  sys.exec_prefix + 'lib/pythonvers/site-packages',
  sys.exec_prefix + 'lib/site-python' ]
```

For each directory in the list, a check is made to see whether the directory exists. If so, it's added to the sys.path variable. Next, a check is made to see whether it contains any path configuration files (files with a .pth suffix). A path configuration file contains a list of directories relative to the location of the path file that should be added to sys.path. For example:

```
# foo package configuration file 'foo.pth'
foo
bar
```

Each directory in the path configuration file must be listed on a separate line. Comments and blank lines are ignored. When the site module loads the file, it checks to see whether each directory exists. If so, the directory is added to sys.path. Duplicated items are added to the path only once.

After all paths have been added to sys.path, an attempt is made to import a module named sitecustomize. The purpose of this module is to perform any additional (and arbitrary) site customization. If the import of sitecustomize fails with an ImportError, the error is silently ignored.

The site module is also responsible for setting the default Unicode encoding. By default, the encoding is set to 'ascii'. However, the encoding can be changed by placing code in sitecustomize.py that calls sys.setdefaultencoding() with a new encoding such as 'utf-8'. If you're willing to experiment, the source code of site can also be modified to automatically set the encoding based on the machine's locale settings.

> **Note**
>
> The automatic import of site can be disabled by running Python with the -S option.

> **See Also:**
>
> sys (p. 166), Chapter 8, "Modules and Packages," and Chapter 10, "Execution Environment"

sys

The sys module contains variables and functions that pertain to the operation of the interpreter and its environment. The following variables are defined:

api_version

An integer representing the C API version of the Python interpreter. Used when working with extension modules.

argv

List of command-line options passed to a program. argv[0] is the name of the program.

builtin_module_names

Tuple containing names of modules built into the Python executable.

byteorder

Native byte-ordering of the machine—'little' for little-endian or 'big' for big-endian.

copyright

String containing copyright message.

__displayhook__

Original value of the displayhook() function.

__excepthook__

Original value of the excepthook() function.

dllhandle

Integer handle for the Python DLL (Windows).

exec_prefix

Directory where platform-dependent Python files are installed.

executable

String containing the name of the interpreter executable.

exitfunc

Function object that's called when the interpreter exits. It can be set to a function taking no parameters. By default, exitfunc is not defined. Direct use of this variable is discouraged. Use the atexit module instead.

See Also:
atexit (p. 149)

hexversion

Integer whose hexadecimal representation encodes the version information contained in
sys.version_info. The value of this integer is always guaranteed to increase with
newer versions of the interpreter.

last_type, last_value, last_traceback

These variables are set when an unhandled exception is encountered and the interpreter
prints an error message. last_type is the last exception type, last_value is the last
exception value, and last_traceback is a stack trace. Note that the use of these variables is not thread-safe. sys.exc_info() should be used instead.

maxint

Largest integer supported by the integer type.

maxunicode

Integer that indicates the largest Unicode character value. The default value is 65535 for
the 16-bit UCS-2 encoding. Will return a larger value if Python has been configured to
use UCS-4 encoding.

modules

Dictionary that maps module names to module objects.

path

List of strings specifying the search path for modules. The first entry is always set to
the directory in which the script used to start Python is located (if available). See
Chapter 8.

platform

Platform identifier string, such as 'linux-i386'.

prefix

Directory where platform-independent Python files are installed.

ps1, ps2

Strings containing the text for the primary and secondary prompts of the interpreter.
Initially, ps1 is set to '>>> ' and ps2 is set to '... '. The str() method of whatever
object is assigned to these values is evaluated to generate the prompt text.

stdin, stdout, stderr

File objects corresponding to standard input, standard output, and standard error. stdin
is used for the raw_input() and input() functions. stdout is used for print and the
prompts of raw_input() and input(). stderr is used for the interpreter's prompts
and error messages. These variables can be assigned to any object that supports a
write() method operating on a single string argument.

__stdin__ , **__stdout__** , **__stderr__**

File objects containing the values of stdin, stdout, and stderr at the start of the interpreter.

tracebacklimit

Maximum number of levels of traceback information printed when an unhandled exception occurs. The default value is 1000. A value of 0 suppresses all traceback information and causes only the exception type and value to be printed.

version

Version string.

version_info

Version information represented as a tuple (*major, minor, micro, releaselevel, serial*). All values are integers except *releaselevel*, which is the string 'alpha', 'beta', 'candidate', or 'final'.

warnoptions

List of warning options supplied to the interpreter with the -W command-line option.

winver

The version number used to form registry keys on Windows.

The following functions are available:

displayhook([value])

This function is called to print the result of an expression when the interpreter is running in interactive mode. By default, the value of repr(*value*) is printed to standard output and *value* is saved in the variable __builtin__._. displayhook can be redefined to provide different behavior if desired.

excepthook(type, value, traceback)

This function is called when an uncaught exception occurs. *type* is the exception class, *value* is the value supplied by the raise statement, and *traceback* is a traceback object. The default behavior is to print the exception and traceback to standard error. However, this function can be redefined to provide alternative handling of uncaught exceptions (which may be useful in specialized applications such as debuggers or CGI scripts).

exc_clear()

Clears all information related to the last exception that occurred. It only clears information specific to the calling thread.

exc_info()

Returns a tuple (*type, value, traceback*) containing information about the exception that's currently being handled. *type* is the exception type, *value* is the exception parameter passed to raise, and *traceback* is a traceback object containing the call stack at the point where the exception occurred. Returns None if no exception is currently being handled.

exit([n])

Exits from Python by raising the SystemExit exception. *n* is an integer exit code indicating a status code. A value of 0 is considered normal (the default); nonzero values are considered abnormal. If a non-integer value is given to *n*, it's printed to sys.stderr and an exit code of 1 is used.

getcheckinterval()

Returns the value of the check interval, which specifies how often the interpreter checks for signals, thread switches, and other periodic events.

getdefaultencoding()

Gets the default string encoding in Unicode conversions. Returns a value such as 'ascii' or 'utf-8'. The default encoding is set by the site module.

getdlopenflags()

Returns the flags parameter that is supplied to the C function dlopen() when loading extension modules on UNIX. See dl module.

getfilesystemencoding()

Returns the character encoding used to map Unicode filenames to filenames used by the underlying operating system. Returns 'mbcs' on Windows or 'utf-8' on Macintosh OS X. On UNIX systems, the encoding depends on locale settings and will return the value of the locale CODESET parameter. May return None, in which case the system default encoding is used.

_getframe([depth])

Returns a frame object from the call stack. If *depth* is omitted or zero, the top-most frame is returned. Otherwise, the frame for that many calls below the current frame is returned. For example, _getframe(1) returns the caller's frame. Raises ValueError if *depth* is invalid.

getrecursionlimit()

Returns the recursion limit for functions.

getrefcount(object)

Returns the reference count of *object*.

getwindowsversion()

Returns a tuple (*major*, *minor*, *build*, *platform*, *text*) that describes the version of Windows being used. *major* is the major version number. For example, a value of 4 indicates Windows NT 4.0, and a value of 5 indicates Windows 2000 and Windows XP variants. *minor* is the minor version number. For example, 0 indicates Windows 2000, whereas 1 indicates Windows XP. *build* is the Windows build number. *platform* identifies the platform and is an integer with one of the following common values: 0 (Win32s on Windows 3.1), 1 (Windows 95,98, or Me), 2 (Windows NT, 2000, XP), 3 (Windows CE). *text* is a string containing additional information such as "Service Pack 3".

setcheckinterval(n)

Sets the number of Python virtual machine instructions that must be executed by the interpreter before it checks for periodic events such as signals and thread context switches. The default value is 100.

setdefaultencoding(enc)

Sets the default encoding. enc is a string such as 'ascii' or 'utf-8'. This function is only defined inside the site module. It can be called from user-definable sitecustomize modules.

See Also:

site (p. 165)

setdlopenflags(flags)

Sets the flags passed to the C dlopen() function, which is used to load extension modules on UNIX. This will affect the way in which symbols are resolved between libraries and other extension modules. flags is the bitwise OR of values that can be found in the dl module (Chapter 19, "Operating System Services")—for example, sys. setdlopenflags(dl.RTLD_NOW | dl.RTLD_GLOBAL).

setprofile(pfunc)

Sets the system profile function that can be used to implement a source code profiler. See Chapter 26, "Debugging, Profiling, and Testing," for information about the Python profiler.

setrecursionlimit(n)

Changes the recursion limit for functions. The default value is 1000. Note that the operating system may impose a hard limit on the stack size, so setting this too high may cause a program to crash.

settrace(tfunc)

Sets the system trace function, which can be used to implement a debugger. See Chapter 26 for information about the Python debugger.

traceback

The traceback module is used to gather and print stack traces of a program after an exception has occurred. The functions in this module operate on traceback objects such as the third item returned by the sys.exc_info() function.

print_tb(traceback [, limit [, file]])

Prints up to limit stack trace entries from traceback to the file file. If limit is omitted, all the entries are printed. If file is omitted, the output is sent to sys.stderr.

print_exception(type, value, traceback [, limit [, file]])

Prints exception information and a stack trace to file. type is the exception type, and value is the exception value. limit and file are the same as in print_tb().

`print_exc([limit [, file]])`

Same as `print_exception()` applied to the information returned by the `sys.exc_info()` function.

`format_exc([limit [, file]])`

Returns a string containing the same information printed by `print_exc()`.

`print_last([limit [, file]])`

Same as `print_exception(sys.last_type, sys.last_value, sys.last_traceback, limit, file)`.

`print_stack([frame [, limit [, file]]])`

Prints a stack trace from the point at which it's invoked. `frame` specifies an optional stack frame from which to start. `limit` and `file` have the same meaning as for `print_tb()`.

`extract_tb(traceback [, limit])`

Extracts the stack trace information used by `print_tb()`. The return value is a list of tuples of the form `(filename, line, funcname, text)` containing the same information that normally appears in a stack trace. `limit` is the number of entries to return.

`extract_stack([frame [, limit]])`

Extracts the same stack trace information used by `print_stack()`, but obtained from the stack frame `frame`. If `frame` is omitted, the current stack frame of the caller is used. `limit` is the number of entries to return.

`format_list(list)`

Formats stack trace information for printing. `list` is a list of tuples as returned by `extract_tb()` or `extract_stack()`.

`format_exception_only(type, value)`

Formats exception information for printing.

`format_exception(type, value, traceback [, limit])`

Formats an exception and stack trace for printing.

`format_tb(traceback [, limit])`

Same as `format_list(extract_tb(traceback, limit))`.

`format_stack([frame [, limit]])`

Same as `format_list(extract_stack(frame, limit))`.

`tb_lineno(traceback)`

Returns the line number set in a traceback object.

Additional details are available in the online documentation.

See Also:

`sys` (p. 166), "Debugging, Profiling, and Testing" (p. 505), Chapter 3, and http://www.python.org/doc/lib/module-traceback.html

types

The types module defines names for all the built-in object types. The contents of this module are often used in conjunction with the built-in isinstance() function and other type-related operations.

Many of the objects in the types module are available as built-ins. For example, the built-in functions int(), long(), complex(), bool(), list(), dict(), tuple(), slice(), str(), unicode(), xrange(), and file() are actually type objects (in fact, they are *exactly the same* objects as referenced in the types module). Therefore, it is never necessary to use the longer name. For instance, writing isinstance(x, int) is the same as isinstance(x, types.IntType).

The module defines the following types:

Variable	Description
BooleanType	Type of Boolean integers True and False. Same as bool.
BuiltinFunctionType	Type of built-in functions.
CodeType	Type of code objects.
ComplexType	Type of complex numbers. Same as complex.
ClassType	Type of user-defined class (old-style classes).
DictType	Type of dictionaries. Same as dict.
DictionaryType	Alternative name for DictType.
EllipsisType	Type of ellipsis.
FileType	Type of file objects. Same as file.
FloatType	Type of floating-point numbers. Same as float.
FrameType	Type of execution frame object.
FunctionType	Type of user-defined functions and lambdas.
GeneratorType	Type of generator-iterator objects.
InstanceType	Type of instances of a user-defined class (old-style classes).
IntType	Type of integers. Same as int.
LambdaType	Alternative name for FunctionType.
ListType	Type of lists. Same as list.
LongType	Type of long integers. Same as long.
MethodType	Type of user-defined class methods.
ModuleType	Type of modules.
NoneType	Type of None.
SliceType	Type of extended slice objects. Returned by slice(). Same as slice.
StringType	Type of strings. Same as str.
StringTypes	Tuple of all string types that can be used for type-checking. (StringType, UnicodeType) by default.
TracebackType	Type of traceback objects.

Variable	Description
TupleType	Type of tuples. Same as tuple.
TypeType	Type of type objects (includes user-defined classes). Same as type.
UnboundMethodType	Alternative name for MethodType.
UnicodeType	Type of unicode strings. Same as unicode.
XRangeType	Type of objects created by xrange(). Same as xrange.

Most of the type objects serve as constructors that can be used to create an object of that type. For example, types.ListType(s) will convert s into a list (this is exactly the same as list(s)). The following list provides the parameters used to create more unconventional objects. Use of these functions is usually only done when objects need to be constructed in a unconventional way (for example, when unpickling) or in the context of defining metaclasses, which is described in Chapter 7. Chapter 3 contains detailed information about the attributes of the objects created and the arguments that need to be supplied to the following functions.

```
FunctionType(code, globals [, name [, defarags [, closure]]])
```

Creates a new function object.

```
ClassType(name, bases, dict)
```

Creates an old-style class object. See Chapter 7 for information about metaclasses.

```
CodeType(argcount, nlocals, stacksize, flags, codestring, constants, names,
varnames, filename, name, firstlineno, lnotab [, freevars [, cellvars ]])
```

Creates a new code object.

```
InstanceType(class [, dict])
```

Creates an instance of an old-style class.

```
MethodType(function, instance, class)
```

Creates a new instance method.

```
ModuleType(name [, doc])
```

Creates a new module object.

```
TypeType(name, bases, dict)
```

Creates a new type object. Used when defining metaclasses, as described in Chapter 7.

Note

The new module contains functions that construct various kinds of built-in objects. However, that module is not needed because objects can already be constructed by simply calling the appropriate type object as a function.

See Also:

Chapter 3 (p. 27)

warnings

The `warnings` module provides functions to issue and filter warning messages. Unlike exceptions, warnings are intended to alert the user to potential problems, but without generating an exception or causing execution to stop. One of the primary uses of the warnings module is to inform users about deprecated language features that may not be supported in future versions of Python. For example:

```
>>> import regex
__main__:1: DeprecationWarning: the regex module is deprecated;  use the re
module
>>>
```

Like exceptions, warnings are organized into a class hierarchy that describes general categories of warnings. The following table lists the currently supported categories:

Column1	Column2
Warning	Base class of all warning types
UserWarning	User-defined warning
DeprecationWarning	Warning for use of a deprecated feature
SyntaxWarning	Potential syntax problem
RuntimeWarning	Potential runtime problem
FutureWarning	Warning that the semantics of a particular feature will change in a future release

Each of these classes is available in the `__builtin__` module as well as the `exceptions` module. In addition, they are also instances of `Exception`. This makes it possible to easily convert warnings into errors.

Warnings are issued using the `warn()` function. For example:

```
warnings.warn("feature X is deprecated.")
warnings.warn("feature Y might be broken.", RuntimeWarning)
```

If desired, warnings can be filtered. The filtering process can be used to alter the output behavior of warning messages, to ignore warnings, or to turn warnings into exceptions. The `filterwarnings()` function is used to add a filter for a specific type of warning. For example:

```
warnings.filterwarnings(action="ignore",
                        message=".*regex.*",
                        category=DeprecationWarning)
import regex      # Warning message disappears
```

Limited forms of filtering can also be specified using the `-W` option to the interpreter. For example:

```
% python -Wignore:the\ regex:DeprecationWarning
```

The following functions are defined in the warnings module:

`warn(message[, category[, stacklevel]])`

Issues a warning. `message` is a string containing the warning message, `category` is the warning class (such as DeprecationWarning), and `stacklevel` is an integer that specifies the stack frame from which the warning message should originate. By default, `category` is UserWarning and `stacklevel` is 1.

warn_explicit(*message*, *category*, *filename*, *lineno*[, *module*[, *registry*]])

This is a low-level version of the warn() function. *message* and *category* have the same meaning as for warn(). *filename*, *lineno*, and *module* explicitly specify the location of the warning. *registry* is an object representing all the currently active filters. If *registry* is omitted, the warning message is not suppressed.

showwarning(*message*, *category*, *filename*, *lineno*[, *file*])

Writes a warning to a file. If *file* is omitted, the warning is printed to sys.stderr.

formatwarning(*message*, *category*, *filename*, *lineno*)

Creates the formatted string that is printed when a warning is issued.

filterwarnings(*action*[, *message*[, *category*[, *module*[, *lineno*[, *append*]]]]])

Adds an entry to the list of warning filters. *action* is one of 'error', 'ignore', 'always', 'default', 'once', or 'module'. The following table provides an explanation of each:

Action	Description
'error'	Convert the warning into an exception.
'ignore'	Ignore the warning.
'always'	Always print a warning message.
'default'	Print the warning once for each location where the warning occurs.
'module'	Print the warning once for each module in which the warning occurs.
'once'	Print the warning once regardless where it occurs.

message is a regular expression string that is used to match against the warning message. *category* is a warning class such as DeprecationError. *module* is a regular expression string that is matched against the module name. *lineno* is a specific line number or 0 to match against all lines. *append* specifies that the filter should be appended to the list of all filters (checked last). By default, new filters are added to the beginning of the filter list. If any argument is omitted, it defaults to a value that matches all warnings.

resetwarnings()

Resets all the warning filters. This discards all previous calls to filterwarnings() as well as options specified with -W.

Notes

- The list of currently active filters is found in the warnings.filters variable.
- When warnings are converted to exceptions, the warning category becomes the exception type. For instance, an error on DeprecationWarning will raise a DeprecationWarning exception.
- The -W option can be used to specify a warning filter on the command line. The general format of this option is

-W*action*:*message*:*category*:*module*:*lineno*

where each part has the same meaning as for the `filterwarning()` function. However, in this case, the *message* and *module* fields specify substrings (instead of regular expressions) for the first part of the warning message and module name to be filtered, respectively.

weakref

The `weakref` module is used to provide support for weak references. Normally, a reference to an object causes its reference count to increase—effectively keeping the object alive until the reference goes away. A weak reference, on the other hand, provides a way of referring to an object without increasing its reference count. This can be useful in certain kinds of applications that must manage objects in unusual ways. For example, a distributed object system might use weak references so that it can keep track of objects without becoming involved with the low-level details of memory management.

A weak reference is created using the `weakref.ref()` function as follows:

```
>>> class A: pass
>>> a = A()
>>> ar = weakref.ref(a)        # Create a weak reference to a
>>> print ar
<weakref at 0x135a24; to 'instance' at 0x12ce0c>
```

Once a weak reference is created, the original object can be obtained from the weak reference by simply calling it as a function with no arguments. If the underlying object still exists, it will be returned. Otherwise, None is returned to indicate that the original object no longer exists. For example:

```
>>> print ar()                 # Print original object
<__main__.A instance at 12ce0c>
>>> del a                      # Delete the original object
>>> print ar()                 # a is gone, so this now returns None
None
>>>
```

The following functions are defined by the `weakref` module:

ref(*object*[, *callback*])

Creates a weak reference to *object*. *callback* is an optional function that will be called when *object* is about to be destroyed. If supplied, this function should accept a single argument, which is the corresponding weak reference object. More than one weak reference may refer to the same object. In this case, the callback functions will be called in order from the most recently applied reference to the oldest reference. *object* can be obtained from a weak reference by calling the returned weak reference object as a function with no arguments. If the original object no longer exists, None will be returned. `ref()` actually defines a type, `ReferenceType`, that can be used for type-checking and subclasses.

proxy(*object*[, *callback*])

Creates a proxy using a weak reference to *object*. The returned proxy object is really a wrapper around the original object that provides access to its attributes and methods. As long as the original object exists, manipulation of the proxy object will transparently mimic the behavior of the underlying object. On the other hand, if the original object has been destroyed, operations on the proxy will raise a `weakref.ReferenceError` to indicate that the object no longer exists. *callback* is a callback function with the same meaning as for the `ref()` function. The type of a proxy object is either `ProxyType` or `CallableProxyType`, depending on whether or not the original object is callable.

`getweakrefcount(object)`

Returns the number of weak references and proxies that refer to *object*.

`getweakrefs(object)`

Returns a list of all weak reference and proxy objects that refer to *object*.

`WeakKeyDictionary([dict])`

Creates a dictionary in which the keys are referenced weakly. When there are no more strong references to a key, the corresponding entry in the dictionary is automatically removed. If supplied, the items in *dict* are initially added to the returned `WeakKeyDictionary` object. Because only certain types of objects can be weakly referenced, there are numerous restrictions on acceptable key values. In particular, built-in strings cannot be used as weak keys. However, instances of user-defined classes that define a `__hash__()` method can be used as keys.

`WeakValueDictionary([dict])`

Creates a dictionary in which the values are reference weakly. When there are no more strong references to a value, corresponding entries in the dictionary will be discarded. If supplied, the entries in *dict* are added to the returned `WeakValueDictionary`.

`ProxyTypes`

This is a tuple `(ProxyType, CallableProxyType)` that can be used for testing if an object is one of the two kinds of proxy objects created by the `proxy()` function—for example, `isinstance(object, ProxyTypes)`.

Example

One application of weak references is to create caches of recently computed results. For instance, if a function takes a long time to compute a result, it might make sense to cache these results and to reuse them as long as they are still in use someplace in the application. For example:

```
_resultcache = { }
def foocache(x):
    if resultcache.has_key(x):
        r = _resultcache[x]()        # Get weak ref and dereference it
        if r is not None: return r
    r = foo(x)
    _resultcache[x] = weakref.ref(r)
    return r
```

Notes

- Only class instances, functions, methods, sets, frozen sets, files, generators, type objects, and certain object types defined in library modules (for example, sockets, arrays, regular expression patterns) support weak references. Built-in functions and most built-in types such as lists, dictionaries, strings, and numbers cannot be used.

- If iteration is ever used on a `WeakKeyDictionary` or `WeakValueDictionary`, great care should be taken to ensure that the dictionary does not change size because this may produce bizarre side effects such as items mysteriously disappearing from the dictionary for no apparent reason.

- If an exception occurs during the execution of a callback registered with `ref()` or `proxy()`, the exception is printed to standard error and ignored.

- Weak references are hashable as long as the original object is hashable. Moreover, the weak reference will maintain its hash value after the original object has been deleted provided that the original hash value is computed while the object still exists.

- Weak references can be tested for equality, but not for ordering. If the objects are still alive, references are equal if the underlying objects have the same value. Otherwise, references are equal if they are the same reference.

UserDict, UserList, **and** UserString

The `UserDict`, `UserList`, and `UserString` modules provide classes that implement wrappers around the built-in dictionary, list, and string objects, respectively. Historically, these wrappers were used as base classes for classes that wanted to override or add new methods to these types. Because modern versions of Python allow built-in types to be subclassed directly, use of this module is rarely needed. However, you may see this module in use in older Python code. Each module defines the class `UserDict`, `UserList`, and `UserString`, respectively.

UserDict([initialdata])

Returns a class instance that simulates a dictionary. *initialdata* is an optional dictionary whose contents are used to populate the newly created `UserDict` instance.

IterableUserDict([initialdata])

A subclass of `UserDict` that supports iteration.

UserList([list])

Returns a class instance that simulates a list. *list* is an optional list that will be used to set the initial value. If omitted, the list will be set to `[ ]`.

UserString([sequence])

Returns a class instance that simulates a string. The initial value of the string is set to the value of `str(sequence)`.

In all cases, the real dictionary, list, or string object can be accessed in the `data` attribute of the instance.

Example

```
# A dictionary with case-insensitive keys
from UserDict import UserDict
import string

class MyDict(UserDict):
    # Perform a case-insensitive lookup
    def __getitem__(self,key):
```

```
        return self.data[key.lower()]
    def __setitem__(self,key,value):
        self.data[key.lower()] = value
    def __delitem__(self,key):
        del self.data[key.lower()]
    def has_key(self,key):
        return self.data.has_key(key.lower())

# Use new dictionary-like class
d = MyDict()
d['Content-Type'] = 'text/html'
print d['content-type']          # Returns 'text/html'
```

It is important to note that Python already allows built-in types to be subclassed. Therefore, the use of UserDict is probably unnecessary. For example, the preceding code could be easily rewritten by defining MyDict as class MyDict(dict) instead.

Although the UserDict class is deprecated, the UserDict module defines a class, DictMixin, that may be more useful. If you have created an object that implements a small subset of the mapping interface (__getitem__(), __setitem__(), __delitem__(), and keys()), the DictMixin class provides the rest of the common dictionary methods, such as has_key(), items(), and so forth. To use DictMixin, you simply inherit from it.

The UserString module also defines a class, MutableString, that provides an implementation of mutable strings. For example:

```
a = UserString.MutableString("Hello World!")
a[1] = 'a'      # a = "Hallo World!"
a[6:] = 'Welt!' # a = "Hallo Welt!"
```

Although mutable strings are a frequently requested Python feature, the implementation provided by MutableString has a number of drawbacks. First, the standard string methods, such as s.replace() and s.upper(), return new strings as opposed to modifying the string in place. Second, mutable strings cannot be used as dictionary keys. Finally, the mutable string implementation does not provide extra memory efficiency or runtime performance as you might expect. For instance, all changes to a MutableString object involve a full memory copy of the underlying string as opposed to simply modifying the contents in place.

Notes

- Use of the MutableString class should generally be discouraged because it provides no significant benefit over the use of standard strings. In fact, it will probably make your application run slower.

- Subclasses of UserList should provide a constructor that takes one or no arguments.

14

Mathematics

THIS CHAPTER DESCRIBES MODULES FOR PERFORMING various kinds of mathematical operations. In additional, the `decimal` module, which provides generalized support for decimal floating-point numbers, is described.

cmath

The `cmath` module provides mathematical functions for complex numbers. All the following functions accept and return complex numbers:

Function	Description
`acos(x)`	Returns the arccosine of x
`acosh(x)`	Returns the arc hyperbolic cosine of x
`asin(x)`	Returns the arcsine of x
`asinh(x)`	Returns the arc hyperbolic sine of x
`atan(x)`	Returns the arctangent of x
`atanh(x)`	Returns the arc hyperbolic tangent of x
`cos(x)`	Returns the cosine of x
`cosh(x)`	Returns the hyperbolic cosine of x
`exp(x)`	Returns e ** x
`log(x [,base])`	Returns the logarithm of x in the given *base*. If *base* is omitted, the natural logarithm is computed.
`log10(x)`	Returns the base 10 logarithm of x
`sin(x)`	Returns the sine of x
`sinh(x)`	Returns the hyperbolic sine of x
`sqrt(x)`	Returns the square root of x
`tan(x)`	Returns the tangent of x
`tanh(x)`	Returns the hyperbolic tangent of x

The following constants are defined:

Constant	Description
pi	Mathematical constant pi, as a real
e	Mathematical constant e, as a real

See Also:
math (p. 190)

decimal

On most systems, the Python `float` data type is represented using a binary floating-point encoding such as the IEEE 754 standard. A subtle consequence of the binary encoding is that decimal values such as 0.1 can't be represented exactly. Instead, the value is 0.10000000000000001. This inexactness carries over to calculations involving floating-point numbers and can sometimes lead to unexpected results (for example, `3*0.1 == 0.3` evaluates as `False`).

The `decimal` module provides generalized support for decimal floating-point numbers. These numbers allow for exact representation of decimals. In addition, parameters such as precision, significant digits, and rounding behavior can be controlled.

The `decimal` module defines two basic data types: a `Decimal` type that represents a decimal number, and a `Context` type that represents various parameters concerning computation such as precision and round-off error-handling.

The following creates a new decimal number:

`Decimal([value [, context]])`

Here, `value` is the value of the number specified as either an integer, a string containing a decimal value such as `'4.5'`, or a tuple `(sign, digits, exponent)`. If a tuple is supplied, `sign` is 0 for positive, 1 for negative; `digits` is a tuple of digits specified as integers; and `exponent` is an integer exponent. The special strings `'Infinity'`, `'-Infinity'`, `'NaN'`, and `'sNaN'` may be used to specify positive and negative infinity as well as Not a Number (NaN). `'sNaN'` is a variant of NaN that results in an exception if it is ever subsequently used in a calculation. An ordinary `float` object may *not* be used as the initial value because that value may not be exact (which defeats the purpose of using `decimal` in the first place). The `context` parameter is a `Context` object, which is described later. If supplied, `context` determines what happens if the initial value is not a valid number—raising an exception or returning a decimal with the value NaN.

The following examples show how to create various decimal numbers:

```
a = decimal.Decimal(42)              # Creates Decimal("42")
b = decimal.Decimal("37.45")         # Creates Decimal("37.45")
c = decimal.Decimal((1,(2,3,4,5),-2)) # Creates Decimal("-23.45")
d = decimal.Decimal("Infinity")
e = decimal.Decimal("NaN")
```

Decimal objects are immutable and have all the usual numeric properties of the built-in `int` and `float` types. They can also be used as dictionary keys, placed in sets, sorted, and so forth.

Various properties of decimal numbers, such as rounding and precision, are controlled through the use of a `Context` object:

```
Context(prec=None, rounding=None, traps=None, flags=None,
 Emin=None, Emax=None, capitals=1)
```

This creates a new decimal context. The parameters should be specified using keyword arguments with the names shown. *prec* is an integer that sets the number of digits of precision for arithmetic operations, *rounding* determines the rounding behavior, and *traps* is a list of signals that produce a Python exception when certain events occur during computation (such as division by zero). *flags* is a list of signals that indicate the initial state of the context (such as overflow). Normally, *flags* is not specified. *Emin* and *Emax* are integers representing the minimum and maximum range for exponents, respectively. *capitals* is a Boolean flag that indicates whether to use `'E'` or `'e'` for exponents. The default is 1 (`'E'`).

Normally, new `Context` objects aren't created directly. Instead, the function `getcontext()` is used to return the currently active `Context` object. That object is then modified as needed. Examples of this appear later in this section. However, in order to better understand those examples, it is necessary to explain the preceding context parameters in further detail.

Rounding behavior is determined by setting the *rounding* parameter to one of the following values:

Constant	Description
ROUND_CEILING	Rounds toward positive infinity. For example, 2.52 rounds up to 2.6, and -2.58 rounds up to -2.5.
ROUND_DOWN	Rounds toward zero. For example, 2.58 rounds down to 2.5, and -2.58 rounds up to -2.5.
ROUND_FLOOR	Rounds toward negative infinity. For example, 2.58 rounds down to 2.5, and -2.52 rounds down to -2.6.
ROUND_HALF_DOWN	Rounds away from zero if the fractional part is greater than half; otherwise, rounds toward zero. For example, 2.58 rounds up to 2.6, 2.55 rounds down to 2.5, -2.55 rounds up to -2.5, and -2.58 rounds down to -2.6.
ROUND_HALF_EVEN	The same as ROUND_HALF_DOWN except that if the fractional part is exactly half, the result is rounded down if the preceding digit is even and rounded up if the preceding digit is odd. For example, 2.65 is rounded down to 2.6, and 2.55 is rounded up to 2.6.
ROUND_HALF_UP	The same as ROUND_HALF_DOWN except that if the fractional part is exactly half, it is rounded away from zero. For example 2.55 rounds up to 2.6, and -2.55 rounds down to -2.6.
ROUND_UP	Rounds away from zero. For example, 2.52 rounds up to 2.6, and -2.52 rounds down to -2.6.

The *traps* and *flags* parameters of `Context()` are lists of signals. A signal represents a type of arithmetic exception that may occur during computation. Unless listed in *traps*, signals are ignored. Otherwise, an exception is raised. The following signals are defined:

- **Clamped**—Exponent adjusted to fit the allowed range.
- **DivisionByZero**—Division of non-infinite number by 0.
- **Inexact**—Rounding error occurred.
- **InvalidOperation**—Invalid operation performed.
- **Overflow**—Exponent exceeds *Emax* after rounding. Also generates Inexact and Rounded.
- **Rounded**—Rounding occurred. May occur even if no information was lost (for example, "1.00" rounded to "1.0").
- **Subnormal**—Exponent is less that *Emin* prior to rounding.
- **Underflow**—Numerical underflow. Result rounded to 0. Also generates Inexact and Subnormal.

These signal names correspond to Python exceptions that can be used for error checking. Here's an example:

```
try:
    x = a/b
except decimal.DivisionByZero:
    print "Division by zero"
```

Like exceptions, the signals are organized into a hierarchy:

```
ArithmeticError (built-in exception)
        DecimalException
                Clamped
                DivisionByZero
        Inexact
                Overflow
                Underflow
        InvalidOperation
        Rounded
                Overflow
                Underflow
        Subnormal
                Underflow
```

The Overflow and Underflow signals appear more than once in the table because those signals also result in the parent signal (for example, an Underflow also signals Subnormal). The decimal.DivisionByZero signal also derives from the built-in DivisionByZero exception.

In many cases, arithmetic signals are silently ignored. For instance, a computation may produce a round-off error but generate no exception. In this case, the signal names can be used to check a set of sticky flags that indicate computation state. Here's an example:

```
ctxt = decimal.getcontext()      # Get current context
x = a + b
if ctxt.flags[decimal.Rounded]:
    print "Result was rounded!"
```

When flags get set, they stay set until they are cleared using the clear_flags() method. Thus, one could perform an entire sequence of calculations and only check for errors at the end.

The remainder of this section describes methods available on `Decimal` and `Context` objects as well as other built-ins in the `decimal` module.

A `Decimal` number, *d*, supports the following methods:

d.adjusted()

Returns the adjusted exponent of *d* by shifting all digits to the right until only one digit appears before the decimal point. For example, the adjusted exponent of 123e+2 is 4 (taken from rewriting the value as 1.23e+4).

d.as_tuple()

Returns a tuple (*sign, digits, exponent*) representing the value. *sign* is 0 or 1, indicating positive or negative. *digits* is a tuple representing the digits, and *exponent* is an integer exponent.

d.compare(*other* [, *context*])

Compares *d* and *other* but returns `Decimal("-1")` if *d* < *other*, `Decimal("1")` if *d* > *other*, `Decimal("0")` if *d* == *other*, or `Decimal("NaN")` if either *d* or *other* is NaN. *context* determines the context in which the comparison is performed. If omitted, the default context is used.

d.max(*other* [, *context*])

Computes the maximum value of *d* and *other* and applies context rounding rules and signal handling to the return value. The default context is used unless *context* is supplied.

d.min(*other* [, *context*])

Computes the minimum value of *d* and *other* and applies context rounding rules and signal handling to the return value.

d.normalize([*context*])

Strips trailing zeroes and normalizes *d* to a canonical value. For example, 42.5000, would become 42.5.

d.quantize(*exp* [, *rounding* [, *context* [, *watchexp*]]])

Rounds *d* to a fixed exponent determined by the decimal number *exp*. *rounding* specifies a rounding method. If not specified, the rounding method of *context* or the current context will be used. If *watchexp* is True, an error will be returned if the exponent of the result is out of range. For example, `Decimal("1.2345").quantize(Decimal("0.01"), ROUND_DOWN)` returns `Decimal("1.23")`.

d.remainder_near(*other* [, *context*])

Computes the smallest remainder (the remainder closest to zero in absolute value) of *d* % *other*. For example, `Decimal("8").remainder_near(Decimal("5"))` is `Decimal("-2")`. It may be easier to think of the result as being the distance away from the closest multiple of *other*. In this case, 8 is closer to 10 than it is to 5. Thus, the result is –2. If *d* is equally close to multiples of *other*, the result has the same sign as *d*.

d.same_quantum(*other* [, *context*])

Returns True if *d* and *other* have the same exponent or if both are NaN.

d.sqrt([*context*])

Computes square root.

d.to_eng_string([*context*])

Converts *d* to an engineering-style string in which the exponent is a multiple of three and up to three digits may appear to the left of the decimal point. For example, "1.2345", "12.345", "123.45", "1.2345E+3", "12.345E+3", and so on.

d.to_integral([*rounding* [, *context*]])

Rounds *d* to the nearest integer. *rounding* specifies the rounding rule, if any. If not specified, the rounding behavior of the context is used. Does not generate signals for Inexact or Rounded.

Context objects control various parameters concerning decimal computation. At any given time, there is a default context that is set and retrieved using the following functions:

getcontext()

Returns the current decimal context of the calling thread.

setcontext(*context*)

Sets the decimal context of the calling thread to *context*.

A Context object, *c*, has the following attributes and methods:

c.capitals

Flag set to 1 or 0 that determines whether to use "E" or "e" as the exponent character.

c.Emax

Integer specifying maximum exponent.

c.Emin

Integer specifying minimum exponent.

c.prec

Integer specifying digits of precision.

c.flags

Dictionary containing current flag values corresponding to signals. For example, *c*.flags[Rounded] returns the current flag value for the Rounded signal.

c.rounding

Rounding rule in effect. An example is ROUND_HALF_EVEN.

c.traps

Dictionary containing True/False settings for the signals that result in Python exceptions. For example, *c*.traps[DivisionByZero] is usually True, whereas *c*.traps[Rounded] is False.

`c.abs(x)`

Absolute value of x in context c.

`c.add(x,y)`

Adds x and y in context c.

`c.clear_flags()`

Resets all sticky flags (clears `c.flags`).

`c.compare(x,y)`

Compares x and y in context c. Returns the result as a `Decimal` object.

`c.copy()`

Returns a copy of context c.

`c.create_decimal(value)`

Creates a new `Decimal` object using c as the context. This may be useful in generating numbers whose precision and rounding behavior override that of the default context.

`c.divide(x,y)`

Divides x by y in context c.

`c.divmod(x,y)`

Returns the integer part of the division x / y in context c.

`c.Etiny()`

Returns the minimum exponent for subnormal results. The value is `Emin - prec + 1`.

`c.Etop()`

Returns the maximum exponent without losing precision. The value is `Emax - prec +1`.

`c.max(x, y)`

Returns the maximum of x and y in context c.

`c.min(x, y)`

Returns the minimum of x and y in context c.

`c.minus(x)`

Returns $-x$ in context c.

`c.multiply(x, y)`

Returns x * y in context c.

`c.normalize(x)`

Normalizes x in context c.

`c.plus(x)`

Returns x + y in context c.

`c.power(x, y [, modulo])`

Returns x ** y or (x ** y) % $modulo$ in context c.

`c.quantize(x, y)`

Returns x.quantize(y) in context c.

`c.remainder(x, y)`

Returns x.remainder(y) in context c.

`c.remainder_near(x, y)`

Returns x.remainder_near(y) in context c.

`c.same_quantum(x, y)`

Returns x.same_quantum(y) in context c.

`c.sqrt(x)`

Returns sqrt(x) in context c.

`c.subtract(x, y)`

Returns x - y in context c.

`c.to_eng_string(x)`

Converts x to an engineering-style string in context c.

`c.to_integral(x)`

Converts x to an integer in context c.

`c.to_sci_string(x)`

Converts x to a string in scientific notation.

Finally, the decimal module provides the following constants and variables:

`Inf`

The same as Decimal("Infinity").

`negInf`

The same as Decimal("-Infinity").

`NaN`

The same as Decimal("NaN").

`BasicContext`

A pre-made context with nine digits of precision. Rounding is ROUND_HALF_UP, Emin is -999999999, Emax is 999999999, and all traps are enabled except for Inexact, Rounded, and Subnormal.

`ExtendedContext`

A pre-made context with nine digits of precision. Rounding is ROUND_HALF_EVEN, Emin is -999999999, Emax is 999999999, and all traps are disabled. Never raises exceptions. Instead, results may be set to NaN or Infinity.

DefaultContext

The default context used when creating new contexts (the values stored here are used as default values for the new context). Defines 28 digits of precision, ROUND_HALF_EVEN rounding, and traps for Overflow, InvalidOperation, and DivisionByZero.

Examples

Here's the basic usage of decimal numbers:

```
>>> a = Decimal("42.5")
>>> b = Decimal("37.1")
>>> a + b
Decimal("79.6")
>>> a / b
Decimal("1.145552560646900269541778976")
>>> divmod(a,b)
(Decimal("1"), Decimal("5.4"))
>>> max(a,b)
Decimal("42.5")
>>> c = [Decimal("4.5"), Decimal("3"), Decimal("1.23e3")]
>>> sum(c)
Decimal("1237.5")
>>> [10*x for x in c]
[Decimal("45.0"), Decimal("30"), Decimal("1.230e4")]
>>> float(a)
42.5
>>> str(a)
'42.5'
```

Here's an example of changing parameters in the context:

```
>>> getcontext().prec = 4
>>> a = Decimal("3.4562384105")
>>> a
Decimal("3.4562384105")
>>> b = Decimal("5.6273833")
>>> getcontext().flags[Rounded]
0
>>> a + b
9.084
>>> getcontext().flags[Rounded]
1
>>> a / Decimal("0")
Traceback (most recent call last):
  File "<stdin>", line 1, in ?
decimal.DivisionByZero: x / 0
>>> getcontext().traps[DivisionByZero] = False
>>> a / Decimal("0")
Decimal("Infinity")
```

The following code shows how to round a result to a specific level of precision:

```
>>> f = Decimal("1.23456789")

>>> f.quantize(Decimal("0.01"))
Decimal("1.23")
>>> f.quantize(Decimal("0.00001"), ROUND_DOWN)
Decimal("1.23456")
>>> f.quantize(Decimal("0.00001"), ROUND_HALF_UP)
Decimal("1.23457")
```

Notes

- The decimal context is unique to each thread. Changes to the context only affect that thread and not others.

- A special number, `Decimal("sNaN")`, may be used as a signaled `NaN`. This number is never generated by any of the built-in functions. However, if it appears in a computation, an error is always signaled. You can use this to indicate invalid computations that must result in an error and must not be silently ignored. For example, a function could return `sNaN` as a result.

- The value of 0 may be positive or negative (that is, `Decimal(0)` and `Decimal("-0")`). The distinct zeros still compare as equals.

- This module is probably unsuitable for high-performance scientific computing due to the significant amount of overhead involved in calculations. Also, there is little practical benefit in using decimal floating point over binary floating point in such applications.

- A full mathematical discussion of floating point representation and error analysis is beyond the scope of this book. Readers should consult a book on numerical analysis for further details.

- The IBM General Decimal Arithmetic Specification contains more information and can be easily located online through search engines.

math

The `math` module defines the following standard mathematical functions. These functions operate on integers and floats, but don't work with complex numbers. The return value of all functions is a float. All trigonometric functions assume the use of radians.

Function	Description
`acos(x)`	Returns the arccosine of x.
`asin(x)`	Returns the arcsine of x.
`atan(x)`	Returns the arctangent of x.
`atan2(y, x)`	Returns the `atan(y / x)`.
`ceil(x)`	Returns the ceiling of x.
`cos(x)`	Returns the cosine of x.
`cosh(x)`	Returns the hyperbolic cosine of x.
`degrees(x)`	Converts x from radians to degrees.
`radians(x)`	Converts x from degrees to radians.
`exp(x)`	Returns `e ** x`.
`fabs(x)`	Returns the absolute value of x.
`floor(x)`	Returns the floor of x.
`fmod(x, y)`	Returns x % y as computed by the C `fmod()` function.
`frexp(x)`	Returns the positive mantissa and exponent of x as a tuple.
`hypot(x, y)`	Returns the Euclidean distance, `sqrt(x * x + y * y)`.

Function	Description
ldexp(x, i)	Returns $x * (2 ** i)$.
log(x [, base])	Returns the logarithm of x to the given *base*. If *base* is omitted, this function computes the natural logarithm.
log10(x)	Returns the base 10 logarithm of x.
modf(x)	Returns the fractional and integer parts of x as a tuple. Both have the same sign as x.
pow(x, y)	Returns $x ** y$.
sin(x)	Returns the sine of x.
sinh(x)	Returns the hyperbolic sine of x.
sqrt(x)	Returns the square root of x.
tan(x)	Returns the tangent of x.
tanh(x)	Returns the hyperbolic tangent of x.

The following constants are defined:

Constant	Description
pi	Mathematical constant pi
e	Mathematical constant e

See Also:
cmath (p. 181)

random

The random module provides a variety of functions for generating pseudo-random numbers as well as functions for randomly generating values according to various distributions on the real numbers. Most of the functions in this module depend on the function random(), which generates uniformly distributed numbers in the range [0.0, 1.0) using the Mersenne Twister generator.

The following functions are used to control the state of the underlying random number generator:

seed([x])

Initializes the random number generator. If x is omitted or None, the system time is used to seed the generator. Otherwise, if x is an integer or long integer, its value is used. If x is not an integer, it must be a hashable object and the value of hash(x) is used as a seed.

getstate()

Returns an object representing the current state of the generator. This object can later be passed to setstate() to restore the state.

`setstate(state)`

Restores the state of the random number generator from an object returned by `getstate()`.

`jumpahead(n)`

Quickly changes the state of the generator to what it would be if `random()` were called *n* times in a row. *n* must be a nonnegative integer.

`getrandbits(k)`

Creates a long integer containing *k* random bits.

The following functions can be used to generate random integers:

`randrange(start,stop [,step])`

Returns a random integer in `range(start,stop,step)`. Does not include the endpoint.

`randint(a,b)`

Returns a random integer, *x*, in the range `a <= x <= b`.

The following functions can be used to randomly manipulate sequences:

`choice(seq)`

Returns a random element from the nonempty sequence *seq*.

`shuffle(x [,random])`

Randomly shuffles the items in the list *x* in place. *random* is an optional argument that specifies a random generation function. If supplied, it must be a function that takes no arguments and returns a floating-point number in the range [0.0, 1.0).

`sample(s, len)`

Returns a sequence length, *len*, containing elements chosen randomly from the sequence *s*. The elements in the resulting sequence are placed in the order in which they were selected.

The following functions generate random numbers on real numbers. Parameter names correspond to the names in the distribution's standard mathematical equation.

`random()`

Returns a random number in the range [0.0, 1.0).

`uniform(a,b)`

Returns a uniformly distributed random number in the range [a, b).

`betavariate(alpha, beta)`

Returns a value between 0 and 1 from the Beta distribution. `alpha > -1` and `beta > -1`.

`cunifvariate(mean, arc)`

Circular uniform distribution. `mean` is the mean angle, and `arc` is the range of the distribution, centered around the mean angle. Both of these values must be specified in radians in the range between 0 and `pi`. Returned values are in the range `(mean - arc/2, mean + arc/2)`.

expovariate(`lambd`)

Exponential distribution. `lambd` is `1.0` divided by the desired mean. Returns values in the range `[0, +Infinity)`.

gammavariate(`alpha`, `beta`)

Gamma distribution. `alpha > -1, beta > 0`.

gauss(`mu`, `sigma`)

Gaussian distribution with mean `mu` and standard deviation `sigma`. Slightly faster than `normalvariate()`.

lognormvariate(`mu`, `sigma`)

Log normal distribution. Taking the natural logarithm of this distribution results in a normal distribution with mean `mu`, standard deviation `sigma`.

normalvariate(`mu`, `sigma`)

Normal distribution with mean `mu` and standard deviation `sigma`.

paretovariate(`alpha`)

Pareto distribution with shape parameter `alpha`.

vonmisesvariate(`mu`, `kappa`)

The von Mises distribution, where `mu` is the mean angle in radians between `0` and `2 * pi`, and `kappa` is a nonnegative concentration factor. If `kappa` is zero, the distribution reduces to a uniform random angle over the range `0` to `2 * pi`.

weibullvariate(`alpha`, `beta`)

Weibull distribution with scale parameter `alpha` and shape parameter `beta`.

Notes

- The `Numeric` extension also provides a number of efficient generators for large samples and creating independent random-number streams.
- The functions in this module are not thread-safe. If you are generating random numbers in different threads, you should use locking to prevent concurrent access.
- The period of the random number generator (before numbers start repeating) is `2**19937-1`.
- The random numbers generated by this module are deterministic and should not be used for cryptography.
- New types of random number generators can be created by subclassing `random.Random` and implementing the `random()`, `seed()`, `getstate()`, and `jumpahead()` methods. All the other functions in this module are actually internally implemented as methods of `Random`. Thus, they could be accessed as methods of an instance of the new random number generator.
- The module provides two alternative random number generators classes— `WichmannHill` and `SystemRandom`—that are used by instantiating the appropriate class and calling the preceding functions as methods. The `WichmannHill` class

implements the Wichmann–Hill generator that was used in earlier Python releases. The `SystemRandom` class generates random numbers using the system random number generator `os.urandom()`.

15

Data Structures and Algorithms

T HE MODULES IN THIS CHAPTER ARE PRIMARILY related to different kinds of common data structures (arrays, queues, and so on) as well as algorithms used for searching and iteration.

array

The array module defines a new object type, array, that works almost exactly like other sequence types, except that its contents are constrained to a single type. The type of an array is determined at the time of creation, using one of the following type codes:

Type Code	Description	C Type	Minimum Size (in Bytes)
'c'	8-bit character	char	1
'b'	8-bit integer	signed char	1
'B'	8-bit unsigned integer	unsigned char	1
'u'	Unicode character	PY_UNICODE	2 or 4
'h'	16-bit integer	short	2
'H'	16-bit unsigned integer	unsigned short	2
'i'	Integer	int	4 or 8
'I'	Unsigned integer	unsigned int	4 or 8
'l'	Long integer	long	4 or 8
'L'	Unsigned long integer	unsigned long	4 or 8
'f'	Single-precision float	float	4
'd'	Double-precision float	double	8

The representation of integers and long integers is determined by the machine architecture (they may be 32 or 64 bits). When values stored as 'L' or 'I' are returned, they're returned as Python long integers.

The module defines the following function:

array(*typecode* [, *initializer*])

Creates an array of type *typecode*. *initializer* is a string or list of values used to initialize values in the array. The following attributes and methods apply to an array object, a:

Item	Description
a.typecode	Type code character used to create the array.
a.itemsize	Size of items stored in the array (in bytes).
a.append(x)	Appends x to the end of the array.
a.buffer_info()	Returns (address, length), giving the memory location and length of the buffer used to store the array.
a.byteswap()	Swaps the byte ordering of all items in the array from big-endian to little-endian, or vice versa. This is only supported for integer values.
a.count(x)	Returns the number of occurrences of x in a.
a.extend(b)	Appends b to the end of array a. b can be an array or an iterable object whose elements are the same type as in a.
a.fromfile(f, n)	Reads n items (in binary format) from the file object f and appends to the end of the array. f must be a file object. Raises EOFError if fewer than n items can be read.
a.fromlist(list)	Appends items from list to the end of the array. list can be any iterable object.
a.fromstring(s)	Appends items from string s, where s is interpreted as a string of binary values—same as would have been read using fromfile().
a.index(x)	Returns the index of the first occurrence of x in a. Raises ValueError if not found.
a.insert(i, x)	Inserts x before position i.
a.pop([i])	Removes item i from the array and returns it. If i is omitted, the last element is removed.
a.remove(x)	Removes the first occurrence of x from the array. Raises ValueError if not found.
a.reverse()	Reverses the order of the array.
a.tofile(f)	Writes all items to file f. Data is saved in native binary format.
a.tolist()	Converts the array to an ordinary list of values.
a.tostring()	Converts to a string of binary data—the same data as would be written using tofile().
a.tounicode()	Converts the array to a Unicode string. Raises ValueError if the array is not of type 'u'.

When items are inserted into an array, a TypeError exception is generated if the type of the item doesn't match the type used to create the array.

Notes

- This module is used to create large lists in a storage-efficient manner. The resulting arrays are not suitable for numeric work. For example, the addition operator doesn't add the corresponding elements of the arrays; instead, it appends one array to the other. To create storage- and calculation-efficient arrays, use the Numeric extension available at http://numpy.sourceforge.net/. Note that the Numeric API is completely different.

- The type of an array object is array. The type ArrayType is an alias for array.
- The += operator can be used to append the contents of another array. The *= operator can be used to repeat an array.

See Also:
struct **(p. 228),** xdrlib **(p. 473)**

bisect

The bisect module provides support for keeping lists in sorted order. It uses a bisection algorithm to do most of its work.

bisect(*list*, *item* [, *low* [, *high*]])

Returns the index of the insertion point for *item* to be placed in *list* in order to maintain *list* in sorted order. *low* and *high* are indices specifying a subset of the list to examine. If *items* is already in the list, the insertion point will always be to the right of existing entries in the list.

bisect_left(*list*, *item* [, *low* [, *high*]])

Returns the index of the insertion point for *item* to be placed in *list* in order to maintain *list* in sorted order. *low* and *high* are indices specifying a subset of the list to examine. If *items* is already in the list, the insertion point will always be to the left of existing entries in the list.

bisect_right(*list*, *item* [, *low* [, *high*]])

The same as bisect().

insort(*list*, *item* [, *low* [, *high*]])

Inserts *item* into *list* in sorted order. If *item* is already in the list, the new entry is inserted to the right of any existing entries.

insort_left(*list*, *item* [, *low* [, *high*]])

Inserts *item* into *list* in sorted order. If *item* is already in the list, the new entry is inserted to the left of any existing entries.

insort_right(*list*, *item* [, *low* [, *high*]])

The same as insort().

collections

The collections module contains high-performance implementations of various container data types. This is a relatively new Python module that only contains a single object as of this writing. However, it may be expanded in future releases.

`deque([iterable])`

Creates a double-ended queue (deque) object. `iterable` is an iterable object used to populate the `deque`. A *deque* allows items to be inserted or removed from either end of the queue. The implementation has been optimized so that the performance of these operations is approximately the same (`O(1)`). This is slightly different from a list where operations at the front of the list may require shifting of all the elements that follow.

An instance, *d*, of deque has the following methods:

`d.append(x)`

Adds *x* to the right side of *d*.

`d.appendleft(x)`

Adds *x* to the left side of *d*.

`d.clear()`

Removes all items from *d*.

`d.extend(iterable)`

Extends *d* by adding all the items in `iterable` on the right.

`d.extendleft(iterable)`

Extends *d* by adding all the items in `iterable` on the left. Due to the sequence of left appends that occur, items in `iterable` will appear in reverse order in *d*.

`d.pop()`

Returns and removes an item from the right side of *d*. Raises `IndexError` if *d* is empty.

`d.popleft()`

Returns and removes an item from the left side of *d*. Raises `IndexError` if *d* is empty.

`d.rotate(n)`

Rotates all the items *n* steps to the right. If *n* is negative, items are rotated to the left.

Notes

- A deque supports the sequence operator `in` and indexing such as `d[i]`. Deques can also be used with built-in functions such as `len()` and `reversed()`. They support iteration as well.
- Deques can be pickled using the `pickle` module.
- Deques are thread-safe.

heapq

The heapq module implements a priority queue using a heap. *Heaps* are simply lists of ordered items in which the heap condition has been imposed. Specifically, $heap[n] <= heap[2*n+1]$ and $heap[n] <= heap[2*n+2]$ for all *n*, starting with $n = 0$. $heap[0]$ always contains the smallest item.

heapify(x)

Converts a list, *x*, into a heap, in place.

heappop(heap)

Returns and removes the smallest item from *heap*, preserving the heap condition. Raises IndexError if *heap* is empty.

heappush(heap, item)

Adds *item* to the heap, preserving the heap condition.

heapreplace(heap, item)

Returns and removes the smallest *item* from the heap. At the same time, a new *item* is added. The heap condition is preserved in the process. This function is more efficient that calling heappop() and heappush() in sequence. In addition, the returned value is obtained prior to adding the new item. Therefore, the return value could be larger than *item*. Raises IndexError if *heap* is empty.

nlargest(n, iterable)

Creates a list consisting of the *n* largest items in *iterable*. The largest item appears first in the returned list.

nsmallest(n, iterable)

Creates a list consisting of the *n* smallest items in *iterable*. The smallest item appears first in the returned list.

> **Note**
>
> The theory and implementation of heap queues can be found in most books on algorithms.

itertools

The itertools module contains functions for creating efficient iterators, useful for looping over data in various ways. All the functions in this module return iterators that can be used with the for statement and other functions involving iterators.

chain(iter1, iter2, ..., iterN)

Given a group of iterators (*iter1*, ... , *iterN*), this function creates a new iterator that chains all the iterators together. The returned iterator produces items from *iter1* until it is exhausted. Then items from *iter2* are produced. This continues until all the items in *iterN* are exhausted.

count([n])

Creates an iterator that produces consecutive integers starting with *n*. If *n* is omitted, counting starts at 0. (Note that this iterator does not support long integers. If *sys.maxint* is exceeded, the counter overflows and continues to count starting with *-sys.maxint - 1*.)

`cycle(iterable)`

Creates an iterator that cycles over the elements in `iterable` over and over again. Internally, a copy of the elements in `iterable` is made. This copy is used to return the repeated items in the cycle.

`dropwhile(predicate, iterable)`

Creates an iterator that discards items from `iterable` as long as the function `predicate(item)` is True. Once `predicate` returns False, that item and all subsequent items in `iterable` are produced.

`groupby(iterable [, key])`

Creates an iterator that groups consecutive items produced by `iterable`. The grouping process works by looking for duplicate items. For instance, if `iterable` produces the same item on several consecutive iterations, that defines a group. If this is applied to a sorted list, the groups would define all the unique items in the list. `key`, if supplied, is a function that is applied to each item. If present, the return value of this function is used to compare successive items instead of the items themselves. The iterator returned by this function produces tuples `(key, group)`, where `key` is the key value for the group and `group` is an iterator that yields all the items that made up the group.

`ifilter(predicate, iterable)`

Creates an iterator that only produces items from `iterable` for which `predicate(item)` is True. If `predicate` is None, all the items in `iterable` that evaluate as True are returned.

`ifilterfalse(predicate, iterable)`

Creates an iterator that only produces items from `iterable` for which `predicate(item)` is False. If `predicate` is None, all the items in `iterable` that evaluate as False are returned.

`imap(function, iter1, iter2, ..., iterN)`

Creates an iterator that produces items `function(i1,i2, ... iN)`, where `i1, i2, ...`, `iN` are items taken from the iterators `iter1, iter2, ..., iterN` respectively. If `function` is None, the tuples of the form `(i1, i2, ..., iN)` are returned. Iteration stops whenever one of the supplied iterators no longer produces any values.

`islice(iterable, [start,] stop [, step])`

Creates an iterator that produces items in a manner similar to what would be returned by a slice, `iterable[start:stop:step]`. The first `start` items are skipped and iteration stops at the position specified in `stop`. `step` specifies a stride that's used to skip items. Unlike slices, negative values may not be used for any of `start`, `stop`, or `step`.

`izip(iter1, iter2, ... iterN)`

Creates an iterator that produces tuples `(i1, i2, ..., iN)`, where `i1, i2, ..., iN` are taken from the iterators `iter1, iter2, ..., iterN` respectively. Iteration stops whenever one of the supplied iterators no longer produces any values. This function produces the same values as the built-in `zip()` function.

repeat(*object* [, *count*])

Creates an iterator that repeatedly produces *object*. *count*, if supplied, specifies a repeat count. Otherwise, the object is returned indefinitely.

starmap(*func* [, *iterable*])

Creates an iterator that produces the values *func*(**item*), where *item* is taken from *iterable*. This only works if *iterable* produces tuples suitable for calling a function in this manner.

takewhile(*predicate* [, *iterable*])

Creates an iterator that produces items from *iterable* as long as *predicate*(*item*) is True. Iteration stops immediately once *predicate* evaluates as False.

tee(*iterable* [, *n*])

Creates *n* independent iterators from *iterable*. The created iterators are returned as a n-tuple. The default value of *n* is 2. This function works with any iterable object. However, in order to clone the original iterator, the items produced are cached and used in all the newly created iterators. Great care should be taken not to use the original iterator *iterable* after tee() has been called. Otherwise, the caching mechanism may not work correctly.

Examples

```
from itertools import *
# Iterate over the numbers 0,1,...,10,9,8,...,1 in an endless cycle
for i in cycle(chain(xangre(10),xrange(10,0,-1))):
    print i

# Create a list of unique items in a
a = [1,4,5,4,9,1,2,3,4,5,1]
a.sort()
b = [k for k,g in groupby(a)]    # b = [1,2,3,4,5,9]

# Iterate over all possible combinations of pairs of values from x and y
x = [1,2,3,4,5]
y = [10,11,12]
for a,b in izip(chain(*(repeat(i,len(y)) for i in x)), cycle(y)):
    print a,b
# Produces output 1 10
#                 1 11
#                 1 12
#                 2 10
#                 ...
#                 5 12
```

## 16

String and Text Handling

THIS CHAPTER DESCRIBES PYTHON MODULES RELATED to basic string and text processing. The focus of this chapter is on the most common string operations, such as processing text, regular expression pattern matching, and text formatting. In addition, a variety of modules related to Unicode and internationalization are described.

codecs

The `codecs` module provides an interface for accessing different string encoding and decoding functions (*codecs*) as well as a collection of base classes that can be used to define new codecs. The following functions are available:

register(*search_function*)

Registers a new codec search function. This function should take a single argument in the form of an encoding string (for example, `'utf-8'`) and return a tuple of functions `(encoder, decoder, streamreader, streamwriter)`.

lookup(*encoding*)

Looks up a codec in the codec registry. *encoding* is a string such as `'utf-8'`. Returns a tuple of functions `(encoder, decoder, streamreader, streamwriter)`. Internally, this function keeps a cache of previously used encodings. If a match is not found in the cache, all the registered search functions are invoked until a match is found. If no match is found, `LookupError` is raised. A list of support codecs is found at the end of this section.

getdecoder(*encoding*)

Returns the decoder function for *encoding*. This is the same as `lookup(encoding)[1]`.

getencoder(*encoding*)

Returns the encoder function for *encoding*. This is the same as `lookup(encoding)[0]`.

getreader(*encoding*)

Returns the `StreamReader` class for *encoding*. This is the same as `lookup(encoding)[2]`.

`getwriter(encoding)`

Returns the `StreamWriter` class for `encoding`. This is the same as `lookup(encoding)[3]`.

`open(filename, mode[, encoding[, errors[, buffering]]])`

Opens `filename` in the given `mode` and provides transparent data encoding/decoding according to the encoding specified in `encoding`. `errors` is one of `'strict'`, `'ignore'`, `'replace'`, `'backslashreplace'`, or `'xmlcharrefreplace'`. The default is `'strict'`. `buffering` has the same meaning as for the built-in `open()` function.

`register_error(name, handler)`

Registers a new error-handling function for use during encoding and decoding. `name` is the name of the error handler that will be used in `decode()` and `encode()` calls (for example, `'strict'`, `'backslashreplace'`, and so on). `handler` is a function that receives a single argument of type `UnicodeError` that contains information about the error. `handler` returns a tuple `(replacement, pos)`, where `replacement` is a string that contains the replacement text and `pos` is the position where encoding/decoding should continue.

`lookup_error(name)`

Returns the error-handling function `name`.

`strict_errors(exc)`

Default error handler for `'strict'`. `exc` is an instance of `UnicodeError`.

`replace_errors(exc)`

Default error handler for `'replace'`.

`ignore_errors(exc)`

Default error handler for `'ignore'`.

`backslashreplace_errors(exc)`

Default error handler for `'backslashreplace'`.

`xmlcharrefreplace_errors(exc)`

Default error handler for `'xmlcharrefreplace'`.

`EncodedFile(file, inputenc[, outputenc [, errors]])`

A class that provides an encoding wrapper around a file object, `file`. Data written to the file is first interpreted according to the input encoding `inputenc` and then written to the file using the output encoding `outputenc`. Data read from the file is decoded according to `inputenc`. If `outputenc` is omitted, it defaults to `inputenc`. `errors` has the same meaning as for `open()` and defaults to `'strict'`.

To define new codecs, the `codecs` module provides a base class, `Codec`, that is subclassed when defining encoders and decoders. The interface to a `Codec` object, `c`, is as follows:

`c.encode(self, input [, errors])`

Encodes input and returns a tuple `(output, length)` where `length` is the length of the data in `input` that was consumed in the encoding. `errors` is one of `'strict'`,

'ignore', 'replace', 'backslashreplace', or 'xmlcharrefreplace' and defaults
to 'strict'.

c.decode(*self,input* [,*errors*])

Decodes input and returns a tuple (*output, length*) where *length* is the length of
the data that was consumed in the decoding. *errors* defaults to 'strict'.

    Neither the encode() nor the decode() method should maintain internal state. In
addition, both methods must be able to operate with zero-length input, producing a
zero-length output object of the proper type.

    In addition, the codecs module provides base classes for four different types of I/O
interfaces. All of these classes are subclasses of Codec.

StreamWriter(stream [, errors])

Provides a wrapper around *stream* for producing an encoded output stream. An
instance, w, of StreamWriter provides the same methods as *stream*. In addition, the
following methods are defined:

w.write(*object*)

Writes an encoded version of *object* to w.

w.writelines(*list*)

Writes a concatenated list of strings to w.

w.reset()

Flushes the output buffers and resets the internal encoding state.

StreamReader(*stream* [, *errors*])

Provides a wrapper around *stream* for reading an encoded input stream. An instance, r,
of StreamReader provides the same methods as *stream* in addition to the following
methods:

r.read([*size*])

Reads decoded data from r. *size* is the approximate number of bytes to read. The
decoder may adjust this value slightly to accommodate the underlying encoding. If
size is omitted, all data is read and decoded.

r.readline([*size*])

Reads a single line of input using the underlying stream's readline() method and
returns as decoded data. *size* is simply passed to the underlying readline() method.

r.readlines([*size*])

Reads all lines and returns as a list of decoded lines.

r.reset()

Resets the codec buffers. This is usually used to recover from decoding errors.

StreamReaderWriter(*stream, reader, writer* [, *errors*])

Provides a wrapper around a stream that provides both encoding and decoding. *stream*
is any file object. *reader* must be a factory function or class implementing the
StreamReader interface. *writer* must be a factory function or class implementing the

StreamWriter interface. A StreamWriter instance provides the combined interface of
StreamReader and StreamWriter.

StreamRecoder(*stream, encode, decode, reader, writer* [,*errors*])

Provides a wrapper around *stream* that allows for conversion between two different
encodings (for example, UTF-8 to and from UTF-16). *stream* may be any file-like
object. The *encode* and *decode* arguments define the encoding and decoding functions
that are returned or accepted by the read() and write() methods, respectively (that is,
data returned by read() is encoded according to *encode*, and data given to write() is
decoded according to *decode*). *reader* and *writer* are the StreamReader and
StreamWriter classes used to read and write the actual contents of the data stream. A
StreamRecoder object provides the combined interface of StreamReader and
StreamWriter.

codecs also defines the following byte-order marker constants that can be used to
help interpret platform-specific files:

Constant	Description
BOM	Native byte-order marker for the machine
BOM_BE	Big-endian byte-order marker ('\xfe\xff')
BOM_LE	Little-endian byte-order marker ('\xff\xfe')
BOM_UTF8	UTF-8 marker ('\xef\xbb\xbf')
BOM_UTF16_BE	16-bit UTF-16 big-endian marker ('\xfe\xff')
BOM_UTF16_LE	16-bit UTF-16 little-endian marker ('\xff\xfe')
BOM_UTF32_BE	32-bit UTF-32 big-endian marker ('\x00\x00\xfe\xff')
BOM_UTF32_LE	32-bit UTF-32 little-endian marker ('\xff\xfe\x00\x00')

Example

The following example illustrates the implementation of a new encoding using encryption based on simple exclusive OR (XOR). This only works for 8-bit strings, but it
could be extended to support Unicode:

```
# xor.py: Simple encryption using XOR
import codecs

# Encoding/decoding function (works both ways)
def xor_encode(input, errors = 'strict', key=0xff):
    output = "".join([chr(ord(c) ^ key) for c in input])
    return (output,len(input))

# XOR Codec class
class Codec(codecs.Codec):
    key = 0xff
    def encode(self,input, errors='strict'):
        return xor_encode(input,errors,self.key)
    def decode(self,input, errors='strict'):
        return xor_encode(input,errors,self.key)
```

```
# StreamWriter and StreamReader classes
class StreamWriter(Codec,codecs.StreamWriter):
    pass

class StreamReader(Codec,codecs.StreamReader):
    pass

# Factory functions for creating StreamWriter and
# StreamReader objects with a given key value.

def xor_writer_factory(stream,errors,key=0xff):
    s = StreamWriter(stream,errors)
    s.key = key
    return s;

def xor_reader_factory(stream,errors,key=0xff):
    r = StreamReader(stream,errors)
    r.key = key
    return r

# Function registered with the codecs module.  Recognizes any
# encoding of the form 'xor-hh' where hh is a hexadecimal number.

def lookup(s):
    if (s[:4] == 'xor-'):
        key = int(s[4:],16)
        # Create some functions with key set to desired value
        e = lambda x,err='strict',key=key:xor_encode(x,err,key)
        r = lambda x,err='strict',key=key:xor_reader_factory(x,err,key)
        w = lambda x,err='strict',key=key:xor_writer_factory(x,err,key)
        return (e,e,r,w)

# Register with the codec module
codecs.register(lookup)
```

Now, here's a short program that uses the encoding:

```
import xor, codecs
f = codecs.open("foo","w","xor-37")
f.write("Hello World\n")          # Writes an "encrypted" version
f.close()

(enc,dec,r,w) = codecs.lookup("xor-ae")
a = enc("Hello World")
# a = ('\346\313\302\302\301\216\371\301\334\302\312', 11)
```

Standard Encodings

The following is a list of the standard encodings currently supported by Python. The encoding name is what you would pass to functions such as open() or lookup() when specifying an encoding. Some additional information about these encodings, including name aliases, can be found in the online documentation at http://www.python.org/doc/current/lib/standard-encodings.html. More information is also available at http://www.unicode.org.

Codec Name	Description
ascii	English
big5	Traditional Chinese
big5hkscs	Traditional Chinese
cp037	English
cp424	Hebrew
cp437	English
cp500	Western Europe
cp737	Greek
cp775	Baltic languages
cp850	Western Europe
cp852	Central and Eastern Europe
cp855	Bulgarian, Byelorussian, Macedonian, Russian, Serbian
cp856	Hebrew
cp857	Turkish
cp860	Portuguese
cp861	Icelandic
cp862	Hebrew
cp863	Canadian
cp864	Arabic
cp865	Danish, Norwegian
cp866	Russian
cp869	Greek
cp874	Thai
cp875	Greek
cp932	Japanese
cp949	Korean
cp950	Traditional Chinese
cp1006	Urdu
cp1026	Turkish
cp1140	Western Europe
cp1250	Central and Eastern Europe
cp1251	Bulgarian, Byelorussion, Macedonian, Russian, Serbian
cp1252	Western Europe
cp1253	Greek
cp1254	Turkish
cp1255	Hebrew
cp1256	Arabic

Codec Name	Description
cp1257	Baltic languages
cp1258	Vietnamese
euc_jp	Japanese
euc_jis_2004	Japanese
euc_jisx0213	Japanese
euc_kr	Korean
gb2312	Simplified Chinese
gbk	Unified Chinese
gb18030	Unified Chinese
hz	Simplified Chinese
iso2022_jp	Japanese
iso2022_jp_1	Japanese
iso2022_jp2_2	Japanese, Korean, Simplified Chinese, Western Europe, Greek
iso2022_jp_2004	Japanese
iso2022_jp_3	Japanese
iso2022_jp_ext	Japanese
iso2022_kr	Korean
latin-1	Western Europe
iso8859_2	Central and Eastern Europe
iso8859_3	Esperanto, Maltese
iso8859_4	Baltic languages
iso8859_5	Bulgarian, Byelorussian, Macedonia, Russian, Serbian
iso8859_6	Arabic
iso8859_7	Greek
iso8859_8	Hebrew
iso8859_9	Turkish
iso8859_10	Nordic languages
iso8859_13	Baltic languages
iso8859_14	Celtic languages
iso8859_15	Western Europe
johab	Korean
koi8_r	Russian
koi8_u	Ukrainian
mac_cyrillic	Bulgarian, Byelorussian, Macedonian, Russian, Serbian
mac_greek	Greek
mac_iceland	Icelandic

Codec Name	Description
mac_latin2	Central and Eastern Europe
mac_roman	Western Europe
mac_turkish	Turkish
ptcp153	Kazakh
shift_jis	Japanese
shift_jis_2004	Japanese
shift_jisx0213	Japanese
utf-16	UTF-16
utf-16-be	UTF-16 big endian
utf-16-le	UTF-16 little endian
utf-7	UTF-7
utf-8	UTF-8

The following codecs are specific to Python but can be used to perform various kinds of data encodings useful in Internet data encoding and file handling.

Codec Name	Description
base64	MIME base-64 encoding
bz2	bz2 compression
hex	Hexadecimal
idna	Internationalize domain names
mbcs	Windows
palmos	PalmOS 3.5
punycode	RFC 3492
quopri	MIME quoted printable
raw_unicode_escape	Python raw Unicode literal string
rot_13	ROT-13 encoding
string_escape	Python literal string
unicode_escape	Python Unicode literal string
uu	Uuencoding
zlib	Zip compression

Notes

- Further use of the codecs module is described in Chapter 9, "Input and Output."
- Most of the built-in encodings are provided to support Unicode string encoding. In this case, the encoding functions produce 8-bit strings, and the decoding functions produce Unicode strings.

difflib

The difflib module provides functions and classes for computing differences between lists of strings. The module duplicates the functionality provided by many variants of the popular Unix diff command that's used to compare files.

```
context_diff(a, b [, fromfile [, tofile [, fromfiledate [, tofiledate
[, n [, lineterm]]]]]])
```

Given two lists of strings, a and b, this function returns a generator object that produces output corresponding to a context-sensitive difference. The output produced by this function is similar to the following:

```
*** fromfile fromfiledate
--- tofile tofiledate
***************
*** 1,9 ****
  context
  context
  context
! modified line
  context
- deleted line
  context
  context
  context
--- 1,9 ----
  context
  context
  context
! modified line
  context
+ added lined
  context
  context
  context
```

The optional parameters supply values for some of the filename and date fields that appear in the output. n specifies the number of lines of context to print (default value is 3). lineterm specifies the line-termination character to use on output lines that are not part of the original input (for example, on the header lines and separators, such as '*** 1,9 ****').

```
get_close_matches(word, possibilities [, n [, cutoff]])
```

Given a string, word, and a list of possible strings in possibilities, this function tries to determine close matches. The return value is a list of strings in possibilities that are equal to or close to word. This list is sorted in descending order of closeness (the best match appears first). n specifies the maximum number of close matches to return. cutoff is a floating-point number in the range 0.0 to 1.0 that controls the meaning of "closeness." Higher values force matches to be more similar. The default value is 0.6. For two words, w and v, their closeness is computed as $2*M/(len(w)+len(v))$, where M is the combined length of all matching subsequences. For example, the words "hello" and "hallo" have a similarity of 0.8.

`ndiff(a, b [, linejunk [, charjunk ]]))`

Given two lists of strings, a and b, this function returns a generator object that produces lines showing the differences between a and b. Each line of output starts with a two-letter code, as follows:

Code	Description
'_ '	Line is unique to sequence a.
'+ '	Line is unique to sequence b.
' '	Line is common to both a and b.
'? '	Line is not part of either a or b.

linejunk is an optional filter function used to filter out input lines that might be junk (for example, blank lines, lines containing special characters, and so on). As input, linejunk takes a string and returns True if the line should be ignored. charjunk is a filter function that filters out input characters. It accepts a single character as input and returns True if the character should be ignored. By default, linejunk is None and charjunk is set to IS_CHARACTER_JUNK(), a function that filters out spaces and tabs.

`restore(ndiffgen, which)`

Given a generator object, ndiffgen, returned by ndiff(), this function returns a generator that can be used to generate either of the original input sequences. If which is 1, the first input sequence is produced. If which is 2, the second input sequence is produced.

`unified_diff(a, b [, fromfile [, tofile [, fromfiledate [, tofiledate [, n [, lineterm]]]]]])`

Given two lists of strings, a and b, this function returns a generator object that produces output corresponding to a unified difference. The parameters of this function have the same meaning as for context_diff(). Only the output format is different. It looks similar to the following:

```
--- fromfile fromfiledate
*** tofile tofiledate
@@ -1,6 _+1,6 @@
 context
 context
 context
+added line
 context
-deleted line
 context
 context
 context
```

The difflib module also defines the following class, HtmlDiff, which may be useful in certain applications:

`HtmlDiff([tabsize [, wrapcolumn [, linejunk [, charjunk]]]])`

This creates an HtmlDiff object that can be used to display differences in the form of an HTML table. tabsize specifies tab spacing and defaults to 8. wrapcolumn specifies the maximum column width (lines wider than this will be wrapped). linejunk and charjunk are filter functions with the same meaning as with ndiff().

An instance, h, of HtmlDiff has the following methods:

h.make_file(*a, b* [, *fromdesc* [, *todesc* [, *context* [, *n*]]]])

Creates a complete HTML file that compares lists of strings provided in *a* and *b*. The HTML file is returned as a string. *fromdesc* provides a description of *a*, and *todesc* provides a description of *b*. *context* is a flag that specifies whether or not a contextual diff should be shown. If True, *n* specifies the number of context lines to display. If False, *n* specifies the number of lines that will be shown at the top of the browser window after "next" hyperlinks are followed in the generated HTML.

h.make_table(*a, b* [, *fromfile* [, *tofile* [, *context* [, *n*]]]])

The same as make_file() except that only an HTML table is created and returned as a string. This can be used to embed differences into other HTML pages (generated elsewhere).

Notes

- Python provides a program, Tools/scripts/diff.py, that provides a command line front-end to the functionality of this module. This tool could be used to provide diff functionality on non-UNIX platforms.

- Low-level access to the algorithm used to generate diffs is also provided in this module through Differ and SequenceMatcher classes. The SequenceMatcher class is primarily used to find matching subsequences within two sequence objects. The Differ class is used to produce output similar to the ndiff() function and is commonly used to implement various diff algorithms. These classes can be used to perform different kinds of comparisons and can even be used to compare sequences not involving strings. Refer to the online documentation for more details.

gettext

The gettext module provides an interface to the GNU gettext library, which is used to provide support for internationalization (i18n). The primary use of gettext is to provide translation of selected program text in a way that's easy to extend and that's mostly transparent to the programmer. For example, if you're writing a program that prompts a user for a password, you might want it to print password in English, passwort in German, contraseña in Spanish, and so forth.

gettext works by making simple string substitutions of selected program text. To do this, it consults a specially constructed locale database that contains mappings of the original program text to translated versions in various languages. This database is application-specific and must be constructed with special tools (described shortly).

The standard interface to gettext relies on the following functions, which are used to both locate the translation database and produce translated strings:

bindtextdomain(*domain* [, *localedir*])

Sets the location of the locale directory for a given domain. *domain* is typically the name of the application, and *localedir* is a path such as /usr/local/share/locale. When searching for translation text, gettext looks for a file in the directory *localdir*/*language*/LC_MESSAGES/*domain*.mo, where *language* is a language name such as en, de, fr, and so on. Normally, the value of *language* is determined according to one of the following environment variables: $LANGUAGE, $LANG, $LC_MESSAGES, or $LC_ALL. The *language* parameter and environment variables can also be a colon-separated list of acceptable languages. If *localedir* is omitted, the current binding for *domain* is returned.

bind_textdomain_codeset(*domain* [, *codeset*])

Binds *domain* to *codeset*. This function determines the encoding of strings returned by other gettext functions. If *codeset* is omitted, this function returns the current codeset binding.

textdomain([*domain*])

Sets the domain that will be used for subsequent text translations. If *domain* is omitted, the name of the current domain is returned.

gettext(*message*)

Returns the translated version of *message* according to the values of the current domain, locale database location, and language. If no suitable translation can be found, *message* is returned unmodified. This function is usually aliased to _() as described in the next section.

lgettext(*message*)

The same as gettext(), but the returned string is encoded using the codeset supplied to the bind_textdomain_codeset() function. If no codeset is specified, the string is encoded in the default system encoding.

dgettext(*domain*, *message*)

Like gettext(), but *message* is looked up in the specified *domain*.

ldgettext(*domain*, *message*)

The same as dgettext(), but the returned string is encoded using the codeset supplied to the bind_textdomain_codeset() function.

ngettext(*singular*, *plural*, *n*)

Returns the translated version of a string, but considers plurality. *n* is a number, *singular* is the singular text, and *plural* is the plural text. The default behavior of this function returns a translated version of *singular* if *n* is 1. Otherwise, a translated version of *plural* is returned. However, the translation process is more complicated than this might imply. The number *n* is actually given to a translation formula that generates catalog indices, which allows for an arbitrary number of plural forms.

lngettext(*singular*, *plural*, *n*)

The same as ngettext(), but the returned string is encoded using the codeset supplied to the bind_textdomain_codeset() function.

dngettext(*domain*, *singular*, *plural*, *n*)

The same as ngettext(), but looks up text in *domain*.

ldngettext(*domain*, *singular*, *plural*, *n*)

The same as lngettext(), but looks up text in *domain*.

Example

The following example shows how the gettext module is used in an application and how a programmer can construct the translation database:

```
# myapp.py
import getpass
import gettext

gettext.bindtextdomain("myapp","./locale")  # Set locale directory
gettext.textdomain("myapp")                 # Enabled 'myapp'
_ = gettext.gettext                         # Alias _() to gettext()

pw = getpass.getpass(_("password:"))
if pw != "spam":
    print _("Authorization failed.\n");
    raise SystemExit
```

The use of the _() alias is a critical feature of the application. For one thing, this shortens the amount of code that needs to be typed. More importantly, in order to construct the translation database, automatic tools are used to extract translation text from program source by looking for special sequences such as _("..."). For Python, the program pygettext.py (found in the Tools/i18n directory of the Python distribution) is used to do this. For example:

```
% pygettext.py -o myapp.po myapp.py
```

The output of pygettext.py is a human-readable .po file that contains information about the translation strings marked by _("...") in the original source. To support a new language, the entries of this file are edited by supplying a foreign language translation. For example, an edited version of myapp.po might look like this:

```
#: myapp.py:8
msgid "Password:"
msgstr "Passwort:"

#: myapp.py:10
msgid  "Authorization failed.\n"
msgstr "Authorisierung fehlgeschlagen.\n"
```

Once the translations for a specific language are entered, the myapp.po file is converted to a binary form using the special msgfmt.py program (found in the same directory as pygettext.py). For example:

```
% msgfmt.py myapp
```

This produces a file, myapp.mo, that can be copied to an appropriate subdirectory with the locale directory (for example, locale/de/LC_MESSAGES/myapp.mo). At this point, you can test the translation by setting the $LANGUAGE environment variable to the string "de" and running the application. You should now see translated text being printed instead of the original program text.

Class-based Interface

In addition to the standard gettext interface, Python provides a class-based interface that offers better support for Unicode and is more flexible. The following functions are used for this interface:

`find(domain[, localedir[, languages [, all]]])`

Locates the appropriate translation file (.mo file) based on the given domain, locale directory, and languages setting. *domain* and *localedir* are the same strings as used with the `bindtextdomain()` function. *languages* is a list of language strings to be searched. If *localedir* and *languages* are omitted, they default to the same values as `bindtextdomain()`. Returns the filename of the translation file on success or None if no match is found. If *all* is supplied, a list of all matching filenames is returned.

`install(domain[, localedir[, unicode [, codeset]]])`

Installs the _() function in the built-in namespace using the settings of *domain* and *localedir*. The *unicode* flag makes translation strings return as Unicode strings. The *codeset* parameter specifies the codeset used to encode the translated strings.

`translation(domain[,localedir[,languages[, class_ [, fallback [, codeset]]]]])`

Returns an instance of a translation object for the given *domain*, *localedir*, and *languages* parameters. *domain* and *localedir* are strings, and *languages* is a list of language names. The *class_* parameter specifies alternative translation implementations and is primarily reserved for future expansion. The default value is GNUTranslations. *fallback* is a Boolean flag. If no translation object can be found and *fallback* is False, an IOError is raised. If *fallback* is True, a NullTranslations object is returned instead. *codeset* specifies the codeset used to encode translated strings.

The translation object *t* returned by `translation()` supports the following methods and attributes:

`t.add_fallback(fallback)`

Adds a fallback object to *t*. If *t* is unable to provide a translation for a particular message using one of the following methods, it forwards the request to the fallback object.

`t.gettext(message)`

Returns the translated version of *message* as a standard string.

`t.lgettext(message)`

Returns the translated version of *message* encoded according to the codeset.

`t.ugettext(message)`

Returns the translated version of *message* as a Unicode string.

`t.ngettext(singular, plural, n)`

Returns the translated version of a plural form.

`t.lngettext(singular, plural, n)`

Returns the translated version of a plural form encoded according to codeset.

`t.ungettext(singular, plural, n)`

Returns the translated version of a plural form as a Unicode string.

`t.info()`

Returns a dictionary containing metadata about the translation, including the character set, author, creation date, and so forth.

t.install([*unicode*])

This function installs the special _() function that's commonly used by gettext. If *unicode* is False, _() is bound to *t*.gettext(). Otherwise, _() is bound to *t*.ugettext(). Use of this function changes the binding of _ in the built-in name-space, affecting all application modules.

t.charset()

Returns the character set encoding for the translation, such as 'ISO-8859-1'.

t.output_charset()

Returns the character set encoding used when returning translated messages.

t.set_output_charset()

Sets the character set encoding used when returning translated messages.

Example

The following example illustrates the use of the class-based interface:

```
# myapp.py
import getpass
import gettext

gettext.install("myapp","./locale")
pw = getpass.getpass(_("password:"))
if pw != "spam":
    print _("Authorization failed.\n");
    raise SystemExit
```

Alternatively, you can directly control a translation instance as follows:

```
import gettext
t = gettext.translation("myapp","./locale", ["de"])
a = t.gettext("password:")
```

Notes

- Currently, only the GNU gettext format is supported by this module. However, the module may be modified to support alternative translation encoding at a later date.

- When Python is run interactively, the _ variable is used to hold the result of the last evaluated expression. This has the potential to clash with the _() function installed by the gettext module. However, such clashes are probably unlikely in practice.

re

The re module is used to perform regular-expression pattern matching and replacement in strings. Both ordinary and Unicode strings are supported. Regular-expression patterns are specified as strings containing a mix of text and special-character sequences. Because patterns often make extensive use of special characters and the backslash, they're usually written as "raw" strings, such as r'(?P<int>\d+)\.(\d*)'. For the remainder of this section, all regular-expression patterns are denoted using the raw string syntax.

The following special-character sequences are recognized in regular expression patterns:

Character(s)	Description
text	Matches the literal string text.
.	Matches any character except newline.
^	Matches the start of a string.
$	Matches the end of a string.
*	Matches zero or more repetitions of the preceding expression, matching as many repetitions as possible.
+	Matches one or more repetitions of the preceding expression, matching as many repetitions as possible.
?	Matches zero repetitions or one repetition of the preceding expression.
*?	Matches zero or more repetitions of the preceding expression, matching as few repetitions as possible.
+?	Matches one or more repetitions of the preceding expression, matching as few repetitions as possible.
??	Matches zero or one repetitions of the preceding expression, matching as few repetitions as possible.
{m}	Matches exactly m repetitions of the preceding expression.
{m, n}	Matches from m to n repetitions of the preceding expression, matching as many repetitions as possible. If m is omitted, it defaults to 0. If n is omitted, it defaults to infinity.
{m, n}?	Matches from m to n repetitions of the preceding expression, matching as few repetitions as possible.
[...]	Matches a set of characters such as r'[abcdef]' or r'[a-zA-z]'. Special characters such as * are not active inside a set.
[^...]	Matches the characters not in the set, such as r'[^0-9]'.
A|B	Matches either A or B, where A and B are both regular expressions.
(...)	Matches the regular expression inside the parentheses as a group and saves the matched substring. The contents of a group can be obtained using the group() method of MatchObject objects obtained while matching.
(?iLmsux)	Interprets the letters "i", "L", "m", "s", "u", and "x" as flag settings corresponding to the re.I, re.L, re.M, re.S, re.U, re.X flag settings given to re.compile().

Character(s)	Description
`(?:...)`	Matches the regular expression inside the parentheses, but discards the matched substring.
`(?P<name>...)`	Matches the regular expression in the parentheses and creates a named group. The group name must be a valid Python identifier.
`(?P=name)`	Matches the same text that was matched by an earlier named group.
`(?#...)`	A comment. The contents of the parentheses are ignored.
`(?=...)`	Matches the preceding expression only if followed by the pattern in the parentheses. For example, `r'Hello (?=World)'` matches `'Hello '` only if followed by `'World'`.
`(?!...)`	Matches the preceding expression only if it's *not* followed by the pattern in parentheses. For example, `r'Hello (?!World)'` matches `'Hello '` only if it's not followed by `'World'`.
`(?<=...)`	Matches the following expression if it's preceded by a match of the pattern in parentheses. For example, `r'(?<=abc)def'` matches `'def'` only if it's preceded by `'abc'`.
`(?<!...)`	Matches the following expression only if it's *not* preceded by a match of the pattern in parentheses. For example, `r'(?<!abc)def'` matches `'def'` only if it's not preceded by `'abc'`.
`(?(id|name)ypat|npat)`	Checks to see whether the regular expression group identified by *id* or *name* exists. If so, the regular expression *ypat* is matched. If not, the optional expression *npat* is matched. For example, the pattern `r'(Hello)?(?(1) World|Howdy)'` matches the string `'Hello World'` or the string `'Howdy'`.

Standard character escape sequences such as `'\n'` and `'\t'` are recognized as standard characters in a regular expression (for example, `r'\n+'` would match one or more newline characters). In addition, literal symbols that normally have special meaning in a regular expression can be specified by preceding them with a backslash. For example, `r'\*'` matches the character `*`. In addition, a number of backslash sequences correspond to special sets of characters:

Character(s)	Description
`\number`	Matches the text that was matched by a previous group number. Groups are numbered from 1 to 99, starting from the left.
`\A`	Matches only at the start of the string.

Character(s)	Description
\b	Matches the empty string at the beginning or end of a word. A *word* is a sequence of alphanumeric characters terminated by whitespace or any other nonalphanumeric character.
\B	Matches the empty string not at the beginning or end of a word.
\d	Matches any decimal digit. Same as `r'[0-9]'`.
\D	Matches any nondigit character. Same as `r'[^0-9]'`.
\s	Matches any whitespace character. Same as `r'[\t\n\r\f\v]'`.
\S	Matches any nonwhitespace character. Same as `r'[^\t\n\r\f\v]'`.
\w	Matches any alphanumeric character.
\W	Matches any character not contained in the set defined by \w.
\Z	Matches only at the end of the string.
\\	Matches a literal backslash.

The \d, \D, \s, \S, \w, and \W special characters are interpreted differently if matching Unicode strings. In this case, they match all Unicode characters that match the described property. For example, \d matches any Unicode character that is classified as a digit, such as European, Arabic, and Indic digits, which each occupy a different range of Unicode characters

The following functions are used to perform pattern matching and replacement:

compile(*str* [, *flags*])

Compiles a regular-expression pattern string into a regular-expression object. This object can be passed as the pattern argument to all the functions that follow. The object also provides a number of methods that are described shortly. *flags* is the bitwise OR of the following:

Flag	Description
I or IGNORECASE	Performs non-case-sensitive matching.
L or LOCALE	Uses locale settings for \w, \W, \b, and \B.
M or MULTILINE	Makes ^ and $ apply to each line in addition to the beginning and end of the entire string. (Normally ^ and $ apply only to the beginning and end of an entire string.)
S or DOTALL	Makes the dot (.) character match all characters, including the newline.
U or UNICODE	Uses information from the Unicode character properties database for \w, \W, \b, and \B.
X or VERBOSE	Ignores unescaped whitespace and comments in the pattern string.

search(*pattern*, *string* [, *flags*])

Searches *string* for the first match of *pattern*. *flags* has the same meaning as for compile(). Returns a MatchObject on success or None if no match was found.

`match(pattern, string [, flags])`

Checks whether zero or more characters at the beginning of `string` match `pattern`. Returns a `MatchObject` on success, or `None` otherwise. `flags` has the same meaning as for `compile()`.

`split(pattern, string [, maxsplit = 0])`

Splits `string` by the occurrences of `pattern`. Returns a list of strings including the text matched by any groups in the pattern. `maxsplit` is the maximum number of splits to perform. By default, all possible splits are performed.

`findall(pattern, string [,flags])`

Returns a list of all non-overlapping matches of `pattern` in `string`, including empty matches. If the pattern has groups, a list of the text matched by the groups is returned. If more than one group is used, each item in the list is a tuple containing the text for each group. `flags` has the same meaning as for `compile()`.

`finditer(pattern, string, [, flags])`

The same as `findall()`, but returns an iterator object instead. The iterator returns items of type `MatchObject`.

`sub(pattern, repl, string [, count = 0])`

Replaces the leftmost non-overlapping occurrences of `pattern` in `string` by using the replacement `repl`. `repl` can be a string or a function. If it's a function, it's called with a `MatchObject` and should return the replacement string. If `repl` is a string, back references such as `'\6'` are used to refer to groups in the pattern. The sequence `'\g<name>'` is used to refer to a named group. `count` is the maximum number of substitutions to perform. By default, all occurrences are replaced. Although these functions don't accept a `flags` parameter like `compile()`, the same effect can be achieved by using the `(?iLmsux)` notation described earlier in this section.

`subn(pattern, repl, string [, count = 0])`

Same as `sub()`, but returns a tuple containing the new string and the number of substitutions.

`escape(string)`

Returns a string with all nonalphanumerics backslashed.

A compiled regular-expression object, `r`, created by the `compile()` function has the following methods and attributes:

`r.search(string [, pos] [, endpos])`

Searches `string` for a match. `pos` and `endpos` specify the starting and ending positions for the search. Returns a `MatchObject` for a match and returns `None` otherwise.

`r.match(string [, pos] [, endpos])`

Checks whether zero or more characters at the beginning of `string` match. `pos` and `endpos` specify the range of `string` to be searched. Returns a `MatchObject` for a match and returns `None` otherwise.

`r.split(string [, maxsplit = 0])`

Identical to the `split()` function.

`r.findall(string [, pos [, endpos]])`

Identical to the findall() function. *pos* and *endpos* specify the starting and ending positions for the search.

`r.finditer(string [, pos [, endpos]])`

Identical to the finditer() function. *pos* and *endpos* specify the starting and ending positions for the search.

`r.sub(repl, string [, count = 0])`

Identical to the sub() function.

`r.subn(repl, string [, count = 0])`

Identical to the subn() function.

`r.flags`

The flags argument used when the regular expression object was compiled, or 0 if no flags were specified.

`r.groupindex`

A dictionary mapping symbolic group names defined by r'(?P<id>)' to group numbers.

`r.pattern`

The pattern string from which the regular expression object was compiled.

The MatchObject instances returned by search() and match() contain information about the contents of groups as well as positional data about where matches occurred. A MatchObject instance, *m*, has the following methods and attributes:

`m.expand(template)`

Returns a string that would be obtained by doing regular-expression backslash substitution on the string *template*. Numeric back-references such as "\1" and "\2" and named references such as "\g<n>" and "\g<name>" are replaced by the contents of the corresponding group. Note that these sequences should be specified using raw strings or with a literal backslash character such as r'\1' or '\\1'.

`m.group([group1, group2, ...])`

Returns one or more subgroups of the match. The arguments specify group numbers or group names. If no group name is given, the entire match is returned. If only one group is given, a string containing the text matched by the group is returned. Otherwise, a tuple containing the text matched by each of the requested groups is returned. An IndexError is raised if an invalid group number or name is given.

`m.groups([default])`

Returns a tuple containing the text matched by all groups in a pattern. *default* is the value returned for groups that didn't participate in the match (the default is None).

`m.groupdict([default])`

Returns a dictionary containing all the named subgroups of the match. *default* is the value returned for groups that didn't participate in the match (the default is None).

`m.start([group])`
`m.end([group])`

Returns the indices of the start and end of the substring matched by a group. If *group* is omitted, the entire matched substring is used. Returns None if the group exists but didn't participate in the match.

`m.span([group])`

Returns a 2-tuple (`m.start(group)`, `m.end(group)`). If *group* didn't contribute to the match, this returns (None, None). If *group* is omitted, the entire matched substring is used.

`m.pos`

The value of *pos* passed to the search() or match() function.

`m.endpos`

The value of *endpos* passed to the search() or match() function.

`m.lastindex`

The numerical index of the last group that was matched. It's None if no groups were matched.

`m.lastgroup`

The name of the last named group that was matched. It's None if no named groups were matched or present in the pattern.

`m.re`

The regular-expression object whose match() or search() method produced this MatchObject instance.

`m.string`

The string passed to match() or search().

When pattern strings don't specify a valid regular expression, the re.error exception is raised.

Examples

```
import re
s = open('foo').read()          # Read some text

# Replace all occurrences of 'foo' with 'bar'
t = re.sub('foo','bar',s)

# Get the title of an HTML document
tmatch = re.search(r'<title>(.*?)</title>',s, re.IGNORECASE)
if tmatch: title = tmatch.group(1)

# Extract a list of possible e-mail addresses from s
pat = re.compile(r'([a-zA-Z][\w-]*@[\w-]+(?:\.[\w-]+)*)')
addrs = re.findall(pat,s)

# Replace strings that look like URLs such as 'http://www.python.org'
# with an HTML anchor tag of the form
# <a href="http://www.python.org">http://www.python.org</a>
```

```
pat = re.compile(r'((ftp|http)://[\w-]+(?:\.[\w-]+)*(?:/[\w-]*)*)')
t = pat.sub('<a href="\\1">\\1</a>', s)
```

Notes

- Detailed information about the theory and implementation of regular expressions can be found in textbooks on compiler construction. The book *Mastering Regular Expressions* by Jeffrey Friedl (O'Reilly & Associates, 1997) may also be useful.
- The re module is 8-bit clean and can process strings that contain null bytes and characters whose high bit is set. Regular expression patterns cannot contain null bytes, but can specify the null bytes as `'\000'`.

See Also:
string (this page)

string

The string module contains a number of useful constants and functions for manipulating strings. Most of the functionality of this module is also available in the form of string methods. The following constants are defined:

Constant	Description
ascii_letters	A string containing all lowercase and uppercase ASCII letters.
ascii_lowercase	The string `'abcdefghijklmnopqrstuvwxyz'`.
ascii_uppercase	The string `'ABCDEFGHIJKLMNOPQRSTUVWXYZ'`.
digits	The string `'0123456789'`.
hexdigits	The string `'0123456789abcdefABCDEF'`.
letters	Concatenation of lowercase and uppercase.
lowercase	String containing all lowercase letters specific to the current locale setting.
octdigits	The string `'01234567'`.
punctuation	String of ASCII punctuation characters.
printable	String of printable characters. A combination of letters, digits, punctuation, and whitespace.
uppercase	String containing all uppercase letters specific to the current locale setting.
whitespace	String containing all whitespace characters. This usually includes space, tab, linefeed, return, formfeed, and vertical tab.

Note that some of these constants (for example, letters and uppercase) will vary depending on the locale settings of the system.

The string module additionally defines a new string type, Template, that simplifies certain string substitutions. An example can be found in Chapter 9.

The following creates a new template string object:

`Template(s)`

Here, *s* is a string and Template is defined as a class.

A Template object, *t*, supports the following methods:

`t.substitute(m [, **kwargs])`

This method takes a mapping object, *m* (for example, a dictionary), or a list of keyword arguments and performs a keyword substitution on the string *t*. This substitution replaces the string '$$' with a single '$' and the strings '$*key*' or '${*key*}' with *m*['*key*'] or *kwargs*['*key*'] if keyword arguments were supplied. *key* must spell a valid Python identifier. If the final string contains any unresolved '$*key*' patterns, a KeyError exception is raised.

`t.safe_substitute(m [, **kwargs])`

The same as substitute() except that no exceptions or errors will be generated. Instead, unresolved $*key* references will be left in the string unmodified.

`t.template`

Contains the original strings passed to Template().

The behavior of the Template class can be modified by subclassing it and redefining the attributes delimiter and idpattern. For example, this code changes the escape character $ to @ and restricts key names to letters only:

```
class MyTemplate(string.Template):
    delimiter = '@'          # Literal character for escape sequence
    idpattern = '[A-Z]*'     # Identifier regular expression pattern
```

The string module also defines a number of functions for manipulating strings. Most of these methods are deprecated and are only provided for backward compatibility. Use string methods instead.

`atof(s)`

Converts string *s* to a floating-point number. See the built-in float() function.

`atoi(s [, base])`

Converts string *s* to an integer. *base* is an optional integer specifying the base. See the built-in int() function.

`atol(s [, base])`

Converts string *s* to a long integer. *base* is an optional integer specifying the base. See the built-in long() function.

`capitalize(s)`

Capitalizes the first character of *s*. Same as s.capitalize().

`capwords(s)`

Capitalizes the first letter of each word in *s*, replaces repeated whitespace characters with a single space, and removes leading and trailing whitespace.

`count(s, sub [, start [, end]])`

Counts the number of non-overlapping occurrences of *sub* in *s*[*start*:*end*]. Same as *s*.count(*sub*, *start*, *end*).

`expandtabs(s [, tabsize=8])`

Expands tabs in string *s* with whitespace. *tabsize* specifies the number of characters between tab stops. Same as *s*.expandtab(*tabsize*).

`find(s, sub [, start [, end]])`
`index(s, sub [, start [, end]])`

Return the first index in *s*[*start*:*end*] where the substring *sub* is found. If *start* and *end* are omitted, the entire string is searched. find() returns -1 if not found, whereas index() raises a ValueError exception. Same as *s*.find(*sub*, *start*, *end*) and *s*.index(*sub*, *start*, *end*).

`rfind(s, sub [, start [, end]])`
`rindex(s, sub [, start [, end]])`

Like find() and index(), but these find the highest index. Same as *s*.rfind(*sub*, *start*, *end*) and *s*.rindex(*sub*, *start*, *end*).

`lower(s)`

Converts all uppercase characters in *s* to lowercase. Same as *s*.lower().

`maketrans(from, to)`

Creates a translation table that maps each character in *from* to the character in the same position in *to*. *from* and *to* must be the same length.

`split(s [, sep [, maxsplit]])`
`splitfields(s [, sep [, maxsplit]])`

Return a list of words in *s*. If *sep* is omitted, the words are separated by whitespace. Otherwise, the string in *sep* is used as a delimiter. *maxsplit* specifies the maximum number of splits that can occur. The remainder of the string will be returned as the last element. split() is the same as *s*.split(*sep*, *maxsplit*).

`join(words [, sep])`
`joinfields(words [, sep])`

Concatenate a sequence of words into a string, with words separated by the string in *sep*. If omitted, the words are separated by whitespace. Same as *sep*.join(*words*).

`lstrip(s)`
`rstrip(s)`
`strip(s)`

Strip leading and/or trailing whitespace from *s*. Same as *s*.lstrip(), *s*.rstrip(), and *s*.strip().

`swapcase(s)`

Changes uppercase to lowercase and lowercase to uppercase in *s*. Same as *s*.swapcase().

translate(*s*, *table* [, *delchars*])

Deletes all characters from *s* that are in *delchars* and translates the remaining characters using *table*. *table* must be a 256-character string mapping characters to characters as created by maketrans(). Same as *s*.translate(*table*, *delchars*).

upper(*s*)

Converts all lowercase characters in *s* to uppercase. Same as *s*.upper().

ljust(*s*, *width*)
rjust(*s*, *width*)
center(*s*, *width*)

Respectively left-aligns, right-aligns, and centers *s* in a field of width *width*. Same as *s*.ljust(*width*), *s*.rjust(*width*), and *s*.center(*width*).

zfill(*s*, *width*)

Pads a numeric string on the left with 0 digits, up to the given width.

replace(*str*, *old*, *new* [, *max*])

Replaces *max* occurrences of *old* with *new* in *str*. If *max* is omitted, all occurrences are replaced. Same as *s*.replace(*old*, *new*, *max*).

Notes

- The string-manipulation functions in this module are considered to be deprecated due to the addition of string methods in Python 2.0, but they are still used in some existing Python programs.
- Unicode and standard strings are supported by the module, but standard strings are coerced to Unicode when necessary.

See Also:
re **(p. 217)** and Chapter 3, "Types and Objects"

StringIO **and** cStringIO

The StringIO and cStringIO modules define an object that behaves like a file but reads and writes data from a string buffer.

The following creates a new StringIO object, where *s* is the initial value (by default, the empty string):

StringIO([*s*])

A StringIO object supports all the standard file operations—read(), write(), and so on—as well as the following methods:

`s.getvalue()`

Returns the contents of the string buffer before `close()` is called.

`s.close()`

Releases the memory buffer.

Notes

- The `StringIO` module defines `StringIO` as a Python class. `cStringIO` defines it as an extension type (implemented in C) and provides significantly faster performance.
- If an initial argument, `s`, is given to `cStringIO.StringIO(s)`, the resulting object only supports read-only access—reading data from `s`.

See Also:

The "Files and File Objects" section of Chapter 9 (for file methods), p.112

struct

The `struct` module is used to convert data between Python and binary data structures (represented as Python strings). These data structures are often used when interacting with functions written in C or with binary network protocols.

`pack(fmt, v1, v2, ...)`

Packs the values `v1`, `v2`, and so on into a string according to the format string in `fmt`.

`unpack(fmt, string)`

Unpacks the contents of `string` according to the format string in `fmt`. Returns a tuple of the unpacked values.

`calcsize(fmt)`

Calculates the size in bytes of the structure corresponding to a format string, `fmt`.

The format string is a sequence of characters with the following interpretations:

Format	C Type	Python Type
`'x'`	pad byte	No value
`'c'`	char	String of length 1
`'b'`	signed char	Integer
`'B'`	unsigned char	Integer
`'h'`	short	Integer
`'H'`	unsigned short	Integer
`'i'`	int	Integer
`'I'`	unsigned int	Integer
`'l'`	long	Integer
`'L'`	unsigned long	Integer

Format	C Type	Python Type
'q'	long long	Long
'Q'	unsigned long long	Long
'f'	float	Float
'd'	double	Float
's'	char[]	String
'p'	char[]	String with length encoded in the first byte
'P'	void *	Integer

Each format character can be preceded by an integer to indicate a repeat count (for example, '4i' is the same as 'iiii'). For the 's' format, the count represents the maximum length of the string, so '10s' represents a 10-byte string. A format of '0s' indicates a string of zero length. The 'p' format is used to encode a string in which the length appears in the first byte, followed by the string data. This is useful when dealing with Pascal code, as is sometimes necessary on the Macintosh. Note that the length of the string in this case is limited to 255 characters.

When the 'I' and 'L' formats are used to unpack a value, the return value is a Python long integer. In addition, the 'P' format may return an integer or long integer, depending on the word size of the machine.

The first character of each format string can also specify a byte ordering and alignment of the packed data, as shown here:

Format	Byte Order	Size and Alignment
'@'	Native	Native
'='	Native	Standard
'<'	Little-endian	Standard
'>'	Big-endian	Standard
'!'	Network (big-endian)	Standard

Native byte ordering may be little-endian or big-endian, depending on the machine architecture. The native sizes and alignment correspond to the values used by the C compiler and are implementation-specific. The standard alignment assumes that no alignment is needed for any type. The standard size assumes that short is 2 bytes, int is 4 bytes, long is 4 bytes, float is 32 bits, and double is 64 bits. The 'P' format can only use native byte ordering.

Notes

- Sometimes it's necessary to align the end of a structure to the alignment requirements of a particular type. To do this, end the structure-format string with the code for that type with a repeat count of zero. For example, the format 'llh0l' specifies a structure that ends on a 4-byte boundary (assuming that longs are aligned on 4-byte boundaries). In this case, two pad bytes would be inserted after the short value specified by the 'h' code. This only works when native size and alignment are being used—standard size and alignment don't enforce alignment rules.

- The 'q' and 'Q' formats are only available if the C compiler used to build Python supports the `long long` data type.

See Also:

`array` (p. 195), `xdrlib` (p. 473)

textwrap

The `textwrap` module can be used to wrap text in order to fit a specified column width. The following functions are provided:

```
fill(text [, width=70 [, initial_indent='' [, subsequent_indent=''
[,expand_tabs=True [, replace_whitespace=True [, fix_sentence_endings=False
 [, break_long_words=True]]]]]]])
```

Wraps the paragraph in *text* so that no line is more than *width* characters wide. The additional parameters control various aspects of the wrapping process and should be specified as keyword arguments using the names listed here. If *expand_tabs* is True (the default), tab characters are replaced by whitespace. If *replace_whitespace* is True, then all characters in `string.whitespace` (defined in the `string` module) will be replaced by a single space. If *fix_sentence_endings* is True, sentence endings will be fixed so that a lowercase letter followed by a period, question mark, or exclamation mark is always followed by two spaces. If *break_long_words* is True, words longer than *width* will be broken to make sure no lines are longer than *width*. Otherwise, long words are put on a line by themselves. The return value of this function is a single string containing the wrapped text.

```
wrap(text [, width=70 [, expand_tabs=True [, replace_whitespace=True
[, initial_indent='' [, subsequent_indent='' [, fix_sentence_endings=False]]]]]])
```

The same as `fill()` except that the return value is a list of strings representing the wrapped lines.

```
dedent(text)
```

Removes all whitespace that can be uniformly removed from the left side of each line.

```
TextWrapper([ width=70 [, expand_tabs=True [, replace_whitespace=True
[, initial_indent='' [, subsequent_indent='' [, fix_sentence_endings=False]]]]]])
```

Creates a `TextWrapper` object that can be used to repeatedly wrap text. The arguments have the same meaning as for `fill()`.

An instance, *t*, of `TextWrapper` provides the following methods and attributes:

```
t.width
```

Maximum line width.

```
t.expand_tabs
```

Replaces tabs with spaces if True.

```
t.replace_whitespace
```

Replaces whitespace characters with a space if True.

`t.initial_indent`

String prepended to the first line of wrapped text.

`t.subsequent_indent`

String prepended to all lines of wrapped text except the first line.

`t.fix_sentence_endings`

Fixes sentence endings if `True`.

`t.break_long_words`

Enables or disables the breaking of long words. `True` by default.

`t.fill(text)`

Returns wrapped `text` as a single string.

`t.wrap(text)`

Returns wrapped `text` as a list of strings representing each wrapped line.

> **Note**
>
> This module is really only intended for simple text formatting. Some of the algorithms used in the implementation don't account for special cases. For example, the algorithm that fixes sentence endings doesn't correctly deal with common abbreviations that might appear in a sentence, such as "Dr." in "Dr. Evil's fiendish plan."

unicodedata

The `unicodedata` module provides access to the Unicode character database, which contains character properties for all Unicode characters.

`bidirectional(unichr)`

Returns the bidirectional category assigned to `unichr` as a string, or an empty string if no such value is defined. Returns one of the following:

Value	Description
L	Left-to-Right
LRE	Left-to-Right Embedding
LRO	Left-to-Right Override
R	Right-to-Left
AL	Right-to-Left Arabic
RLE	Right-to-Left Embedding
RLO	Right-to-Left Override
PDF	Pop Directional Format
EN	European Number
ES	European Number Separator
ET	European Number Terminator

Value	Description
AN	Arabic Number
CS	Common Number Separator
NSM	Non-Spacing Mark
BN	Boundary Neutral
B	Paragraph Separator
S	Segment Separator
WS	Whitespace
ON	Other Neutrals

category(*unichr*)

Returns a string describing the general category of *unichr*. The returned string is one of the following values:

Value	Description
Lu	Letter, Uppercase
Ll	Letter, Lowercase
Lt	Letter, Title case
Mn	Mark, Non-Spacing
Mc	Mark, Spacing Combining
Me	Mark, Enclosing
Nd	Number, Decimal Digit
Nl	Number, Letter
No	Number, Other
Zs	Separator, Space
Zl	Separator, Line
Zp	Separator, Paragraph
Cc	Other, Control
Cf	Other, Format
Cs	Other, Surrogate
Co	Other, Private Use
Cn	Other, Not Assigned
Lm	Letter, Modifier
Lo	Letter, Other
Pc	Punctuation, Connector
Pd	Punctuation, Dash
Ps	Punctuation, Open
Pe	Punctuation, Close
Pi	Punctuation, Initial Quote

Value	Description
Pf	Punctuation, Final Quote
Po	Punctuation, Other
Sm	Symbol, Math
Sc	Symbol, Currency
Sk	Symbol, Modifier
So	Symbol, Other

combining(`unichr`)

Returns an integer describing the combining class for `unichr`, or 0 if no combining class is defined. One of the following values is returned:

Value	Description
0	Spacing, split, enclosing, reordrant, and Tibetan subjoined
1	Overlays and interior
7	Nuktas
8	Hiragana/Katakana voicing marks
9	Viramas
10-199	Fixed position classes
200	Below left attached
202	Below attached
204	Below right attached
208	Left attached
210	Right attached
212	Above left attached
214	Above attached
216	Above right attached
218	Below left
220	Below
222	Below right
224	Left
226	Right
228	Above left
230	Above
232	Above right
233	Double below
234	Double above
240	Below (iota subscript)

`decimal(`*unichr*`[, `*default*`])`

Returns the decimal integer value assigned to the character *unichr*. If *unichr* is not a decimal digit, *default* is returned or `ValueError` is raised.

`decomposition(`*unichr*`)`

Returns a string containing the decomposition mapping of *unichr*, or the empty string if no such mapping is defined. Typically, characters containing accent marks can be decomposed into multicharacter sequences. For example, `decomposition(u"\u00fc")` ("ü") returns the string `"0075 0308"` corresponding to the letter *u* and the umlaut (¨) accent mark. The string returned by this function may also include the following strings:

Value	Description
`<font>`	A font variant (for example, a blackletter form)
`<noBreak>`	A nonbreaking version of a space or hyphen
`<initial>`	An initial presentation form (Arabic)
`<medial>`	A medial presentation form (Arabic)
`<final>`	A final presentation form (Arabic)
`<isolated>`	An isolated presentation form (Arabic)
`<circle>`	An encircled form
`<super>`	A superscript form
`<sub>`	A subscript form
`<vertical>`	A vertical layout presentation form
`<wide>`	A wide (or zenkaku) compatibility character
`<narrow>`	A narrow (or hankaku) compatibility character
`<small>`	A small variant form (CNS compatibility)
`<square>`	A CJK squared-font variant
`<fraction>`	A vulgar fraction form
`<compat>`	Otherwise unspecified compatibility character

`digit(`*unichr*`[, `*default*`])`

Returns the integer digit value assigned to the character *unichr*. If *unichr* is not a digit, *default* is returned or `ValueError` is raised. This function differs from `decimal()` in that it works with characters that may represent digits, but that are not decimal digits.

`east_asian_width(`*unichr*`)`

Returns the east Asian width assigned to *unichr*.

`lookup(`*name*`)`

Looks up a character by name. For example, `lookup('COPYRIGHT SIGN')` returns the corresponding Unicode character. Common names can be found at http://www.unicode.org/charts.

mirrored(*unichr*)

Returns 1 if *unichr* is a "mirrored" character in bidirectional text and returns 0 otherwise. A mirrored character is one whose appearance might be changed to appear properly if text is rendered in reverse order. For example, the character "(" is mirrored because it might make sense to flip it to ")" in cases where text is printed from right to left.

name(*unichr* [, *default*])

Returns the name of a Unicode character, *unichr*. Raises ValueError if no name is defined or returns *default* if provided. For example, name(u'\xfc') returns 'LATIN SMALL LETTER U WITH DIAERESIS'.

normalize(*form*, *unistr*)

Normalizes the Unicode string *unistr* according to normal form *form*. *form* is one of 'NFC', 'NFKC', 'NFD', or 'NFKD'. The normalization of a string partly pertains to the composition and decomposition of certain characters. For example, the Unicode string for the word "resumé" could be represented as u'resum\u00e9' or as the string u'resume\u0301'. In the first string, the accented character é is represented as a single character. In the second string, the accented character is represented by the letter *e* followed by a combining accent mark (´). 'NFC' normalization converts the string *unistr* so that all of the characters are fully composed (for example, é is a single character). 'NFD' normalization converts *unistr* so that characters are decomposed (for example, é is the letter *e* followed by an accent). 'NFKC' and 'NFKD' perform the same function as 'NFC' and 'NFD' except that they additionally transform certain characters that may be represented by more than one Unicode character value into a single standard value. For example, Roman numerals have their own Unicode character values, but are also just represented by the Latin letters *I*, *V*, *M*, and so on. 'NFKC' and 'NFKD' would convert the special Roman numeral characters into their Latin equivalents.

numeric(*unichr*[, *default*])

Returns the value assigned to the Unicode character *unichr* as a floating-point number. If no numeric value is defined, *default* is returned or ValueError is raised. For example, the numeric value of U+2155 (the character for the fraction "1/5") is 0.2.

unidata_version

A string containing the Unicode database version used (for example '3.2.0').

> **Note**
>
> For further details about the Unicode character database, see http://www.unicode.org.

17

Data Management and Object Persistence

THE MODULES IN THIS CHAPTER ARE USED TO store data in a variety of DBM-style database formats. These databases operate like a large disk-based hash table in which objects are stored and retrieved using unique keys represented by standard strings. Most of these modules are optional Python extensions that require third-party libraries and must be enabled when Python is built. See Chapter 27, "Extending and Embedding Python," for further details.

Introduction

Most of the databases in this chapter are opened using a variation of the open() function (defined in each database module):

```
open(filename [, flag [, mode]])
```

This function opens the database file *filename* and returns a database object. *flag* is 'r' for read-only access, 'w' for read-write access, 'c' to create the database if it doesn't exist, or 'n' to force the creation of a new database. *mode* is the integer file-access mode used when creating the database (the default is 0666 on UNIX).

The object returned by the open() function supports the following dictionary-like operations:

Operation	Description
d[key] = value	Inserts *value* into the database
value = d[key]	Gets data from the database
del d[key]	Removes a database entry
d.close()	Closes the database
d.has_key(key)	Tests for a key
d.keys()	Returns a list of keys

In all cases, *key* must be a standard string. In addition, *value* must be a standard string for all the database modules except the shelve module. Unicode strings cannot be used for keys in any of the modules and cannot be used for values in any module except shelve.

> **Note**
> Most of the database packages described rely on third-party libraries that must be installed in addition to Python.

anydbm

The `anydbm` module provides a generic interface that's used to open a database without knowing which of the lower-level database packages are actually installed and available. When imported, it looks for one of the `bsddb`, `gdbm`, or `dbm` modules. If none are installed, the `dumbdbm` module is loaded.

A database object is created using the `open()` function:

open(*filename* [, *flag*='r' [, *mode*]])

This function opens the database file *filename* and returns a database object. If the database already exists, the `whichdb` module is used to determine its type and the corresponding database module to use. If the database doesn't exist, an attempt is made to create it using the first installed module in the preceding list of database modules. *flags* and *mode* are as described earlier in this chapter, in the "Introduction" section.

error

A tuple containing the exceptions that can be raised by each of the supported database modules.

Programs wanting to catch errors should use this tuple as an argument to `except`. For example:

```
try:
    d = anydbm.open('foo','r')
except anydbm.error:
    # Handle error
```

> **Note**
> If the `dumbdbm` module is the only installed database module, attempts to reopen a previously created database with `anydbm` will fail. Use `dumbdbm.open()` instead.

> **See Also:**
> `dumbdbm` (p. 240), `whichdb` (p. 243).

bsddb

The `bsddb` module provides an interface to the Berkeley DB library. Hash, Btree, or record-based files can be created using the appropriate `open()` call:

hashopen(*filename* [, *flag*='r' [, *mode*]])

Opens the hash format file named *filename*. The parameters have the same meaning as for `open()`, as described in the chapter introduction.

`btopen(`*`filename`* `[,` *`flag`*`='r'` `[,` *`mode`*`]])`

Opens the Btree format file named *filename*.

`rnopen(`*`filename`* `[,` *`flag`*`='r'` `[,` *`mode`*`]])`

Opens a DB record format file named *filename*.

Databases created by this module behave like dictionaries, as described in the "Introduction" section, and additionally provide the following methods for moving a "cursor" through records:

Method	Description
`d.set_location(`*`key`*`)`	Sets the cursor to the item indicated by the key and returns it.
`d.first()`	Sets the cursor to the first item in the database and returns it.
`d.next()`	Sets the cursor to the next item in the database and returns it.
`d.previous()`	Sets the cursor to the previous item in the DB file and returns it. Not supported on hash table databases.
`d.last()`	Sets the cursor to the last item in the DB file and returns it. Not supported on hash table databases.
`d.sync()`	Synchronizes the database on disk.

`error`

Exception raised on non-key-related database errors.

Notes

- This module uses the version 3.2 API of the Berkeley DB package, available at http://www.sleepycat.com. Some versions of Python may have a module, `bsddb185`, that provides the same functionality but uses version 1.85 of the Berkeley DB package.

- All the `open()` functions accept additional optional arguments that are rarely used. Consult the online documentation for details.

- Consult New Riders' *Berkeley DB Reference* (ISBN 0735710643).

See Also:
dbhash (next), http://www.python.org/doc/lib/module-bsddb.html

dbhash

The `dbhash` module is used to open databases using the `bsddb` module, but with an interface that closely matches the interface of the other database modules.

`open(`*`filename`* `[,`*`flag`*`='r'` `[,` *`mode`*`])`

Opens a DB database and returns the database object. A database object, *d*, returned by `open()` behaves like a dictionary and also provides the following methods:

Method	Description
`d.first()`	Returns the first key in the database
`d.last()`	Returns the last key in a database traversal
`d.next(key)`	Returns the next key following *key* in the database
`d.previous(key)`	Returns the item that comes before *key* in a forward traversal of the database
`d.sync()`	Writes unsaved data to the disk

error

Exception raised on database errors other than `KeyError`. Same as `bsddb.error`.

See Also:
bsddb (p. 238)

dbm

The `dbm` module provides an interface to the UNIX dbm library.

open(*filename* [, *flag*='r' [, *mode*]])

Opens a dbm database and returns a dbm object. Here, *filename* is the name of the database file (without the `.dir` or `.pag` extension). The returned object behaves like a dictionary, as described in the "Introduction" section earlier in this chapter.

error

Exception raised for dbm-specific errors other than `KeyError`.

Note
This module should work with a variety of different UNIX databases, including ndbm databases, BSD DB compatibility interfaces, and the GNU GDBM compatibility interface.

See Also:
anydbm (p. 238), gdbm (p. 241)

dumbdbm

The `dumbdbm` module is a simple DBM-style database implemented in Python. It should only be used when no other DBM database modules are available.

open(*filename* [, *flag* [, *mode*]])

Opens the database file *filename*. Note that *filename* should not include a suffix such as .dat or .dir. The returned database object behaves like a dictionary, as described in the "Introduction" section earlier in this chapter.

error

Exception raised for database-related errors other than KeyError.

See Also:
anydbm (**p. 238**), whichdb (**p. 243**)

gdbm

The gdbm module provides an interface to the GNU DBM library.

open(*filename* [, *flag*='r' [, *mode*]])

Opens a gdbm database with filename *filename*. Appending 'f' to the flag opens the database in fast mode. In this mode, altered data is not automatically written to disk after every change, resulting in better performance. If this flag is used, the sync() method should be used to force unwritten data to be written to disk on program termination.

A gdbm object, *d*, behaves like a dictionary, as described in the section "Introduction" earlier in this chapter, but it also supports the following methods:

Method	Description
d.firstkey()	Returns the starting key in the database.
d.nextkey(*key*)	Returns the key that follows *key* in a traversal of the database.
d.reorganize()	Reorganizes the database and reclaims unused space. This can be used to shrink the size of the gdbm file after a lot of deletions have occurred.
d.sync()	Forces unwritten data to be written to disk.

error

Exception raised for gdbm-specific errors.

Note
The GNU DBM library is available at www.gnu.org/software/gdbm/gdbm.html.

See Also:
anydbm (**p. 238**), whichdb (**p. 243**)

shelve

The `shelve` module provides support for persistent objects using a special "shelf" object. This object behaves like a dictionary except that all the objects it contains are stored on disk using a database such as dbm or gdbm. A shelf is created using the `shelve.open()` function.

open(*filename* [,*flag*='c' [, protocol [, writeback]]])

Opens a shelf file. If the file doesn't exist, it's created. *filename* should be the database filename and should not include a suffix. *flag* has the same meaning as described in the chapter introduction and is one of `'r'`, `'w'`, `'c'`, or `'n'`. If the database file doesn't exist, it is created. *protocol* specifies the protocol used to pickle objects stored in the database. It has the same meaning as described in the `pickle` module. *writeback* controls the caching behavior of the database object. If `True`, all accessed entries are cached in memory and only written back when the shelf is closed. The default value is `False`. It returns a shelf object.

Once a shelf is opened, the following dictionary operations can be performed on it:

Operation	Description
d[*key*] = data	Stores data at *key*. Overwrites existing data.
data = d[*key*]	Retrieves data at *key*.
del d[*key*]	Deletes data at *key*.
d.has_key(*key*)	Tests for the existence of *key*.
d.keys()	Returns all keys.
d.close()	Closes the shelf.
d.sync()	Writes unsaved data to disk.

The key values for a shelf must be strings. The objects stored in a shelf must be serializable using the `pickle` module.

Shelf(*dict* [, protocol [, writeback]])

A mix-in class that implements the functionality of a shelf on top of a dictionary object, *dict*. When this is used, objects stored in the returned shelf object will be pickled and stored in the underlying dictionary *dict*. One use of this function is to create shelf objects that utilize a preferred database engine—for example, s = `Shelf(gdbm.open("foo","c"))`. Both *protocol* and *writeback* have the same meaning as for `shelve.open()`.

BsdDbShelf(*dict* [, protocol [, writeback]])

A mix-in class that performs the same function as `Shelf()`, but also exposes the `first()`, `next()`, `previous()`, `last()`, and `set_location()` methods available in the `bsddb` module. The *dict* object must also support these methods and is usually an object created using a function such as `bsddb.hashopen()`.

DbfilenameShelf(*filename* [, flag [, protocol [, writeback]]])

The same as `Shelf()`, but opens the specified file *filename* using `anydbm.open()` and uses the returned object as the dictionary. *flags*, *protocol*, and *writeback* have the same meaning as for `open()`.

Notes

- The `shelve` module differs from other database modules in that it allows almost any Python object to be stored.

- The `pickle` module is used to marshal Python objects to and from the underlying database.

See Also:
`pickle` (p. 162), Chapter 9

whichdb

The `whichdb` module provides a function that attempts to guess which of the several simple database modules (`dbm`, `gdbm`, or `dbhash`) should be used to open a database file.

whichdb(*filename*)

filename is a filename without any suffixes. Returns `None` if the file cannot be opened because it's unreadable or doesn't exist. Returns the empty string if the file format cannot be guessed. Otherwise, a string containing the required module name is returned, such as `'dbm'` or `'gdbm'`.

See Also:
`anydbm` (p. 238)

18

File Handling

THIS CHAPTER DESCRIBES PYTHON MODULES for high-level file handling. Topics include modules for processing various kinds of file formats, such as zip files, tar files, and bzip2 files. In addition, modules for working with files and directories are described. Low-level operating-system calls related to files are covered in Chapter 19, "Operating System Services."

bz2

The `bz2` module is used to read and write data compressed according to the bzip2 compression algorithm.

BZ2File(`filename` [, `mode` [, `buffering` [, `compresslevel`]]])

Opens a `.bz2` file, `filename`, and returns a file-like object. `mode` is `'r'` for reading or `'w'` for writing. Universal newline support is also available by specifying a mode of `'rU'`. `buffering` specifies the buffer size in bytes with a default value of 0 (no buffering). `compresslevel` is a number between 1 and 9. A value of 9 (the default) provides the highest level of compression, but consumes the most processing time. The returned object supports all the common file operations, including `close()`, `read()`, `readline()`, `readlines()`, `seek()`, `tell()`, `write()`, and `writelines()`.

BZ2Compressor([`compresslevel`])

Creates a compressor object that can be used to sequentially compress a sequence of data blocks. `compresslevel` specifies the compression level as a number between 1 and 9 (the default).

An instance, `c`, of `BZ2Compressor` has the following two methods:

c.compress(`data`)

Feeds new string data to the compressor object, `c`. Returns a string of compressed data if possible. Because compression involves chunks of data, the returned string may not include all the data and may include compressed data from previous calls to `compress()`. The `flush()` method should be used to return any remaining data stored in the compressor after all input data has been supplied.

`c.flush()`

Flushes the internal buffers and returns a string containing the compressed version of all remaining data. After this operation, no further `compress()` calls should be made on the object.

`BZ2Decompressor()`

Creates a decompressor object.

An instance, *d*, of `BZ2Decompressor` supports just one method:

`d.decompress(data)`

Given a chunk of compressed data in the string *data*, this method returns uncompressed data. Because data is processed in chunks, the returned string may or may not include a decompressed version of everything supplied in *data*. Repeated calls to this method will continue to decompress data blocks until an end-of-stream marker is found in the input. If subsequent attempts are made to decompress data after that, an `EOFError` exception will be raised.

`compress(data [, compresslevel])`

Returns a compressed version of the data supplied in the string *data*. *compresslevel* is a number between 1 and 9 (the default).

`decompress(data)`

Returns a string containing the decompressed data in the string *data*.

CSV

The csv module is used to read and write files consisting of comma-separated values (CSV). A CSV file consists of rows of text, each row consisting of values separated by a delimiter character, typically a comma (,) or a tab. Here's an example:

```
Blues,Elwood,"1060 W Addison","Chicago, IL 60613","B263-1655-2187",116,56
```

Variants of this format commonly occur when working with databases and spreadsheets. For instance, a database might export tables in CSV format, allowing the tables to be read by other programs. Subtle complexities arise when fields contain the delimiter character. For instance, in the preceding example, one of the fields contains a comma and must be placed in quotes.

`reader(csvfile [, dialect  [, **fmtparams])`

Returns a reader object that produces the values for each line of input of the input file *csvfile*. *csvfile* is any iterable object that produces a string each time its next() method is called. The returned reader object is an iterator that produces a list of strings each time its next() method is called. The *dialect* parameter is either a string containing the name of a dialect or a `Dialect` object. The purpose of the *dialect* parameter is to account for differences between different CSV encodings. The only built-in dialect supported by this module is `'excel'` (which is the default value), but others can be defined by the user as described later in this section. *fmtparams* is a set of keyword arguments that customize various aspects of the dialect. The following keyword arguments can be specified as *fmtparams*:

Keyword Argument	Description
delimiter	Character used to separate fields (the default is ',').
doublequote	Boolean flag that determines how the quote character (quotechar) is handled when it appears in a field. If True, the character is simply doubled. If False, an escape character (escapechar) is used as a prefix. The default is True.
escapechar	Character used as an escape character when the delimiter appears in a field and quoting is QUOTE_NONE. The default value is None.
lineterminator	Line termination sequence ('\r\n' is the default).
quotechar	Character used to quote fields that contain the delimiter ('"' is the default).
skipinitialspace	If True, whitespace immediately following the delimiter is ignored (False is the default).

writer(*csvfile* [, *dialect* [, **fmtparam]]))

Returns a writer object that can be used to create a CSV file. *csvfile* is any file-like object that supports a write() method. *dialect* has the same meaning as for reader() and is used to handle differences between various CSV encodings. *fmtparams* has the same meaning as for readers. However, one additional keyword argument is available:

Keyword Argument	Description
quoting	Controls the quoting behavior of output data. It's set to one of QUOTE_ALL (quotes all fields), QUOTE_MINIMAL (only quote fields that contain the delimiter or start with the quote character), QUOTE_NONNUMERIC (quote all nonnumeric fields), or QUOTE_NONE (never quote fields). The default value is QUOTE_MINIMAL.

A writer instance, *w*, supports the following methods:

w.writerow(*row*)

Writes a single row of data to the file. *row* must be a sequence of strings or numbers.

w.writerows(*rows*)

Writes multiple rows of data. *rows* must be a sequence of rows as passed to the writerow() method.

DictReader(*csvfile* [, *fieldnames* [, *restkey* [, *restval* [, *dialect* [, **fmtparams]]]]])

Returns a reader object that operates like the ordinary reader, but returns dictionary objects instead of lists of strings when reading the file. *fieldnames* provides a list of field names used as keys in the returned dictionary. If omitted, the dictionary key names are taken from the first row of the input file. *restkey* provides the name of a dictionary key that's used to store excess data—for instance, if a row has more data fields than field names. *restval* is a default value that's used as the value for fields that are missing from the input. For instance, if a row does not have enough fields. The default value of *restkey* and *restval* is None. *dialect* and *fmtparams* have the same meaning as for reader().

DictWriter(*csvfile*, *fieldnames* [, *restval* [, *extrasaction* [, *dialect* [, **fmtparams]]]])

Returns a writer object that operates like the ordinary writer, but writes dictionaries into output rows. *fieldnames* specifies the order and names of attributes that will be written to the file. *restval* is the value that's written if the dictionary being written is missing one of the field names in *fieldnames*. *extrasaction* is a string that specifies what to do if a dictionary being written has keys not listed in *fieldnames*. The default value of *extrasaction* is 'raise', which raises a ValueError exception. A value of 'ignore' may be used, in which case extra values in the dictionary are ignored. *dialect* and *fmtparams* have the same meaning as with writer().

A DictWriter instance, *w*, supports the following methods:

w.writerow(*row*)

Writes a single row of data to the file. *row* must be a dictionary that maps field names to values.

w.writerows(*rows*)

Writes multiple rows of data. *rows* must be a sequence of rows as passed to the writerow() method.

Sniffer()

Creates a Sniffer object that is used to try and automatically detect the format of a CSV file.

A Sniffer instance, *s*, has the following methods:

s.sniff(*sample* [, *delimiters*])

Looks at data in *sample* and returns an appropriate Dialect object representing the data format. *sample* is a portion of a CSV file containing at least one row of data. *delimiters*, if supplied, is a string containing possible field delimiter characters.

s.has_header(*sample*)

Looks at the CSV data in *sample* and returns True if the first row looks like a collection of column headers.

Dialects

Many of the functions and methods in the csv module involve a special dialect parameter. The purpose of this parameter is to accommodate different formatting conventions of CSV files (for which there is no official "standard" format). For example, differences between comma-separated values and tab-delimited values, quoting conventions, and so forth.

Dialects are defined by inheriting from the class Dialect and defining the same set of attributes as the formatting parameters given to the reader() and writer() functions (delimiter, doublequote, escapechar, lineterminator, quotechar, quoting, skipinitialspace).

The following utility functions are used to manage dialects:

`register_dialect(name, dialect)`

Registers a new Dialect object, *dialect*, under the name *name*.

`unregister_dialect(name)`

Removes the Dialect object with name *name*.

`get_dialect(name)`

Returns the Dialect object with name *name*.

`list_dialects()`

Returns a list of all registered dialect names. Currently, there are only two built-in dialects: `'excel'` and `'excel-tab'`.

Example

```
# Read a basic CSV file
f = open("scmods.csv","rb")
for r in csv.reader(f):
    print r

# Write a basic CSV file
data = [
  ['Blues','Elwood','1060 W Addison','Chicago','IL','60613' ],
  ['McGurn','Jack','4802 N Broadway','Chicago','IL','60640' ],
]
f = open("address.csv","wb")
w = csv.writer(f)
w.writerows(data)
f.close()

# Using a DictReader instead
f = open("address.csv")
r = csv.DictReader(f,['lastname','firstname','street','city','zip'])
for a in r:
    print a["firstname"], a["lastname"], a["street"], a["city"], z["zip"]
```

filecmp

The `filecmp` module provides the following functions, which can be used to compare files and directories:

`cmp(file1, file2[, shallow])`

Compares the files *file1* and *file2* and returns True if they're equal, False if not. By default, files that have identical attributes as returned by `os.stat()` are considered to be equal. If the *shallow* parameter is specified and is False, the contents of the two files are compared to determine equality.

`cmpfiles(dir1, dir2, common[, shallow])`

Compares the contents of the files contained in the list *common* in the two directories *dir1* and *dir2*. Returns a tuple containing three lists of filenames (*match*, *mismatch*, *errors*). *match* lists the files that are the same in both directories, *mismatch* lists the files that don't match, and *errors* lists the files that could not be compared for some reason. The *shallow* parameter has the same meaning as for cmp().

dircmp(*dir1*, *dir2* [, *ignore*[, *hide*]])

Creates a directory comparison object that can be used to perform various comparison operations on the directories *dir1* and *dir2*. *ignore* is a list of filenames to ignore and has a default value of ['RCS', 'CVS', 'tags']. *hide* is a list of filenames to hide and defaults to the list [os.curdir, os.pardir] (['.', '..'] on UNIX).

A directory object, *d*, returned by dircmp() has the following methods and attributes:

d.report()

Compares directories *dir1* and *dir2* and prints a report to sys.stdout.

d.report_partial_closure()

Compares *dir1* and *dir2* and common immediate subdirectories. Results are printed to sys.stdout.

d.report_full_closure()

Compares *dir1* and *dir2* and all subdirectories recursively. Results are printed to sys.stdout.

d.left_list

Lists the files and subdirectories in *dir1*. The contents are filtered by *hide* and *ignore*.

d.right_list

Lists the files and subdirectories in *dir2*. The contents are filtered by *hide* and *ignore*.

d.common

Lists the files and subdirectories found in both *dir1* and *dir2*.

d.left_only

Lists the files and subdirectories found only in *dir1*.

d.right_only

Lists the files and subdirectories found only in *dir2*.

d.common_dirs

Lists the subdirectories that are common to *dir1* and *dir2*.

d.common_files

Lists the files that are common to *dir1* and *dir2*.

d.common_funny

Lists the files in *dir1* and *dir2* with different types or for which no information can be obtained from os.stat().

d.same_files

Lists the files with identical contents in *dir1* and *dir2*.

d.diff_files

Lists the files with different contents in *dir1* and *dir2*.

d.funny_files

Lists the files that are in both *dir1* and *dir2*, but that could not be compared for some reason (for example, insufficient permission to access).

d.subdirs

A dictionary that maps names in *d*.common_dirs to additional dircmp objects.

> **Note**
>
> The attributes of a dircmp object are evaluated lazily and not determined at the time the dircmp object is first created. Thus, if you're interested in only some of the attributes, there's no added performance penalty related to the other unused attributes.

fileinput

The fileinput module iterates over a list of input files and reads their contents line by line. The main interface to the module is the following function:

input([*files* [, *inplace* [, *backup*]]])

Creates an instance of the FileInput class. *files* is an optional list of filenames to be read (a single filename is also permitted). If omitted, the filenames are read from the command line in sys.argv[1:]. An empty list implies input from stdin, as does a filename of '-'. If *inplace* is set to True, each input file is moved to a backup file and sys.stdout is redirected to overwrite the original input file. The backup file is then removed when the output is closed. The *backup* option specifies a filename extension such as .bak that is appended to each filename in order to create the names of backup files. When given, the backup files are not deleted. By default, *backup* is the empty string and no backup files are created.

All FileInput instances have the following methods. These methods are also available as functions that apply to the last instance created by the input() function.

Method	Description
filename()	Returns the name of the file currently being read
lineno()	Returns the cumulative line number just read
filelineno()	Returns the line number in the current file
isfirstline()	Returns True if the line just read was the first line of a file
isstdin()	Returns True if the input is stdin
nextfile()	Closes the current file and skips to the next file
close()	Closes the file sequence

In addition, the FileInput instance returned by input() can be used as an iterator for reading all input lines.

Example

The following code reads and prints all the input lines from a list of files supplied on the command line:

```
import fileinput
for line in fileinput.input():
    print '%5d %s' % (fileinput.lineno(), line),
```

Notes

- All files opened by this module are opened in text mode.
- An IOError is raised if a file cannot be opened.
- Empty files are opened and closed immediately.
- All lines returned include trailing newlines, except possibly the last line of the input file (for example, if the last line doesn't end with a newline).
- This module should not be used on older MS-DOS/Windows file systems that only support short filenames (eight characters plus a three-letter suffix).

See Also:
glob (p. 253), fnmatch (this page)

fnmatch

The fnmatch module provides support for matching filenames using UNIX shell-style wildcard characters:

Character(s)	Description
*	Matches everything
?	Matches any single character
[seq]	Matches any character in seq
[!seq]	Matches any character not in seq

The following functions can be used to test for a wildcard match:

fnmatch(filename, pattern)

Returns True or False depending on whether filename matches pattern. Case sensitivity depends on the operating system (and may be non–case sensitive on certain platforms such as Windows).

fnmatchcase(filename, pattern)

Performs a case-sensitive comparison of filename against pattern.

Example

```
fnmatch('foo.gif', '*.gif')            # Returns True
fnmatch('part37.html', 'part3[0-5].html') # Returns False
```

See Also:
glob (this page)

glob

The glob module returns all filenames in a directory that match a pattern specified using the rules of the UNIX shell (as described in the fnmatch module).

glob(*pattern*)

Returns a list of pathnames that match pattern.

Example

```
glob('*.html')
glob('image[0-5]*.gif')
```

Note

Tilde (~) and shell variable expansion are not performed. Use os.path.expanduser() and os.path.expandvars(), respectively, to perform these expansions prior to calling glob().

See Also:
fnmatch (p. 252), os.path (p. 326)

gzip

The gzip module provides a class, GzipFile, that can be used to read and write files compatible with the GNU gzip program. GzipFile objects work like ordinary files except that data is automatically compressed or decompressed.

GzipFile([*filename* [, *mode* [, *compresslevel* [, *fileobj*]]]])

Opens a GzipFile. *filename* is the name of a file, and *mode* is one of 'r', 'rb', 'a', 'ab', 'w', or 'wb'. The default is 'rb'. *compresslevel* is an integer from 1 to 9 that controls the level of compression. 1 is the fastest and produces the least compression; 9 is the slowest and produces the most compression (the default). *fileobj* is an existing file object that should be used. If supplied, it's used instead of the file named by *filename*.

open(*filename* [, *mode* [, *compresslevel*]])

Same as GzipFile(*filename, mode, compresslevel*). The default mode is 'rb'. The default *compresslevel* is 9.

Notes

- Calling the close() method of a GzipFile object doesn't close files passed in *fileobj*. This allows additional information to be written to a file after the compressed data.

- Files produced by the UNIX `compress` program are not supported.
- This module requires the `zlib` module.

See Also:
`zlib` (p. 261), `zipfile` (p. 258)

tarfile

The `tarfile` module is used to manipulate tar archive files. Using this module, it is possible to read and write tar files, with or without compression.

`is_tarfile(name)`

Returns `True` if `name` appears to be a valid tar file that can be read by this module.

`open([name [, mode [, fileobj [, bufsize]]]])`

Creates a new `TarFile` object with the pathname `name`. `mode` is a string that specifies how the tar file is to be opened. The `mode` string is a combination of a file mode and a compression scheme specified as `'filemode[:compression]'`. Valid combinations include the following:

Mode	Description
`'r'`	Open for reading. If the file is compressed, it is decompressed transparently. This is the default mode.
`'r:'`	Open for reading without compression.
`'r:gz'`	Open for reading with gzip compression.
`'r:bz2'`	Open for reading with bzip2 compression.
`'a'`, `'a:'`	Open for appending with no compression.
`'w'`, `'w:'`	Open for writing with no compression.
`'w:gz'`	Open for writing with gzip compression.
`'w:bz2'`	Open for writing with bzip2 compression.

The following modes are used when creating a `TarFile` object that only allows sequential I/O access (no random seeks):

Mode	Description
`'r|'`	Open a stream of uncompressed blocks for reading.
`'r|gz'`	Open a gzip compressed stream for reading.
`'r|bz2'`	Open a bzip2 compressed stream for reading.
`'w|'`	Open an uncompressed stream for writing.
`'w|gz'`	Open a gzip compressed stream for writing.
`'w|bz2'`	Open a bzip2 compressed stream for writing.

If the parameter `fileobj` is specified, it must be an open `file` object. In this case, the file overrides any filename specified with `name`. `bufsize` specifies the block size used in a tar file. The default is 20*512 bytes.

A `TarFile` instance, `t`, returned by `open()` supports the following methods:

t.add(*name* [, *arcname* [, *recursive*]])

Adds a new file to the tar archive. *name* is the name of any kind of file (directory, symbolic link, and so on). *arcname* specifies an alternative name to use for the file inside the archive. *recursive* is a Boolean flag that indicates whether or not to recursively add the contents of directories. By default, it is set to `True`.

t.addfile(*tarinfo* [, *fileobj*])

Adds a new object to the tar archive. *tarinfo* is a `TarInfo` structure that contains information about the archive member. *fileobj* is an open file object from which data will be read and saved in the archive. The amount of data to read is determined by the `size` attribute of *tarinfo*.

t.close()

Closes the tar archive, writing two zero blocks to the end if the archive was opened for writing.

t.debug

Controls the amount of debugging information produced, with 0 producing no output and 3 producing all debugging messages. Messages are written to `sys.stderr`.

t.dereference

If this method is set to `True`, symbolic and hard links and dereferenced, and the entire contents of the referenced file are added to the archive. If it's set to `False`, just the link is added.

t.errorlevel

Determines how errors are handled when an archive member is being extracted. If this method is set to 0, errors are ignored. If it's set to 1, errors result in `OSError` or `IOError` exceptions. If it's set to 2, nonfatal errors additionally result in `TarError` exceptions.

t.extract(*member* [, *path*])

Extracts a member from the archive, saving it to the current directory. *member* is either an archive member name or a `TarInfo` instance. *path* is used to specify a different destination directory.

t.extractfile(*member*)

Extracts a member from the archive, returning a read-only file-like object that can be used to read its contents using `read()`, `readline()`, `readlines()`, `seek()`, and `tell()` operations. *member* is either an archive member name or a `TarInfo` object. If *member* refers to a link, an attempt will be made to open the target of the link.

t.getmember(*name*)

Looks up archive member *name* and returns a `TarInfo` object containing information about it. Raises `KeyError` if no such archive member exists. If member *name* appears more than once in the archive, information for the last entry is returned (which is assumed to be the more recent).

t.getmembers()

Returns a list of TarInfo objects for all members of the archive.

t.getnames()

Returns a list of all archive member names.

t.gettarinfo([*name* [, *arcname* [, *fileobj*]]])

Returns a TarInfo object corresponding to a file, *name*, on the file system or an open file object, *fileobj*. *arcname* is an alternative name for the object in the archive. The primary use of this function is to create an appropriate TarInfo object for use in methods such as add().

t.ignore_zeros

If this method is set to True, empty blocks are skipped when reading an archive. If it's set to False (the default), an empty block signals the end of the archive. Setting this method to True may be useful for reading a damaged archive.

t.list([*verbose*])

Lists the contents of the archive to sys.stdout. *verbose* determines the level of detail. If this method is set to False, only the archive names are printed. Otherwise, full details are printed (the default).

t.next()

A method used for iterating over the members of an archive. Returns the TarInfo structure for the next archive member or None.

t.posix

If this method is set to True, the tar file is created according to the POSIX 1003.1–1990 standard. This places restrictions on filename lengths and file size (filenames must be less than 256 characters and files must be less than 8GB in size). If this method is set to False, the archive is created using GNU extensions that lift these restrictions. The default value is False.

An instance, *ti*, of TarInfo as returned by many of the preceding methods has the following methods and attributes:

ti.isfile()

Returns True if the object is a regular file.

ti.isreg()

Same as isfile().

ti.isdir()

Returns True if the object is a directory.

ti.issym()

Returns True if the object is a symbolic link.

ti.islnk()

Returns True if the object is a hard link.

ti.ischr()

Returns True if the object is a character device.

ti.isblk()

Returns True if the object is a block device.

ti.isfifo()

Returns True if the object is a FIFO.

ti.isdev()

Returns True if the object is a device (character device, block device, or FIFO).

ti.name

Archive member name.

ti.size

Size in bytes.

ti.mtime

Last modification time.

ti.mode

Permission bits

ti.type

File type. It's one of the constants REGTYPE, AREGTYPE, LNKTYPE, SYMTYPE, DIRTYPE, FIFOTYPE, CONTTYPE, CHRTYPE, BLKTYPE, or GNUTYPE_SPARSE.

ti.linkname

Target filename of hard and symbolic links.

ti.uid

User ID.

ti.gid

Group ID.

ti.uname

Username.

ti.gname

Group name.

Exceptions

TarError

Base class for the following exceptions.

ReadError

Raised when an error occurs while opening a tar file (for example, when opening an invalid file).

CompressionError

Raised when data can't be decompressed.

StreamError

Raised when an unsupported operation is performed on a stream-like `TarFile` object (for instance, an operation that requires random access).

ExtractError

Raised for nonfatal errors during extraction. This is only raised if `errorlevel` is set to 2.

Example

```
# Open a tar file and iterate over all of its members
t = tarfile.open("foo.tar")
for f in t:
    print f.name, f.size

# Scan a tar file and print the contents of "README" files
t = tarfile.open("foo.tar")
for f in t:
    if os.path.basename(f.name) == "README":
        data = t.extractfile(f).read()
        print "**** %s ****" % f.name
        print data
```

zipfile

The `zipfile` module is used to manipulate files encoded in the popular zip format (originally known as PKZIP, although now supported by a wide variety of programs). The following functions are available:

is_zipfile(*filename*)

Tests *filename* to see if it's a valid zip file. Returns `True` if *filename* is a zip file; returns `False` otherwise.

ZipFile(*filename* [, *mode* [, *compression*]])

Opens a zip file, *filename*, and returns a `ZipFile` instance. *mode* is `'r'` to read from an existing file, `'w'` to truncate the file and write a new file, or `'a'` to append to an existing file. For `'a'` mode, if *filename* is an existing zip file, new files are added to it. If *filename* is not a zip file, the archive is simply appended to the end of the file. *compression* is the zip compression method used when writing to the archive and is either `ZIP_STORED` or `ZIP_DEFLATED`. The default is `ZIP_STORED`.

PyZipFile(*filename* [, *mode*[, *compression*]])

Opens a zip file like `ZipFile()`, but returns a special `PyZipFile` instance with one extra method, `writepy()`, used to add Python source files to the archive.

ZipInfo([*filename* [, *date_time*]])

Manually creates a new `ZipInfo` instance, used to contain information about an archive member. Normally, it's not necessary to call this function except when using the `z.writestr()` method of a `ZipFile` instance (described later). The *filename* and *date_time* arguments supply values for the *filename* and *date_time* attributes described later.

An instance, *z*, of `ZipFile` or `PyZipFile` supports the following methods and attributes:

z.close()

Closes the archive file. This must be called in order to flush records to the zip file before program termination.

z.getinfo(*name*)

Returns information about the archive member name as a `ZipInfo` instance (described shortly).

z.infolist()

Returns a list of `ZipInfo` objects for all the members of the archive.

z.namelist()

Returns a list of the archive member names.

z.printdir()

Prints the archive directory to `sys.stdout`.

z.read(*name*)

Reads archive contents for member *name* and returns the data as a string.

z.testzip()

Reads all the files in the archive and verifies their CRC checksums. Returns the name of the first corrupted file or `None` if all files are intact.

z.write(*filename*[, *arcname*[, *compress_type*]])

Writes *filename* to the archive with the archive name *arcname*. *compress_type* is the compression parameter and is either `ZIP_STORED` or `ZIP_DEFLATED`. By default, the compression parameter given to the `ZipFile()` or `PyZipFile()` function is used. The archive must be opened in `'w'` or `'a'` mode for writes to work.

z.writepy(*pathname*)

This method, available only with `PyZipFile` instances, is used to write Python source files (`*.py` files) to a zip archive and can be used to easily package Python applications for distribution. If *pathname* is a file, it must end with `.py`. In this case, one of the corresponding `.pyo`, `.pyc`, or `.py` files will be added (in that order). If *pathname* is a directory and the directory is not a Python package directory, all the corresponding `.pyo`, `.pyc`, or `.py` files are added at the top level. If the directory is a package, the files are added under the package name as a file path. If any subdirectories are also package directories, they are added recursively.

z.writestr(*arcinfo*, *s*)

Writes the string *s* into the zip file. *arcinfo* is either a filename within the archive in which the data will be stored or it is a `ZipInfo` instance containing a filename, date, and time.

z.debug

Debugging level in the range of 0 (no output) to 3 (most output).

ZipInfo instances returned by the ZipInfo(), *z*.getinfo(), and *z*.infolist() functions have the following attributes:

zinfo.filename

Archive member name.

zinfo.date_time

Tuple (*year*, *month*, *day*, *hours*, *minutes*, *seconds*) containing the last modification time. *month* and *day* are numbers in the range 1–12 and 1–31, respectively. All other values start at 0.

zinfo.compress_type

Compression type for the archive member. Only ZIP_STORED and ZIP_DEFLATED are currently supported by this module.

zinfo.comment

Archive member comment.

zinfo.extra

Expansion field data, used to contain additional file attributes. The data stored here depends on the system that created the file.

zinfo.create_system

Integer code describing the system that created the archive. Common values include those in the following table:

Value	Description
0	MS-DOS (FAT/VFAT/FAT32 file systems)
3	UNIX
7	Macintosh
10	Windows NTFS

zinfo.create_version

Integer pkzip version code that created the zip archive.

zinfo.extract_version

Minimum pkzip version needed to extract the archive.

zinfo.reserved

Reserved field. Currently set to 0.

zinfo.flag_bits

Zip flag bits that describe the encoding of the data, including encryption and compression.

zinfo.volume

Volume number of the file header.

zinfo.internal_attr

Describes the internal structure of the archive contents. If the low-order bit is 1, the data is ASCII text. Otherwise, binary data is assumed.

zinfo.external_attr

External file attributes. Operating system dependent.

zinfo.header_offset

Byte offset to the file header.

zinfo.file_offset

Byte offset to the start of the file data.

zinfo.CRC

CRC-32 checksum of the uncompressed file.

zinfo.compress_size

Size of the compressed file data.

zinfo.file_size

Size of the uncompressed file.

Notes

- This module requires the use of the zlib module.
- Detailed documentation about the internal structure of zip files can be found as a PKZIP Application Note at http://www.pkware.com/appnote.html.

zlib

The zlib module supports data compression by providing access to the zlib library.

adler32(*string* [, *value*])

Computes the Adler-32 checksum of *string*. *value* is used as the starting value (which can be used to compute a checksum over the concatenation of several strings). Otherwise, a fixed default value is used.

compress(*string* [, *level*])

Compresses the data in *string*, where *level* is an integer from 1 to 9 controlling the level of compression. 1 is the least (fastest) compression, and 9 is the best (slowest) compression. The default value is 6. Returns a string containing the compressed data or raises error if an error occurs.

compressobj([*level*])

Returns a compression object. *level* has the same meaning as in the compress() function.

`crc32(`*`string`* `[,` *`value`*`])`

Computes a CRC checksum of *string*. If *value* is present, it's used as the starting value of the checksum. Otherwise, a fixed value is used.

`decompress(`*`string`* `[,` *`wbits`* `[,` *`buffsize`*`]])`

Decompresses the data in *string*. *wbits* controls the size of the window buffer, and *buffsize* is the initial size of the output buffer. Raises `error` if an error occurs.

`decompressobj([`*`wbits`*`])`

Returns a compression object. The *wbits* parameter controls the size of the window buffer.

A compression object, *c*, has the following methods:

`c.compress(`*`string`*`)`

Compresses *string*. Returns a string containing compressed data for at least part of the data in *string*. This data should be concatenated to the output produced by earlier calls to `c.compress()` to create the output stream. Some input data may be stored in internal buffers for later processing.

`c.flush([`*`mode`*`])`

Compresses all pending input and returns a string containing the remaining compressed output. *mode* is Z_SYNC_FLUSH, Z_FULL_FLUSH, or Z_FINISH (the default). Z_SYNC_FLUSH and Z_FULL_FLUSH allow further compression and are used to allow partial error recovery on decompression. Z_FINISH terminates the compression stream.

A decompression object, *d*, has the following methods and attributes:

`d.decompress(`*`string`* `[,`*`max_length`*`])`

Decompresses *string* and returns a string containing uncompressed data for at least part of the data in *string*. This data should be concatenated with data produced by earlier calls to `decompress()` to form the output stream. Some input data may be stored in internal buffers for later processing. *max_length* specifies the maximum size of returned data. If exceeded, unprocessed data will be placed in the *d*.unconsumed_tail attribute.

`d.flush()`

All pending input is processed, and a string containing the remaining uncompressed output is returned. The decompression object cannot be used again after this call.

`d.unconsumed_tail`

String containing data not yet processed by the last `decompress()` call. This would contain data if decompression needs to be performed in stages due to buffer size limitations. In this case, this variable would be passed to subsequent `decompress()` calls.

`d.unused_data`

String containing extra bytes that remain past the end of the compressed data.

Exception

`error`

Exception raised on compression and decompression errors.

Note

The zlib library is available at http://www.zlib.net.

See Also:

gzip (p. 253)

19

Operating System Services

THE MODULES IN THIS CHAPTER PROVIDE ACCESS to a wide variety of operating system services with an emphasis on files, process management, and the operating environment. A separate chapter on file management contains information on modules related to reading various kinds of file formats, and working with filenames.

A general familiarity with basic operating system concepts is assumed in this section. Furthermore, a number of modules provide advanced functionality, which is beyond the scope of this book to introduce, but is presented for readers who know what they're doing.

Most of Python's operating system modules are based on POSIX interfaces. POSIX is a standard that defines a core set of operating system interfaces. Most UNIX systems support POSIX, and other platforms such as Windows support large portions of the interface. Throughout this chapter, functions and modules that only apply to a specific platform are noted as such. UNIX systems include both Linux and Mac OS X. Windows systems include all versions of Windows unless otherwise noted.

Readers may want to supplement the material presented here with additional references. *The C Programming Language, Second Edition* by Brian W. Kernighan and Dennis M. Ritchie (Prentice Hall, 1989) provides a good overview of files, file descriptors, and the low-level interfaces on which many of the modules in this section are based. More advanced readers may want to consult a book such as *Advanced Programming in the UNIX Environment, 2nd Edition by W. Richard Stevens and Stephen Rago* (Addison Wesley, 2005). Background material regarding operating system concepts can be found in a text such as *Operating Systems Concepts, 7th Edition* by Abraham Silberschatz, Peter Baer Galvin, and Greg Gagne (John Wiley & Sons, 2004). Threads and network programming are presented in separate chapters.

commands

The commands module is used to execute system commands as a string and return their output as a string. This module is only available on UNIX systems.

getoutput(*cmd*)

Executes *cmd* in a shell and returns a string containing both the standard output and standard error streams of the command.

getstatus(*filename*)

Returns the output of `'ls -ld *filename*'` as a string.

getstatusoutput(*cmd*)

Like getoutput(), except that a 2-tuple (*status, output*) is returned, where *status* is the exit code, as returned by the os.wait() function, and *output* is the string returned by getoutput().

mkarg(*str*)

Turns *str* into an argument that can be safely used within a command string (using quoting rules of the shell).

Notes

- The os.popen2() call is used to execute commands. This module is available on most UNIX systems, but is not supported on all versions of Windows.
- The returned output strings don't include a trailing newline.

See Also:
os (p. 308), popen2 (p. 331), subprocess (p. 340)

crypt

The crypt module provides an interface to the UNIX crypt() routine that is used to encrypt passwords on many UNIX systems.

crypt(*word*, *salt*)

Encrypts *word* using a modified DES algorithm. *salt* is a two-character seed used to initialize the algorithm. Returns the encrypted word as a string. Only the first eight characters of *word* are significant.

Example

The following code reads a password from the user and compares it against the value in the system password database:

```
import getpass
import pwd
import crypt
uname  = getpass.getuser()            # Get username from environment
pw     = getpass.getpass()            # Get entered password
realpw = pwd.getpwnam(uname)[1]       # Get real password
entrpw = crypt.crypt(pw,realpw[:2])   # Encrypt
if realpw == entrpw:                  # Compare
     print 'Password Accepted'
else:
     print 'Get lost.'
```

Note
Many modern UNIX systems use MD5 or other cryptographic hashing algorithms to store passwords. In those cases, this module would not be so useful in password checking.

See Also:
pwd (p. 332), getpass (p. 283)

datetime

The datetime module provides a variety of classes for representing and manipulating dates and times. Date manipulation is a complex subject, and readers would be strongly advised to consult Python's online documentation for an introductory background concerning the design of this module.

date Objects

date(*year, month, day*)

Creates a new date object. *year* is an integer in the range datetime.MINYEAR to datetime.MAXYEAR. *month* is an integer in the range 1 to 12, and *day* is an integer in the range 1 to the number of days in the given month. The returned date object is immutable and has the attributes *year*, *month*, and *day* corresponding to the values of the supplied arguments.

date.today()

A class method that returns a date object corresponding to the current date.

date.fromtimestamp(timestamp)

A class method that returns a date object corresponding to the timestamp *timestamp*. *timestamp* is a value returned by the time.time() function.

date.fromordinal(ordinal)

A class method that returns a date object corresponding to an *ordinal* number of days from the minimum allowable date (January 1 of year 1 has ordinal value 1 and January 1, 2006 has ordinal value 732312).

date.min

Class attribute representing the earliest date that can be represented (datetime.date(1,1,1)).

date.max

Class attribute representing the latest possible date (datetime.date(9999,12,31)).

date.resolution

Smallest resolvable difference between non-equal date objects (datetime. timedelta(1)).

An instance, *d*, of date provides the following methods:

d.replace([*year* [, *month* [, *day*]]])

Returns a new date object with one or more of the supplied components replaced by a new value. For example, d.replace(month=4) returns a new date where the month has been replaced by 4.

d.timetuple()

Returns a time.struct_time object suitable for use by functions in the time module. Values related to the time of day (hours, minutes, seconds) will be set to 0.

d.toordinal()

Converts d to an ordinal value. January 1 of year 1 has ordinal value 1.

d.weekday()

Returns the day of the week in the range 0 (Monday) to 6 (Sunday).

d.isoweekday()

Returns the day of the week in the range 1 (Monday) to 7 (Sunday).

d.isocalendar()

Returns the date as a tuple (iso_year, iso_week, iso_weekday), where iso_week is in the range 1 to 53 and iso_weekday is the range 1 (Monday) to 7 (Sunday). The first iso_week is the first week of the year that contains a Thursday. The range of values for the three tuple components is determined by the ISO 8601 standard.

d.isoformat()

Returns an ISO 8601–formatted string of the form 'YYYY-MM-DD' representing the date.

d.ctime()

Returns a string representing the date in the same format as normally used by the time.ctime() function.

d.strftime(format)

Returns a string representing the date formatted according to the same rules as the time.strftime() function. This function only works for dates later than the year 1900. Moreover, format codes for components missing from date objects (such as hours, minutes, and so on) should not be used.

time **Objects**

time(hour [, minute [, second [, microsecond [, tzinfo]]]])

Creates a time object representing a time where $0 <= hour < 24, 0 <= minute < 60, 0 <= second < 60$, and $0 <= microsecond < 1000000$. tzinfo provides time zone information and is an instance of the tzinfo class. The returned time object has the attributes hour, minute, second, microsecond, and tzinfo, which hold the corresponding values supplied as arguments.

time.min

Class attribute representing the minimum representable time (datetime.time(0,0)).

time.max

Class attribute representing the maximum representable time (datetime.time(23,59, 59, 999999)).

`time.resolution`

Smallest resolvable difference between non-equal `time` objects
(`datetime.timedelta(0,0,1)`).

An instance, `t`, of a `time` object has the following methods:

`t.replace([hour [, minute [, second [, microsecond [, tzinfo ]]]]])`

Returns a new `time` object, where one or more components have been replaced by the
supplied values. For example, `t.replace(second=30)` changes the seconds field to 30
and returns a new `time` object. The arguments have the same meaning as those supplied
to the `time()` function.

`t.isoformat()`

Returns a string representing the time as `'HH:MM:SS.mmmmmm'`. If the microseconds are
0, that part of the string is omitted. If time zone information has been supplied, the
time may have an offset added to it (for example, `'HH:MM:SS.mmmmmm+HH:MM'`).

`t.strftime(format)`

Returns a string formatted according to the same rules as the `time.strftime()` function in the `time` module. Because date information is unavailable, only the formatting
codes for time-related information should be used.

`t.utcoffset()`

Returns the value of `t.tzinfo.utcoffset(None)`. The returned object is a
`timedelta` object. If no time zone has been set, `None` is returned.

`t.dst()`

Returns the value of `t.tzinfo.dst(None)`. The returned object is a `timedelta`
object. If no time zone is set, `None` is returned.

`t.tzname()`

Returns the value of `t.tzinfo.tzname()`. If no time zone is set, `None` is returned.

datetime **Objects**

`datetime(year, month, day [, hour [, minute [, second`
`[, microsecond [, tzinfo]]]]])`

Creates a new `datetime` object that combines all the features of `date` and `time`
objects. The arguments have the same meaning as arguments provided to `date()` and
`time()`.

A `datetime` object supports all the class methods and attributes of both `date` and
`time` objects. In addition, the following class methods are available:

`datetime.now([tz])`

Creates a `datetime` object from the current local date and time. `tz` provides optional
time zone information and is an instance of `tzinfo`.

`datetime.utcnow()`

Creates a `datetime` object from the current UTC date and time.

`datetime.fromtimestamp(timestamp [, tz])`

Creates a datetime object from a timestamp returned by the time.time() function. tz provides optional time zone information and is a tzinfo instance.

`datetime.utcfromtimestamp(timestamp)`

Creates a datetime object from a timestamp typically returned by time.gmtime().

`datetime.fromordinal(ordinal)`

Creates a datetime object given an ordinal day. The time components are all set to 0, and tzinfo is set to None.

`datetime.combine(date,time)`

Creates a datetime object by combining the contents of a date object, date, and a time object, time.

`datetime.min`

Earliest representable date and time (datetime.datetime(1,1,1,0,0)).

`datetime.max`

Latest representable date and time (datetime.datetime(9999,12,31,23,59, 59,999999)).

`datetime.resolution`

Smallest resolvable difference between non-equal datetime objects (datetime.timedelta(0,0,1)).

An instance, d, of a datetime object supports the same methods as date and time objects. In additional, the following methods are available:

`d.date()`

Returns a date object with the same date.

`d.time()`

Returns a time object with the same time. The resulting time object has no time zone information set.

`d.timetz()`

Returns a time object with the same time and time zone information.

`d.replace([year [, month [, day [, hour [, minute [, second [, microsecond [, tzinfo]]]]]]]])`

Returns a new datetime object with one or more of the listed parameters replaced by new values. Use keyword arguments to replace an individual value.

`d.astimezone(tz)`

Returns a new datetime object but in a different time zone, tz. The members of the new object will be adjusted to represent the same UTC time, but in the time zone tz.

`d.utctimetuple()`

Returns a time.struct_time object containing date and time information normalized to UTC time.

timedelta **Objects**

timedelta([*days* [, *seconds* [, *microseconds* [, *milliseconds* [, *minutes*
[, *hours* [, *weeks*]]]]]]])

Creates a timedelta object that represents the difference between two dates and times.
The only significant parameters are *days*, *seconds*, and *microseconds*, which are used
internally to represent a difference. The other parameters, if supplied, are converted into
days, seconds, and microseconds. The attributes days, seconds, and microseconds of
the returned timedelta object contain these values.

timedelta.min

The most negative timedelta object that can be represented (timedelta(-
999999999)).

timedelta.max

The most positive timedelta object that can be represented
(timedelta(days=999999999, hours=23, minutes=59, seconds=59,
microseconds=999999)).

timedelta.resolution

A timedelta object representing the smallest resolvable difference between non-equal
timedelta objects (timedelta(microseconds=1)).

An instance, *td*, of timedelta has the following attributes:

td.days

Number of days.

td.seconds

Number of seconds.

td.microseconds

Number of microseconds.

Mathematical Operations Involving Dates

A significant feature of the datetime module is that it supports mathematical operations involving dates. Both date and datetime objects support the following operations:

Operation	Description
td = *date1* - *date2*	Returns a timedelta object
date2 = *date1* + *td*	Adds a timedelta to a date
date2 = *date1* - *td*	Subtracts a timedelta from a date
date1 < *date2*	Date comparison
date1 <= *date2*	Date comparison
date1 == *date2*	Date comparison
date1 != *date2*	Date comparison
date1 > *date2*	Date comparison
date1 >= *date2*	Date comparison

When comparing dates, you must use care when time zone information has been supplied. If a date includes `tzinfo` information, that date can only be compared with other dates that include `tzinfo`. Otherwise, a `TypeError` is generated. When two dates in different time zones are compared, they are first adjusted to UTC before being compared.

`timedelta` objects also support a variety of mathematical operations:

Operation	Description
`td3 = td2 + td1`	Adds two time deltas
`td3 = td2 - td1`	Subtracts two time deltas
`td2 = td1 * i`	Multiplication by an integer
`td2 = i * td2`	
`td2 = td1 // i`	Floor division by an integer, `i`
`td2 = -td1`	Unary subtraction, addition
`td2 = +td1`	
`abs(td)`	Absolute value
`td1 < td2`	Comparison
`td1 <= td2`	
`td1 == td2`	
`td1 != td2`	
`td1 > td2`	
`td1 >= td2`	

Here are some examples:

```
>>> today = datetime.datetime.now()
>>> today.ctime()
'Thu Oct 20 11:10:10 2005'
>>> oneday = datetime.timedelta(days=1)
>>> tomorrow = today + oneday
>>> tomorrow.ctime()
'Fri Oct 21 11:10:10 2005'
>>>
```

In addition to these operations, all `date`, `datetime`, `time`, and `timedelta` objects are immutable. This means that they can be used as dictionary keys, placed in sets, and used in a variety of other operations.

`tzinfo` Objects

Many of the methods in the `datetime` module manipulate special `tzinfo` objects that represent information about a time zone. `tzinfo` is merely a base class. Individual time zones are created by inheriting from `tzinfo` and implementing the following methods:

`tz.utcoffset(dt)`

Returns a `timedelta` object representing the offset of local time from UTC in minutes east of UTC. The offset incorporates all elements that make up the local time, including daylight savings time if applicable. The argument `dt` is either a `datetime` object or None.

tz.dst(dt)

Returns a `timedelta` object representing daylight savings time adjustments, if applicable. Returns `None` if no information is known about DST. The argument `dt` is either a `datetime` object or `None`.

tz.tzname(dt)

Returns a string with the name of the time zone (for example, `"US/Central"`). `dt` is either a `datetime` object or `None`.

tz.fromutc(dt)

Converts a `datetime` object, `dt`, from UTC time to the local time zone and returns a new `datetime` object. This method is called by the `astimezone()` method on `datetime` objects. A default implementation is already provided by `tzinfo`, so it's usually not necessary to redefine this method.

The following example shows a basic prototype of how one would define a time zone.

```
# Variables that must be defined
# TZOFFSET   - Timezone offset in hours from UTC. For
#              example, US/CST is -6 hours
# DSTNAME    - Name of timezone when DST is in effect
# STDNAME    - Name of timezone when DST not in effect

class SomeZone(datetime.tzinfo):
        def utcoffset(self,dt):
                return datetime.timedelta(hours=TZOFFSET) + self.dst(dt)
        def dst(self,dt):
                # is_dst() is a function you must implement to see
                # whether DST is in effect according to local timezone rules.
                if is_dst(dt):
                        return datetime.timedelta(hours=1)
                else:
                        return datetime.timedelta(0)
        def tzname(self,dt):
                if is_dst(dt):
                        return DSTNAME
                else:
                        return STDNAME
```

A number of examples of defining time zones can also be found in the online documentation for `datetime`.

See also:

`time` (p. 348)

dl

The `dl` module provides access to the dynamic loader on UNIX platforms. There is rarely any need to use this module directly. However, the contents of this module may be of some use for programmers who work with C/C++ extensions to Python.

`open(name [, mode])`

Opens a shared object file, *name*, and returns a handle object. *mode* is the bitwise OR of flags that control how symbols are solved in the loaded library. Here are the common flag values:

Flag Value	Description
RTLD_GLOBAL	External symbols in the loaded library added to the global namespace and used to resolve symbols in subsequently loaded libraries.
RTLD_LAZY	Use late-binding of symbols.
RTLD_LOCAL	Symbols in the loaded library are private.
RTLD_NODELETE	Do not remove the library from memory after the object file handle has been closed.
RTLD_NOLOAD	If the object file is already part of the process address space, return a valid handle to it. Otherwise, return nothing.
RTLD_NOW	Immediate binding of symbols.

The returned handle object, *h*, supports the following methods:

`h.close()`

Closes the object file or library, releasing all resources except memory unless the `RTLD_NODELETE` flag was supplied.

`h.sym(name)`

Tests *h* for the presence of a symbol, *name*. Returns a nonzero number (corresponding to a C function pointer value) if *name* exists. Returns 0 otherwise.

`h.call(name [, arg1 [, arg2 ... ]])`

Calls function *name* with the specified arguments. The arguments in this case are only allowed to be integers or strings. For integers, the arguments are converted to the C `int` data type. For strings, the string data is passed as a C `char *`. At most, 10 arguments may be supplied. Moreover, the function's return value is assumed to be a C `long` data type, which is converted into a Python integer.

Notes

- This module can only be used to call functions in C/C++ libraries in a limited capacity. The most common, and preferred, way to do this is to write a Python extension module instead.

- The flags supplied to the `open()` function may be of some use for extension programmers. The function `sys.setdlopenflags()` is used to set the flags used when loading extension modules into Python via the `import` statement. Sometimes problems related to the resolution of symbols can be resolved by changing the flag's setting—for instance, making all symbols global using the `RTLD_GLOBAL` flag.

errno

The errno module defines symbolic names for the integer error codes returned by various operating system calls. These codes are typically found in the errno attribute of an OSError or IOError exception. The os.strerror() function can be used to translate an error code into a string error message. The following dictionary can also be used to translate an integer error code into its symbolic name:

errorcode

This dictionary maps errno integers to symbolic names (such as 'EPERM').

The following list shows the POSIX symbolic names for many system error codes. Not all names are available on all machines. Some platforms may define additional codes. The codes U, W, M, and A are used to indicate the availability of the following codes for UNIX, Windows, Macintosh, and all platforms, respectively.

Error Code	Platform	Description
E2BIG	A	Arg list too long.
EACCES	A	Permission denied.
EADDRINUSE	A	Address already in use.
EADDRNOTAVAIL	A	Cannot assign requested address.
EADV	U	Advertise error.
EAFNOSUPPORT	A	Address family not supported by protocol.
EAGAIN	A	Try again.
EALREADY	A	Operation already in progress.
EBADE	U	Invalid exchange.
EBADF	A	Bad file number.
EBADFD	U	File descriptor in bad state.
EBADMSG	U	Not a data message.
EBADR	U	Invalid request descriptor.
EBADRQC	U	Invalid request code.
EBADSLT	U	Invalid slot.
EBFONT	U	Bad font file format.
EBUSY	A	Device or resource busy.
ECHILD	A	No child processes.
ECHRNG	U	Channel number out of range.
ECOMM	U	Communication error on send.
ECONNABORTED	A	Software caused connection abort.
ECONNREFUSED	A	Connection refused.
ECONNRESET	A	Connection reset by peer.
EDEADLK	A	Resource deadlock would occur.
EDEADLOCK	U, W	File-locking deadlock error.

Error Code	Platform	Description
EDESTADDRREQ	A	Destination address required.
EDOM	A	Math argument out of domain of function.
EDOTDOT	U	RFS-specific error.
EDQUOT	A	Quota exceeded.
EEXIST	A	File exists.
EFAULT	A	Bad address.
EFBIG	A	File too large.
EHOSTDOWN	A	Host is down.
EHOSTUNREACH	A	No route to host.
EIDRM	U	Identifier removed.
EILSEQ	A	Illegal byte sequence.
EINPROGRESS	A	Operation now in progress.
EINTR	A	Interrupted system call.
EINVAL	A	Invalid argument.
EIO	A	I/O error.
EISCONN	A	Transport endpoint is already connected.
EISDIR	A	Is a directory.
EISNAM	U	Is a named type file.
EL2HLT	U	Level 2 halted.
EL2NSYNC	U	Level 2 not synchronized.
EL3HLT	U	Level 3 halted.
EL3RST	U	Level 3 reset.
ELIBACC	U	Cannot access a needed shared library.
ELIBBAD	U	Accessing a corrupted shared library.
ELIBEXEC	U	Cannot exec a shared library directly.
ELIBMAX	U	Attempting to link in too many shared libraries.
ELIBSCN	U	.lib section in a.out corrupted.
ELNRNG	U	Link number out of range.
ELOOP	A	Too many symbolic links encountered.
EMFILE	A	Too many open files.
EMLINK	A	Too many links.
EMSGSIZE	A	Message too long.
EMULTIHOP	U	Multihop attempted.
ENAMETOOLONG	U, M	Filename too long.
ENAVAIL	U	No XENIX semaphores available.

Error Code	Platform	Description
ENETDOWN	A	Network is down.
ENETRESET	A	Network dropped connection because of reset.
ENETUNREACH	A	Network is unreachable.
ENFILE	A	File table overflow.
ENOANO	U	No anode.
ENOBUFS	A	No buffer space available.
ENOCSI	U	No CSI structure available.
ENODATA	U	No data available.
ENODEV	A	No such device.
ENOENT	A	No such file or directory.
ENOEXEC	A	Exec format error.
ENOLCK	A	No record locks available.
ENOLINK	U	Link has been severed.
ENOMEM	A	Out of memory.
ENOMSG	U, M	No message of desired type.
ENONET	U	Machine is not on the network.
ENOPKG	U	Package not installed.
ENOPROTOOPT	A	Protocol not available.
ENOSPC	A	No space left on device.
ENOSR	U	Out of streams resources.
ENOSTR	U	Device not a stream.
ENOSYS	A	Function not implemented.
ENOTBLK	U, M	Block device required.
ENOTCONN	A	Transport endpoint is not connected.
ENOTDIR	A	Not a directory.
ENOTEMPTY	A	Directory not empty.
ENOTNAM	U	Not a XENIX named type file.
ENOTSOCK	A	Socket operation on non-socket.
ENOTTY	A	Not a terminal.
ENOTUNIQ	U	Name not unique on network.
ENXIO	A	No such device or address.
EOPNOTSUPP	A	Operation not supported on transport endpoint.
EOVERFLOW	U, M	Value too large for defined data type.
EPERM	A	Operation not permitted.
EPFNOSUPPORT	A	Protocol family not supported.
EPIPE	A	Broken pipe.

Error Code	Platform	Description
EPROTO	U	Protocol error.
EPROTONOSUPPORT	A	Protocol not supported.
EPROTOTYPE	A	Protocol wrong type for socket.
ERANGE	A	Math result not representable.
EREMCHG	U	Remote address changed.
EREMOTE	A	Object is remote.
EREMOTEIO	U	Remote I/O error.
ERESTART	U	Interrupted system call should be restarted.
EROFS	A	Read-only file system.
ESHUTDOWN	A	Cannot send after transport endpoint shutdown.
ESOCKTNOSUPPORT	A	Socket type not supported.
ESPIPE	A	Illegal seek.
ESRCH	A	No such process.
ESRMNT	U	srmount error.
ESTALE	A	Stale NFS file handle.
ESTRPIPE	U	Streams pipe error.
ETIME	U	Timer expired.
ETIMEDOUT	A	Connection timed out.
ETOOMANYREFS	A	Too many references: Cannot splice.
ETXTBSY	U, M	Text file busy.
EUCLEAN	U	Structure needs cleaning.
EUNATCH	U	Protocol driver not attached.
EUSERS	A	Too many users.
EWOULDBLOCK	A	Operation would block.
EXDEV	A	Cross-device link.
EXFULL	U	Exchange full.
WSAEACCES	W	Permission denied.
WSAEADDRINUSE	W	Address already in use.
WSAEADDRNOTAVAIL	W	Cannot assign requested address.
WSAEAFNOSUPPORT	W	Address family not supported by protocol family.
WSAEALREADY	W	Operation already in progress.
WSAEBADF	W	Invalid file handle.
WSAECONNABORTED	W	Software caused connection abort.
WSAECONNREFUSED	W	Connection refused.
WSAECONNRESET	W	Connection reset by peer.

Error Code	Platform	Description
WSAEDESTADDRREQ	W	Destination address required.
WSAEDISCON	W	Remote shutdown.
WSAEDQUOT	W	Disk quota exceeded.
WSAEFAULT	W	Bad address.
WSAEHOSTDOWN	W	Host is down.
WSAEHOSTUNREACH	W	No route to host.
WSAEINPROGRESS	W	Operation now in progress.
WSAEINTR	W	Interrupted system call.
WSAEINVAL	W	Invalid argument.
WSAEISCONN	W	Socket already connected.
WSAELOOP	W	Cannot translate name.
WSAEMFILE	W	Too many open files.
WSAEMSGSIZE	W	Message too long.
WSAENAMETOOLONG	W	Name too long.
WSAENETDOWN	W	Network is down.
WSAENETRESET	W	Network dropped connection on reset.
WSAENETUNREACH	W	Network is unreachable.
WSAENOBUFS	W	No buffer space is available.
WSAENOPROTOOPT	W	Bad protocol option.
WSAENOTCONN	W	Socket is not connected.
WSAENOTEMPTY	W	Cannot remove non-empty directory.
WSAENOTSOCK	W	Socket operation on non-socket.
WSAEOPNOTSUPP	W	Operation not supported.
WSAEPFNOSUPPORT	W	Protocol family not supported.
WSAEPROCLIM	W	Too many processes.
WSAEPROTONOSUPPORT	W	Protocol not supported.
WSAEPROTOTYPE	W	Protocol wrong type for socket.
WSAEREMOTE	W	Item not available locally.
WSAESHUTDOWN	W	Cannot send after socket shutdown.
WSAESOCKTNOSUPPORT	W	Socket type not supported.
WSAESTALE	W	File handle no longer available.
WSAETIMEDOUT	W	Connection timed out.
WSAETOOMANYREFS	W	Too many references to a kernel object.
WSAEUSERS	W	Quota exceeded.
WSAEWOULDBLOCK	W	Resource temporarily unavailable.
WSANOTINITIALISED	W	Successful WSA startup not performed.
WSASYSNOTREADY	W	Network subsystem not available.
WSAVERNOTSUPPORTED	W	Winsock.dll version out of range.

See Also:
os (p. 308)

fcntl

The `fcntl` module performs file and I/O control on UNIX file descriptors. File descriptors can be obtained using the `fileno()` method of a file or socket object.

`fcntl(fd, cmd [, arg])`

Performs a command, *cmd*, on an open file descriptor, *fd*. *cmd* is an integer command code. *arg* is an optional argument that's either an integer or a string. If *arg* is passed as an integer, the return value of this function is an integer. If *arg* is a string, it's interpreted as a binary data structure, and the return value of the call is the contents of the buffer converted back into a string object. In this case, the supplied argument and return value should be less than 1024 bytes to avoid possible data corruption. The following commands are available:

Command	Description
F_DUPFD	Duplicates a file descriptor. *arg* is the lowest number that the new file descriptor can assume. Similar to the os.dup() system call.
F_SETFD	Sets the close-on-exec flag to *arg* (0 or 1). If set, the file is closed on an exec() system call.
F_GETFD	Returns the close-on-exec flag.
F_SETFL	Sets status flags to *arg*, which is the bitwise OR of the following:
	O_NDELAY—Nonblocking I/O (System V)
	O_APPEND—Append mode (System V)
	O_SYNC—Synchronous write (System V)
	FNDELAY—Nonblocking I/O (BSD)
	FAPPEND—Append mode (BSD)
	FASYNC—Sends SIGIO signal to process group when I/O is possible (BSD)
F_GETFL	Gets status flags as set by F_SETFL.
F_GETOWN	Gets process ID or process group ID set to receive SIGIO and SIGURG signals (BSD).
F_SETOWN	Sets process ID or process group ID to receive SIGIO and SIGURG signals (BSD).
F_GETLK	Returns flock structure used in file-locking operations.
F_SETLK	Locks a file, returning -1 if the file is already locked.
F_SETLKW	Locks a file, but waits if the lock cannot be acquired.

An IOError exception is raised if the fcntl() function fails. The F_GETLK and F_SETLK commands are supported through the lockf() function.

ioctl(fd, op, arg [, mutate_flag])

This function is like the fcntl() function, except that the operations supplied in *op* are generally defined in the library module termios. The extra *mutate_flag* controls the behavior of this function when a mutable buffer object is passed as an argument. Further details about this can be found in the online documentation. Because the primary use of *ioctl()* is to interact with device drivers and other low-level components of the operating system, its use depends highly on the underlying platform. It should not be used in code that aims to be portable.

flock(fd, op)

Performs a lock operation, *op*, on the file descriptor *fd*. *op* is the bitwise OR of the following constants, which are found in fnctl:

Item	Description
LOCK_EX	Exclusive lock.
LOCK_NB	Nonblocking mode.
LOCK_SH	Shared lock.
LOCK_UN	Unlock.

In nonblocking mode, an IOError exception is raised if the lock cannot be acquired.

lockf(fd, op [, len [, start [, whence]]])

Performs record or range locking on part of a file. *op* is the same as for the flock() function. *len* is the number of bytes to lock. *start* is the starting position of the lock relative to the value of *whence*. *whence* is 0 for the beginning of the file, 1 for the current position, and 2 for the end of the file.

Example

```
import fcntl

# Set the close-on-exec bit for a file object f
fcntl.fcntl(f.fileno(), fcntl.F_SETFD, 1)

# Lock a file (blocking)
fcntl.flock(f.fileno(), fcntl.LOCK_EX)

# Lock the first 8192 bytes of a file (non-blocking)
try:
    fcntl.lockf(f.fileno(), fcntl.LOCK_EX | fcntl.LOCK_NB, 8192, 0, 0)
except IOError,e:
    print "Unable to acquire lock", e
```

Notes

- The set of available fcntl() commands and options is system dependent. The fcntl module may contain well over 100 constants on some platforms.
- Many of the functions in this module can also be applied to the file descriptors of sockets.

See Also:
os (p. 308), socket (p. 375)

getopt

The getopt module is used to parse command-line options (typically passed in sys.argv).

getopt(args, options [, long_options])

Parses the command-line options supplied in the list *args*. *options* is a string of letters corresponding to the single-letter options that a program wants to recognize (for example, '-x'). If an option requires an argument, the option letter must be followed by a colon. If supplied, *long_options* is a list of strings corresponding to long option names. When supplied in *args*, these options are always preceded by a double hyphen (--), such as in '--exclude' (the leading -- is not supplied in *long_options*). Long option names requiring an argument should be followed by an equal sign (=). The function returns a list of (*option*, *value*) pairs matched and a list of program arguments supplied after all the options. The options are placed in the list in the same order in which they were found. Long and short options can be mixed. Option names are returned with a leading hyphen (-) or double hyphen (--). The processing of options stops when the first non-option argument is encountered.

gnu_getopt(args, options [, long_options])

Processes command-line options like getopt(), but allows option and non-option arguments to be mixed. See the second example.

GetOptError

Exception raised when an unrecognized option is found or when an option requiring an argument is given none. The exception argument is a string indicating the cause of the error.

Examples

```
>>> args = ['-a', '-b', 'foo', '-cd', 'blah', '--exclude=bar', 'x1', 'x2']
>>> opts, pargs = getopt.getopt(args, 'ab:cd:', ['exclude='])
>>> opts
[('-a', ''), ('-b', 'foo'), ('-c',''), ('-d','blah'),('--exclude', 'bar')]
>>> pargs
['x1', 'x2']
```

This example shows the difference between getopt() and gnu_getopt().

```
>>> args = ['-a','x1','x2','-b','foo','-cd','blah','--exclude','bar']
>>> opts, pargs = getopt.getopt(args, 'ab:cd:', ['exclude='])
>>> opts
[('-a','')]
>>> pargs
['x1', 'x2', '-b', 'foo', '-cd', 'blah', '--exclude=', 'bar']
>>> opts, pargs = getopt.gnu_getopt(args, 'ab:cd:', ['exclude='])
>>> opts
[('-a',''), ('-b','foo'), ('-c',''), ('-d','blah'), ('--exclude','bar')]
>>> pargs
['x1','x2']
```

Notes

- Only single-letter command-line options can be recognized with a single hyphen (-). For example, '-n 3' is legal, but '-name 3' isn't.

- More than one single-letter option can be combined, provided that all but the last option take no arguments. The '-cd blah' option in the examples illustrates this behavior.

- Long options can often be shortened. For example, if a program defines the option --exclude, it can be specified as --ex or --excl, provided that the shortened version doesn't conflict with other options.

See Also:
optparse (p. 302), sys (p. 166)

getpass

The getpass module provides support for reading passwords and usernames.

getpass([prompt])

Prompts the user with the given prompt for a password without echoing keyboard input. The default prompt is 'Password: '. Returns the entered password as a string.

getuser()

Returns the login name of the user by first checking the environment variables $LOGNAME, $USER, $LNAME, and $USERNAME and then checking the system password database. Raises a KeyError exception if no name can be found (UNIX and Windows).

Notes

- An example of getpass is shown in the documentation for the crypt module.

- On UNIX, the getpass module depends on the termios module, which is disabled by default on some systems. On Windows, getpass uses the msvcrt module.

See Also:
pwd (p. 332), crypt (p. 266)

grp

The grp module provides access to the UNIX group database.

`getgrgid(gid)`

Returns the group database entry for a group ID, `gid`. The returned object is a group structure with the following attributes:

- `gr_name`—The group name
- `gr_passwd`—The group password (if any)
- `gr_gid`—The integer group ID
- `gr_mem`—A list of usernames in the group

The returned object also behaves like a 4-tuple (`gr_name`, `gr_passwd`, `gr_gid`, `gr_mem`). Raises `KeyError` if the group doesn't exist.

`getgrnam(name)`

Same as `getgrgid()`, but looks up a group by name.

`getgrall()`

Returns all available group entries as a list of tuples as returned by `getgrgid()`.

See Also:
pwd (p. 332)

locale

The `locale` module provides access to the POSIX locale database, which allows programmers to handle certain cultural issues in an application without knowing all the specifics of each country where the software is executed. A "locale" defines a set of parameters that describe the representation of strings, time, numbers, and currency. These parameters are grouped into the following category codes:

Category	Description
LC_CTYPE	Character conversion and comparison.
LC_COLLATE	String sorting. Affects `strcoll()` and `strxfrm()`.
LC_TIME	Time formatting. Affects `time.strftime()`.
LC_MONETARY	Formatting of monetary values.
LC_MESSAGES	Message display. This may affect error messages returned by functions such as `os.strerror()`.
LC_NUMERIC	Number formatting. Affects `format()`, `atoi()`, `atof()`, and `str()`.
LC_ALL	A combination of all locale settings.

The following functions are available:

`setlocale(category [, locale])`

If `locale` is specified, this function changes the locale setting for a particular category. `locale` is a string or tuple (`langcode`, `encoding`) that specifies the locale name. If set to 'C', the portable locale is selected (the default). If the string is empty, the default locale from the user's environment is selected. If *locale* is omitted, a string representing the setting for the given category is returned. Raises the exception locale.Error on failure.

localeconv()

Returns the database of local conventions as a dictionary.

nl_langinfo(option)

Returns locale-specific information as a string. *option* is a numeric code that represents a specific item to return. Possible codes are as follows:

Option Code	Description
ABDAY_1–ABDAY_7	Abbreviated day, Sunday through Saturday
ABMON_1–ABMON_12	Abbreviated month, January through December
DAY_1–DAY_7	Non-abbreviated day, Sunday through Saturday
MON_1–MON_12	Non-abbreviated month, January through December
ALT_DIGITS	Alternative symbols for digits used when formatting numbers
AM_STR	String for "a.m." time
PM_STR	String for "p.m." time
D_FMT	Format string for dates
T_FMT	Format string for times
T_FMT_AMPM	Format string for time with a.m./p.m.
D_T_FMT	Format string for dates and times
RADIXCHAR	Radix character (decimal point)
CRNCYSTR	Currency string
YESSTR	Affirmative string
YESEXPR	Regular expression for "yes" character (for example, '^[yY]')
NOSTR	Negative string
NOEXPR	Regular expression for "no" character
CODESET	Name of codeset used (for example, 'US-ASCII')
THOUSEP	Separator for thousands
ERA	Japanese era description segments
ERA_D_FMT	Japanese era date format
ERA_D_T_FMT	Japanese era date and time format
ERA_T_FMT	Japanese era time format

getdefaultlocale([envvars])

Returns a tuple (*langcode, encoding*) with the default locale setting. The determination of the locale is typically performed by examining environment variables for the LANG environment variable and other related variants. *envvars* optionally supplies values for environment variables as a dictionary.

getlocale([category])

Returns the locale setting for category *category*. *category* is one of the LC_* constants defined earlier. If omitted, *category* defaults to LC_CTYPE. Returns a tuple (*langcode, encoding*).

getpreferredencoding([do_setlocale])

Gets the preferred character encoding based on user preferences on the locale machine (environment variables, system settings, and so on). This function may have to invoke setlocale() to determine this information. If *do_setlocale* is set to False, setlocale() will not be called.

normalize(localename)

Returns a normalized locale code for *localename*.

resetlocale([category])

Resets the locale setting for a particular category to the default value. *category* is one of the LC_* constants defined earlier and defaults to LC_ALL.

strcoll(string1, string2)

Compares two strings according to the current LC_COLLATE setting. Returns a negative, positive, or zero value depending on whether *string1* collates before or after *string2* or is equal to it. This function might be used if you wanted to alphabetize a list of strings according to the locale settings.

strxfrm(string)

Transforms a string to one that can be used for the built-in function cmp() and still return locale-aware results.

format(format, val [, grouping])

Formats a number, *val*, according to the current LC_NUMERIC setting. The *format* follows the conventions of the % operator. For floating-point values, the decimal point is modified, if appropriate. If *grouping* is true, the locale grouping is taken into account.

str(float)

Formats a floating-point number using the same format as the built-in function str(float), but takes the decimal point into account.

atof(string)

Converts a string to a floating-point number according to the LC_NUMERIC settings.

atoi(string)

Converts a string to an integer according to the LC_NUMERIC conventions.

Exception

Error

Raised on failure of the `setlocale()` function.

> **Note**
> Additional information about this module is available in the online library reference.

> **See Also:**
> http://www.python.org/doc/lib/module-locale.html.

logging

The `logging` module provides a flexible facility for applications to log events, errors, warnings, and debugging information. This information can be collected, filtered, written to files, sent to the system log, and even sent over the network to remote machines.

Five different levels of information are collected by the `logging` module. These levels have both a symbolic name and a numerical value that is used for filtering:

Level	Value	Description
CRITICAL	50	Critical errors/messages
ERROR	40	Errors
WARNING	30	Warning messages
INFO	20	Informative messages
DEBUG	10	Debugging
NOTSET	0	No level set

Basic Logging

In the most simple case, logging messages are issued by an application and sent to a special `Logging` object known as the *root logger*. By default, the root logger only handles messages at the WARNING level or above. Logging messages are either sent to standard error (`sys.stderr`) or written to a file. The following functions are used to issue logging messages at different levels:

`critical(fmt [, *args [, exc_info]])`

Issues a logging message at the CRITICAL level on the root logger. `fmt` is a format string that specifies the format of the log message. Any remaining arguments serve as arguments for various format specifiers in the format string. A single keyword argument, `exc_info`, may also be supplied. If True, exception information from `sys.exc_info()` is also added to the log message. `exc_info` may also be given an exception tuple as returned by `sys.exc_info()`, in which case that information is used instead. By default, `exc_info` is False.

`error(`*fmt* `[, *args [, exc_info]])`

Issues a logging message at the ERROR level on the root logger.

`exception(`*fmt* `[, *args ])`

Issues a logging message at the ERROR level on the root logger. Includes exception information and can only be used inside exception handlers.

`warning(`*fmt* `[, *args [, exc_info]])`

Issues a logging message at the WARNING level on the root logger.

`info(`*fmt* `[, *args [, exc_info]])`

Issues a logging message at the INFO level on the root logger.

`debug(`*fmt* `[, *args [, exc_info]])`

Issues a logging message at the DEBUG level on the root logger.

`log(`*level*`, fmt [, *args [, exc_info]])`

Issues a logging message at the level specified by *level* on the root logger.

The following function can be used to control the behavior of the root logger:

`basicConfig([**`*kwargs*`])`

Performs basic configuration of the root logger. This function should be called before any logging calls are made. The function accepts a number of keyword arguments:

Keyword Argument	Description
filename	Redirects logging message output to a file with the given filename.
filemode	Specifies the mode used to open the file. By default, mode 'a' (append) is used.
format	Format string used to produce log messages (see the following list).
datefmt	Format string used to output dates and times.
level	Sets the level of the root logger. All log messages with a level equal to or above this level will be processed. Lower-level messages will be silently ignored.
stream	Provides an open file to which log messages are sent. The default stream is sys.stderr. This parameter may not be used simultaneously with the filename parameter.

The format string specified with the format keyword argument controls the actual output of the logger. This format string contains text and the following set of substitutions:

Format	Description
%(name)s	Name of the logger.
%(levelno)s	Numeric logging level.
%(levelname)s	Text name of the logging level.

Format	Description
%(pathname)s	Pathname of the source file where the logging call was executed.
%(filename)s	Filename of the source file where the logging call was executed.
%(module)s	Module name where the logging call executed.
%(lineno)d	Line number where the logging call executed.
%(created)f	Time when the logging call executed. The value is a number as returned by time.time().
%(asctime)s	ASCII-formatted date and time when the logging call was executed.
%(msecs)s	Millisecond portion of the time when the logging call executed.
%(thread)d	Thread ID.
%(threadName)s	Thread name.
%(process)d	Process ID.
%(message)s	The logged message (supplied by user).

The date format string specified with the datefmt keyword argument is a format string in the same form as used by the time.strftime() function.

The following example shows the basic use of the logging module:

```
import logging
logging.basicConfig(
    filename="log.txt",
    format = "%(levelname)-10s %(asctime)s %(message)s"
    level = logging.DEBUG
)
logging.debug("Debugging info")
logging.info("Something wonderful is about to happen")
logging.critical("Creeping death detected.")
```

As output, this would produce log messages in the file log.txt as follows:

```
DEBUG      2005-10-25 20:46:57,125 Debugging info
INFO       2005-10-25 20:46:57,125 Something wonderful is about to happen
CRITICAL   2005-10-25 20:46:57,126 Creeping death detected.
```

Application-Specific Logging

If desired, logging can be custom tailored to a specific application or specific Python modules. The primary means of customization is to create a new Logger object and to customize it as desired. Messages are then sent to this object instead of the root logger.

The following function is used to retrieve or create new logging objects:

getLogger(*logname*)

Returns a Logger object associated with the name *logname*. If no such object exists, a new Logger object is created and returned. *logname* is a string that specifies a name or series of names separated by periods (for example 'appl' or 'appl.ui.visualizer'). Setting *logname* to the empty string ' ' returns the Logger object associated with the root logger.

An instance, L, of Logger supports the following methods for issuing messages:

`L.critical(`*`fmt`* `[, *`*`args`* `[, `*`exc_info`*`]])`

Issues a message at the CRITICAL level. Arguments have the same meaning as the critical() function discussed earlier.

`L.error(`*`fmt`* `[, *`*`args`* `[, `*`exc_info`*`]])`

Issues a message at the ERROR level.

`L.exception(`*`fmt`* `[, *`*`args`* `])`

Issues a message at the ERROR level with exception information.

`L.warning(`*`fmt`* `[, *`*`args`* `[, `*`exc_info`*`]])`

Issues a message at the WARNING level.

`L.info(`*`fmt`* `[, *`*`args`* `[, `*`exc_info`*`]])`

Issues a message at the INFO level.

`L.debug(`*`fmt`* `[, *`*`args`* `[, `*`exc_info`*`]])`

Issues a message at the DEBUG level.

`L.log(`*`level`*`, fmt [, *`*`args`* `[, `*`exc_info`*`]])`

Issues a message at the level in *level*.

The following methods and attributes are used to customize the behavior of the logging object L:

`L.propagate`

Controls the propagation of logging messages to parent logging objects. For example, if the logger L has the name 'foo.bar.spam' and this attribute is True, messages sent to L will also propagate to the logger with the name 'foo.bar'.

`L.setLevel(`*`level`*`)`

Sets the level of L. Only logging messages with a level greater than or equal to *level* will be handled. By default, the level is set to logging.NOTSET when a logger is first created. This level results in the processing of all log messages.

`L.isEnabledFor(`*`level`*`)`

Returns True if a logging message at level *level* would be processed.

`L.getEffectiveLevel()`

Returns the effective level of the logger. If a level has been set using setLevel(), that level is returned. If no level has been explicitly set (the level is logging.NOTSET in this case), this function returns the effective level of the parent logger instead. If none of the parent loggers have a level set, the effective level of the root logger will be returned.

`L.addFilter(`*`filt`*`)`

Adds a filter object, *filt*, to the logger. A filter is an object of type Filter, which is also part of the logging module (described later).

L.removeFilter(*filt*)

Removes a Filter object, *filt*, from the logger.

L.filter(*record*)

Determines whether the logging message *record* would be processed by the logger according to current filter settings. Returns True if the message would be processed. *record* is an object of type LogRecord that contains logging information.

L.addHandler(*handler*)

Adds a Handler object to the logger. A handler is an object responsible for the actual processing of log messages. Different handlers can be defined for writing messages to files, recording information in the system log, and so forth, as described later.

L.removeHandler(*handler*)

Removes the Handler object *handler* from the logger.

L.findCaller()

Returns a tuple (*filename, lineno*) corresponding to the caller's source filename and line number.

L.handle(*record*)

Given a LogRecord object, *record*, containing message information, this function dispatches the record to all the handlers registered with addHandler().

LogRecord

A number of the methods on Logger objects involve objects of type LogRecord. The LogRecord type is merely the internal implementation of the contents of a logging message. It includes information about the log message itself, message level, and origin of the logging call.

LogRecord(*name, level, pathname, line, msg, args, exc_info*)

Creates a LogRecord object that represents the contents of a logging message. *name* is the name of the Logger object (for example, 'appl.ui'), *level* is the numeric level, *pathname* is the name of the source file where the logging message originated, *line* is the line number in that file where the message originated, *msg* is the message text, *args* is a tuple corresponding to the extra arguments supplied to the various message functions, and *exc_info* is an exception tuple obtained from sys.exc_info() or None if no exception information is available.

An instance, *r*, of LogRecord has one method:

r.getMessage()

Returns the message contained in *r* after applying various formatting rules to user-supplied arguments (if any).

The following utility function is used to create a LogRecord object from a dictionary of attributes:

makeLogRecord(*attrdict*)

Given a dictionary containing the attribute names and values of a logging record, this function creates a LogRecord object. The primary use of this function is to create

`LogRecord` objects from logging data that has been received from elsewhere (socket connections, web uploads, and so on).

Handlers

The processing of log messages is normally performed by special handlers that are attached to a `Logger` object using the `addHandler()` method. Each handler is defined as a class that derives from `Handler`. Some handlers are contained in the sub-module `logging.handlers`. Others are just part of the `logging` module. The following handlers are available:

`handlers.DatagramHandler(host,port)`

Sends log messages to a UDP server located on the given *host* and *port*. Log messages are encoded by taking the dictionary of the corresponding `LogRecord` object and encoding it using the `pickle` module. The transmitted network message consists of a 4-byte network order (big-endian) length followed by the pickled record data. To reconstruct the message, the receiver must strip the length header, read the entire message, unpickle the contents, and call `makeLogRecord()`. Because UDP is unreliable, network errors may result in lost log messages.

`FileHandler(filename [, mode])`

Writes log messages to the file *filename*. *mode* is the file mode to use when opening the file and defaults to `'a'`.

`handlers.HTTPHandler(host, url [, method])`

Uploads log messages to an HTTP server using HTTP GET or POST methods. *host* specifies the host machine, *url* is the URL to use, and *method* is either `'GET'` (the default) or `'POST'`. The log message is encoded by taking the dictionary of the corresponding `LogRecord` object and encoding it as a set of URL query-string variables using the `urllib.urlencode()` function.

`handlers.MemoryHandler(capacity [, flushLevel [, target]])`

This handler is used to collect log messages in memory and to flush them to another handler, *target*, periodically. *capacity* is the size of the memory buffer in bytes. *flushLevel* is a numeric logging level that forces a memory flush should a logging message of that level or higher appear. The default value is ERROR. *target* is another `Handler` object that receives the messages. If *target* is omitted, you will need to set a target using the `setTarget()` method of the resulting handler object in order for this handler to do anything.

`handlers.NTEventLogHandler(appname [, dllname [, logtype]])`

Sends messages to the event log on Windows NT, Windows 2000, or Windows XP. *appname* is the name of the application name to use in the event log. *dllname* is a full pathname to a `.DLL` or `.EXE` file that provides message definitions to hold in the log. If omitted, dllname is set to `'win32service.pyd'`. *logtype* is either `'Application'`, `'System'`, or `'Security'`. The default value is `'Application'`. This handler is only available if Win32 extensions for Python have been installed.

handlers.RotatingFileHandler(*filename* [, *mode* [, *maxBytes* [, *backupCount*]]]**)**

Writes log messages to the file *filename*. However, if the file exceeds the size specified by *maxBytes*, the file is rotated to *filename*.1 and a new log file, *filename*, is opened. *backupCount* specifies the maximum number of backup files to create. By default, the value of *backupCount* is 0. However, when specified, backup files are rotated through the sequence *filename*.1, *filename*.2, ... ,*filename*.*N*, where *filename*.1 is always the most recent backup and *filename*.*N* is always the oldest backup. *mode* specifies the file mode to use when opening the log file. The default mode is 'a'. If *maxBytes* is 0 (the default), the log file is never rolled over and is allowed to grow indefinitely.

handlers.SMTPHandler(*mailhost, fromaddr, toaddrs, subject***)**

Sends log messages to a remote host using email. *mailhost* is the address of an SMTP server that can receive the message. The address can be a simple hostname specified as a string or a tuple (*host, port*). *fromaddr* is the from address, *toaddrs* is the destination address, and *subject* is the message subject to use in the message.

handlers.SocketHandler(*host, port***)**

Sends log messages to a remote host using a TCP socket connection. *host* and *port* specify the destination. Messages are sent in the same format as described for DatagramHandler. Unlike DatagramHandler, this handler reliably delivers log messages.

StreamHandler([*fileobj***])**

Writes log messages to an already open file-like object, *fileobj*. If no argument is provided, messages are written to sys.stderr. This handler is the default handler used by the root logger.

handlers.SysLogHandler([*address* [, *facility*]]**)**

Sends log messages to a UNIX system logging daemon. *address* specifies the destination as a (*host, port*) tuple. If omitted, a destination of ('localhost', 514) is used. *facility* is an integer facility code and is set to SysLogHandler.LOG_USER by default. A full list of facility codes can be found in the definition of SysLogHandler.

handlers.TimedRotatingFileHandler(*filename* [, *when* [, *interval* [, *backupCount*]]]**)**

The same as RotatingFileHandler, but the rotation of files is controlled by time instead of filesize. *interval* is a number and *when* is a string that specifies units. Possible values for *when* are 'S' (seconds), 'M' (minutes), 'H' (hours), 'D' (days), 'W' (weeks), and 'midnight' (roll over at midnight). For example, setting *interval* to 3 and *when* to 'D' rolls the log every three days. *backupCount* specifies the maximum number of backup files to keep.

A Handler object, *h*, supports the following methods:

h.createLock()

Initializes an internal thread lock that can be used if the handler is to be used in a threaded environment.

h.acquire()

Acquires the thread lock.

`h.release()`

Releases the thread lock.

`h.setLevel(level)`

Sets the threshold of messages to be handled. `level` is a numeric code such as ERROR or CRITICAL.

`h.setFormatter(formatter)`

Sets the object used for message formatting to `formatter`. `formatter` is an object of type Formatter.

`h.addFilter(filt)`

Adds a Filter object, `filt`, to the handler.

`h.removeFilter(filt)`

Removes a Filter object, `filt`, from the handler.

`h.filter(record)`

Returns True if the logging record `record` would be processed by the handler after applying all filtering rules.

`h.flush()`

Flushes all logging output.

`h.close()`

Closes the handler.

`h.handle(record)`

Emits the logging record `record`. Filtering rules are applied so the record will only be emitted if it passes through all the filters. If a thread lock was created with createLock(), it is used to prevent race conditions. `record` is an object of type LogRecord. If an error occurs while emitting a log record, the record is passed to the handleError() method.

`h.handleError(record)`

This method is called whenever an error occurs during the normal handling of records. `record` is the log record that was being emitted when the error occurred. By default, this method does nothing, thus causing errors to be silently ignored. It can be redefined if you want something else to happen.

`h.format(record)`

Returns a string containing the formatted output of a logging record. `record` is an object of type LogRecord.

`h.emit(record)`

Emits the logging record `record`. This method is actually responsible for producing the logging output. Unlike handle(), it only omits the record; it doesn't provide any locking.

Filters

A number of methods associated with loggers and handlers involve `Filter` objects. A filter provides a mechanism for filtering messages in a manner that's different from the level scheme. The `logging` module defines a class, `Filter`, that is used for simple filtering.

Filter([*name*])

Creates a simple filter object. *name* specifies the name of a logger as a period-separated list of names. For example, setting *name* to `'foo.bar'` will create a filter that only accepts messages directed to loggers such as `'foo.bar'`, `'foo.bar.spam'`, `'foo.bar.blah'` and so forth. Messages sent elsewhere, such as to `'foo.grok'` or `'mondo'`, will be rejected. If *name* is omitted, all messages are accepted.

An instance, *f*, of `Filter` has one method:

f.filter(*record*)

Examines a `LogRecord` object *record* and returns `True` if the record should be logged or `False` if the record should be ignored.

Different kinds of filters can be created by subclassing `Filter` and providing a different implementation of the `filter()` method.

Formatters

The actual formatting of log messages is performed by a special `Formatter` object. A formatter is attached to handlers using the `setFormatter()` method of `Handler`, described earlier.

Formatter([*fmt* [, *datefmt*]])

Creates a new `Formatter` object. *fmt* provides a format string for messages. This format string is the same as that described in the explanation of the `basicConfig()` function earlier. If omitted, *fmt* is set to `'%(message)s'`. *datefmt* is a date format string compatible with the `time.strftime()` function. If omitted, the date format is set to the ISO 8601 format.

A `Formatter` instance, *f*, has the following methods:

f.format(*record*)

Returns a formatted string containing the log message for `LogRecord` object *record*.

f.formatTime(*record* [, *datefmt*])

Returns a string representing the date and time of `LogRecord` object *record*. *datefmt* optionally specifies a format string to use with `time.strftime()`. If omitted, an ISO 8601 time format is used (for example, `'2005-10-25 20:46:57,125'`).

f.formatException(*exc_info*)

Formats exception information. *exc_info* is a tuple containing exception information as returned by `sys.exc_info()`. By default, this method returns the same string as produced by `traceback.print_exception()`.

If special formatting of log message is desired, `Formatter` can be subclassed and modified.

Miscellaneous Utility Functions

The following functions in `logging` control a few other aspects of logging:

`disable(level)`

Globally disables all logging messages below the level specified in `level`. This can be used to turn off logging on a applicationwide basis; for instance, if you want to temporarily disable or reduce the amount of logging output.

`addLevelName(level, levelName)`

Creates an entirely new logging level and name. `level` is a number and `levelName` is a string. This can be used to change the names of the built-in levels or to add more levels than are supported by default.

`getLevelName(level)`

Returns the name of the level corresponding to the numeric value `level`.

`shutdown()`

Shuts down all logging objects, flushing output if necessary.

Examples

Creating a customized logger for an application involves four basic steps:

1. Use `getLogger()` to create a `Logger` object and establish a name associated with that object. Set parameters such as the level, as appropriate.
2. Create a `Handler` object by instantiating one of the various types of handlers (`FileHandler`, `StreamHandler`, `SocketHandler`, and so on) and set an appropriate level.
3. Create a `Formatter` object and attach it to the `Handler` object using the `setFormatter()` method.
4. Attach the `Handler` object to the `Logger` object using the `addHandler()` method.

Once these steps have been performed, messages can be issued to the logger using the basic `critical()`, `error()`, `warning()`, `info()`, and `debug()` methods.

Example 1: Application Logging to Rotating Files

This example shows the basic steps of creating a new logging object and getting it to work:

```
import logging
import logging.handlers

# Create a Logger
log1 = logging.getLogger("mondo")
log1.setLevel(logging.INFO)

# Create a Handler
hand = logging.handlers.RotatingFileHandler("mondo.log", 'a', 100000, 4)

# Create a Formatter
form = logging.Formatter("%(levelname)-10s %(name)-12s %(asctime)s %(message)s")
```

```
# Attach formatter to Handler
hand.setFormatter(form)

# Attach handler to Logger
log1.addHandler(hand)

# Create some log messages
log1.info("MONDO application starting up")
log1.warning("MONDO flag not set")
```

Example 2: Multiple Destinations

Suppose you wanted to modify the last example so that extremely critical messages were handled differently. To do this, simply create a new handler function and attach it to a logger. For example:

```
# Create a critical message handler
crithand = logging.StreamHandler(sys.stderr)
crithand.setLevel(logging.CRITICAL)
crithand.setFormatter(form)
log1.addHandler(crithand)

# A critical message
log1.critical("MONDO OVERLOAD!")
```

It is important to note that in this example, two different handlers have been attached to the same logging object, log1. Whenever a message is issued, it is passed to both handlers, which process the message as appropriate. In this case, a critical message would appear both in the log file and on the standard output. Less critical messages will only appear in the log file.

Example 3: Multiple Loggers and Message Propagation

If an application has many different components, you might divide the logging into multiple loggers. For example:

```
netlog = logging.getLogger("mondo.net")
netlog.info("Networking on port %d", port)
```

When you do this, logging messages issued on 'mondo.net' will propagate up to any loggers defined for 'mondo'. Thus, the preceding message will appear in the log file. However, the message name will identify that it came from 'mondo.net'. For example:

```
CRITICAL   mondo       2005-10-26 09:34:11,900 MONDO OVERLOAD!
INFO       mondo.net   2005-10-26 09:34:11,905 networking on port 31337
```

If desired, additional handlers can be defined for 'mondo.net'. For instance, if you wanted to additionally log network messages to a different file, you could do this:

```
nethand = logging.FileHandler("mondo.net.log")
nethand.setLevel(logging.DEBUG)
nethand.setFormatter(form)
netlog.addHandler(nethand)
```

Now, messages sent to netlog will be written to the file 'mondo.net.log' and will additionally be written to the file 'mondo.log'. Critical messages will go to both places and be additionally displayed on sys.stderr.

Example 4: Remote Logging

The following example shows how to send logging messages to remote machines. For instance, suppose you wanted to send critical messages to a monitoring program running elsewhere.

In clients, messages can be sent remotely by adding a `DatagramHandler` or `SocketHandler`. For example:

```
remotehand = logging.handlers.DatagramHandler("monitorhost", 1234)
remotehand.setLevel(logging.CRITICAL)
log1.addHandler(remotehand)
```

To receive a remote logging message, you would need to write a server to receive it. Typically, this server would receive messages and place them into a log that runs on it. Here is a very simple example:

```
import socket
import logging
import pickle
import string

s = socket.socket(socket.AF_INET, socket.SOCK_DGRAM)
s.bind(("",1234))

logging.basicConfig(
    format = "%(hostname)s %(levelname)-10s %(name)-12s %(asctime)s %(message)s"
)

monitor = logging.getLogger("monitor")
while 1:
    data,address = s.recvfrom(8192)
    size = struct.unpack(">L",data[:4])[0]
    if size == len(data[4:]):
        pdata = pickle.loads(data[4:])
        record = logging.makeLogRecord(pdata)
        # Attach a hostname attribute
        record.hostname = address[0]
        monitor.handle(record)
```

When this example is run, critical messages issued on the client will be propagated to the monitor program running elsewhere.

Notes

- The `logging` module provides a large number of customization options not discussed here. Readers should consult online documentation for further details.
- The use of logger names such as `'myapp.ui.visualizer'` provides a convenient way to locate logging objects. Various program modules can simply call `logging.getLogger()` with that name to obtain the appropriate object without having to worry about passing log objects around among different modules.

mmap

The `mmap` module provides support for a memory-mapped file object. This object behaves both like a file and a string and can be used in most places where an ordinary file or string is expected. Furthermore, the contents of a memory-mapped file are mutable. This means that modifications can be made using index-assignment and slice-assignment operators. Unless a private mapping of the file has been made, such changes directly alter the contents of the underlying file.

A memory-mapping file is created by the mmap() function, which is slightly different on UNIX and Windows.

```
mmap(fileno, length [, flags, [prot [,access]]])
```

(UNIX) Returns an mmap object that maps length bytes from the file with an integer file descriptor, fileno. flags specifies the nature of the mapping and is the bitwise OR of the following:

Flag	Meaning
MAP_PRIVATE	Create a private copy-on-write mapping. Changes to the object will be private to this process.
MAP_SHARED	Share the mapping with all other processes mapping the same areas of the file. Changes to the object will affect all mappings.
MAP_ANON	Used when creating an anonymous shared-memory region on BSD.
MAP_DENYWRITE	Disallow writes (not available on all platforms).
MAP_EXECUTABLE	Map memory as executable (not available on all platforms).

The default flags setting is MAP_SHARED. prot specifies the memory protections of the object and is the bitwise OR of the following:

Setting	Meaning
PROT_READ	Data can be read from the object.
PROT_WRITE	Modifications can be made to the object.
PROT_EXEC	The object can contain executable instructions.

The default value of prot is PROT_READ | PROT_WRITE. The modes specified in prot must match the access permissions used to open the underlying file descriptor fileno. In most cases, this means that the file should be opened in read/write mode (for example, os.open(name, os.O_RDWR)).

The optional access parameter may be used as an alternative to flags and prot. If given, it has one of the following values

Access	Meaning
ACCESS_READ	Read-only access.
ACCESS_WRITE	Read/write access with write-through. Modifications affect the underlying file.
ACCESS_COPY	Read/write access with copy-on-write. Modifications affect memory, but do not change the underlying file.

When access is supplied, it is typically given as a keyword argument—for example, mmap(fileno, length, access=ACCESS_READ). It is an error to supply values for both access and flags/prot.

`mmap(fileno, length[, tagname [,access]])`

(Windows) Returns an mmap object that maps *length* bytes from the file specified by the integer file descriptor *fileno*. If *length* is larger than the current size of the file, the file is extended to *length* bytes. If *length* is 0, the current length of the file is used as the length as long as the file is non-empty (otherwise, an exception will be raised). *tagname* is an optional string that can be used to name the mapping. If *tagname* refers to an existing mapping, that mapping is opened. Otherwise, a new mapping is created. If *tagname* is None, an unnamed mapping is created. *access* is an optional parameter that specifies the access mode. It takes the same values for *access* as described for the UNIX version of mmap(). By default, *access* is ACCESS_WRITE.

A memory-mapped file object, *m*, supports the following methods.

`m.close()`

Closes the file. Subsequent operations will result in an exception.

`m.find(string[, start])`

Returns the index of the first occurrence of *string*. *start* specifies an optional starting position. Returns -1 if no match is found.

`m.flush([offset, size])`

Flushes modifications of the in-memory copy back to the file system. *offset* and *size* specify an optional range of bytes to flush. Otherwise, the entire mapping is flushed.

`m.move(dst,src,count)`

Copies *count* bytes starting at index *src* to the destination index *dst*. This copy is performed using the C memmove() function, which is guaranteed to work correctly when the source and destination regions happen to overlap.

`m.read(n)`

Reads up to *n* bytes from the current file position and returns the data as a string.

`m.read_byte()`

Reads a single byte from the current file position and returns as a string of length 1.

`m.readline()`

Returns a line of input starting at the current file position.

`m.resize(newsize)`

Resizes the memory-mapped object to contain *newsize* bytes.

`m.seek(pos[, whence])`

Sets the file position to a new value. *pos* and *whence* have the same meaning as for the seek() method on file objects.

`m.size()`

Returns the length of the file. This value may be larger than the size of the memory-mapped region.

`m.tell()`

Returns the value of the file pointer.

m.write(*string*)

Writes a string of bytes to the file at the current file pointer.

m.write_byte(*byte*)

Writes a single byte into memory at the current file pointer.

Notes

- Although UNIX and Windows supply slightly different mmap() functions, this module can be used in a portable manner by relying on the optional access parameter that is common to both functions. For example, mmap(*fileno*, *length*, access=ACCESS_WRITE) will work on both UNIX and Windows.

- Certain memory mapping may only work with a length that's a multiple of the system page size, which is contained in the constant mmap.PAGESIZE.

- On UNIX SVR4 systems, anonymous mapped memory can be obtained by calling mmap() on the file /dev/zero, opened with appropriate permissions.

- On UNIX BSD systems, anonymous mapped memory can be obtained by calling mmap() with a negative file descriptor and the flag mmap.MAP_ANON.

msvcrt

The msvcrt module provides access to a number of useful functions in the Microsoft Visual C runtime library. This module is available only on Windows.

getch()

Reads a keypress and returns the resulting character. This call blocks if a keypress is not available. If the pressed key was a special function key, the call returns '\000' or '\xe0' and the next call returns the keycode. This function doesn't echo characters to the console, nor can the function be used to read Ctrl+C.

getche()

Like getch(), except that characters are echoed (if printable).

get_osfhandle(*fd*)

Returns the file handle for file descriptor *fd*. Raises IOError if *fd* is not recognized.

heapmin()

Forces the internal Python memory manager to return unused blocks to the operating system. This works only on Windows NT and raises IOError on failure.

kbhit()

Returns True if a keypress is waiting to be read.

locking(*fd*, *mode*, *nbytes*)

Locks part of a file, given a file descriptor from the C runtime. *nbytes* is the number of bytes to lock relative to the current file pointer. *mode* is one of the following integers:

Setting	Description
0	Unlocks the file region (LK_UNLCK)
1	Locks the file region (LK_LOCK)
2	Locks the file region; nonblocking (LK_NBLCK)
3	Locks for writing (LK_RLCK)
4	Locks for writing; nonblocking (LK_NBRLCK)

Attempts to acquire a lock that take more than approximately 10 seconds result in an IOError exception.

open_osfhandle(handle, flags)

Creates a C runtime file descriptor from the file handle handle. flags is the bitwise OR of os.O_APPEND, os.O_RDONLY, and os.O_TEXT. Returns an integer file descriptor that can be used as a parameter to os.fdopen() to create a file object.

putch(char)

Prints the character char to the console without buffering.

setmode(fd, flags)

Sets the line-end translation mode for file descriptor fd. flags is os.O_TEXT for text mode and os.O_BINARY for binary mode.

ungetch(char)

Causes the character char to be "pushed back" into the console buffer. It will be the next character read by getch() or getche().

> **Note**
> A wide variety of Win32 extensions are available that provide access to the Microsoft Foundation Classes, COM components, graphical user interfaces, and so forth. These topics are far beyond the scope of this book, but detailed information about many of these topics is available in *Python Programming on Win32* by Mark Hammond and Andy Robinson (O'Reilly & Associates, 2000). Also, http://www.python.org maintains an extensive list of contributed modules for use under Windows.

> **See Also:**
> _winreg (p. 351)

optparse

The optparse module provides high-level support for processing command-line options. It provides similar functionality as the getopt module, but adds a considerable number of new features related to configuration, error handling, and option processing. Use of optparse primarily focuses on the OptionParser class.

`OptionParser([**args])`

Creates a new command option parser and returns an `OptionParser` instance. A variety of optional keyword arguments can be supplied to control configuration. These keyword arguments are described in the following list:

Keyword Argument	Description
add_help_option	Specifies whether or not a special help option (`--help` and `-h`) is supported. By default, this is set to `True`.
conflict_handler	Specifies the handling of conflicting command-line options. May be set to either `'error'` (the default value) or `'resolve'`. In `'error'` mode, an `optparse.OptionConflictError` exception will be raised if conflicting option strings are added to the parser. In `'resolve'` mode, conflicts are resolved so that options added later take priority. However, earlier options may still be available if they were added under multiple names and no conflicts exist for at least one of the names.
description	A string that provides a description of the program for display during help. This string will automatically be reformatted to fit the screen when displayed.
formatter	Instance of an `optparse.HelpFormatter` class used to format text when printing help. May be either `optparse.IndentedHelpFormatter` (the default) or `optparse.TitledHelpFormatter`.
option_class	The Python class that's used to hold information about each command line option. The default class is `optparse.Option`.
option_list	A list of options used to populate the parser. By default, this list is empty and options are added using the `add_option()` method instead. If supplied, this list contains objects of type `Option`.
prog	The program name used to replace `'%prog'` in help text.
usage	The usage string that's printed when the `--help` option is used or incorrect options are passed. The default value is the string `'%prog [options]'`, where the `'%prog'` keyword gets replaced with either the value of `os.path.basename(sys.argv[0])` or the value of the `prog` keyword argument (if supplied). The value `optparse.SUPPRESS_USAGE` can be given to suppress the usage message entirely.
version	Version string that's printed when the `-version` option is supplied. By default, `version` is `None` and no `--version` option is added. When this string is supplied, `-version` is automatically added. The special keyword `'%prog'` is replaced by the program name.

Unless you really need to customize option processing in some way, an `OptionParser` will usually be created with no arguments. For example:

```
p = optparse.OptionParser()
```

An instance, `p`, of `OptionParser` supports the following methods:

`p.add_option(name1, ..., nameN [, **parms])`

Adds a new option to `p`. The arguments `name1`, `name2`, and so on are all of the various names for the option. For example, you might include short and long option names such as `'-f'` and `'--file'`. Following the option names, an optional set of keyword arguments is supplied that specifies how the option will be processed when parsed. These keyword arguments are described in the following list:

Keyword Argument	Description
action	Action to perform when the option is parsed. Acceptable values are as follows:
	`'store'`—Option has an argument that is read and stored. This is the default if no action is specified explicitly.
	`'store_const'`—The option takes no arguments, but when the option is encountered, a constant value specified with the `const` keyword argument is stored.
	`'store_true'`—Like `'store_const'`, but stores a boolean `True` when the option is parsed.
	`'store_false'`—Like `'store_true'`, but stores `False` instead.
	`'append'`—Option has an argument that is appended to a list when parsed. This is used if the same command-line option is used to specify multiple values.
	`'count'`—Option takes no arguments, but a counter value is stored. The counter value is increased by one each time the argument is encountered.
	`'callback'`—Invokes a callback function specified with the `callback` keyword argument when the option is encountered.
	`'help'`—Prints a help message when the option is parsed. This is only needed if you want help to be displayed via a different option than the standard -h or --help option.
	`'version'`—Prints the version number supplied to `OptionParser()`, if any. Only used if you want to display version information using an option other than the standard -v or --version option.

Keyword Argument	Description
callback	Specifies a callback function to be invoked when the option is encountered. This callback function is a Python callable object that is invoked as `callback(option, opt_str, value, parser, *args, **kwargs)`. The `option` argument is an instance of optparse.Option, `opt_str` is the option string supplied on the command line that triggered the callback, `value` is the value of the option (if any), `parser` is the instance of OptionParser that's running, `args` are positional arguments supplied using the `callback_args` keyword argument, and `kwargs` are keyword arguments supplied using the `callback_kwargs` keyword argument.
callback_args	Optional positional arguments supplied to a callback function specified with the `callback` argument.
callback_kwargs	Optional keyword arguments supplied to a callback function specified with the `callback` argument.
choices	A list of strings that specifies all possible option values. Used when an option only has a limited set of values (for example, `['small', 'medium', 'large']`).
const	The constant value that's stored with the `'store_const'` action.
default	Sets the default value of the option if not supplied. By default, the default value is None.
dest	Sets the name of the attribute used to store option values during parsing. Normally the name is derived from the option name itself.
help	Help text for this particular option. If this is not supplied, the option will be listed in help without a description. The value optparse.SUPPRESS_HELP can be used to hide an option. The special keyword `'%default'` is replaced by the option default value in the help string.
metavar	Specifies the name of an option argument that's used when printing help text.
nargs	Specifies the number of option arguments for actions that expect arguments. The default value is 1. If a number greater than 1 is used, option arguments will be collected into a tuple that is then used whenever arguments are handled.
type	Specifies the type of an option. Valid types are `'string'` (the default), `'int'`, `'long'`, `'choice'`, `'float'`, and `'complex'`.

`p.disable_interspersed_args()`

Disallows the mixing of simple options with positional arguments. For example, if '-x' and '-y' are options that take no parameters, the options must appear before any arguments (for example, 'prog -x -y arg1 arg2 arg3').

`p.enable_interspersed_args()`

Allows the mixing of options with positional arguments. For example, if '-x' and '-y' are simple options that take no parameters, they may be mixed with the arguments, such as in 'prog -x arg1 arg2 -y arg3'. This is the default behavior.

`p.parse_args([arglist])`

Parses command-line options and returns a tuple (*options*, *args*) where *options* is an object containing the values of all the options and *args* is a list of all the remaining positional arguments left over. The *options* object stores all the option data in attributes with names that match the option name. For example, the option '--output' would have its value stored in *options*.output. If the option does not appear, the value will be None. The name of the attribute can be set using the dest keyword argument to add_option(), described previously. By default, arguments are taken from sys.argv[1:]. However, a different source of arguments can be supplied as an optional argument, *arglist*.

`p.set_defaults(dest=value, ... dest=value)`

Sets the default values of particular option destinations. You simply supply keyword arguments that specify the destinations you wish to set. The name of the keyword arguments should match the names specified using the dest parameter in add_option(), described earlier.

`p.set_usage(usage)`

Changes the usage string displayed in text produced by the --help option.

Example

```
# foo.py
import optparse
p = optparse.OptionParser()

# A simple option, with no arguments
p.add_option("-t", action="store_true", dest="tracing")

# An option that accepts a string argument
p.add_option("-o", "--outfile", action="store", type="string", dest="outfile")

# An option requires an integer argument
p.add_option("-d", "--debuglevel", action="store", type="int", dest="debug")

# An option with a few choices
p.add_option("--speed", action="store", type="choice", dest="speed",
             choices=["slow","fast","ludicrous"])

# An option taking multiple arguments
p.add_option("--coord", action="store", type="int", dest="coord", nargs=2)

# A set of options that control a common destination
p.add_option("--novice", action="store_const", const="novice", dest="mode")
p.add_option("--guru", action="store_const", const="guru", dest="mode")
```

```
# Set default values for the various option destinations
p.set_defaults(tracing=False,
               debug=0,
               speed="fast",
               coord=(0,0),
               mode="novice")

# Parse the arguments
opt, args = p.parse_args()

# Print option values
print "tracing   :", opt.tracing
print "outfile   :", opt.outfile
print "debug     :", opt.debug
print "speed     :", opt.speed
print "coord     :", opt.coord
print "mode      :", opt.mode

# Print remaining arguments
print "args      :", args
```

Here is a short interactive Unix session that shows how the preceding code works:

```
% python foo.py -h
usage: foo.py [options]

options:
  -h, --help              show this help message and exit
  -t
  -o OUTFILE, --outfile=OUTFILE
  -d DEBUG, --debuglevel=DEBUG
  --speed=SPEED
  --coord=COORD
  --novice
  --guru
% python foo.py -t -o outfile.dat -d 3 --coord 3 4 --speed=ludicrous blah
tracing   : True
outfile   : outfile.dat
debug     : 3
speed     : ludicrous
coord     : (3, 4)
mode      : novice
args      : ['blah']
% python foo.py --speed=insane
usage: foo.py [options]

foo.py:error:option --speed:invalid choice:'insane'
    (choose from 'slow', 'fast', 'ludicrous')
```

Notes

- When specifying option names, use a single dash to specify a short name such as
  '-x' and a double-dash to specify a long name such as '--exclude'. An
  OptionError exception will be raised if you attempt to define an option that is a
  mix of the two styles, such as '-exclude'.

- The optparse module contains a considerable number of advanced features
  related to customization and specialized handling of certain kinds of command-
  line options. However, none of these features are required for the most common

types of command-line option parsing. Readers should consult the online library documentation for more details and additional examples.

See Also:
getopt (p. 282)

OS

The os module provides a portable interface to common operating-system services. It does this by searching for an OS-dependent built-in module such as nt or posix and exporting the functions and data as found there. Unless otherwise noted, functions are available on Windows and UNIX. UNIX systems include both Linux and Mac OS X.

The following general-purpose variables are defined:

environ

A mapping object representing the current environment variables. Changes to the mapping are reflected in the current environment.

linesep

The string used to separate lines on the current platform. May be a single character such as '\n' for POSIX or multiple characters such as '\r\n' for Windows.

name

The name of the OS-dependent module imported: 'posix', 'nt', 'dos', 'mac', 'ce', 'java', 'os2', or 'riscos'.

path

The OS-dependent standard module for pathname operations. This module can also be loaded using import os.path.

Process Environment

The following functions are used to access and modify various parameters related to the environment in which a process runs. Process, group, process group, and session IDs are integers unless otherwise noted.

chdir(path)

Changes the current working directory to path.

chroot(path)

Changes the root directory of the current process (UNIX).

ctermid()

Returns a string with the filename of the control terminal for the process (UNIX).

fchdir(fd)

Changes the current working directory. fd is a file descriptor to an opened directory (UNIX).

`getcwd()`

Returns a string with the current working directory.

`getcwdu()`

Returns a Unicode string with the current working directory.

`getegid()`

Returns the effective group ID (UNIX).

`geteuid()`

Returns the effective user ID (UNIX).

`getgid()`

Returns the real group ID of the process (UNIX).

`getgroups()`

Returns a list of integer group IDs to which the process owner belongs (UNIX).

`getpgid(pid)`

Returns the process group ID of the process with process ID *pid*. If *pid* is 0, the process group of the calling process is returned (UNIX).

`getpgrp()`

Returns the ID of the current process group. Process groups are typically used in conjunction with job control. The process group is not necessarily the same as the group ID of the process (UNIX).

`getpid()`

Returns the real process ID of the current process (UNIX and Windows).

`getppid()`

Returns the process ID of the parent process (UNIX).

`getsid(pid)`

Returns the process session identifier of process *pid*. If *pid* is 0, the identifier of the current process is returned (UNIX).

`getuid()`

Returns the real user ID of the current process (UNIX).

`putenv(varname, value)`

Sets environment variable *varname* to *value*. Changes affect subprocesses started with `os.system()`, `popen()`, `fork()`, and `execv()`. Assignments to items in `os.environ` automatically call `putenv()`. However, calls to `putenv()` don't update `os.environ` (UNIX and Windows).

`setgroups(groups)`

Sets the group access list of the current process. *groups* is a sequence of integers specifying group identifiers. Can only be called by root (UNIX).

`setgid(gid)`

Sets the group ID of the current process (UNIX).

`setpgrp()`

Creates a new process group by calling the system call `setpgrp()` or `setpgrp(0, 0)`, depending on which version is implemented (if any). Returns the ID of the new process group (UNIX).

`setpgid(pid, pgrp)`

Assigns process *pid* to process group *pgrp*. If *pid* is equal to *pgrp*, the process becomes a new process group leader. If *pid* is not equal to *pgrp*, the process joins an existing group. If *pid* is 0, the process ID of the calling process is used. If *pgrp* is 0, the process specified by *pid* becomes a process group leader (UNIX).

`setreuid(ruid, euid)`

Sets the real and effective user ID of the calling process (UNIX).

`setregid(rgid, egid)`

Sets the real and effective group ID of the calling process (UNIX).

`setsid()`

Creates a new session and returns the newly created session ID. Sessions are typically associated with terminal devices and the job control of processes that are started within them (UNIX).

`setuid(uid)`

Sets the real user ID of the current process. This function is privileged and often can be performed only by processes running as root (UNIX).

`strerror(code)`

Returns the error message corresponding to the integer error *code* (UNIX and Windows).

See Also:
`errno` (p. 275)

`umask(mask)`

Sets the current numeric umask and returns the previous umask. The umask is used to clear permissions bits on files created by the process (UNIX and Windows).

See Also:
`open(file [, flags [, mode]])` (p. 312)

`uname()`

Returns a tuple of strings (`sysname`, `nodename`, `release`, `version`, `machine`) identifying the system type (UNIX).

```
unsetenv(name)
```

Unsets the environment variable *name*.

File Creation and File Descriptors

The following functions provide a low-level interface for manipulating files and pipes. In these functions, files are manipulated in terms of an integer file descriptor, *fd*. The file descriptor can be extracted from a file object by invoking its `fileno()` method.

```
close(fd)
```

Closes the file descriptor *fd* previously returned by `open()` or `pipe()`.

```
dup(fd)
```

Duplicates file descriptor *fd*. Returns a new file descriptor that's the lowest-numbered unused file descriptor for the process. The new and old file descriptors can be used interchangeably. Furthermore, they share state, such as the current file pointer and locks (UNIX and Windows).

```
dup2(oldfd, newfd)
```

Duplicates file descriptor *oldfd* to *newfd*. If *newfd* already corresponds to a valid file descriptor, it's closed first (UNIX and Windows).

```
fdopen(fd [, mode [, bufsize]])
```

Creates an open file object connected to file descriptor *fd*. The *mode* and *bufsize* arguments have the same meaning as in the built-in `open()` function.

```
fpathconf(fd, name)
```

Returns configurable pathname variables associated with the open file with descriptor *fd*. *name* is a string that specifies the name of the value to retrieve. The values are usually taken from parameters contained in system header files such as `<limits.h>` and `<unistd.h>`. POSIX defines the following constants for *name*:

Constant	Description
`"PC_ASYNC_IO"`	Indicates whether asynchronous I/O can be performed on *fd*.
`"PC_CHOWN_RESTRICTED"`	Indicates whether the `chown()` function can be used. If *fd* refers to a directory, this applies to all files in the directory.
`"PC_FILESIZEBITS"`	Maximum size of a file.
`"PC_LINK_MAX"`	Maximum value of the file's link count.
`"PC_MAX_CANON"`	Maximum length of a formatted input line. *fd* refers to a terminal.
`"PC_MAX_INPUT"`	Maximum length of an input line. *fd* refers to a terminal.
`"PC_NAME_MAX"`	Maximum length of a filename in a directory.
`"PC_NO_TRUNC"`	Indicates whether an attempt to create a file with a name longer than PC_NAME_MAX for a directory will fail with an ENAMETOOLONG error.

Constant	Description
`"PC_PATH_MAX"`	Maximum length of a relative pathname when the directory *fd* is the current working directory.
`"PC_PIPE_BUF"`	Size of the pipe buffer when *fd* refers to a pipe or FIFO.
`"PC_PRIO_IO"`	Indicates whether priority I/O can be performed on *fd*.
`"PC_SYNC_IO"`	Indicates whether synchronous I/O can be performed on *fd*.
`"PC_VDISABLE"`	Indicates whether *fd* allows special-character processing to be disabled. *fd* must refer to a terminal.

Not all names are available on all platforms, and some systems may define additional configuration parameters. However, a list of the names known to the operating system can be found in the dictionary os.pathconf_names. If a known configuration name is not included in os.pathconf_names, its integer value can also be passed as *name*. Even if a name is recognized by Python, this function may still raise an OSError if the host operating system doesn't recognize the parameter or associate it with the file *fd*. This function is only available on some versions of UNIX.

fstat(fd)

Returns the status for file descriptor *fd*. Returns the same values as the os.stat() function (UNIX and Windows).

fstatvfs(fd)

Returns information about the file system containing the file associated with file descriptor *fd*. Returns the same values as the os.statvfs() function (UNIX).

ftruncate(fd, length)

Truncates the file corresponding to file descriptor *fd* so that it's at most *length* bytes in size (UNIX).

fsync(fd)

Forces any unwritten data on *fd* to be written to disk. Note that if you are using an object with buffered I/O (for example, a Python file object), you should first flush the data before calling fsync(). Available on UNIX and Windows.

lseek(fd, pos, how)

Sets the current position of file descriptor *fd* to position *pos*. Values of *how* are as follows: 0 sets the position relative to the beginning of the file, 1 sets it relative to the current position, and 2 sets it relative to the end of the file.

open(file [, flags [, mode]])

Opens the file *file*. *flags* is the bitwise OR of the following constant values:

Value	Description
O_RDONLY	Open the file for reading.
O_WRONLY	Open the file for writing.
O_RDWR	Open for reading and writing (updates).

Value	Description
O_APPEND	Append bytes to the end of the file.
O_CREAT	Create the file if it doesn't exist.
O_NONBLOCK	Don't block on open, read, or write (UNIX).
O_NDELAY	Same as O_NONBLOCK (UNIX).
O_DSYNC	Synchronous writes (UNIX).
O_NOCTTY	When opening a device, don't set controlling terminal (UNIX).
O_TRUNC	If the file exists, truncates to zero length.
O_RSYNC	Synchronous reads (UNIX).
O_SYNC	Synchronous writes (UNIX).
O_EXCL	Error if O_CREAT and the file already exists.
O_TEXT	Text mode (Windows).
O_BINARY	Binary mode (Windows).
O_NOINHERIT	File not inherited by child processes (Windows).
O_SHORT_LIVED	Hint to system that the file is used for short-term storage (Windows).
O_TEMPORARY	Delete file when closed (Windows).
O_RANDOM	Hint to system that file will be used for random access (Windows).
O_SEQUENTIAL	Hint to system that file will be accessed sequentially (Windows).

Synchronous I/O modes (O_SYNC, O_DSYNC, O_RSYNC) force I/O operations to block until they've been completed at the hardware level (for example, a write will block until the bytes have been physically written to disk). The mode parameter contains the file permissions represented as the bitwise OR of the following octal values (which are defined as constants in the stat module as indicated):

Mode	Meaning
0100	User has execute permission (stat.S_IXUSR).
0200	User has write permission (stat.S_IWUSR).
0400	User has read permission (stat.S_IRUSR).
0700	User has read/write/exec permission (stat.S_IRWXU).
0010	Group has execute permission (stat.S_IXGRP).
0020	Group has write permission (stat.S_IWGRP).
0040	Group has read permission (stat.S_IRGRP).
0070	Group has read/write/exec permission (stat.S_IRWXG).
0001	Others have execute permission (stat.S_IXOTH).
0002	Others have write permission (stat.S_IWOTH).
0004	Others have read permission (stat.S_IROTH).
0007	Others have read/write/exec permission (stat.S_IRWXO).

Mode	Meaning
4000	Set UID mode (stat.S_ISUID).
2000	Set GID mode (stat.S_ISGID).
1000	Set the sticky bit (stat.S_ISVTX).

The default mode of a file is (0777 & ~umask), where the umask setting is used to remove selected permissions. For example, a umask of 0022 removes the write permission for groups and others. The umask can be changed using the os.umask() function. The umask setting has no effect on Windows.

openpty()

Opens a psuedo-terminal and returns a pair of file descriptors (*master*, *slave*) for the PTY and TTY. Available on some versions of UNIX.

pipe()

Creates a pipe that can be used to establish unidirectional communication with another process. Returns a pair of file descriptors (*r*, *w*) usable for reading and writing, respectively. This function is usually called prior to executing a fork() function. After the fork(), the sending process closes the read end of the pipe and the receiving process closes the write end of the pipe. At this point, the pipe is activated and data can be sent from one process to another using read() and write() functions (UNIX).

read(*fd*, *n*)

Reads at most *n* bytes from file descriptor *fd*. Returns a string containing the bytes read.

tcgetpgrp(*fd*)

Returns the process group associated with the control terminal given by *fd* (UNIX).

tcsetpgrp(*fd*, *pg*)

Sets the process group associated with the control terminal given by *fd* (UNIX).

ttyname(*fd*)

Returns a string that specifies the terminal device associated with file descriptor *fd*. If *fd* is not associated with a terminal device, an OSError exception is raised (UNIX).

write(*fd*, *str*)

Writes the string *str* to file descriptor *fd*. Returns the number of bytes actually written.

Files and Directories

The following functions and variables are used to manipulate files and directories on the file system. To handle variances in file-naming schemes, the following variables contain information about the construction of pathnames:

Variable	Description
altsep	An alternative character used by the OS to separate pathname components, or None if only one separator character exists. This is set to '/' on DOS and Windows systems, where *sep* is a backslash.
curdir	The string used to refer to the current working directory: '.' for UNIX and Windows and ':' for the Macintosh.
devnull	The path of the null device (for example, /dev/null).
extsep	Character that separates the base filename from its type (for example the '.' in 'foo.txt').
pardir	The string used to refer to the parent directory: '..' for UNIX and Windows and '::' for the Macintosh.
pathsep	The character used to separate search path components (as contained in the $PATH environment variable): ':' for UNIX and ';' for DOS and Windows.
sep	The character used to separate pathname components: '/' for UNIX and Windows and ':' for the Macintosh.

The following functions are used to manipulate files:

access(*path*, *accessmode*)

Checks read/write/execute permissions for this process to access the file *path*. *accessmode* is R_OK, W_OK, X_OK, or F_OK for read, write, execute, or existence, respectively. Returns 1 if access is granted, 0 if not.

chmod(*path*, *mode*)

Changes the mode of *path*. *mode* has the same values as described for the open() function (UNIX and Windows).

chown(*path*, *uid*, *gid*)

Changes the owner and group ID of *path* to the numeric *uid* and *gid*. Setting *uid* or *gid* to -1 causes that parameter to remain unmodified (UNIX).

lchown(*path*, *uid*, *gid*)

The same as chown(), but doesn't follow symbolic links (UNIX).

link(*src*, *dst*)

Creates a hard link named *dst* that points to *src* (UNIX).

listdir(*path*)

Returns a list containing the names of the entries in the directory *path*. The list is returned in arbitrary order and doesn't include the special entries of '.' and '..'. If *path* is Unicode, the resulting list will contain Unicode strings.

lstat(*path*)

Like stat(), but doesn't follow symbolic links (UNIX).

`makedev(major,minor)`

Creates a raw device number given major and minor device numbers (UNIX).

`major(devicenum)`

Returns the major device number from a raw device number *devicenum*, created by `makedev()`.

`minor(devicenum)`

Returns the minor device number from a raw device number *devicenum*, created by `makedev()`.

`makedirs(path [, mode])`

Recursive directory-creation function. Like `mkdir()`, but makes all the intermediate-level directories needed to contain the leaf directory. Raises an `OSError` exception if the leaf directory already exists or cannot be created.

`mkdir(path [, mode])`

Creates a directory named *path* with numeric mode *mode*. The default mode is `0777`. On non-UNIX systems, the mode setting may have no effect or be ignored.

`mkfifo(path [, mode])`

Creates a FIFO (a named pipe) named *path* with numeric mode *mode*. The default mode is `0666` (UNIX).

`mknod(path [, mode, device])`

Creates a device-special file. *path* is the name of the file, *mode* specifies the permissions and type of file, and *device* is the raw device number created using `os.makedev()`. The *mode* parameter accepts the same parameters as `open()` when setting the file's access permissions. In addition, the flags `stat.S_IFREG`, `stat.S_IFCHR`, `stat.S_IFBLK`, and `stat.S_IFIFO` are added to *mode* to indicate a file type (UNIX).

`pathconf(path, name)`

Returns configurable system parameters related to the pathname *path*. *name* is a string that specifies the name of the parameter and is the same as described for the `fpathconf()` function (UNIX).

See Also:
`fpathconf` (p. 311)

`readlink(path)`

Returns a string representing the path to which a symbolic link, *path*, points (UNIX).

`remove(path)`

Removes the file *path*. This is identical to the `unlink()` function.

`removedirs(path)`

Recursive directory-removal function. Works like `rmdir()` except that, if the leaf directory is successfully removed, directories corresponding to the rightmost path segments will be pruned away until either the whole path is consumed or an error is raised (which is ignored, because it generally means that a parent directory isn't empty). Raises an OSError exception if the leaf directory could not be removed successfully.

rename(*src*, *dst*)

Renames the file or directory *src* to *dst*.

renames(*old*, *new*)

Recursive directory-renaming or file-renaming function. Works like rename() except it first attempts to create any intermediate directories needed to make the new pathname. After the rename, directories corresponding to the rightmost path segments of the old name will be pruned away using removedirs().

rmdir(*path*)

Removes the directory *path*.

stat(*path*)

Performs a stat() system call on the given *path* to extract information about a file. The return value is an object whose attributes contain file information. Common attributes include

Attribute	Description
st_mode	Inode protection mode
st_ino	Inode number
st_dev	Device the inode resides on
st_nlink	Number of links to the inode
st_uid	User ID of the owner
st_gid	Group ID of the owner
st_size	File size in bytes
st_atime	Time of last access
st_mtime	Time of last modification
st_ctime	Time of last status change

However, additional attributes may be available depending on the system. The object returned by stat() also looks like a 10-tuple containing the parameters (*st_mode*, *st_ino*, *st_dev*, *st_nlink*, *st_uid*, *st_gid*, *st_size*, *st_atime*, *st_mtime*, *st_ctime*). This latter form is provided for backward compatibility. The stat module defines constants that are used to extract files from this tuple.

stat_float_times([*newvalue*])

Returns True if the times returned by stat() are floating-point numbers instead of integers. The behavior can be changed by supplying a Boolean value for *newvalue*.

statvfs(*path*)

Performs a statvfs() system call on the given *path* to get information about the file system. The return value is an object whose attributes describe the file system. Common attributes include

Attribute	Description
f_bsize	Preferred system block size
f_frsize	Fundamental file system block size
f_blocks	Total number of blocks in the file system
f_bfree	Total number of free blocks
f_bavail	Free blocks available to a non-superuser
f_files	Total number of file inodes
f_ffree	Total number of free file inodes
f_favail	Free nodes available to a non-superuser
f_flag	Flags (system dependent)
f_namemax	Maximum filename length

The returned object also behaves like a tuple containing these attributes in the order listed. The standard module statvfs defines constants that can be used to extract information from the returned statvfs data (UNIX).

symlink(*src, dst*)

Creates a symbolic link named *dst* that points to *src*.

tempnam([*dir* [, *prefix*]])

Creates a unique path name. *dir* provides a location in which the name should be created. If *dir* is omitted, the path will correspond to a system default location (for example, /tmp on UNIX). *prefix* is a string that's prepended to the generated filename. This function does not actually create a temporary file, only a name that can be used for one. If you're working with temporary files, consider using the tempfile module instead.

tmpnam()

Creates a unique pathname. The pathname is created in a system default location (for example, /tmp on UNIX). If you're working with temporary files, consider using the tempfile module instead. The variable os.TMP_MAX contains the number of unique names that will be generated before names are repeated.

unlink(*path*)

Removes the file *path*. Same as remove().

utime(*path*, (*atime, mtime*))

Sets the access and modified time of the file to the given values. (The second argument is a tuple of two items.) The time arguments are specified in terms of the numbers returned by the time.time() function.

walk(*top* [, *topdown* [, *onerror*]])

Creates a generator object that walks through a directory tree. *top* specifies the top of the directory and *topdown* is a Boolean that indicates whether to traverse directories in a top-down (the default) or bottom-up order. The returned generator produces tuples (*dirpath*, *dirnames*, *filenames*) where *dirpath* is a string containing the path to the directory, *dirnames* is a list of all subdirectories in *dirpath*, and *filenames* is a list of the files in *dirpath*, not including directories.

The *onerror* parameter is a function accepting a single argument. If any errors occur during processing, this function will be called with an instance of os.error. The default behavior is to ignore errors. If a directory is walked in a top-down manner, modifications to *dirnames* will affect the walking process. For example, if directories are removed from *dirnames*, those directories will be skipped. This function does not follow symbolic links.

Process Management

The following functions and variables are used to create, destroy, and manage processes:

abort()

Generates a SIGABRT signal that's sent to the calling process. Unless the signal is caught with a signal handler, the default is for the process to terminate with an error.

defpath

This variable contains the default search path used by the exec*p*() functions if the environment doesn't have a 'PATH' variable.

execl(*path, arg0, arg1, ...*)

Equivalent to execv(*path*, (*arg0*, *arg1*, ...)). Available on UNIX and Windows.

execle(*path, arg0, arg1, ..., env*)

Equivalent to execve(*path*, (*arg0*, *arg1*, ...), *env*). Available on UNIX and Windows.

execlp(*path, arg0, arg1, ...*)

Equivalent to execvp(*path*, (*arg0*, *arg1*, ...)). Available on UNIX and Windows.

execv(*path, args*)

Executes the program *path* with the argument list *args*, replacing the current process (that is, the Python interpreter). The argument list may be a tuple or list of strings (UNIX and Windows).

execve(*path, args, env*)

Executes a new program like execv(), but additionally accepts a dictionary, *env*, that defines the environment in which the program runs. *env* must be a dictionary mapping strings to strings (UNIX and Windows).

execvp(*path, args*)

Like execv(*path*, *args*), but duplicates the shell's actions in searching for an executable file in a list of directories. The directory list is obtained from environ['PATH']. Available on UNIX and Windows.

execvpe(*path, args, env*)

Like execvp(), but with an additional environment variable as in the execve() function (UNIX and Windows).

_exit(n)

Exits immediately to the system with status n, without performing any cleanup actions. This is typically only done in child processes created by fork(). This is also different than calling sys.exit(), which performs a graceful shutdown of the interpreter. The exit code n is application dependent, but a value of 0 usually indicates success, whereas a nonzero value indicates an error of some kind. Depending on the system, a number of standard exit code values may be defined:

Value	Description
EX_OK	No errors.
EX_USAGE	Incorrect command usage.
EX_DATAERR	Incorrect input data.
EX_NOINPUT	Missing input.
EX_NOUSER	User doesn't exist.
EX_NOHOST	Host doesn't exist.
EX_NOTFOUND	Not found.
EX_UNAVAILABLE	Service unavailable.
EX_SOFTWARE	Internal software error.
EX_OSERR	Operating system error.
EX_OSFILE	File system error.
EX_CANTCREAT	Can't create output.
EX_IOERR	I/O error.
EX_TEMPFAIL	Temporary failure.
EX_PROTOCOL	Protocol error.
EX_NOPERM	Insufficient permissions.
EX_CONFIG	Configuration error.

fork()

Creates a child process. Returns 0 in the newly created child process and the child's process ID in the original process. The child process is a clone of the original process and shares many resources such as open files (UNIX).

forkpty()

Creates a child process using a new pseudo-terminal as the child's controlling terminal. Returns a pair (*pid*, *fd*) in which *pid* is 0 in the child and *fd* is a file descriptor of the master end of the pseudo-terminal. This function is available only in certain versions of UNIX.

kill(*pid*, *sig*)

Sends the process *pid* the signal *sig*. A list of signal names can be found in the signal module (UNIX).

killpg(*pgid*, *sig*)

Sends the process group *pgid* the signal *sig*. A list of signal names can be found in the signal module (UNIX).

`nice(`*`increment`*`)`

Adds an increment to the scheduling priority (the "niceness") of the process. Returns the new niceness. Typically, users can only decrease the priority of a process, because increasing the priority requires root access. The effect of changing the priority is system dependent, but decreasing the priority is commonly done to make a process run in the background in a way such that it doesn't noticeably impact the performance of other processes (UNIX).

`plock(`*`op`*`)`

Locks program segments into memory, preventing them from being swapped. The value of *op* is an integer that determines which segments are locked. The value of *op* is platform-specific, but is typically one of UNLOCK, PROCLOCK, TXTLOCK, or DATLOCK. These constants are not defined by Python but might be found in the `<sys/lock.h>` header file. This function is not available on all platforms and often can be performed only by a process with an effective user ID of 0 (root). Available in UNIX.

`popen(`*`command`* `[,` *`mode`* `[,` *`bufsize`*`]])`

Opens a pipe to or from a command. The return value is an open file object connected to the pipe, which can be read or written depending on whether *mode* is `'r'` (the default) or `'w'`. *bufsize* has the same meaning as in the built-in `open()` function. The exit status of the command is returned by the `close()` method of the returned file object, except that when the exit status is zero, None is returned.

`popen2(`*`cmd`*`[,` *`bufsize`*`[,` *`mode`*`]])`

Executes *cmd* as a subprocess and returns the file objects (*child_stdin,* *child_ stdout*). *bufsize* is the buffer size. *mode* is `'t'` or `'b'` to indicate text or binary mode, which is needed on Windows.

`popen3(`*`cmd`*`[,` *`bufsize`*`[,` *`mode`*`]])`

Executes *cmd* as a subprocess and returns three file objects (*child_stdin, child_stdout, child_stderr*).

`popen4(`*`cmd`*`[,` *`bufsize`*`[,` *`mode`*`]])`

Executes *cmd* as a subprocess and returns two file objects (*child_stdin, child_ stdout_stderr*), in which the standard output and standard error of the child are combined.

`spawnv(`*`mode, path, args`*`)`

Executes the program *path* in a new process, passing the arguments specified in *args* as command-line parameters. *args* can be a list or a tuple. The first element of *args* should be the name of the program. *mode* is one of the following constants:

Constant	Description
P_WAIT	Executes the program and waits for it to terminate. Returns the program's exit code.
P_NOWAIT	Executes the program and returns the process handle.
P_NOWAITO	Same as P_NOWAIT.

Constant	Description
P_OVERLAY	Executes the program and destroys the calling process (same as the exec functions).
P_DETACH	Executes the program and detaches from it. The calling program continues to run but cannot wait for the spawned process.

spawnv() is available on Windows and some versions of UNIX.

spawnve(mode, path, args, env)

Executes the program path in a new process, passing the arguments specified in args as command-line parameters and the contents of the mapping env as the environment. args can be a list or a tuple. mode has the same meaning as described for spawnv(). Available on Windows and UNIX.

spawnl(mode, path, arg1, ..., argn)

The same as spawnv() except that all the arguments are supplied as extra parameters (UNIX and Windows).

spawnle(mode, path, arg1, ... , argn, env)

The same as spawnve() except that the arguments are supplied as parameters. The last parameter is a mapping containing the environment variables (UNIX and Windows).

spawnlp(mode, file, arg1, ... , argn)

The same as spawnl(), but looks for file using the settings of the PATH environment variable (UNIX).

spawnlpe(mode, file, arg1, ... , argn, env)

The same as spawnle(), but looks for file using the settings of the PATH environment variable (UNIX).

spawnvp(mode, file, args)

The same as spawnv(), but looks for file using the settings of the PATH environment variable (UNIX).

spawnvpe(mode, file, args, env)

The same as spawnve(), but looks for file using the settings of the PATH environment variable (UNIX).

startfile(path)

Launches the application associated with the file path. This performs the same action as would occur if you double-clicked the file in Windows Explorer. The function returns as soon as the application is launched. Furthermore, there is no way to wait for completion or to obtain exit codes from the application. path is a relative to the current directory (Windows).

system(command)

Executes command (a string) in a subshell. On UNIX, the return value is the exit status of the process as returned by wait(). On Windows, the exit code is always 0 (UNIX and Windows).

`times()`

Returns a 5-tuple of floating-point numbers indicating accumulated times in seconds. On UNIX, the tuple contains the user time, system time, children's user time, children's system time, and elapsed real time in that order. On Windows, the tuple contains the user time, system time, and zeros for the other three values. Available on UNIX and Windows, but not supported on Windows 95/98.

`wait()`

Waits for completion of a child process and returns a tuple containing its process ID and exit status. The exit status is a 16-bit number whose low byte is the signal number that killed the process and whose high byte is the exit status (if the signal number is zero). The high bit of the low byte is set if a core file was produced.

`waitpid(`*`pid, options`*`)`

Waits for a change in the state of a child process given by process ID *pid*, and returns a tuple containing its process ID and exit status indication, encoded as for `wait()`. *options* should be 0 for normal operation or `WNOHANG` to avoid hanging if no child process status is available immediately. This function can also be used to gather information about child processes that have only stopped executing for some reason. Setting *options* to `WCONTINUED` gathers information from a child when it resumes operation after being stopped via job control. Setting *options* to `WUNTRACED` gathers information from a child that has been stopped, but from which no status information has been reported yet.

The following functions take a process status code as returned by `waitpid()` and are used to examine the state of the process (UNIX only).

`WCOREDUMP(`*`status`*`)`

Returns `True` if the process dumped core.

`WIFEXITED(`*`status`*`)`

Returns `True` if the process exited using the `exit()` system call.

`WEXITSTATUS(`*`status`*`)`

If `WIFEXITED(`*`status`*`)` is true, the integer parameter to the `exit()` system call is returned. Otherwise, the return value is meaningless.

`WIFCONTINUED(`*`status`*`)`

Returns `True` if the process has resumed from a job-control stop.

`WIFSIGNALED(`*`status`*`)`

Returns `True` if the process exited due to a signal.

`WIFSTOPPED(`*`status`*`)`

Returns `True` if the process has been stopped.

`WSTOPSIG(`*`status`*`)`

Returns the signal that caused the process to stop.

`WTERMSIG(`*`status`*`)`

Returns the signal that caused the process to exit.

System Configuration

The following functions are used to obtain system configuration information:

`confstr(name)`

Returns a string-valued system configuration variable. *name* is a string specifying the name of the variable. The acceptable names are platform-specific, but a dictionary of known names for the host system is found in `os.confstr_names`. If a configuration value for a specified name is not defined, the empty string is returned. If *name* is unknown, `ValueError` is raised. An `OSError` may also be raised if the host system doesn't support the configuration name. The parameters returned by this function mostly pertain to the build environment on the host machine and include paths of system utilities, compiler options for various program configurations (for example, 32-bit, 64-bit, and large-file support), and linker options (UNIX).

`getloadavg()`

Returns a 3-tuple containing the average number of items in the system run-queue over the last 1, 5, and 15 minutes (UNIX).

`sysconf(name)`

Returns an integer-valued system-configuration variable. *name* is a string specifying the name of the variable. The names defined on the host system can be found in the dictionary `os.sysconf_names`. Returns `-1` if the configuration name is known but the value is not defined. Otherwise, a `ValueError` or `OSError` may be raised. Some systems may define well over 100 different system parameters. However, the following list details the parameters defined by POSIX.1 that should be available on most UNIX systems:

Parameter	Description
`"SC_ARG_MAX"`	Maximum length of the arguments that can be used with `exec()`.
`"SC_CHILD_MAX"`	Maximum number of processes per user ID.
`"SC_CLK_TCK"`	Number of clock ticks per second.
`"SC_NGROUPS_MAX"`	Maximum number of simultaneous supplementary group IDs.
`"SC_STREAM_MAX"`	Maximum number of streams a process can open at one time.
`"SC_TZNAME_MAX"`	Maximum number of bytes in a time zone name.
`"SC_OPEN_MAX"`	Maximum number of files a process can open at one time.
`"SC_JOB_CONTROL"`	System supports job control.
`"SC_SAVED_IDS"`	Indicates whether each process has a saved set-user-ID and a saved set-group-ID.

`urandom(n)`

Returns a string containing *n* random bytes generated by the system (for example, `/dev/urandom` on UNIX). The returned bytes are suitable for cryptography.

Exception

error

Exception raised when a function returns a system-related error. This is the same as the built-in exception OSError. The exception carries two values: errno and strerr. The first contains the integer error value as described for the errno module. The latter contains a string error message. For exceptions involving the file system, the exception also contains a third attribute, filename, which is the filename passed to the function.

Example

The following example uses the os module to implement a minimalistic UNIX shell that can run programs and perform I/O redirection:

```
import os, sys, string
print 'Welcome to the Python Shell!'
while 1:
    cmd = string.split(raw_input('pysh % '))
    if not cmd: continue
    progname = cmd[0]
    outfile = None
    infile = None
    args = [progname]
    for c in cmd[1:]:
        if c[0] == '>':
            outfile = c[1:]
        elif c[0] == '<':
            infile = c[1:]
        else:
            args.append(c)
    # Check for a change in working directory
    if progname == 'cd':
        if len(args) > 1:
            try:
                os.chdir(args[1])
            except OSError,e:
                print e
        continue
    # Exit from the shell
    if progname == 'exit':
        sys.exit(0)
    # Spawn a process to run the command
    pid = os.fork()
    if not pid:
        # Open input file (redirection)
        if infile:
            ifd = os.open(infile,os.O_RDONLY)
            os.dup2(ifd,sys.stdin.fileno())
        # Open output file (redirection)
        if outfile:
            ofd = os.open(outfile,os.O_WRONLY | os.O_CREAT | os.O_TRUNC)
            os.dup2(ofd,sys.stdout.fileno())
        # Run the command
        os.execvp(progname, args)
    else:
        childpid,ec = os.wait()
        if ec:
            print 'Exit code ',ec
```

Note

The os.popen2(), os.popen3(), and os.popen4() functions can also be found in the popen2 module. However, the order of the returned file objects is different.

See Also:

os.path (this page), stat (p. 338), statvfs (p. 339), time (p. 348), popen2 (p. 331), signal (p. 336), fcntl (p. 280)

os.path

The os.path module is used to manipulate pathnames in a portable manner. It's imported by the os module.

abspath(*path*)

Returns an absolute version of the pathname *path*, taking the current working directory into account. For example, abspath('../Python/foo') might return '/home/beazley/Python/foo'.

basename(*path*)

Returns the base name of pathname *path*. For example, basename('/usr/local/python') returns 'python'.

commonprefix(*list*)

Returns the longest string that's a prefix of all strings in *list*. If *list* is empty, the empty string is returned.

dirname(*path*)

Returns the directory name of pathname *path*. For example, dirname('/usr/local/python') returns '/usr/local'.

exists(*path*)

Returns True if *path* refers to an existing path. Returns False if *path* refers to a broken symbolic link.

expanduser(*path*)

Replaces pathnames of the form '~user' with a user's home directory. If the expansion fails or *path* does not begin with '~', the path is returned unmodified.

expandvars(*path*)

Expands environment variables of the form '$name' or '${name}' in *path*. Malformed or nonexistent variable names are left unchanged.

getatime(*path*)

Returns the time of last access as the number of seconds since the epoch (see the time module). The return value may be a floating-point number if os.stat_float_times() returns True.

getctime(*path*)

Returns the time of last modification on UNIX and the time of creation on Windows. The time is returned as the number of seconds since the epoch (see the `time` module). The return value may be a floating-point number in certain cases (see `getatime()`).

getmtime(*path*)

Returns the time of last modification as the number of seconds since the epoch (see the `time` module). The return value may be a floating-point number in certain cases (see `getatime()`).

getsize(*path*)

Returns the file size in bytes.

isabs(*path*)

Returns `True` if *path* is an absolute pathname (begins with a slash).

isfile(*path*)

Returns `True` if *path* is a regular file. This function follows symbolic links, so both `islink()` and `isfile()` can be true for the same path.

isdir(*path*)

Returns `True` if *path* is a directory. Follows symbolic links.

islink(*path*)

Returns `True` if *path* refers to a symbolic link. Returns `False` if symbolic links are unsupported.

ismount(*path*)

Returns `True` if *path* is a mount point.

join(*path1* [, *path2* [, ...]])

Intelligently joins one or more path components into a pathname. For example, `join('/ home', 'beazley', 'Python')` returns `'/home/beazley/Python'`.

lexists(*path*)

Returns `True` if *path* exists. Returns `True` for all symbolic links, even if the link is broken.

normcase(*path*)

Normalizes the case of a pathname. On non–case-sensitive file systems, this converts *path* to lowercase. On Windows, forward slashes are also converted to backslashes.

normpath(*path*)

Normalizes a pathname. This collapses redundant separators and up-level references so that `'A//B'`, `'A/./B'`, and `'A/foo/../B'` all become `'A/B'`. On Windows, forward slashes are converted to backslashes.

realpath(*path*)

Returns the real path of *path*, eliminating symbolic links if any (UNIX).

samefile(*path1, path2*)

Returns True if *path1* and *path2* refer to the same file or directory (UNIX).

sameopenfile(*fp1, fp2*)

Returns True if the open file objects *fp1* and *fp2* refer to the same file (UNIX).

samestat(*stat1, stat2*)

Returns True if the stat tuples *stat1* and *stat2* as returned by fstat(), lstat(), or stat() refer to the same file (UNIX).

split(*path*)

Splits *path* into a pair (*head, tail*), where *tail* is the last pathname component and *head* is everything leading up to that. For example, '/home/user/foo' gets split into ('/home/user', 'foo'). This tuple is the same as would be returned by (dirname(), basename()).

splitdrive(*path*)

Splits *path* into a pair (*drive, filename*) where *drive* is either a drive specification or the empty string. *drive* is always the empty string on machines without drive specifications.

splitext(*path*)

Splits a pathname into a base filename and suffix. For example, splitext('foo.txt') returns ('foo', '.txt').

splitunc(*path*)

Splits a pathname into a pair (*unc, rest*) where *unc* is a UNC (Universal Naming Convention) mount point and *rest* the remainder of the path (Windows).

supports_unicode_filenames

Variable set to True if the file system allows Unicode filenames.

walk(*path, visitfunc, arg*)

This function recursively walks all the directories rooted at *path* and calls the user-supplied function *visitfunc(arg, dirname, names)* for each directory. *dirname* specifies the visited directory, and *names* is a list of the files in the directory as retrieved using os.listdir(*dirname*). The *visitfunc* function can modify the contents of names to alter the search process if necessary. This function does not follow symbolic links.

> **Note**
> On Windows, some care is required when working with filenames that include a drive letter (for example, 'C:spam.txt'). In most cases, filenames are interpreted as being relative to the current working directory. For example, if the current directory is 'C:\Foo\', then the file 'C:spam.txt' is interpreted as the file 'C:\Foo\C:spam.txt', not the file 'C:\spam.txt'.

See Also:
fnmatch (**p. 252**), glob (**p. 253**), os (**p. 308**).

platform

The platform module contains functions for querying various aspects of the underlying platform on which Python is running. Unless specifically noted, these functions are available with all versions of Python.

architecture([executable, [bits [, linkage]]])

Returns a tuple (*bits*, *linkage*) containing information about how Python was built, where *bits* is a string containing information about the word size (for example, '32bit' or '64bit') and *linkage* contains information about linking of the Python executable. The *executable* parameter specifies a path to the Python interpreter and is sys.executable by default. The *bits* and *linkage* parameters specify default values to be returned if no information is available.

dist([distname [, version [, id [, supported_dists]]]])

Returns a tuple (*distname*, *version*, *id*) containing information about a Linux distribution—for example, ('debian','3.1',''). Available on UNIX only.

java_ver([release [, vendor [, vminfo [,osinfo]]]])

Returns a tuple (*release*, *vender*, *vminfo*, *osinfo*) containing version information related to JPython. *vminfo* is a tuple (*vm_name*, *vm_release*, *vm_vendor*) and *osinfo* is a tuple (*os_name*, *os_version*, *os_arch*). The parameters simply provide default values that are used if no information can be determined (Java only).

libc_ver([executable [, lib [, version [, chunksize]]]])

Returns information about the C library used by the Python interpreter. Returns a tuple such as ('glibc','2.3'). *executable* is a path to the Python interpreter and defaults to sys.executable. *lib* and *version* provide default values for the return result. Version information is obtained by reading the Python executable itself. *chunksize* determines the block size used for reading. Available on UNIX only and may only work if Python has been built using gcc.

mac_ver([release [, versioninfo [, machine]]])

Returns Macintosh version information as a tuple (*release*, *versioninfo*, *machine*), where *versioninfo* is a tuple (*version*, *dev_stage*, *non_release_version*). Available on Macintosh only.

machine()

Returns a string representing the machine type (for example, 'Power Macintosh', 'i686', or an empty string if it can't be determined).

node()

Returns a string with the hostname or an empty string if can't be determined.

`platform([`*`aliased`* `[,` *`terse`*`]])`

Returns a descriptive string representing the platform, such as `'Darwin-8.2.0-`
`Power_Macintosh-powerpc-32bit'`. If *`aliased`* is True, an alternative system name
may be used instead (for example, `'Solaris'` instead of `'SunOS''SunOS'`). If *`terse`* is
True, a shortened string is returned (for example `'Darwin-8.2.0'`).

`popen(`*`cmd,`* `[`*`mode`* `[,` *`bufsize`*`]])`

A portable implementation of the popen() system call for use on Windows 95/98. See
os.popen() for more details.

`processor()`

Returns a string describing the processor (for example, `'powerpc'`).

`python_build()`

Returns a tuple (*`buildnum,`* *`builddate`*) describing Python build information—for
example (2, `'Mar 31 2005 00:05:10'`).

`python_compiler()`

Returns a string describing the compiler used to build Python—for example, `'GCC 3.3`
`20030304 (Apple Computer, Inc. build 1666)'`.

`python_version()`

Returns a string describing the Python version (for example, `'2.4.1'`).

`python_version_tuple()`

Returns Python version information as a list containing version number components
(for example, `['2','4','1']`).

`release()`

Returns the system release number as a string (for example, `'8.2.0'` or `'XP'`).

`system()`

Returns the name of the operating system (for example, `'Windows'`, `'Darwin'`, or
`'Linux'`).

`system_alias(`*`system, release, version`*`)`

Takes system, release, and version information and converts it to commonly used system
names more associated with marketing (for example, `'SunOS'` vs. `'Solaris'`). Returns
a tuple (*`system, release, version`*) with updated information, if any.

`version()`

Returns a string representing system release information (for example, `'Darwin`
`Kernel Version 8.2.0: Fri Jun 24 17:46:54 PDT 2005; root:xnu-`
`792.2.4.obj~3/RELEASE_PPC'`).

`win32_ver([`*`release`* `[,` *`version`* `[,` *`csd`* `[,` *`ptype`* `]]]])`

Returns version information related to Windows (PythonWin only).

uname()

Returns a tuple (*system, node, release, version, machine, processor*) with system information. Entries that can't be determined are set to the empty string `''`. Similar to the `os.uname()` function.

popen2

The popen2 module is used to spawn processes and connect to their input/output/ error streams using pipes on UNIX and Windows. Note that these functions are also available in the os module with slightly different return values.

popen2(cmd [, bufsize [, mode]])

Executes *cmd* as a subprocess and returns a pair of file objects (*child_stdout, child_stdin*) corresponding to the input and output streams of the subprocess. *bufsize* specifies the buffer size for the I/O pipes. *mode* is one of `'t'` or `'b'` to indicate text or binary data, which is needed on Windows.

popen3(cmd [, bufsize [, mode]])

Executes cmd as a subprocess like popen2(), but returns a triple (*child_stdout, child_stdin, child_stderr*) that includes the standard error stream.

popen4(cmd [, bufsize [.mode]])

Executes *cmd* as a subprocess like popen2(), but returns a pair of file objects (*child_stdout_stderr, child_stdin*) in which the standard output and standard error streams have been combined.

In addition to the functions just described, the UNIX version of this module provides the following classes that can be used to control processes:

Popen3(cmd [, capturestderr [, bufsize]])

This class represents a child process. *cmd* is the shell command to execute in a subprocess. The *capturestderr* flag, if true, specifies that the object should capture standard error output of the child process. *bufsize* is the size of the I/O buffers (UNIX).

Popen4(cmd [, bufsize])

Like the class Popen3, but combines standard output and standard error (UNIX).

An instance, *p*, of the Popen3 or Popen4 class has the following methods and attributes:

p.poll()

Returns the exit code of the child or -1 if the child process has not finished yet.

p.wait()

Waits for the child process to terminate and returns its exit code.

p.fromchild

A file object that captures the output of the child process.

p.tochild

A file object that sends input to the child process.

p.**childerr**

A file object that captures the standard error stream of the child process. May be None.

p.**pid**

Process ID of the child.

> **Note**
> The order of file objects returned by popen2(), popen3(), and popen4() differ from the standard UNIX ordering of stdin, stdout, and stderr. The versions in the os module correct this.

> **See Also:**
> commands (p. 265), os.popen (p. 321), subprocess (p. 340)

pwd

The pwd module provides access to the UNIX password database.

getpwuid(*uid*)

Returns the password database entry for a numeric user ID, *uid*. Returns a password structure with the following attributes:

- pw_name—The login name
- pw_passwd—The encrypted password (optional)
- pw_uid—The numerical user ID
- pw_gid—The numerical group ID
- pw_gecos—The username or comment field
- pw_dir—The user home directory
- pw_shell—The user shell

For backward compatibility, the returned object also behaves like a 7-tuple (*pw_name*, *pw_passwd*, *pw_uid*, *pw_gid*, *pw_gecos*, *pw_dir*, *pw_shell*). KeyError is raised if the entry cannot be found.

getpwnam(*name*)

Returns the password database entry for a username.

getpwall()

Returns a list of all available password database entries. Each entry is a tuple as returned by getpwuid().

Example

```
>>> import pwd
>>> pwd.getpwnam('beazley')
('beazley', 'x', 100, 1, 'David M. Beazley', '/home/beazley',
 '/usr/local/bin/tcsh')
>>>
```

> **See Also:**
> `grp` (p. 283), `getpass` (p. 283), `crypt` (p. 266)

resource

The `resource` module is used to measure and control the system resources used by a program on UNIX systems. Resource usage is limited using the `setrlimit()` function. Each resource is controlled by a soft limit and a hard limit. The soft limit is the current limit and may be lowered or raised by a process over time. The hard limit can be lowered to any value greater than the soft limit, but never raised (except by the superuser).

getrlimit(*resource*)

Returns a tuple (*soft*, *hard*) with the current soft and hard limits of a resource. *resource* is one of the following symbolic constants:

Constant	Description
RLIMIT_CORE	The maximum core file size (in bytes).
RLIMIT_CPU	The maximum CPU time (in seconds). If exceeded, a SIGXCPU signal is sent to the process.
RLIMIT_FSIZE	The maximum file size that can be created.
RLIMIT_DATA	The maximum size (in bytes) of the process heap.
RLIMIT_STACK	The maximum size (in bytes) of the process stack.
RLIMIT_RSS	The maximum resident set size.
RLIMIT_NPROC	The maximum number of processes that can be created.
RLIMIT_NOFILE	The maximum number of open file descriptors.
RLIMIT_OFILE	The BSD name for RLIMIT_NOFILE.
RLIMIT_MEMLOC	The maximum memory size that can be locked in memory.
RLIMIT_VMEM	The largest area of mapped memory that can be used.
RLIMIT_AS	The maximum area (in bytes) of address space that can be used.

setrlimit(*resource*, *limits*)

Sets new limits for a resource. *resource* is one of the constants described for `getrlimit()`. *limits* is a tuple (*soft*, *hard*) of two integers describing the new limits. A value of -1 can be used to specify the maximum possible upper limit.

getrusage(*who*)

This function returns an object that describes the resources consumed by either the current process or its children. *who* is one of the following values:

Value	Description
RUSAGE_SELF	Information about the current process
RUSAGE_CHILDREN	Information about child processes
RUSAGE_BOTH	Information about both current and child processes

The returned object r has the following attributes:

Attribute	Resource
r.ru_utime	Time in user mode (float)
r.ru_stime	Time in system mode (float)
r.ru_maxrss	Maximum resident set size (pages)
r.ru_ixrss	Shared memory size (pages)
r.ru_idrss	Unshared memory size (pages)
r.ru_isrss	Unshared stack size (pages)
r.ru_minflt	Page faults not requiring I/O
r.ru_majflt	Page faults requiring I/O
r.ru_nswap	Number of swapouts
r.ru_inblock	Block input operations
r.ru_oublock	Block output operations
r.ru_msgsnd	Messages sent
r.ru_msgrcv	Messages received
r.ru_nsignals	Signals received
r.ru_nvcsw	Voluntary context switches
r.ru_nivcsw	Involuntary context switches

For backward compatibility, the returned value r also behaves like a 16-tuple containing the fields in the same order as listed here.

`getpagesize()`

Returns the number of bytes in a system page.

Exception

`error`

Exception raised for unexpected failures of the `getrlimit()` and `setrlimit()` system calls.

Note
Not all resource names are available on all systems.

See Also:
UNIX man pages for `getrlimit(2)`

shutil

The `shutil` module is used to perform high-level file operations such as copying, removing, and renaming.

`copy(src,dst)`

Copies the file `src` to the file or directory `dst`, retaining file permissions. `src` and `dst` are strings.

`copy2(src, dst)`

Like `copy()`, but also copies the last access and modification times.

`copyfile(src, dst)`

Copies the contents of `src` to `dst`. `src` and `dst` are strings.

`copyfileobj(f1, f2 [, length])`

Copies all data from open file object `f1` to open file object `f2`. `length` specifies a maximum buffer size to use. A negative length will attempt to copy the data entirely with one operation (that is, all data will be read as a single chunk and then written).

`copymode(src, dst)`

Copies the permission bits from `src` to `dst`.

`copystat(src, dst)`

Copies the permission bits, last access time, and last modification time from `src` to `dst`. The contents, owner, and group of `dst` are unchanged.

`copytree(src, dst [, symlinks])`

Recursively copies an entire directory tree rooted at `src`. The destination directory `dst` will be created (and should not already exist). Individual files are copied using `copy2()`. If `symlinks` is true, symbolic links in the source tree are represented as symbolic links in the new tree. If `symlinks` is false or omitted, the contents of linked files are copied to the new directory tree. If an error occurs, the `Error` exception is raised.

`move(src, dst)`

Moves file or directory `src` to `dst`. Will recursively copy `src` if it is being moved to a different file system.

`rmtree(path [, ignore_errors [, onerror]])`

Deletes an entire directory tree. If `ignore_errors` is true, errors will be ignored. Otherwise, errors are handled by the `onerror` function (if supplied). This function must accept three parameters (`func`, `path`, and `excinfo`), where `func` is the function that caused the error (`os.remove()` or `os.rmdir()`), `path` is the pathname passed to the function, and `excinfo` is the exception information returned by `sys.exc_info()`. If an error occurs and `onerror` is omitted, an exception is raised.

Exception

`Error`

Exception raised when errors occur during operations involving multiple files. The exception argument is a list of tuples containing (`srcname, dstname, exception`).

See Also:
os.path (p. 326)

signal

The signal module is used to write signal handlers in Python. Signals usually correspond to asynchronous events that are sent to a program due to the expiration of a timer, arrival of incoming data, or some action performed by a user. The signal interface emulates that of UNIX, although parts of the module are supported on other platforms.

alarm(*time*)

If *time* is nonzero, a SIGALRM signal is scheduled to be sent to the program in *time* seconds. Any previously scheduled alarm is canceled. If *time* is zero, no alarm is scheduled and any previously set alarm is canceled. Returns the number of seconds remaining before any previously scheduled alarm, or zero if no alarm was scheduled (UNIX).

getsignal(*signalnum*)

Returns the signal handler for signal *signalnum*. The returned object is a callable Python object. The function may also return SIG_IGN for an ignored signal, SIG_DFL for the default signal handler, or None if the signal handler was not installed from the Python interpreter.

pause()

Goes to sleep until the next signal is received (UNIX).

signal(*signalnum, handler*)

Sets a signal handler for signal *signalnum* to the function *handler*. *handler* must be a callable Python object taking two arguments: the signal number and frame object. SIG_IGN or SIG_DFL can also be given to ignore a signal or use the default signal handler, respectively. The return value is the previous signal handler, SIG_IGN, or SIG_DFL. When threads are enabled, this function can only be called from the main thread. Otherwise, a ValueError exception is raised.

Individual signals are identified using symbolic constants of the form SIG*. These names correspond to integer values that are machine-specific. Typical values are as follows:

Signal Name	Description
SIGABRT	Abnormal termination
SIGALRM	Alarm
SIGBUS	Bus error
SIGCHLD	Change in child status
SIGCLD	Change in child status
SIGCONT	Continue
SIGFPE	Floating-point error
SIGHUP	Hang up
SIGILL	Illegal instruction

Signal Name	Description
SIGINT	Terminal interrupt character
SIGIO	Asynchronous I/O
SIGIOT	Hardware fault
SIGKILL	Terminate
SIGPIPE	Write to pipe, no readers
SIGPOLL	Pollable event
SIGPROF	Profiling alarm
SIGPWR	Power failure
SIGQUIT	Terminal quit character
SIGSEGV	Segmentation fault
SIGSTOP	Stop
SIGTERM	Termination
SIGTRAP	Hardware fault
SIGTSTP	Terminal stop character
SIGTTIN	Control TTY
SIGTTOU	Control TTY
SIGURG	Urgent condition
SIGUSR1	User defined
SIGUSR2	User defined
SIGVTALRM	Virtual time alarm
SIGWINCH	Window size change
SIGXCPU	CPU limit exceeded
SIGXFSZ	File size limit exceeded

In addition, the module defines the following variables:

Variable	Description
SIG_DFL	Signal handler that invokes the default signal handler
SIG_IGN	Signal handler that ignores a signal
NSIG	One more than the highest signal number

Example

The following example illustrates a timeout on establishing a network connection:

```
import signal, socket
def handler(signum, frame):
    print 'Timeout!'
    raise IOError, 'Host not responding.'
sock = socket.socket(socket.AF_INET, socket.SOCK_STREAM)
signal.signal(signal.SIGALRM, handler)
signal.alarm(5)                        # 5-second alarm
sock.connect('www.python.org', 80)     # Connect
signal.alarm(0)                        # Clear alarm
```

Notes

- Signal handlers remain installed until explicitly reset, with the exception of SIGCHLD (whose behavior is implementation-specific).
- It's not possible to temporarily disable signals.
- Signals are only handled between the atomic instructions of the Python interpreter. The delivery of a signal can be delayed by long-running calculations written in C (as might be performed in an extension module).
- If a signal occurs during an I/O operation, the I/O operation may fail with an exception. In this case, the errno value is set to errno.EINTR to indicate an interrupted system call.
- Certain signals such as SIGSEGV cannot be handled from Python.
- Python installs a small number of signal handlers by default. SIGPIPE is ignored, SIGINT is translated into a KeyboardInterrupt exception, and SIGTERM is caught in order to perform cleanup and invoke sys.exitfunc.
- Extreme care is needed if signals and threads are used in the same program. Currently, only the main thread of execution can set new signal handlers or receive signals.
- Signal handling on Windows is of only limited functionality. The number of supported signals is extremely limited on this platform.

See Also:
thread (p. 356), errno (p. 275)

stat

The stat module defines constants and functions for interpreting the results of os.stat(), os.fstat(), and os.lstat(). These functions return a 10-tuple containing file information. The following variables define the indices within the tuple for certain items and are listed in the order in which they commonly appear in the tuple:

Variable	Description
ST_MODE	Inode protection mode
ST_INO	Inode number
ST_DEV	Device the inode resides on
ST_NLINK	Number of links to the inode
ST_UID	User ID of the owner
ST_GID	Group ID of the owner
ST_SIZE	File size in bytes
ST_ATIME	Time of last access
ST_MTIME	Time of last modification
ST_CTIME	Time of last status change

The following functions can be used to test file properties given the mode value returned using os.stat(path)[stat.ST_MODE]:

Function	Description
S_ISDIR(*mode*)	Returns nonzero if *mode* is from a directory.
S_ISCHR(*mode*)	Returns nonzero if *mode* is from a character-special device file.
S_ISBLK(*mode*)	Returns nonzero if *mode* is from a block-special device file.
S_ISREG(*mode*)	Returns nonzero if *mode* is from a regular file.
S_ISFIFO(*mode*)	Returns nonzero if *mode* is from a FIFO (named pipe).
S_ISLNK(*mode*)	Returns nonzero if *mode* is from a symbolic link.
S_ISSOCK(*mode*)	Returns nonzero if *mode* is from a socket.
S_IMODE(*mode*)	Returns the portion of the file's mode that can be set by os.chmod(). This is the file's permission bits, sticky bit, set-group-ID, and set-user-ID bits.
S_IFMT(*mode*)	Returns the portion of the file's mode that describes the file type (used by the S_IS*() functions, discussed earlier).

Note

Much of the functionality in this module is also provided in a more portable form by the os.path module.

See Also:

os (p. 308), os.path (p. 326), statvfs (p. 339)

statvfs

The statvfs module defines constants used to interpret the result of the os.statvfs() function on UNIX. The constants defined in this module define the indices into the tuple returned by os.statvfs() for specific information. Constants are listed in the order that items commonly appear in the statvfs tuple.

Constant	Description
F_BSIZE	Preferred file system block size
F_FRSIZE	Fundamental file system block size
F_BLOCKS	Total number of blocks in the file system
F_BFREE	Total number of free blocks
F_BAVAIL	Free blocks available to a non-superuser
F_FILES	Total number of file nodes
F_FFREE	Total number of free file nodes

Constant	Description
F_FAVAIL	Free nodes available to a non-superuser
F_FLAG	Flags (system-dependent)
F_NAMEMAX	Maximum filename length

See Also:
os (p. 308), stat (p. 338)

subprocess

The subprocess module contains functions and objects that generalize the task of creating new processes, controlling input and output streams, and handling return codes. The module centralizes functionality contained in a variety of other modules such as os, popen2, and commands.

Popen(*args*, ***parms*)

Executes a new command as a subprocess and returns a Popen object representing the new process. The command is specified in *args* as either a string, such as 'ls -l', or as a list of strings, such as ['ls', '-l']. *parms* represents a collection of keyword arguments that can be set to control various properties of the subprocess. The following keyword parameters are understood:

Keyword	Description
bufsize	Specifies the buffering behavior, where 0 is unbuffered, 1 is line-buffered, a negative value uses the system default, and other positive values specify the approximate buffer size. The default value is 0.
close_fds	If True, all file descriptors except 0, 1, and 2 are closed prior to execution of the child process. The default value is False.
creation_flags	Specifies process-creation flags on Windows. The only flag currently available is CREATE_NEW_CONSOLE. The default value is 0.
cwd	The directory in which the command will execute. The current directory of the child process is changed to cwd prior to execution. The default value is None, which uses the current directory of the parent process.
env	Dictionary of environment variables for the new process. The default value is None, which uses the environment variables of the parent process.
executable	Specifies the name of the executable program to use. This is rarely needed because the program name is already included in *args*. If shell has been given, this parameter specifies the name of the shell to use. The default value is None.

Keyword	Description
preexec_fn	Specifies a function that will be called in the child process just before the command is executed. The function should take no arguments.
shell	If True, the command is executed using the UNIX shell like the os.system() function. The default shell is /bin/sh, but this can be changed by also setting executable. The default value of shell is None.
startupinfo	Provides startup flags used when creating processes on Windows. The default value is None. Possible values include STARTF_USESHOWWINDOW and STARTF_USESTDHANDLERS.
stderr	File object representing the file to use for stderr in the child process. May be a file object created via open(), an integer file descriptor, or the special value PIPE, which indicates that a new pipe should be created. The default value is None.
stdin	File object representing the file to use for stdin in the child process. May be set to the same values as stderr. The default value is None.
stdout	File object representing the file to use for stdout in the child process. May be set to the same values as stderr. The default value is None.
universal_newlines	If True, the files representing stdin, stdout, and stderr are opened in text mode with universal newline mode enabled. See the open() function for a full description.

call(*args*, **parms*)

This function is exactly the same as Popen(), except that it simply executes the command and returns its return code instead (that is, it does not return a Popen object). This function is useful if you just want to execute a command but are not concerned with capturing its output or controlling it in other ways. The parameters have the same meaning as with Popen().

The Popen object *p* returned by Popen() has a variety of methods and attributes that can be used for interacting with the subprocess.

p.communicate([*input*])

Communicates with the child process by sending the data supplied in *input* to the standard input of the process. Once data is sent, the method waits for the process to terminate while collecting output received on standard output and standard error. Returns a tuple (*stdout*, *stderr*) where *stdout* and *stderr* are strings. If no data is sent to the child process, *input* is set to None (the default).

p.poll()

Checks to see if *p* has terminated. If so, the return code is returned. Otherwise, None is returned.

p.wait()

Waits for *p* to terminate and returns the return code.

p.pid

Process ID of the child process.

p.returncode

Numeric return code of the process. If None, the process has not terminated yet. If negative, it indicates the process was terminated by a signal (UNIX).

p.stdin, p.stdout, p.stderr

These three attributes are set to open file objects whenever the corresponding I/O stream is opened as a pipe (for example, setting the *stdout* argument in Popen() to PIPE). These file objects are provided so that the pipe can be connected to other subprocesses. These attributes are set to None if pipes are not in use.

Examples

```
# Execute a basic system command.  Like os.system()
ret = subprocess.call("ls -l", shell=True)

# Execute a system command, but capture the output
p = subprocess.Popen("ls -l", shell=True, stdout=subprocess.PIPE)
out = p.stdout.read()

# Execute a command, but send input and receive output
p = subprocess.Popen("wc", shell=True, stdin=subprocess.PIPE,
                     stdout=subprocess.PIPE, stderr=subprocess.PIPE)
out, err = p.communicate(s)    # Send string s to the process

# Create two subprocesses and link them together via pipe
p1 = subprocess.Popen("ls -l", shell=True, stdout=subprocess.PIPE)
p2 = subprocess.Popen("wc",shell=True, stdin=p1.stdout,
                     stdout=subprocess.PIPE)
out = p2.stdout.read()
```

tempfile

The tempfile module is used to generate temporary filenames and files.

mkdtemp([suffix [,prefix [, dir]]])

Creates a temporary directory accessible only by the owner of the calling process and returns its absolute pathname. *suffix* is an optional suffix that will be appended to the directory name, *prefix* is an optional prefix that will be inserted at the beginning of the directory name, and *dir* is a directory where the temporary directory should be created.

mkstemp([suffix [,prefix [, dir [,text]]]])

Creates a temporary file and returns a tuple (*fd, pathname*) where *fd* is an integer file descriptor returned by os.open() and *pathname* is absolute pathname of the file. *suffix* is an optional suffix appended to the filename, *prefix* is an optional prefix inserted at the beginning of the filename, *dir* is the directory in which the file should be created, and *text* is a Boolean flag that indicates whether to open the file in text mode or binary mode (the default). The creation of the file is guaranteed to be atomic (and secure) provided that the system supports the `O_EXCL` flag for `os.open()`.

mktemp([suffix [, prefix [,dir]]])

Returns a unique temporary filename. `suffix` is an optional file suffix to append to the filename, `prefix` is an optional prefix inserted at the beginning of the filename, and `dir` is the directory in which the file is created. This function only generates a unique filename and doesn't actually create or open a temporary file. Because this function generates a name before the file is actually opened, it introduces a potential security problem. To address this, consider using `mkstemp()` instead.

gettempdir()

Returns the directory in which temporary files are created.

gettempprefix()

Returns the prefix used to generate temporary files. Does not include the directory in which the file would reside.

TemporaryFile([mode [, bufsize [, suffix [,prefix [, dir]]]]])

Creates a temporary file using `mkstemp()` and returns a file-like object that supports the same methods as an ordinary file object. `mode` is the file mode and defaults to `'w+b'`. `bufsize` specifies the buffering behavior and has the same meaning as for the `open()` function. `suffix`, `prefix`, and `dir` have the same meaning as for `mkstemp()`. The object returned by this function is only a wrapper around a built-in file object that's accessible in the file attribute. The file created by this function is automatically destroyed when the temporary file object is destroyed.

NamedTemporaryFile([mode [, bufsize [, suffix [,prefix [, dir]]]]])

Creates a temporary file just like `TemporaryFile()`, but makes sure the filename is visible on the file system. The filename can be obtained by accessing the name attribute of the returned file object. Note that certain systems may prevent the file from being re-opened using this name until the temporary file has been closed.

Two global variables are used to construct temporary names. They can be assigned to new values if desired. Their default values are system-dependent.

Variable	Description
tempdir	The directory in which filenames returned by mktemp() reside.
template	The prefix of filenames generated by mktemp(). A string of decimal digits is added to template to generate unique filenames.

> **Note**
>
> By default, the `tempfile` module creates files by checking a few standard locations. For example, on UNIX, files are created in one of `/tmp`, `/var/tmp`, or `/usr/tmp`. On Windows, files are created in one of `C:\TEMP`, `C:\TMP`, `\TEMP`, or `\TMP`. These directories can be overridden by setting one or more of the TMPDIR, TEMP, and TMP environment variables. If, for whatever reason, temporary files can't be created in any of the usual locations, they will be created in the current working directory.

termios

The `termios` module provides a POSIX-style interface for controlling the behavior of TTYs and other serial communication devices on UNIX systems. All the functions operate on integer file descriptors such as those returned by the `os.open()` function or the `fileno()` method of a file object. In addition, the module relies on a large collection of constants that are also defined in this module.

tcgetattr(fd)

Returns a list [`iflag`, `oflag`, `cflag`, `lflag`, `ispeed`, `ospeed`, `cc`] of TTY attributes for a file descriptor, `fd`. The meaning of these fields is as follows:

Field	Description
iflag	Input modes (integer)
oflag	Output modes (integer)
cflag	Control modes (integer)
lflag	Local modes (integer)
ispeed	Input speed (integer)
ospeed	Output speed (integer)
cc	A list of control characters (as strings)

The mode fields `iflag`, `oflag`, `cflag`, and `lflag` are bit fields that are interpreted using constants that appear in the tables that follow.

Input Modes

The following constants are used to interpret the `iflag` bit field:

Mode	Description
IGNBRK	Ignore break condition on input.
BRKINT	Generate SIGINT signal on break if IGNBRK is not set.
IGNPAR	Ignore framing and parity errors.
PARMRK	Mark characters with a parity error.
INPCK	Enable input parity checking.
ISTRIP	Strip off the eighth bit.
INLCR	Translate newlines to carriage returns.
IGNCR	Ignore carriage returns.
ICRNL	Translate carriage returns to newlines.
IUCLC	Map uppercase characters to lowercase.
IXON	Enable XON/XOFF flow control on output.
IXANY	Enable any character to restart output.
IXOFF	Enable XON/XOFF flow control on input.
IXMAXBEL	Ring bell when the input queue is full.

Output Modes

The following constants are used to interpret the *oflag* bit field:

Mode	Description
OPOST	Implementation-defined output processing.
OLCUC	Map lowercase to uppercase on output.
ONLCR	Map newlines to carriage returns.
OCRNL	Map carriage returns to newlines.
ONLRET	Don't output carriage returns.
OFILL	Send fill characters for delay.
OFDEL	Set the fill character to ASCII DEL.
NLDLY	Newline delay mask. Values are NL0 and NL1.
CRDLY	Carriage return delay mask. Values are CR0, CR1, CR2, and CR3.
TABDLY	Horizontal tab delay mask: TAB0, TAB1, TAB2, TAB3, or XTABS.
BSDLY	Backspace delay mask: BS0 or BS1.
VTDLY	Vertical tab delay mask: VT0 or VT1.
FFDLY	Formfeed delay mask: FF0 or FF1.

Control Modes

The following constants are used to interpret the *cflag* bit field:

Mode	Description
CSIZE	Character size mask: CS5, CS6, CS7, or CS8.
CSTOPB	Set two stop bits.
CREAD	Enable receiver.
PARENB	Enable parity generation and checking.
PARODD	Use odd parity.
HUPCL	Lower modem control lines when device is closed.
CLOCAL	Ignore modem control lines.
CRTSCTS	Flow control.

Local Modes

The following constants are used to interpret the *lflag* bit field:

Mode	Description
ISIG	Generate corresponding signals when INTR, QUIT, SUSP, or DSUSP characters are received.
ICANON	Enable canonical mode.
XCASE	Perform case conversion if ICANON is set.
ECHO	Echo input characters.

Mode	Description
ECHOE	If ICANON is set, the ERASE character erases the preceding input character. WERASE erases the preceding word.
ECHOK	If ICANON is set, the KILL character erases the current line.
ECHONL	If ICANON is set, echo newline (NL) characters.
ECHOCTL	If ECHO is set, echo control characters as ^X.
ECHOPRT	Print characters as they're erased.
ECHOKE	Echo KILL by erasing each character one at a time.
FLUSHO	Output is being flushed.
NOFLSH	Disable flushing the input/output queues when generating the SIGINT and SIGQUIT signals.
TOSTOP	Send the SIGTTOU signal to the process group of a background process that writes its controlling terminal.
PENDIN	Reprint all characters in the input queue when the next character is typed.
IEXTEN	Enable implementation-defined input processing.

Speeds

Speeds are defined by constants such as B0, B50, B75, and B230400 indicating a baud rate. The available values are implementation-specific.

Control Characters

The following constants are indices into the cc list. These can be used to change various key bindings.

Character	Description
VINTR	Interrupt character (typically Ctrl+C).
VQUIT	Quit.
VERASE	Erase the preceding character (typically Del).
VWERASE	Erase the preceding word (Ctrl+W).
VKILL	Delete the entire line.
VREPRINT	Reprint all characters that have not been read yet.
VEOF	End of file (Ctrl+D).
VNL	Line delimiter (line feed).
VSUSP	Suspend (Ctrl+Z).
VSTOP	Stop output (Ctrl+S).
VSTART	Start output (Ctrl+Q).

tcsetattr(fd, when, attributes)

Sets the TTY attributes for a file descriptor, fd. attributes is a list in the same form as returned by tcgetattr(). The when argument determines when the changes take effect and is one of the following constants:

Argument	Description
TCSANOW	Changes take place immediately.
TCSADRAIN	After transmitting queued output.
TCSAFLUSH	After transmitting queued output and discarding queued input.

`tcsendbreak(fd, duration)`

Sends a break on file descriptor `fd`. A duration of zero sends a break for approximately 0.25–0.5 seconds. A nonzero duration is implementation-defined.

`tcdrain(fd)`

Waits until all output written to file descriptor `fd` has been transmitted.

`tcflush(fd, queue)`

Discards queued data on file descriptor `fd`. `queue` determines which data to discard and is one of the following constants:

Queue	Description
TCIFLUSH	Input queue
TCOFLUSH	Output queue
TCIOFLUSH	Both queues

`tcflow(fd, action)`

Suspends or resumes input or output on file descriptor `fd`. `action` is one of the following:

Action	Description
TCOOFF	Suspends output
TCOON	Restarts output
TCIOFF	Suspends input
TCION	Restarts input

Example

The following function prompts for a password with local echoing turned off:

```
def getpass():
    import termios, sys
    fd = sys.stdin.fileno()
    tc = termios.tcgetattr(fd)
    old = tc[3] & termios.ECHO
    tc[3] = tc[3] & ~termios.ECHO          # Disable echo
    try:
        termios.tcsetattr(fd, termios.TCSADRAIN, tc)
        passwd = raw_input('Password: ')
    finally:
        tc[3] = tc[3] | old                # Restore old echo setting
        termios.tcsetattr(fd, termios.TCSADRAIN, tc)
    return passwd
```

See Also:
tty (p. 351), getpass (p. 283), signal (p. 336)

time

The time module provides various time-related functions. In Python, time is measured as the number of seconds since the "epoch." The epoch is the beginning of time (the point at which time = 0 seconds). The epoch is January 1, 1970 on UNIX and can be determined by calling time.gmtime(0) on other systems.

The following variables are defined:

accept2dyear

A Boolean value that indicates whether two-digit years are accepted. Normally this is True, but it's set to False if the environment variable $PYTHONY2K is set to a non-empty string. The value can be changed manually as well.

altzone

The time zone used during daylight saving time (DST), if applicable.

daylight

Is set to a nonzero value if a DST time zone has been defined.

timezone

The local (non-DST) time zone.

tzname

A tuple containing the name of the local time zone and the name of the local daylight saving time zone (if defined).

The following functions can be used:

asctime([*tuple*])

Converts a tuple representing a time as returned by gmtime() or localtime() to a string of the form 'Mon Jul 12 14:45:23 1999'. If no arguments are supplied, the current time is used.

clock()

Returns the current CPU time in seconds as a floating-point number.

ctime([*secs*])

Converts a time expressed in seconds since the epoch to a string representing local time. ctime(*secs*) is the same as asctime(localtime(*secs*)). If *secs* is omitted or None, the current time is used.

gmtime([*secs*])

Converts a time expressed in seconds since the epoch to a time in UTC Coordinated Universal Time (a.k.a. Greenwich Mean Time). This function returns a struct_time object with the following attributes:

Attribute	Value
tm_year	A four-digit value such as 1998
tm_mon	1-12
tm_mday	131
tm_hour	023
tm_min	059
tm_sec	061
tm_wday	06 (0=Monday)
tm_yday	1366
tm_isdst	-1, 0, 1

The tm_isdst attribute is 1 if daylight saving time is in effect, 0 if not, and -1 if no information is available. If *secs* is omitted or None, the current time is used. For backward compatibility, the returned struct_time object also behaves like a 9-tuple containing the preceding attribute values in the same order as listed.

localtime([*secs*])

Returns a struct_time object as with gmtime(), but corresponding to the local time zone. If *secs* is omitted or None, the current time is used.

mktime(*tuple*)

This function takes a struct_time object or tuple representing a time in the local time zone (in the same format as returned by localtime()) and returns a floating-point number representing the number of seconds since the epoch. An OverflowError exception is raised if the input value is not a valid time.

sleep(*secs*)

Puts the current process to sleep for *secs* seconds. *secs* is a floating-point number.

strftime(*format* [, *tm*])

Converts a struct_time object *tm* representing a time as returned by gmtime() or localtime() to a string. (For backward compatibility, tm may also be a tuple representing a time value.) *format* is a format string in which the following format codes can be embedded:

Directive	Meaning
%a	Locale's abbreviated weekday name
%A	Locale's full weekday name
%b	Locale's abbreviated month name
%B	Locale's full month name
%c	Locale's appropriate date and time representation
%d	Day of the month as a decimal number [01-31]
%H	Hour (24-hour clock) as a decimal number [00-23]
%I	Hour (12-hour clock) as a decimal number [01-12]
%j	Day of the year as a decimal number [001-366]

Directive	Meaning
%m	Month as a decimal number [01-12]
%M	Minute as a decimal number [00-59]
%p	Locale's equivalent of either AM or PM
%S	Seconds as a decimal number [00-61]
%U	Week number of the year [00-53] (Sunday as first day)
%w	Weekday as a decimal number [0-6] (0 = Sunday)
%W	Week number of the year (Monday as first day)
%x	Locale's appropriate date representation
%X	Locale's appropriate time representation
%y	Year without century as a decimal number [00-99]
%Y	Year with century as a decimal number
%Z	Time zone name (or by no characters if no time zone exists)
%%	The % character

The format codes can include a width and precision in the same manner as used with the % operator on strings. ValueError is raised if any of the tuple fields are out of range. If *tuple* is omitted, the time tuple corresponding to the current time is used.

strptime(*string* [, *format*])

Parses a string representing a time and returns a struct_time object as returned by localtime() or gmtime(). The *format* parameter uses the same specifiers as used by strftime() and defaults to '%a %b %d %H:%M:%S %Y'. This is the same format as produced by the ctime() function. If the string cannot be parsed, a ValueError exception is raised.

time()

Returns the current time as the number of seconds since the epoch in UTC (Coordinated Universal Time).

tzset()

Resets the time zone setting based on the value of the TZ environment variable on UNIX. For example:

```
os.environ['TZ'] = 'US/Mountain'
time.tzset()

os.environ['TZ'] = "CST+06CDT,M4.1.0,M10.5.0"
time.tzset()
```

Notes

- When two-digit years are accepted, they're converted to four-digit years according to the POSIX X/Open standard, where the values 69-99 are mapped to 1969-1999 and the values 0-68 are mapped to 2000-2068.

- The accuracy of the time functions is often much less than what might be suggested by the units in which time is represented. For example, the operating system might only update the time 50–100 times a second.

- The functions in this module are not intended to handle dates and times far in the past or future. In particular, dates before the epoch are illegal, as are dates beyond the maximum time (2^{31} seconds since the epoch on many machines).

See Also:
datetime **(p. 267)**, locale **(p. 284)**

tty

The tty module provides functions for putting a TTY into cbreak and raw modes on UNIX systems. Raw mode forces a process to receive every character on a TTY with no interpretation by the system. Cbreak mode enables system processing for special keys such as the interrupt and quit keys (which generate signals).

setraw(*fd* [, *when*])

Changes the mode of the file descriptor *fd* to raw mode. *when* specifies when the change occurs and is termios.TCSANOW, termios.TCSADRAIN, or termios.TCSAFLUSH (the default). Refer to the termios module for more description of these constants.

setcbreak(*fd* [, *when*])

Changes the mode of file descriptor *fd* to cbreak mode. *when* has the same meaning as in setraw().

Note
The tty module requires the termios module.

See Also:
termios **(p. 344)**

_winreg

The _winreg module provides a low-level interface to the Windows registry. The registry is a large hierarchical tree in which each node is called a *key*. The children of a particular key are known as *subkeys* and may contain additional subkeys or values. For example, the setting of the Python sys.path variable is typically contained in the registry as follows:

\HKEY_LOCAL_MACHINE\Software\Python\PythonCore\2.0\PythonPath

In this case, Software is a subkey of HKEY_LOCAL_MACHINE, Python is a subkey of Software, and so forth. The value of the PythonPath key contains the actual path setting.

Keys are accessed through open and close operations. Open keys are represented by special handles (which are wrappers around the integer handle identifiers normally used by Windows).

CloseKey(*key*)

Closes a previously opened registry key with handle *key*.

ConnectRegistry(*computer_name, key*)

Returns a handle to a predefined registry key on another computer. *computer_name* is the name of the remote machine as a string of the *computername*. If *computer_name* is None, the local registry is used. *key* is a predefined handle such as HKEY_CURRENT_USER or HKEY_ USERS. Raises EnvironmentError on failure. The following list shows all HKEY_* values defined in the _winreg module:

- HKEY_CLASSES_ROOT
- HKEY_CURRENT_CONFIG
- HKEY_CURRENT_USER
- HKEY_DYN_DATA
- HKEY_LOCAL_MACHINE
- HKEY_PERFORMANCE_DATA
- HKEY_USERS

CreateKey(*key, sub_key*)

Creates or opens a key and returns a handle. *key* is a previously opened key or a predefined key defined by the HKEY_* constants. *sub_key* is the name of the key that will be opened or created. If *key* is a predefined key, *sub_key* may be None, in which case *key* is returned.

DeleteKey(*key, sub_key*)

Deletes *sub_key*. *key* is an open key or one of the predefined HKEY_* constants. *sub_key* is a string that identifies the key to delete. *sub_key* must not have any subkeys; otherwise, EnvironmentError is raised.

DeleteValue(*key, value*)

Deletes a named value from a registry key. *key* is an open key or one of the predefined HKEY_* constants. *value* is a string containing the name of the value to remove.

EnumKey(*key, index*)

Returns the name of a subkey by index. *key* is an open key or one of the predefined HKEY_* constants. *index* is an integer that specifies the key to retrieve. If *index* is out of range, an EnvironmentError is raised.

EnumValue(*key, index*)

Returns a value of an open key. *key* is an open key or a predefined HKEY_* constant. *index* is an integer specifying the value to retrieve. The function returns a tuple (*name*, *data*, *type*) in which *name* is the value name, *data* is an object holding the value data, and *type* is an integer that specifies the type of the value data. The following type codes are currently defined:

Code	Description
REG_BINARY	Binary data
REG_DWORD	32-bit number
REG_DWORD_LITTLE_ENDIAN	32-bit little-endian number
REG_DWORD_BIG_ENDIAN	32-bit number in big-endian format
REG_EXPAND_SZ	Null-terminated string with unexpanded references to environment variables
REG_LINK	Unicode symbolic link
REG_MULTI_SZ	Sequence of null-terminated strings
REG_NONE	No defined value type
REG_RESOURCE_LIST	Device driver resource list
REG_SZ	Null-terminated string

FlushKey(*key*)

Writes the attributes of *key* to the registry, forcing changes to disk. This function should only be called if an application requires absolute certainty that registry data is stored on disk. Does not return until data is written. It is not necessary to use this function under normal circumstances.

RegLoadKey(*key*, *sub_key*, *filename*)

Creates a subkey and stores registration information from a file into it. *key* is an open key or a predefined HKEY_* constant. *sub_key* is a string identifying the subkey to load. *filename* is the name of the file from which to load data. The contents of this file must be created with the SaveKey() function and the calling process must have SE_RESTORE_PRIVILEGE for this to work. If *key* was returned by ConnectRegistry(), *filename* should be a path that's relative to the remote computer.

OpenKey(*key*, *sub_key*[, *res* [, *sam*]])

Opens a key. *key* is an open key or an HKEY_* constant. *sub_key* is a string identifying the subkey to open. *res* is a reserved integer that must be zero (the default). *sam* is an integer defining the security access mask for the key. The default is KEY_READ. Here are the other possible values for *sam*:

- KEY_ALL_ACCESS
- KEY_CREATE_LINK
- KEY_CREATE_SUB_KEY
- KEY_ENUMERATE_SUB_KEYS
- KEY_EXECUTE
- KEY_NOTIFY
- KEY_QUERY_VALUE

- KEY_READ
- KEY_SET_VALUE
- KEY_WRITE

OpenKeyEx()

Same as OpenKey().

QueryInfoKey(*key*)

Returns information about a key as a tuple (*num_subkeys*, *num_values*, *last_modified*) in which *num_subkeys* is the number of subkeys, *num_values* is the number of values, and *last_modified* is a long integer containing the time of last modification. Time is measured from January 1, 1601, in units of 100 nanoseconds.

QueryValue(*key*, *sub_key*)

Returns the unnamed value for a key as a string. *key* is an open key or an HKEY_* constant. *sub_key* is the name of the subkey to use, if any. If omitted, the function returns the value associated with *key* instead. This function returns the data for the first value with a null name. However, the type is returned (use QueryValueEx instead).

QueryValueEx(*key*, *value_name*)

Returns a tuple (*value*, *type*) containing the data value and type for a key. *key* is an open key or HKEY_* constant. *value_name* is the name of the value to return. The returned type is one of the integer codes as described for the EnumValue() function.

SaveKey(*key*, *filename*)

Saves *key* and all its subkeys to a file. *key* is an open key or a predefined HKEY_* constant. *filename* must not already exist and should not include a filename extension. Furthermore, the caller must have backup privileges for the operation to succeed.

SetValue(*key*, *sub_key*, *type*, *value*)

Sets the value of a key. *key* is an open key or HKEY_* constant. *sub_key* is the name of the subkey with which to associate the value. *type* is an integer type code, currently limited to REG_SZ. *value* is a string containing the value data. If *sub_key* does not exist, it is created. *key* must have been opened with KEY_SET_VALUE access for this function to succeed.

SetValueEx(*key*, *value_name*, *reserved*, *type*, *value*)

Sets the value field of a key. *key* is an open key or an HKEY_* constant. *value_name* is the name of the value. *type* is an integer type code as described for the EnumValue() function. *value* is a string containing the new value. When the values of numeric types (for example, REG_DWORD) are being set, *value* is still a string containing the raw data. This string can be created using the struct module. *reserved* is currently ignored and can be set to anything (the value is not used).

20

Threads

THIS CHAPTER DESCRIBES MODULES THAT CAN be used to develop multithreaded applications. First, a little terminology and background.

Thread Basics

A running program is called a *process*. Associated with each process is a system state, which includes memory, lists of open files, a program counter that keeps track of the instruction being executed, and a call stack used to hold the local variables of functions. Normally, a process executes statements in a single sequence of control flow. This sequence is sometimes called a *thread* (or *main thread*).

When a program creates new processes by using the os.system(), os.fork(), os.spawnv(), and similar system calls, these processes run as independent programs— each with its own set of system resources and main thread of execution. However, it's also possible for a program to create additional threads of execution that exist inside the calling process and share data and system resources with the original thread of execution. Threads are particularly useful when an application wants to perform tasks concurrently without spawning child processes, or when subtasks need to read and write shared data.

A multithreaded program executes by dividing its processing time between all active threads. For example, a program with 10 active threads of execution would allocate approximately 1/10th of its CPU time to each thread and cycle between threads in rapid succession.

Because threads share the same data, an extreme degree of caution is required whenever shared data structures are updated by one of the threads. In particular, attempts to update a data structure by multiple threads at approximately the same time can lead to a corrupted and inconsistent program state (a problem formally known as a *race condition*). To fix these problems, threaded programs need to lock critical sections of code by using mutual-exclusion locks and other similar synchronization primitives.

More information regarding the theory and implementation of threads and locks can be found in most operating system textbooks.

Python Threads

Python supports threads on Windows, Mac OS X, Linux, Solaris, and systems that support the POSIX threads library (pthreads).

The scheduling of threads and thread switching is tightly controlled by a global interpreter lock that allows only a single thread of execution to be running in the interpreter at once. Furthermore, thread switching can only occur between the execution of individual bytecodes in the interpreter. The frequency with which the interpreter checks for thread switching is set by the sys.setcheckinterval() function. By default, the interpreter checks for thread switching after every 100 bytecode instructions.

When working with extension modules, the interpreter may invoke functions written in C. Unless specifically written to interact with a threaded Python interpreter, these functions block the execution of all other threads until they complete execution. Thus, a long-running calculation in an extension module may limit the effectiveness of using threads. However, most of the I/O functions in the standard library have been written to work in a threaded environment.

Finally, programmers need to be aware that threads can interact strangely with signals and interrupts. For instance, the KeyboardInterrupt exception can be received by an arbitrary thread, while signals used in conjunction with the signal module are only received by the main thread. In addition, many of Python's most popular extensions, such as Tkinter, may not work properly in a threaded environment.

thread

The thread module provides the following low-level functions for working with threads. This module is available only on UNIX and Windows.

allocate_lock()

Creates a new lock object of type LockType. Locks are initially unlocked.

exit()

Raises the SystemExit exception. Forces a thread to exit.

get_ident()

Returns the integer "thread identifier" of the current thread.

interrupt_main()

Raises a KeyboardInterrupt exception in the main thread.

start_new_thread(func, args [, kwargs])

Executes the function func in a new thread. func is called using apply(func, args, kwargs). On success, control is immediately returned to the caller. When the function func returns, the thread exits silently. If the function terminates with an unhandled exception, a stack trace is printed and the thread exits (other threads continue to run, however).

A lock object, lck, returned by allocate_lock() has the following methods:

lck.acquire([waitflag])

Acquires the lock, waiting until the lock is released by another thread if necessary. If waitflag is omitted, the function returns None when the lock is acquired. If waitflag is set to 0, the lock is acquired only if it can be acquired immediately without waiting. If waitflag is nonzero, the method blocks until the lock is released. When waitflag is supplied, the function returns 1 if the lock was acquired successfully and 0 otherwise.

lck.**release()**

Releases the lock.

lck.**locked()**

Returns the lock status: 1 if locked, 0 if not.

Example

The following example shows a simple thread that prints the current time every 5 seconds:

```
import thread
import time
def print_time(delay):
    while 1:
        time.sleep(delay)
        print time.ctime(time.time())

# Start the new thread
thread.start_new_thread(print_time,(5,))
# Now go do something else while the thread runs
while 1:
    pass
```

Exception

The error exception is raised on thread-specific errors.

Notes

- Calling sys.exit() or raising the SystemExit exception is equivalent to calling thread.exit().
- The acquire() method on a lock cannot be interrupted.
- When the main thread exits, whether the other threads survive depends on the system. On most systems, they're killed immediately without executing any cleanup. Furthermore, the cleanup actions of the main thread are somewhat limited. In particular, standard I/O files are not flushed, nor are object destructors invoked.
- If the thread module is unavailable, the dummy_thread module can be imported to supply its API. This may allow certain programs that use thread-related functions to operate provided that those programs don't deadlock (for example, waiting for other threads or performing blocking I/O operations).

See Also:
threading (p. 358)

threading

The threading module provides high-level thread support with a Thread class and classes for various synchronization primitives. It's built using the lower-level thread module.

The following utility functions are available:

activeCount()

Returns the number of currently active Thread objects.

currentThread()

Returns the Thread object corresponding to the caller's thread of control.

enumerate()

Returns a list of all currently active Thread objects.

local()

Returns a local object that allows for the storage of thread-local data. This object is guaranteed to be unique in each thread.

setprofile(*func*)

Sets a profile function that will be used for all threads created. *func* is passed to sys.setprofile() before each thread starts running.

settrace(*func*)

Sets a tracing function that will be used for all threads created. *func* is passed to sys.settrace() before each thread starts running.

Thread **Objects**

The Thread class is used to represent a separate thread of control. A new thread can be created as follows:

Thread(*group*=None, *target*=None, *name*=None, *args*=(), *kwargs*={})

This creates a new Thread instance. *group* is None and is reserved for future extensions. *target* is a callable object invoked by the run() method when the thread starts. By default, it's None, meaning that nothing is called. *name* is the thread name. By default, a unique name of the form "Thread-*N*" is created. *args* is a tuple of arguments passed to the *target* function. *kwargs* is a dictionary of keyword arguments passed to *target*.

A Thread object, *t*, supports the following methods:

t.start()

Starts the thread by invoking the run() method in a separate thread of control. This method can be invoked only once.

t.run()

This method is called when the thread starts. By default, it calls the target function passed in the constructor. This method can also be redefined in subclasses of Thread.

`t.join([`*`timeout`*`])`

Waits until the thread terminates or a timeout occurs. *timeout* is a floating-point number specifying a timeout in seconds. A thread cannot join itself, and it's an error to join a thread before it has been started.

`t.getName()`

Returns the thread name.

`t.setName(name)`

Sets the thread name.

`t.isAlive()`

Returns `True` if the thread is alive and `False` otherwise. A thread is alive from the moment the `start()` method returns until its `run()` method terminates.

`t.isDaemon()`

Returns the thread's daemon flag.

`t.setDaemon(daemonic)`

Sets the thread's daemon flag to the Boolean value `daemonic`. This must be called before `start()` is called. The initial value is inherited from the creating thread. The entire Python program exits when no active non-daemon threads are left.

A thread can be flagged as a "daemon thread" using the `setDaemon()` method. If only daemon threads remain, a program will exit. All programs have a main thread that represents the initial thread of control. It's not a daemon thread.

In some cases, dummy thread objects are created. These are threads of control started outside the `threading` module, such as from a C extension module. Dummy threads are always considered alive, active, and daemonic, and they cannot be joined. Furthermore, they're never deleted, so it's impossible to detect the termination of such threads.

As an alternative to explicitly creating a `Thread` object, the `Thread` class can also be subclassed. If this approach is used, the `run()` method can be overridden to perform the activity of the thread. The constructor can also be overridden, but it's very important to invoke the base class constructor `Thread.__init__()` in this case. It's an error to override any other methods of the `Thread` class.

`Timer` **Objects**

A `Timer` object is used to execute a function at some later time.

`Timer(`*`interval, func`* `[,` *`args`* `[,` *`kwargs`*`]])`

Creates a `Timer` object that runs the function *func* after *interval* seconds have elapsed. *args* and *kwargs* provide the arguments and keyword arguments passed to *func*. The timer does not start until the `start()` method is called.

A `Timer` object, *t,* has the following methods:

`t.start()`

Starts the timer. The function *func* supplied to `Timer()` will be executed after the specified timer interval.

```
t.cancel()
```

Cancels the timer if the function has not executed yet.

Lock **Objects**

A *primitive lock* (or *mutual exclusion lock*) is a synchronization primitive that's in either a "locked" or "unlocked" state. Two methods, `acquire()` and `release()`, are used to change the state of the lock. If the state is locked, attempts to acquire the lock are blocked until the lock is released. If more than one thread is waiting to acquire the lock, only one is allowed to proceed when the lock is released. The order in which waiting threads proceed is undefined.

A new Lock instance is created using the constructor.

```
Lock()
```

Creates a new Lock object that's initially unlocked.

A Lock object, `lck`, supports the following methods:

```
lck.acquire([blocking = 1])
```

Acquires the lock, blocking until the lock is released if necessary. If blocking is supplied and set to zero, the function returns immediately with a value of 0 if the lock could not be acquired, or 1 if locking was successful.

```
lck.release()
```

Releases a lock. It's an error to call this method when the lock is in an unlocked state.

RLock

A *reentrant lock* is a synchronization primitive that's similar to a Lock object, but it can be acquired multiple times by the same thread. This allows the thread owning the lock to perform nested `acquire()` and `release()` operations. In this case, only the outermost `release()` operation resets the lock to its unlocked state.

A new RLock object is created using the following constructor:

```
RLock()
```

Creates a new reentrant lock object.

An RLock object, `rlck`, supports the following methods:

```
rlck.acquire([blocking = 1])
```

Acquires the lock, blocking until the lock is released if necessary. If no thread owns the lock, it's locked and the recursion level is set to 1. If this thread already owns the lock, the recursion level of the lock is increased by one and the function returns immediately.

```
rlck.release()
```

Releases a lock by decrementing its recursion level. If the recursion level is zero after the decrement, the lock is reset to the unlocked state. Otherwise, the lock remains locked. This function should only be called by the thread that currently owns the lock.

Condition Variables

A *condition variable* is a synchronization primitive, built on top of another lock, that's used when a thread is interested in a particular change of state or event occurring. A typical use is a producer-consumer problem where one thread is producing data to be consumed by another thread. A new `Condition` instance is created using the following constructor:

`Condition([lock])`

Creates a new condition variable. *lock* is an optional `Lock` or `RLock` instance. If not supplied, a new `RLock` instance is created for use with the condition variable.

A condition variable, *cv*, supports the following methods:

`cv.acquire(*args)`

Acquires the underlying lock. This method calls the corresponding `acquire(*args)` method on the underlying lock and returns its return value.

`cv.release()`

Releases the underlying lock. This method calls the corresponding `release()` method on the underlying lock.

`cv.wait([timeout])`

Waits until notified or until a timeout occurs. This method is called after the calling thread has already acquired the lock. When called, the underlying lock is released, and the thread goes to sleep until it's awakened by a `notify()` or `notifyAll()` call performed on the condition variable by another thread. Once awakened, the thread reacquires the lock and the method returns. `timeout` is a floating-point number in seconds. If this time expires, the thread is awakened, the lock reacquired, and control returned.

`cv.notify([n])`

Wakes up one or more threads waiting on this condition variable. This method is called only after the calling thread has acquired the lock, and it does nothing if no threads are waiting. *n* specifies the number of threads to awaken and defaults to 1. Awakened threads don't return from the `wait()` call until they can reacquire the lock.

`cv.notifyAll()`

Wakes up all threads waiting on this condition.

Examples

The following examples show a producer-consumer problem using condition variables:

```
# Consume one item
def consumer():
    cv.acquire()
    while not an_item_is_available():
        cv.wait()  # Wait for item
    cv.release()

# Produce one item
def produce():
    cv.acquire()
    make_an_item_available()
    cv.notify()    # Notify the consumer
    cv.release()
```

Semaphore and Bounded Semaphore

A *semaphore* is a synchronization primitive based on a counter that's decremented by each acquire() call and incremented by each release() call. If the counter ever reaches zero, the acquire() method blocks until some other thread calls release().

Semaphore([value])

Creates a new semaphore. *value* is the initial value for the counter. If omitted, the counter is set to a value of 1.

A Semaphore instance, *s*, supports the following methods:

s.acquire([blocking])

Acquires the semaphore. If the internal counter is larger than zero on entry, this method decrements it by one and returns immediately. If it's zero, this method blocks until another thread calls release(). The blocking argument has the same behavior as described for Lock and RLock objects.

s.release()

Releases a semaphore by incrementing the internal counter by one. If the counter is zero and another thread is waiting, that thread is awakened. If multiple threads are waiting, only one will be returned from its acquire() call. The order in which threads are released is not deterministic.

BoundedSemaphore([value])

Creates a new semaphore. *value* is the initial value for the counter. If *value* is omitted, the counter is set to a value of 1. A BoundedSemaphore works exactly like a Semaphore except the number of release() operations cannot exceed the number of acquire() operations.

Events

Events are used to communicate between threads. One thread signals an "event," and one or more other threads wait for it. An Event instance manages an internal flag that can be set to true with the set() method and reset to false with the clear() method. The wait() method blocks until the flag is true.

Event()

Creates a new Event instance with the internal flag set to false. An Event instance, *e*, supports the following methods:

e.isSet()

Returns true only if the internal flag is true.

e.set()

Sets the internal flag to true. All threads waiting for it to become true are awakened.

e.clear()

Resets the internal flag to false.

e.wait([timeout])

Blocks until the internal flag is true. If the internal flag is true on entry, this method returns immediately. Otherwise, it blocks until another thread calls set() to set the flag to true, or until the optional timeout occurs. *timeout* is a floating-point number specifying a timeout period in seconds.

Example

The following example illustrates the use of the `threading` module by fetching a collection of URLs in separate threads. In this example, threads are defined by subclassing the `Thread` class.

```
import threading
import urllib
class FetchUrlThread(threading.Thread):
    def __init__(self, url,filename):
            threading.Thread.__init__(self)
            self.url = url
            self.filename = filename
    def run(self):
            print self.getName(), 'Fetching ', self.url
            urllib.urlretrieve(self.url,self.filename)
            print self.getName(), 'Saved in ', self.filename
urls = [ ('http://www.python.org','/tmp/index.html'),
        ('ftp://ftp.python.org/pub/python/src/py152.tgz','/tmp/py152.tgz'),
        ('ftp://ftp.swig.org/pub/swig1.1p5.tar.gz','/tmp/swig1.1p5.tar.gz'),
        ('http://www.pud.com','/tmp/pud.html')
      ]
# Go fetch a bunch of URLs in separate threads
for url,file in urls:
    t = FetchUrlThread(url,file)
    t.start()
```

> **Note**
>
> If the `threading` module is unavailable, the module `dummy_threading` can be imported solely for the purpose of providing its API. This may allow programs that use thread-related functions to operate as long as there is no deadlock (for example, if one thread waits on another thread).

> **See Also:**
> `thread` **(p. 356)**, `Queue` **(p. 363)**

Queue

The `Queue` module implements a multiproducer, multiconsumer FIFO queue that can be used to safely exchange information between multiple threads of execution. It's available only if thread support has been enabled.

The `Queue` module defines the following class:

Queue(*maxsize*)

Creates a new queue in which *maxsize* is the maximum number of items that can be placed in the queue. If *maxsize* is less than or equal to zero, the queue size is infinite.

A `Queue` object, *q*, has the following methods:

q.qsize()

Returns the approximate size of the queue. Because other threads may be updating the queue, this number is not entirely reliable.

q.empty()

Returns True if the queue is empty and returns False otherwise.

q.full()

Returns True if the queue is full and returns False otherwise.

q.put(*item* [, *block* [, *timeout*]])

Puts *item* into the queue. If optional argument *block* is True (the default), the caller blocks until a free slot is available. Otherwise (*block* is False), the Full exception is raised if the queue is full. *timeout* supplies an optional timeout value in seconds. If a timeout occurs, the Full exception is raised.

q.put_nowait(*item*)

Equivalent to q.put(*item*, False).

q.get([*block* [, *timeout*]])

Removes and returns an item from the queue. If optional argument *block* is True (the default), the caller blocks until an item is available. Otherwise (*block* is False), the Empty exception is raised if the queue is empty. *timeout* supplies an optional timeout value in seconds. If a timeout occurs, the Empty exception is raised.

q.get_nowait()

Equivalent to get(0).

Exceptions

Exception	Description
Empty	The exception raised when nonblocking get() or get_nowait() is called on a Queue object that's empty or locked.
Full	The exception raised when nonblocking put() or put_nowait() is called on a Queue object that's full or locked.

See Also:

thread (p. 356), threading (p. 358)

## 21

Network Programming

THIS CHAPTER DESCRIBES THE MODULES USED to implement low-level network servers and clients. Python provides extensive network support, ranging from access to low-level network interfaces to high-level clients and frameworks for writing network applications. To begin, a very brief (and admittedly terse) introduction to network programming is presented. Readers are advised to consult a book such as *UNIX Network Programming, Volume 1: Networking APIs: Sockets and XTI*, by W. Richard Stevens (Prentice Hall, 2003, ISBN 0131411551) for many of the advanced details.

Introduction

Python's network programming modules primarily support two Internet protocols: TCP and UDP. The TCP protocol is a reliable connection-oriented protocol used to establish a two-way communications stream between machines. UDP is a lower-level packet-based protocol (connectionless) in which machines send and receive discrete packets of information without formally establishing a connection. Unlike TCP, UDP communication is unreliable and thus inherently more complicated to manage in applications that require reliable communications. Consequently, most Internet protocols utilize TCP connections.

Both network protocols are handled through a programming abstraction known as a *socket*. A socket is an object similar to a file that allows a program to accept incoming connections, make outgoing connections, and send and receive data. Before two machines can establish a connection, both must create a socket object.

Furthermore, the machine receiving the connection (the server) must bind its socket object to a port. A port is a 16-bit number in the range 0–65535 that's managed by the operating system and used by clients to uniquely identify servers. Ports 0–1023 are reserved by the system and used by common network protocols. The following table shows the port assignments for a number of common protocols (a more complete list can be found at http://www.iana.org/assignments/port-numbers):

Service	Port Number
FTP-Data	20
FTP-Control	21
SSH	22
Telnet	23
SMTP (Mail)	25

Service	Port Number
Finger	79
HTTP (WWW)	80
POP3	110
NNTP (News)	119
IMAP	143
HTTPS (Secure WWW)	443

The process of establishing a TCP connection involves a precise sequence of steps on both the server and client, as shown in Figure 21.1.

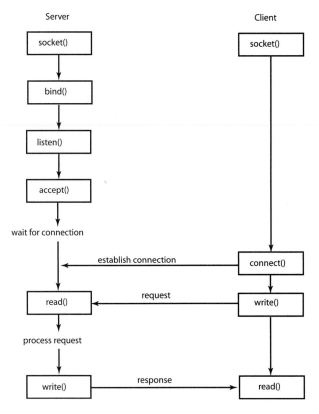

Figure 21.1   TCP connection protocol.

For TCP servers, the socket object used to receive connections is not the same socket used to perform subsequent communication with the client. In particular, the accept () system call returns a new socket object that's actually used for the connection. This allows a server to manage connections from a large number of clients simultaneously.

UDP communication is performed in a similar manner, except that clients and servers don't establish a "connection" with each other, as shown in Figure 21.2.

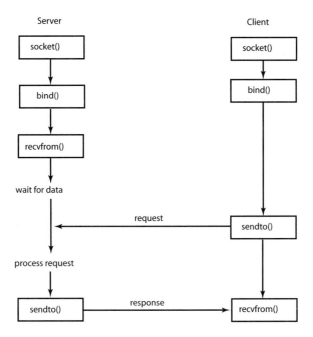

Figure 21.2   UDP connection protocol.

The following example illustrates the TCP protocol with a client and server written using the socket module. In this case, the server simply returns the current time to the client as a string.

```
# Time server program
from socket import *
import time

s = socket(AF_INET, SOCK_STREAM)    # Create a TCP socket
s.bind(('',8888))                   # Bind to port 8888
s.listen(5)                         # Listen, but allow no more than
                                    # 5 pending connections.
while 1:
    client,addr = s.accept()        # Get a connection
    print 'Got a connection from ',addr
    client.send(time.ctime(time.time()))   # Send back to client
    client.close()
```

Here's the client program:

```
# Time client program
from socket import *
s = socket(AF_INET,SOCK_STREAM)     # Create a TCP socket
s.connect(('foo.bar.com', 8888))    # Connect to the server
tm = s.recv(1024)                   # Receive no more than 1024 bytes
s.close()
print 'The time is ', tm
```

An example of establishing a UDP connection appears later in this chapter.

The remainder of this chapter describes modules that are related to low-level socket programming. Chapter 22, "Internet Application Protocols," describes higher-level modules that provide support for various Internet applications such as email and the Web.

asynchat

The `asynchat` module simplifies the implementation of applications that implement asynchronous networking using the `asyncore` module. This module extends the capabilities of the `dispatcher` class in `asyncore` by adding some features that make it easier to handle protocols based on a simple request/response mechanism (for example, HTTP).

To use this module, you must define a class that inherits from `async_chat`. Within this class, you must define two methods: `collect_incoming_data()` and `found_terminator()`. The first method is invoked whenever data is received on the network connection. Typically, it would simply take the data and store it someplace. The `found_terminator()` method is called when the end of a command request has been detected. For example, in HTTP, requests are terminated by a blank line.

For data output, `async_chat` maintains a producer FIFO queue. If you need to output data, it is simply added to this queue. Then, whenever writes are possible on the network connection, data is transparently taken from this queue.

async_chat([*sock*])

Base class used to define new handlers. `async_chat` inherits from `asyncore.dispatcher` and provides the same methods. *sock* is a socket object that's used for communication.

An instance, `a`, of `async_chat` has the following methods in addition to those already provided by the `asyncore.dispatcher` base class:

a.close_when_done()

Signals an end-of-file on the outgoing data stream by pushing None onto the producer FIFO queue. When this is reached by the writer, the channel will be closed.

a.collect_incoming_data(*data*)

Called whenever data is received on the channel. *data* is the received data and is typically stored for later processing. This method must be implemented by the user.

a.discard_buffers()

Discards all data held in input/output buffers and the producer FIFO queue.

a.found_terminator()

Called when the termination condition set by `set_terminator()` holds. This method must be implemented by the user. Typically, it would process data previously collected by the `collect_incoming_data()` method.

a.get_terminator()

Returns the terminator for the channel.

a.push(*data*)

Pushes data onto the channel's outgoing producer FIFO queue. *data* is a string containing the data to be sent.

a.push_with_producer(*producer*)

Pushes a producer object, *producer*, onto the producer FIFO queue. *producer* may be any object that has a simple method, more(). The more() method should produce a string each time it is invoked. An empty string is returned to signal the end of data. Internally, the async_chat class repeatedly calls more() to obtain data to write on the outgoing channel. More than one producer object can be pushed onto the FIFO by calling push_with_producer() repeatedly.

a.set_terminator(*term*)

Sets the termination condition on the channel. *term* may either be a string, an integer, or None. If *term* is a string, the method found_terminator() is called whenever that string appears in the input stream. If *term* is an integer, it specifies a byte count. After many bytes have been read, found_terminator() will be called. If *term* is None, data is collected forever.

> **Note**
>
> The asynchat module is typically used in conjunction with the asyncore module. For instance, asyncore is used to set up the high-level server, which accepts incoming connections. asynchat is then used to implement handlers for each connection.

Example

The following example shows how to use this module. The example omits a lot of error checking and details, but should be enough to get you started. Readers should compare this example to the example in the asyncore module, later in this chapter.

```
# An asynchronous HTTP server
import asynchat
import asyncore
import socket
import rfc822
import mimetypes
import cStringIO

class async_http(asyncore.dispatcher):
    def __init__(self,port):
        asyncore.dispatcher.__init__(self)
        self.create_socket(socket.AF_INET,socket.SOCK_STREAM)
        self.bind(('',port))
        self.listen(5)
    def handle_accept(self):
        client,addr = self.accept()
        return async_http_handler(client)

class async_http_handler(asynchat.async_chat):
    def __init__(self,conn=None):
        asynchat.async_chat.__init__(self,conn)
        self.data = []
        self.got_header = 0
```

```
            self.processing = 0
            self.set_terminator("\r\n\r\n")
    # Get incoming data and append to data buffer
    def collect_incoming_data(self,data):
        self.data.append(data)
    # Got a terminator. It is either a blank line (\r\n) or the end of
    # additional data supplied via the POST method.
    def found_terminator(self):
        if not self.got_header:
            header_data = "".join(self.data)
            self.parse_headers(header_data)
            self.got_header = 1
            if self.op == "POST":
                size = self.headers.getheader("content-length")
                self.set_terminator(int(size))
                self.data = []
            else:
                self.set_terminator(None)
                self.data = []
                self.process_request()
        elif not self.processing:
            self.set_terminator(None)
            self.post_data = "".join(self.data)
            self.data = []
            self.process_request()
    # Parse HTTP headers and save information
    def parse_headers(self,hdata):
        hlines = hdata.splitlines()
        request = hlines[0].split()
        self.op = request[0]
        self.url = request[1]
        self.type, self.encoding = mimetypes.guess_type(self.url)
        self.headers = rfc822.Message(
                         cStringIO.StringIO("".join(hlines[1:])))
    # Process the request
    def process_request(self):
        self.processing = 1
        if self.op == "GET":
            data = open(self.url).read()
            self.push('HTTP/1.0 200 OK\r\n')
            self.push('Content-length: %d\r\n' % len(data))
            self.push('Content-type: %s\r\n' % self.type)
            self.push('\r\n')
            self.push(data)
            self.close_when_done()

a = async_http(8080)
asyncore.loop()
```

asyncore

The asyncore module is used to build network applications in which network activity
is handled asynchronously as a series of events dispatched by an event loop, built using
the select() system call. Such an approach is useful in network programs that want to
provide concurrency, but without the use of threads or processes. This method can also
provide high performance for short transactions. All the functionality of this module is
provided by the dispatcher class, which is a thin wrapper around an ordinary socket
object.

`dispatcher([`*`sock`*`])`

A base class defining an event-driven nonblocking socket object. *sock* is an existing socket object. If omitted, a socket must be created using the `create_socket()` method (described shortly). Once it's created, network events are handled by special handler methods. In addition, all open dispatcher objects are saved in an internal list that's used by a number of polling functions.

The following methods of the `dispatcher` class are called to handle network events. They should be defined in classes derived from dispatcher.

d`.handle_read()`

Called when new data is available to be read from a socket.

d`.handle_write()`

Called when an attempt to write data is made.

d`.handle_expt()`

Called when out-of-band data for a socket is received.

d`.handle_connect()`

Called when a connection is made.

d`.handle_close()`

Called when the socket is closed.

d`.handle_accept()`

Called on listening sockets when a new connection arrives.

d`.handle_error()`

Called when an uncaught Python exception occurs.

d`.readable()`

This function is used by the `select()` loop to see whether the object is willing to read data. Returns 1 if so, 0 if not. This method is called to see if the `handle_read()` method should be called with new data.

d`.writable()`

Called by the `select()` loop to see if the object wants to write data. Returns 1 if so, 0 otherwise. This method is always called to see whether the `handle_write()` method should be called to produce output.

In addition to the preceding methods, the following methods are used to perform low-level socket operations. They're similar to those available on a socket object.

d`.create_socket(`*`family, type`*`)`

Creates a new socket. Arguments are the same as for `socket.socket()`.

d`.connect(`*`address`*`)`

Makes a connection. *address* is a tuple (*host, port*).

d`.send(`*`data`*`)`

Sends data. *data* is a string.

d.recv(*size*)

Receives at most *size* bytes. An empty string indicates the client has closed the channel.

d.listen([*backlog*])

Listens for incoming connections. *backlog* is an integer that is passed to the underlying socket.listen() function.

d.bind(*address*)

Binds the socket to *address*. *address* is typically a tuple (*host*, *port*), but this depends on the address family being used.

d.accept()

Accepts a connection. Returns a pair (*client*, *addr*) where *client* is a socket object used to send and receive data on the connection and *addr* is the address of the client.

d.close()

Closes the socket.

The dispatcher class also defines the following attributes that may be modified:

d.ac_in_buffer_size

Input buffer size. Default is 4096 bytes.

d.ac_out_buffer_size

Output buffer size. Default is 4096 bytes.

The following function is used to handle events:

loop([*timeout* [, *use_poll* [, *map* [, *count*]]]])

Polls for events indefinitely. The select() function is used for polling unless the *use_poll* parameter is True, in which case poll() is used instead. *timeout* is the timeout period and is set to 30 seconds by default. *map* is a dictionary containing all the channels to monitor. *count* specifies how many polling operations to perform before returning. If *count* is None (the default), loop() polls forever until all channels are closed. If *count* is 1, the function will execute a single poll for events and return.

Example

The following example implements a minimalistic web server using asyncore. It implements two classes—asynhttp for accepting connections and asynclient for processing client requests.

```
# A minimal HTTP server with no error checking.
import asyncore, socket
import string, os, stat, mimetypes
# Class that does nothing but accept connections
class asynhttp(asyncore.dispatcher):
    def __init__(self, port):
        asyncore.dispatcher.__init__(self)
        self.create_socket(socket.AF_INET,socket.SOCK_STREAM)
        self.bind(('',port))
        self.listen(5)
    # Accept an incoming connection and create a client
    def handle_accept(self):
        client,addr = self.accept()
```

```
              print 'Connection from ', addr
              return asynclient(client)
# Handle clients
class asynclient(asyncore.dispatcher):
    def __init__(self, sock = None):
        asyncore.dispatcher.__init__(self,sock)
        self.got_request = 0          # Read HTTP request?
        self.request_data = []
        self.responsef = None         # Response file
        self.sent_headers = 0         # Send HTTP headers?
        self.clientf = sock.makefile('r+',0)   # Request file
    # Only readable if request header not read
    def readable(self):
        if not self.got_request: return 1
    # Read request header (until blank line)
    def handle_read(self):
        data = string.strip(self.clientf.readline())
        if data:
            self.request_data.append(data)
            return
        self.got_request = 1
        request = string.split(self.request_data[0])
        if request[0] == 'GET':
            filename = request[1][1:]
            self.responsef = open(filename)
            self.content_type,enc = mimetypes.guess_type(filename)
            self.content_length = os.stat(filename)[stat.ST_SIZE]
        else:
            self.close()
    # Only writable if a response is ready
    def writable(self):
        if self.responsef: return 1
        return 0
    # Write response data
    def handle_write(self):
        # Send HTTP headers if not sent yet
        if not self.sent_headers:
            self.send('HTTP/1.0 200 OK\n')
            if not self.content_type:
                    self.content_type = 'text/plain'
            self.send('Content-type: %s\n' % (self.content_type,))
            self.send('Content-length: %d\n\n' % (self.content_length,))
            self.sent_headers = 1
        # Read some data and send it
        data = self.responsef.read(8192)
        if data:
            sent = self.send(data)
            # Adjust for unsent data
            self.responsef.seek(sent-len(data),1)
        else:
            self.responsef.close()
            self.close()
# Create the server
a = asynhttp(80)
# Poll forever
asyncore.loop()
```

Note

This module requires the select module.

See Also:
socket (p. 375), select (p. 374), httplib (p. 415), SocketServer (p. 388)

select

The select module provides access to the select() and poll() system calls. select() is typically used to implement polling or to multiplex processing across multiple input/output streams without using threads or subprocesses. On UNIX, it works for files, sockets, pipes, and most other file types. On Windows, it only works for sockets.

select(*iwtd, owtd, ewtd* [, *timeout*])

Queries the input, output, and exceptional status of a group of file descriptors. The first three arguments are lists containing either integer file descriptors or objects with a method, fileno(), that can be used to return a file descriptor. The *iwtd* parameter specifies objects waiting for input, *owtd* specifies objects waiting for output, and *ewtd* specifies objects waiting for an exceptional condition. Each list may be empty. *timeout* is a floating-point number specifying a timeout period in seconds. If *timeout* is omitted, the function waits until at least one file descriptor is ready. If it's 0, the function merely performs a poll and returns immediately. The return value is a tuple of lists containing the objects that are ready. These are subsets of the first three arguments. If none of the objects is ready before the timeout occurs, three empty lists are returned. If an error occurs, a select.error exception raised. Its value is the same as that returned by IOError and OSError.

poll()

Creates a polling object that utilizes the poll() system call. This is only available on systems that support poll().

A polling object, *p*, returned by poll() supports the following methods:

p.register(*fd* [, *eventmask*])

Registers a new file descriptor, *fd*. *fd* is either an integer file descriptor or an object that provides the fileno() method from which the descriptor can be obtained. *eventmask* is the bitwise OR of the following flags, which indicate events of interest:

Constant	Description
POLLIN	Data is available for reading.
POLLPRI	Urgent data is available for reading.
POLLOUT	Ready for writing.
POLLERR	Error condition.
POLLHUP	Hang up.
POLLNVAL	Invalid request.

If *eventmask* is omitted, the POLLIN, POLLPRI, and POLLOUT events are checked.

p.unregister(*fd*)

Removes the file descriptor *fd* from the polling object. Raises `KeyError` if the file is not registered.

p.poll([*timeout*])

Polls for events on all the registered file descriptors. *timeout* is an optional timeout specified in milliseconds. Returns a list of tuples (*fd*, *event*), where *fd* is a file descriptor and event is a bitmask indicating events. The fields of this bitmask correspond to the constants `POLLIN`, `POLLOUT`, and so on. For example, to check for the `POLLIN` event, simply test the value using *event* & `POLLIN`. If an empty list is returned, it means a timeout occurred and no events occurred.

Example

The following code shows how `select()` could be used in an event loop that wants to periodically query a collection of sockets for an incoming connection:

```
import socket, select
# Create a few sockets
s1 = socket.socket(socket.AF_INET, socket.SOCK_STREAM)
s1.bind(("",8888))
s1.listen(5)
s2 = socket.socket(socket.AF_INET, socket.SOCK_STREAM)
s2.bind(("",8889))
s2.listen(5)
# Event loop
while 1:
    ... processing ...
    # Poll the sockets for activity
    input,output,exc = select.select([s1,s2],[],[],0)
    # Loop over all of the sockets that have pending input
    for sock in input:
        # Accept an incoming connection
        client = sock.accept()
        ... handle client ...
        client.close()
    # Done. Carry on.
    ... more processing ...
```

Note

There's usually an upper limit on the number of file selectors that can be given to `select()`. It's often 64 for Windows and 256 for UNIX.

See Also:

asyncore (p. 370), socket (p. 375), os (p. 308)

socket

The socket module provides access to the standard BSD socket interface. Although it's based on UNIX, this module is available on all platforms. The socket interface is designed to be generic and is capable of supporting a wide variety of networking protocols (Internet, IPX, Appletalk, and so on). However, the most common protocol is the Internet Protocol (IP), which includes both TCP and UDP. Python supports both IPv4 and IPv6, although IPv4 is far more common.

It should be noted that this module is relatively low-level, providing direct access to the network functions provided by the operating system. If you are writing a network application, it may be easier to use modules described in Chapter 22, "Internet Application Protocols," or the SocketServer module described at the end of this chapter.

Protocol Families

Many of the socket functions require the specification of a protocol family, sometimes referred to as an *address family*. The family specifies what kind of network protocol is being used. The following constants are used to specify the family:

Constant	Description
AF_INET	IPv4 protocols (TCP, UDP)
AF_INET6	IPv6 protocols (TCP, UDP)
AF_UNIX	UNIX domain protocols

Socket Types

Many of the socket functions also require the specification of a socket type. The socket type specifies the type of communications to be used. The following constants specify the socket type:

Constant	Description
SOCK_STREAM	A reliable connection-oriented byte stream (TCP)
SOCK_DGRAM	Datagrams (UDP)
SOCK_RAW	Raw socket
SOCK_RDM	Reliable datagrams
SOCK_SEQPACKET	Sequenced connection-mode transfer of records

The most common socket types are SOCK_STREAM and SOCK_DGRAM because they correspond to TCP and UDP in the Internet Protocol suite. SOCK_RDM and SOCK_SEQPACKET are used to support some less common communication models and may not be supported on all systems. SOCK_RAW is used to provide low-level access to the network and is used to send ICMP messages, implement packet sniffers, and perform other similar tasks. Use of SOCK_RAW is usually restricted to programs running with superuser or administrator access.

Internet Addresses

For Internet applications, many socket functions require an address to be given. An address identifies a specific host and port on the network. For IPv4, an address is given as a tuple (*host*, *port*). Here are two examples:

```
('www.python.org', 80)
```

```
('66.113.130.182', 25)
```

If *host* is the empty string, it has the same meaning as INADDR_ANY, which means any address. This is typically used by servers when creating sockets that any client can connect to. If *host* is set to '<broadcast>', it has the same meaning as the INADDR_BROADCAST constant in the socket API.

For IPv6, addresses are specified as a four-tuple (*host*, *port*, *flowinfo*, *scopeid*). With IPv6, the *host* and *port* components work in the same way as IPv4, except that the numerical form of an IPv6 host address is typically specified by a string of eight colon-separated hexadecimal numbers, such as 'FEDC:BA98:7654:3210:FEDC:BA98:7654:3210' or '080A::4:1' (in this case the double colon fills in a range of address components with 0s).

The *flowinfo* parameter is a 32-bit number consisting of a 24-bit flow label (the low 24 bits), a 4-bit priority (the next 4 bits), and 4 reserved bits (the high 4 bits). A flow label is typically only used when a sender wants to enable special handling by routers. Otherwise, *flowinfo* is set to 0.

The *scopeid* parameter is a 32-bit number that's only needed when working with link-local and site-local addresses. A link-local address always starts with the prefix 'FE80:...' and is used between machines on the same LAN (routers will not forward link-local packets). In this case, *scopeid* an interface index that identifies a specific network interface on the host. This information can be viewed using a command such as 'ifconfig' on UNIX or 'ipv6 if' on Windows. A site-local address always starts with the prefix 'FEC0:...' and is used between machines within the same site (for example, all machines on a given subnet). In this case, *scopeid* is a site-identifier number.

If no data is given for *flowinfo* or *scopeid*, an IPv6 address can be given as the tuple (*host*, *port*), as with IPv4.

Functions

The socket module defines the following functions:

fromfd(*fd, family, socktype* [, *proto*])

Creates a socket object from an integer file descriptor, *fd*. The address family, socket type, and protocol number are the same as for socket(). The file descriptor must refer to a previously created socket. Returns an instance of SocketType.

getaddrinfo(*host, port* [,*family* [, *socktype* [, *proto* [, *flags*]]]])

Given *host* and *port* information about a host, this function returns a list of tuples containing information needed to open up a socket connection. *host* is a string containing a hostname or numerical IP address. *port* is a number or a string representing a service name (for example, "http", "ftp", "smtp"). Each returned tuple consists of five elements (*family*, *socktype*, *proto*, *canonname*, *sockaddr*). The *family*, *socktype*, and *proto* items have the same values as would be passed to the socket() function. *canonname* is a string representing the canonical name of the host. *sockaddr* is a tuple containing a socket address as described in the earlier section on Internet addresses. Here's an example:

```
>>> socket.getaddrinfo("www.python.org",80)
[(2,2,17,'',('194.109.137.226',80)), (2,1,6,'',('194.109.137.226'),80))]
```

In this example, getaddrinfo() has returned information about two possible socket connections. The first one (*proto*=17) is a UDP connection, and the second one (`proto=6`) is a TCP connection. The additional parameters to `getaddrinfo()` can be used to narrow the selection. For instance, this example returns information about establishing an IPv4 TCP connection:

```
>>> socket.getaddrinfo("www.python.org",80,socket.AF_INET,socket.SOCK_STREAM)
[(2,1,6,'',('194.109.137.226',80))]
```

The special constant `AF_UNSPEC` can be used for the address family to look for any kind of connection. For example, this code gets information about any TCP-like connection and may return information for either IPv4 or IPv6:

```
>>> socket.getaddrinfo("www.python.org","http",socket.AF_UNSPEC,
socket.SOCK_STREAM)
[(2,1,6,'',('194.109.137.226',80))]
```

`getaddrinfo()` is intended for a very generic purpose and is applicable to all support-ed network protocols (IPv4, IPv6, and so on). Use it if you are concerned about com-patibility and supporting future protocols, especially if you intend to support IPv6.

getdefaulttimeout()

Returns the default socket timeout in seconds. A value of `None` indicates that no time-out has been set.

getfqdn([name])

Returns the fully qualified domain name of *name*. If *name* is omitted, the local machine is assumed. For example, `getfqdn("foo")` might return `"foo.quasievil.org"`.

gethostbyname(hostname)

Translates a hostname such as `'www.python.org'` to an IPv4 address. The IP address is returned as a string, such as `'132.151.1.90'`. Does not support IPv6.

gethostbyname_ex(hostname)

Translates a hostname to an IPv4 address, but returns a triple (*hostname*, *aliaslist*, *ipaddrlist*) in which *hostname* is the primary hostname, *aliaslist* is a list of alternative hostnames for the same address, and *ipaddrlist* is a list of IPv4 addresses for the same interface on the same host. For example, `gethostbyname_ex('www.python.org')` returns something like (`'fang.python.org'`, [`'www.python.org'`], [`'194.109.137.226'`]). This function does not support IPv6.

gethostname()

Returns the hostname of the local machine.

gethostbyaddr(ip_address)

Returns the same information as `gethostbyname_ex()`, given an IP address such as `'132.151.1.90'`. If *ip_address* is an IPv6 address such as `'FEDC:BA98:7654:3210:FEDC:BA98:7654:3210'`, information regarding IPv6 will be returned.

getnameinfo(address, flags)

Given a socket address, *address*, this function translates the address into a 2-tuple (*host*, *port*), depending on the value of *flags*. The *address* parameter is a tuple specifying an address—for example, (`'www.python.org',80`). *flags* is the bitwise OR of the following constants:

Constant	Description
NI_NOFQDN	Don't use fully qualified name for local hosts.
NI_NUMERICHOST	Return the address in numeric form.
NI_NAMEREQD	Require a hostname. Returns an error if *address* has no DNS entry.
NI_NUMERICSERV	The returned *port* is returned as a string containing a port number.
NI_DGRAM	Specifies that the service being looked up is a datagram service (UDP) instead of TCP (the default).

The main purpose of this function is to get additional information about an address. Here's an example:

```
>>> socket.getnameinfo(('194.109.137.226',80),0)
('fang.python.org', 'http')
>>> socket.getnameinfo(('194.109.137.226',80),socket.NI_NUMERICSERV)
('fang.python.org','80')
```

getprotobyname(*protocolname*)

Translates an Internet protocol name (such as `'icmp'`) to a protocol number (such as the value of IPPROTO_ICMP) that can be passed to the third argument of the `socket()` function. Raises `socket.error` if the protocol name isn't recognized.

getservbyname(*servicename* [, *protocolname*])

Translates an Internet service name and protocol name to a port number for that service. For example, `getservbyname('ftp', 'tcp')` returns 21. The protocol name, if supplied, should be `'tcp'` or `'udp'`. Raises `socket.error` if *servicename* doesn't match any known service.

getservbyport(*port* [, *protocolname*])

This is the opposite of `getservbyname()`. Given a numeric port number, *port*, this function returns a string giving the service name, if any. For example, `getservbyport(21, 'tcp')` returns `'ftp'`. The protocol name, if supplied, should be `'tcp'` or `'udp'`. Raises `socket.error` if no service name is available for *port*.

htonl(*x*)

Converts 32-bit integers from host to network byte order (big endian).

htons(*x*)

Converts 16-bit integers from host to network byte order (big endian).

inet_aton(*ip_string*)

Converts an IPv4 address provided as a string (for example, `'135.128.11.209'`) to a 32-bit packed binary format for use as the raw-encoding of the address. The returned value is a four-character string containing the binary encoding. This may be useful if passing the address to C or if the address must be packed into a data structure passed to other programs. Does not support IPv6.

`inet_ntoa(packedip)`

Converts a binary-packaged IPv4 address into a string that uses the standard dotted representation (for example, `'135.128.11.209'`). `packedip` is a four-character string containing the raw 32-bit encoding of an IP address. The function may be useful if an address has been received from C or is being unpacked from a data structure. Does not support IPv6.

`ntohl(x)`

Converts 32-bit integers from network (big-endian) to host byte order.

`ntohs(x)`

Converts 16-bit integers from network (big-endian) to host byte order.

`setdefaulttimeout(timeout)`

Sets the default timeout for newly created socket objects. `timeout` is a floating-point number specified in seconds. A value of `None` may be supplied to indicate no timeout (this is the default).

`ssl(sock, key_file, cert_file)`

Creates a client-side secure socket. `sock` is an existing socket instance that has already established a connection using its `connect()` method. `key_file` is the name of a client private-key file. `cert_file` is the name of a client certificate file. `key_file` and `cert_file` must both be set to `None` or set to the names of PEM format files containing the client key and certificate. This function is available only if Python has been configured with OpenSSL support. In addition, this function cannot be used to create server-side secure sockets.

`socket(family, type [, proto])`

Creates a new socket using the given address family, socket type, and protocol number. `family` is the address family, and `type` is the socket type, as discussed in the first part of this section.
The protocol number is usually omitted (and defaults to 0). It's usually used only in conjunction with raw sockets (`SOCK_RAW`) and is set to one of the constants listed here when used.

Constant	Description
IPPROTO_AH	IPv6 authentication header
IPPROTO_DSTOPTS	IPv6 destination options
IPPROTO_EGP	Exterior gateway protocol
IPPROTO_EON	ISO CNLP (Connectionless Network Protocol)
IPPROTO_ESP	IPv6 Encapsulating security payload
IPPROTO_FRAGMENT	IPv6 fragmentation header
IPPROTO_GGP	Gateway to Gateway Protocol (RFC823)
IPPROTO_GRE	Generic Routing Encapsulation (RFC1701)

Constant	Description
IPPROTO_HELLO	Fuzzball HELLO protocol
IPPROTO_HOPOPTS	IPv6 hop-by-hop options
IPPROTO_ICMP	IPv4 ICMP
IPPROTO_ICMPV6	IPv6 ICMP
IPPROTO_IDP	XNS IDP
IPPROTO_IGMP	Group management protocol
IPPROTO_IP	IPv4
IPPROTO_IPCOMP	IP Payload compression protocol
IPPROTO_IPIP	IP inside IP
IPPROTO_IPV4	IPv4 header
IPPROTO_IPV6	IPv6 header
IPPROTO_ND	Netdisk protocol
IPPROTO_NONE	IPv6 no next header
IPPROTO_PIM	Protocol Independent Multicast
IPPROTO_PUP	Xerox PARC Universal Packet (PUP)
IPPROTO_RAW	Raw IP packet
IPPROTO_ROUTING	IPv6 routing header
IPPROTO_RSVP	Resource reservation
IPPROTO_TCP	TCP
IPPROTO_TP	OSI Transport Protocol (TP-4)
IPPROTO_UDP	UDP
IPPROTO_XTP	eXpress Transfer Protocol

To open a TCP connection, use socket(AF_INET, SOCK_STREAM). To open a UDP connection, use socket(AF_INET, SOCK_DGRAM). To open a raw IP socket, use socket(AF_INET, SOCK_RAW). Access to raw sockets is privileged and will only succeed if a program is running with administrator or root access. The function returns an instance of SocketType (described shortly).

socketpair([family [, type [, proto]]])

Creates a pair of connected socket objects using the given *family*, *type*, and *proto* options, which have the same meaning as for the socket() function. This function only applies to UNIX domain sockets (*family*=AF_UNIX). *type* may be either SOCK_DGRAM or SOCK_STREAM. If *type* is SOCK_STREAM, an object known as a *stream pipe* is created. *proto* is usually 0 (the default). The primary use of this function would be to set up interprocess communication between processes created by os.fork(). For example, the parent process would call socketpair() to create a pair of sockets and call os.fork(). The parent and child processes would then communicate with each other using these sockets. Available only on UNIX.

Sockets are represented by an instance of type SocketType. The following methods are available on a socket, *s*:

`s.accept()`

Accepts a connection and returns a pair (*conn*, *address*), where *conn* is a new socket object that can be used to send and receive data on the connection, and *address* is the address of the socket on the other end of the connection.

`s.bind(address)`

Binds the socket to an address. The format of *address* depends on the address family. In most cases, it's a tuple of the form (*hostname*, *port*). For IP addresses, the empty string represents `INADDR_ANY`, and the string `'<broadcast>'` represents `INADDR_BROADCAST`. The `INADDR_ANY` hostname (the empty string) is used to indicate that the server allows connections on any Internet interface on the system. This is often used when a server is multihomed. The `INADDR_BROADCAST` hostname (`'<broadcast>'`) is used when a socket is being used to send a broadcast message.

`s.close()`

Closes the socket. Sockets are also closed when they're garbage-collected.

`s.connect(address)`

Connects to a remote socket at *address*. The format of *address* depends on the address family, but it's normally a tuple (*hostname*, *port*). Raises `socket.error` if an error occurs.

If you're connecting to a server on the same computer, you can use the name `'localhost'` as the first argument to `s.connect()`.

`s.connect_ex(address)`

Like `connect(address)`, but returns 0 on success or the value of `errno` on failure.

`s.fileno()`

Returns the socket's file descriptor.

`s.getpeername()`

Returns the remote address to which the socket is connected. Usually the return value is a tuple (*ipaddr*, *port*), but this depends on the address family being used. Not supported on all systems.

`s.getsockname()`

Returns the socket's own address. Usually this is a tuple (*ipaddr*, *port*).

`s.getsockopt(level, optname [, buflen])`

Returns the value of a socket option. *level* defines the level of the option and is `SOL_SOCKET` for socket-level options or a protocol number such as `IPPROTO_IP` for protocol-related options. *optname* selects a specific option. If *buflen* is omitted, an integer option is assumed and its integer value is returned. If *buflen* is given, it specifies the maximum length of the buffer used to receive the option. This buffer is returned as a string, where it's up to the caller to decode its contents using the `struct` module or other means. The following tables list the socket options defined by Python. Most of these options are considered part of the Advanced Sockets API and control low-level details of the network. You will need to consult other documentation to find more detailed descriptions. Not all options are available on all machines.

The following are commonly used option names for level `SOL_SOCKET`:

Option Name	Value	Description
SO_ACCEPTCONN	0, 1	Determines whether or not the socket is accepting connections.
SO_DEBUG	0, 1	Determines whether or not debugging information is being recorded.
SO_KEEPALIVE	0, 1	Periodically probes the other end of the connection and terminates if it's half-open.
SO_RCVBUF	int	Size of receive buffer (in bytes).
SO_SNDBUF	int	Size of send buffer (in bytes).
SO_REUSEADDR	0, 1	Allows local address reuse.
SO_RCVLOWAT	int	Number of bytes read before select() returns the socket as readable.
SO_SNDLOWAT	int	Number of bytes available in send buffer before select() returns the socket as writable.
SO_RCVTIMEO	tvalue	Timeout on receive calls in seconds.
SO_SNDTIMEO	tvalue	Timeout on send calls in seconds.
SO_OOBINLINE	0, 1	Places out-of-band data into the input queue.
SO_LINGER	linger	Lingers on close() if the send buffer contains data.
SO_DONTROUTE	0, 1	Bypasses routing table lookups.
SO_ERROR	int	Gets error status.
SO_BROADCAST	0, 1	Allows sending of broadcast datagrams.
SO_TYPE	int	Gets socket type.
SO_USELOOPBACK	0, 1	Routing socket gets copy of what it sends.

tvalue is a binary structure that's decoded as (*second*, *microsec*) = struct.unpack("ll", *tvalue*).

linger is a binary structure that's decoded as (*linger_onoff*, *linger_sec*) = struct.unpack("ii", *linger*).

The following options are available for level IPPROTO_IP:

Option Name	Value	Description
IP_ADD_MEMBERSHIP	ipmreg	Join multicast group (set only).
IP_DEFAULT_MULTICAST_LOOP	uchar	Loopback.
IP_DEFAULT_MULTICAST_TTL	uchar	Time to live.
IP_DROP_MEMBERSHIP	ipmreg	Leave a multicast group (set only).
IP_HDRINCL	int	IP header included with data.
IP_MAX_MEMBERSHIPS	int	Maximum number of multicast groups.
IP_MULTICAST_IF	inaddr	Outgoing interface.

Option Name	Value	Description
IP_MULTICAST_LOOP	uchar	Loopback.
IP_MULTICAST_TTL	uchar	Time to live.
IP_OPTIONS	char[44]	IP header options.
IP_RECVDSTADDR	0,1	Receive IP destination address with datagram.
IP_RECVOPTS	0,1	Receive all IP options with datagram.
IP_RECVRETOPTS	0,1	Receive IP options with response.
IP_RETOPTS	ipopts	Set/get IP per-packet options.
IP_TOS	int	Type of service.
IP_TTL	int	Time to live.

inaddr is a 32-bit binary structure containing an IP address (struct.unpack('bbbb', *inaddr*)). *ipmreg* is a 64-bit binary structure containing two IP addresses in the same format as *inaddr*. *uchar* is a 1-byte unsigned integer as created by struct.pack('b', *uvalue*). *char[44]* is a string containing at most 44 bytes.

The following options are available for level IPPROTO_IPV6:

Option Name	Value	Description
IPV6_CHECKSUM	0,1	Have system compute checksum.
IPV6_JOIN_GROUP		Join multicast group.
IPV6_LEAVE_GROUP		Leave multicast group.
IPV6_MULTICAST_HOPS	int	Hop-limit for multicast packets.
IPV6_MULTICAST_IF		Interface for outgoing multicast packets.
IPV6_MULTICAST_LOOP	0,1	Deliver outgoing multicast packets back to local application.
IPV6_PKTINFO	pktinfo	Packet information structure.
IPV6_HOPLIMIT	int	Hop limit.
IPV6_NEXTHOP	addr	Next hop address.
IPV6_HOPOPTS	impl	Hop-by-hop options.
IPV6_DSTOPTS	impl	Destination options.
IPV6_RTHDR	rthdr	Routing header.
IPV6_UNICAST_HOPS	int	Hop limit for unicast packets.
IPV6_V6ONLY	0,1	Only connect to other IPV6 nodes.

pktinfo is an IPV6 packet information structure that contains an IPv6 address and an integer interface index (see the definition of in6_pktinfo in <netinet/in.h> in C). *rthdr* is an IPv6 routing header used for source routing (see RFC 2460). *addr* is an IPv6 address, and *impl* means that the data is implementation specific.

The following options are available for level SOL_TCP:

Option Name	Value	Description
TCP_CORK	0,1	Don't send out partial frames if set.
TCP_DEFER_ACCEPT	0,1	Awake listener only when data arrives on socket.
TCP_INFO	*tcp_info*	Returns a structure containing information about the socket. *tcp_info* is implementation specific.
TCP_KEEPCNT	int	Maximum number of keepalive probes TCP should send before dropping a connection.
TCP_KEEPIDLE	int	Time in seconds the connection should be idle before TCP starts sending keepalive probes if the TCP_KEEPALIVE option has been set.
TCP_KEEPINTVL	int	Time in seconds between keepalive probes.
TCP_LINGER2	int	Lifetime of orphaned FIN_WAIT2 state sockets.
TCP_MAXSEG	int	Maximum segment size for outgoing TCP packets.
TCP_NODELAY	0,1	If set, disables the Nagle algorithm.
TCP_QUICKACK	0,1	If set, ACKs are sent immediately. Disables the TCP delayed ACK algorithm.
TCP_SYNCNT	int	Number of SYN retransmits before aborting a connection request.
TCP_WINDOW_CLAMP	int	Sets an upper bound on the advertised TCP window size.

s.gettimeout()

Returns the current timeout value if any. Returns a floating point number in seconds or None if no timeout is set.

s.listen(*backlog*)

Starts listening for incoming connections. *backlog* specifies the maximum number of pending connections the operating system should queue before connections are refused. The value should be at least 1, with 5 being sufficient for most applications.

s.makefile([*mode* [, *bufsize*]])

Creates a file object associated with the socket. *mode* and *bufsize* have the same meaning as with the built-in open() function. The file object uses a duplicated version of the socket file descriptor, created using os.dup(), so the file object and socket object can be closed or garbage-collected independently.

s.recv(*bufsize* [, *flags*])

Receives data from the socket. The data is returned as a string. The maximum amount of data to be received is specified by *bufsize*. *flags* provides additional information about the message and is usually omitted (in which case it defaults to zero). If used, it's usually set to one of the following constants (system-dependent):

Constant	Description
MSG_PEEK	Look at data, but don't discard (receive only)
MSG_WAITALL	Don't return until the requested number of bytes have been read (receive only)
MSG_OOB	Receive/send out-of-band data
MSG_DONTWAIT	Nonblocking operation.
MSG_DONTROUTE	Bypass routing table lookup (send only)

s.recvfrom(*bufsize* [, *flags*])

Like the recv() method, except that the return value is a pair (*data*, *address*) in which *data* is a string containing the data received and *address* is the address of the socket sending the data. The optional *flags* argument has the same meaning as for recv(). This function is primarily used in conjunction with the UDP protocol.

s.send(*string* [, *flags*])

Sends data in *string* to a connected socket. The optional *flags* argument has the same meaning as for recv(), described earlier. Returns the number of bytes sent, which may be fewer than the number of bytes in *string*. Raises an exception if an error occurs.

s.sendall(*string* [, *flags*])

Sends data in *string* to a connected socket, except that an attempt is made to send all of the data before returning. Returns None on success; raises an exception on failure. *flags* has the same meaning as for send().

s.sendto(*string* [, *flags*], *address*)

Sends data to the socket. *flags* has the same meaning as for recv(). *address* is a tuple of the form (*host*, *port*), which specifies the remote address. The socket should not already be connected. Returns the number of bytes sent. This function is primarily used in conjunction with the UDP protocol.

s.setblocking(*flag*)

If *flag* is zero, the socket is set to nonblocking mode. Otherwise, the socket is set to blocking mode (the default). In nonblocking mode, if a recv() call doesn't find any data or if a send() call cannot immediately send the data, the socket.error exception is raised. In blocking mode, these calls block until they can proceed.

s.setsockopt(*level*, *optname*, *value*)

Sets the value of the given socket option. *level* and *optname* have the same meaning as for getsockopt(). The value can be an integer or a string representing the contents of a buffer. In the latter case, it's up to the caller to ensure that the string contains the proper data. See getsockopt() for socket option names, values, and descriptions.

`s.settimeout(timeout)`

Sets a timeout on socket operations. `timeout` is a floating-point number in seconds. A value of `None` means no timeout. If a timeout occurs, a `socket.timeout` exception is raised. As a general rule, timeouts should be set as soon as a socket is created because they can be applied to operations involved in establishing a connection (such as `connect()`).

`s.shutdown(how)`

Shuts down one or both halves of the connection. If `how` is 0, further receives are disallowed. If `how` is 1, further sends are disallowed. If `how` is 2, further sends and receives are disallowed.

Exceptions

`error`

This exception is raised for socket- or address-related errors. It returns a pair (`errno`, `mesg`) with the error returned by the underlying system call.

`herror`

Error raised for address-related errors. Returns a tuple (`herrno`, `hmesg`) containing an error number and error message.

`gaierror`

Error raised for address-related errors in the `getaddrinfo()` and `getnameinfo()` functions. The error value is a tuple (`errno`, `mesg`), where `errno` is an error number and `mesg` is a string containing a message. `errno` is set to one of the following constants defined in the `socket` module:

Constant	Description
EAI_ADDRFAMILY	Address family not supported.
EAI_AGAIN	Temporary failure in name resolution.
EAI_BADFLAGS	Invalid flags.
EAI_BADHINTS	Bad hints.
EAI_FAIL	Nonrecoverable failure in name resolution.
EAI_FAMILY	Address family not supported by host.
EAI_MEMORY	Memory allocation failure.
EAI_NODATA	No address associated with node name.
EAI_NONAME	No node name or service name provided.
EAI_PROTOCOL	Protocol not supported.
EAI_SERVICE	Service name not supported for socket type.
EAI_SOCKTYPE	Socket type not supported.
EAI_SYSTEM	System error.

`timeout`

Exception raised when a socket operation times out. This only occurs if a timeout has been set using the `setdefaulttimeout()` function or `settimeout()` method of a socket object. Exception value is a string, `'timeout'`.

Example

A simple example of a TCP connection is shown earlier in this chapter. The following example illustrates a simple UDP client and server:

```
# UDP message server
# Receive small packets from anywhere and print them out
import socket
s = socket.socket(socket.AF_INET, socket.SOCK_DGRAM)
s.bind(("",10000))
while 1:
    data, address = s.recvfrom(256)
    print address[0], "said : ", data

# UDP message client
# Send a message packet to the server
import socket
s = socket.socket(socket.AF_INET, socket.SOCK_DGRAM)
while 1:
    msg = raw_input("Say something : ")
    if msg:
        s.sendto(msg, ("servername",10000))
    else:
        break
s.close()
```

Notes

- Not all constants and socket options are available on all platforms. If portability is your goal, you should only rely on options that are documented in major sources such as the W. Richard Stevens' book *UNIX Network Programming*, cited at the beginning of this chapter.

- There is a subtle difference between nonblocking socket operations and operations involving a timeout. When a socket function is used in nonblocking mode, it will return immediately with an error if the operation would have blocked. When a timeout is set, a function returns an error only if the operation doesn't complete within a specified timeout.

See Also:

SocketServer (p. 388), asyncore (p. 370), select (p. 374)

SocketServer

The `SocketServer` module is used to write TCP, UDP, and UNIX domain socket servers. Rather than having to implement servers using the low-level socket module, this module provides four classes that implement these protocols:

`TCPServer(`*`address, handler`*`)`

A server supporting the TCP protocol using IPv4. *address* is a tuple of the form
(*host, port*). *handler* is an instance of a subclass of the `BaseRequestHandler` class
described later.

`UDPServer(`*`address, handler`*`)`

A server supporting the Internet UDP protocol using IPv4. *address* and *handler* are
the same as for `TCPServer()`.

`UnixStreamServer(`*`address, handler`*`)`

A server implementing a stream-oriented protocol using UNIX domain sockets.
Inherits from `TCPServer`.

`UnixDatagramServer(`*`address, handler`*`)`

A server implementing a datagram protocol using UNIX domain sockets. Inherits from
`UDPServer`.

Instances of all four server classes have the following methods and attributes:

`s``.fileno()`

Returns the integer file descriptor for the server socket.

`s``.handle_request()`

Waits for a request and handles it by creating an instance of the `handler` class
(described shortly) and invoking its `handle()` method.

`s``.serve_forever()`

Handles an infinite number of requests.

`s``.address_family`

The protocol family of the server, either `socket.AF_INET`, `socket.AF_INET6`, or
`socket.AF_UNIX`.

`s``.RequestHandlerClass`

The user-provided request handler class that was passed to the server constructor.

`s``.server_address`

The address on which the server is listening, such as the tuple (`'127.0.0.1', 80`).

`s``.socket`

The socket object being used for incoming requests.

In addition, the server classes define the following class attributes (*Server* should be
filled in with the name of one of the four available classes):

`Server``.allow_reuse_address`

Allows a socket to reuse an address. This is useful when you want to immediately restart
a server on the same port after a program has terminated (otherwise you have to wait a
few minutes). The default value is `False`.

***Server*.request_queue_size**

The size of the request queue that's passed to the socket's `listen()` method. The default value is 5.

***Server*.socket_type**

The socket type used by the server, such as `socket.SOCK_STREAM` or `socket.SOCK_DGRAM`.

Requests are handled by defining a subclass of the class `BaseRequestHandler`. When the server receives a connection, it creates an instance, *h*, of the `handler` class and invokes the following methods:

***h*.finish()**

Called to perform cleanup actions after the `handle()` method has completed. By default, it does nothing. It's not called if either the `setup()` or `handle()` method generates an exception.

***h*.handle()**

This method is called to perform the actual work of a request. It's called with no arguments, but several instance variables are set to useful values. `h.request` contains the request, `h.client_address` contains the client address, and `h.server` contains an instance of the server that called the handler. For stream services such as TCP, the `h.request` attribute is a socket object. For datagram services, it's a string containing the received data.

***h*.setup()**

This method is called before the `handle()` method to perform initialization actions. By default, it does nothing.

The process of creating a server involves the following steps:

1. Define a request handler class by subclassing `BaseRequestHandler`.

2. Create an instance of one of the server classes by passing the server's address and the request handler class.

3. Call the `handle_request()` or `serve_forever()` method of the server to process connections.

The following code illustrates the process for a very simple HTTP server that simply echoes the HTTP request back in a web page:

```
import SocketServer
import socket
import string
# Read an HTTP request from a client and bounce it back in a Web page
class EchoHandler(SocketServer.BaseRequestHandler):
    def handle(self):
        f = self.request.makefile()
        self.request.send("HTTP/1.0 200 OK\r\n")
        self.request.send("Content-type: text/plain\r\n\r\n")
        self.request.send("Received connection from %s\r\n\r\n" %
                        (self.client_address,))
        while 1:
            line = f.readline()
            self.request.send(line)
            if not string.strip(line):
```

```
            break
        f.close()
# Create the server and start serving
serv = SocketServer.TCPServer(("",80),EchoHandler)
serv.serve_forever()
```

By default, the server classes process requests one at a time in a synchronous manner.
The servers can alternatively handle requests in a subprocess, using os.fork(), or as a
separate thread by instantiating one of the following server classes instead of the four
classes listed earlier:

- ForkingUDPServer(*address, handler*)
- ForkingTCPServer(*address, handler*)
- ThreadingUDPServer(*address, handler*)
- ThreadingTCPServer(*address, handler*)

These classes are actually composed using the following mix-in classes, which are also
defined in the SocketServer module:

- ThreadingMixIn
- ForkingMixIn

For instance, the ForkingTCPServer class is defined as follows:

```
class ForkingTCPServer(ForkingMixIn, TCPServer): pass
```

If you define your own server classes by inheriting from one of the existing servers, the
mix-in classes can be used in a similar way to provide threaded and forking variants.
    Finally, two additional classes can be used as base classes for handlers:
StreamRequestHandler and DatagramRequestHandler. When used, these classes
override the setup() and finish() methods of the handle to provide two file attributes, self.rfile and self.wfile, that can be used to read and write data to and
from the client, respectively. For example:

```
# Read an HTTP request from a client and bounce it back
class EchoHandler(SocketServer.StreamRequestHandler):
    def handle(self):
        self.wfile.write("HTTP/1.0 200 OK\r\n")
        self.wfile.write("Content-type: text/plain\r\n\r\n")
        self.wfile.write("Received connection from %s\r\n\r\n" %
                         (self.client_address,))
        while 1:
            line = self.rfile.readline()
            self.wfile.write(line)
            if not string.strip(line):
                break
```

Notes

- All the server classes can be specialized by inheritance.
- To support different network protocols, inherit from an appropriate base class and
  change the address_family attribute. For example:

```
class ThreadingTCP6Server(ThreadingTCPServer):
    address_family = socket.AF_INET6
```

See Also:

socket (p. 375), BaseHTTPServer (p. 313), SimpleHTTPServer (p. 428),
CGIHTTPServer (p. 402), thread (p. 356), os (p. 308).

## 22

Internet Application Protocols

T HIS CHAPTER DESCRIBES MODULES USED TO write Internet applications. The primary focus is on application-level network protocols such as HTTP, FTP, and NNTP. In addition, this chapter covers modules that are commonly used in web applications such as modules related to CGI scripting. Low-level network programming with sockets is covered in Chapter 21, "Network Programming." Information related to data formats commonly used in Internet applications is covered in Chapter 23, "Internet Data Handling and Encoding."

BaseHTTPServer

The BaseHTTPServer module defines two base classes used to implement standalone HTTP servers. This module is used by a number of other modules, including SimpleHTTPServer, CGIHTTPServer, and SimpleXMLRPCServer.

HTTPServer(*server_address, request_handler*)

Creates a new HTTPServer object. *server_address* is a tuple of the form (*host*, *port*) on which the server will listen. *request_handler* is a factory function that is used to create instances of BaseHTTPRequestHandler objects, described later. These handler objects are used to handle the details of each connection that is made to the server.

The HTTPServer class is derived from SocketServer.TCPServer and supports the same methods. In particular, the following functions are most relevant:

Function	Description
h.handle_request()	Processes a single request
h.serve_forever()	Handles an infinite number of requests

Requests are handled by defining a handler derived from the following class:

BaseHTTPRequestHandler(*request, client_address, server*)

This class is used to handle HTTP requests. When a connection is received, the request and HTTP headers are parsed. An attempt is then made to execute a method of the form do_*REQUEST* based on the request type. For example, a 'GET' method invokes do_GET() and a 'POST' method invokes do_POST. By default, this class does nothing, so these methods must be defined in subclasses.

The following class variables are defined for BaseHTTPRequestHandler:

BaseHTTPRequestHandler.server_version

Specifies the server software version string that the server reports to clients—for example, `'ServerName/1.2'`.

BaseHTTPRequestHandler.sys_version

Python system version, such as `'Python/2.0'`.

BaseHTTPRequestHandler.error_message_format

Format string used to build error messages sent to the client. The format string is applied to a dictionary containing the attributes `code`, `message`, and `explain`. For example:

```
'''<head>
  <title>Error response</title>
  </head>
  <body>
  <h1>Error response</h1>
  <p>Error code %(code)d.
  <p>Message: %(message)s.
  <p>Error code explanation: %(code)s = %(explain)s.
  </body>'''
```

BaseHTTPRequestHandler.protocol_version

HTTP protocol version used in responses. The default is `'HTTP/1.0'`.

BaseHTTPRequestHandler.MessageClass

Class used to parse HTTP headers. The default is `mimetools.Message`.

BaseHTTPRequestHandler.responses

Mapping of integer HTTP error codes to two-element tuples (`message`, `explain`) that describe the problem. For example, the integer code 404 is mapped to (`"Not Found"`, `"Nothing matches the given URI"`). The integer code and strings in this mapping are used when creating error messages as defined in the `error_message_format` attribute.

An instance, b, of `BaseHTTPRequestHandler` has the following attributes:

Attribute	Description
b.client_address	Client address as a tuple (host, port)
b.command	Request type, such as `'GET'`, `'POST'`, `'HEAD'`, and so on
b.path	Contains the request path
b.request_version	HTTP version string from the request, such as `'HTTP/1.0'`
b.headers	HTTP headers, typically represented as a mimetools.Message object
b.rfile	Input stream for optional input data. This is used when a client is uploading data (for example, during a POST request).
b.wfile	Output stream for writing a response back to the client

The following methods are used:

b.`handle`()

Request dispatcher. Parses the request and calls a method of the form do_*().

b.`send_error`(*code* [, *message*])

Sends an error reply to the client. *code* is the numeric HTTP response code. *message* is an optional error message.

b.`send_response`(*code* [, *message*])

Sends a response header. The HTTP response line is sent, followed by `Server` and `Date` headers. *code* is an HTTP response code, and *message* is an optional message.

b.`send_header`(*keyword*, *value*)

Writes a MIME header entry to the output stream. *keyword* is the header keyword, and *value* is its value.

b.`end_headers`()

Sends a blank line to signal the end of the MIME headers.

b.`log_request`([*code* [, *size*]])

Logs a successful request. *code* is the HTTP code, and *size* is the size of the response in bytes (if available).

b.`log_error`(*format*, ...)

Logs an error message. By default, `log_message`() is called.

b.`log_message`(*format*, ...)

Logs an arbitrary message to `sys.stderr`. *format* is a format string applied to any additional arguments passed. The client address and current time are prefixed to every message.

b.`version_string`()

Returns the server software's version string—a combination of the `server_version` and `sys_version` variables.

b.`date_time_string`()

Returns the current date and time, formatted for a header.

b.`log_date_time_string`()

Returns the current date and time, formatted for logging.

b.`address_string`()

Performs a name lookup on the client's IP address and returns a hostname formatted for logging.

Example

The following example handles GET methods and simply echoes the request back to the client on a web page:

```
import BaseHTTPServer
class EchoHandler(BaseHTTPServer.BaseHTTPRequestHandler):
    # Echo the request information back on a Web page
    def do_GET(self):
            self.send_response(200)
            self.send_header('Content-type','text/html')
            self.end_headers()
            self.wfile.write('''
<html><head><title>Your Request</title></head>
<body>
<pre>
You requested the following : %s
The request headers were :
%s
</pre></body></html>
''' % (self.path, self.headers))

server = BaseHTTPServer.HTTPServer(('',80),EchoHandler)
server.serve_forever()
```

> **Note**
>
> The contents of this module are rarely used directly. Instead, the module is used in the implementa-
> tion of other servers. For example, see the `SimpleHTTPServer` and `CGIHTTPServer` modules.

> **See Also:**
>
> `SimpleHTTPServer` (p. 428), `CGIHTTPServer` (p. 402), `SimpleXMLRPCServer` (p.429),
> `SocketServer` (p. 388), `httplib` (p. 415)

cgi

The `cgi` module is used to implement CGI scripts in web applications. CGI scripts are
programs executed by a web server when it wants to process user input submitted
through an HTML form such as the following:

```
<FORM ACTION='/cgi-bin/foo.cgi' METHOD='GET'>
Your name : <INPUT type='Text' name='name' size='30'>
Your email address: <INPUT type='Text' name='email' size='30'>
<INPUT type='Submit' name='submit-button' value='Subscribe'>
</FORM>
```

When the form is submitted, the web server executes the CGI program `foo.cgi`. CGI
programs receive input from two sources: `sys.stdin` and environment variables set by
the server. The following list details common environment variables set by web servers:

Variable	Description
AUTH_TYPE	Authentication method
CONTENT_LENGTH	Length of data passed in `sys.stdin`
CONTENT_TYPE	Type of query data
DOCUMENT_ROOT	Document root directory
GATEWAY_INTERFACE	CGI revision string

Variable	Description
HTTP_ACCEPT	MIME types accepted by the client
HTTP_COOKIE	Netscape persistent cookie value
HTTP_FROM	Email address of client (often disabled)
HTTP_REFERER	Referring URL
HTTP_USER_AGENT	Client browser
PATH_INFO	Extra path information passed
PATH_TRANSLATED	Translated version of PATH_INFO
QUERY_STRING	Query string
REMOTE_ADDR	Remote IP address of the client
REMOTE_HOST	Remote hostname of the client
REMOTE_IDENT	User making the request
REMOTE_USER	Authenticated username
REQUEST_METHOD	Method ('GET' or 'POST')
SCRIPT_NAME	Name of the program
SERVER_NAME	Server hostname
SERVER_PORT	Server port number
SERVER_PROTOCOL	Server protocol
SERVER_SOFTWARE	Name and version of the server software

As output, a CGI program writes to standard output sys.stdout. The gory details of CGI programming can be found in a book such as *CGI Programming with Perl, 2nd Edition*, by Shishir Gundavaram (O'Reilly & Associates, 2000). For our purposes, there are really only two things to know. First, the contents of an HTML form are passed to a CGI program in a sequence of text known as a *query string*. In Python, the contents of the query string are accessed using the FieldStorage class. For example:

```
import cgi
form = cgi.FieldStorage()
name = form.getvalue('name')     # Get 'name' field from a form
email = form.getvalue('email')   # Get 'email' field from a form
```

Second, the output of a CGI program consists of two parts: an HTTP header and the raw data (which is typically HTML). A blank line always separates these two components. A simple HTTP header looks like this:

```
print 'Content-type: text/html'   # HTML Output
print                             # Blank line (required!)
```

The rest of the output is the raw output. For example:

```
print '<TITLE>My CGI Script</TITLE>'
print '<H1>Hello World!</H1>'
print 'You are %s (%s)' % (name, email)
```

If you need to signal an error, that is done by including a special 'Status:' header in the output. For example:

```
print 'Status: 401 Forbidden'    # HTTP Error code
print 'Content-type: text/plain'
```

```
print                           # Blank line (required)
print 'You're not worthy of accessing this page!'
```

Most of the work in the `cgi` module is performed by creating an instance of the `FieldStorage` class. This class reads the contents of a form by reading and parsing the query string passed in an environment variable or standard input. Because input can be read from standard input, only one instance should be created. An instance, `f`, of `FieldStorage` has the following attributes:

Attribute	Description
`f.name`	The field name, if specified
`f.filename`	Client-side filename used in uploads
`f.value`	Value as a string
`f.file`	File-like object from which data can be read
`f.type`	Content type
`f.type_options`	Dictionary of options specified on the content-type line of the HTTP request
`f.disposition`	The `'content-disposition'` field; None if not specified
`f.disposition_options`	Dictionary of disposition options
`f.headers`	A dictionary-like object containing all the HTTP header contents

Values from a form can be extracted using the following methods:

f.getvalue(*fieldname* **[,** *default* **])**

Returns the value of a given field with the name *fieldname*. If a field is defined twice, this function will return a list of all values defined. If *default* is supplied, it specifies the value to return if the field is not present.

f.getfirst(*fieldname* **[,** *default* **])**

Returns the first value defined for a field with the name *fieldname*. If *default* is supplied, it specifies the value to return if the field is not present.

f.getlist(*fieldname* **)**

Returns a list of all values defined for *fieldname*. Always returns a list, even if only one value is defined. Returns an empty list if no values exist.

In addition, the `cgi` module defines a class, `MiniFieldStorage`, that contains only the attribute's name and value. This class is used to represent individual fields of a form passed in the query string, whereas `FieldStorage` is used to contain multiple fields and multipart data.

Instances of `FieldStorage` are accessed like a Python dictionary, where the keys are the field names on the form. When accessed in this manner, the objects returned are themselves an instance of `FieldStorage` for multipart data (content type is `'multipart/form-data'`) or file uploads, an instance of `MiniFieldStorage` for simple fields (content type is `'application/x-www-form-urlencoded'`), or a list of such instances in cases where a form contains multiple fields with the same name. For example:

```
form = cgi.FieldStorage()
if not form.has_key("name"):
    print "<b>Please enter your name</b>"
    return
name = form['name'].value     # Get 'name' field from a form
email = form['email'].value   # Get 'email' field from a form
```

If a field represents an uploaded file, accessing the value attribute reads the entire file into memory as a string. Because this may consume a large amount of memory on the server, it may be preferable to read uploaded data in smaller pieces by reading from the file attribute directly. For instance, the following example reads uploaded data line by line:

```
fileitem = form['userfile']
if fileitem.file:
    # It's an uploaded file; count lines
    linecount = 0
    while 1:
        line = fileitem.file.readline()
        if not line: break
        linecount = linecount + 1
```

The following functions provide a more low-level CGI interface:

escape(s [, quote])

Converts the characters '&', '<', and '>' in string s to HTML-safe sequences such as '&', '<', and '>'. If the optional flag quote is true, the double-quote character (") is also translated to '"'.

parse([fp [, environ [, keep_blank_values [, strict_parsing]]]])

Parses a form into a dictionary. fp is a file object from which data is read (defaults to stdin). environ is a dictionary containing environment variables (defaults to os.environ). keep_blank_values, if set to True, instructs the parser to map blank entries into empty strings. Otherwise, blank entries are ignored (the default). The strict_parsing option is a Boolean flag that specifies what to do with parsing errors. By default, errors are ignored. If set to True, parsing errors result in a ValueError exception. Returns a dictionary mapping field names to lists of values.

parse_header(string)

Parses the data supplied after an HTTP header field such as 'content-type'. The data is split into a primary value and a dictionary of secondary parameters that are returned in a tuple. For example, the command

```
parse_header('text/html; a=hello; b="world"')
```

returns this result:

```
('text/html', {'a':'hello', 'b':'world'}).
```

parse_multipart(fp,pdict)

Parses input of type 'multipart/form-data' as is commonly used with file uploads. fp is the input file, and pdict is a dictionary containing parameters of the content-type header. Returns a dictionary mapping field names to lists of values. This function doesn't work with nested multipart data. The FieldStorage class should be used instead.

```
parse_qs(qs [, keep_blank_values [, strict_parsing]]):
```

Parses a query string, *qs*. *keep_blank_values* and *strict_parsing* have the same meaning as in parse(). Returns a dictionary mapping field names to lists of values.

```
parse_qsl(qs [, keep_blank_values [, strict_parsing]])
```

Like parse_qs(), except that a list of (*name*, *value*) pairs is returned.

```
print_directory()
```

Formats the name of the current working directory in HTML and prints it out. The resulting output will be sent back to the browser, which can be useful for debugging.

```
print_environ()
```

Creates a list of all environment variables formatted in HTML. Used for debugging.

```
print_environ_usage()
```

Prints a more selected list of useful environment variables in HTML. Used for debugging.

```
print_form(form)
```

Formats the data supplied on a form in HTML. *form* must be an instance of FieldStorage. Used for debugging.

```
test()
```

Writes a minimal HTTP header and prints all the information provided to the script in HTML format. Primarily used for debugging.

Notes

- The process of installing a CGI program varies widely according to the type of web server being used. Typically programs are placed in a special cgi-bin directory. A server may also require additional configuration. You should consult the documentation for the server or the server's administrator for more details.

- On UNIX, Python CGI programs may require appropriate execute permissions to be set and a line such as the following to appear as the first line of the program:

```
#!/usr/local/bin/python
import cgi
...
```

- To simplify debugging, import the cgitb module—for example, import cgitb; cgitb.enable(). This modifies exception handling so that errors are displayed in the web browser.

- If you invoke an external program—for example, via the os.system() or os.popen() function—be careful not to pass arbitrary strings received from the client to the shell. This is a well-known security hole that hackers can use to execute arbitrary shell commands on the server (because the command passed to these functions is first interpreted by the UNIX shell as opposed to being executed directly). In particular, never pass any part of a URL or form data to a shell command unless it has first been thoroughly checked by making sure that the string contains only alphanumeric characters, dashes, underscores, and periods.

- On UNIX, don't give a CGI program setuid mode. This is a security liability and not supported on all machines.
- Don't use 'from cgi import *' with this module. The cgi module defines a wide variety of names and symbols that you probably don't want in your namespace.

- The original CGI specification can be found at http://hoohoo.ncsa.uiuc.edu/cgi/interface.html.

See Also:
CGIHTTPServer (p. 402)

cgitb

This module provides an alternative exception handler that displays a detailed report whenever an uncaught exception occurs. The report contains source code, values of parameters, and local variables. Originally, this module was developed to help debug CGI scripts, but it can be used in any application.

enable([*display* [, *logdir* [, *context* [, *format*]]]])

Enables special exception handling. *display* is a flag that determines whether any information is displayed when an error occurs. The default value is 1. *logdir* specifies a directory in which error reports will be written to files instead of printed to standard output. When *logdir* is given, each error report is written to a unique file created by the tempfile.mkstemp() function (see **p. 342**). *context* is an integer specifying the number of lines of source code to display around lines upon which the exception occurred. *format* is a string that specifies the output format. A format of 'html' specifies HTML (the default). Any other value results in plain-text format.

handle([*info*])

Handles an exception using the default settings of the enable() function. *info* is a tuple (*exctype*, *excvalue*, *tb*) where *exctype* is an exception type, *excvalue* is an exception value, and *tb* is a traceback object. This tuple is normally obtained using sys.exc_info(). If *info* is omitted, the current exception is used.

Note

To enable special exception handling in CGI scripts, include the line import cgitb; enable() at the beginning of the script.

CGIHTTPServer

The CGIHTTPServer module provides a simple standalone HTTP server handler that can run CGI scripts. The server is defined by the following request handler class, intended for use with the BaseHTTPServer module:

CGIHTTPRequestHandler(*request, client_address, server*)

Serves files from the current directory and all its subdirectories. In addition, the handler will run a file as a CGI script if it's located in a special CGI directory (defined by the cgi_directories attribute). The handler supports both GET and POST methods.

The list of valid CGI directories is contained in the following attribute:

CGIHTTPRequestHandler.cgi_directories

List of CGI directories. Defaults to ['/cgi-bin', '/htbin'].

Example

```
from BaseHTTPServer import HTTPServer
from CGIHTTPServer import CGIHTTPRequestHandler
import os
# Change to the document root
os.chdir('/home/httpd/html')
# Start the CGI server
serv = HTTPServer(('',80),CGIHTTPRequestHandler)
serv.serve_forever()
```

Notes

- A log of requests is printed to sys.stdout. This output can be redirected elsewhere by simply replacing sys.stdout with an appropriate file object.
- For security, CGI scripts are executed with a UID of user nobody.
- Problems with the CGI script will be translated to HTTP error 403.
- Requests are handled using the do_GET and do_POST methods, both of which can be redefined in subclasses.
- To prevent problems in the execution of CGI scripts, it is usually a good idea to use CGI directory names that do not contain any embedded whitespace.

See Also:

BaseHTTPServer (p. 393), SimpleHTTPServer (p. 428), cgi (p. 396), httplib (p. 415)

Cookie

The Cookie module provides support for server-side management of HTTP cookies. Cookies are used to provide state management in CGI scripts that implement sessions, user logins, shopping carts, and related features. To drop a cookie on a user's browser, an HTTP server typically adds an HTTP header similar to the following to an HTTP response (see the httplib module):

```
Set-Cookie: session=8273612; expires=Sun, 18-Feb-2001 15:00:00 GMT; \
            path=/; domain=foo.bar.com
```

Alternatively, a cookie can be set by embedding JavaScript in the <head> section of an HTML document:

```
<SCRIPT LANGUAGE="JavaScript">
document.cookie = "session=8273612; expires=Sun, 18-Feb-2001 15:00:00 GMT; \
    Feb 17; Path=/; Domain=foo.bar.com;"
</SCRIPT>
```

The Cookie module simplifies the task of generating cookie values by providing a special dictionary-like object that stores and manages collections of cookie values known as *morsels*. Each morsel has a name, a value, and a set of optional attributes containing metadata to be supplied to the browser (expires, path, comment, domain, max-age, secure, version). The name is usually a simple identifier such as "name" and must not be the same as one of the metadata names such as "expires" or "path". The value is usually a short string. To create a cookie, simply create a cookie object like this:

```
c = Cookie.SimpleCookie()
```

Next, cookie values (morsels) can be set using ordinary dictionary assignment:

```
c["session"] = 8273612
c["user"] = "beazley"
```

Additional attributes of a specific morsel are set as follows:

```
c["session"]["path"] = "/"
c["session"]["domain"] = "foo.bar.com"
c["session"]["expires"] = "18-Feb-2001 15:00:00 GMT"
```

To output the cookie data as a set of HTTP headers, use the c.output() method. For example:

```
print c.output()
# Produces two lines of output
# Set-Cookie: session=8273612; expires=...; path=/; domain=...
# Set-Cookie: user=beazley
```

When a browser sends a cookie back to an HTTP server, it is encoded as a string of *key=value* pairs, such as "session=8273612; user=beazley". Optional attributes such as expires, path, and domain are not returned. The cookie string can usually be found in the HTTP_COOKIE environment variable, which can be read by CGI applications. To recover cookie values, use code similar to the following:

```
c = Cookie.SimpleCookie(os.environ["HTTP_COOKIE"])
session = c["session"].value
user    = c["user"].value
```

In the preceding examples, SimpleCookie is a class that derives from BaseCookie.

SimpleCookie([input])

Defines a cookie object in which cookie values are interpreted as simple strings. The c.value_decode() method is the identity function, and the c.value_encode() method uses the str() function to generate encoded values.

A cookie instance, c, provides the following methods:

`c.value_decode(val)`

Takes a string, `val`, and returns a decoded cookie value. This function is used to interpret a cookie value returned to a server by a browser.

`c.value_encode(val)`

Takes an object, `val`, and returns it as an encoded string suitable for use in an HTTP header. A server would use this to encode cookie values being sent to the browser.

`c.output([attrs [,header [,sep]]])`

Generates a string suitable for use in setting cookie values in HTTP headers. `attrs` is an optional list of the optional attributes to include (`"expires"`, `"path"`, `"domain"`, and so on). By default, all cookie attributes are included. `header` is the HTTP header to use (`'Set-Cookie: '` by default). `sep` is the character used to join the headers together and is a newline by default.

`c.js_output([attrs])`

Generates a string containing JavaScript code that will set the cookie if executed on a browser supporting JavaScript. `attrs` is an optional list of the attributes to include.

`c.load(rawdata)`

Loads the cookie `c` with data found in `rawdata`. If `rawdata` is a string, it's assumed to be in the same format as the `HTTP_COOKIE` environment variable in a CGI program. If `rawdata` is a dictionary, each `key-value` pair is interpreted by setting `c[key]=value`.

   Internally, the `key/value` pairs used to store a cookie value are instances of a `Morsel` class. An instance, `m`, of `Morsel` behaves like a dictionary and allows the optional `"expires"`, `"path"`, `"comment"`, `"domain"`, `"max-age"`, `"secure"`, and `"version"` keys to be set. In addition, the morsel `m` has the following methods and attributes:

`m.value`

A string containing the raw value of the cookie.

`m.coded_value`

A string containing the encoded value of the cookie that would be sent to or received from the browser.

`m.key`

The cookie name.

`m.set(key, value, coded_value)`

Sets the values of `m.key`, `m.value`, and `m.coded_value` above.

`m.isReservedKey(k)`

Tests whether `k` is a reserved keyword, such as `"expires"`, `"path"`, `"domain"`, and so on.

`m.output([attrs [,header]])`

Produces the HTTP header string for this morsel. `attrs` is an optional list of the additional attributes to include (`"expires"`, `"path"`, and so on). `header` is the header string to use (`'Set-Cookie: '` by default).

`m.js_output([attrs])`

Outputs JavaScript code that sets the cookie when executed.

`m.OutputString([attrs])`

Returns the cookie string without any HTTP headers or JavaScript code.

Exceptions

If an error occurs during the parsing or generation of cookie values, a `CookieError` exception is raised.

Notes

- More information about persistent cookies can be found in almost any book on CGI programming. An official specification can be found in RFC-2109.
- The `Cookie` module also defines the classes `SerialCookie` and `SmartCookie`. However, these classes are deprecated and should not be used for security reasons.
- Most browsers place limits on the size and number of cookie values. You should limit the size of cookie data to a few hundred bytes at most.

> **See Also:**
> `cgi` (p. 396), `httplib` (p. 415)

cookielib

The `cookielib` module provides client-side support for managing HTTP cookies. The primary use of this module is in conjunction with the `urllib2` module, which is used to access documents on the Internet. For instance, the `cookielib` module can be used to capture cookies and to retransmit them on subsequent connection requests. It can also be used to work with files containing cookie data such as files created by various browsers.

`CookieJar([policy])`

Creates a new `CookieJar` instance that is responsible for holding HTTP cookie values, storing cookies received as a result of HTTP requests, and adding cookies to outgoing HTTP requests. `policy` is an instance of `CookiePolicy`. The purpose of `policy` is to define various handling rules regarding cookies (for example, protocols, domain restrictions, and so on). See the description of `CookiePolicy`, later in this section, for more information.

An instance, `c`, of `CookieJar` provides the following methods. Many of these methods are rarely called directly by a user. Instead, they are used by modules such as `urllib2` when working with cookies.

`c.add_cookie_header(request)`

Given an outgoing HTTP request, `request`, this method adds all the appropriate cookie-related headers according to whatever policy has been set on `c`. Normally, `request` is an instance of `urllib2.Request`.

c.extract_cookies(*response*, *request*)

Given an outgoing HTTP request, *request*, and the received response, *response*, this function extracts received cookies and stores them as determined by the policy set on *c*. *response* is normally the result of a function such as urllib2.urlopen(). *request* is normally an instance of urllib2.Request.

c.set_policy(*policy*)

Sets the cookie policy on *c*. *policy* is an instance of CookiePolicy, described later in this section.

c.make_cookies(*response*, *request*)

Given an outgoing request, *request*, and the associated response, *response*, this function creates a sequence of Cookie objects that have been extracted from *response*. This can be used if you actually want to examine received cookies for some reason.

c.set_cookie_if_ok(*cookie*, *request*)

Stores a cookie, *cookie*, if it's allowed by the current policy. *request* is an associated HTTP request. This is necessary because cookies are always associated with specific domains. *cookie* is an instance of Cookie, and *request* is an instance of urllib2.Request.

c.set_cookie(*cookie*)

Unconditionally stores a cookie, *cookie*, in *c*. *c* is an instance of Cookie.

c.clear([*domain* [, *path* [, *name*]]])

Clears cookies associated with a specific domain, path, and name. If no arguments are given, all cookies are cleared. If only a domain is supplied, then all the cookies associated with that domain are cleared. If only a domain and path is given, then all cookies with that domain and path are cleared. If all three arguments are given, then only that specific cookie is cleared.

c.clear_session_cookies()

Clears all session cookies.

The following object is used to interact with cookies that have been saved on disk by the client:

FileCookieJar(*filename* [, *delayload* [, *policy*]])

Creates a FileCookieJar instance that retrieves and stores cookie information to a file. *filename* is the name of the file. *delayload*, if True, enables lazy access to the file. That is, the file won't be read or stored except by demand. *policy* is an instance of CookiePolicy.

An instance, *f*, of FileCookieJar supports the same methods as CookieJar. In addition, the following methods are supported:

f.save([*filename* [, *ignore_discard* [, *ignore_expires*]]])

Saves the contents of *f* to the file. *filename* provides an alternative filename (if different from the filename used when creating *f*). If *ignore_discard* is True, all cookies are saved, even if cookies are marked to be discarded. If *ignore_expires* is True, expired cookies are written to the file. The default value for *ignore_discard* and *ignore_expires* is `False`. Keyword arguments may be used if you only need to supply values for some of the arguments.

f.load([*filename* [, *ignore_discard* [, *ignore_expires*]]])

Loads cookies from a file. Old cookies are preserved unless overwritten by the file contents. The arguments have the same meaning as for the save() method.

f.revert([*filename* [, *ignore_discard* [, *ignore_expires*]]])

Discards all cookies and reloads values from the file. The arguments have the same meaning as for save().

f.filename

Filename used by default for loading/saving cookies. This is the same as supplied to the FileCookieJar() constructor.

The following functions create FileCookieJar objects corresponding to specific file formats:

MozillaCookieJar(*filename* [, *delayload* [, *policy*]])

Creates a FileCookieJar instance that is compatible with the Mozilla cookies.txt file.

LWPCookieJar(*filename* [, *delayload* [, *policy*]])

Creates a FileCookieJar instance that is compatible with the libwww-perl Set-Cookie3 file format.

Cookies are managed according to a specific policy. Policies control various aspects of cookies, such as blocking certain domains, imposing security constraints, and so forth. Policies are implemented by creating a class that inherits from CookiePolicy. This base class defines the following general methods and attributes that apply to any CookiePolicy instance, *p*:

p.set_ok(*cookie, request*)

Returns `True` if storing *cookie* is allowed. *cookie* is a Cookie instance. *request* is an instance of urllib2.Request and contains information about the domain and path.

p.return_ok(*cookie, request*)

Returns `True` if *cookie* can be returned to the server described by *request*. *cookie* is an instance of Cookie. *request* is an instance of urllib2.Request.

p.domain_return_ok(*domain, request*)

Returns `True` if cookies should be returned from a given domain. *domain* is a string, and *request* is an instance of urllib2.Request.

p.path_return_ok(*path, request*)

Returns `True` if cookies should be returned from a given path. *path* is a string, and *request* is an instance of urllib2.Request.

p.netscape

Set to `True` if the policy implements the Netscape cookie protocol.

p.rfc2965

Set to `True` if the policy implements the RFC-2965 cookie protocol.

p.hide_cookie2

Set to `True` if `Cookie2:` headers should never be added to HTTP requests.

One almost never instantiates `CookiePolicy` directly. Instead, the `DefaultCookiePolicy` object is used instead. This object provides some basic policies and adds these methods:

```
DefaultCookiePolicy(blocked_domains=None, allowed_domains=None, netscape=True,
rfc2965=False, hide_cookie2=False, strict_domain=False,
strict_rfc2965_unveriable=True, strict_ns_unverifiable=False,
strict_ns_domain=DefaultCookiePolicy.DomainLiberal,
strict_ns_set_initial_dollar=False, strict_ns_set_path=False)
```

Creates a `DefaultCookiePolicy` object. The arguments specify default values for the attributes listed next and are specified using keyword arguments:

d.blocked_domains()

Returns a tuple of domains blocked by the policy.

d.set_blocked_domains(blocked_domains)

Sets the domains blocked by the policy. *blocked_domains* is a sequence of domain names.

d.is_blocked(domain)

Returns `True` if *domain* is blocked.

d.allowed_domains()

Returns a tuple of allowed domains set for the policy.

d.set_allowed_domains(allowed_domains)

Sets the set of domains allowed by the policy. *allowed_domains* is a sequence of domain names.

d.is_not_allowed(domain)

Returns `True` if *domain* is not allowed according to the allowed domains setting.

d.strict_domain

Set to `True` to prevent sites from setting two-component domains where one of the domains is a country code (for example '.co.uk').

d.strict_rfc2965_unverifiable

Set to `True` to enforce RFC-2965 rules on unverifiable transactions.

d.strict_ns_unverifiable

Set to `True` to enforce RFC-2965 rules on unverifiable transactions to Netscape cookies.

d.strict_ns_domain

Determines the strictness of domain-matching rules with Netscape cookies. This is the bitwise OR of `DomainStrictNoDots`, `DomainStrictNonDomain`, and

`DomainRFC2965Match`. The constant `DomainLiberal` turns off all flags, and `DomainStrict` turns on all flags.

d.strict_ns_set_initial_dollar

If `True`, cookie names that start with `'$'` are ignored.

d.strict_ns_set_path

If `True`, cookie paths must match the request URL.

Cookie values are represented by instances of `Cookie`. An instance, `c`, of `Cookie` has the following attributes:

c.version

Number representing the type of cookie. Netscape cookies have a value of 0 and RFC-2965 cookies have a value of 1.

c.name

The cookie name.

c.value

String containing the cookie value.

c.port

String containing port information or `None`.

c.path

Cookie path.

c.secure

Set to `True` if the cookie should only be sent over a secure connection.

c.expires

Cookie expiration date represented in seconds since the epoch.

c.discard

Set to `True` if the cookie is a session cookie.

c.comment

String containing cookie comment (if any).

c.comment_url

String containing URL from server that explains the purpose of a cookie (if any).

c.port_specified

Set to `True` if a server explicitly specified port information.

c.domain_specified

Set to `True` if a server explicitly specified a domain.

c.domain_initial_dot

Set to `True` if the domain specified by the server begins with a dot (.).

An instance, `c`, of `Cookie` also has the following methods:

`c.has_nonstandard_attr(name)`

Returns `True` if the cookie has a nonstandard attribute named *name*.

`c.get_nonstandard_attr(name [, default])`

Returns the value of a nonstandard cookie attribute, *name*. If not found, `None` or the value of *default* is returned (if supplied).

`c.set_nonstandard_attr(name, value)`

Sets the value of a nonstandard cookie attribute, *name*.

`c.is_expired([now])`

Returns `True` if a cookie has expired. *now* optionally supplies a time, in which case the expiration check will be performed with that value instead of the current time.

Example

The following example shows how this module is most commonly used, in conjunction with the `urllib2` module:

```
import cookielib, urllib2

# Create a cookiejar object
jar = cookielib.CookieJar()

# Create a URL opener and attach the cookie jar
o = urllib2.build_opener(urllib2.HTTPCookieProcessor(jar))

# Now use the opener normally
r = o.open("http://www.python.org")
```

See Also:

Cookie **(p. 402)**, `urllib2` **(p. 435)**, RFC-2965

DocXMLRPCServer

The `DocXMLRPCServer` module provides an extended version of the functions in the XML-RPC server module `SimpleXMLRPCServer`. This module enhances an XML-RPC server with a documentation feature that responds to HTTP GET requests (normally sent by a browser). This gives XML-RPC servers a dual nature. If XML-RPC requests are made, they are handled normally. However, if you connect to the XML-RPC server with a browser, you will get a documentation page showing all the functions supported by the server.

`DocXMLRPCServer(addr [, requestHandler [, logRequest]])`

Creates a standalone XML-RPC server at socket address *addr* (for example, (`'localhost'`, 8080)). *requestHandler* is a factory function for creating request handler objects and defaults to `DocXMLRPCRequestHandler`. Normally, it's not necessary to specify this. *logRequest* is a flag that indicates whether requests are logged.

DocCGIXMLRPCRequestHandler()

Creates an XML-RPC request handler suitable for use when the XML-RPC server runs as a CGI script.

An instance, `d`, of `DocXMLRPCServer` or `DocCGIXMLRPCRequestHandler` supports the same methods as `SimpleXMLRPCServer` and `CGIXMLRPCRequestHandler` in the `SimpleXMLRPCServer` module. In addition, the following methods are supported:

d.set_server_title(*server_title*)

Sets the title of the server in HTML documentation. The string is placed in the HTML `<title>` tag.

d.set_server_name(*server_name*)

Sets the name of the server in HTML documentation. The string appears at the top of the page in an `<h1>` tag.

d.set_server_documentation(*server_documentation*)

Adds a descriptive paragraph to the generated HTML output. This string is added right after the server name, but before a description of the XML-RPC functions.

Example

This module is used in the same way as the `SimpleXMLRPCServer` module. For example:

```
import DocXMLRPCServer
import math

def add(x,y):
    "Adds two numbers"
    return x+y


s = DocXMLRPCServer.DocXMLRPCServer(("localhost",8080))
s.register_function(add)
s.register_instance(math)
s.serve_forever()
```

> **See Also:**
>
> `SimpleXMLRPCServer` **(p. 429)**, `xmlrpclib` **(p. 442)**

encodings.idna

The `encodings.idna` module contains a few functions for handling internationalized domain names. Whenever an internationalized domain name contains non-ASCII characters, they are converted into an ASCII-compatible encoding for the purpose of interacting with systems such as DNS.

nameprep(*name*)

Returns a prepared version of *name*. This normalizes characters and converts characters to a common case.

ToASCII(name)

Converts *name* to an ASCII-compatible encoding.

ToUnicode(name)

Converts *name* from an ASCII-compatible encoding back into Unicode.

Notes

- Details of the encoding process are described in RFC-3490 and RFC-3492.
- The encoding/decoding can also be performed by specifying `'idna'` to the `encode()` and `decode()` method of strings—for example, `name.encode('idna')`.
- Most Python modules that use hostnames (`socket`, `httplib`, `ftplib`, and so on) implicitly use this module and already accept Unicode hostnames.

ftplib

The `ftplib` module is used to implement the client side of the FTP protocol. It's rarely necessary to use this module directly because the `urllib` and `urllib2` modules provide a higher-level interface. However, this module may still be useful if you want to have more control over the low-level details of an FTP connection. In order to use this module, it may be helpful to know some of the details of the FTP protocol, which is described in Internet RFC 959.

A single class is defined for establishing an FTP connection:

FTP([host [, user, passwd]])

Creates an object representing an FTP connection. *host* is a string specifying a hostname. *user* and *passwd* optionally specify a username and password. If used, both arguments must be supplied together. If no arguments are given, the `connect()` and `login()` methods must be called explicitly to initiate the actual connection. If *host* is given, `connect()` is automatically invoked. If *user* and *passwd* are given, `login()` is invoked.

An instance, *f*, of FTP has the following methods:

f.abort()

Attempts to abort a file transfer that is in progress. This may or may not work depending on the remote server.

f.close()

Closes the FTP connection. After this has been invoked, no further operations can be performed on the FTP object, *f*.

f.connect(host [, port])

Opens an FTP connection to a given host and port. *host* is a string specifying the hostname. *port* is the integer port number of the FTP server and defaults to port 21. It is not necessary to call this if a hostname was already given to `FTP()`.

f.cwd(pathname)

Changes the current working directory on the server to *pathname*.

`f.delete(filename)`

Removes the file `filename` from the server.

`f.dir([dirname [, ... [, callback]]])`

Generates a directory listing as produced by the `'LIST'` command. `dirname` optionally supplies the name of a directory to list. Also, if any additional arguments are supplied, they are simply passed as additional arguments to `'LIST'`. If the last argument `callback` is a function, it is used as a callback function to process the returned directory listing data. This callback function works in the same way as the callback used by the `retrlines()` method. By default, this method prints the directory list to sys.stdout.

`f.login([user, [passwd])`

Logs into the server using the specified username and password. `user` is a string giving the username and defaults to `'anonymous'`. `passwd` is a string containing the password and defaults to the empty string `' '`. It is not necessary to call this method if a username and password were already given to FTP().

`f.mkd(pathname)`

Creates a new directory on the server.

`f.ntransfercmd(command [, rest])`

The same as transfercmd(), except that a tuple `(sock, size)` is returned where `sock` is a socket object corresponding to the data connection and `size` is the expected size of the data in bytes or None if the size could not be determined.

`f.pwd()`

Returns a string containing the current working directory on the server.

`f.quit()`

Closes the FTP connection by sending the `'QUIT'` command to the server.

`f.rename(oldname,newname)`

Renames a file on the server.

`f.retrbinary(command, callback [, blocksize [, rest]])`

Returns the results of executing a command on the server using binary transfer mode. `command` is a string that specifies the appropriate file-retrieval command and is almost always `'RETR filename'`. `callback` is a callback function that is invoked each time a block of data is received. This callback function is invoked with a single argument, which is the received data in the form of a string. `blocksize` is the maximum block size to use and defaults to 8192 bytes. `rest` is an optional offset into the file. If supplied, this specifies the position in the file where you want to start the transfer. However, this is not supported by all FTP servers, so this may result in an error_reply exception.

`f.retrlines(command [, callback])`

Returns the results of executing a command on the server using text-transfer mode. `command` is a string that specifies the command and is usually something like `'RETR filename'`. `callback` is a callback function that is invoked each time a line of data is received. This callback function is called with a single argument, which is a string

containing the received data. If *callback* is omitted, the returned data is printed to
sys.stdout.

f.rmd(*pathname*)

Removes a directory from the server.

f.sendcmd(*command*)

Sends a simple command to the server and returns the server response. *command* is a
string containing the command. This method should only be used for commands that
don't involve the transfer of data.

f.set_pasv(*pasv*)

Sets passive mode. *pasv* is a Boolean flag that turns passive mode on if True or off if
False. By default, passive mode is on.

f.size(*filename*)

Returns the size of *filename* in bytes. Returns None if the size can't be determined for
some reason.

f.storbinary(*command*, *file* [, *blocksize*])

Executes a command on the server and transmits data using binary transfer mode.
command is a string that specifies the low-level command. It is almost always set to
'STOR *filename*', where *filename* is the name of a file you want to place on the
server. *file* is an open file object from which data will be read using
file.read(*blocksize*) and transferred to the server. *blocksize* is the block size to
use in the transfer. By default, it is 8192 bytes.

f.storlines(*command*, *file*)

Executes a command on the server and transfers data using text-transfer mode. *command*
is a string that specifies the low-level command. It is usually 'STOR *filename*'. *file*
is an open file object from which data will be read using file.readline() and sent to
the server.

f.transfercmd(*command* [, *rest*])

Initiates a transfer over the FTP data connection. If active mode is being used, this sends
a 'PORT' or 'EPRT' command and accepts the resulting connection from the server. If
passive mode is being used, this sends an 'EPSV' or 'PASV' command followed by a
connection to the server. In either case, once the data connection has been established,
the FTP command in *command* is then issued. This function returns a socket object corresponding to the open data connection. The optional *rest* parameter specifies a starting byte offset into files requested on the server. However, this is not supported on all
servers and could result in an error_reply exception.

Example

The following example illustrates the use of this module:

```
>>> import ftplib
>>> ftp = ftplib.FTP('ftp.python.org')
>>> ftp.login()
>>> ftp.retrlines('LIST')
total 40
drwxrwxr-x  12 root     4127       512 Apr  6 19:57 .
drwxrwxr-x  12 root     4127       512 Apr  6 19:57 ..
```

```
drwxrwxr-x   2 root      4127       512 Aug 25  1998 RCS
lrwxrwxrwx   1 root      bin         11 Jun 29 18:34 README -> welcome.msg
drwxr-xr-x   3 root      wheel      512 May 19  1998 bin
...
>>> f = open("README","wb")
>>> ftp.retrbinary('RETR README', f.write)
'226 Transfer complete.'
>>> f.close()
>>> ftp.quit()
```

See Also:

urllib (p. 433), http://www.python.org/doc/lib/module-ftplib.html, Internet RFC-959

httplib

This module implements the client side of the Hypertext Transfer Protocol (HTTP) used in web applications. Both the HTTP/1.0 and HTTP/1.1 protocols are supported. In addition, if Python is configured with OpenSSL support, connections can be made using secure sockets. This module is not normally used directly; instead, you should consider using urllib or urllib2. However, HTTP is such an important protocol, this module is covered in some detail in this section. For more details about HTTP, consult RFC 2616 (HTTP/1.1) and RFC 1945 (HTTP/1.0).

The HTTP protocol is a simple text-based protocol that works as follows:

1. A client makes a connection to a web server and sends a request header of the following form:

```
GET /document.html HTTP/1.0
Connection: Keep-Alive
User-Agent: Mozilla/4.61 [en](X11; U; SunOS 5.6 sun4u)
Host: rustler.cs.uchicago.edu:8000
Accept: image/gif, image/x-xbitmap, image/jpeg, image/pjpeg, image/png, */*
Accept-Encoding: gzip
Accept-Language: en
Accept-Charset: iso-8859-1,*,utf-8

(optional data)
...
```

The first line defines the request type, document (the selector), and protocol version. Following the request line is a series of header lines containing various information about the client, such as passwords, cookies, cache preferences, and client software. Following the header lines, a single blank line indicates the end of the header lines. After the header, data may appear in the event that the request is sending information from a form or uploading a file. Each of the lines in the header should be terminated by a carriage return and a newline ('\r\n').

2. The server sends a response of the following form:

```
HTTP/1.0  200  OK
Content-type: text/html
Content-length:  72883 bytes
...
Header: data

Data
...
```

The first line of the server response indicates the HTTP protocol version, a success code, and return message. Following the response line is a series of header fields that contain information about the type of the returned document, the document size, web server software, cookies, and so forth. The header is terminated by a single blank line followed by the raw data of the requested document.

The following request methods are the most common:

Method	Description
GET	Get a document.
POST	Post data to a form.
HEAD	Return header information only.
PUT	Upload data to the server.

The response codes detailed in Table 22.1 are most commonly returned by servers.

Table 22.1   **Response Codes Commonly Returned by Servers**

Code	Description
Success Codes (2xx)	
200	OK
201	Created
202	Accepted
204	No content
Redirection (3xx)	
300	Multiple choices
301	Moved permanently
302	Moved temporarily
303	Not modified
Client Error (4xx)	
400	Bad request
401	Unauthorized
403	Forbidden
404	Not found
Server Error (5xx)	
500	Internal server error
501	Not implemented
502	Bad gateway
503	Service unavailable

A wide range of optional header fields can appear in both the request and response headers. These headers are specified in a format known as RFC-822, in which headers are specified in the form *Header: data*. For example:

```
Date: Fri, 16 Jul 1999 17:09:33 GMT
Server: Apache/1.3.6 (Unix)
Last-Modified: Mon, 12 Jul 1999 19:08:14 GMT
ETag: "741d3-44ec-378a3d1e"
Accept-Ranges: bytes
Content-Length: 17644
Connection: close
Content-Type: text/html
```

The following classes can be used to establish an HTTP connection with a server:

HTTPConnection(*host* [,*port*])

Creates an HTTP connection. *host* is the hostname, and *port* is the remote port number. The default port is 80. Returns an HTTPConnection instance.

HTTPSConnection(*host* [, *port* [, key_file=*kfile* [, cert_file=*cfile*]]])

Creates an HTTP connection but uses a secure socket. The default port is 443. key_file and cert_file are optional keyword arguments that specify client PEM-formatted private-key and certificate chain files, should they be needed for client authentication. Returns an HTTPSConnection instance.

An instance, *h*, of HTTPConnection or HTTPSConnection supports the following methods:

h.connect()

Initializes the connection to the host and port given to HTTPConnection() or HTPPSConnection().

h.close()

Closes the connection.

h.send(*str*)

Sends a string, *str*, to the server. Direct use of this function is discouraged, because it may break the underlying response/request protocol. It's most commonly used to send data to the server after *h*.endheaders() has been called.

h.putrequest(*method, selector* [, *skip_host* [, *skip_accept_encoding*]])

Sends a request to the server. *method* is the HTTP method, such as 'GET' or 'POST'. *selector* specifies the object to be returned, such as '/index.html'. The *skip_host* and *skip_accept_encoding* parameters are flags that disable the sending of Host: and Accept-Encoding: headers in the HTTP request. By default, both of these arguments are False. Because the HTTP/1.1 protocol allows multiple requests to be sent over a single connection, a CannotSendRequest exception may be raised if the connection is in a state that prohibits new requests from being issued.

h.putheader(*header, value, ...*)

Sends an RFC-822–style header to the server. It sends a line to the server, consisting of the header, a colon and a space, and the value. Additional arguments are encoded as continuation lines in the header. Raises a CannotSendHeader exception if *h* is not in a state that allows headers to be sent.

h.endheaders()

Sends a blank line to the server, indicating the end of the header lines.

h.request(*method*, *url* [, *body* [, *headers*]])

Sends a complete HTTP request to the server. *method* and *url* have the same meaning as for *h*.putrequest(). *body* is an optional string containing data to upload to the server after the request has been sent. If *body* is supplied, the Context-length: header will automatically be set to an appropriate value. *headers* is a dictionary containing *header:value* pairs to be given to the *h*.putheader() method.

h.getresponse()

Gets a response from the server and returns an HTTPResponse instance that can be used to read data. Raises a ResponseNotReady exception if *h* is not in a state where a response would be received.

An HTTPResponse instance, *r*, as returned by the getresponse() method, supports the following methods:

r.read([*size*])

Reads up to *size* bytes from the server. If *size* is omitted, all the data for this request is returned.

r.getheader(*name* [,*default*])

Gets a response header. *name* is the name of the header. *default* is the default value to return if the header is not found.

r.getheaders()

Returns a list of (*header*, *value*) tuples.

An HTTPResponse instance, *r*, also has the following attributes:

r.version

HTTP version used by the server.

r.status

HTTP status code returned by the server.

r.msg

An instance of mimetools.Message containing the response headers.

r.reason

HTTP error message returned by the server.

r.length

Number of bytes left in the response.

Constants

The httplib module defines the following constants corresponding to port identifiers and status codes:

HTTP_PORT

Default port for HTTP (80).

HTTPS_PORT

Default port for HTTPS (443).

HTTP status codes are represented by the following constants and values. Links to further information concerning these codes can be found in online documentation for the httplib module:

Constant	Value
CONTINUE	100
SWITCHING_PROTOCOLS	101
PROCESSING	102
OK	200
CREATED	201
ACCEPTED	202
NON_AUTHORITATIVE_INFORMATION	203
NO_CONTENT	204
RESET_CONTENT	205
PARTIAL_CONTENT	206
MULTI_STATUS	207
IM_USED	226
MULTIPLE_CHOICES	300
MOVED_PERMANENTLY	301
FOUND	302
SEE_OTHER	303
NOT_MODIFIED	304
USE_PROXY	305
TEMPORARY_REDIRECT	307
BAD_REQUEST	400
UNAUTHORIZED	401
PAYMENT_REQUIRED	402
FORBIDDEN	403
NOT_FOUND	404
METHOD_NOT_ALLOWED	405
NOT_ACCEPTABLE	406
PROXY_AUTHENTICATION_REQUIRED	407
REQUEST_TIMEOUT	408
CONFLICT	409
GONE	410
LENGTH_REQUIRED	411
PRECONDITION_FAILED	412
REQUEST_ENTITY_TOO_LARGE	413

Constant	Value
REQUEST_URI_TOO_LONG	414
UNSUPPORTED_MEDIA_TYPE	415
REQUESTED_RANGE_NOT_SATISFIABLE	416
EXPECTATION_FAILURE	417
UNPROCESSABLE_ENTITY	422
LOCKED	423
FAILED_DEPENDENCY	424
UPGRADE_REQUIRED	426
INTERNAL_SERVER_ERROR	500
NOT_IMPLEMENTED	501
BAD_GATEWAY	502
SERVICE_UNAVAILABLE	503
GATEWAY_TIMEOUT	504
HTTP_VERSION_NOT_SUPPORTED	505
INSUFFICIENT_STORAGE	507
NOT_EXTENDED	510

Exceptions

The following exceptions may be raised in the course of handling HTTP connections:

HTTPException

Base class of all HTTP-related errors.

NotConnected

Raised if requests are made, but no connection established.

InvalidURL

Bad URL or port number given.

UnknownProtocol

Unknown HTTP protocol.

UnknownTransferEncoding

Unknown transfer encoding.

UnimplementedFileMode

Unimplemented file mode.

IncompleteRead

Incomplete data received.

BadStatusLine

Unknown status code received.

The following exceptions are related to the state of HTTP/1.1 connections. Because HTTP/1.1 allows multiple requests/responses to be sent over a single connection, extra rules are imposed as to when requests can be sent and responses received. Trying to do things in the wrong order will generate an exception.

ImproperConnectionState

Base class for all exceptions related to HTTP connection state.

CannotSendRequest

Can't send a request. A subclass of `ImproperConnectionState`.

CannotSendHeader

Can't send headers. A subclass of `ImproperConnectionState`.

ResponseNotReady

Can't read a response. A subclass of `ImproperConnectionState`.

Example

The following example shows how the `HTTPConnection` class can be used to open an HTTP/1.1 connection and fetch several files:

```
import httplib

files = [ '/index.html', '/doc/index.html', '/News.html' ]
h = httplib.HTTPConnection("www.python.org",80)
h.connect()

for f in files:
    h.request('GET',f)
    r = h.getresponse()
    if r.status == httplib.OK:
        data = r.read()
        print ":::: %s ::::" % f
        print data

h.close()
```

Notes

- This module is used by the `urllib` module, which provides a higher-level interface for accessing URLs.
- Secure HTTP is not available unless Python has also been compiled with OpenSSL support.

See Also:

`urllib` (p. 433), `mimetools` (p. 501), `asyncore` (p. 370), `BaseHTTPServer` (p. 393), `SimpleHTTPServer` (p. 428), `CGIHTTPServer` (p. 402), RFC 2616, RFC 1945

imaplib

The `imaplib` module provides a low-level client-side interface for connecting to an IMAP4 mail server using the IMAP4rev1 protocol. Documents describing the protocol, as well as sources and binaries for servers implementing it, can be found at the University of Washington's IMAP Information Center website at http://www.cac. washington.edu/imap.

The following example shows how the module is used by opening a mailbox and printing all messages:

```
import getpass, imaplib, string
m = imaplib.IMAP4()
m.login(getpass.getuser(), getpass.getpass())
m.select()
typ, data = m.search(None, 'ALL')
for num in string.split(data[0]):
    typ, data = m.fetch(num, '(RFC822)')
    print 'Message %s\n%s\n' % (num, data[0][1])
m.logout()
```

> **See Also:**
>
> `poplib` **(p. 426)**, http://www.python.org/doc/lib/module-imaplib.html,
> http://www.cac.washington.edu/imap, Internet RFC-1730, RFC-2060

nntplib

The `nntplib` module provides a low-level interface to the client side of NNTP (Network News Transfer Protocol). NNTP is described in RFC 977, which may be useful in understanding the fine detail. The module defines the following class:

NNTP(*host* [, *port* [, *user* [, *password* [, *readermode* [, *usenetrc*]]]]])

Establishes an NNTP connection with the NNTP server at *host*. *port* specifies the NNTP port and defaults to 119. *user* and *password* provide user-authentication information if required. *readermode* is a Boolean flag. If `True`, the special command "mode reader" is sent to the server before authentication. By default, *readermode* is `False`. *usenetrc* is a Boolean flag that reads authentication information from an `.netrc` file, if present. The default value is `True`. An `NNTPError` is raised on failure.

An instance, *n*, of `NNTP` supports the following methods:

n.getwelcome()

Returns the welcome message of the NNTP server as a string.

n.set_debuglevel(*level*)

Determines the amount of debugging information printed, where a *level* of 0 produces no output and a *level* of 2 produces the maximum amount of debugging information.

n.newgroups(*date*, *time* [, *file*])

Returns a list of all newsgroups created since the specified *date* and *time*. *date* is a string of the form `"yymmdd"`, and *time* is a string of the form `"hhmmss"`. The returned value is a tuple (*response*, *grouplist*) where *response* is the server response and *grouplist* is a list of strings of the form "*group last first post*". In this case, *group* is the group name, *last* is the last message number, *first* is the first message number, and *post* is 'y' or 'n', indicating whether posting is allowed. If the *file* parameter is supplied, the result is written to that location. *file* may either be a filename or an open file object.

n.newnews(*group, date, time* [, *file*])

Returns a list of all new message identifiers since the specified *date* and *time*. The returned value is a tuple (*response*, *idlist*) where *response* is the server response and *idlist* is a list of message identifiers. Message identifiers are strings of the form '*<message-id-string>*'. If *file* is supplied, the list of message identifiers is written to that destination instead.

n.list([*file*])

Returns a list of all groups on the server. The return value is a tuple (*response*, *grouplist*) where *response* is the server response string and *grouplist* is a list of tuples of the form (*groupname, last, first, postallowed*). *groupname* is the group name, *last* is the last message number (as a string), *first* is the first message number, and *postallowed* indicates whether posting is allowed. If *file* is supplied, the list of newsgroups is written to that destination instead.

n.description(*group*)

Returns a short description of the newsgroup *group*. The return value is a string containing the description.

n.descriptions(*grouppattern*)

Returns a list of descriptions for all the groups that match *grouppattern*. *grouppattern* is a simple text pattern that is similar to filename matching (see the glob module). The return value is a tuple (*response*, *descriplist*) where *response* is the server response string and *descriplist* is a list of tuples (*groupname, description*).

n.group(*name*)

Returns information about the newsgroup *name*. Returns a tuple (*response, count, first, last, name*) where *response* is the server response string, *count* is the number of messages, *first* is the first message number, *last* is the last message number, and *name* is the newsgroup name. The numbers are represented as strings. The method also sets the currently active group that will be used for subsequent operations such as stat() and body().

n.help([*file*])

Returns the output of the HELP command on the server. The returned value is a tuple (*response, helplist*) where *response* is the server response string and *helplist* is a list of strings containing the output. If *file* is specified, the result is written to that location instead.

n.stat(*id*)

Returns information about message *id*. The return value is a tuple (*response, number, msgid*) where *response* is the server response string, *number* is the message number as a string, and `msgid` is the message identifier. The `id` parameter is either a message identifier (for example, '`<message-id>`') or a message number as a string. If a message number is supplied, it corresponds to a message in the current active group set by the `group()` method. This method also sets the current article pointer on the server. This pointer is used by operations such as `next()` and `last()`.

`n.next()`

Moves the current article pointer to the next message in the currently active group and performs a `stat()` operation. The return value is the same as for `stat()`.

`n.last()`

Moves to the previous article and performs a `stat()` operation. The return value is the same as for `stat()`.

`n.head(id)`

Returns the message headers of message `id`, where `id` is either a message identifier (for example, '`<message-id>`') or a message number in the current group. Returns a tuple (`response, number, msgid, headerlist`) where `response` is the server response string, `number` is the message number as a string, `msgid` is the message identifier, and `headerlist` is a list of strings containing the message headers.

`n.body(id [, file])`

Returns the message body of message `id`, where `id` is a message identifier (for example, '`<message-id>`') or a message number (given as a string) in the current group. Returns a tuple (`response, number, msgid, bodylist`) where `response` is the server response string, `number` is the message number (as a string), `msgid` is the message identifier, and `bodylist` is a list of strings that make up the message body. `file` is either a filename or an open file object. If supplied, the message body will be written to the file instead of being returned in `bodylist`.

`n.article(id)`

Returns both the article headers and body of message `id`. The return value is the same as for `head()` or `body()`.

`n.slave()`

Indicates to the remote server that this connection is being made by a slave news server as opposed to a news client. The effect of this command is implementation specific—it may be ignored or it may result in different performance properties (the remote machine may give higher or lower priority to the connection).

`n.xhdr(header, msgid [, file])`

Returns a specific header from messages identified by `msgid`. `header` is the name of an article header (for example, '`subject`'). `msgid` is either a message identifier string, a message number, or a range of message numbers. If a range is specified, it is specified as a string such as '`1234-1290`' or '`1234-`'. The return value is a tuple (`response, headerlist`) where `response` is the server response string and `headerlist` is a list of tuples of the form (`messagenum, header`). `file` is either a filename or an open file object. If supplied, the header data is written to the file instead of being returned in `headerlist`.

***n*.post(*file*)**

Posts a message. *file* is an open file object that is read until an end-of-file is received. The message read should be a properly formatted news message including all headers and the message body.

***n*.ihave(*id, file*)**

Instructs the server that the client has the message with identifier *id*. *file* is a file object containing the message. Depending on the server response, the message will be posted (for example, a server may choose to ignore the request if it already has a copy of the message).

***n*.date()**

Returns the current date and time on the server. The return value is a tuple (*response, date, time*) where *response* is the server response string, *date* is a string of the form '*yymmdd*', and *time* is a string of the form '*hhmmss*'.

***n*.xover(*start, end* [, *file*])**

Returns a list of extended information about a range of article numbers specified by *start* and *end* (both numbers specified as strings). Returns a tuple of the form (*response, list*) where *response* is the server response string and *list* is a list of tuples of the form (*number, subject, poster, date, id, references, size, lines*). All elements of the tuple are strings except for *references*, which is a list of message identifier strings.

***n*.xpath(*id*)**

Returns the directory path of an article with identifier *id*. The return value is a tuple (*response, path*), where *response* is the server response string and *path* is the path.

***n*.quit()**

Shuts down the NNTP connection.

Exceptions

NNTPError

Base class of all exceptions generated by the nntplib module.

NNTPDataError

Error in response data.

NNTPPermanentError

Exception raised when a NNTP error code in the range 500–599 is received from the server.

NNTPProtocolError

Raised if there is a protocol with the NNTP protocol itself. For example, a malformed server response.

NNTPReplyError

Unexpected reply from server.

`NNTPTemporaryError`

Exception raised when an NNTP error code in the range 400–499 is received from the server.

Example

```
# print the last 5 articles posted on comp.lang.python
import nntplib
n = nntplib.NNTP('nntp.someserver.com')

resp, count, first, last, name = n.group("comp.lang.python")
m = n.stat(last)
for i in range(0,5):
    resp, num, msgid, lines = n.article(m[2])
    print "\n".join(lines)
    print "-"*80
    m = n.last()

n.quit()
```

See Also:
http://www.python. org/doc/lib/module-nntplib.html, Internet RFC 977

poplib

The `poplib` module provides a low-level client-side connection to a POP3 mail server. POP3 is described in RFC 1725, which may be a useful reference when using this module.

Two objects are defined by this module:

`POP3(host [, port])`

Creates a connection to a POP3 server at *host*. *port* is an optional port number and defaults to 110.

`POP3_SSL(host [, port [, keyfile [, certfile]]])`

Creates a secure connection to a POP3 server at *host*. *port* is an optional port number and defaults to 995. *keyfile* and *certfile* specify PEM-formatted private key and certificate files for client authentication if required.

An instance, `p`, of POP3 or POP3_SSL supports the following methods:

`p.apop(user, secret)`

Logs in to the POP3 server using APOP authentication. *user* is the username, and *secret* is a string containing a secret shared by both the client and server.

`p.dele(msgid)`

Marks message *msgid* for deletion.

`p.getwelcome()`

Returns the welcome message sent by the server.

p.list([msgid])

Returns a tuple of the form (*response*, *msglist*, *size*) containing information about the mailbox. *response* is the server response code, *msglist* is a list of strings of the form 'msgid size', and *size* is the size of the response in bytes. *msgid*, if supplied, specifies the message to list.

p.pass_(password)

Sends a password. The return value is a status string containing the server response and information about the current mailbox (number of messages and size).

p.quit()

Quits the session.

p.retr(msgid)

Retrieves message *msgid*. The return value is a tuple of the form (*response*, *lines*, *size*) where *response* is the server response, *lines* is a list of message lines, and *size* is the size of the message.

p.rpop(user)

Authenticates a user using RPOP authentication. *user* is the username.

p.rset()

Removes deletion marks for the mailbox.

p.set_debuglevel(level)

Sets the debugging level. By default, no debugging information is printed (level 0). Level 1 prints some debugging information, and level 2 prints the maximum amount of debugging.

p.stat()

Returns the mailbox status as a tuple (*message_count*, *size*).

p.top(msgid, lines)

Returns the first *lines* of message text for message *msgid*. The return value is a tuple (*response*, *lines*, *size*) where *response* is the server response string, *lines* is a list of lines, and *size* is the number of bytes.

p.uidl([msgid])

Returns the message digest list. If *msgid* is given, information for that message is returned. Otherwise, information for all messages is returned.

p.user(username)

Sends a username to the server.

The following example opens a mailbox and retrieves all messages:

```
import getpass, poplib
M = poplib.POP3('localhost')
M.user(getpass.getuser())
M.pass_(getpass.getpass())
numMessages = len(M.list()[1])
for i in range(numMessages):
    for j in M.retr(i+1)[1]:
        print j
```

See Also:
http://www. python.org/doc/lib/module-poplib.html, Internet RFC 1725.

robotparser

The robotparser module provides a class that can be used to fetch and query information contained in the robots.txt files that websites use to instruct web crawlers and spiders. The contents of this file typically look like this:

```
# robots.txt
User-agent: *
Disallow: /warheads/designs    # Don't allow robots here
```

RobotFileParser()

Creates an object that can be used to read and query a single robots.txt file.
    An instance, r, of RobotFileParser has the following attributes and methods:

r.set_url(url)

Sets the URL of the robots.txt file.

r.read()

Reads the robots.txt file and parses it.

r.parse(lines)

Parses a list of lines obtained from a robots.txt file. The resulting data is saved internally for use with other methods.

r.can_fetch(useragent, url)

Returns True if useragent is allowed to fetch url.

r.mtime()

Returns the time at which the robots.txt file was last fetched.

r.modified()

Sets the time at which robots.txt was last fetched to the current time.

Note
Details about the robots.txt format can be found at http://info.webcrawler.com/ mak/projects/robots/norobots.html.

SimpleHTTPServer

The SimpleHTTPServer module provides a simple HTTP server handler that can serve files from the current directory. The module defines the following handler class, intended for use with the BaseHTTPServer module:

SimpleHTTPRequestHandler(request, client_address, server)

Serves files from the current directory and all its subdirectories. The class implements the do_HEAD() and do_GET() methods to support HEAD and GET requests, respectively.

All IOError exceptions result in a 404 File not found error. Attempts to access a directory result in a 403 Directory listing not supported error.

The following class attributes are available:

SimpleHTTPRequestHandler.server_version

Server version string.

SimpleHTTPRequestHandler.extensions_map

A dictionary mapping suffixes to MIME types. Unrecognized file types are considered to be of type 'text/plain'.

SimpleHTTPRequestHandler inherits from BaseHTTPRequestHandler, so documentation for the BaseHTTPServer module should be consulted for additional attributes and methods.

Example

```
from BaseHTTPServer import HTTPServer
from SimpleHTTPServer import SimpleHTTPRequestHandler
import os
# Change to the document root
os.chdir("/home/httpd/html")
# Start the SimpleHTTP server
serv = HTTPServer(("",80),SimpleHTTPRequestHandler)
serv.serve_forever()
```

> **See Also:**
> BaseHTTPServer (p. 393), CGIHTTPServer (p. 402), httplib (p. 415)

SimpleXMLRPCServer

The SimpleXMLRPCServer module is used to write servers supporting the XML-RPC protocol. XML-RPC is a remote procedure call mechanism that uses XML for data encoding and HTTP as a transport mechanism. This module supports two basic kinds of XML-RPC servers. The first type of server operates as a standalone HTTP server that listens for incoming requests on a socket and responds accordingly. The second type of server responds to XML-RPC requests received through the CGI mechanism of another web server.

SimpleXMLRPCServer(addr [, requestHandler [, logRequests]])

Creates a new XML-RPC server listening on the socket address addr (for example, ('localhost',8080)). requestHandler is factory function that creates handler request objects when connections are received. By default, it is set to SimpleXMLRPCRequestHandler, which is currently the only available handler. logRequests is a Boolean flag that indicates whether or not to log incoming requests. The default value is True.

An instance, s, of SimpleXMLRPCServer has the following methods:

s.register_function(func [, name])

Registers a new function, func, with the XML-RPC server. name is an optional name to use for the function. If name is supplied, it's the name clients will use to access the function. This name may contain characters that are not part of valid Python identifiers, including periods (.). If *name* is not supplied, then the actual function name of *func* is used instead.

s.register_instance(*instance* [, *allow_dotted_names*])

Registers an object that's used to resolve method names not registered with the register_function() method. If the instance *instance* defines the method _dispatch(*self, methodname, params*), it is called to process requests. *methodname* is the name of the method, and *params* is a tuple containing arguments. The return value of _dispatch() is returned to clients. If no _dispatch() method is defined, the instance is checked to see if the method name matches the names of any methods defined for *instance*. If so, the method is called directly. The *allow_dotted_names* parameter is a flag that indicates whether a hierarchical search should be performed when checking for method names. For example, if a request for method 'foo.bar.spam' is received, this determines whether or not a search for *instance*.foo.bar.spam is made. By default, this is False. It should not be set to True unless the client has been verified. Otherwise, it opens up a security hole that can allow intruders to execute arbitrary Python code. Note that, at most, only one instance can be registered at a time.

s.register_introspection_functions()

Adds XML-RPC introspection functions system.listMethods(), system.methodHelp(), and system.methodSignature() to the XML-RPC server. system.methodHelp() returns the documentation string for a method (if any). The system.methodSignature() function simply returns a message indicating that the operation is unsupported (since Python is dynamically typed, type information is available).

s.register_multicall_functions()

Adds XML-RPC multicall function support by adding the system.multicall() function to the server.

XML-RPC can be handled inside CGI scripts using the following function:

CGIXMLRPCRequestHandler()

Creates a CGIXMLRPCRequestHandler object for processing XML-RPC requests received through a CGI script.

An instance, *c*, of CGIXMLRPCRequestHandler has the following methods. These methods have the same behavior as for SimpleXMLRPCServer.

c.register_function(*func* [, *name*])

Adds a new function, *func*, to the XML-RPC server.

c.register_instance(*instance* [, *allow_dotted_names*])

Registers an instance, *instance*, with the XMl-RPC server.

c.register_introspection_functions()

Adds XML-RPC introspection functions.

c.register_multicall_functions()

Adds XML-RPC multicall functionality.

c.**handle_request**([*request_text*])

Processes an XML-RPC request. By default, the request is read from standard input. If *request_text* is supplied, it contains the request data in the form received by an HTTP POST request.

Examples

Here is an very simple example of writing a standalone server. It adds a single function, add. In addition, it adds the entire contents of the math module as an instance, exposing all the functions it contains.

```
import SimpleXMLRPCServer
import math

def add(x,y):
    "Adds two numbers"
    return x+y

s = SimpleXMLRPCServer.SimpleXMLRPCServer(("localhost",8080))
s.register_function(add)
s.register_instance(math)
s.register_introspection_functions()
s.serve_forever()
```

Here is the same functionality implemented as CGI-script:
```
import SimpleXMLRPCServer
import math

def add(x,y):
    "Adds two numbers"
    return x+y

s = SimpleXMLRPCServer.CGIXMLRPChandler()
s.register_function(add)
s.register_instance(math)
s.register_introspection_functions()
s.handle_request()
```

To access XML-RPC functions from other Python programs, use the xmlrpclib module. Here is a short interactive session that shows how it works:

```
>>> import xmlrpclib
>>> s = xmlrpclib.ServerProxy("http://localhost:8080")
>>> s.add(3,5)
8
>>> s.system.listMethods()
['acos', 'add', 'asin', 'atan', 'atan2', 'ceil', 'cos', 'cosh', 'degrees', 'exp',
'fabs', 'floor', 'fmod', 'frexp', 'hypot', 'ldexp', 'log', 'log10', 'modf',
'pow', 'radians', 'sin', 'sinh', 'sqrt', 'system.listMethods',
'system.methodHelp', 'system.methodSignature', 'tan', 'tanh']
>>> s.system.methodHelp("tan")
'tan(x)\n\nReturn the tangent of x (measured in radians).'
>>> s.tan(4.5)
4.6373320545511847
>>>
```

Here is a possibly questionable example of registering an instance that makes use of a _dispatch() method:

```
import SimpleXMLRPCServer

class ModuleExporter(object):
    def __init__(self,*modules):
        self.modules = modules
    def _dispatch(self,name,args):
        names = name.split(".",1)
        modname = names[0]
        funcname = names[1]
        for m in self.modules:
            if m.__name__ == modname:
                f = getattr(m,funcname)
                return f(*args)
        raise NameError, "No such module"

s = SimpleXMLRPCServer.SimpleXMLRPCServer(("localhost",8080))

import math, string
s.register_instance(ModuleExporter(math,string))
s.serve_forever()
```

Now, try it out:

```
>>> import xmlrpclib
>>> s = xmlrpclib.ServerProxy("http://localhost:8080")
>>> s.math.sin(3)
0.1411200805986721
>>> s.string.lower("FOOBAR")
'foobar'
>>>
```

Notes

- SimpleXMLRPCServer inherits from SocketServer.TCPServer and can be customized in the same way (for instance, adding support for processing requests in separate threads or processes).
- The HTTP transport mechanism is implemented using the BaseHTTPServer module.
- Great care should be taken when implementing public XML-RPC servers. Oversight of potential security problems can make it possible for intruders to execute arbitrary code on the machine running the server. For example, you probably wouldn't want to expose functions in the os module.

See Also:
xmlrpclib (p. 442), DocXMLRPCServer (p. 410)

smtplib

The smtplib module provides a low-level SMTP client interface that can be used to send mail using the SMTP protocol, described in RFC 821 and RFC 1869. This module contains a number of low-level functions and methods that are described in detail in the online documentation. However, the following covers the most useful parts of this module:

SMTP([*host* [, *port*]])

Creates an object representing a connection to an SMTP server. If *host* is given, it specifies the name of the SMTP server. *port* is an optional port number. The default port is 25. If *host* is supplied, the connect() method is called automatically. Otherwise, you will need to manually call connect() on the returned object to establish the connection.

An instance, *s*, of SMTP has the following methods:

s.connect([*host* [, *port*]])

Connects to the SMTP server on *host*. If *host* is omitted, a connection is made to the local host ('127.0.0.1'). *port* is an optional port number that defaults to 25 if omitted. It is not necessary to call connect() if a hostname was given to SMTP().

s.login(user, password)

Logs in to the server if authentication is required. *user* is a username, and *password* is a password.

s.quit()

Terminates the session by sending a 'QUIT' command to the server.

s.sendmail(fromaddr, toaddrs, message)

Sends a mail message to the server. *fromaddr* is a string containing the email address of the sender. *toaddrs* is a list of strings containing the email addresses of recipients. *message* is a string containing a completely formatted RFC 822–compliant message. The email module is commonly used to create such messages.

Example

The following example shows how the module can be used to send a message:

```
import smtplib

fromaddr = "someone@some.com"
toaddrs = ["recipient@other.com"]
msg = "From: %s\r\nTo: %s\r\n\r\n" % (fromaddr, ",".join(toaddrs))
msg += """
We will deny your mortgage application in 15 seconds!!!
"""

server = smtplib.SMTP('localhost')
server.sendmail(fromaddr, toaddrs, msg)
server.quit()
```

> **See Also:**
>
> poplib (**p. 426**), imaplib (**p. 422**), email (**p. 449**), http://www.python.org/doc/lib/module-smtplib.html, Internet RFC-821 (Simple Mail Transfer Protocol), Internet RFC-1869 (SMTP Service Extensions).

urllib

The urllib module is used to fetch data from the Web. This module is relatively simple and easy to use. However, if you need more advanced capabilities, such as dealing with cookies or user authentication, you should use the urllib2 module instead.

`urlopen(url [, data])`

Given the uniform resource locator `url`, such as `'http://www.python.org'` or `'ftp://foo.com/pub/foo.tar'`, this function opens a network connection and returns a file-like object. If the URL doesn't have a scheme identifier such as `ftp:` or `http:`, or if it's `file:`, a local file is opened. If a connection cannot be made or an error occurs, an `IOError` exception is raised. If the URL is an HTTP request, the optional `data` argument specifies that the request should be made using a `POST` method, in which case the data is uploaded to the server. In this case, the data must be encoded in an `'application/x-www-form-urlencoded'` format, as produced by the `urlencode()` function.

`urlretrieve(url [, filename [, hook]])`

Opens a URL and copies its data to a local file, if necessary. If `url` is a local file or a cached copy of the data exists, no copying is performed. `filename` specifies the name of the local file in which data will be saved. If this is omitted, a temporary filename will be generated. `hook` is a function called after a connection has been made and after each block of data has been read. It's called with three arguments: the number of blocks transferred so far, the block size in bytes, and the total size of the file in bytes. The function returns a tuple `(filename, headers)` in which `filename` is the name of the local file where the data was saved and `headers` is the information returned by the `info()` method as described for `urlopen()`. If the URL corresponds to a local file or if a cached copy was used, `headers` will be `None`. Raises an `IOError` if an error occurs.

`urlcleanup()`

Clears the local cache created by `urlretrieve()`.

`quote(string [, safe])`

Replaces special characters in `string` with escape sequences suitable for including in a URL. Letters, digits, and the underscore (_), comma (,), period (.), and hyphen (-) characters are unchanged. All other characters are converted into escape sequences of the form `'%xx'`. `safe` provides a string of additional characters that should not be quoted and is `'/'` by default.

`quote_plus(string [, safe])`

Calls `quote()` and additionally replaces all spaces with plus signs. `string` and `safe` are the same as in `quote()`.

`unquote(string)`

Replaces escape sequences of the form `'%xx'` with their single-character equivalent.

`unquote_plus(string)`

Like `unquote()`, but also replaces plus signs with spaces.

`urlencode(dict)`

Converts a dictionary to a URL-encoded string suitable for use as the `data` argument of the `urlopen()` function. The resulting string is a series of `'key=value'` pairs separated by `'&'` characters, where both `key` and `value` are quoted using `quote_plus()`.

The file-like object u returned by urlopen() supports the following methods:

Method	Description
u.read([nbytes])	Reads nbytes of data.
u.readline()	Reads a single line of text.
u.readlines()	Reads all input lines and returns a list.
u.fileno()	Returns the integer file descriptor.
u.close()	Closes the connection.
u.info()	Returns the mimetools.Message object containing meta-information associated with the URL. For HTTP, the HTTP headers included with the server response are returned. For FTP, the headers include 'content-length'. For local files, the headers include a date, 'content-length', and 'content-type' field.
u.geturl()	Returns the real URL of the returned data, taking into account any redirection that may have occurred.

Notes

- The only supported protocols are HTTP, FTP, Gopher, and local files. If Python is configured with OpenSSL; secure HTTP (https://name) is additionally supported.
- Although the httplib module supports HTTP/1.1, this module uses HTTP/1.0 to retrieve documents.
- The urlopen() function works transparently with proxies that don't require authentication. On UNIX and Windows, proxy servers should be set with the $http_proxy, $ftp_proxy, and $gopher_proxy environment variables.
- Caching is currently not implemented.
- If a URL points to a local file but the file cannot be opened, the URL is opened using the FTP protocol.

See Also:
urllib2 (p. 435), httplib (p. 415), ftplib (p. 412), urlparse (p. 440), mimetools (p. 501)

urllib2

The urllib2 module provides an extensible framework for opening URLs on the Internet. Unlike the urllib module, urllib2 is capable of handling more complicated connection scenarios, including those involving HTTP cookies, redirection, and password authorization.

urllib2 defines the following functions:

`urlopen(url [, data])`

Opens the URL `url` and returns a file-like object that can be used to read the returned data. `url` may either be a string containing a URL or an instance of the `Request` class, described later. `data` is a URL-encoded string containing data to be uploaded to the server. When data is given, the HTTP `'POST'` method is used instead of `'GET'` (the default). Data is generally created using a function such as `urllib.urlencode()`.

The file-like object `u` returned by `urlopen()` supports all the usual file operations in addition to the following two methods:

`u.geturl()`

Returns the URL of the data retrieved.

`u.info()`

Returns a dictionary-like object containing metadata. Typically this contains information from returned HTTP headers.

The following two functions are used to create and install different objects responsible for opening URLs:

`install_opener(opener)`

Installs a different opener object for use as the global URL opener used by `urlopen()`. `opener` is an instance of `OpenerDirector`.

`build_opener([handler1 [, handler2, ... ]])`

This function builds an opener object of type `OpenerDirector`. The arguments `handler1`, `handler2`, and so on are all instances of type `BaseHandler`. The purpose of these handlers is to add various capabilities to the resulting opener object. The following lists all the available handler objects:

Handler	Description
CacheFTPHandler	FTP handler with persistent FTP connections
FileHandler	Opens local files
FTPHandler	Opens URLs via FTP
GopherHandler	Opens URLs via Gopher
HTTPBasicAuthHandler	Basic HTTP authentication handling
HTTPCookieProcessor	Processing of HTTP cookies
HTTPDefaultErrorHandler	Handles HTTP errors by raising an HTTPError exception
HTTPDigestAuthHandler	HTTP digest authentication handling
HTTPHandler	Opens URLs via HTTP
HTTPRedirectHandler	Handles HTTP redirects
HTTPSHandler	Opens URLs via secure HTTP
ProxyHandler	Redirects requests through a proxy
ProxyBasicAuthHandler	Basic proxy authentication
ProxyDigestAuthHandler	Digest proxy authentication
UnknownHandler	Handler that deals with all unknown URLs

By default, an opener is always created with the handlers `ProxyHandler`, `UnknownHandler`, `HTTPHandler`, `HTTPSHandler`, `HTTPDefaultErrorHandler`, `HTTPRedirectHandler`, `FTPHandler`, `FileHandler`, and `HTTPErrorProcessor`. These handlers provide a basic level of functionality. Extra handlers supplied as arguments are added to this list. However, if any of the extra handlers are of the same type as the defaults, they take precedence. For example, if you added an instance of `HTTPHandler` or some class that derived from `HTTPHandler`, it would be used instead of the default. The returned object of type `OpenerDirector` has a method, `open()`, that can be used to open URLs according to all the rules provided by the various handlers. This object can also be made the default using the `install_opener()` function.

The following example briefly shows how the `build_opener()` function is used:

```
import urllib2
o = urllib2.build_opener(urllib2.HTTPCookieProcessor())    # Add cookie support

# Open a page
f = o.open("http://www.somesite.com/index.html")
```

More examples appear in sections that follow.

Password Authentication

To handle requests involving password authentication, you must create a password manager instance. This is done using the following two functions:

`HTTPPasswordMgr()`

Creates a password manager that maps (*realm*, *uri*) to (*user*, *password*) information. The *realm* is a name or description associated with the authentication. Its value depends on the remote server. However, it's usually a common name associated with a collection of related web pages. *uri* is a base URL associated with the authentication. Typical values for *realm* and *uri* might be something like (`'Administrator'`, `'http://www.somesite.com'`). *user* and *password* specify a username and password, respectively.

`HTTPPasswordMgrWithDefaultRealm()`

The same as `HTTPPasswordMgr()`, but adds a default realm that is checked if no other matches are found.

An instance, *p*, of either password manager provides two methods:

`p.add_password(realm, uri, user, passwd)`

Adds user and password information for a given realm and URI. All parameters are strings. *uri* can optionally be a sequence of URIs, in which case the user and password information is applied to all the URIs in the sequence. See the description of `HTTPPasswordMgr()` for more information on the other arguments.

`p.find_user_password(realm, uri)`

Looks up a username and password given a specific realm and URI. Returns a tuple (*user*, *passwd*) if found or (`None`,`None`).

A password manager is used with all the handlers involving authentication. This includes `HTTPBasicAuthHandler`, `HTTPDigestAuthHandler`, `ProxyBasicAuthHandler`, and `ProxyDigestAuthHandler`. By default, these handlers create an instance of `HTTPPasswordMgr` unless an alternative is supplied as an argument to the handler constructor. All the handlers expose the `add_password()` method, which can be used to add passwords.

Here is an example of how to set up authentication:

```
auth = urllib2.HTTPBasicAuthHandler()
auth.add_password("Administrator","http://www.secretlair.com","drevil","12345")

# Create opener with authentication added
o = urllib2.build_opener(auth)

# Open URL
f = o.open("http://www.secretlair.com/evilplan.html")
```

HTTP Cookies

To manage HTTP cookies, create an opener object with an `HTTPCookieProcessor` handler added to it. For example:

```
cookiehand = urllib2.HTTPCookieProcessor()
o = urllib2.build_opener(cookiehand)
f = o.open("http://www.somewhere.com/")
```

By default, the `HTTPCookieProcessor` uses the `CookieJar` object found in the `cookielib` module. Different types of cookie processing can be supported by supplying a different `CookieJar` object as an argument to `HTTPCookieProcessor`. For example:

```
cookiehand = urllib2.HTTPCookieProcessor(
              cookielib.MozillaCookieJar("cookies.txt")
            )
o = urllib2.build_opener(cookiehand)
f = o.open("http://www.somewhere.com/")
```

Proxies

If requests need to be redirected through a proxy, create an instance of `ProxyHandler`.

ProxyHandler([proxies])

Creates a proxy handler that routes requests through a proxy. The argument *proxies* is a dictionary that maps protocol names (for example, `'http'`, `'ftp'`, and so on) to the URLs of the corresponding proxy server.

The following example shows how to use this:

```
phand = urllib2.ProxyHandler({'http': 'http://someproxy.com:8080/'}
pauth = urllib2.HTTPBasicAuthHandler()
pauth.add_password("realm","host", "username", "password")
o = urllib2.build_opener(phand,pauth)

f = o.open("http://www.somewhere.com/doc.html")
```

Request Objects

The `urllib2` module defines a `Request` object that contains request information and is used in the implementation.

Request(url [, data [, headers [, origin_req_host [, unverifiable]]]])

Creates a new `Request` instance. *uri* specifies the URI (for example, `'http://www.foo.bar/spam.html'`). *data* is URL-encoded data to be uploaded to the server in HTTP requests. When this is supplied, it changes the HTTP request type from 'GET' to 'POST'. *headers* is a dictionary containing key-value mappings. *origin_req_host* is set to the request-host of the transaction—typically it's the host-name from which the request is originating. *unverifiable* is set to True if the request is for an unverifiable URL. An unverifiable URL is informally defined as a URL not directly entered by the user; for instance, a URL embedded within a page that loads an image. The default value of *unverifiable* is False.

`r.add_data(data)`

Adds data to a request. If the request is an HTTP request, the method is changed to 'POST'. *data* is URL-encoded data, as described for Request().

`r.add_header(key, val)`

Adds header information to the request. *key* is the header name, and *val* is the header value. Both arguments are strings.

`r.add_unredirected_header(key, val)`

Adds header information to a request that will not be added to redirected requests. *key* and *val* have the same meaning as for add_header().

`r.get_data()`

Returns requests data (if any).

`r.get_full_url()`

Returns the full URL of a request.

`r.get_host()`

Returns the host to which the request will be sent.

`r.get_method()`

Returns the HTTP method, which is either 'GET' or 'POST'.

`r.get_origin_req_host()`

Returns the request-host of the originating transaction.

`r.get_selector()`

Returns the selector part of the URL (for example, '/index.html').

`r.get_type()`

Returns the URL type (for example, 'http').

`r.has_data()`

Returns True if data is part of the request.

`r.is_unverifiable()`

Returns True if the request is unverifiable.

`r.has_header(header)`

Returns True if the request has header *header*.

r.set_proxy(*host, type*)

Prepares the request for connecting to a proxy server. This replaces the original host with *host* and the original type of the request with *type*. The selector part of the URL is set to the original URL.

Exceptions

The following exceptions are defined:

GopherError

An error raised by the GopherHandler.

HTTPError

Raised to indicate problems with the HTTP protocol. This error may be used to signal events such as authentication required. This exception can also be used as a file object to read the data returned by the server that's associated with the error. This is a subclass of URLError.

URLError

Error raised by handlers when a problem is detected. This is a subclass of IOError.

Notes

- The urllib2 module contains a wide variety of customization options and support for writing new handlers. Refer to the online documentation for more details.
- Information about unverifiable URLs can be found in RFC-2965.

See Also:
cookielib (p. 405), urllib (p. 433)

urlparse

The urlparse module is used to manipulate URL strings such as "http://www.python.org". The general form of a URL is "*scheme://netloc/path;parameters?query#fragment*".

urlparse(*urlstring* [, *default_scheme* [, *allow_fragments*]])

Parses the URL in urlstring and returns a tuple (*scheme, netloc, path, parameters, query, fragment*). *default_scheme* specifies the scheme ("http", "ftp", and so on) to be used if none is present in the URL. If *allow_fragments* is zero, fragment identifiers are not allowed.

urlunparse(*tuple*)

Constructs a URL string from a tuple as returned by urlparse().

urljoin(*base, url* [, *allow_fragments*])

Constructs an absolute URL by combining a base URL, *base*, with a relative URL, *url*. *allow_fragments* has the same meaning as for urlparse(). If the last component of the base URL is not a directory, it's stripped.

Examples

```
>>> urlparse("http://www.python.org/index.html")
('http', 'www.python.org', '/index.html', '', '', '')

>>> urlunparse(('http', 'www.python.org', '/index.html', '', '', ''))
'http://www.python.org/index.html'

>>> urljoin("http://www.python.org/index.html","Help.html")
'http://www.python.org/Help.html'
```

See Also:

urllib (p. 433), Internet RFC-1738, Internet RFC-1808

webbrowser

The webbrowser module provides functions for opening documents in a web browser in a platform-independent manner. The module tries to determine the current browser using the environment settings of the local machine.

open(*url* [, *new*])

Displays *url* with the default browser. If *new* is True, a new browser window is opened.

open_new(*url*)

Displays *url* in a new window of the default browser. The same as open(*url*, True).

get([*name*])

Returns a controller object for manipulating a browser. *name* is the name of the browser type and is typically a string such as 'netscape', 'mozilla', 'kfm', 'grail', 'windows-default', 'internet-config', or 'command-line'. The returned controller object has the methods open() and open_new(), which accept the same arguments and perform the same operation as the two previous functions. If *name* is omitted, a controller object for the default browser is returned.

register(*name, constructor*[, *controller*])

Registers a new browser type for use with the get() function. *name* is the name of the browser. *constructor* is called without arguments to create a controller object for opening pages in the browser. *controller* is a controller instance to use instead. If supplied, *constructor* is ignored and may be None.

A controller instance, *c*, returned by the get() function has the following methods:

c.open(*url*[, *new*])

Same as the open() function.

c.open_new(*url*)

Same as the open_new() function.

Notes

If set, the $BROWSER environment variable determines the name of the default browser.

xmlrpclib

The xmlrpclib module provides client-side support for XML-RPC. XML-RPC is a remote procedure call mechanism that uses XML for data encoding and HTTP as a transport mechanism. This module handles most of the details automatically. Therefore, it is not necessary to worry about the underlying encoding or transport of data.

To use the module, you create an instance of ServerProxy:

ServerProxy(*uri* [, *transport* [, *encoding* [, *verbose* [, *allow_none*]]]])

uri is the location of the remote XML-RPC server—for example, "http://www.foo. com/RPC2". If necessary, basic authentication information can be added to the URI using the format "http://users:pass@host:port/path", where user:pass is the username and password encoded in base-64 format. If Python is configured with OpenSSL support, HTTPS can also be used. *transport* specifies a transport factory instance. This argument is only used if XML-RPC is being used over some kind of connection other than HTTP or HTTPS. It is almost never necessary to supply this argument in normal use (consult the online documentation for details). *encoding* specifies the encoding, which is UTF-8 by default. *verbose* displays some debugging information if True. *allow_none*, if True, allows the value None to be sent to remote servers. By default, this is disabled because it's not universally supported.

An instance, *s*, of ServerProxy transparently exposes all the methods on the remote server. The methods are accessed as attributes of *s*. For example, this code gets the current time from a remote server providing that service:

```
>>> s = xmlrpclib.ServerProxy("http://www.xmlrpc.com/RPC2")
>>> s.currentTime.getCurrentTime()
<DateTime u'20051102T20:08:24' at 2c77d8>
>>>
```

For the most part, RPC calls work just like ordinary Python functions. However, only a limited number of argument types and return values are supported by the XML-RPC protocol:

XML-RPC Type	Python Equivalent
boolean	True and False
integer	int
float	float
string	string or unicode (must only contain characters valid in XML)
array	Any sequence containing valid XML-RPC types
structure	Dictionary containing string keys and values of valid types
dates	Date and time (xmlrpclib.DateTime)
binary	Binary data (xmlrpclib.Binary)

If you make an RPC call with arguments involving invalid types, you may get a `TypeError` or an `xmlrpclib.Fault` exception.

If the remote XML-RPC server supports introspection, the following methods may be available:

_s_.system.listMethods()

Returns a list of strings listing all the methods provided by the XML-RPC server.

_s_.methodSignatures(_name_)

Given the name of a method, _name_, returns a list of possible calling signatures for the method. Each signature is a list of types in the form of a comma-separated string (for example, `'string, int, int'`), where the first item is the return type and the remaining items are argument types. Multiple signatures may be returned due to overloading. In XML-RPC servers implemented in Python, signatures are typically empty because functions and methods are dynamically typed.

_s_.methodHelp(_name_)

Given the name of a method, _name_, returns a documentation string describing the use of that method. Documentation strings may contain HTML markup. An empty string is returned if no documentation is available.

The following utility functions are available in the `xmlrpclib` module:

boolean(_value_)

Creates an XML-RPC boolean object from _value_. This function predates the existence of the Python boolean type, so you may see it used in older code.

binary(_data_)

Creates an XML-RPC object containing binary data. _data_ is a string containing the raw data. Returns a `Binary` instance. The returned `Binary` instance is transparently encoded/decoded using base 64 during transmission. To extract binary from `Binary` instance _b_, use _b_.data.

dumps(_params_ [, _methodname_ [, _methodresponse_ [, _encoding_ [, _allow_none_]]]])

Converts _params_ into an XML-RPC request or response, where _params_ is either a tuple of arguments or an instance of the `Fault` exception. _methodname_ is the name of the method as a string. _methodresponse_ is a Boolean flag. If `True`, then the result is an XML-RPC response. In this case, only one value can be supplied in _params_. _encoding_ specifies the text encoding in the generated XML and defaults to UTF-8. _allow_none_ is a flag that specifies whether or not `None` is supported as a parameter type. `None` is not explicitly mentioned by the XML-RPC specification, but many servers support it. By default, _allow_none_ is `False`.

loads(_data_)

Converts _data_ containing an XML-RPC request or response into a tuple (_params_, _methodname_) where _params_ is a tuple of parameters and _methodname_ is a string containing the method name. If the request represents a fault condition instead of an actual value, then the `Fault` exception is raised.

MultiCall(*server*)

Creates a `MultiCall` object that allows multiple XML-RPC requests to be packaged together and sent as a single request. This can be a useful performance optimization if many different RPC requests need to be made on the same server. *server* is an instance of `ServerProxy`, representing a connection to a remote server. The returned `MultiCall` object is used in exactly the same way as `ServerProxy`. However, instead of immediately executing the remote methods, the method calls as queued until the `MultiCall` object is called as a function. Once this occurs, the RPC requests are transmitted. The return value of this operation is a generator that yields the return result of each RPC operation in sequence. Note that `MultiCall()` only works if the remote server provides a `system.multicall()` method.

Here is an example that illustrates the use of `MultiCall`:

```
multi = xmlrpclib.MultiCall(server)
multi.foo(4,6,7)                    # Remote method foo
multi.bar("hello world")            # Remote method bar
multi.spam()                        # Remote method spam
# Now, actually send the XML-RPC request and get return results
foo_result, bar_result, spam_result = multi()
```

Exceptions

The following exceptions are defined in `xmlrpclib`:

Fault

Indicates an XML-RPC fault. The `faultCode` attribute contains a string with the fault type. The `faultString` attribute contains a descriptive message related to the fault.

ProtocolError

Indicates a problem with the underlying networking—for example, a bad URL or a connection problem of some kind. The `url` attribute contains the URI that triggered the error. The `errcode` attribute contains an error code. The `errmsg` attribute contains a descriptive string. The `headers` attribute contains all the HTTP headers of the request that triggered the error.

Notes

- More information about XML-RPC can be obtained at http://www.xmlrpc.com.
- An example of writing an XML-RPC server can be found in the section on the `SimpleXMLRPCServer` module.

23

Internet Data Handling and Encoding

THE MODULES IN THIS SECTION ARE USED TO ENCODE and decode data in formats that are widely used by Internet applications and protocols, including email, HTTP, and remote procedure call.

base64

The base64 module is used to encode and decode data using base 64, base 32, or base 16 encoding. Base 64 is commonly used to embed binary data in mail attachments.

Base 64 encoding works by grouping the data to be encoded into groups of 24 bits (3 bytes). Each 24-bit group is then subdivided into four 6-bit components. Each 6-bit value is then represented by a printable ASCII character from the following alphabet:

Value	Encoding
0–25	ABCDEFGHIJKLMNOPQRSTUVWXYZ
26–51	abcdefghijklmnopqrstuvwxyz
52–61	0123456789
62	+
63	/
pad	=

If the number of bytes in the input stream is not a multiple of 3 (24 bits), the data is padded to form a complete 24-bit group. The extra padding is then indicated by special '=' characters that appear at the end of the encoding. For example, if you encode a 16-byte character sequence, there are five 3-byte groups with 1 byte left over. The remaining byte is padded to form a 3-byte group. This group then produces two characters from the base 64 alphabet (the first 12 bits, which include 8 bits of real data), followed by the sequence '==', representing the bits of extra padding. A valid base 64 encoding will only have none, one (=), or two (==) padding characters at the end of the encoding.

Base 32 encoding works by grouping binary data into groups of 40 bits (5 bytes). Each 40-bit group is subdivided into eight 5-bit components. Each 5-bit value is then encded using the following alphabet:

Value	Encoding
0–25	ABCDEFGHIJKLMNOPQRSTUVWXYZ
26–31	2–7

Like with base 64, if the end of the input stream does not form a 40-bit group, it is padded to 40 bits and the '=' character is used to represent the extra padding in the output. At most, there will be six padding characters ('======'), which occurs if the final group only includes 1 byte of data.

Base 16 encoding is the standard hexadecimal encoding of data. Each 4-bit group is represented by the digits '0'–'9' and the letters 'A'–'F'. There is no extra padding or pad characters for base 16 encoding.

`b64encode(s [, altchars])`

Encodes string s using base 64 encoding. `altchars`, if given, is a two-character string that specifies alternative characters to use for '+' and '/' characters that normally appear in base 64 output. This is useful if base 64 encoding is being used with filenames or URLs.

`b64decode(s [, altchars])`

Decodes string s, which is encoded as base64. `altchars`, if given, is a two-character string that specifies the alternative characters for '+' and '/' that normally appear in base 64 encoded data. TypeError is raised if the input s contains extraneous characters or is incorrectly padded.

`standard_b64encode(s)`

Encodes string s using the standard base 64 encoding.

`standard_b64decode(s)`

Decodes string s using standard base 64 encoding.

`urlsafe_b64encode(s)`

Encodes string s using base 64, but uses the characters '-' and '_' instead of '+' and '/', respectively. The same as b64encode(s, '-_').

`urlsafe_b64decode(s)`

Decodes string s encoded with a URL-safe base 64 encoding.

`b32encode(s)`

Encodes string s using base 32 encoding.

`b32decode(s [, casefold [, map01]])`

Decodes string s using base 32 encoding. If `casefold` is True, both uppercase and lowercase letters are accepted. Otherwise, only uppercase letters may appear (the default). `map01`, if present, specifies which letter the digit 1 maps to (for example, the letter 'I' or the letter 'L'). If this argument is given, the digit '0' is also mapped to the letter 'O'. A TypeError is raised if the input string contains extraneous characters or is incorrectly padded.

`b16encode(s)`

Encodes string s using base 16 (hex) encoding.

`b16decode(s [,casefold])`

Decodes string s using base 16 (hex) encoding. If casefold is True, letters may be uppercase or lowercase. Otherwise, hexadecimal letters 'A'–'F' must be uppercase (the default). Raises TypeError if the input string contains extraneous characters or is malformed in any way.

The following functions are part of an older base 64 module interface that you may see used in older Python code:

`decode(input, output)`

Decodes base 64–encoded data. input is a filename or a file object open for reading. output is a filename or a file object open for writing.

`decodestring(s)`

Decodes a base 64–encoded string, s. Returns a string containing the decoded binary data.

`encode(input, output)`

Encodes data using base 64. input is a filename or a file object open for reading. output is a filename or a file object open for writing.

`encodestring(s)`

Encodes a string, s, using base64.

Example

```
>>> import base64
>>> s = "Hello World"
>>> base64.b64encode(s)
'SGVsbG8gV29ybGQ='
>>> base64.b32encode(s)
'JBSWY3DPEBLW64TMMQ======'
>>> base64.b16encode(s)
'48656C6C6F20576F726C64'
>>>
```

See Also:
binascii (p. 447), Internet RFC-3548 and RFC-1421

binascii

The binascii module is used to convert data between binary and a variety of ASCII encodings, such as base 64, binhex, and uuencoding.

`a2b_uu(string)`

Converts a line of uuencoded data to binary. Lines normally contain 45 (binary) bytes, except for the last line which may be less. Line data may be followed by whitespace.

448   Chapter 23   Internet Data Handling and Encoding

b2a_uu(data)

Converts a string of binary data to a line of uuencoded ASCII characters. The length of data should not be more than 45 bytes. Otherwise, the Error exception is raised.

a2b_base64(string)

Converts a string of base 64–encoded data to binary.

b2a_base64(data)

Converts a string of binary data to a line of base 64–encoded ASCII characters. The length of data should not be more than 57 bytes if the resulting output is to be transmitted through email (otherwise it might get truncated).

a2b_hex(string)

Converts a string of hexadecimal digits to binary data. This function is also called as unhexlify(string).

b2a_hex(data)

Converts a string of binary data to a hexadecimal encoding. This function is also called as hexlify(data).

a2b_hqx(string)

Converts a string of binhex 4–encoded data to binary without performing RLE decompression.

rledecode_hqx(data)

Performs an RLE (Run-Length Encoding) decompression of the binary data in data. Returns the decompressed data unless the data input is incomplete, in which case the Incomplete exception is raised.

rlecode_hqx(data)

Performs a binhex 4 RLE compression of data.

b2a_hqx(data)

Converts the binary data to a string of binhex 4–encoded ASCII characters. data should already be RLE-coded. Also, unless data is the last data fragment, the length of data should be divisible by three.

crc_hqx(data, crc)

Computes the binhex 4 CRC checksum of the data. crc is a starting value of the checksum.

crc32(data [, crc])

Computes the CRC-32 checksum of data. crc is an optional initial CRC value. If omitted, crc defaults to 0.

Exceptions

Error

Exception raised on errors.

`Incomplete`

Exception raised on incomplete data. This exception occurs when multiple bytes of data are expected, but the input data has been truncated.

See Also:
`base64` (p. 445), `binhex` (p. 449), `uu` (p. 473)

binhex

The `binhex` module is used to encode and decode files in binhex 4, a format commonly used when transferring files on older Macintosh systems.

`binhex(input, output)`

Converts a binary file with name *input* to a binhex file. *output* is a filename or an open file-like object that supports the `write()` and `close()` methods.

`hexbin(input [, output])`

Decodes a binhex file. *input* is either a filename or a file-like object with `read()` and `close()` methods. *output* is the name of the output file. If omitted, the output name is taken from the binhex file.

Exceptions

`Error`

Raised when data can't be encoded as binhex format or when input can't be properly decoded.

Notes

- Both the data and resource forks are handled on the Macintosh.
- Only the data fork is handled on other platforms.

See Also:
`binascii` (p. 447)

email

The `email` package provides a wide variety of functions and objects for representing, parsing, and manipulating email messages encoded according to the MIME standard. The package itself is composed of several submodules. The following list briefly outlines the most commonly used submodules. However, it should be noted that the module contains additional submodules not described here. Consult the online documentation for full details.

Module	Description
email.Message	Representation of email messages
email.FeedParser	Incremental parsing of email messages
email.Encoders	Encoding of email messages
email.Header	Support for internationalized email headers
email.Utils	Useful utility functions
email.Iterators	Iterators for various aspects of email
email.MIME*	Various types of basic messages
email.Errors	Exceptions

At the top level, the email module provides just two utility functions for parsing messages:

message_from_file(f)

Creates an email.Message.Message object by reading an email message from the file f. f is a file-like object created by a function such as open(). The input message should be a complete MIME-encoded email message, including all headers, text, and attachments.

message_from_string(str)

Creates an email.Message.Message object by reading an email message from the string str.

The remaining functionality of the module is contained in the submodules, each of which is now described in a separate section.

email.Message

The email.Message module defines a class, Message, that represents the contents of an email message, including message headers and content.

Message()

Creates a new Message object. The newly created object is entirely empty. Various methods must be used to add components to the message.

An instance, m, of Message supports the following methods:

m.add_header(name, value, **params)

Adds a new message header. name is the name of the header, value is the value of the header, and params is a set of keyword arguments that supply additional optional parameters. For example, add_header('Foo', 'Bar', spam='major') adds the header line 'Foo: Bar; spam="major"' to the message.

m.as_string([unixfrom])

Converts the entire message to a string. unixfrom is a Boolean flag. If this is set to True, a UNIX-style 'From ...' line appears as the first line. By default, unixfrom is False.

m.attach(*payload*)

Adds an attachment to a multipart message. *payload* must be another Message object (for example, email.MIMEText.MIMEText). Internally, *payload* is appended to a list that keeps track of the different parts of the message. If the message is not a multipart message, use set_payload() to set the body of a message to a simple string.

m.del_param(*param* [, *header* [, *requote*]])

Deletes the parameter *param* from header *header*. For example, if a message has the header 'Foo: Bar; spam="major"', del_param('spam','Foo') would delete the 'spam="major"' portion of the header. If *requote* is True (the default), all remaining values are quoted when the header is rewritten. If *header* is omitted, the operation is applied to the 'Content-type' header.

m.get_all(*name* [, *default*])

Returns a list of all values for a header with name *name*. Returns *default* if no such header exists.

m.get_boundary([*default*])

Returns the boundary parameter found within the 'Content-type' header of a message. Typically the boundary is a string such as '===============0995017162==' that's used to separate the different subparts of a message. Returns *default* if no boundary parameter could be found.

m.get_charset()

Returns the character set associated with the message payload (for instance, 'iso-8859-1').

m.get_charsets([*default*])

Returns a list of all character sets that appear in the message. For multipart messages, the list will represent the character set of each subpart. The character set of each part is taken from 'Content-type' headers that appear in the message. If no character set is specified or the content-type header is missing, the character set for that part is set to the value of *default* (which is None by default).

m.get_content_charset([*default*])

Returns the character set from the first 'Content-type' header in the message. If the header is not found or no character set is specified, *default* is returned.

m.get_content_maintype()

Returns the main content type (for example, 'text' or 'multipart').

m.get_content_subtype()

Returns the subcontent type (for example, 'plain' or 'mixed').

m.get_content_type()

Returns a string containing the message content type (for example, 'multipart/mixed' or 'text/plain').

m.get_default_type()

Returns the default content type (for example, 'text/plain' for simple messages).

m.get_filename([*default*])

Returns the `filename` parameter from a `'Content-Disposition'` header, if any. Returns *default* if the header is missing or does not have a `filename` parameter.

m.get_param(*param* [, *default* [, *header* [, *unquote*]]])

Returns the value of a specific header parameter. *param* is a parameter name, *default* is a default value to return if the parameter is not found, *header* is the name of the header, and *unquote* specifies whether or not to unquote the parameter. If no value is given for *header*, parameters are taken from the `'Content-type'` header. The default value of *unquote* is `True`. The return value is either a string or a 3-tuple (*charset*, *language*, *value*) in the event the parameter was encoded according to RFC-2231 conventions. In this case, *charset* is a string such as `'iso-8859-1'`, *language* is a string containing a language code such as `'en'`, and *value* is the parameter value.

m.get_params([*default* [, *header* [, *unquote*]]])

Returns all parameters for *header* as a list. *default* specifies the value to return if the header isn't found. If *header* is omitted, the `'Content-type'` header is used. *unquote* is a flag that specifies whether or not to unquote values (`True` by default). The contents of the returned list are tuples (*name*, *value*) where *name* is the parameter name and *value* is the value as returned by the get_param() method.

m.get_payload([*i* [, *decode*]])

Returns the payload of a message. If the message is a simple message, a string containing the message body is returned. If the message is a multipart message, a list containing all the subparts is returned. For multipart messages, *i* specifies an optional index in this list. If supplied, only that message component will be returned. If *decode* is `True`, the payload is decoded according to the setting of any `'Content-Transfer-Encoding'` header that might be present (for example, `'quoted-printable'`, `'base64'`, and so on). To decode the payload of a simple non-multipart message, set *i* to `None` and *decode* to `True` or specify *decode* using a keyword argument.

m.get_unixfrom()

Returns the UNIX-style `'From ...'` line, if any.

m.is_multipart()

Returns `True` if *m* is a multipart message.

m.replace_header(*name*, *value*)

Replaces the value of the first occurrence of the header *name* with value *value*. Raises `KeyError` if the header is not found.

m.set_boundary(*boundary*)

Sets the boundary parameter of a message to the string *boundary*. This string gets added as the boundary parameter to the `'Content-type'` header in the message. Raises `HeaderParseError` if the message has no content-type header.

m.set_charset(*charset*)

Sets the default character set used by a message. *charset* may be a string such as `'iso-8859-1'` or `'euc-jp'`. An instance of `email.Charset.Charset` may also be passed (refer to the online documentation for details). Setting a character set normally

adds a parameter to the 'Content-type' header of a message (for example,
'Content-type: text/html; charset="iso-8859-1"').

m.set_default_type(*ctype*)

Sets the default message content type to *ctype*. *ctype* is a string containing a MIME
type such as 'text/plain' or 'message/rfc822'. This type is not stored in the
'Content-type' header of the message.

m.set_param(*param, value* [, *header* [, *requote* [, *charset* [, *language*]]]])

Sets the value of a header parameter. *param* is the parameter name, and *value* is the
parameter value. *header* specifies the name of the header and defaults to
'Content-type'. *requote* specifies whether or not to requote all the values in the
header after adding the parameter. By default, this is True. *charset* and *language*
specify optional character set and language information. If these are supplied, the
parameter is encoded according to RFC-2231. This produces parameter text such as
param*="'iso-8859-1'en-us'some%20value".

m.set_payload(*payload* [, *charset*])

Sets the entire message payload to *payload*. For simple messages, *payload* can be a
string containing the message body. For multipart messages, *payload* is a list of
Message objects. *charset* optionally specifies the default character set (see
set_charset).

m.set_type(*type* [, *header* [, *requote*]])

Sets the type used in the 'Content-type' header. *type* is a string specifying the type,
such as 'text/plain' or 'multipart/mixed'. *header* specifies an alternative header
other than the default 'Content-type' header. *requote* quotes the value of any
parameters already attached to the header. By default, this is True.

m.set_unixfrom(*unixfrom*)

Sets the text of the UNIX-style 'From ...' line. *unixfrom* is a string containing the
complete text including the 'From' text. This text is only output if the *unixfrom*
parameter of m.as_string() is set to True.

m.walk()

Creates a generator that iterates over all the subparts of a message. The iteration is a
depth-first traversal of the message. Typically, this function could be used to process all
the components of a multipart message.

Message objects support a number of dictionary methods that are used to access
message headers. The following operations are supported:

Operation	Description
m[*name*]	Returns the value of header *name*.
m[*name*] = *value*	Adds a header *name* with value *value*. This does not overwrite any existing header with the given name.
del m[*name*]	Deletes all headers with name *name* from the message.
m.has_key(*name*)	Tests for the presence of header *name*.
m.keys()	Returns a list of all message header names.

Operation	Description
m.values()	Returns a list of message header values.
m.items()	Returns a list of tuples containing message header names and values.
m.get(name [,def])	Returns a header value for header name. def specifies a default value to return if not found.
len(m)	Returns the number of message headers.
str(m)	Turns the message into a string. The same as the as_string() method.
name in m	Returns True if name is the name of a header in the message.

Finally, a Message object has a few attributes, typically set when messages have been parsed.

m.preamble

Any text that appears in a multipart message between the blank line that signals the end of the headers and the first occurrence of the multipart boundary string that marks the first subpart of the message.

m.epilogue

Any text in the message that appears after the last multipart boundary string and the end of the message.

m.defects

A list of all message defects found when parsing the message. See email.Errors for more details.

The following example illustrates how the Message class is used while parsing an email message. The following code reads an email message, prints a short summary of useful headers, prints the plain-text portions of the message, and saves any attachments.

```
import email
import sys

f = open(sys.argv[1])              # Open message file
m = email.message_from_file(f)     # Parse message

# Print short summary of sender/recipient
print "From    :", m["from"]
print "To      :", m["to"]
print "Subject :", m["subject"]
print

if not m.is_multipart():
    # Simple message. Just print the payload
    print m.get_payload()
else:
    # Multipart message.
    # Walk over subparts and save attachments.  Print any text/plain
    # portions that weren't attachments.
    for s in m.walk():
        filename = s.get_filename()
        if filename:
            print "Saving attachment: ", filename
```

```
        data = s.get_payload(decode=True)
        open(filename,"wb").write(data)
    else:
        if s.get_content_type() == 'text/plain':
            print s.get_payload()
```

email.FeedParser

The email.FeedParser module provides a parser that can incrementally process email messages when the data that makes up the message is supplied in chunks. This can be useful when processing email messages that are received over network connections instead of being read from files. The class described in this section would be used an alternative to the message_from_file() and message_from_string() functions normally used to parse email messages.

FeedParser()

Creates a new FeedParser object.
    An instance, f, of FeedParser has the following methods:

f.feed(data)

Feeds data to the parser. data is a string containing lines of input data. data will be joined with previously fed data (if any).

f.close()

Closes the parser and returns an email.Message.Message object representing the parsed message.

email.Encoders

The email.Encoders module contains functions that take a message and encode its payload according to different encoding schemes. In the process, the message is adjusted accordingly by setting the appropriate headers related to the encoding selected.

encode_quopri(msg)

Encodes the payload of message msg using quoted-printable encoding.

encode_base64(msg)

Encodes the payload of message msg using base 64 encoding.

encode_7or8bit(msg)

Examines the message payload and sets the 'Content-Transfer-Encoding' header to '7bit' or '8bit' as appropriate.

email.MIME*

The following Message objects are used to create email messages of various content types. Each object is contained in a package of the same name. For instance, MIMEText is contained in the module email.MIMEText. These message objects are suitable for use in creating multipart MIME messages. For instance, you would create a new message and attach different parts using the attach() method of Message.

`MIMEAudio(data [, subtype [, encoder [, **params]]])`

Creates a message containing audio data. `data` is a string containing the raw binary audio data. `subtype` specifies the type of the data and is a string such as `'mpeg'` or `'wav'`. If no subtype is provided, the audio type will be guessed by looking at the data using the `sndhdr` module. `encoder` is an optional encoding function from the `email.Encoders` module. By default, audio data is encoded using base 64 encoding. `params` represents optional keyword arguments and values that will be added to the `'Content-type'` header of the message.

`MIMEImage(data [, subtype [, encoder [, **parms]]])`

Creates a message containing image data. `data` is a string containing the raw image data. `subtype` specifies the image type and is a string such as `'jpg'` or `'png'`. If no `subtype` is provided, the type will be guessed using a function in the `imghdr` module. `encoder` is an optional encoding function from the `email.Encoders` module. By default, image data is encoded using base 64 encoding. `params` represents optional keyword arguments and values that are added to the `'Content-type'` header of the message.

`MIMEMessage(msg [, subtype])`

Creates a new non-multipart MIME message. `msg` is a message object containing the initial payload of the message. `subtype` is the type of the message and defaults to `'rfc822'`.

`MIMEMultipart([subtype [, boundary [, subparts [, **params]]]])`

Creates a new MIME multipart message. `subtype` specifies the optional subtype to be added to the 'Content-type: multipart/`subtype`' header. By default, `subtype` is `'mixed'`. `boundary` is a string that specifies the boundary separator used to make each message subpart. If this is set to None or omitted, a suitable boundary is determined automatically. `subparts` is a sequence of Message objects that make up the contents of the message. `params` represents optional keyword arguments and values that are added to the `'Content-type'` header of the message. Once a multipart message has been created, additional subparts can be added using the `Message.attach()` method.

`MIMEText(data [, subtype [, charset]])`

Creates a message containing textual data. `data` is a string containing the message payload. `subtype` specifies the text type and is a string such as `'plain'` (the default) or `'html'`. `charset` is the character set, which defaults to `'us-ascii'`. The message may be encoded depending on the contents of the message.

The following example shows how to compose and send an email message using the classes in this section.

```
mport email
import smtplib
from email.MIMEText import MIMEText
from email.MIMEMultipart import MIMEMultipart
from email.MIMEAudio import MIMEAudio

sender  = "jon@nogodiggydie.net"
receiver= "dave@dabeaz.com"
subject = "Faders up!"
```

```
body    = "I never should have moved out of Texas. -J.\n"
audio   = "TexasFuneral.mp3"

m = MIMEMultipart()
m["to"]       = receiver
m["from"]     = sender
m["subject"]  = subject

m.attach(MIMEText(body))
apart = MIMEAudio(open(audio,"rb").read(),"mpeg")
apart.add_header("Content-Disposition","attachment",filename=audio)
m.attach(apart)

# Send the email message
s = smtplib.SMTP()
s.connect()
s.sendmail(sender, [receiver],m.as_string())
s.close()
```

email.Header

The email.Header module is used to support internationalized email headers. You would use this module if you needed to generate an email header that contains non-ASCII text (for example, a subject line).

Header([s [, charset [, maxlinelen [, header_name [, continuation_ws [, errors]]]]]])

Creates a Header instance representing a header value. s is a string with the value. charset specifies the character set (for example, 'iso-8859-1'). maxlinelen specifies the maximum line length to use. header_name is the name of the header, which is only used if the first line needs to be split to a shorter length. continuation_ws is white-space added to continuation lines.

A Header object can be used anywhere a header value is used in the email module. For example:

```
from email.Message import Message
from email.Header import Header
m = Message()
m['Subject'] = Header("some subject", "iso-8859-1")
```

Instances of Header can be compared using the usual equality operators (==, !=). In addition, an instance, h, of Header has the following methods:

h.append(s [, charset [, errors]])

And appends the string s to the header. charset specifies the character set if any (if omitted, it defaults to the same character set of h). errors specifies how errors are to be handled when encoding the header. It has the same meaning as the errors parameter given to various Unicode encode() and decode() methods.

h.encode([splitchars])

Encodes the header into a string. splitchars specifies characters on which long lines can be split.

The following utility functions are provided in email.Header:

decode_header(*header*)

Decodes a raw internationalized header. Returns a list of tuples of the form (*value*, *charset*) where *value* is the decoded value and *charset* is the character set used. If a header contains multiple encoded parts, the returned list contains an entry for each part.

make_header(*decoded_seq* [, *maxlinelen* [, *header_name* [, *continuation_ws*]]])

Takes a list of tuples of the form (*value*, *charset*), as returned by decode_header(), and creates a Header instance. The input list is supplied in the *decoded_seq* parameter. The other parameters have the same meaning as for Header.

email.Iterators

The email.Iterators module defines some functions that create iterators for looping over the contents of a message.

body_line_iterator(*msg* [, *decode*])

Returns an iterator that iterates over all the subparts of the message *msg* and returns all the lines that contain text. Lines containing information related to the message encoding (boundary separators, and so on) are skipped. In addition, any subpart whose type does not correspond to a Python string are skipped. The *decode* parameter is passed to msg.get_payload(), which is used for getting payload information.

typed_subpart_iterator(*msg* [, *maintype* [, *subtype*]])

Creates an iterator that iterates over all the subparts of a multipart message. The iterator returns Message objects corresponding to the subparts. The *maintype* and *subtype* parameters act as a filter. If supplied, then only the subparts of the message whose type match '*maintype*/*subtype*' are returned. The default value of *maintype* is 'text'.

email.Utils

The email.Utils module provides utility functions that are generally useful when working with email-related data.

collapse_rfc2231_value(*value* [, *errors* [, *fallback_charset*]])

Given a 3-tuple *value* containing (*charset*, *language*, *value*), creates a Unicode string representing the value. Typically, *value* is returned by the method Message.get_param() when an RFC-2231 encoded header is encountered. *errors* is the Unicode error-handling method to use, which defaults to 'replace'. *fallback_charset* specifies the character set to be used if the one specified in *charset* is unknown. The default value is 'us-ascii'.

decode_rfc2231(*str*)

Decodes a string encoded according to the rules of RFC-2231. RFC-2231 is a specification for encoding parameter values that involve different language and character set encodings.

encode_rfc2231(*str* [, *charset* [, *language*]])

Encodes a string according the rules of RFC-2231. *charset* and *language* specify the character set and language, respectively.

formataddr(*addr*)

Given a tuple (*realname*, *email*), creates a string value suitable for use in headers such as 'To:' and 'Cc:'. *realname* is an individual's real name, and *email* is the email address. The created string typically looks like 'realname <email>'.

formatdate([*timeval* [, *localtime* [, *usegmt*]]])

Formats a time value *timeval* in RFC-2822 format for use in a message. *timeval* is a floating point as returned by time.gmtime() or time.localtime(). If omitted, the current time is used. If *localtime* is True, the time is interpreted relative to the current time zone instead of UTC. The default value is False. *usegmt* is a flag that outputs the date with the time zone set as the string 'GMT'. This only applies if *localtime* is False. The default value of *usegmt* is False.

getaddresses(*fieldvalues*)

Returns a list of addresses, each in the format returned by parseaddr(). *fieldvalues* is a list of raw address values as stored in the message. Typically, this list is obtained using a method such as *m*.get_all('To').

make_msgid([*idstring*])

Creates a string suitable for use in a 'Message-ID' header. If *idstring* is provided, it is used as part of the generated message identifier.

mktime_tz(*tuple*)

Converts a 10-tuple as returned by parsedate_tz() into a UTC timestamp.

parseaddr(*address*)

Parses an email address into a 2-tuple (*realname*, *email*).

parsedate(*date*)

Parses a date value encoded in RFC-2822 format, such as "Fri, 4 Nov 2005 14:13:05 -0500". Returns a 9-element time tuple compatible with the time.mktime() function in the time module. However, the last three items of this tuple (the tm_wday, tm_yday, and tm_isdst fields) are not set.

parsedate_tz(*date*)

The same as parsedate(), but returns a 10-tuple containing the date and information about the time zone. The first nine items of the tuple are the same as returned by parsedate(). A time zone offset is stored in the tenth item of the returned tuple (if found). If no time zone is defined, the tenth item of the returned tuple is None.

quote(*str*)

Returns a string where backslashes have been replaced by two backslashes and double quotes have been replaced by a backslash-quote.

unquote(*str*)

Returns an unquoted version of *str*. If *str* starts and ends with double quotes (") or angle brackets (<>), they are removed.

email.Errors

The email.Errors module defines exceptions that occur within the email package. In addition, classes representing defects encountered while parsing are also defined.

The following exceptions are defined:

MessageError

Base class of all exceptions raised by the email package.

MessageParseError

Base class of an exception raised while parsing email messages.

HeaderParseError

A MessageParseError exception that is raised when an error occurs while parsing email headers.

BoundaryError

A MessageParseError exception that is raised when the boundaries can't be located in a multipart email message.

MultipartConversionError

A MessageError exception that is raised when attachments are added to a message, but the message is not a multipart message.

The following classes are used to describe defects that occur while parsing messages. Defects are found in the defects attribute of a Message object. Defects are not exceptions. Instead, they are more informational. For example, a message with a defect still might be parsed in some way. However, if the resulting content appears to be malformed, the defects attribute could be inspected to see if any problems with the message were detected by the parser.

MessageDefect

Base class of all the following defects.

NoBoundaryInMultipartDefect

Message was of type multipart, but doesn't define a boundary separator.

StartBoundaryNotFoundDefect

Message was of type multipart, but the boundary separator it specified never appeared in the message.

FirstHeaderLineIsContinuationDefault

The first header line of the message was a header-continuation line.

MisplacedEnvelopeHeaderDefect

A UNIX "From " header appeared while parsing other email headers.

MalformedHeaderDefect

Malformed header.

MultipartInvariantViolationDefect

A message was of type multipart, but it didn't contain any subparts.

Notes

- The email module provides much of the same functionality of the rfc822 module, but is more modern and powerful.

- A number of advanced customization and configuration options have not been discussed. Readers should consult the online documentation for advanced uses of this module.

- Additional examples can also be found in the online documentation.

See Also:

rfc822 **(p. 470)**, mimetypes **(p. 464)**

HTMLParser

The HTMLParser module defines a class, HTMLParser, that can be used to parse HTML and XHTML documents. To use this module, you define your own class that inherits from HTMLParser and redefines methods as appropriate.

HTMLParser()

This is a base class that is used to create HTML parsers. It is initialized without any arguments.

An instance, *h*, of HTMLParser has the following methods:

***h*.close()**

Closes the parser and forces the processing of any remaining unparsed data. This method is called after all HTML data has been fed to the parser.

***h*.feed(*data*)**

Supplies new data to the parser. This data will be immediately parsed. However, if the data is incomplete (for example, it ends with an incomplete HTML element), the incomplete portion will be buffered and parsed the next time feed() is called with more data.

***h*.getpos()**

Returns the current line number and character offset into that line as a tuple (*line*, *offset*).

***h*.get_starttag_text()**

Returns the text corresponding to the most recently opened start tag.

***h*.handle_charref(*name*)**

This handler method is called whenever a character reference such as '&#*ref*;' is encountered. *name* is a string containing the name of the reference. For example, when parsing 'å', *name* will be set to '229'.

h.handle_comment(*data*)

This handler method is called whenever a comment is encountered. *data* is a string containing the text of the comment. For example, when parsing the comment '`<!--comment-->`', *data* will contain the text '*comment*'.

h.handle_data(*data*)

This handler is called to process data that appears between tags. *data* is a string containing text.

h.handle_decl(*decl*)

This handler is called to process declarations such as '`<!DOCTYPE HTML ...>`'. *decl* is a string containing the text of the declaration, not including the leading '`<!`' and trailing '`>`'.

h.handle_endtag(*tag*)

This handler is called whenever end tags are countered. *tag* is the name of the tag converted to lowercase. For example, if the end tag is '`</BODY>`', *tag* is the string '`body`'.

h.handle_entityref(*name*)

This handler is called to handle entity references such as '`&name;`'. *name* is a string containing the name of the reference. For example, if parsing '`&lt;`', *name* will be set to '`lt`'.

h.handle_pi(*data*)

This handler is called to handle processing instructions such as '`<?processing instruction>`'. *data* is a string containing the text of the processing instruction, not including the leading '`<?`' and trailing '`>`'. When called on XHTML-style instructions of the form '`<?...?>`', the last '`?`' will be included in *data*.

h.handle_startendtag(*tag*, *attrs*)

This handler processes XHTML-style empty tags such as '`<tag name="value" ... />`'. *tag* is a string containing the name of the tag. *attrs* contains attribute information and is a list of tuples of the form (*name*, *value*) where *name* is the attribute name converted to lowercase and *value* is the attribute value. For example, if parsing '`<a href="http://www.foo.com"/>`', *tag* is '`a`' and *attrs* is [('`href`','`http://www.foo.com`')]. If not defined in derived classes, the default implementation of this method simply calls handle_starttag() and handle_endtag().

h.handle_starttag(*tag*, *attrs*)

This handler processes start tags such as '`<tag name="value" ...>`'. *tag* and *attrs* have the same meaning as described for handle_startendtag().

h.reset()

Resets the parser, discarding any unprocessed data.

The following exception is provided:

HTMLParserError

Exception raised as a result of parsing errors. The exception has three attributes. The msg attribute contains a message describing the error, the lineno attribute is line number where the parsing error occurred, and the offset attribute is the character off-set into the line.

Example

The following example fetches an HTML document using the urllib module and prints out all links that have been specified with '<a href="...">' declarations:

```
# printlinks.py
import HTMLParser
import urllib
import sys

class PrintLinks(HTMLParser.HTMLParser):
    def handle_starttag(self,tag,attrs):
        if tag == 'a':
            for name,value in attrs:
                if name == 'href':  print value

m = PrintLinks()
m.feed(urllib.urlopen(sys.argv[1]).read())
m.close()
```

mailcap

The mailcap module is used to read UNIX mailcap files. Mailcap files are used to tell mail readers and web browsers how to process files with different MIME types. The contents of a mailcap file typically look something like this:

```
video/mpeg; xmpeg %s
application/pdf; acroread %s
```

When data of a given MIME type is encountered, the mailcap file is consulted to find an application for handling that data.

getcaps()

Reads all available mailcap files and returns a dictionary mapping MIME types to a mailcap entry. mailcap files are read from $HOME/.mailcap, /etc/mailcap, /usr/etc/mailcap, and /usr/local/etc/mailcap.

findmatch(*caps, mimetype* [, *key* [, *filename* [, *plist*]]])

Searches the dictionary *caps* for a mailcap entry matching *mimetype*. The *caps* dictionary is created by getcaps(). *key* is a string indicating an action and is typically 'view', 'compose', or 'edit'. *filename* is the name of the file that's substituted for the %s keyword in the mailcap entry. *plist* is a list of named parameters given as strings of the form '*name=value*' (for example, ['foo=3', 'bar=hello']). These parameters are used to replace parameters that appear in the mailcap entry as '%{*name*}'. Returns a tuple (*cmd, mailcap*) containing the command from the mailcap file and the raw mailcap entry.

Example

```
import mailcap
import urllib
import os
# Go fetch a document
urllib.urlretrieve("http://www.swig.org/Doc1.1/PDF/Python.pdf",
```

```
                         "/tmp/tmp1234")
caps = mailcap.getgaps()
cmd, mc = mailcap.findmatch(caps,'application/pdf','view','/tmp/tmp1234')
if cmd:
    os.system(cmd + " &")
else:
    print "No application for type application/pdf"
```

See Also:

mimetypes (this page), http://www.python.org/doc/lib/module-mailcap.html, Internet RFC-1524.

mimetypes

The mimetypes module is used to guess the MIME type associated with a file, based on its filename extension. It also converts MIME types to their standard filename extensions. MIME types consist of a type/subtype pair. The following list shows the MIME types recognized by Python 2.4:

File Suffix	MIME Type
.a	application/octet-stream
.ai	application/postscript
.aif	audio/x-aiff
.aifc	audio/x-aiff
.aiff	audio/x-aiff
.au	audio/basic
.avi	video/x-msvideo
.bat	text/plain
.bcpio	application/x-bcpio
.bin	application/octet-stream
.bmp	image/x-ms-bmp
.c	text/plain
.cdf	application/x-netcdf
.cpio	application/x-cpio
.csh	application/x-csh
.css	text/css
.dll	application/octet-stream
.doc	application/msword
.dot	application/msword
.dvi	application/x-dvi
.eml	message/rfc822
.eps	application/postscript
.etx	text/x-setext

File Suffix	MIME Type
.exe	application/octet-stream
.gif	image/gif
.gtar	application/x-gtar
.h	text/plain
.hdf	application/x-hdf
.htm	text/html
.html	text/html
.ief	image/ief
.jpe	image/jpeg
.jpeg	image/jpeg
.jpg	image/jpeg
.js	application/x-javascript
.ksh	text/plain
.latex	application/x-latex
.m1v	video/mpeg
.man	application/x-troff-man
.me	application/x-troff-me
.mht	message/rfc822
.mhtml	message/rfc822
.mid	audio/midi (non-standard)
.midi	audio/midi (non-standard)
.mif	application/x-mif
.mov	video/quicktime
.movie	video/x-sgi-movie
.mp2	audio/mpeg
.mp3	audio/mpeg
.mpa	video/mpeg
.mpe	video/mpeg
.mpeg	video/mpeg
.mpg	video/mpeg
.ms	application/x-troff-ms
.nc	application/x-netcdf
.nws	message/rfc822
.o	application/octet-stream
.obj	application/octet-stream
.oda	application/oda
.p12	application/x-pkcs12

File Suffix	MIME Type
.p7c	application/pkcs7-mime
.pbm	image/x-portable-bitmap
.pdf	application/pdf
.pfx	application/x-pkcs12
.pgm	image/x-portable-graymap
.pic	image/pict (non-standard)
.pict	image/pict (non-standard)
.pl	text/plain
.pnm	image/x-portable-anymap
.png	image/png
.pot	application/vnd.ms-powerpoint
.ppa	application/vnd.ms-powerpoint
.ppm	image/x-portable-pixmap
.pps	application/vnd.ms-powerpoint
.ppt	application/vnd.ms-powerpoint
.ps	application/postscript
.pwz	application/vnd.ms-powerpoint
.py	text/x-python
.pyc	application/x-python-code
.pyo	application/x-python-code
.qt	video/quicktime
.ra	audio/x-pn-realaudio
.ram	application/x-pn-realaudio
.ras	image/x-cmu-raster
.rdf	application/xml
.rgb	image/x-rgb
.roff	application/x-troff
.rtf	application/rtf (non-standard)
.rtx	text/richtext
.sgm	text/x-sgml
.sgml	text/x-sgml
.sh	application/x-sh
.shar	application/x-shar
.snd	audio/basic
.so	application/octet-stream
.src	application/x-wais-source
.sv4cpio	application/x-sv4cpio

File Suffix	MIME Type
.sv4crc	application/x-sv4crc
.swf	application/x-shockwave-flash
.t	application/x-troff
.tar	application/x-tar
.tcl	application/x-tcl
.tex	application/x-tex
.texi	application/x-texinfo
.texinfo	application/x-texinfo
.tif	image/tiff
.tiff	image/tiff
.tr	application/x-troff
.tsv	text/tab-separated-values
.txt	text/plain
.ustar	application/x-ustar
.vcf	text/x-vcard
.wav	audio/x-wav
.wiz	application/msword
.xbm	image/x-xbitmap
.xlb	application/vnd.ms-excel
.xls	application/vnd.ms-excel
.xml	text/xml
.xpm	image/x-xpixmap
.xsl	application/xml
.xul	text/xul (non-standard)
.xwd	image/x-xwindowdump
.zip	application/zip

guess_type(*filename* [, *strict*])

Guesses the MIME type of a file based on its filename or URL. Returns a tuple
(*type*, *encoding*) in which *type* is a string of the form type/subtype and *encoding*
is the program used to encode the data (for example, compress or gzip). Returns
(None, None) if the type cannot be guessed. If *strict* is True (the default), then only
official MIME types registered with IANA are recognized. Otherwise, some common,
but unofficial MIME types are also recognized.

guess_extension(*type* [, *strict*])

Guesses the standard file extension for a file based on its MIME type. Returns a string
with the filename extension including the leading dot (.). Returns None for unknown
types. If *strict* is True (the default), then only official MIME types are recognized.

guess_all_extensions(type [, strict])

The same as guess_extension(), but returns a list of all possible filename extensions.

init([files])

Initializes the module. *files* is a sequence of filenames that are read to extract type information. These files contain lines that map a MIME type to a list of acceptable file suffixes such as the following:

```
image/jpeg:   jpe jpeg jpg
text/html:    htm html
...
```

read_mime_types(filename)

Loads type mapping from a given filename. Returns a dictionary mapping filename extensions to MIME type strings. Returns None if *filename* doesn't exist or cannot be read.

add_type(type, ext [, strict])

Adds a new MIME type to the mapping. *type* is a MIME type such as 'text/plain', *ext* is a filename extension such as '.txt', and *strict* is a Boolean indicating whether the type is an officially registered MIME type. By default, *strict* is True.

The following variables contain configuration information related to this module:

knownfiles

List of common names for mime.types files.

suffix_map

Dictionary mapping suffixes to suffixes. This is used to allow recognition of encoded files for which the encoding and the type are indicated by the same extension. For example, the .tgz extension is mapped to .tar.gz to allow the encoding and type to be recognized separately.

encodings_map

Dictionary mapping filename extensions to encoding types.

types_map

Dictionary mapping filename extensions to MIME types.

common_types

Dictionary mapping filename extensions to nonstandard MIME types.

The mimetypes module also defines a class that can be used to manage different databases of MIME types.

MimeTypes([filenames])

Creates a new database of MIME types populated with the same information already provided by the mimetypes module. *filenames* is a list of filenames from which to read additional MIME type information (which is added to the database).

An instance, *m*, of MimeTypes has the attributes and methods *m*.suffix_map, *m*.encodings_map, *m*.types_map, *m*.common_types, *m*.guess_extension(), and *m*.guess_type(), which have the same usage as the global functions already described. In addition, the following methods are available:

m.read(*path*)

Reads MIME information from the file *path*.

m.readfp(*file*)

Reads MIME information from the open file object *file*.

quopri

The quopri module performs quoted-printable transport encoding and decoding. This format is used primarily to encode text files that are mostly readable but may contain a small number of special characters (for example, control characters or non-ASCII characters). The following rules describe how the quoted-printable encoding works:

- Any printable non-whitespace ASCII character, with the exception of '=', is represented as is.

- The '=' character is used as an escape character. When followed by two hexadecimal digits, it represents a character with that value (for example, '=0C'). The equals sign is represented by '=3D'. If '=' appears at the end of a line, it denotes a soft line break. This only occurs if a long line of input text must be split into multiple output lines.

- Spaces and tabs are left as is, but may not appear at the end of line.

It is fairly common to see this format used when documents make use of special characters in the extended ASCII character set. For example, if a document contained the text "Copyright © 2005," this would be represented by the Python string 'Copyright \xa9 2005'. The quoted-printed version of the string is 'Copyright =A9 2005', where the special character '\xa9' has been replaced by the escape sequence '=A9'.

decode(*input, output* [, *header*])

Decodes. *input* and *output* are file objects. If header is True, then the underscore (_) will be interpreted as a space. Otherwise, it is left alone. This is used when decoding MIME headers that have been encoded. By default, *header* is False.

decodestring(*s* [, *header*])

Decodes string *s*. *header* has the same meaning as with decode().

encode(*input, output, quotetabs* [, *header*])

Encodes. *input* and *output* are file objects. *quotetabs*, if set to True, forces tab characters to be quoted in addition to the normal quoting rules. Otherwise, tabs are left as is. By default, *quotetabs* is False. *header* has the same meaning as for decode().

encodestring(*s* [, *quotetabs* [, *header*]])

Encodes string *s*. *quotetabs* and *header* have the same meaning as with encode().

See Also:

binascii (**p. 447**), Internet RFC-1521

rfc822

The `rfc822` module is used to parse email headers presented in a format defined by the Internet standards RFC-822 and RFC-2822. Headers of this form are used in a number of contexts, including mail handling and in the HTTP protocol. A collection of RFC-822 headers looks like this:

```
Return-Path: <beazley@cs.uchicago.edu>
Date: Sun, 15 Apr 03:18:21 -0500 (CDT)
Message-Id: <199907171518.KAA24322@gargoyle.cs.uchicago.edu>
Reply-To: beazley@cs.uchicago.edu
References: <15065.6056.897223.775915@empire-builder.cs.uchicago.edu>
        <20010415041130.008D1D1D8@smack.cs.uchicago.edu>
Mime-Version: 1.0 (generated by tm-edit 7.78)
Content-Type: text/plain; charset=US-ASCII
From: David Beazley <beazley@cs.uchicago.edu>
To: techstaff@cs
Subject: Modem problem

I'm having some trouble running MPI over the ultra-scalable modem
array on our Beowulf cluster. Can someone take a look at it?
```

Each header line is of the form '`headername: values`' and may span multiple lines, provided that additional lines are indented with whitespace. Header names are not case sensitive, so a field name of '`Content-Type`' is the same as '`content-type`'. A list of headers is terminated by a single blank line.

RFC-822 headers are parsed by creating an instance of the `Message` class.

Message(*file* [, *seekable*])

Reads RFC-822 headers from the file-like object *file* and returns a *Message* object. Headers are read using *file*.`readline()` until a blank line is encountered. *seekable* is a flag that's set to zero if *file* is unseekable (such as a file created from a socket).

A `Message` object, *m*, behaves like a dictionary, except that its key values are not case sensitive and it doesn't support certain dictionary operations, including `update()` and `clear()`. The following operations are supported:

Method	Description
m[*name*]	Returns the value for the header name.
m[*name*]=*value*	Adds a header.
m.keys()	Returns a list of header names.
m.values()	Returns a list of header values.
m.items()	Returns a list of header (*name*, *value*) pairs.
m.has_key(*name*)	Tests for the existence of a header name.
m.get(*name* [, *default*])	Gets a header value. Returns *default* if not found.
len(*m*)	Returns the number of headers.
str(*m*)	Converts headers to an RFC-822–formatted string.

In addition, the following methods are available:

`m.getallmatchingheaders(name)`

Returns a list of all lines with headers that match *name*, including continuation lines (if any). Returns an empty list if no matches are found.

`m.getfirstmatchingheader(name)`

Returns the list of lines for the first header matching *name*, including any continuation lines. Returns None if *name* doesn't match any headers.

`m.getrawheader(name)`

Returns a string containing the raw text after the colon for the first header matching *name*. Returns None if no match is found.

`m.getheader(name [, default])`

Like getrawheader(*name*), but strips all leading and trailing whitespace. *default* specifies a default value to return if no matching header is found.

`m.getaddr(name)`

Returns a pair (*full_name, email_address*) for a header containing an email address. If no header matches *name*, (None, None) is returned.

`m.getaddrlist(name)`

Parses a header containing a list of email addresses and returns a list of tuples as returned by the getaddr() method. If multiple headers match the named header, all are parsed for addresses (for example, multiple 'cc' headers).

`m.getdate(name)`

Parses a header containing a date and returns a 9-tuple compatible with time.mktime(). Returns None if no match is found or the date cannot be parsed.

`m.getdate_tz(name)`

Parses a header containing a date and returns a 10-tuple in which the first nine elements are the same as returned by getdate() and the tenth is a number with the offset of the date's time zone from UTC (Greenwich Mean Time). Returns None if no match is found or the date is unparsable.

`m.rewindbody()`

Seeks to the beginning of the message body. Only applicable if the underlying file object is seekable.

Finally, messages have two instance attributes:

`m.headers`

A list containing the entire set of header lines.

`m.fp`

The file-like object passed when the Message was created.

In addition to Message, the rfc822 module defines the following utility functions:

`dump_address_pair(pair)`

Given an email address specified as a tuple (*name, emailaddr*), returns a string suitable for use in an address field of an email message (for example, "To:", "Cc:", and so on). If the *name* part of *pair* is empty or None, then the returned string is simply *emailaddr*.

parseaddr(*address*)

Parses an email address specified as a string and returns a tuple (*name*, *emailaddr*) where *name* is the real name and *emailaddr* is the email address.

parsedate(*date*)

Parses an RFC-822–formatted date such as 'Mon, 16 Apr 2001 17:30:08 -0600' and returns a 9-tuple that's compatible with the time.mktime() function. Returns None if *date* cannot be parsed.

parsedate_tz(*date*)

Parses a date, but returns a 10-tuple where the first nine elements are the same as returned by parsedate() and the tenth item is the offset of the date's time zone from UTC. Returns None if *date* cannot be parsed.

mktime_tz(*tuple*)

Turns a 10-tuple as returned by parsedate_tz() into a UTC timestamp. If the time zone item is None, local time is assumed.

quote(*str*)

Returns a string where all the backslashes and double quotes in *str* have been escaped by backslashes.

unquote(*str*)

Returns a string that is an unquoted version of *str*. If the text in *str* is surrounded by quotes or angle brackets, they are removed. Backslash escapes such as '\\' and '\"' are also replaced.

AddressList(*addrlist*)

Converts a string containing a comma-separated list of email addresses into an AddressList object. The following operations can be performed on AddressList objects:

Operation	Description
len(a)	Number of addresses in a list
str(a)	Converts a back into a string of email addresses
a + b	Combines two lists of addresses, removing duplicates
a - b	Removes all addresses in list b from list a

Example

```
import rfc822
# Open a mail message
f = open("mailmessage")
# Read the headers
m = rfc822.Message(f)
# Extract a few fields
m_from = m["From"]
m_to = m.getaddr("To")
m_subject = m["Subject"]
```

Notes

- Much of the functionality of this module has been superceded by that in the email module. However, the rfc822 module is used in a wide variety of existing code.

- The Message class defines a few additional methods that can be specialized in a subclass. Refer to the online documentation at http://www.python.org/doc/lib/module-rfc822.html for details.

See Also:

email (p. 449), mimetypes (p. 464), mailcap (p. 463), Internet RFC-822, Internet RFC-2822, http://www.python.org/doc/lib/module-rfc822.html

uu

The uu module is used to encode and decode files in uuencode format, a data encoding sometimes used when transferring binary data over an ASCII-only connection.

`encode(input, output [, name [, mode]])`

Uuencodes a file. *input* is a file object opened for reading or a filename. *output* is a file object opened for writing or a filename. *name* specifies the name of the file that's encoded in the uuencoded file. *mode* specifies the mode of the file. By default, *name* and *mode* are taken from the input file.

`decode(input [, output [, mode [, quiet]]])`

Decodes a uuencoded file. *input* is a file object opened for reading or a filename. *output* is a file object opened for writing or a filename. *mode* is used to set permission bits and overrides the setting encoded in the input file. Raises the exception uu.Error if the output file already exists or the input stream contains corrupted data. In certain cases, Python may be able to recover from encoding errors, but will print a warning message. The *quiet* option, if True, silences these messages.

See Also:

binascii (p. 447)

xdrlib

xdrlib is used to encode and decode data in the Sun XDR (External Data Representation) format. XDR is often used as a portable way to encode binary data for use in networked applications. It's used extensively in applications involving remote procedure calls (RPCs).

Encoding and decoding is controlled through the use of two classes:

`Packer()`

Creates an object for packing data into an XDR representation.

`Unpacker(data)`

Creates an object for unpacking XDR-encoded data. `data` is a string containing XDR-encoded data values.

An instance, p, of the `Packer` class supports the following methods:

`p.get_buffer()`

Returns the current pack buffer as a string.

`p.reset()`

Resets the pack buffer to the empty string.

`p.pack_uint(x)`

Packs a 32-bit unsigned integer x.

`p.pack_int(x)`

Packs a 32-bit signed integer x.

`p.pack_enum(x)`

Packs an enumeration x (an integer).

`p.pack_bool(x)`

Packs a Boolean value x.

`p.pack_uhyper(x)`

Packs a 64-bit unsigned integer x.

`p.pack_hyper(x)`

Packs a 64-bit signed integer x.

`p.pack_float(x)`

Packs a single-precision floating-point number x.

`p.pack_double(x)`

Packs a double-precision floating-point number x.

`p.pack_fstring(n, s)`

Packs a fixed-length string s of length n.

`p.pack_fopaque(n, data)`

Packs a fixed-length opaque data stream. Similar to `pack_fstring()`.

`p.pack_string(s)`

Packs a variable-length string s.

`p.pack_opaque(data)`

Packs a variable-length opaque data string `data`. Similar to `pack_string()`.

`p.pack_bytes(bytes)`

Packs a variable-length byte stream `bytes`. Similar to `pack_string()`.

p.pack_list(*list, pack_func*)

Packs a list of homogeneous items. *pack_func* is the function called to pack each data item (for example, p.pack_int). For each item in the list, an unsigned integer, 1, is packed first, followed by the data item. An unsigned integer, 0, is packed at the end of the list.

p.pack_farray(*n, array, pack_func*)

Packs a fixed-length list of homogeneous items. *n* is the list length, *array* is a list containing the data, and *pack_func* is the function called to pack each data item.

p.pack_array(*list, pack_func*)

Packs a variable-length list of homogeneous items by first packing its length and then calling the pack_farray() method.

An instance, u, of the Unpacker class supports the following methods:

u.reset(*data*)

Resets the string buffer with the given data.

u.get_position()

Returns the current unpack position in the data buffer.

u.set_position(*position*)

Sets the data buffer unpack position to *position*.

u.get_buffer()

Returns the current unpack data buffer as a string.

u.done()

Indicates unpack completion. Raises an Error exception if all the data has not been unpacked.

In addition, every data type that can be packed with a Packer can be unpacked with an Unpacker. Unpacking methods are of the form unpack_*type*() and usually take no arguments. They return the unpacked object.

u.unpack_int()

Unpacks and returns a 32-bit signed integer.

u.unpack_uint()

Unpacks and returns a 32-bit unsigned integer. If the unsigned value is larger than sys.maxint, it is returned as an unsigned long integer.

u.unpack_enum()

Unpacks and returns an enumeration (an integer).

u.unpack_bool()

Unpacks a Boolean value and returns it as an integer.

u.unpack_hyper()

Unpacks and returns a 64-bit signed integer as a Python long integer.

`u.unpack_uhyper()`

Unpacks and returns a 64-bit unsigned integer as a Python long integer.

`u.unpack_float()`

Unpacks and returns a single-precision floating-point number. The value will be converted to double precision when it is returned as a Python floating-point number.

`u.unpack_double()`

Unpacks and returns a double-precision floating-point number.

`u.unpack_fstring(n)`

Unpacks and returns a fixed-length string. n is the number of characters expected.

`u.unpack_fopaque(n)`

Unpacks and returns a fixed-length opaque data stream, similarly to `unpack_fstring()`.

`u.unpack_string()`

Unpacks and returns a variable-length string.

`u.unpack_opaque()`

Unpacks and returns a variable-length opaque data string.

`u.unpack_bytes()`

Unpacks and returns a variable-length byte stream.

`u.unpack_list(unpack_func)`

Unpacks and returns a list of homogeneous items as packed by `pack_list()`. `unpack_func` is the function called to perform the unpacking for each item (for example, `unpack_int`).

`u.unpack_farray(n, unpack_func)`

Unpacks and returns (as a list) a fixed-length array of homogeneous items. n is the number of list elements to expect and `unpack_func` is the function used to unpack each item.

`u.unpack_array(unpack_func)`

Unpacks and returns a variable-length list of homogeneous items. `unpack_func` is the function used to unpack each item.

Exceptions

`Error`

The base exception class. `Error` has a single public data member, `msg`, containing the description of the error.

`ConversionError`

Class derived from `Error`. Contains no additional instance variables.

Note

Objects created with xdrlib can be pickled using the `pickle` module.

> **See Also:**
> `struct` (**p. 228**), `array` (**p. 195**), Internet RFC 1014

xml

Python includes a number of modules for processing XML data. The topic of XML processing is large and full coverage is beyond the scope of this book. However, modules related to basic XML parsing are covered. This section assumes the reader is already familiar with basic XML concepts. A book such as *Inside XML* by Steve Holzner (New Riders) or *XML In a Nutshell* by Elliotte Harold and W. Scott Means (O'Reilly and Associates) will be useful in explaining basic XML concepts. Several books discuss XML processing with Python, including *Python & XML* by Christopher Jones (O'Reilly and Associates) and *XML Processing with Python* by Sean McGrath (Prentice Hall).

There are two common approaches for parsing XML documents. The first approach, SAX (Simple API for XML), is based on event handling. With SAX, an XML document is read sequentially. As the document is read, each XML element triggers a handler function that is responsible for handling that part of the document. The second approach, DOM (Document Object Model), builds a tree structure representing an entire XML document. Once the tree has been built, DOM provides an interface for traversing the tree and extracting data.

Each parsing approach is described in a separate section that follows.

Readers are advised that the coverage here is really only focused on basic handling of XML data. Python also includes XML modules related to implementing new kinds of parsers, building XML documents from scratch, and so forth. In addition, a variety of third-party extensions extend Python's capabilities with additional XML features such as support for XSLT and XPATH. Links to further information can be found at http://www.python.org.

xml.dom

The `xml.dom` module defines some objects and exceptions that are used by parsers that implement the Document Object Model. With DOM, documents are parsed into a tree structure representing the document structure. The tree structure can then be traversed and manipulated as necessary.

As an example of the tree structure, consider the following XML document:

```
<?xml version="1.0" encoding="iso-8859-1"?>

   <!DOCTYPE recipe [
   <!-- The RECIPE DTD appears here -->
     <!ELEMENT recipe (title, description?, ingredients, directions)>
     <!ELEMENT ingredients (item+)>
     <!ELEMENT title (#PCDATA)>
     <!ELEMENT description (#PCDATA)>
     <!ELEMENT item (#PCDATA)>
     <!ELEMENT directions (#PCDATA)>
     <!ATTLIST item num     CDATA     #REQUIRED
                    units  (C | tsp | tbl | bottles | none )  "none">
   ]>
   <!-- End of DTD -->
<recipe>
   <title>
```

```
      Famous Guacamole
      </title>
      <description>
      A southwest favorite!
      </description>
      <ingredients>
           <item num="4"> Large avocados, chopped </item>
           <item num="1"> Tomato, chopped </item>
           <item num="1/2" units="C"> White onion, chopped </item>
           <item num="2" units="tbl"> Fresh squeezed lemon juice </item>
           <item num="1"> Jalapeno pepper, diced </item>
           <item num="1" units="tbl"> Fresh cilantro, minced </item>
           <item num="1" units="tbl"> Garlic, minced </item>
           <item num="3" units="tsp"> Salt </item>
           <item num="12" units="bottles"> Ice-cold beer </item>
      </ingredients>
      <directions>
      Combine all ingredients and hand whisk to desired consistency.
      Serve and enjoy with ice-cold beers.
      </directions>
</recipe>
```

When parsed using DOM, the document is turned into a tree with the following structure:

```
Document
     DocumenType
     Comment
     Element(recipe)
         Text ("")
         Element (title)
             Text ("Famous Guacamole")
         Element (description)
              Text ("A Southwest Favorite")
         Element (ingredients)
              Text ("")
              Element (item)
                    Text ("Large avocados, chopped")
              Element (item)
                    Text ("Tomato, chopped")
              ...
         Element (directions)
              Text ("Combine all ingredients...")
```

Each node of a DOM tree is of type xml.dom.Node. An instance, *n*, of Node has the following attributes that define various properties of the node and the underlying tree structure:

n.nodeType

An integer that specifies the node type. It is set to one of the following values, which are class variables of the Node class: ATTRIBUTE_NODE, CDATA_SECTION_NODE, COMMENT_NODE, DOCUMENT_FRAGMENT_NODE, DOCUMENT_NODE, DOCUMENT_TYPE_NODE, ELEMENT_NODE, ENTITY_NODE, ENTITY_REFERENCE_NODE, NOTATION_NODE, PROCESSING_INSTRUCTION_NODE, or TEXT_NODE. Descriptions of each node type and examples can be found in the section on the xml.dom.minidom module that appears later.

n.parentNode

A reference to the parent node or None if the node is the top of the tree.

n.attributes

A mapping that contains attribute values, if any. This is only defined for element nodes. Otherwise, the value is None.

n.previousSibling

The node that appears before *n* in the tree and has the same parent. If *n* is the first child, it is None.

n.nextSibling

The node that appears after *n* in the tree and has the same parent. If *n* is the last child, it is None.

n.childNodes

A list of all child nodes of *n*.

n.firstChild

The first child of *n*.

n.lastChild

The last child of *n*.

n.localName

The local tag name of an element. If a colon appears in the tag (for example, '<foo:bar ...>'), then this only contains the part after the colon.

n.prefix

Part of a tag name that appears before a colon, if any. For example, the element '<foo:bar ...>' would have a prefix of 'foo'.

n.namespaceURI

The namespace associated with *n*, if any.

n.nodeName

The name of the node. The meaning of the name depends on the DOM node type.

n.nodeValue

The value of the node. The meaning of the value depends on the DOM node type.
    The following methods are used to manipulate nodes. Typically, these are used to manipulate the tree structure.

n.appendChild(*child*)

Adds a new child node, *child*, to *n*. The new child is added at the end of any other children.

n.cloneNode(*deep*)

Make a copy of the node *n*. If *deep* is True, all child nodes are also cloned.

n.hasAttributes()

Returns True if the node has any attributes.

`n.hasChildNodes()`

Returns True if the node has any children.

`n.insertBefore(newchild, ichild)`

Inserts a new child, `newchild`, before another child, `ichild`. `ichild` must already be a child of `n`.

`n.isSameNode(other)`

Returns True if the node `other` refers to the same DOM node as `n`.

`n.normalize()`

Joins adjacent text nodes into a single text node.

`n.removeChild(child)`

Removes child `child` from `n`.

`n.replaceChild(newchild,oldchild)`

Replaces the child `oldchild` with `newchild`. `oldchild` must already be a child of `n`.

Exceptions

The following exceptions are defined in `xml.dom` and used by parsers in other modules:

`DOMException`

Base class of all DOM exceptions.

`DomStringSizeErr`

Exception raised when a string is too large to fit into a string. Never raised by Python-only implementations of DOM because Python strings don't have size limits.

`HierarchyRequestErr`

Exception raised when the type of a node being inserted is not allowed at the point of insertion.

`IndexSizeErr`

Exception raised when an index or size parameter is out of range.

`InuseAttributeErr`

Exception raised when an attempt is made to insert an attribute node, but the node is already used elsewhere in the document.

`InvalidAccessErr`

Exception raised if an operation is not supported by a node.

`InvalidCharacterErr`

Exception raised when a string parameter contains an invalid character.

`InvalidModificationErr`

Exception raised if an attempt is made to change the type of a node.

`InvalidStateErr`

Exception raised if an attempt is made to use a node that is no longer defined or usable.

NamespaceErr

Exception raised if an object is changed in a way that is not permitted according to namespace rules.

NotFoundErr

Exception raised if a node does not exist.

NotSupportedErr

Exception raised if the DOM implementation does not support a particular feature or operation.

NoDataAllowedErr

Exception raised if data is supplied to a node type that does not support data.

NoModificationAllowedErr

Exception raised if modifications are attempted on read-only values.

SyntaxErr

Exception raised if an invalid or illegal string is specified for certain node parameters.

WrongDocumentErr

Exception raised if a node is inserted into a different document than the one to which it currently belongs.

xml.dom.minidom

The xml.dom.minidom module provides a simple parser for creating DOM trees.

parse(*file* [, *parser*])

Parses the contents of *file* and returns a Document node representing the top of the document tree. *file* is a filename or an already-open file object. *parser* is an optional SAX2-compatible parser object that will be used to construct the tree. If omitted, a default parser will be used.

parseString(*string* [, *parser*])

The same as parse(), except that the input data is supplied in a string instead of a file.

Both of these parsing methods return the top node of a DOM tree. The tree can be traversed using the standard attributes and methods for nodes described in the xml.dom module. The xml.dom.minidom module adds a few additional methods to each node:

n.toprettyxml([*indent* [, *newl*]])

Creates a nicely formatted string containing the XML represented by node *n* and its children. *indent* specifies an indentation string and defaults to a tab ('\t'). *newl* specifies the newline character and defaults to '\n'.

n.toxml([*encoding*])

Creates a string containing the XML represented by node *n* and its children. *encoding* specifies the encoding (for example, 'utf-8'). If no encoding is given, none is specified in the output text.

`n.unlink()`

Prepares a node, *n*, for garbage collection by breaking all the internal cycles (that is, links between nodes that would interfere with garbage collection). This can be used on a node when it is no longer needed. This operation affects all descendents of *n* as well.

`n.writexml(`*writer* [, *indent* [, *addindent* [, *newl*]]]`)`

Writes XML to *writer*. *writer* can be any object that provides a `write()` method that is compatible with the file interface. *indent* specifies the indentation of *n*. It is a string that is prepended to the start of node *n* in the output. *addindent* is a string that specifies the incremental indentation to apply to child nodes of *n*. *newl* specifies the newline character.

Parse Trees

A variety of different node types and objects are used to represent objects in the DOM tree created by the parsing functions. The following set of objects is used for this purpose:

`Attr()`

The `Attr` type is used to represent attributes as a `Node` object. `Attr` objects are returned by methods such as `getAttributeNode()` on `Element` objects.

An instance, `a`, of `Attr` is a `Node` and shares the same attributes and methods. For instance, the value of an attribute can be obtained in the `nodeValue` attribute. In addition, the following attributes are specific to the attribute name:

`a.name`

The name of the attribute. If a document is using XML namespaces, the name will have colons in it.

`a.localName`

When XML namespaces are used, this contains the part of the attribute name after the separating colon.

`a.prefix`

When XML namespaces are used, this contains the part of the attribute name before the last colon (if any).

`CDATASection()`

A `CDATASection` object is used to store information in XML CDATA sections. Data is stored in the `data` attribute. It should be noted that XML parsers may break up large CDATA sections into multiple `CDATASection` objects.

`Comment()`

A `Comment` object is used to store information in XML comments. Comment text is stored in the `data` attribute. The comment text does not include the leading `'<!--'` or trailing `'-->'` characters.

`Document()`

The `Document` type is a node that represents an entire XML document.

An instance, *d*, of Document has the following attributes and methods. Methods that create new node types merely return the newly created node and do not insert the node into the document. The insertion process should be done using other methods such as appendChild().

d.documentElement

Contains the root element of the entire document.

d.createElement(*tagname*)

Creates and returns a new element node. *tagname* is the name of the new element.

d.createElementNS(*namespaceuri*, *tagname*)

Creates and returns a new element node with a namespace. *namespaceuri* is a string containing the namespace and is usually a URL such as 'http://www.foo.com/bar'. *tagname* is the name of the element.

d.createTextNode(*data*)

Creates and returns a new text node. *data* is a string containing the text.

d.createComment(*data*)

Creates and returns a new comment node. *data* is a string containing the comment text.

d.createProcessingInstruction(*target*, *data*)

Creates and returns a new processing instruction node. *target* is a string specifying the target of the instruction, and *data* is a string containing the processing information.

d.createAttribute(*name*)

Creates and returns a new attribute node. *name* is the name of the attribute.

d.createAttributeNS(*namespaceuri*, *qualifiedname*)

Creates and returns a new attribute node with a namespace.

d.getElementsByTagName(*tagname*)

Searches all child nodes and returns a list of elements with a given tag name *tagname*. The returned list is an object of type NodeList.

d.getElementsByTagNameNS(*namespaceuri*, *localname*)

Searches all child nodes and returns a list of elements with a given namespace URI and local name. The returned list is an object of type NodeList.

DocumentType()

A DocumentType object is used to contain information about notation and entity declarations defined in the '<!DOCTYPE ...>' portion of an XML document.

dt.publicId

Public identifier for the external subset of the document type definition. For example, if the declaration is '<!DOCTYPE foo PUBLIC "-//EVILCORP//FOO DTD//EN" "..dtds/foo.dtd">', this attribute contains '-//EVILCORP//FOO DTD//EN'.

dt.systemId

The system identifier for the external subset of the document type definition. For example, if the declaration is '<!DOCTYPE foo SYSTEM "../dtds/foo.dtd">', this attribute contains '../dtds/foo.dtd'.

dt.internalSubset

A string that contains everything defined within the internal portion of the '<!DOCTYPE ...[*internalSubset*]>' declaration. Does not include the enclosing '<!DOCTYPE' text or brackets.

dt.name

Document type name. For example, if the declaration '<!DOCTYPE foo [...' appears, the name is 'foo'.

dt.entities

A mapping containing definitions of external entities. This is an object of type NamedNodeMap.

dt.notations

A mapping containing definitions of notations. This is an object of type NamedNodeMap.

Element()

An Element object represents an XML document element.

An instance, e, of Element provides the following attributes and methods:

e.tagName

The tag name of the element. For example, if the element is defined by '<foo ...>', the tag name is 'foo'.

e.getElementsByTagName(*tagname*)

Returns a list of all children with a given tag name. The returned object is an object of type NodeList.

e.getElementsByTagNameNS(*namespaceuri, localname*)

Returns a list of all children with a given tag name in a namespace. *namespaceuri* and *localname* are strings that specify the namespace and tag name. If a namespace has been declared using a declaration such as '<foo xmlns:foo="http://www.spam.com/foo">', *namespacuri* is set to 'http://www.spam.com/foo'. If searching for a subsequent element, '<foo:bar>', *localname* is set to 'bar'. The returned object is of type NodeList.

e.hasAttribute(*name*)

Returns True if an element has an attribute with name *name*.

e.hasAttributeNS(*namespaceuri, localname*)

Returns True if an element has an attribute named by *namespaceuri* and *localname*. The arguments have the same meaning as described for getElementsByTagNameNS().

e.getAttribute(*name*)

Returns the value of attribute *name*. The return value is a string. If the attribute doesn't exist, an empty string is returned.

e.`getAttributeNode(`*name*`)`

Returns attribute *name* as an `Attr` node.

e.`getAttributeNS(`*namespaceuri*`, `*localname*`)`

Returns the value of the attributed named by *namespaceuri* and *localname*. The return value is a string. An empty string is returned if the attribute does not exist. The arguments are the same as described for `getElementsByTagNameNS()`.

e.`getAttributeNodeNS(`*namespaceuri*`, `*localname*`)`

Returns the attribute named by *namespaceuri* and *localname* as an `Attr` node. The arguments are the same as described for `getElementsByTagNameNS()`.

e.`removeAttribute(`*name*`)`

Removes the named attribute from the element.

e.`removeAttributeNode(`*attr*`)`

Removes the `Attr` node *attr* from the element.

e.`removeAttributeNS(`*namespaceuri*`, `*localname*`)`

Removes the attribute named by *namespaceuri* and *localname*. The arguments are the same as described for `getElementsByTagNameNS()`.

e.`setAttribute(`*name*`, `*value*`)`

Sets the value of an attribute *name* from the string *value*.

e.`setAttributeNode(`*newattr*`)`

Attaches the `Attr` node *newattr* to the element, replacing any existing attribute with the same name. Returns the old attribute if a replacement occurs.

e.`setAttributeNodeNS(`*newattr*`)`

Attaches the `Attr` node *newattr* to the element using the `namespaceURI` and `localName` attributes. Replaces and returns any existing attribute with the same names.

e.`setAttributeNS(`*namespaceuri*`, `*qname*`, `*value*`)`

Sets the value of an attribute from a *namespaceuri* and qualified name *qname*. *qname* is the entire name of the attribute and is not the same as *localname* (discussed previously). *value* is a string.

`NodeList()`

`NodeList` objects are used to represent lists of nodes returned by methods such as `getElementsByTagName()`.

A `NodeList` instance, *n*, supports the standard Python list operations such as indexing, slicing, and length. In addition, it supports the following interface:

n.`item(`*i*`)`

Returns item *i* from the list. *i* is an integer.

n.`length`

The length of the list.

`NamedNodeMap()`

`NamedNodeMap` objects are used to represent collections of named values such as the `entities` and `notations` attributes of `DocumentType` objects.

An instance, *n*, supports a minimal set Python dictionary operations, such as looking up values using *n*[*key*]. In addition, the following interface is supported:

`n.item(i)`

Returns item *i* from the node map where *i* is an integer. The name of the item is obtained by reading from the `nodeName` attribute of the returned object.

`n.length`

Number of items in the node map.

`ProcessingInstruction()`

Object used to represent an XML processing instruction such as `'<?xml-stylesheet href="mystyle.css" type="text/css"?>'`.

An instance, *p*, of `ProcessingInstruction` has the following attributes:

`p.target`

The text of the processing instruction up to the first whitespace character (for example, `'xml-stylesheet'`).

`p.data`

The remaining text of the processing instruction (for example, `'href="mystyle.css" type="text/css"'`).

`Text()`

`Text` objects are used to represent text data. Text data is stored in the `data` attribute of a `Text` object.

Parsing Example

The following examples show how to go about using the basic features of the `minidom` module:

```
# Parse a document and print out the entire parse tree
import sys
from xml.dom import minidom
doc = minidom.parse(sys.argv[1])

def print_tree(n, indent=0):
    while n:
        print " "*indent, n
        print_tree(n.firstChild,indent+4)
        n = n.nextSibling

print_tree(doc)

# Get all document elements matching a given tag
items = doc.getElementsByTagName("item")    # Get all <item ...> elements

# Loop over all items extracting an attribute and text data
for i in items:
    quantity = i.getAttribute("num")
    text = ""
    t = i.firstChild:
```

```
# Collect text from immediate children
    while t:
            if t.nodeType == t.TEXT_NODE:
                    text += t.data
        t= t.nextSibling
print quantity, t
```

xml.sax

The xml.sax module provides support for parsing XML documents using the SAX2 API.

make_parser([parser_list])

Creates a new SAX parser object. To use the parser, you must set a content handler using the setContentHandler() method and then call the parse() method. The optional argument parser_list specifies a list of module names (as strings) that implement low-level XML parsers. It is rarely necessary to supply this.

parse(file, handler [, error_handler])

Parses an XML document, file. file is either the name of a file or an open file object. handler is a content handler object. error_handler is a SAX error-handler object. If omitted, errors result in a SAXParseException exception. This function works by creating a new SAX parser (using make_parser(), discussed previously), attaching the content and error handlers, and parsing the file.

parseString(string, handler [, error_handler])

The same as parse(), but parses XML data contained in a string instead.

XMLReader Objects

The parser object p created by the make_parser() function is an instance of the type xml.sax.xmlreader.XMLReader. The following methods are provided:

p.getContentHandler()

Returns the current content handler object.

p.getDTDHandler()

Returns the current DTD handler object.

p.getEntityResolver()

Returns the current entity resolver object.

p.getErrorHandler()

Returns the current error handler object.

p.getFeature(featurename)

Returns the value of feature flag featurename. featurename is a string identifying standard SAX2 feature names—for example, 'http://xml.org/sax/feature/namespaces' or 'http://xml.org/sax/feature/validation'. Feature names can also be specified using one of the feature_* constants defined in the xml.sax.handler module (for example, feature_namespaces, feature_validation, and so on). Raises SAXNotRecognizedException if the feature name is not recognized.

p.getProperty(*propertyname*)

Returns the value of the property *propertyname*. *propertyname* is a string identifying standard SAX2 property names—for example, 'http://xml.org/sax/property/ document-xml-version'. Property names can also be specified using one of the property_* constants defined in the xml.sax.handler module (for example, property_encoding, propery_declaration_handler, and so on). Raises SAXNotRecognizedException if the property name is not recognized. Refer to the online documentation for more details.

p.parse(*source*)

Parses XML data contained in *source*. *source* may be a filename, a file object, or an instance of xml.sax.InputSource. xml.sax.InputSource is described later.

p.setContentHandler(*handler*)

Sets the content handler object used by the parser. *handler* is an instance of xml.sax.handler.ContentHandler.

p.setDTDHandler(*handler*)

Sets the DTD handler object used by the parser. *handler* is an instance of xml.sax.handler.DTDHandler.

p.setEntityResolver(*handler*)

Sets the entity resolver object used by the parser. *handler* is an instance of xml.sax.handler.EntityResolver.

p.setErrorHandler(*handler*)

Sets the error handler object used by the parser. *handler* is an instance of xml.sax.handler.ErrorHandler.

p.setFeature(*featurename*, *value*)

Sets the value of the SAX feature flag *featurename*. *value* is a Boolean value. *featurename* is a string containing a standard SAX2 feature name—for example, 'http://xml.org/sax/feature/namespaces'. *featurename* can also be set to one of the feature_* constants defined in xml.sax.handler.

p.setLocale(*locale*)

Sets the locale for error messages and warnings.

p.setProperty(*propertyname*, *value*)

Sets the value of the SAX property *propertyname*. *value* is the property value. *propertyname* is a string containing a standard SAX2 property name—for example, 'http://xml.org/sax/property/document-xml-version'. *propertyname* can also be set to one of the property_* constants defined in xml.sax.handler.

Handler Objects

SAX parsing relies on different handler objects for content handling, DTD handling, entity resolution, and error handling. These objects are typically defined by the user by inheriting from objects found in the xml.sax.handler module. The following objects are defined in xml.sax.handler:

`ContentHandler()`

Base class used to define new content handlers. To parse an XML document, you inherit from this class and define the following methods as needed.

An instance, `c`, of `ContentHandler` defines the following methods, which are called during the parsing process:

`c.characters(content)`

Called to receive raw character data. `content` is a string containing the characters.

`c.endDocument()`

Called when the end of the document is reached.

`c.endElement(name)`

Called when the end of element `name` is reached. For example, if `'</foo>'` is parsed, this method is called with `name` set to `'foo'`.

`c.endElementNS(name, qname)`

Called when the end of an element involving an XML namespace is reached. `name` is a tuple of strings `(uri, localname)` and `qname` is the fully qualified name. Usually `qname` is None unless the SAX `namespace-prefi XEs` feature has been enabled. For example, if the element is defined as `'<foo:bar xmlns:foo="http://spam.com">'`, then the `name` tuple is `(u'http://spam.com', u'bar')`.

`c.endPrefixMapping(prefix)`

Called when the end of an XML namespace is reached. `prefix` is the name of the namespace.

`c.ignorableWhitespace(whitespace)`

Called when ignorable whitespace is encountered in a document. `whitespace` is a string containing the whitespace.

`c.processingInstruction(target, data)`

Called when an XML processing instruction enclosed in `<? ... ?>` is encountered. `target` is the type of instruction, and `data` is the instruction data. For example, if the instruction is `'<?xml-stylesheet href="mystyle.css" type="text/css"?>`, `target` is set to `'xml-stylesheet'` and `data` is the remainder of the instruction text `'href="mystyle.css" type="text/css"'`.

`c.setDocumentLocator(locator)`

Called by the parser to supply a locator object that can be used for tracking line numbers, columns, and other information. The primary purpose of this method is simply to store the locator someplace so that you can use it later—for instance, if you needed to print an error message. The locator object supplied in `locator` provides four methods—`getColumnNumber()`, `getLineNumber()`, `getPublicId()`, and `getSystemId()`—that can be used to get location information.

`c.skippedEntity(name)`

Called whenever the parser skips an entity. `name` is the name of the entity that was skipped.

`c.startDocument()`

Called at the start of a document.

`c.startElement(name, attrs)`

Called whenever a new XML element is encountered. `name` is the name of the element, and `attrs` is an object containing attribute information. For example, if the XML element is `'<foo bar="whatever" spam="yes">'`, `name` is set to `'foo'` and `attrs` contains information about the bar and spam attributes. The `attrs` object provides a number of methods for obtaining attribute information:

`attrs.getLength()`	Returns the number of attributes
`attrs.getNames()`	Returns a list of attribute names
`attrs.getType(name)`	Gets the type of attribute `name`
`attrs.getValue(name)`	Gets the value of attribute `name`

`c.startElementNS(name, qname, attrs)`

Called when a new XML element is encountered and XML namespaces are being used. `name` is a tuple `(uri, localname)` and qname is a fully qualified element name (normally set to `None` unless the SAX2 namespace-prefixes feature has been enabled). `attrs` is an object containing attribute information. For example, if the XML element is `'<foo:bar xmlns:foo="http://spam.com" blah="whatever">'`, then `name` is `(u'http://spam.com', u'bar')`, qname is `None`, and `attrs` contains information about the attribute blah. The `attrs` object has the same methods as used in when accessing attributes in the aforementioned `startElement()` method. In addition, the following additional methods are added to deal with namespaces:

`attrs.getValueByQName(qname)`	Return value for qualified name.
`attrs.getNameByQName(qname)`	Returns `(namespace, localname)` tuple for a name.
`attrs.getQNameByName(name)`	Returns qualified name for `name` specified as a tuple `(namespace, localname)`.
`attrs.getQNames()`	Returns qualified names of all attributes.

`c.startPrefixMapping(prefix, uri)`

Called at the start of an XML namespace declaration. For example, if an element is defined as `'<foo:bar xmlns:foo="http://spam.com">'`, then `prefix` is set to `'foo'` and `uri` is set to `'http://spam.com'`.

`DTDHandler()`

Base class used to define handlers for processing DTD information. You would inherit from this class and redefine the following methods to use it.

An instance, `d`, of `DTDHandler` has the following methods:

`d.notationDecl(name, publicId, systemId)`

Called to process `'<!NOTATION ...>'` declarations in a DTD. `name` is the name of the notation, `publicId` is the public identifiers, and `systemId` is a system identifier. For example, if the declaration `'<!NOTATION GIF SYSTEM "Compuserve Graphics`

Interchange Format 87a">' is parsed, *name* is 'GIF', *publicId* is None, and *systemId* is 'Compuserve Graphics Interchange Format 87a'.

d.unparsedEntityDecl(name, publicId, systemid, ndata)

Called to process '<!ENTITY ...'> declarations in a DTD. *name* is the name of the entity, *publicId* is the public identifier, *systemId* is the system identifier, and *ndata* is the notation type. For example, the declaration '<!ENTITY FooImage SYSTEM "foo.gif" NDATA GIF>' has *name* set to 'FooImage', *publicId* set to None, *systemId* set to 'foo.gif', and *ndata* set to 'GIF'.

EntityResolver()

A base class used to define handlers for dealing with external entities that appear in an XML document. For example, if a document defines an entity using '<!ENTITY FooImage ...>' and then later refers to it as '&FooImage;', methods of this class are invoked to handle the entity reference.

An instance, *e*, of EntityResolver has the following method:

e.resolveEntity(publicId, systemId)

Called to resolve an external entity with public identifier *publicId* and system identifier *systemId*. For example, if an entity was defined as '<!ENTITY FooImage SYSTEM "foo.gif" NDATA GIF>', the entity reference '&FooImage;' causes this method to be invoked with *publicId* set to None and *systemId* set to 'foo.gif'.

ErrorHandler()

Base class used to define error handlers. You inherit from this class to define your own error handling.

An instance, *err*, of ErrorHandler has the following methods:

err.error(exception)

Called when the parser encounters a recoverable error (for example, an undeclared attribute discovered by a validating parser). *exception* is an exception object of type SAXParseException raised by the parser. If discarded, parsing will continue.

err.fatalError(exception)

Called when the parser encounters a fatal error (for example, a missing closing element or unresolved entity). *exception* is an exception object of type SAXParseException raised by the parser. Normally, parsing should terminate after this method is called. This is accomplished by raising an exception of some kind.

err.warning(exception)

Called when the parser wants to report minor warning information. *exception* is an object of type SAXParseException and parsing continues after this function is invoked.

Exceptions

The following exceptions are defined by the xml.sax module:

SAXException(*msg* [, *exception*])

Encapsulation of an XML error or warning message. *msg* is a string containing a description of the error. *exception* is another exception object that contains more information. This exception is also used as a base class for the other SAX-related exceptions.

SAXParseException(*msg*, *exception*, *locator*)

Exception raised for parsing errors. *msg* is a descriptive message, *exception* is an exception object containing more information about the parsing error, and *locator* is a locator object that can be used to determine where the error occurred.

SAXNotRecognizedException(*msg* [, *exception*])

Exception raised for unrecognized features or properties. *msg* is a descriptive message, and *exception* is an exception object containing more information.

SAXNotSupportedException(*msg* [, *exception*])

Exception raised when an attempt is made to set an unsupported feature or property value. *msg* is a descriptive message, and *exception* is an exception object containing more information.

Example

The following example shows how to set up a SAX-based parser, including the creation of the parsing object and attachment of the handler objects. The example merely prints out element and DTD information for simple XML documents:

```python
import sys
from xml.sax import make_parser
from xml.sax import handler

# A simple content handler
class SimpleHandler(handler.ContentHandler):
    def startElement(self,name,attrs):
        print "Start: ", name
        for aname in attrs.getNames():
            print "    attribute : %s = %s" % (aname, attrs.getValue(aname))
    def endElement(self,name):
        print "End: ", name
    def characters(self,data):
        print "characters: ", data

# A simple DTD handler
class SimpleDTDHandler(handler.DTDHandler):
    def notationDecl(self,name,publicid,systemid):
        print "Notation: ", name, publicid, systemid
    def unparsedEntityDecl(self,name,publicid,systemid,ndata):
        print "UnparsedEntity: ", name, publicid, systemid, ndata

# Make the parser and attach handlers
p = make_parser()
p.setContentHandler(SimpleHandler())
p.setDTDHandler(SimpleDTDHandler())

# Parse file supplied on command line
p.parse(sys.argv[1])
```

xml.sax.saxutils

The `xml.sax.saxutils` module defines some utility functions and objects that may be useful when writing SAX-based XML parsers.

escape(*data* [, *entities*])

Given a string, *data*, this function replaces certain characters with escape sequences. For example, `'<'` gets replaced by `'&lt;'`. *entities* is an optional dictionary that maps characters to the escape sequences. For example, setting *entities* to `{ u'\xf1' : '&ntilde;' }` would replace occurs of ñ with `'&ntilde;'`.

unescape(*data* [, *entities*])

Unescapes special escape sequences that appear in *data*. For instance, `'&lt;'` is replaced by `'<'`. *entities* is an optional dictionary mapping entities to unescaped character values. *entities* is the inverse of the dictionary used with `escape()`—for example, `{ '&ntilde;' : u'\xf1' }`.

quoteattr(*data* [, *entities*])

Escapes the string *data*, but performs additional processing that allows the result value to be used as an XML attribute value. The return value can be printed directly as an attribute value—for example, `print "<element attr=%s>" % quoteattr(somevalue)`. *entities* is a dictionary compatible for use with the `escape()` function.

XMLGenerator([*out* [, *encoding*]])

This is a `ContentHandler` object that merely echoes parsed XML data back to the output stream as an XML document. This re-creates the original XML document. *out* is the output document and defaults to `sys.stdout`. *encoding* is the character encoding to use and defaults to `'iso-8859-1'`.

XMLFilterBase(*base*)

Defines a class that can be used to intercept requests sent between an `XMLReader` object and its various handler functions.

prepare_input_source(*source* [, *base*])

Creates an `InputSource` object that can be used as a data source in the `parse()` method of a SAX parser. *source* can be a filename, a file object, or another `InputSource` object. *base* is an optional base URL.

24

Cryptographic Services

THIS CHAPTER DESCRIBES BUILT-IN MODULES that are useful in implementing applications involving cryptography. The modules are primarily used to compute digital signatures and message authentication codes.

hmac

The hmac module provides support for HMAC (Keyed-Hashing for Message Authentication). HMAC is a mechanism used for message authentication that is built upon cryptographic hashing functions such as MD5 and SHA-1.

new(*key* [, *msg* [, *digest*]])

Creates a new HMAC object. *key* is a string containing the starting key for the hash, *msg* contains initial data to process, and *digest* is a module that should be used for cryptographic hashing. By default, *digest* is md5. Normally, the initial key value is determined at random using a cryptographically strong random number generator.

An HMAC object, *h*, has the following methods:

h.update(*msg*)

Adds the string *msg* to the HMAC object.

h.digest()

Returns the digest of all data processed so far and returns a string that may contain binary data. The length of the string depends on the underlying hashing function. For MD5, it is 16 characters; for SHA-1, it is 20 characters.

h.hexdigest()

Returns the digest as a string of hexadecimal digits.

h.copy()

Makes a copy of the HMAC object.

Example

```
import hmac
# Create a seed value.  This is a string of random bytes, that are computed
# somehow--usually involving the use of a crypographically strong random number
# generator such as the os.urandom() function
seed = compute_seed()
```

```
# Create an HMAC object and use it.
h = hmac.new(seed)
h.update("Hello")
h.update("World")
d = h.digest()          # Get the digest value
```

> **Note**
>
> The hmac module is more than just a wrapper around the low-level MD5 and SHA-1 modules. Data
> is packaged differently and the result of calling digest() yields a different result than calling
> digest() on an MD5 or SHA-1 object with the same data. The HMAC algorithm is described in
> more detail in RFC 2104.

> **See Also:**
>
> md5 (this page), sha (p. 497), RFC 2104

md5

The md5 module implements RSA's MD5 message-digest algorithm. MD5 takes a
sequence of input text and produces a 128-bit hash value. To compute the hash value,
create an md5 object using the new() function, feed data to it using the update()
method, and then call the digest() method to get the hash value.

new([string])

Returns a new md5 object. If *string* is present, update(*string*) is called.
    An md5 object, *m*, has the following methods:

m.update(arg)

Updates the md5 object *m* with the string *arg*.

m.digest()

Returns the digest of all data passed to the object using the update() method and
returns a 16-byte string that may contain nonprintable characters, including null bytes.

m.hexdigest()

Returns the digest as a string of 32 hexadecimal digits.

m.copy()

Returns a copy of the md5 object.

Example

```
import md5
m = md5.new()           # Create a new MD5 object
m.update("Hello")
m.update("World")
d = m.digest()          # Get the digest
```

The following shortcut can also be used:

```
d = md5.new("Hello World").digest()
```

See Also:
sha (this page), Internet RFC 1321

sha

The sha module implements the secure hash algorithm (SHA). SHA takes a sequence of input text and produces a 160-bit hash value. To compute the hash value, create an sha object using the new() function and feed data to it.

new([string])

Returns a new sha object. If string is present, update(*string*) is called.
    An instance, *s*, of an sha object has the following methods:

***s*.update(arg)**

Updates the sha object with the string arg.

***s*.digest()**

Returns the digest of all data passed to the object using the update() method and returns a 20-byte string that may contain nonprintable characters, including null bytes.

***s*.copy()**

Returns a copy of the sha object.

***s*.hexdigest()**

Returns the digest value as a string of hexadecimal digits.

Note
The SHA algorithm is defined by NIST document FIPS PUB 180-1: Secure Hash Standard. It's available online at http://csrc.nist.gov/fips/fip180-1.ps.

See Also:
md5 (p. 496)

## 25

Miscellaneous Modules

THE MODULES LISTED IN THIS SECTION ARE not covered in detail in this book, but have descriptions in the online library reference and elsewhere. These modules have mostly been omitted because they are either extremely low level and of limited use, restricted to very specific platforms, obsolete, or so complicated that coverage would require a book of their own. Although these modules have been omitted from this book, online documentation is available for each module at http://www.python.org/doc/current/lib/module-*modname*.html. An index of all modules is also available at http://www.python.org/doc/current/modindex.html.

Python Services

The following modules provide additional services related to the execution of the Python interpreter. Many of these modules are related to parsing and compilation of Python source code.

Module	Description
codeop	Compiles Python code
compileall	Byte-compiles Python files in a directory
dis	Disassembler
distutils	Distribution of Python modules (see Chapter 27)
fpectl	Floating-point exception control
imp	Provides access to the implementation of the import statement
keyword	Tests whether a string is a Python keyword
linecache	Retrieves lines from files
modulefinder	Finds modules used by a script
parser	Accesses parse trees of Python source code
pickletools	Tools for pickle developers
pkgutil	Package extension utility
pprint	Prettyprinter for objects
pyclbr	Extracts information for class browsers
py_compile	Compiles Python source to bytecode files

Module	Description
repr	Alternate implementation of the `repr()` function
symbol	Constants used to represent internal nodes of parse trees
tabnanny	Detection of ambiguous indentation
test	Regression testing package
token	Terminal nodes of the parse tree
tokenize	Scanner for Python source code
user	User configuration file parsing
zipimport	Import modules from zip archives

String Processing

The following are some older modules, now obsolete, used for string processing.

Module	Description
fpformat	Floating-point number formatting
regex	Regular expression matching (obsolete)
regsub	Regular expression substitution (obsolete)

Operating System Modules

These modules provide additional operating system services. In some cases, the functionality of a module listed here is already incorporated into the functionality of other modules covered in Chapter 19, "Operating System Services."

Module	Description
curses	Curses library interface
dircache	Directory cache
mutex	Mutual exclusion locks
pty	Pseudo terminal handling
pipes	Interface to shell pipelines
posixfile	File locking
nis	Interface to Sun's NIS
readline	Access to GNU readline library
rlcompleter	Completion function for GNU readline
sched	Event scheduler
statcache	Caching version of `stat()` function
syslog	Interface to UNIX syslog daemon

Network

The following modules provide support for lesser-used network protocols.

Module	Description
gopherlib	Gopher protocol
smtpd	SMTP server
telnetlib	Telnet protocol

Internet Data Handling

The following modules provide additional support for Internet data processing. Many of these modules are obsolete, having been replaced by more modern modules described in Chapter 23, "Internet Data Handling and Encoding." Others provide advanced functionality beyond the scope of this book.

Module	Description
formatter	Generic output formatting
htmlentitydefs	Definitions of HTML general entities
htmllib	HTML parsing (see HTMLParser instead)
mailbox	Reading various mailbox formats
mhlib	Access to MH mailboxes
mimetools	Tools for parsing MIME messages
MimeWriter	Generic MIME file writer
mimify	MIME processing of mail messages
multifile	Support for multipart mail messages
netrc	Netrc file processing
sgmllib	Simple SGML parsing
xml.parsers.expat	XML parsing with Expat
xml.dom.pulldom	Building of partial DOM trees
xmllib	Simple XML parsing (obsolete)

Multimedia Services

The following modules provide support for handling various kinds of multimedia files.

Module	Description
audioop	Manipulates raw audio data
imageop	Manipulates raw image data
aifc	Reads and writes AIFF and AIFC files
sunau	Reads and writes Sun AU files
wave	Reads and writes WAV files
chunk	Reads IFF chunked data
colorsys	Conversions between color systems
rgbimg	Reads and writes SGI RGB files
imghdr	Determines the type of an image

Module	Description
sndhdr	Determines the type of a sound file
ossaudiodev	Access to OSS-compatible audio devices

Miscellaneous

Module	Description
Bastion	Restricted access to objects
cmd	Line-oriented command interpreters
ConfigParser	Configuration file parser
calendar	Calendar-generation functions
rexec	Restriction execution
shlex	Simple lexical analysis module
Tkinter	Python interface to Tcl/Tk
whrandom	Random number generation
winsound	Playing sounds on Windows
xreadlines	Efficient iteration over a file

26

Debugging, Profiling, and Testing

T HIS CHAPTER DESCRIBES MODULES RELATED TO debugging, profiling, and testing Python programs.

doctest

The doctest module examines documentation strings for text fragments that look like interactive Python sessions. These fragments are then executed and verified to see if they produce the output shown. Here is a short example:

```
def gcd(x,y):
    """
    Computes the greatest common divisor of x and y.  For example:
    >>> gcd(40,16)
    8
    >>> gcd(24,15)
    3
    >>> gcd(12,85)
    1

    Both arguments must be positive integers.

    >>> gcd(3.5,4.2)
    Traceback (most recent call last):
    ...
    TypeError: Arguments must be integers
    >>> gcd(-4,7)
    Traceback (most recent call last):
    ...
    ValueError: Arguments must be positive integers

    Long integers may also be used. In this case, the returned value is also a
long.

    >>> gcd(23748928388L, 6723884L)
    4L

    """
    if not (isinstance(x,(int,long)) and isinstance(y,(int,long))):
        raise TypeError, "Arguments must be integers"
    if x <= 0 or y <= 0:
        raise ValueError, "Arguments must be positive integers"
```

```
        g = y
        while x > 0:
            g = x
            x = y % x
            y = g
        return g

def _test():
    import doctest
    doctest.testmod()

if __name__ == "__main__":
    _test()
```

The documentation string for gcd() contains many interactive examples. These examples form a series of tests. These tests are executed by the doctest.testmod() function used at the bottom of the example.

To run the tests on this example, you simply run Python on the module itself, as shown here:

```
% python gcd.py
```

If all the tests are working, no output will be produced. Verbose testing output can be obtained by supplying the -v option to the interpreter. This will display information about each test that is attempted, expected output, and the results of the test. For example:

```
% python gcd.py -v
Trying:
    gcd(40,16)
Expecting:
    8
ok
Trying:
    gcd(24,15)
Expecting:
    3
ok
Trying:
    gcd(12,85)
Expecting:
    1
ok
Trying:
    gcd(3.5,4.2)
Expecting:
    Traceback (most recent call last):
    ...
    TypeError: Arguments must be integers
ok
Trying:
    gcd(-4,7)
Expecting:
    Traceback (most recent call last):
    ...
    ValueError: Arguments must be positive integer
ok
Trying:
    gcd(23748928388L, 6723884L)
Expecting:
    4L
ok
```

```
2 items had no tests:
    __main__
    __main__._test
1 items passed all tests:
    6 tests in __main__.gcd
6 tests in 3 items.
6 passed and 0 failed.
Test passed.
```

The following functions are most commonly used in the doctest module:

testfile(*filename* [, **kwargs])

Runs tests on the docstrings in the file *filename*. Returns a tuple (*failure_count*, *test_count*). This function also accepts a large number of optional keyword arguments that control various aspects of testing. However, none of these options are necessary to use this function in the common case. Consult the online documentation for further details.

testmod([*module* [, **kwargs]])

Runs tests on the module *module*. Returns a tuple (*failure_count*, *test_count*). If *module* is omitted, it defaults to the same module as the caller. Like testfile(), this function also accepts a number of optional keyword arguments that control various aspects of testing. Consult the online documentation for further details.

> **Note**
>
> Examples of using the doctest module can often be found in the Python standard library. The library file test/test_doctest.py also contains a variety of examples that may be useful.

hotshot

The hotshot module provides high-performance profiling information. Because the module is written primarily in C, it should be much faster than the profile module.

Profile(*filename* [, *lineevents* [, *linetimings*]])

Creates a Profile object. *filename* is the name of a file to which profile data will be logged. *lineevents* is a Boolean flag that indicates whether to log each line of source code or just function calls. The default value is False. *linetimings* is a Boolean flag that indicates whether or not to record timing information. The default value is True.

An instance, *p*, of Profile has the following methods:

_p_.addinfo(*key*, *value*)

Adds a labeled value to the profile output.

_p_.close()

Closes the profiler.

_p_.fileno()

Returns the file number of the profile log file.

p.run(*cmd*)

Runs a command and logs profile information. *cmd* is a command suitable for execution using the exec statement.

p.runcall(*func*, **args*, ***kwargs*)

Runs a function call and logs profile information. *func* is a callable object. Additional arguments are passed along to the function. The return value is the same as the return value of *func*.

p.runctx(*cmd*, *globals*, *locals*)

Runs a command using exec in the environment defined by the dictionaries in *globals* and *locals*.

p.start()

Starts the profiler.

p.stop()

Stops the profiler.

The data recorded by hotshot can be analyzed using the pstats module, which is also used to analyze data recorded using the profile module. To analyze data, use the following function, which is located in the hotshot.stats module:

load(*filename*)

Reads profile data recorded by the hotshot module and returns a pstats.Stats object.

Example

```
import hotshot, hotshot.stats
p = hotshot.Profile("foo.prof")
p.runcall(foo)
p.close()
s = hotshot.stats.load("foo.prof")
s.print_stats()
```

Note

The hotshot module should not be used with programs that utilize threads.

pdb

The Python debugger is loaded by importing the pdb module. The pdb module provides an interactive source code debugger that allows post-mortem debugging, inspection of stack frames, breakpoints, single-stepping of source lines, and code evaluation.

The debugger is started by loading the pdb module and issuing one of the following functions:

run(*statement* [, *globals* [, *locals*]])

Executes the string *statement* under debugger control. The debugger prompt will appear immediately before any code executes. Typing 'continue' will force it to run.

globals and *locals* define the global and local namespaces, respectively, in which the code runs.

runeval(*expression* [, *globals* [, *locals*]])

Evaluates the *expression* string under debugger control. The debugger prompt will appear before any code executes so you will need to type 'continue' to force it to execute as with run(). On success, the value of the expression is returned.

runcall(*function* [, *argument*, ...])

Calls a function within the debugger. *function* is a callable object. Additional arguments are supplied as the arguments to *function*. The debugger prompt will appear before any code executes. The return value of the function is returned upon completion.

set_trace()

Starts the debugger at the point at which this function is called. This can be used to hard-code a debugger breakpoint into a specific code location.

post_mortem(*traceback*)

Starts post-mortem debugging of a traceback object. traceback is typically obtained using a function such as sys.exc_info() or the variable sys.last_traceback if running interactively.

pm()

Enters post-mortem debugging using the traceback in sys.last_traceback.

When the debugger starts, it will present a prompt such as the following:

```
>>> import pdb
>>> import buggymodule
>>> pdb.run('buggymodule.start()')
> <string>(0)?()
(Pdb)
```

(Pdb) is the debugger prompt at which the following commands are recognized. Note that some commands have a short and a long form. In this case, parentheses are used to indicate both forms. For example, h(elp) means that either h or help is acceptable.

h(elp) [*command*]

Shows the list of available commands. Specifying a command returns help for that command.

w(here)

Prints a stack trace.

d(own)

Moves the current frame one level down in the stack trace.

u(p)

Moves the current frame one level up in the stack trace.

b(reak) [*loc* [, *condition*]]

Sets a breakpoint at location *loc*. *loc* is one of the following:

Setting	**Description**
`n`	A line number in the current file
`filename:n`	A line number in another file
`function`	A function name in the current file
`filename:function`	A function name in another file

If `loc` is omitted, all the current breakpoints are printed. `condition` is an expression that must evaluate to true before the breakpoint is honored. All breakpoints are assigned numbers that are printed as output upon the completion of this command. These numbers are used in a number of other debugger commands that follow.

`tbreak [loc [, condition]]`

Sets a temporary breakpoint that's removed after its first hit.

`cl(ear) [bpnumber [bpnumber ...]]`

Clears a list of breakpoint numbers. If breakpoints are specified, all breaks are cleared.

`disable [bpnumber [bpnumber ...]]`

Disables the set of specified breakpoints. Unlike with `clear`, they can be reenabled later.

`enable [bpnumber [bpnumber ...]]`

Enables a specified set of breakpoints.

`ignore bpnumber [count]`

Ignores a breakpoint for `count` executions.

`condition bpnumber [condition]`

Places a condition on a breakpoint. `condition` is an expression that must evaluate to true before the breakpoint is recognized. Omitting the condition clears any previous condition.

`s(tep)`

Executes a single source line and stops inside called functions.

`n(ext)`

Executes until the next line of the current function. Skips the code contained in function calls.

`r(eturn)`

Runs until the current function returns.

`c(ont(inue))`

Continues execution until the next breakpoint is encountered.

`j(ump) lineno`

Sets the next line to execute. This can only be used to move between statements in the same execution frame. Moreover, you can't jump into certain statements such as statements in the middle of a loop.

l(ist) [*first* [, *last*]]

Lists source code. Without arguments, this command lists 11 lines around the current line (five lines before and five lines after). With one argument, it lists 11 lines around that line. With two arguments, it lists lines in a given range. If *last* is less than *first*, it's interpreted as a count.

a(rgs)

Prints the argument list of the current function.

p *expression*

Evaluates the expression in the current context and prints its value.

pp *expression*

The same as the p command, but the result is formatted using the pretty-printing module (pprint).

alias [*name* [*command*]]

Creates an alias called *name* that executes *command*. Within the *command* string, the substrings '%1', '%2', and so forth are replaced by parameters when the alias is typed. '%*' is replaced by all parameters. If no command is given, the current alias list is shown. Aliases can be nested and can contain anything that can be legally typed at the Pdb prompt. For example:

```
#Print instance variables (usage "pi classInst")
alias pi for k in %1.__dict__.keys(): print "%1.",k,"=",%1.__dict__[k]
#Print instance variables in self
alias ps pi self
```

unalias *name*

Deletes the specified alias.

[!]*statement*

Executes the (one-line) *statement* in the context of the current stack frame. The exclamation point may be omitted, but it must be used to avoid ambiguity if the first word of the statement resembles a debugger command. To set a global variable, you can prefix the assignment command with a "global" command on the same line:

```
(Pdb) global list_options; list_options = ['-1']
(Pdb)
```

q(uit)

Quits from the debugger.

Debugging from the Command Line

An alternative method for running the debugger is to invoke it on the command line. Here's an example:

```
% python -m pdb someprogram.py
```

In this case, the debugger is launched automatically if the supplied program terminates abnormally with an exception. Moreover, once you quit the debugger, the program will be restarted. When restarting, debugging parameters such as breakpoints are preserved.

Notes

- Entering a blank line repeats the last command entered.

- Commands that the debugger doesn't recognize are assumed to be Python statements and are executed in the context of the program being debugged.

- If a .pdbrc file exists in the user's home directory or in the current directory, it's read in and executed as if it had been typed at the debugger prompt. This can be useful for specifying debugging commands that you want to execute each time the debugger is started (as opposed to having to interactively type the commands each time).

profile

The `profile` module is used to collect profiling information.

`run(command [, filename])`

Executes the contents of `command` using the exec statement under the profiler. `filename` is the name of a file in which raw profiling data is saved. If it's omitted, a report such as the following is printed to standard output:

```
126 function calls (6 primitive calls) in 5.130 CPU seconds
Ordered by: standard name
ncalls  tottime  percall  cumtime   percall filename:lineno(function)
    1    0.030    0.030    5.070     5.070 <string>:1(?)
  121/1   5.020    0.041    5.020     5.020 book.py:11(process)
    1    0.020    0.020    5.040     5.040 book.py:5(?)
    2    0.000    0.000    0.000     0.000 exceptions.py:101(__init__)
    1    0.060    0.060    5.130     5.130 profile:0(execfile('book.py'))
    0    0.000             0.000           profile:0(profiler)
```

Different parts of the report generated by `run()` are interpreted as follows:

Section	Description
primitive calls	Number of nonrecursive function calls
ncalls	Total number of calls (including self-recursion)
tottime	Time spent in this function (not counting subfunctions)
percall	tottime/ncalls
cumtime	Total time spent in the function
percall	cumtime/(primitive calls)
filename:lineno(function)	Location and name of each function

When there are two numbers in the first column (for example, "121/1"), the latter is the number of primitive calls, and the former is the actual number of calls.

Profiling from the Command Line

An entire script can be profiled by launching the profiler from the command line. For example:

```
% python -m profile someprogram.py
```

Notes

- Analysis of saved profile data is performed by the pstats module.
- To obtain accurate information, it may be necessary to calibrate the profiler. Refer to http://www.python.org/doc/lib/profile.html for details.

pstats

The pstats module defines a class, Stats, that's used to analyze the data saved by the profile module.

Stats(filename)

Reads profiling data from filename—a file previously created by the profile.run() function and returns a statistics object that can be used to print reports.

A statistics object, s, has the following methods:

s.strip_dirs()

Removes leading path information from filenames.

s.add(filename [, ...])

Accumulates additional profiling information into the current profile. filename is the name of a file containing data previously saved by profile.run().

s.dump_stats(filename)

Writes statistics information to the file filename.

s.sort_stats(key [, ...])

Sorts statistics according to the criteria specified by key. Additional keys may be specified to further refine the sort order. Each key can be one of the following values:

Key Name	Description
'calls'	Call count
'cumulative'	Cumulative time
'file'	Filename
'module'	Filename
'pcalls'	Primitive call count
'line'	Line number
'name'	Function name
'nfl'	Name/file/line
'stdname'	Standard name
'time'	Internal time

Time values and call counts are sorted in descending order. Line numbers and filenames are sorted in ascending order.

`s.print_stats(restriction [, ...])`

Prints a profile report to standard output. The order is the same as produced by the last `sort_stats()` method. The arguments are used to eliminate entries in the report. Each restriction can be an integer to select a maximum line count, a decimal to select a percentage of the lines, or a regular expression to pattern-match against the names that are printed.

`s.print_callers(restrictions [, ...])`

Prints a list of all functions that called each function in the profile database. The ordering is identical to `print_stats()`. `restrictions` has the same meaning as for `print_stats()`.

`s.print_callees(restrictions [, ...])`

Prints a list of functions that were called by each function. `restrictions` has the same meaning as for `print_stats()`.

timeit

The `timeit` module is used to time simple Python code.

`Timer([statement [, setup [, timer]]])`

Creates a `Timer` object. `statement` is a string containing a Python statement to be timed. `setup` is an optional string containing a Python statement that is executed prior to the timing of `statement`. `timer` is a platform-specific timing function such as `time.time()` or `time.clock()` in the `time` module. Normally, this does not need to be supplied.

An instance, `t`, of `Timer` has the following methods:

`t.print_exc([file])`

Prints execution information for exceptions that occur in timed code. To use this, enclose the `timeit()` method in a `try` block and use `print_exc` in an except clause.

`t.repeat([repeat [, number]])`

Executes the `timeit()` method multiple times and returns timing information as a list. `repeat` specifies the repeat count. `number` is passed to the `timeit()` method.

`t.timeit([number])`

Times the execution of the statement supplied to the `Timer` object, `t`. `number` is the number of times to execute the statement and defaults to `1000000` (one million). The `setup` statement passed to `Timer` is executed once, prior to timing. The return value is a floating-point number.

Example

```
>>> import timeit
>>> t = timeit.Timer("math.sqrt(10.0)","import math")
>>> print "%s seconds" % t.timeit(1000000)
1.60450792313 seconds
>>> t = timeit.Timer("sqrt(10.0)","from math import sqrt")
```

```
>>> print "%s seconds" % t.timeit(1000000)
0.980136156082 seconds
```

Command-line Interface

The `timeit` module can also be used from the command line:

```
% python -m timeit.py [-n N] [-r N] [-s setup] [-t] [-c] [-v] [-h] [statement ...]
```

The options are as follows:

Option	Description
-n *N*	Number of times to execute the statement.
-r N	Number of times to repeat the timer.
-s setup	Setup statement to be performed.
-t	Use time.time() as the timer function.
-c	Use time.clock() as the timer function.
-v	Verbose output.
-h	Print help.

Here is an example that illustrates the command-line interface:

```
% python -m timeit -n 1000000 -s "import math" "math.sqrt(10.0"
1000000 loops, best of 3: 1.33 usec per loop
%
```

Notes

- On Unix, the default timer function is `time.time()`. On Windows, it is `time.clock()`.
- The default timing measurements are based on wall-clock time and will be affected by other running processes.
- In the command-line interface, multiline statements can be given by simply specifying multiple statements as arguments—they will be concatenated together on separate lines. Similarly, multiline setup statements can be specified using the `-s` option multiple times in a row.

unittest

The `unittest` module is used to perform unit testing. With unit testing, a developer writes a collection of isolated test cases for each element that makes up a program (for example, individual functions, methods, classes, and modules). These tests are then run to verify correct behavior. As programs grow in size, unit tests for various components can be combined to create large testing frameworks and testing tools. This can greatly simplify the task of verifying correct behavior as well isolating and fixing problems when they do occur. Use of the module is best illustrated by an example. For instance, suppose you had the following Python module:

```
# module: gcd.py
def gcd(x,y):
    if not (isinstance(x,(int,long)) and isinstance(y,(int,long))):
        raise TypeError, "Arguments must be integers"
    if x <= 0 or y <= 0:
        raise ValueError, "Arguments must be positive integer"
    g = y
    while x > 0:
        g = x
        x = y % x
        y = g
    return g
```

Now, suppose you wanted to write unit tests for testing various aspects of the gcd()
function. To do this, you might write a separate module, testgcd, as follows:

```
# testgcd.py
import gcd
import unittest

class TestGCDFunction(unittest.TestCase):
    def setUp(self):
        # Perform set up actions (if any)
        pass
    def tearDown(self):
        # Perform clean-up actions (if any)
        pass
    def testsimple(self):
        # Test with simple integer arguments
        g = gcd.gcd(40,16)
        self.assertEqual(g,8)
    def testfloat(self):
        # Test with floating point arguments. Should get an exception
        self.assertRaises(TypeError, gcd.gcd, 3.5, 4.2)
    def testlong(self):
        # Test with long integers
        g = gcd.gcd(23748928388L, 6723884L)
        self.assertEqual(g,4L)
        self.assert_(type(g) is long)

if __name__ == '__main__':
    unittest.main()
```

To run tests, simply run Python on the file testgcd.py. For example:

```
% python testgcd.py
...
------------------------------
Ran 3 tests in 0.014s

OK
```

Basic use of unittest involves defining a class that inherits from unittest.TestCase.
Within this class, individual tests are defined by methods starting with the name
'test'—for example, 'testsimple', 'testfloat', and so on. (It is important to
emphasize that the names are entirely up to you as long as they start with 'test'.)
Within each test, various assertions are used to check for different conditions.

An instance, t, of unittest.TestCase has the following methods that are used
when writing tests and for controlling the testing process:

`t.setUp()`

Called to perform set-up steps prior to running any of the testing methods.

`t.tearDown()`

Called to perform clean-up actions after running the tests.

`t.assert_(expr [, msg])`
`t.failUnless(expr [, msg])`

Signals a test failure if `expr` evaluates as `False`. `msg` is a message giving an explanation for the failure (if any).

`t.assertEqual(x, y [,msg])`
`t.failUnlessEqual(x, y [, msg])`

Signal a test failure if `x` and `y` are not equal to each other. `msg` is a message explaining the failure (if any).

`t.assertNotEqual(x, y [, msg])`
`t.failIfEqual(x, y, [, msg])`

Signal a test failure if `x` and `y` are equal to each other. `msg` is a message explaining the failure (if any).

`t.assertAlmostEqual(x, y [, places [, msg]])`
`t.failUnlessAlmostEqual(x, y, [, places [, msg]])`

Signal a test failure if numbers `x` and `y` are not within `places` decimal places of each other. This is checked by computing the difference of `x` *and* `y` and rounding the result to the given number of places. If the result is zero, `x` and `y` are almost equal. `msg` is a message explaining the failure (if any).

`t.assertNotAlmostEqual(x, y, [, places [, msg]])`
`t.failIfAlmostEqual(x, y [, places [, msg]])`

Signal a test failure if `x` and `y` are not at least `places` decimal places apart. `msg` is a message explaining the failure (if any).

`t.assertRaises(exc, callable, ...)`
`t.failUnlessRaises(exc, callable, ...)`

Signal a test failure if the callable object `callable` does not raise the exception `exc`. Remaining arguments are passed as arguments to `callable`. Multiple exceptions can be checked by using a tuple of exceptions as `exc`.

`t.failIf(expr [, msg])`

Signals a test failure if `expr` evaluates as `True`. `msg` is a message explaining the failure (if any).

`t.fail([msg])`

Signals a test failure. `msg` is a message explaining the failure (if any).

`t.failureException`

This attribute is set to the last exception caught in a test. This may be useful if you not only want to check that an exception was raised, but that the exception raises an appropriate value.

Note

- The unittest module contains a large number of advanced customization options for grouping tests, creating test suites, and controlling the way in which tests are run. These features are not needed to effectively use the module. However, readers should consult the online documentation for more advanced unit-testing examples.
- The test directory of the Python standard library contains a large number of examples of the unittest module.

Extending and Embedding

27

Extending and Embedding Python

THIS CHAPTER COVERS THE C API USED TO BUILD extension modules and embed the Python interpreter into other applications. It's not intended to be a tutorial, so readers may want to consult the "Embedding and Extending the Python Interpreter" document available at http://www.python.org/doc/ext, as well as the "Python/C API Reference Manual" available at http://www.python.org/doc/api.

The primary focus of this chapter is to cover the most common cases. Advanced extension-building techniques such as defining entirely new Python types is not covered. This omission is intentional; most advanced extension-building problems are better handled by extension-building tools such as Boost Python and SWIG. References to these and other tools can be found at the end of this chapter.

Extension Module Example

Extension modules are used to extend the Python interpreter with functions in C. For example, suppose you had some C code in a file spam.c that you wanted to access from Python as a module named spam. To do this, you first need to know something about the original C code. The following listing shows some sample C functions that we are going to access from Python:

```
/* file: spam.c */
/* Compute the greatest common divisor of positive
   integers x and y */
int gcd(int x, int y) {
    int g;
    g = y;
    while (x > 0) {
        g = x;
        x = y % x;
        y = g;
    }
    return g;
}
/* Print some data */
void print_data(char *name, char *email, char *phone) {
    printf("Name     : %s\n", name);
    printf("Email    : %s\n", email);
    printf("Phone    : %s\n", phone);
}
```

To access these functions as a Python extension module, you must write some additional C code, such as that in Listing 27.1. Typically this code is put into a separate file, such as spamwrapper.c.

Listing 27.1 **Accessing Functions from an Extension Module**

```
/* file: spamwrapper.c */
/* Defines a "spam" Python extension module */

/* Include the Python C API */
#include "Python.h"

/* External declarations to functions in spam.c */
extern int gcd(int,int);
extern void print_data(char *, char *, char *);

/* Wrapper for the gcd() function */
PyObject *spam_gcd(PyObject *self, PyObject *args) {
    int x, y, g;
    /* Get Python arguments */
    if (!PyArg_ParseTuple(args,"ii",&x,&y)) {
        return NULL;
    }
    /* Call the C function */
    g = gcd(x,y);
    return Py_BuildValue("i",g);
}

/* Wrapper for the print_data() function */
PyObject *
spam_print_data(PyObject *self, PyObject *args, PyObject *kwargs)
{
    char *name = "None";
    char *email = "None";
    char *phone = "None";
    static char *argnames[] = {"name","email","phone",null};

    /* Get Python arguments */
    if (!PyArg_ParseTupleAndKeywords(args,kwargs,"|sss",argnames,
        &name,&email,&phone)) {
        return NULL;
    }
    /* Call the C function */
    print_data(name,email,phone);
    return Py_BuildValue("");        /* Return None */
}
/* Method table mapping names to wrappers */
static PyMethodDef spammethods[] = {
    {"gcd", spam_gcd, METH_VARARGS},
    {"print_data", spam_print_data, METH_VARARGS | METH_KEYWORDS },
    {NULL, NULL}
};
/* Module initialization function */
void initspam() {
    Py_InitModule("spam", spammethods);
}
```

Extension modules always need to include "Python.h". For each C function to be accessed, a wrapper function is written. These wrapper functions accept either two arguments (self and args, both of type PyObject *) or three arguments (self, args, and kwargs, all of type PyObject *). The self parameter is used when the wrapper function is implementing a built-in method to be applied to an instance of some object. In this case, the instance is placed in the `self` parameter. Otherwise, `self` is set to `NULL`. `args` is a tuple containing the function arguments passed by the interpreter. `kwargs` is a dictionary containing keyword arguments.

Arguments are converted from Python to C using the `PyArg_ParseTuple()` or `PyArg_ParseTupleAndKeywords()` function. Similarly, the `Py_BuildValue()` function is used to construct an acceptable return value. These functions are described in later sections.

Functions signal an error by returning `NULL`. If a function has no return value (that is, `void`), the `None` object must be returned. For example:

```
PyObject *wrap_foo(PyObject *self, PyObject *args) {
    ...
    /* Return None */
    return Py_BuildValue("");
}
```

None can also be returned as follows:

```
PyObject *wrap_foo(PyObject *self, PyObject *args) {
    ...
    /* Return None */
    Py_INCREF(Py_None);
    return Py_None;
}
```

This latter technique utilizes the macro `Py_INCREF` for manipulating reference counts. Because this interacts with Python's memory manager, some care is in order. Refer to the section "Reference Counting" for further details.

The method table `spammethods` in Listing 27.1 is used to associate Python names with the C wrapper functions. These are the names used to call the function from the interpreter. The `METH_VARARGS` flag indicates the calling conventions for a wrapper. In this case, only positional arguments in the form of a tuple are accepted. It can also be set to `METH_VARARGS | METH_KEYWORDS` to indicate a wrapper function accepting keyword arguments.

The module initialization function `initspam` is used to initialize the contents of the module. In this case, the `Py_InitModule("spam", spammethods)` function creates a module, `spam`, and populates it with built-in function objects corresponding to the functions listed in the method table.

Compilation of Extensions

Extension modules are usually compiled into shared libraries or DLLs that can be dynamically loaded by the interpreter. The low-level details of this process vary on every machine, but the `distutils` module in the Python library can be used to simplify the process. To create an extension module using `distutils`, follow these steps:

1. Create a file called `setup.py` that starts with the following code:

   ```
   # setup.py
   from distutils.core import setup, Extension
   ```

2. Next, add some source information about your extension, as follows:

   ```
   setup(name="spam", version="1.0",
         ext_modules=[Extension("spam", ["spam.c", "spamwrapper.c"])])
   ```

3. Now, to build your extension, type the following:

```
python setup.py build
```

At this point, a shared library such as `spammodule.so` (or some variant of this name, such as `spammodule.sl` or `spammodule.dll`) will be created in a special "build" directory. If you want to install the extension, you can type **python setup.py install**. This will copy the shared library to the `site-packages` directory (for example, `/usr/local/lib/python2.4/site-packages`).

If you need to supply additional build information, such as include directories, libraries, and preprocessor macros, they can also be included in `setup.py`, as follows:

```
setup(name="spam", version="1.0",
   ext_modules=[
     Extension(
       "spam",
       ["spam.c", "spamwrapper.c"],
       include_dirs = ["/usr/include/X11","/opt/include"],
       define_macros = [('DEBUG',1'),
                          ('MONDO_FLAG',1)],
       undef_macros = ['HAVE_FOO','HAVE_NOT'],
       library_dirs= ["/usr/lib/X11", "/opt/lib"],
       libraries = [ "X11", "Xt", "blah" ]
     )
   ]
)
```

At this point, it is worth noting that the `distutils` module can more generally be used to create Python packages suitable for distribution and installation by other users. For instance, it allows packages to be distributed as a mix of scripts and compiled extensions. It also knows how to create RPM spec files and self-extracting zip files on Windows. Further details about `distutils` are available at http://www.python.org/doc/current/dist/dist.html.

In some situations, you may want to build an extension module manually. This almost always requires advanced knowledge of various compiler and linker options. The following is an example on Linux:

```
linux % gcc -c -fpic -I/usr/local/include/python2.4 spam.c spamwrapper.c
linux % gcc -shared spam.o spamwrapper.o -o spammodule.so
```

When you're building a module, it's important to note that the name of the shared library must match the name of the module used in the wrapper code. For example, if the module is named spam, the initialization function must be named `initspam` and the shared library must be called `spammodule.so` (possibly with a different file extension, depending on your machine).

Once compiled, an extension module is used like any other module, by simply using the `import` statement:

```
>>> import spam
>>> spam.gcd(63,56)
7
>>> spam.gcd(71,89)
1
>>> spam.print_data(name="Dave",phone="555-1212")
Name   : Dave
Email  : None
Phone  : 555-1212
>>>
```

When searching for an extension module, Python uses the same search path as it does for .py files. Thus, for Python to properly find an extension module, it should be located in the current working directory or in one of the directories in sys.path.

Converting Data from Python to C

The following C functions are used to convert arguments passed from Python to C. Their prototypes are defined by including the Python.h header file.

```
int PyArg_ParseTuple(PyObject *args, char *format, ...);
```

Parses a tuple of objects in *args* into a series of C variables. *format* is a format string containing zero or more of the specifier strings from Table 27.1, which describes the expected contents of *args*. All the remaining arguments contain the addresses of C variables into which the results will be placed. The order and types of these arguments must match the specifiers used in *format* and use the C data types listed in Table 27.1. Zero is returned if the arguments could not be parsed.

```
int PyArg_ParseTupleAndKeywords(PyObject *args, PyObject *kwdict,
                                char *format, char **kwlist, ...);
```

Parses both a tuple of arguments and a dictionary containing keyword arguments contained in *kwdict*. *format* has the same meaning as for PyArg_ParseTuple(). The only difference is that *kwlist* is a null-terminated list of strings containing the names of all the arguments. Returns 1 on success, 0 on error.

Note that in Table 27.1, results of a conversion (for example, in char *r or char **r) are always placed in the parameter labeled *r*. When applicable, a length is stored in *len*.

Table 27.1 **Base Format Specifiers and Associated C Data Types for PyArg_Parse***

Format	Python Type	C Type
"s"	String or Unicode	char **r
"s#"	String or Unicode	char **r, int *len
"z"	String, Unicode, or None	char **r
"z#"	String, Unicode, or None	char **r, int *len
"u"	Unicode	Py_UNICODE **r
"u#"	Unicode	Py_UNICODE **r, int *len
"es"	String or Unicode	const char *enc, char **r
"es#"	String or Unicode	const char *enc, char **r, int *len
"et"	String or Unicode	const char *enc, char **r, int *len
"et#"	String or Unicode	const char *enc, char **r, int *len
"b"	Integer	char *r
"B"	Integer	unsigned char *r
"h"	Integer	short *r
"H"	Integer	unsigned short *r
"i"	Integer	int *r

Table 27.1 **Continued**

Format	Python Type	C Type
`"I"`	Integer	`unsigned int *r`
`"l"`	Integer	`long int *r`
`"k"`	Integer	`unsigned long *r`
`"L"`	Integer	`long long *r`
`"K"`	Integer	`unsigned long long *r`
`"c"`	String of length 1	`char *r`
`"f"`	Float	`float *r`
`"d"`	Float	`double *r`
`"D"`	Complex	`Py_complex *r`
`"O"`	Any	`PyObject **r`
`"O!"`	Any	`PyTypeObject *type, PyObject **r`
`"O&"`	Any	`int (*converter)(PyObject *, void *), void *r`
`"S"`	String	`PyObject **r`
`"U"`	Unicode	`PyObject **r`
`"t#"`	Read-only buffer	`char **r, int *len`
`"w"`	Read-write buffer	`char **r`
`"w#"`	Read-write buffer	`char **r, int *len`

When integer values are converted, an `OverflowError` exception is raised if the Python integer is too large to fit into the requested C data type. However, the `"k"` and `"K"` conversions are special cases that convert integers without overflow checking. Long integers may also be used anyplace an integer is expected, provided that they're small enough to fit.

When strings are converted with the `"s"`, `"s#"`, `"z"`, and `"z#"` specifiers, both standard and Unicode strings may be used. The `"z"` specifier also allows `None` to be passed, in which case a null pointer is returned. In both cases, it's unnecessary to allocate space for the returned string—a pointer to the raw string data stored in the Python interpreter is returned. When Unicode strings are passed, they're first converted to an 8-bit string using the default Unicode encoding. The `"u"` and `"u#"` specifiers require a Unicode string and return a pointer to raw Unicode string data, where each character is of type `Py_UNICODE` (which is currently the same as the C `wchar_t` type). The `"s#"`, `"z#"`, and `"u#"` specifiers return the string length in addition to the string data.

The `"es"`, `"es#"`, `"et"`, and `"et#"` specifiers are used to read a string or Unicode string that has been encoded according to a specific encoding rule. For example:

```
char *buffer;
PyArg_ParseTuple(args,"es","utf-8",&buffer);
```

In this case, `PyArg_ParseTuple()` first reads an encoding name and then returns a pointer to a buffer in which an encoded version of the string has been placed. This buffer contains dynamically allocated memory and must be explicitly deallocated using `PyMem_Free()` after the caller has finished using the encoded contents. The `"es#"` specifier optionally accepts a buffer length. In this case, a user can pass the address and length of a preallocated buffer in which encoded string data will be placed. The `len` parameter is always set to the actual length of the encoded data upon return. The `"et"` conversions differ from the `"es"` conversions in that if an 8-bit string is given, it is passed through without any modification.

The `"t#"`, `"w"`, and `"w#"` specifiers are similar to the string-conversion specifiers, but return a pointer to byte-oriented data stored in a Python object implementing the buffer interface. String and Unicode objects provide this interface, as do selected types in the standard library, such as arrays created with the `array` module and `mmap` objects created by the `mmap` module.

The `"O"`, `"S"`, and `"U"` specifiers return raw Python objects of type `PyObject *`. `"S"` and `"U"` restrict this object to be a string or Unicode string, respectively.

The `"O!"` conversion requires two C arguments: a pointer to a Python type object and a pointer to a `PyObject *` into which a pointer to the object is placed. A `TypeError` is raised if the type of the object doesn't match the type object. For example:

```
/* Parse a List Argument */
PyObject *listobj1;
PyArg_ParseTuple(args,"O!", &PyList_Type, &listobj1);
```

The `"O&"` conversion takes two arguments (`converter`, `addr`) and uses a function to convert a `PyObject *` to a C data type. `converter` is a pointer to a function with the prototype int `converter(PyObject *obj, void *addr)`, where `obj` is the passed Python object and `addr` is the address supplied as the second argument. `converter()` should return 1 on success, 0 on failure. On error, the converter should also raise an exception. For example:

```
struct Point {
    int x;
    int y;
};

int convert_point(PyObject *obj, void *addr) {
    Point *p = (Point *) addr;
    return PyArg_ParseTuple(obj,"ii", &p->x, &p->y);
}
...
PyObject *wrapper(PyObject *self, PyObject *args) {
    Point p;
    ...
    /* Get a point */
    if (!PyArg_ParseTuple(args,"O&",convert_point, &p))
        return NULL;
    ...
}
```

Table 27.2 lists format modifers that can also be used in format strings.

Table 27.2 **Format String Modifiers**

Format String	Description
`"(items)"`	A tuple of objects.
`"|"`	Start of optional arguments.
`":"`	End of arguments. The remaining text is the function name.
`";"`	End of arguments. The remaining text is the error message.

The modifier " | " specifies that all remaining arguments are optional. This can appear only once in a format specifier and cannot be nested. The modifier " : " indicates the end of the arguments. Any text that follows is used as the function name in any error messages. The modifier " ; " signals the end of the arguments. Any following text is used as the error message. Note that only one of : and ; should be used. Here are some examples:

```
int       ival, ival2, len;
double    dval;
char      *sval;
PyObject *o1, *o2;

/* Parse an integer, double, and a string */
PyArg_ParseTuple(args,"ids", &ival, &dval, &sval);

/* Parse a string and length */
PyArg_ParseTuple(args,"s#", &sval, &len);

/* Parse optional arguments */
PyArg_ParseTuple(args,"id|s", &ival, &dval, &sval);

/* Parse with an error message */
PyArg_ParseTuple(args,"ii; gcd requires 2 integers", &ival, &ival2);

/* Parse two tuples */
PyArg_ParseTuple(args,"(ii)(ds)", &ival, &ival2, &dval, &sval);

/* Parse two raw Python objects */
PyArg_ParseTuple(args,"OO", &o1, &o2);
```

The following functions are also available for receiving and processing Python objects. However, they are not used as often as `PyArg_ParseTuple()`.

int PyArg_VaParse(PyObject *args, char *format, va_list vargs);

The same as `PyArg_ParseTuple()`, but accepts a `va_list` structure instead of variable-length arguments.

int PyArg_VaParseTupleAndKeywords(PyObject *args, PyObject *kw, char *format, char **kwlist, va_list vargs)

The same as `PyArg_ParseTupleAndKeywords()`, but accepts a `va_list` structure instead of variable-length arguments.

int PyArg_UnpackTuple(Pyobject *args, char *name, int min, int max, ...);

Unpacks a tuple of arguments, *args*, without any interpretation of the arguments. The arguments are simply placed into variables of type `PyObject *`, which are supplied as extra arguments. *name* is the name of the function to use in error messages. *min* is the minimum number of arguments that must be unpacked. *max* is the maximum number of arguments that can be unpacked. This function is similar to using `PyArg_ParseTuple()` with a format string containing the "O" conversion for all parameters.

Converting Data from C to Python

The following C function is used to convert the values contained in C variables to a Python object:

`PyObject *Py_BuildValue(char *format, ...)`

This constructs a Python object from a series of C variables. `format` is a string describing the desired conversion. The remaining arguments are the values of C variables to be converted.

The `format` specifier is similar to that used with the `PyArg_ParseTuple*` functions, as shown in Table 27.3.

Table 27.3   **Format Specifiers for** `Py_BuildValue()`

Format	Python Type	C Type	Description
`"s"`	String	`char *`	Null-terminated string. If the C string pointer is NULL, None is returned.
`"s#"`	String	`char *, int`	String and length. May contain null bytes. If the C string pointer is NULL, None is returned.
`"z"`	String or None	`char *`	Same as `"s"`.
`"z#"`	String or None	`char *, int`	Same as `"s#"`.
`"u"`	Unicode	`Py_UNICODE *`	Null-terminated Unicode string. If the string pointer is NULL, None is returned.
`"u#"`	Unicode	`Py_UNICODE *`	Unicode string and length.
`"b"`	Integer	`char`	8-bit integer.
`"h"`	Integer	`short`	Short 16-bit integer.
`"i"`	Integer	`int`	Integer.
`"l"`	Integer	`long`	Long integer.
`"c"`	String	`char`	Single character. Creates a Python string of length 1.
`"f"`	Float	`float`	Single-precision floating point.
`"d"`	Float	`double`	Double-precision floating point.
`"O"`	Any	`PyObject *`	Any Python object. The object is unchanged except for its reference count, which is incremented by 1. If a NULL pointer is given, a NULL pointer is returned.
`"O&"`	Any	`converter, any`	C data processed through a converter function.
`"S"`	String	`PyObject *`	Same as `"O"`.
`"U"`	Unicode	`PyObject *`	Same as `"O"`.
`"N"`	Any	`PyObject *`	Same as `"O"` except that the reference count is not incremented.

Table 27.3 **Continued**

Format	Python Type	C Type	Description
`"(items)"`	Tuple	*vars*	Creates a tuple of items. *items* is a string of format specifiers from this table. *vars* is a list of C variables corresponding to the items in *items*.
`"[items]"`	List	*vars*	Creates a list of items. *items* is a string of format specifiers. *vars* is a list of C variables corresponding to the items in *items*.
`"{items}"`	Dictionary	*vars*	Creates a dictionary of items.

Some examples follow:

```
Py_BuildValue("")                        None
Py_BuildValue("i",37)                    37
Py_BuildValue("ids",37,3.4,"hello")      (37, 3.5, "hello")
Py_BuildValue("s#","hello",4)            "hell"
Py_BuildValue("()")                      ()
Py_BuildValue("(i)",37)                  (37,)
Py_BuildValue("[ii]",1,2)                [1,2]
Py_BuildValue("[i,i]",1,2)               [1,2]
Py_BuildValue("{s:i,s:i}","x",1,"y",2)   {'x':1, 'y':2}
```

Error Handling

Errors are indicated by returning NULL to the interpreter. Prior to returning NULL, an exception should be set or cleared using one of the following functions:

void PyErr_Clear()

Clears any previously raised exceptions.

PyObject *PyErr_Occurred()

Checks to see whether an error has been generated. If so, returns the current exception object. Otherwise, it returns NULL.

int PyErr_ExceptionMatches(Pyobject *exc)

Returns 1 if the current exception matches the exception *exc*. Otherwise, it returns 0. This function applies the same exception-matching rules as in Python code. Therefore, *exc* could be a superclass of the current exception. It can also be a tuple of exception objects.

int PyErr_GivenExceptionMatches(PyObject *given, PyObject *exc)

Returns 1 if the exception in *given* matches the exception *exc*. Otherwise, it returns 0.

`void PyErr_NoMemory()`

Raises a `MemoryError` exception.

`void PyErr_SetFromErrno(PyObject *exc)`

Raises an exception. *exc* is an exception object. The value of the exception is taken from the `errno` variable in the C library.

`void PyErr_SetFromErrnoWithFilename(PyObject *exc, char *filename)`

Like `PyErr_SetFromErrno()`, but includes the filename in the exception value as well.

`void PyErr_SetObject(PyObject *exc, PyObject *val)`

Raises an exception. *exc* is an exception object, and *val* is an object containing the value of the exception.

`void PyErr_SetString(PyObject *exc, char *msg)`

Raises an exception. *exc* is an exception object, and *msg* is a message describing what went wrong.

The *exc* argument in these functions can be set to one of the following:

C Name	Python Exception
PyExc_ArithmeticError	ArithmeticError
PyExc_AssertionError	AssertionError
PyExc_AttributeError	AttributeError
PyExc_EnvironmentError	EnvironmentError
PyExc_EOFError	EOFError
PyExc_Exception	Exception
PyExc_FloatingPointError	FloatingPointError
PyExc_ImportError	ImportError
PyExc_IndexError	IndexError
PyExc_IOError	IOError
PyExc_KeyError	KeyError
PyExc_KeyboardInterrupt	KeyboardInterrupt
PyExc_LookupError	LookupError
PyExc_MemoryError	MemoryError
PyExc_NameError	NameError
PyExc_NotImplementedError	NotImplementedError
PyExc_OSError	OSError
PyExc_OverflowError	OverflowError
PyExc_ReferenceError	ReferenceError
PyExc_RuntimeError	RuntimeError
PyExc_StandardError	StandardError
PyExc_StopIteration	StopIteration
PyExc_SyntaxError	SyntaxError

C Name	Python Exception
PyExc_SystemError	SystemError
PyExc_SystemExit	SystemExit
PyExc_TypeError	TypeError
PyExc_UnicodeError	UnicodeError
PyExc_UnicodeEncodeError	UnicodeEncodeError
PyExc_UnicodeDecodeError	UnicodeDecodeError
PyExc_UnicodeTranslateError	UnicodeTranslateError
PyExc_ValueError	ValueError
PyExc_WindowsError	WindowsError
PyExc_ZeroDivisionError	ZeroDivisionError

The following example shows how an exception is typically set and an error returned
in extension code:

```
PyErr_SetString(PyExc_ValueError,"Expected a positive value!");
return NULL;
```

Warnings can be issued using the following function:

```
PyObject *PyErr_Warn(PyObject *category, char *message)
```

This issues a warning message that is normally printed to sys.stderr. *category* is a
warning category that is normally set to one of the following values:

C Name	Python Warning
PyExc_Warning	Warning
PyExc_UserWarning	UserWarning
PyExc_DeprecationWarning	DeprecationWarning
PyExc_PendingDeprecationWarning	PendingDeprecationWarning
PyExc_RuntimeWarning	RuntimeWarning
PyExc_FutureWarning	FutureWarning

An extension module can define a new exception type by using the following function:

```
PyObject *PyErr_NewException(char *excname, PyObject *base, PyObject *dict)
```

This creates a new exception object. *excname* is the name of the exception in the form
"*modulename.excname*", *base* is an optional base class for the exception, and *dict* is
an optional dictionary used as the __dict__ attribute of the resulting exception class.
Both of these arguments are normally set to NULL. The returned object is a class object.

The following example shows how a new exception is created in an extension
module:

```
static PyObject *SpamError;
...

/* Module initialization function */
void  initspam() {
    PyObject *m, *d;
    m= Py_InitModule("spam",SpamMethods);
    d= PyModule_GetDict(m);
```

```
    SpamError = PyErr_NewException("spam.error", NULL, NULL);
    PyDict_SetItemString(d,"error",SpamError);
    ...
}
```

Reference Counting

Unlike programs written in Python, C extensions occasionally have to manipulate the reference count of Python objects. This is done using the following macros:

Macro	Description
Py_INCREF(*obj*)	Increments the reference count of *obj*, which must be non-null
Py_DECREF(*obj*)	Decrements the reference count of *obj*, which must be non-null
Py_XINCREF(*obj*)	Increments the reference count of *obj*, which may be null
Py_XDECREF(*obj*)	Decrements the reference count of *obj*, which may be null

Manipulating the reference count of Python objects in C is a delicate topic, and readers are strongly advised to consult the "Extending and Embedding the Python Interpreter" document available at http://www.python.org/doc/ext before proceeding any further. With this in mind, all Python objects are manipulated in C through the use of pointers of type PyObject *. Furthermore, these pointers are classified into two categories: owned references and borrowed references. An *owned reference* is a pointer to a Python object in which the reference count of that object has been updated to reflect the fact that some piece of C code or a C data structure is holding a pointer to it. A *borrowed reference*, on the other hand, is simply a bare pointer to a Python object in which the reference count of the object has not been updated.

Owned references are most commonly created by functions that create new Python objects, such as Py_BuildValue(), PyInt_FromLong(), and PyList_New(). When these functions are called, a new Python object is created and the object is said to be *owned* by the calling function. Borrowed references often appear when a function obtains a pointer to a Python object from elsewhere or when the contents of Python objects such as lists and dictionaries are extracted. For example, the self and args parameters of a wrapper function are borrowed references, as is the pointer returned by functions such as PyList_GetItem().

The owner of a reference must either give up ownership using the Py_DECREF() macro or transfer ownership elsewhere. For example, temporary objects created inside a wrapper function should be destroyed using Py_DECREF(), whereas the return value of a wrapper is an owned reference that's given back to the interpreter. Likewise, the holder of a borrowed reference can obtain ownership using the Py_INCREF() macro. However, special care is in order. For example, decrementing the reference count of a borrowed reference may cause the interpreter to crash with a segmentation fault at a later time during execution. Likewise, failure to release an owned reference or inadvertently increasing the reference count of an object will lead to memory leaks.

Figuring out Python's reference-counting scheme is tricky because there are several inconsistencies in its treatment of references. However, here are a few general rules:

- Functions that create new Python objects always return owned references.
- If you want to save a reference to a Python object, use `Py_INCREF()` to increase the reference count.
- To dispose of an owned reference, use `Py_DECREF()`.
- Many (but not all) functions that return pointers to objects contained in sequences and mapping objects return owned references.
- Many (but not all) functions that store objects in containers such as sequences and mappings increase the reference count of objects they contain.
- All C wrapper functions must return an owned reference.

Exceptions to these rules are noted in later sections of this chapter.

Calling Python from C

Sometimes it's useful to call Python functions from C programs. To do this, the following functions can be used:

```
PyObject *PyEval_CallObject(PyObject *func, PyObject *args)
```

Calls `func` with arguments `args`. `func` is a Python callable object (function, method, class, and so on). `args` is a tuple of arguments.

```
PyObject *PyEval_CallObjectWithKeywords(PyObject *func, PyObject *args,
                                        PyObject *kwargs)
```

Calls `func` with positional arguments `args` and keyword arguments `kwargs`. `func` is a callable object, `args` is a tuple, and `kwargs` is a dictionary.

The following example illustrates the use of these functions:

```
/* Call a python function */

PyObject *func;     /* Callable object. */
PyObject *args;
PyObject *result;
int       arg1, arg2;

func = get_python_function()  /* See below */
args = Py_BuildValue("(ii)", arg1, arg2);  /* Build argument list */
result = PyEval_CallObject(func,args);     /* Call function        */
```

The only remaining problem is that C code, at compile time, cannot know the address of a Python object that has not yet been created given that Python is dynamic. One approach is to let Python create the function object and then register the address with a callback function. To deal with this, you can use extension code such as the following to set the callback function:

```
static PyObject *func = 0;    /* Callback function */

static PyObject *
set_callback(PyObject *self, PyObject *args) {
    PyObject *f;
    if (PyArg_ParseTuple(args,"O",&f)) {
        if (!PyCallable_Check(f)) {
            PyErr_SetString(PyExc_TypeError, "expected a callable");
            return NULL;
        }
```

```
         Py_XINCREF(f);        /* Save reference to callback */
         Py_XDECREF(func);     /* Release any previous callback */
         func = f;
         Py_INCREF(Py_None);
         return Py_None;
     }
     return NULL;
}
```

This function would then be invoked from the interpreter as follows:

```
# Some function
def foo(x,y):
    return x+y
...
set_callback(foo)
```

Alternatively, it might be possible to obtain Python callable objects using functions in the embedding API, described later in this chapter.

Abstract Object Layer

The functions in Tables 27.4 through 27.9 are used to manipulate objects from C, much in the same manner as from the interpreter. All the functions in this section that return an int return -1 if an error occurs. Likewise, functions that return a PyObject * return NULL on failure. Note that an "error" in this context is not the same as the false result of a test. For instance, the PyNumber_Check(PyObject *obj) function returns 0 if obj is not a number, but this isn't the same as an error. Finally, unless otherwise noted, all functions in this section that return a PyObject * return ownership with the object. It's up to the caller to decrement the reference count of the returned object if necessary.

Most of the functions in this section mirror the operation of various built-in Python functions and operators. Unless otherwise noted, arguments of type PyObject * accept the same types of arguments as in Python code. For instance, the built-in function isinstance(o,cls) accepts either a class object or a tuple of class objects as the cls argument. In C, the function PyObject_IsInstance() implements this operation and accepts exactly the same kinds of arguments.

Table 27.4   **Objects**

Type	Function
int	PyObject_AsFileDescriptor(PyObject *o)
int	PyCallable_Check(PyObject *o)
PyObject *	PyObject_CallFunction(PyObject *callable, char *format,...)
PyObject *	PyObject_CallFunctionObjArgs(PyObject *callable, ...)
PyObject *	PyObject_CallMethod(PyObject *o, char *methodname, char *format, ...)
PyObject *	PyObject_CallMethodObjArgs(PyObject *callable, ...)

Table 27.4 **Continued**

Type	Function
PyObject *	PyObject_CallObject(PyObject *callable, PyObject *args)
void	PyObject_ClearWeakRefs(PyObject *obj)
int	PyObject_Cmp(PyObject *o1, PyObject *o2, int *result)
int	PyObject_Compare(PyObject *o1, PyObject *o2)
int	PyObject_DelAttr(PyObject *o, PyObject *attr_name)
int	PyObject_DelAttrString(PyObject *o, char *attr_name)
int	PyObject_DelItem(PyObject *o, PyObject *key)
PyObject *	PyObject_Dir(PyObject *o)
PyObject *	PyObject_GetAttr(PyObject *o, PyObject *attr_name)
PyObject *	PyObject_GetAttrString(PyObject *o, char *attr_name)
PyObject *	PyObject_GetItem(PyObject *o, PyObject *key)
PyObject *	PyObject_GetIter(PyObject *o)
int	PyObject_HasAttr(PyObject *o, PyObject *attr_name)
int	PyObject_HasAttrString(PyObject *o, char *attr_name)
int	PyObject_Hash(PyObject *o)
int	PyObject_IsInstance(PyObject *o, PyObject *cls)
int	PyObject_IsSubclass(PyObject *o, PyObject *cls)
int	PyObject_IsTrue(PyObject *o)
int	PyObject_Length(PyObject *o)
int	PyObject_Print(PyObject *o, FILE *fp, int flags)
PyObject *	PyObject_Repr(PyObject *o)
PyObject *	PyObject_RichCompare(PyObject *o1, PyObject *o2, int op);
int	PyObject_RichCompareBool(PyObject *o1, PyObject *o2, int op);
int	PyObject_SetAttr(PyObject *o, PyObject *attr_name, PyObject *v)
int	PyObject_SetAttrString(PyObject *o, char *attr_name, PyObject *v)
int	PyObject_SetItem(PyObject *o, PyObject *key, PyObject *v)
int	PyObject_Size(PyObject *o)
PyObject *	PyObject_Str(PyObject *o)
PyObject *	PyObject_Type(PyObject *o)
int	PyObject_TypeCheck(PyObject *o, PyTypeObject *type)

The *flags* argument of PyObject_Print() is used to select printing options. Currently, the only option is Py_PRINT_RAW, which forces PyObject_Print() to produce output using PyObject_Str() as opposed to PyObject_Repr() (the default).

PyObject_Hash() and PyObject_Length() return a positive integer result on success and -1 on error.

The op argument to PyObject_RichCompare() and PyObject_RichCompareBool() is one of Py_EQ, Py_NE, Py_LT, Py_GT, Py_GE, or Py_LE.

Table 27.5 **Numbers**

Type	Function
PyObject *	PyNumber_Absolute(PyObject *o)
PyObject *	PyNumber_Add(PyObject *o1, PyObject *o2)
PyObject *	PyNumber_And(PyObject *o1, PyObject *o2)
int	PyNumber_Check(PyObject *o)
PyObject *	PyNumber_Coerce(PyObject **p1, PyObject **p2)
PyObject *	PyNumber_Divide(PyObject *o1, PyObject *o2)
PyObject *	PyNumber_Divmod(PyObject *o1, PyObject *o2)
PyObject *	PyNumber_Float(PyObject *o)
PyObject *	PyNumber_FloorDivide(PyObject *o1, PyObject *o2)
PyObject *	PyNumber_Int(PyObject *o)
PyObject *	PyNumber_Invert(PyObject *o)
PyObject *	PyNumber_Long(PyObject *o)
PyObject *	PyNumber_Lshift(PyObject *o1, PyObject *o2)
PyObject *	PyNumber_Multiply(PyObject *o1, PyObject *o2)
PyObject *	PyNumber_Negative(PyObject *o)
PyObject *	PyNumber_Or(PyObject *o1, PyObject *o2)
PyObject *	PyNumber_Positive(PyObject *o)
PyObject *	PyNumber_Power(PyObject *o1, PyObject *o2, PyObject *o3)
PyObject *	PyNumber_Remainder(PyObject *o1, PyObject *o2)
PyObject *	PyNumber_Rshift(PyObject *o1, PyObject *o2)
PyObject *	PyNumber_Subtract(PyObject *o1, PyObject *o2)
PyObject *	PyNumber_TrueDivide(PyObject *o1, PyObject *o2)
PyObject *	PyNumber_Xor(PyObject *o1, PyObject *o2)
PyObject *	PyNumber_InPlaceAdd(PyObject *o1, PyObject *o2)
PyObject *	PyNumber_InPlaceSubtract(PyObject *o1, PyObject *o2)
PyObject *	PyNumber_InPlaceMultiply(PyObject *o1, PyObject *o2)
PyObject *	PyNumber_InPlaceDivide(PyObject *o1, PyObject *o2)
PyObject *	PyNumber_InPlaceFloorDivide(PyObject *o1, PyObject *o2)

Table 27.5   **Continued**

Type	Function
PyObject *	PyNumber_InPlaceTrueDivide(PyObject *o1, PyObject *o2)
PyObject *	PyNumber_InPlaceRemainder(PyObject *o1, PyObject *o2)
PyObject *	PyNumber_InPlacePower(PyObject *o1, PyObject *o2)
PyObject *	PyNumber_InPlaceLshift(PyObject *o1, PyObject *o2)
PyObject *	PyNumber_InPlaceRshift(PyObject *o1, PyObject *o2)
PyObject *	PyNumber_InPlaceAnd(PyObject *o1, PyObject *o2)
PyObject *	PyNumber_InPlaceXor(PyObject *o1, PyObject *o2)
PyObject *	PyNumber_InPlaceOr(PyObject *o1, PyObject *o2)

Table 27.6   **Sequences**

Type	Function
int	PySequence_Check(PyObject *o)
PyObject *	PySequence_Concat(PyObject *o1, PyObject *o2)
int	PySequence_Contains(PyObject *o, PyObject *value);
int	PySequence_Count(PyObject *o, PyObject *value)
int	PySequence_DelItem(PyObject *o, int i)
int	PySequence_DelSlice(PyObject *o, int i1, int i2)
PyObject *	PySequence_GetItem(PyObject *o, int i)
PyObject *	PySequence_GetSlice(PyObject *o, int i1, int i2)
int	PySequence_In(PyObject *o, PyObject *value)
int	PySequence_Index(PyObject *o, PyObject *value)
int	PySequence_Length(PyObject *o)
PyObject *	PySequence_List(PyObject *o)
PyObject *	PySequence_Repeat(PyObject *o, int count)
int	PySequence_SetItem(PyObject *o, int i, PyObject *v)
int	PySequence_SetSlice(PyObject *o, int i1, int i2, PyObject *v)
int	PySequence_Size(PyObject *o)
PyObject *	PySequence_Tuple(PyObject *o)
PyObject *	PySequence_InPlaceConcat(PyObject *o1, PyObject *o2)
PyObject *	PySequence_InPlaceRepeat(PyObject *o1, int count)

Table 27.7   **Mappings**

Type	Function
int	PyMapping_Check(PyObject *o)
int	PyMapping_Clear(PyObject *o)
int	PyMapping_DelItem(PyObject *o, PyObject *key)
int	PyMapping_DelItemString(PyObject *o, char *key)
PyObject *	PyMapping_GetItemString(PyObject *o, char *key)
int	PyMapping_HasKey(PyObject *o, PyObject *key)
int	PyMapping_HasKeyString(PyObject *o, char *key)
PyObject *	PyMapping_Items(PyObject *o)
PyObject *	PyMapping_Keys(PyObject *o)
int	PyMapping_Length(PyObject *o)
int	PyMapping_SetItemString(PyObject *o, char *key, PyObject *v)
PyObject *	PyMapping_Values(PyObject *o)

Table 27.8   **Iterator Interface**

Type	Function
int	PyIter_Check(PyObject *o)
PyObject *	PyIter_Next(PyObject *o)

Table 27.9   **Buffer Interface**

Type	Function
int	PyObject_AsCharBuffer(PyObject *o, const char **buffer, int *len)
int	PyObject_AsReadBuffer(PyObject *o, const void **buffer, int *len)
int	PyObject_AsWriteBuffer(PyObject *o, void **buffer, int *len)
int	PyObject_CheckReadBuffer(PyObject *o)

The buffer interface is used by objects to that want to expose the raw bytes used to store data to the caller without having to make a copy. Typically this is only used by strings, Unicode strings, and arrays as created in the array module. The size and interpretation of the data depends on the underlying object.

Low-level Functions on Built-in Types

The functions in Tables 27.10 through 27.22 can be used to manipulate specific built-in types. Functions of the form Py<type>_Check() are used to check the type of an

object and return 1 if an object is the correct type, 0 otherwise. Functions of the form
`Py<type>_CheckExact()` perform the same task, but make sure that the object is
exactly the appropriate type—not a type that has been derived via inheritance.
Functions of the form `Py<type>_From<type>` are used to create a Python object from
a C data type. Functions of the form `Py<type>_As<type>` are used to convert from
Python to C.

Only the most commonly used functions are presented here. Readers should consult
the Python C API documentation for full coverage of all functions.

The functions in this section are presented without further description.

Table 27.10   **Integers**

Type	Function
long	`PyInt_AsLong(PyObject *iobj);`
int	`PyInt_Check(PyObject *obj)`
int	`PyInt_CheckExact(PyObject *obj)`
PyObject *	`PyInt_FromLong(long);`
long	`PyInt_GetMax();`

Table 27.11   **Booleans**

Type	Function
int	`PyBool_Check(PyObject *obj)`
PyObject *	`PyBool_FromLong(long v)`
PyObject *	`Py_False`
PyObject *	`Py_True`

The `Py_False` and `Py_True` objects represent the values `False` and `True` in the interpreter.

Table 27.12   **Long Integers**

Type	Function
double	`PyLong_AsDouble(PyObject *lobj)`
long	`PyLong_AsLong(PyObject *lobj)`
long long	`PyLong_AsLongLong(PyObject *lobj)`
unsigned long	`PyLong_AsUnsignedLong(PyObject *lobj)`
unsigned long long	`PyLong_AsUnsignedLongLong(PyObject *lobj)`
int	`PyLong_Check(PyObject *obj)`
int	`PyLong_CheckExact(PyObject *obj)`
PyObject *	`PyLong_FromDouble(double)`
PyObject *	`PyLong_FromLong(long)`
PyObject *	`PyLong_FromLongLong(long long)`

Table 27.12   **Continued**

Type	Function
PyObject *	PyLong_FromUnsignedLong(unsigned long)
PyObject *	PyLong_FromUnsignedLongLong(unsigned long long)

Table 27.13   **Floats**

Type	Function
double	PyFloat_AsDouble(PyObject *fobj)
int	PyFloat_Check(PyObject *obj)
int	PyFloat_CheckExact(PyObject *obj)
PyObject *	PyFloat_FromDouble(double)

Table 27.14   **Complex**

Type	Function
Py_complex	PyComplex_AsCComplex(PyObject *cobj)
int	PyComplex_Check(PyObject *obj)
int	PyComplex_CheckExact(PyObject *obj)
PyObject *	PyComplex_FromCComplex(Py_complex *cobj)
PyObject *	PyComplex_FromDoubles(double real, double imag)
double	PyComplex_ImagAsDouble(PyObject *cobj)
double	PyComplex_RealAsDouble(PyObject *cobj)

The Py_complex structure returned by PyComplex_AsCComplex() is defined as follows:

```
typedef struct {
    double real;
    double imag;
} Py_complex;
```

Table 27.15   **Strings**

Type	Function
char *	PyString_AsString(PyObject *str);
int	PyString_Check(PyObject *obj);
int	PyString_CheckExact(PyObject *obj)
void	PyString_Concat(PyObject **str, PyObject *newpart)

Table 27.15   **Continued**

Type	Function
void	PyString_ConcatAndDel(PyObject **str, PyObject *newpart)
PyObject *	PyString_Decode(const char *s, int size, const char *encoding, const char *errors)
PyObject *	PyString_Encode(const Py_UNICODE *s, int size, const char *encoding, const char *errors)
PyObject *	PyString_Format(PyObject *format, PyObject *args);
PyObject *	PyString_FromFormat(const char *fmt, ...)
PyObject *	PyString_FromFormatV(const char *fmt, va_list vargs)
PyObject *	PyString_FromString(char *str);
PyObject *	PyString_FromStringAndSize(char *str, int len);
int	PyString_Resize(PyObject **str, int newsize)
int	PyString_Size(PyObject *str);

Note

The Encode and Decode functions expect encoding and error parameters that are the same as the built-in unicode() function.

Table 27.16   **Unicode**

Type	Function
int	PyUnicode_AsWideChar(PyObject *o, wchar_t *buf, int maxlen)
Py_UNICODE *	PyUnicode_AsUnicode(PyObject *o)
int	PyUnicode_Check(PyObject *o)
int	PyUnicode_CheckExact(PyObject *o)
PyObject *	PyUnicode_FromUnicode(Py_UNICODE *, int size)
PyObject *	PyUnicode_FromEncodedObject(PyObject *obj, const char *encoding, const char *errors)
PyObject *	PyUnicode_FromObject(PyObject *o)
PyObject *	PyUnicode_FromWideChar(const wchar_t *, int size)
int	PyUnicode_GetSize(PyObject *o)

Table 27.17 **Lists**

Type	Function
int	PyList_Append(PyObject *list, PyObject *obj)
PyObject *	PyList_AsTuple(PyObject *list)
int	PyList_Check(PyObject *obj)
int	PyList_CheckExact(PyObject *obj)
PyObject *	PyList_GetItem(PyObject *list, int index)
PyObject *	PyList_GetSlice(PyObject *list, int i, int j)
int	PyList_Insert(PyObject *list, int index, PyObject *obj)
PyObject *	PyList_New(int size)
int	PyList_Reverse(PyObject *list)
int	PyList_SetItem(PyObject *list, int index, PyObject *obj)
int	PyList_SetSlice(PyObject *list, int i, int j, PyObject *slc)
int	PyList_Size(PyObject *list)
int	PyList_Sort(PyObject *list)

Note

PyList_GetItem() returns a borrowed reference.

Table 27.18 **Tuples**

Type	Function
int	PyTuple_Check(PyObject *obj)
int	PyTuple_CheckExact(PyObject *obj)
PyObject *	PyTuple_GetItem(PyObject *tup, int index)
PyObject *	PyTuple_GetSlice(PyObject *tup, int i, int j)
PyObject *	PyTuple_New(int size)
PyObject *	PyTuple_Pack(int n, PyObject *o1, ...)
int	PyTuple_SetItem(PyObject *tup, int index, PyObject *obj)
int	PyTuple_Size(PyObject *tup)

Note

PyTuple_SetItem() increments the reference count of obj even if it fails, and
PyTuple_GetItem() returns a borrowed reference.

Table 27.19 **Dictionaries**

Type	Function
int	PyDict_Check(PyObject *obj)
int	PyDict_CheckExact(PyObject *obj)
void	PyDict_Clear(PyObject *dict)
PyObject *	PyDict_Copy(PyObject *dict)
int	PyDict_DelItem(PyObject *dict, PyObject *key)
int	PyDict_DelItemString(PyObject *dict, char *key)
PyObject *	PyDict_GetItem(PyObject *dict, PyObject *key)
PyObject *	PyDict_GetItemString(PyObject *dict, char *key)
PyObject *	PyDict_Items(PyObject *dict)
PyObject *	PyDict_Keys(PyObject *dict)
PyObject *	PyDict_New()
int	PyDict_SetItem(PyObject *dict, PyObject *key, PyObject *value)
int	PyDict_SetItemString(PyObject *dict, char *key, PyObject *value)
int	PyDict_Size(PyObject *dict)
int	PyDict_Update(PyObject *dict1, PyObject *dict2)
PyObject *	PyDict_Values(PyObject *dict)

Note

PyDict_GetItem() and PyDict_GetItemString() return borrowed references.

Table 27.20 **Buffer Objects**

Type	Function
int	PyBuffer_Check(PyObject *o)
PyObject *	PyBuffer_FromObject(PyObject *base, int offset, int size)
PyObject *	PyBuffer_FromMemory(void *ptr, int size)
PyObject *	PyBuffer_FromReadWriteMemory(void *ptr, int size)
PyObject *	PyBuffer_FromReadWriteObject(PyObject *base, int offset, int size)
PyObject *	PyBuffer_New(int size)

Table 27.21   **Files**

Type	Function
FILE *	PyFile_AsFile(PyObject *file)
int	PyFile_Check(PyObject *obj)
int	PyFile_CheckExact(PyObject *obj)
PyObject *	PyFile_FromFile(FILE *, char *, char *, int (*)(FILE *))
PyObject *	PyFile_FromString(char *name, char *mode)
PyObject *	PyFile_GetLine(PyObject *file, int)
PyObject *	PyFile_Name(PyObject *file)
void	PyFile_SetBufSize(PyObject *file, int size)
int	PyFile_SoftSpace(PyObject *file, int)
int	PyFile_WriteObject(PyObject *file, PyObject *obj, int)
int	PyFile_WriteString(char *str, PyObject *file)

Table 27.22   **Modules**

Type	Function
int	PyModule_AddIntConstant(PyObject *mod, char *name, long value)
int	PyModule_AddObject(PyObject *mod, char *name, PyObject *value)
int	PyModule_AddStringConstant(PyObject *mod, char *name, char *value)
int	PyModule_Check(PyObject *obj)
int	PyModule_CheckExact(PyObject *obj)
PyObject *	PyModule_GetDict(PyObject *mod)
char *	PyModule_GetFilename(PyObject *mod)
char *	PyModule_GetName(PyObject *mod)
PyObject *	PyModule_New(char *name)

Threads

A global interpreter lock is used to prevent more than one thread from executing in the interpreter at once. If a function written in an extension module executes for a long time, it will block the execution of other threads until it completes. This is because the lock is held whenever an extension function is invoked. If the extension module is thread-safe, the following macros can be used to release and reacquire the global interpreter lock:

`Py_BEGIN_ALLOW_THREADS`

Releases the global interpreter lock and allows other threads to run in the interpreter. The C extension must not invoke any functions in the Python C API while the lock is released.

`Py_END_ALLOW_THREADS`

Reacquires the global interpreter lock. The extension will block until the lock can be acquired successfully in this case.

The following example illustrates the use of these macros:

```
PyObject *spamfunction(PyObject *self, PyObject *args) {
        ...
        PyArg_ParseTuple(args, ...)
        Py_BEGIN_ALLOW_THREADS
        result = run_long_calculation(args);
        Py_END_ALLOW_THREADS
        ...
        return Py_BuildValue(fmt,result);
}
```

Many more subtle aspects of threads are not covered here. Readers are strongly advised to consult the C API Reference Manual. In addition, you may need to take steps to make sure that your C extension is thread-safe, as it could be invoked by other Python threads shortly after the interpreter lock is released.

Embedding

The Python interpreter can also be embedded into other applications. When embedding the interpreter on UNIX, you must include the file `config.c` (usually found in a place such as `<python>/lib/python2.4/config/config.c`, where `<python>` is the directory in which Python was installed) and link against the library `libpython2.4.a`. (A comparable but more complex process is required on Windows and the Macintosh. Consult the online documentation for details.)

The following functions are used to call the interpreter to execute code and control its operation:

`int PyRun_AnyFile(FILE *fp, char *filename)`

If *fp* is an interactive device such as tty in Unix, this function calls `PyRun_InteractiveLoop()`. Otherwise, `PyRun_SimpleFile()` is called. *filename* is a string that gives a name for the input stream. This name will appear when the interpreter reports errors. If *filename* is NULL, a default string of `"???"` is used as the filename.

`int PyRun_SimpleString(char *command)`

Executes *command* in the __main__ module of the interpreter. Returns 0 on success, -1 if an exception occurred.

`int PyRun_SimpleFile(FILE *fp, char *filename)`

Similar to `PyRun_SimpleString()`, except that the program is read from the file *fp*.

`int PyRun_InteractiveOne(FILE *fp, char *filename)`

Executes a single interactive command.

```
int PyRun_InteractiveLoop(FILE *fp, char *filename)
```

Runs the interpreter in interactive mode.

```
int PyRun_String(char *str, int start, PyObject *globals, PyObject *locals)
```

Executes the code in `str` in the global and local namespaces defined by `globals` and `locals`, both of which must be dictionary objects. `start` is a start token to use when parsing the source code. Returns the result of execution or NULL if an error occurred.

```
int PyRun_File(FILE *fp, char *filename, int start, PyObject *globals,
               PyObject *locals)
```

Like `PyRun_String()`, except that code is read from the file `fp`.

```
PyObject *Py_CompileString(char *str, char *filename, int start)
```

Compiles code in `str` into a code object. `start` is the starting token, and `filename` is the filename that will be set in the code object and used in tracebacks. Returns a code object on success, NULL on error.

```
void Py_Initialize()
```

Initializes the Python interpreter. This function should be called before using any other functions in the C API, with the exception of `Py_SetProgramName()`, `PyEval_InitThreads()`, `PyEval_ReleaseLock()`, and `PyEval_AcquireLock()`.

```
int Py_IsInitialized()
```

Returns 1 if the interpreter has been initialized, 0 if not.

```
void Py_Finalize()
```

Cleans up the interpreter by destroying all the sub-interpreters and objects that were created since calling `Py_Initialize()`. Normally, this function frees all the memory allocated by the interpreter. However, circular references and extension modules may introduce memory leaks that cannot be recovered by this function.

```
void Py_SetProgramName(char *name)
```

Sets the program name that's normally found in the `argv[0]` argument of the `sys` module. This function should only be called before `Py_Initialize()`.

```
char *Py_GetProgramName()
```

Returns the program name as set by `Py_SetProgramName()`.

```
char *Py_GetPrefix()
```

Returns the prefix for installed platform-independent files. This is the same value as found in `sys.prefix`.

```
char *Py_GetExecPrefix()
```

Returns the exec-prefix for installed platform-dependent files. This is the same value as found in `sys.exec_prefix`.

```
char *Py_GetProgramFullPath()
```

Returns the full pathname of the Python executable.

```
char *Py_GetPath()
```

Returns the default module search path. The path is returned as a string consisting of directory names separated by a platform-dependent delimiters (: on UNIX, ; on DOS/Windows).

```
const char *Py_GetVersion()
```

Returns the version of the interpreter as a string.

```
const char *Py_GetPlatform()
```

Returns the platform identifier string for the current platform.

```
const char *Py_GetCopyright()
```

Returns the official copyright string.

```
const char *Py_GetCompiler()
```

Returns the compiler string.

```
const char *Py_GetBuildInfo()
```

Returns build information about the interpreter.

```
int PySys_SetArgv(int argc, char **argv)
```

Sets command-line options used to populate the value of sys.argv. This should only be called by Py_Initialize().

Defining New Python Types

One of the most advanced topics in extension building is defining new Python types in C/C++. Just as it is possible to add new functions to Python, one can add entirely new objects that behave similarly to the other built-in types, such as lists, tuples, and dictionaries.

The steps involved in adding a new type to Python are considerable and are not discussed further here. However, in practice, it rarely seems necessary to manually add a new type. For one, most of Python's built-in types can be subclassed directly in Python. Therefore, if your only goal is to slightly modify one of the existing types, that can already be done without resorting to a C extension module. Second, a huge number of third-party extension modules are already available for Python. Therefore, instead of resorting to the arduous task of creating a new type, it may be easier to first check if someone else has already done the work. For example, there is no good reason to implement a new Matrix type when several implementations already exist. Finally, advanced extension-building problems may be better handled through the use of extension-building tools, as briefly discussed in the next section. These tools can automate the process of creating very complicated extension modules—even modules that make use of fairly advanced C++ features (such as templates).

Extension Building Tools

A number of tools are available to simplify the construction of Python extensions. Many of these tools hide all or most of the underlying details of connecting C/C++ to Python. For instance, a tool might generate a Python extension by simply reading a

C++ header file or having you write code in a higher-level language. Full coverage of these tools would require a dedicated book. Therefore, only a brief description and links to more information have been provided.

Boost Python Library

The Boost Python Library, created by David Abrahams, provides a tool for wrapping C++ libraries into Python extensions. The library provides a number of advanced features, including support for overloaded functions and operators. Details are available at http://www.boost.org/libs/python/doc/index.html.

CXX

The CXX extension, developed by Paul Dubois, simplifies the process of creating extension modules in C++ by providing an easy-to-use C++ API to Python. It is available at http://cxx.sourceforge.net.

f2py

f2py is a Fortran-to-Python interface generator developed by Pearu Peterson. Details are available at http://cens.ioc.ee/projects/f2py2e/.

pyfort

pyfort, also developed by Paul Dubois, can be used to build Python extension modules from Fortran code. Details are available at http://pyfortran.sourceforge.net.

psyco

psyco isn't an extension-building tool per se, but it's an extension module that can dramatically speed up existing Python programs using techniques related to just-in-time compilation. If you are considering the use of a C extension module for performance reasons, you might consider the use of psyco first. Details are available at http://psyco.sourceforge.net.

Pyrex

Pyrex is a special-purpose language for writing Python extension modules. The language has the special feature of looking almost exactly like Python, making it very easy to migrate existing Python code to a C module. Details are available at http://www.cosc.canterbury.ac.nz/~greg/python/Pyrex.

Weave

Weave is an extension tool that allows C/C++ code to be inlined into Python programs. Further details are available at http://www.scipy.org.

SWIG

SWIG (Simplified Wrapper and Interface Generator), developed by the author and available at http://www.swig.org, can be used to create Python extensions automatically from annotated C header files.

Index

Symbols & Numbers

( ) tuple, 11, 23

- (hyphen) character on command-line, 124

- operator, set difference, 12, 63

- subtraction operator, 57

- unary minus operator, 57

_ variable, interactive mode, 125, 135

_() function, gettext module, 215

! command, Python debugger, 509

!= not equal to, 58

(comment), 5, 20

#! in UNIX shell script, 126

#! in Unix shell script, 6

% modulo operator, 57

% (string format operator), 7, 53, 59, 61–62, 115
    and unicode, 67

%= assignment operator, 64

& bitwise and operator, 57

& operator, set intersection, 12, 63

&= assignment operator, 64

* multiplication operator, 57
    sequence replication, 59

* symbol in function arguments, 80

* wildcard character in import, 18, 104

** power operator, 57

** symbol in function arguments, 80

**= assignment operator, 64

*= assignment operator, 64

+ addition operator, 57
    lists, 10, 59
    sequence concatenation, 59

strings, 10, 59

tuples, 59

+ unary plus operator, 57

+= assignment operator, 64

. dot operator, 27, 47, 64, 93

... (Ellipsis), 44, 50

... prompt, 125, 167

/ division operator, 57

// floor division operator, 57

//= assignment operator, 64

/= assignment operator, 64

<> not equal to, 58

> greater than, 58

^= assignment operator, 64

| bitwise or operator, 58

| operator, set union, 12, 63

; (semicolon), 20

< less than, 58

<< left shift operator, 57

<<= assignment operator, 64

<= less than or equal to, 58

-= assignment operator, 64

== equal to, 58

== equality operator, 68

>= greater than or equal to, 58

>> modifier to print, 9, 115

>> right shift operator, 57

>>= assignment operator, 64

>>> prompt, 5, 125, 167

@ symbol (decorators), 88

[ ] (brackets) list, 11, 23

^ bitwise exclusive-or operator, 58

^ operator, set symmetric difference, 12, 63

A

B

C

E

of SocketServer objects, 389

of urlopen objects, 435

file_offset attribute, of ZipInfo objects, 261

files, 8

access modes, 313

C API, 543

capturing output in a string, 227

changing access permission, 315

changing owner, 315

close() method, 112

comma separated, 246

copying, 335

creating temporary, 342

fileno() method, 113

flush() method, 112

globbing, 253

I/O, 112

integer file descriptors, 311

isatty() method, 112

iteration, 113

large file support, 113

locking, 280-281

logging events to, 292

modes, 112

modification time, 326

moving, 335

next() method, 113

opening, 141

read() method, 112

readline() method, 112

readlines() method, 112

shell operations, 335

testing for existence, 326

truncate() method, 113

type, 42

universal newlines, 112-113

write() method, 112

writelines() method, 112

xreadlines() method, 112

file_size attribute, of ZipInfo objects, 261

FileType type, 172

fill() function, textwrap module, 230

fill() method, of TextWrapper objects, 231

Filter object, logging module, 295

filter() function, 85, 138

filter() method

of Filter objects, 295

of Handler objects, 294

of Logger objects, 291

filterwarnings() function, warnings module, 175

finalization of objects, 155

finally statement, 74-75

find() function

gettext module, 216

string module, 226

find() method

of mmap objects, 300

of strings, 35

findall() function, re module, 221

findall() method, of regular expression objects, 222

findCaller() method, of Logger objects, 291

finditer() function, re module, 221

finditer() method, of regular expression objects, 222

findmatch() function, mailcap module, 463

find_user_password() method, of HTTPPasswordMgr objects, 437

finish() method, of BaseRequestHandler objects, 390

first() method

of bsddb objects, 239

of dbhash objects, 240

firstChild attribute, of Node objects, 479

first-class objects, 83

FirstHeaderLineIsContinuationDefect, email package, 460

firstkey() method, of dbm objects, 241

H

I

isupper() method, of strings, 35

is_zipfile() function, zipfile module, 258

item assignment, in lists, 33

item deletion, in lists, 33

item() method
  of NamedNodeMap objects, 486
  of NodeList objects, 485

itemgetter() function, operator module, 162

items() method
  of dictionary, 37
  of Message objects, 470

itemsize attribute, of Array objects, 196

iter() function, 140

__iter__() method, 72, 140
  iterators, 50

__iter__() special method, 14

IterableUserDict() function, UserDict module, 178

iteration, 8, 13, 50, 71
  and files, 113
  and generator expressions, 87
  and weak references, 178
  email messages, 458
  on files, 9
  over directory, 318
  over list of input files, 251
  protocol, 14, 50, 71-72
  sets, 38
  use of a sentinel, 140
  utility functions, 199

iterators
  and regular expression matching, 221-222
  duplicating, 201

iteritems() method, of dictionary, 37

iterkeys() method, of dictionary, 37

itertools module, 199

itervalues() method, of dictionary, 37

__itruediv__() method, 52

__ixor__() method, 52

izip() function, itertools module, 200

J-K

java_ver() function, platform module, 329

join() function
  os.path module, 327
  string module, 226

join() method
  of strings, 35
  of Thread objects, 359

joinfields() function, string module, 226

js_output() method
  of Cookie objects, 404
  of Morsel objects, 405

j(ump) command, Python debugger, 508

jumpahead() function, random module, 192

kbhit() function, msvcrt module, 301

key attribute, of Morsel objects, 404

key index operator, 37

key values in dictionaries, 63

KEY_ALL_ACCESS constant, _winreg module, 353

KeyboardInterrupt exception, 75, 114, 146, 529
  and threads, 356

KEY_CREATE_LINK constant, _winreg module, 353

KEY_CREATE_SUB_KEY constant, _winreg module, 353

KEY_ENUMERATE_SUB_KEYS constant, _winreg module, 353

KeyError exception, 37, 62, 75, 146, 529

KEY_EXECUTE constant, _winreg module, 353

KEY_NOTIFY constant, _winreg module, 353

KEY_QUERY_VALUE constant, _winreg module, 353

KEY_READ constant, _winreg module, 354

keys() method
  of Database objects, 237
  of dictionary, 13, 37

minimum value of a sequence, 140

minor() function, os module, 316

minus() method, of Context objects, 187

mirrored character, unicode, 235

mirrored() function, unicodedata module, 235

MisplacedEnvelopeHeaderDefect, email package, 460

mixed-type operations, 53

mixing positional and keyword arguments, 80

mixing standard and unicode strings, 67

mkarg() function, commands module, 266

mkd() method, of FTP objects, 413

mkdir() function, os module, 316

mkdtemp() function, tempfile module, 342

mkfifo() function, os module, 316

mknod() function, os module, 316

mkstemp() function, tempfile module, 342

mktemp() function, tempfile module, 343

mktime() function, time module, 349

mktime_tz() function

email module, 459

rfc822 module, 472

mmap module, 298

mmap object, mmap module, 300

mmap() function, mmap module, 299

mmap, portable use of, 301

mod() function, operator module, 161

__mod__() method, 51

mode attribute

of files, 113

of TarInfo objects, 257

modf() function, math module, 191

modified() method, of RobotFileParser objects, 428

'module' action, warnings module, 175

module() function, new module, 160

modules, 17, 41, 103

modules variable, sys module, 167

modules

.py files, 105-106

.pyc files, 106

.pyo files, 106

attributes of, 42

C API, 543

case sensitivity of import, 106

compilation into byte code, 106

controlling exported symbols, 104

extensions, 106

importing, 103

importing from zip files, 105

loading, 105-106

__main__, 104-105

namespace, 41, 103

reloading, 106, 142

running as a script, 124

search path, 105, 165

ModuleType type, 31, 172

modulo operator (%), 57

Morsel object, Cookie module, 404

move() function, shutil module, 335

move() method, of mmap objects, 300

MozillaCookieJar() function, cookielib module, 407

__mro__ attribute, 95

msg attribute, of HTTPResponse objects, 418

msgfmt.py utility, 215

msvcrt module, 301

mtime attribute, of TarInfo objects, 257

mtime() method, of RobotFileParser objects, 428

mul() function, operator module, 161

__mul__() method, 51

and sequences, 50

MultiCall() function, xmlrpclib module, 444

multifile module, 501

O

P

omitting trailing newline, 9, 115

softspace attribute, of files, 114

printable variable, string module, 224

print_callees() method, of Stats objects, 512

print_callers() method, of Stats objects, 512

printdir() method, of ZipFile objects, 259

print_directory() function, cgi module, 400

print_environ() function, cgi module, 400

print_environ_usage() function, cgi module, 400

print_exc() function, traceback module, 171

print_exc() method, of Timer objects, 512

print_exception() function, traceback module, 170

printf(), 7, 61

print_form() function, cgi module, 400

printing a traceback, 170

print_last() function, traceback module, 171

print_stack() function, traceback module, 171

print_stats() method, of Stats objects, 512

print_tb() function, traceback module, 170

priority queue, 198

private class members, 20, 97

private symbols in modules, 20

process

aborting, 319

creation of, 320, 331, 340

environment, 308

management, 319

resource limits, 333

threads, 355

ProcessingInstruction object, xml.dom.minidom module, 486

processingInstruction() method, of ContentHandler objects, 489

processor() function, platform module, 330

producer-consumer problem, 361

profile module, 510

Profile() function, hotshot module, 505

profiling, 505, 510

from the command line, 511

of statements, 512

program termination, 126, 169

garbage collection, 127

NameError exception, 127

setting cleanup actions, 149

program testing, 503

prompting for a password, 283

prompts, 125

propagate attribute, of Logger objects, 290

properties, 48, 91-93, 141

property() function, 48, 141

PROT_EXEC constant, mmap module, 299

ProtocolError exception, xmlrpclib module, 444

protocol_version attribute, of BaseHTTPRequestHandler objects, 394

PROT_READ constant, mmap module, 299

PROT_WRITE constant, mmap module, 299

proxy server, in urllib2 module, 438

proxy() function, weakref module, 176

ProxyBasicAuthHandler, urllib2 module, 436

ProxyDigestAuthHandler, urllib2 module, 436

ProxyHandler() function, urllib2 module, 438

ProxyHandler, urllib2 module, 436

ProxyTypes type, 177

Q

REMOTE_USER environment variable, 397

remove() function, os module, 316

remove() method
of Array objects, 196
of lists, 33
of sets, 39

removeAttribute() method, of Element objects, 485

removeAttributeNode() method, of Element objects, 485

removeAttributeNS() method, of Element objects, 485

removeChild() method, of Node objects, 480

removedirs() function, os module, 316

removeFilter() method
of Handler objects, 294
of Logger objects, 291

removeHandler() method, of Logger objects, 291

removing a directory, 335

removing directories, 317

removing files, 318

rename() function, os module, 317

rename() method, of FTP objects, 413

renames() function, os module, 317

reorganize() method, of dbm objects, 241

repeat() function
itertools module, 201
operator module, 161

repeat() method, of Timer objects, 512

'replace' error handling, encoding, 66, 117

replace() function, string module, 227

replace() method
of date objects, 267
of datetime objects, 270
of strings, 35
of time objects, 269

replaceChild() method, of Node objects, 480

replace_errors() function, codecs module, 204

replace_header() method, of Message objects, 452

replacement character, 66, 117

replace_whitespace attribute, of TextWrapper objects, 230

replacing a slice, 61

report() method, of directory objects, 250

report_full_closure() method, of directory objects, 250

report_partial_closure() method, of directory objects, 250

repr module, 500

repr() function, 10, 65, 142
and eval(), 46
and str(), 46
and unicode, 67

__repr__() method, 46
example of, 97

__repr__(), difference from __str__(), 98

Request object, urllib2 module, 439

Request() function, urllib2 module, 438

request() method, of HTTPConnection objects, 418

RequestHandlerClass attribute, of SocketServer objects, 389

REQUEST_METHOD environment variable, 397

request_queue_size attribute, of SocketServer objects, 390

request_version attribute, of BaseHTTPRequestHandler objects, 394

reserved attribute, of ZipInfo objects, 260

reserved network ports, 365

reserved words, 20

reset() method
of HTMLParser objects, 462
of Packer objects, 474

stack trace, 159

stack() function, inspect module, 159

standard encodings, list of, 207

standard error, 114

standard I/O streams, 167

standard input, 114, 124

standard library, 131

standard output, 114

standard_b64decode() function, base64 module, 446

standard_b64encode() function, base64 module, 446

StandardError exception, 75, 145, 529

starmap() function, itertools module, 201

start() method
    of match objects, 223
    of Profile objects, 506
    of Thread objects, 358
    of Timer objects, 359

StartBoundaryNotFoundDefect, email package, 460

startDocument() method, of ContentHandler objects, 490

startElement() method, of ContentHandler objects, 490

startElementNS() method, of ContentHandler objects, 490

startfile() function, os module, 322

start_new_thread() function, thread module, 356

startPrefixMapping() method, of ContentHandler objects, 490

startswith() method, of strings, 36

stat module, 313, 338

stat() function, os module, 317

stat() method
    of NNTP objects, 423
    of POP3 objects, 427

statcache module, 500

stat_float_times() function, os module, 317

static method, 39

static methods, 16, 92

@staticmethod decorator, 16, 92, 143

staticmethod() function, 92, 143

ST_ATIME constant, stat module, 338

Stats object, pstats module, 511

Stats() function, pstats module, 511

status attribute, of HTTPResponse objects, 418

statvfs module, 339

statvfs() function, os module, 317

ST_CTIME constant, stat module, 338

stderr attribute, of Popen objects, 342

stderr variable, sys module, 114, 167

__stderr__ variable, sys module, 114, 168

ST_DEV constant, stat module, 338

stdin attribute, of Popen objects, 342

stdin variable, sys module, 114, 167

__stdin__ variable, sys module, 114, 168

stdout attribute, of Popen objects, 342

stdout variable, sys module, 114, 167

__stdout__ variable, sys module, 114, 168

s(tep) command, Python debugger, 508

stes, removing items, 12

ST_GID constant, stat module, 338

ST_INO constant, stat module, 338

ST_MODE constant, stat module, 338

ST_MTIME constant, stat module, 338

ST_NLINK constant, stat module, 338

stop() method, of Profile objects, 506

StopIteration exception, 14, 50, 72, 75, 147, 529
    and generators, 87

storbinary() method, of FTP objects, 414

storlines() method, of FTP objects, 414

str type, 30, 172

str() function, 10, 65, 143
    and print, 115
    and repr(), 46
    and unicode, 67
    locale module, 286

template strings, 116, 225

template variable, tempfile module, 343

Template() function, string module, 225

tempnam() function, os module, 318

temporary filename, 318

temporary files, 342
  location of, 343

TemporaryFile() function, tempfile
  module, 343

terminals, 344

terminating program execution, 169

termios module, 344

ternary power-modulo function, 58

test module, 500

test() function, cgi module, 400

TestCase object, unittest module, 514

testfile() function, doctest module, 505

testing, 503
  unit testing, 513

testmod() function, doctest module, 505

testzip() method, of ZipFile objects, 259

text file mode, 112

text filling, 230

Text() function, xml.dom.minidom
  module, 486

textdomain() function, gettext module,
  214

textwrap module, 230

TextWrapper object, textwrap module,
  230

thread module, 356

Thread object, threading module, 358

Thread objects, threading module, 358

threaded network server, 391

threading module, 358

ThreadingMixIn class, SocketServer
  module, 391

ThreadingTCPServer() function,
  SocketServer module, 391

ThreadingUDPServer() function,
  SocketServer module, 391

threads, 355
  and deque objects, 198
  and exception handling, 77
  and random number generation, 193
  blocking in C functions, 356
  context switching, 170, 355
  daemonic, 359
  exceptions, 167
  extension modules, 543
  in Python, 356
  KeyboardInterrupt exception, 356
  locking, 356
  main thread, 357
  processes, 355
  queueing, 363
  signals, 338, 356
  switching, 356
  termination, 357

thread-safe queue, 363

time and date manipulation, 267

time module, 348

time object, datetime module, 268

time() function
  datetime module, 268
  time module, 350

time() method, of datetime objects, 270

timedelta object, datetime module, 271

TimedRotatingFileHandler, logging
  module, 293

timeit module, 512

timeit() method, of Timer objects, 512

timeout variable, socket module, 388

timeouts, 336

Timer object
  threading module, 359
  timeit module, 512

Timer objects, threading module, 359

times() function, os module, 323

timetuple() method, of date objects, 268

timetz() method, of datetime objects,
  270

V

How can we make this index more useful? Email us at indexes@samspublishing.com

X-Y-Z